# Clinician's
# Guide to
# Cultural
# Psychiatry

# Clinician's Guide to Cultural Psychiatry

*Wen-Shing Tseng*

Department of Psychiatry
University of Hawaii
Honolulu, Hawaii

## ACADEMIC PRESS
An imprint of Elsevier Science

Amsterdam   Boston   London   New York   Oxford   Paris
San Diego   San Francisco   Singapore   Sydney   Tokyo

Copyright © 2003, Elsevier Science (USA).

All Rights Reserved.
No part of this publication may be reproduced or transmitted in any form or by any
means, electronic or mechanical, including photocopy, recording, or any information
storage and retrieval system, without permission in writing from the publisher.

Permissions may be sought directly from Elsevier's Science & Technology Rights
Department in Oxford, UK: phone: (+44) 1865 843830, fax: (+44) 1865 853333,
e-mail: permissions@elsevier.com.uk. You may also complete your request on-line
via the Elsevier Science homepage (http://elsevier.com), by selecting "Customer
Support" and then "Obtaining Permissions."

Academic Press
*An imprint of Elsevier Science*
525 B Street, Suite 1900, San Diego, California 92101-4495, USA
http://www.academicpress.com

Academic Press
84 Theobald's Road, London WC1X 8RR, UK
http://www.academicpress.com

Library of Congress Catalog Card Number: 2003102256

International Standard Book Number: 0-12-701633-3

PRINTED IN THE UNITED STATES OF AMERICA
03   04   05   06   07       8   7   6   5   4   3   2   1

# Contents

# 3  *Culture and Psychopathology: Specific Phenomena*

# 4  *Culture and Psychopathology: General Disorders*

## 5  *Culturally Competent Clinical Assessment*

# 6   Culturally Competent Clinical Care

# 7   Culturally Competent Psychotherapy

# 8 *Ethnicity, Culture, and Drug Therapy*

# 9 *Culture and Therapy with Special Subgroups*

# 10 *Culture-Oriented Care of Different Ethnic Groups*

# 11 *Some Social Phenomena and Therapeutic Considerations*

# *Preface*

Modern psychiatry has made remarkable progress in understanding human behavior and psychopathology through a well-balanced orientation toward biological, psychological, and sociocultural aspects. This is necessary both in training and in clinical practice. Associated with the awareness that clinical work needs to consider the diverse ethnic-cultural backgrounds of the patients, there is an increased demand for culturally competent psychiatric service. This is becoming a reality for clinicians working in multiethnic/cultural societies such as the United States and many other societies around the world.

Associated with this increased awareness of the need for culture-oriented clinical practice, there is a demand for a book to use in training and practice. This book, *Clinician's Guide to Cultural Psychiatry*, is written to fill that vacancy. The book serves as a practical guide for clinicians in the application of cultural psychiatry to their work, and may also be useful as a text for teaching psychiatrists and clinical psychologists in training. The contents derive largely from the more comprehensive and in depth *Handbook of Cultural Psychiatry* published by Academic Press in 2001. The contents in *Clinician's Guide* have been restricted to the most relevant information to clinical practice, with case vignettes added for clinical illustration. Material has been updated and restructured to be of most use to clinicians in practice and student clinicians. Additional chapters not in the original *Handbook* are included, discussing culturally competent clinical care in a variety of clinical services and settings (Chapter 6) and addressing the culture-oriented care of different ethnic groups in the United States (Chapter 10). For more theoretical issues or detailed research matters, the reader is advised to refer to the *Handbook*.

Throughout this book, there are many photo illustrations to enhance the material presented. Many thanks are due to colleagues and friends who were kind enough to contribute their valuable photographs, which add a very special quality to the book. Also, a total of 29 actual case vignettes are inserted in various chapters for clinical illustration. The examples were contributed by many practitioners and scholars, and also by residents: Todd Elwyn, Eileen Ha, Shae Locke, Lillian Jones, and Sonia Patel. Based on their actual clinical encounters, these cases have been presented in conferences or seminars at the department of psychiatry at the University of Hawaii, where the author is involved in teaching. In addition, the residents, Tiffany Bender-Niide, Nalani Blaisdell-Brennan, Bettina Haerer, and Brian Tsuzaki studied and presented various major religions during cultural psychiatry seminars in the academic year 2001–2002. Their discussion contributes to the expansion of Chapter 11 on the subject of religion to meet the current demand for clinicians to pay attention to the religious and spiritual lives of the patients. The contribution of these psychiatric residents toward achieving the goal of preparing this book for use in clinical application is much appreciated.

This book focuses heavily on clinical situations in the United States. It aims to meet the new and formal requirement in the United States for cultural competence in psychiatric training. However, as the material is also derived from various cultural settings around the world, this book will still be useful for many societies beyond the United States, and suitable for readers around the world.

When the author was preparing the *Handbook*, preceding this book, more than 30 national and international experts were consulted on various topics. They are (in alphabetical order): Renato D. Alarcón, Goffredo Bartocci, Richard W. Brislin, Joseé Cañive, Ajita Chakraborty, Edmond Chiu, Juris G. Draguns, Keisuke Ebata, F. M. El-Islam, Armando R. Favazza, Edward F. Foulks, Ezra Griffith, Jing Hsu, Wolfgang Jilek, Kwang-Iel Kim, J. David Kinzie, Laurence J, Kirmayer, Joan D. Koss-Chioino, Takie Sugiyama Lebra, Keh-Ming Lin, Tsung-Yi Lin, Roland Littlewood, Francis G. Lu, Juan E. Mezzich, Masahisa Nishizono, Raymond Prince, Norman Sartorius, Shen Yu-Cun, Ronald C. Simons, Jon Streltzer, Eng-Seong Tan, Vijoy K. Varma, Joseph Westermeyer, and Ronald M. Wintrop. Their vast expertise, insights, and valuable input are greatly appreciated.

Special thanks are due to Academic Press for its vision and commitment in undertaking the timely, needed publication of this book, immediately after the publication of the *Handbook of Cultural Psychiatry*. Much appreciation goes to the publisher, Nikki Levy, for her guidance and assistance in preparing the work.

Throughout this academic and personal undertaking, I am very grateful for the endless encouragement given by my wife, Jing Hsu, M.D., as well as our three children, Chau-Wen Tseng, Ph.D., Chien-Wen Tseng, M.D., and Stephanie Shih-Wen Tseng, M.D. for their enthusiastic support and assistance. I appreciate very much Kathy Luter Reimers for her continuous dedication in editing the manuscript through years. I also thank media specialist Gary F. Belcher for preparing the tables and figures and Christine Yoshida, who provided help with the references and index.

There have also been many colleagues who have provided expertise, shared experiences, and inspired me to broaden my knowledge in the clinical application of cultural psychiatry. I am very grateful for their direct and indirect contributions to this book, which I hope will serve as a useful teaching textbook for clinicians for the further development of competent cultural psychiatry.

*Wen-Shing Tseng*
Honolulu, Hawaii
June 5, 2002

# About the Author: Wen-Shing Tseng

Wen-Shing Tseng, M.D., is a professor of psychiatry at the University of Hawaii School of Medicine. Born in Taiwan in 1935, he was trained in psychiatry at the National Taiwan University in Taipei and later at the Massachusetts Mental Health Center of Harvard Medical School in Boston. He was a research fellow in culture and mental health at the East-West Center from 1970 to 1971, before being recruited as a faculty member of the University of Hawaii School of Medicine, where he became a professor in 1976, and served as training director for the psychiatric residency training program between 1975 and 1982.

As a consultant to the World Health Organization and for teaching and research projects, he has traveled extensively to many countries in Asia and the Pacific, including China, Japan, Singapore, Malaysia, Fiji, and Micronesia. He served as chairman of the Transcultural Psychiatry Section of the World Psychiatric Association for two terms, from 1983 to 1993. In that capacity, he developed a wide network of colleagues around the world in the field of cultural psychiatry. Relating to the subject of culture and mental health, he has coordinated numerous international conferences in Honolulu, Beijing, Tokyo, and Budapest. He has held the position of guest professor at the Institute of Mental Health, Beijing University, since 1987.

He has conducted numerous research projects, mainly relating to the cultural aspects of assessment of psychopathology, child development, family relations, epidemic mental disorders, culture-related specific psychiatric syndromes, folk healing, and psychotherapy. The studies resulted in the publication of more than 80 articles in scientific journals and book chapters.

He has edited/coedited the books: *People and Cultures of Hawaii: A Psychocultural Profile* (University Press of Hawaii, 1980), *Chinese Culture and Mental Health*

(Academic Press, 1985), *Suicidal Behaviour in the Asia-Pacific Region* (Singapore University Press, 1992), *Chinese Societies and Mental Health* (Oxford University Press, 1995), *Migration and Adjustment* (in Japanese) (Nihon Hyoronsha, 1996), *Chinese Mind and Psychotherapy* (in Chinese) (Beijing Medical University Press, 1997), *Culture and Psychopathology* (Brunner/Mazel, 1997) and *Culture and Psychotherapy* (American Psychiatric Press, 2001). He has authored the books: *Culture, Mind and Therapy: Introduction to Cultural Psychiatry* (Brunner/Mazel, 1981), *Culture and Family: Problems and Therapy* (Haworth Press, 1991), *Textbook of Psychiatry* (in Chinese) (Buffalo Book Co., 1994), *Psychotherapy: Theory and Analysis* (in Chinese) (Beijing Medical University Press, 1994), and *Handbook of Cultural Psychiatry* (Academic Press, 2001).

Presently, he is a member of the Board of Directors of the Society for the Study of Psychiatry and Culture and honorable advisor of the Transcultural Psychiatry Section of the World Psychiatric Association. Because of his research, publications, and experience, he has gained a reputation as an expert in cultural psychiatry, at both the national and international levels.

# CHAPTER 1

# Culture, Behavior, and Pathology

## A. WHAT IS CULTURAL PSYCHIATRY?

### 1. Cultural Psychiatry: Definition and Scope

Cultural psychiatry is a special field of psychiatry. It is primarily concerned with the cultural aspects of human behavior, mental health, psychopathology, and treatment (APA, 1969). Culture refers to the unique behavior and lifestyle shared by a group of people, and includes customs, habits, beliefs, and values that shape emotions, behavior, and life pattern. Within the framework of bio-psycho-sociocultural approaches in psychiatry, cultural psychiatry is mainly focused on sociocultural aspects. At the *clinical* level, cultural psychiatry aims to promote culturally competent mental health care for patients of diverse ethnic or cultural backgrounds. This includes culturally relevant assessment and understanding of psychopathologies and psychological problems and culturally appropriate care and treatment. In terms of *research*, cultural psychiatry is interested in how ethnic or cultural factors may influence human behavior and psychopathology, as well as the art of healing. On a *theoretical* level, cultural psychiatry aims to expand our knowledge of human behavior and mental problems transculturally to facilitate the development of more universally applicable and cross-culturally valid theories (Tseng, 2001, pp. 3–19). From actual perspectives the scope of cultural psychiatry covers the following areas:

### a. Studying Cultural Perspectives of Human Behavior

As the basis for investigation for mental health and illness-related behavior, as well as for clinical application, the first concern of cultural psychiatry is to study the impact of culture on human behavior, at both universal and culture-specific levels. More precisely, cultural psychiatry may include the study of the interrelation between culture and child development, personality formation, behavior patterns, marriage and family, socialization patterns, and life cycle. It aims to increase knowledge of how culture influences the mind and behavior. In order to comprehend the social aspects of human life, the scope of study may expand to involve the examination of culture-related social phenomena, such as the mental health perspectives of cultural change, migration, minorities, interracial relations, or even religion. Based on such exploration, clinicians will have a better insight into and understanding of the nature of the sociocultural environment and its impact on human life.

### b. Investigating Mental Stress and Illness Behavior

Clinicians are always concerned with how an individual, a family, or a collective group encounters stress and deals with problems or conflicts. As an area of cultural psychiatry, there is a need to investigate culture-related stresses and/or culture-induced problems that exist in a society and to learn the coping mechanisms provided or sanctioned by the cultural system. It is also necessary to focus on the cultural dimensions of illness behavior: namely, how patients (or their families) perceive, conceptualize, and present their problems; how they seek help; and what kinds of healing systems are available and utilized within each cultural setting.

### c. Examining Psychopathology

It is important clinically to investigate from a descriptive and phenomenological point of view how cultural factors relate to the formation and manifestation of psychopathology, the clinical picture, and the frequency of certain mental illnesses, particularly minor psychiatric disorders and closely related psychological problems, which are influenced predominantly by social and cultural factors (Mezzich et al., 1996). This may also include the study of culture-related specific psychiatric conditions that are heavily influenced by culture. Although descriptive and epidemiological approaches to examining psychopathology are useful, yielding basic information for further investigation, it is important to realize that such approaches are not sufficient from a cultural point of view. A dynamic approach to examining how various factors work integratively for the formation of psychopathology is more meaningful.

### d. Addressing Clinical Practice

Beyond theoretical investigation, it is currently the trend to emphasize the clinical application of cultural psychiatry, regarding evaluation, diagnosis, management, and treatment. The focus on culture is needed when a clinician is dealing not just with patients of minority or other ethnic backgrounds, or from foreign countries but also with patients who are part of the majority population of their own society. This view is based on the assumption that every person's mental life is subject to the influence of culture and that cultural attention is needed even when treating patients from the therapist's own society with the same ethnic-cultural background. Attention is needed not just on the ethnic-cultural background of the patient but equally on the therapist or caregiver. Cultural impact is manifested as a bilateral interaction between the therapist and the patient, rather than a unilateral influence. Thus, the cultural dimensions of communication, relation, and interaction between therapist and patient deserve full attention with every patient a clinician encounters. Every clinician is now expected to provide culturally sensitive, relevant, and effective clinical care and treatment for all of his patients.

## 2. Culturally Competent Psychiatric Practice

It has been recognized that, in addition to ordinary clinical competence, cultural competence is necessary for contemporary clinicians to provide effective, meaningful, and satisfactory care of every patient, whether the patient belongs to an ethnic minority or majority, with whatever ethnic, racial, or cultural background. The qualities for cultural competence include: cultural sensitivity, cultural knowledge, cultural empathy, culture-relevant relations and interaction, and ability for cultural guidance (see Section 5A, The Need for Cultural Competence, for details). The world is becoming more multicultural everywhere, and cultural competence is becoming a formal requirement in the training of future clinicians.

It can be said that cultural psychiatry emerged initially as the result of investigating "other" cultures, which were mainly prescientific, foreign, or exotic (Prince, Okpaku, & Merkel, 1998). The current trend is to expand the scope of cultural psychiatry into clinical application and to focus on our own society. Attention should be given to worldwide and everyday application.

It is important for us to realize that the behavior of every person or group of people, no matter what his or her ethnicity or cultural background, is always influenced by cultural, as well as biological and psychological, perspectives. Cultural orientation and attention are needed in dealing with ethnic minorities

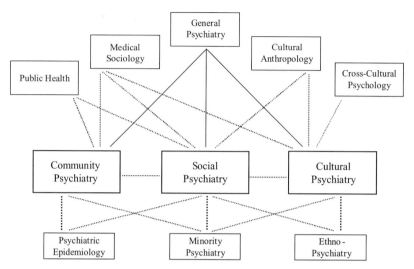

FIGURE 1    Scope of cultural psychiatry and its relation to other fields.

or people from foreign countries, as well as with majority people and people from our own societies.

The cultural aspects of psychiatric practice need more attention. This is because, from a worldwide perspective, there is a continuous increase in international communication, travel, and migration, and many societies are becoming multiethnic. Cultural psychiatry is becoming an essential part of general psychiatry, providing culture-relevant services for people of diverse cultural backgrounds (Favazza & Oman, 1978).

In summary, the core of cultural psychiatry is the analysis of culture and its relation to psychiatry. It is based on the foundation of cultural anthropology, cross-cultural psychology, and medical sociology and exists as a subfield of general psychiatry (see Fig. 1). As a clinical science, cultural psychiatry is interested in scientific research and theoretical investigation, but its final goal is clinical application, providing culturally relevant and competent care for patients of various ethnic/cultural backgrounds.

## B. HOW DOES CULTURE IMPACT MIND AND BEHAVIOR?

### 1. What Is Culture?

In order to explore the field of cultural psychiatry, the concept of culture should first be clarified. Several terms that are closely related in nature, but have differ-

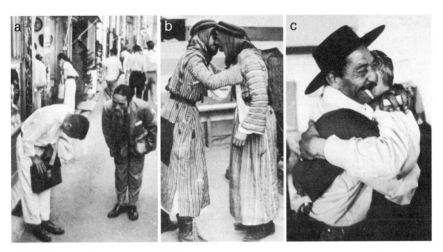

FIGURE 2   Culturally patterned different social greeting behavior. (a) A Japanese student keeps his physical distance and bows deeply to his professor. (b) Two Arab men rub noses. (c) The Latin American *abrazzo* emphasizes emotional expressiveness. [From *Anthropology: The Study of Man*, by E. A. Hoebel. McGraw-Hill, 1972. Courtesy of: (a) Marc Riboud, Magnum Photos; (b) the American Museum of Natural History Library; (c) Rene Burri, Magnum Photos.]

ent meanings, such as race, ethnicity, society, and minority, need to be defined as well.

### a. Definitions of Culture and Related Terms

*Culture.*   From the point of clinical application, the nature of culture can be summarized as follows:

a. Culture refers to the unique behavior patterns and lifestyle shared by a group of people, which distinguish it from others (see Fig. 2).

b. Culture is characterized by a set of views, beliefs, values, and attitudes toward things in life (see Fig. 3). It serves as the core of behavior and is expressed in various means of regulating life, such as rituals, customs, etiquette, taboos, or laws, manifested in daily life, and reflected in cultural products, such as common sayings, legends, drama, plays, art, philosophical thought, and religions.

c. Culture is learned by the process of "enculturation" and is transmitted from generation to generation through family units and social environments. Enculturation occurs and is enforced by personal child-rearing patterns, institutionalized education, and the surrounding social system.

d. Although continuity is a basic characteristic of culture, culture may be subject to transient and subtle or even acute and revolutionary changes, which may occur within the culture itself or as the result of the influence of other cultures.

FIGURE 3 Values emphasized in different cultures. (a) A person-sized stone money in Yap, Micronesia, the most treasured "thing" in that culture. (b) People risked their lives sailing several hundred miles away by canoe to another island, worked hard for several years carving the stone by shell, brought it back to their island, and placed it on the roadside in the village once its credibility was established [Courtesy of Paul Dale, M.D.]. (c) A diamond is admired as a forever "thing" in some cultures, but not necessarily in others [From *Invitation to Anthropology*, by Douglas L. Oliver, copyright 1964. Permission from Doubleday, a division of Random House, Inc.].

   e. The process of "acculturation" may occur when a person contacts a different cultural system and, under the influence of such an encounter, acquires part of the new or foreign culture. Sometimes, a person acquires the new or dominant culture to such an extent that he or she becomes similar to its members. This phenomenon of "assimilation" may occur voluntarily or involuntarily.
   f. Culture shapes people's behavior, but, at the same time, it is molded by the ideas and behavior of the members of the culture. Thus, culture and people influence each other bilaterally and interactionally.

g. Culture exists as a recognizable social or institutional pattern at the macroscopic level, but it also functions as the mode of behavior and the reactions of an individual at the microscopic level, of which the individual may be consciously aware, or which may be operating at a nonconscious level.

*Race.* Race is quite different from culture. In the past, scholars and laymen have used the term "race" to refer to a group of people that is characterized by certain physical features, such as color of skin, eyes, and hair, facial or body features, or physical size, that distinguish it from other groups. Anthropologists have used the term "geographic race" to indicate a human population that has inhabited a continental land mass or an island chain sufficiently long to have developed its own distinctive genetic composition, compared with that of other geographic populations (Hoebel, 1972). Based on such old concepts, in laymen's terms, African (black), American (Native American), Asian (yellow), Australian, European (white), Indian, and Polynesian are some of the major geographic races recognized around the world.

Based on these traditional views, both scholars and the general public have been conditioned to viewing human races as natural and separate divisions within the human species, based on visible physical differences. However, as indicated in the official statement by the American Anthropological Association (1999), with improvements in genetic study, analysis of DNA among members of different races has shown that there are greater variations *within* racial groups than *between* them.

Thus, races are socially and culturally constructed categories that may have little to do with actual biological differences. The validity of race as a biological term has been discredited. There is a final objection to racial classification based on phenotype (Kottak, 1994, pp. 76–85). Also, given what we know about the capacity of normal humans to achieve and function within any culture, it has been concluded that present-day inequalities between so-called racial groups are not consequences of biological inheritance but rather products of historical and contemporary social, economic, educational, and political circumstances (American Anthropological Association, 1999, p. 713).

*Ethnicity.* Ethnicity refers to social groups that distinguish themselves from other groups by a common historical path, behavior norms, and their own group identities. The members of an ethnic group are affiliated with and may share a common language, religion, culture, racial background, or other characteristics that make them identifiable within their own group. American anthropologist George De Vos (1975, p. 9) defined ethnic group as "a self-perceived group of people who hold in common a set of traditions not shared by the others with whom they are in contact. Such traditions typically include 'folk' religious beliefs and practices, language, a sense of historical continuity, and common ancestry or place of origin." For instance, Jewish people, based on their common faith and past history, identify themselves (and are identified by others) as the Jewish ethnic group, even though they may be scattered geographically and inhabit different political institutions. The same can be said of Italians, Irish, Chinese, or Japanese ethnic groups living in various parts of the world, as well as African-Americans in the United States and Hispanic-Americans in many societies in South America. Thus, culture refers to manifested characteristic behavior patterns and value systems, whereas ethnicity refers to a group of people that share a common cultural feature or root culture.

*Society.* Although the term "society" is used in close association with the term "culture," society means something different. A society is a social institution characterized by a particular, visible organizational structure. A society is composed of a collective group of members. It is organized by an administrative structure and is regulated by certain rules or systems. It performs an institutional function, including production, economic, and social functions, and self-protection for the group. Within each society, people may live a certain style of life (referred to as "culture," with a less visible existence). However, the boundaries of society and culture are not the same. Several cultures or subcultures may exist within a single society; whereas a cultural system may be shared by people from several societies. The sizes of societies may vary. They may be small, at a community level, composed of several hundred inhabitants, or large, at a national level, with a population of several billion.

*Social Class.* Social class refers to the social stratification in a society. Sociologists tend to use socioeconomic status (SES) to carry out epidemiological research by dividing the population in a community into different subgroups. Commonly the variables of educational level, occupation, financial income, and ecological area of residence are used for these distinctions. However, some scholars (Wohlfarth & van den Brink, 1998) take the view that "social class" is different from "socioeconomic status," which has different associations with physical or mental health problems. Generally, social class is considered primarily the product of the perceptions and beliefs held by people about the existence of different subgroups in a society, such as upper class, middle working class, and lower class, which are associated with certain lifestyles and values. These classes constitute a long-existing stratification that seldom changes radically. An extreme of such social stratification is the caste system that is still observed in some societies, such as India. A person's caste is inherited and never changes. It is associated with discrimination without negotiation. For example, intermarriage between different castes is forbidden.

In contrast, socioeconomic status is primarily based on practical factors, determined by level of education, nature of occupation, and financial income. Thus, it is changeable (i.e., a person can move up or down the social ladder depending on his social achievement). As pointed out by Vanneman and Cannon (1987), in America, people tend to deny the existence of social class because America is considered a land of opportunity. Instead, racial and ethnic divisions are more prominent. In contrast, European societies, influenced by their feudal pasts, are less concerned with racial or ethnic heterogeneity and are more preoccupied with differences and tensions among social classes.

*Minority.*    Minority refers to a relatively smaller group that is identified against the majority group in the society. The status of a minority may be acquired by a native people after they have been invaded, taken over, or destroyed by militarily, technically, or economically superior outsiders (as illustrated by most of the Native Americans in North America, the Native Hawaiians in Hawaii, and the native aborigines in Australia). It may also derive mainly by racial background and perhaps also be associated with a historical path (as illustrated by African-Americans in the United States, East Indians in the United Kingdom, or Malay-Singaporeans in Singapore), ethnic origin (as exemplified by the Hutterite people in the United States, the Korean-Japanese in Japan, or the Mongolian-Chinese in China), or merely psychological factors associated with historical path (as shown by the untouchable in India or the *burakumin* in Japan) (see Section 11B Minority).

*Subcultures.*    Subcultures refer specifically to parts of the population within a society that hold rather different cultural systems than those of the majority population. The smaller subcultures usually have the same racial background as the majority group, but they choose to have distinctly different sets of beliefs, value systems, and ways of life. They are voluntary in nature and, as such, are different from minorities. However, in daily life, laymen tend to use the terms "minority" and "subculture" indistinguishably.

The best example of a subculture is the old order of Amish in the United States. As described by anthropologist Serena Nanda (1980, p. 42), the Amish number about 60,000 and live mainly as farmers in the states of Pennsylvania, Ohio, and Indiana. Their religious beliefs require a simple life in a church community away from other influences. Their culture emphasizes learning through doing for the welfare of the community rather than individual competition. The Amish reject television, telephones, automobiles, radios, and other modern conveniences. Their distinctive dress and speech and their habit of manual work are symbolic of their cultural separateness, and also contribute to the integration of the community. From a racial perspective, the Amish do belong to the same Caucasian group as the majority of the Anglo-American population, yet they choose to maintain their unique subculture, distinct from the majority culture of the United States as a whole.

### b. Various Experiences with the Cultural System

*Enculturation.*    Enculturation is a professional term used by cultural anthropologists to imply the process through which an individual acquires his culture, mainly early in life. It is a part of learning through introjection and absorption of value systems from his parents, other family members, neighbors, friends, classmates and teachers in school, and the media of the society. The culture incorporated is the cultural system belonging to the person's own society, or the "native" culture. Thus, it is a part of development to become a member of a society—a Russian child is enculturated to become Russian, an Italian child to become Italian (see Section B3 in this chapter: Child Development and Enculturation).

*Acculturation.*    In contrast to enculturation, acculturation refers to the process by which a person acquires a new set of cultural systems, either by contact with a "foreign" culture(s) or through the influence of an "outside" culture. This implies a process that occurs after adulthood, after a person has established his own "native" culture. It is the term usually used to describe how members of a minority acquire the culture of the majority group or how migrants absorb the culture of the host society. However, depending on the size of the minority or the migrants, sometimes the members of the majority or the host society learn and acquire some cultural features of the minority or migrants. This is because bilateral interaction usually occurs when two cultures encounter each other.

*Assimilation.*    Assimilation refers to the process by which a person or a group of people, either voluntarily or by force, incorporates or assumes proportionately significant features of the cultural system of others, often of a majority group or a host society, so that he, or the group, assumes a role as a member of the other culture and, from a cultural point of view, belongs to the nonnative cultural system. In a sense, the term is often used to describe a minority person assimilated into a majority group, colonized people assimilated into the dominant group, or an emigrant assimilated to the host society. Thus, the term has political and social implications.

*Deculturation or Cultural Uprooting.*    Deculturation describes the situation in which a person or a group of people, either by accident or by force, gives up the major features of his or the group's own native cultural system and becomes like a tree that has lost its roots. Therefore, it is also called uprooting. In contrast to the situation of acculturation or assimilation, the original culture is lost or destroyed without proper replacement by the substituted culture, causing a loss of meaning and direction in life.

Deculturation is illustrated in the following instances. Historically, when Hispanic people came to South American or Central American countries, such as Mexico, they purposely destroyed the native people's temples and built churches on the same sites with the materials from the temples they tore down. This was done to destroy the native culture by first abolishing its native faith. Americans who originally came to Hawaii as missionaries or whalers destroyed the Hawaiian monarchy by military force. Under the influence of the Western-ers, native Hawaiians lost their taboos and social etiquette, such as men and women not sitting together for meals, changing the status of men and women. The loss of native culture was accelerated by the remarkable loss of population when they encountered diseases (such as measles and syphilis) brought by the Westerners for which they had no immunological defenses. It was the combined effects of biological, political, and cultural factors that the native Hawaiians encountered that resulted in the loss of their original culture.

*Cultural Change.* The phenomena of enculturation, acculturation, assimila-tion, or deculturation are viewed by people from the standpoint of their cultural systems. In contrast, cultural change or cultural diffusion is viewed from the stand-point of the cultural system itself, indicating how a culture as a whole is con-serving its systems or making changes and how it is reacting to other cultures it encounters. Although culture, by definition, conserves its systems through trans-mission from one generation to another, at the same time, as pointed out by Herskovits (1964, pp. 141–158), culture is seen to constantly and dynamically change to a certain degree, if examined from a historical perspective (see Section 11A, Sociocultural Change, Migration, and Refuge).

*Cultural Diffusion.* Cultural change is stimulated through direct contact with other cultural systems. Cultural elements may diffuse to other cultural units through geographical routes. This spreading of cultural elements is called cultural diffusion. In the past, contact with other cultural systems through traveling, trading, migration, and war has provoked opportunities for cultural influence and diffusion. In the contemporary world, with technological advances in communi-cation, such as movies, TV, and other mass media, culture may be transmitted to people far away, without direct contact. The borrowing of culture from others does not necessarily go in one direction, it can be bilateral. Thus, diffusion of culture can occur on both sides.

### c. Clinical Application of Culture

Although the terms and concepts relating to culture have been examined already, it is necessary to elaborate further on how culture is addressed, ex-pressed, and understood by people in general and by patients and therapists in particular. It is especially important in clinical settings to know how culture is approached.

*Different Levels of Culture Addressed.* In everyday life, culture may be perceived at different levels or in different dimensions. From the standpoint of behavior analysis, it is important to be aware of the different ways of grasping culture. From a clinical point of view, it is important to know to which levels the patient, the patient's family, and the interpreter are referring. Culture can be referred to at the following different levels for description and discussion.

*Ideal cultural behavior* refers to a desirable pattern of life prescribed by a certain group of people. This ideal does not necessarily match the actual behavior observed in the society. Ideal norms are generally selected and described by the members of a society in terms of group well-being, and they are often violated when individual self-interest induces another course of action (Hoebel, 1972).

*Actual cultural behavior* is a norm of behavior actually observed in life. The real culture is what the members of a society do and think in all their activities, in fact (Hoebel, 1972). The gap between the ideal culture and the real culture may be great or small, depending on the society in question.

*Stereotyped cultural behavior* refers to a certain behavior pattern that is described by an outsider to the group, as if it represents the total behavior pattern of the group. The described behavior pattern is usually fragmented, exaggerated, or distorted. It may be merely a product of the outsider's own projection and not reflect the actual culture at all.

*Deviated cultural behavior* refers to behavior patterns that are idiosyncratic and deviate from the pattern of the majority. Such deviated behavior may or may not be pathological.

*How Culture Is Referred To or Identified with.*   Because "culture" is an abstract term, relatively difficult to identify and distinguish, reference is customarily made by laymen to ethnicity or country. For example, Japanese culture refers to the cultural system that is shared by the people of Japan; and Jewish culture, to the cultural system shared by the Jewish ethnic group. However, caution is necessary in such use, as the unit of culture is not necessarily congruent with the unit of ethnicity or country.

A clinician also needs to recognize that a patient has a different level of understanding of his own culture and a different pattern of using culture to explain his behavior. For instance, a patient may have no insight about his own culture, or ignore the dimension of cultural influence and deny the existence of cultural impact on his thought or behavior. This is likely to occur because culture as defined, in contrast to ethnicity, race, or nationality, is a rather abstract concept, difficult for laymen to recognize. No one knows how to describe and identify his own cultural system. Thus, if you were to ask a person, What is your culture? few people would know how to answer you. Even a physician may focus on ethnic background, or religion affiliation, such as Italian-American, Catholic, or Thai people, Buddhism, and so on, at best.

However, some people, or patients, may be fully aware of the influence of ethnicity and/or cultural background and may use them as excuses for problems they have encountered. Many people of minority backgrounds may explain their failures as the result of discrimination by the majority group or claim they are not fairly cared for by their physicians simply because of the color of their skin or their racial heritage. Clinically, it is necessary to assess to what extent these claims represent the actual situation.

### d. Different Perspectives of Examining Culture: Etic and Emic

The terms "etic" and "emic" are derived originally from the linguistic terms "phonetic" (sound of universal language) and "phonemic" (sound of specific language). Etic is used to address things that are considered universal, whereas emic is culture-specific. In the field of cultural research, the etic strategy holds the view that investigation can take place anywhere in the world, as the characteristics to be studied are universal, whereas the emic approach takes the position that the characteristics are indigenous and distinctive and only applicable to certain cultural groups (Draguns, 1989). At another level, the etic approach implies that research is conducted by an outsider; the emic approach, by an insider. Each approach has its own inherent advantages and shortcomings. Observation by an outsider, an etic approach, may be more objective, able to pick up things that may be taken for granted by the culture's own people, but may lose culturally relevant meaning in its interpretation. A study done by an insider, an emic approach, tends to be more subjective, able to explain things from a cultural perspective, but may lose objectivity and be unaware of things that only an outsider would notice.

Applied to the clinical task of assessing psychopathology, defining abnormality, and interpreting dynamics, whether a perspective is etic or emic becomes important, as each can bring about different results. A clinician with an outside cultural background may be advantageous because he has a fresh and objective view but disadvantageous because he may misinterpret the phenomena he observes. In contrast, a clinician with an inside cultural background will have the benefit of knowing how to give culturally meaningful explanations for what has been observed, but may be handicapped by a subjective bias. Thus, the clinician should keep in mind which approach he is undertaking and what possible advantages or handicaps he is facing.

## 2. Marriage and the Family

Marriage between husband and wife is considered a socially approved, formal sexual union that is intended to be permanent. It is the bond on the basis of which a family develops. The family is the basic sociocultural unit. It is a nest for the growth of an individual, a resource for social support, and the institution through which culture is transmitted. Therefore, from a cultural psychiatric point of view, the family is an appropriate arena for examining the cultural aspects of human behavior (Tseng & Hsu, 1991).

The family is a complex institution that can be investigated and understood according to various dimensions, including the individual members of the family, the subsystem of the family, the interaction patterns of the family as a group, the life cycle of the family, and the family as a system.

Although marriage and the formation of families rest on the biological complementarity of male and female and on the biological process of reproduction, both marriage and family are cultural patterns. As such, they differ in form and function in different societies. In order to provide culturally relevant assessment and treatment for families of different cultural backgrounds, it is essential to understand the cultural aspects of marriage and family systems and functions.

### a. Cultural Variations of Marriage

*Marriage Forms.*    Marriage forms concern the number of spouses in a marriage. *Monogamy* permits a person to have only one spouse at any given time, while *polygamy* permits more than one spouse in the marriage. If a man has several wives, it is called *polygyny*, and if a woman is married to more than one man, it is known as *polyandry*.

In societies where monogamy is preferred and marriage is considered closely and exclusively tied to sex and emotion, it is hard for people to understand how polygamous marriage can exist without conflict and jealousy among wives. In fact, much evidence indicates that when a man has many wives, problems usually occur among them. However, as explained by anthropologist Nanda (1980), sexual jealousy among wives might not be a great problem in societies that do not idealize romantic love and exclusive sexual rights in marriage.

Polyandry is basically different in nature from polygamy. Among the Tibetans, the Todas, and other tribes in India, where the practice of polyandry is common, several brothers usually marry the same woman (Hoebel, 1972). In societies where land and property are scarce, the division of assets among siblings can be avoided if brothers form a family by marrying a common wife. Thus, polyandry is frequently practiced as a way of coping with an economic situation (Levine and Sangree, 1980). It is not brought about by a superwoman who wants many husbands, as might be speculated.

*Choice of Mates.*    Every society has certain rules pertaining to the choice of a candidate for marriage. *Exogamy* is when marriage partners must be chosen from outside one's own kin group or community. In contrast, *endogamy* is when a person is obligated to marry within his or her own culturally defined group. An example of caste-elated endogamy is the social rule in India that a person must marry within his or her caste to avoid becoming "polluted" through marriage to someone outside of it.

Associated with the rule of marital choice is the process by which the marital partner is chosen. *Arranged marriage* refers to marriages in which the partners are selected primarily by someone other than the partners themselves, usually by their parents or other kin. In contrast, a marriage partner may be chosen by *self-selection* or through free love, the method preferred by young members of most contemporary societies. The main concerns in arranging a marriage are the compatibility of the family backgrounds and of the prospective partners, as well as the partners' physical condition, health, moral character, working patterns, and ability to produce the next generation (see Fig. 4). In free love, affection and love are the major concerns, even though other factors, such as the character and personal background of the partner, may be taken into consideration.

*Postmarital Residence.*    Another recognized parameter is the choice of residence after marriage. When the married couple lives with or near the husband's parents, it is called *patrilocal* residence. When the married couple lives with or near the wife's parents, it is called *matrilocal* residence. If the married couple lives with or near the parents of only one side, either the wife's parents or the husband's, it is called *bilocal* residence. If the newly married couple lives apart from the relatives of both spouses, choosing a new place of their own, it is described as *neolocal* residence.

FIGURE 4    Arranged marriage between children in a Nepalese family. A girl in childhood is arranged to marry a boy-husband, living with and serving her mother-in-law.

The significance of postmarital choice of residence is obvious, as it affects the pattern of kinship relations as well as the power distribution and respective roles of the spouses. Why do societies practice different patterns of residence? The prime determinants of residence are ecological circumstances (Haviland, 1978). If the man's role in subsistence is predominant, patrilocal residence is the likely result. Matrilocal residence is a likely result if ecological circumstances make the role of the woman predominant in subsistence, as is found most often in horticultural societies, where political complexity is relatively undeveloped and cooperation among women is important. Bilocal residence is particularly well-suited to situations in which resources are limited and the cooperation of more people is needed. Because one can join either the bride's or the groom's family, family membership is flexible, and one can go where the resources look best. Neolocal residence occurs where the independence of the nuclear family is emphasized. Because most economic activity occurs outside the family in modern, industrialized societies, and it is important for people to be able to move to where jobs can be found, neolocal residence is the pattern best suited to this type of society.

### b. Cultural Variations of Family Systems

*Kinship System and Descent Group.*   A kinship system is a system of terms used to classify different kin. It refers to the totality of relationships based on blood and marriage that links individuals through a web of rights and obligations, and the kinds of groups formed in a society on the basis of kinship. Societies differ in the categories of relatives they recognize and the principles by which kin are classified. Generation, relative age, gender, and lineality versus collaterality are some of the categories that are usually distinguished.

In most societies, there is a rule of descent that defines how individuals are affiliated with sets of kin. *Patrilineal* descent affiliates an individual with kinsmen of both sexes through the males. In each generation, children belong to the kin group of the father and carry the father's family name, and lineage is traced through the grandfather, father, son, and grandson. *Matrilineal* descent affiliates an individual with kinsmen only through the females; thus, children belong to the mother's kin group, and lineage is traced through the grandmother, mother, daughter, and granddaughter. *Ambilineal* descent affiliates an individual with kinsmen through either males or females so that some children belong to the kin group of the father and others to the kin group of the mother. Consequently, the descent groups show both female and male genealogical links. According to anthropologists (Hoebel, 1972), patrilineal organization is the most frequent type of descent system, constituting about 45 percent of all societies in the world. Matrilineal organization comprises only about 14 percent.

Although societies with matrilineal descent seem in many respects like mirror images of their patrilineal counterparts, they differ in one important way, namely,

FIGURE 5   Micronesian family following the matrilineal system. Title is transmitted from mother to daughter, and then to granddaughter, but the power is exercised by a woman's husband and her brothers.

who exercises authority. In patrineal systems, where the line of descent passes through the males, it is also the males who exercise authority in the kin groups. Consequently, the lines of descent and of authority converge. In a matrilineal system, however, the line of descent passes through females, but females rarely exercise authority in their kin groups. A female usually allows her husband and her brothers to exercise the power. Thus, unlike the patrilineal system, the lines of authority and descent do not converge (see Fig. 5).

*Household and Family Structure.*   Household refers to all the persons who live in one house. Usually it is implied that they are related either by marriage or blood and share the work, financial responsibilities, and food. Several terms address various forms of households. The *nuclear family* is composed of the basic family members: parents and their (unmarried) children. This is the most frequently observed form of household in most industrialized societies. If a household is composed of a nuclear family plus the parent (or parents) of either the husband or wife, it is called a *stem family*. If, in addition to the stem family, a spouse's unmarried siblings are living with them, it is referred to as a *joint family*. If the married siblings (and their children, if any) are living in the same household (usually with the presence of their parent or parents), it is recognized as an *extended family* (see Figs. 6 and 7).

FIGURE 6    Traditional and contemporary Chinese families. (a) An idealized extended family with members of three generations celebrating a mid-fall festival in the family courtyard, with the children considered their parents' treasures. (b) A model family taking a picture in front of a painting on the street that advocates the one-child-per-couple family policy to avoid a potential population explosion.

*One-parent families*, particularly female-headed households, are found to be widespread in various cultures. Reviewing this type of family household cross-culturally, Bilge and Kaufman (1983) regarded the one-parent family as neither pathological nor inferior. They concluded that whether or not the single-parent

FIGURE 7  Japanese families in a village and in the city. (a) A wife serving food for three generations in a traditional village family. (b) A contemporary nuclear family in the city enjoying dinner together.

household becomes a personal or social disaster depends upon the availability of sufficient material resources and supportive social networks, as well as culturally structured attitudes toward such a household. However, in most developed societies, such as the United States, there are not adequate institutionalized support systems for children of single-parent families, and the social conditions of such families are generally not as good as those of two-parent families. This situation is also reported in European societies, such as Denmark (Koch-Nielsen, 1980) and France (Lefaucheur, 1980).

Along with an increase in divorce and remarriage, the number of *stepfamilies* is rising remarkably in Western societies. As Visher and Visher (1982) observe, stepfamilies differ structurally from biological families in several ways: all step-family members have experienced important losses, all members come with past family histories, parent-child bonds predate the new couple relationship, there is a biological parent elsewhere (either living or deceased), children often are members of two households, and no legal relationship exists between stepparent and stepchild. Thus, from a developmental point of view, step-families need to work on the reintegration of the family.

*Primary Axis.*    From the perspective of loyalty and affection bonds, a partic-ular dyad may be molded culturally as the prominent and recognizable axis in some family systems. According to psychological anthropologist F. L. K. Hsu (1972), the axis may be built on husband-wife (the majority of people of European origin), father-son (the majority of Asian people), mother-son (the majority of people in India and possibly the Muslim groups), brother-brother (the majority of people of Africans south of the Sahara), or brother-sister (the people in Micronesia) dyads. The presence of any particular primary axis can be recognized only when conflict and competition occur between different dyads in a family. Based on the concept of a primary axis, Hsu (1972) hypothesized that the different emphases of the primary dyad result in different family systems, which have specific, varied influences on the individuals reared in them. Consequently, many characteristic thought and behavior patterns shown by family members can be attributed to the existence of different primary bonds within a family system (see Fig. 8).

## 3. Child Development and Enculturation

### a. Cross-Cultural Study of Child Development

Numerous approaches have been taken by anthropologists and behavioral scien-tists concerning child development and the examination of child development from a cross-cultural perspective. These approaches can be divided into field observational studies, child-rearing literature review, examination of fantasies for and about children (in fairy tales and other children's stories), analysis of chil-dren's imaginative productions, interviews with parents and children, and clinical studies (Mead & Wolfenstein, 1955).

Observational study emphasizes the importance of direct observation by the researcher (Whiting & Child, 1953). In order to answer the academic question,

FIGURE 8    A Korean family showing respect for parental authority. Wearing traditional dress, grandchildren bow to their grandparents on new year's day.

Are children brought up in societies with different customs, beliefs, and values radically different from each other? a well-planned field observation was conducted by a team of investigators through Children of Six-Culture Study (Whiting & Whiting, 1975). It studied children of six cultures from selected sites at Taira (Okinawa), Tarong (the Philippines), Khalapur (India), Nyansongo (Kenya), Juxtlahuuaca (Oaxaca), and Orchard Town in New England (United States). This study supports the view that culture has a considerable effect on the social interaction patterns manifested by children of school age.

To investigate how early in the lives of infants, and in what ways, cultural differences become manifest in behavior, an American cultural anthropologist, William Caudill, undertook a cross-cultural investigation of maternal care and infant behavior in Japan and America (Caudill & Weinstein, 1969). The results revealed that there are no significant differences in the amount of time awake, sucking on the breast or a bottle, or intake of food. However, the differences lay in the styles in which the infants and mothers behaved in the two cultures. The American mothers seemed to take more lively and stimulating approaches to their babies, positioning the infant's body and looking at and chatting with the infant more. The Japanese mothers, in contrast, were present more with the baby, in general, and seemed to have more soothing and quieting approaches, as indicated by greater lulling and more carrying in the arms and rocking. According to their observations, the Japanese babies seemed passive and usually lay quietly, with occasional unhappy vocalizations, while the mothers tried to sooth and quiet them, communicating with them physically rather than verbally. However, the

American infants were more active, happily vocal, and explored their environments more, while their mothers did more looking at and chatting with their babies. They seemed to stimulate their babies to activity and vocal response. Caudill explained that such patterns of mother–infant interaction correlated with cultural patterns.

Recently, a new subject has gained considerable attention and provoked investigation among scholars in the field of child development: child temperament. It has been discovered that, even in infancy, a baby demonstrates a certain temperament. For instance, by subjectively comparing the behavior of Chinese-American and Caucasian-American newborns in New York (Freedman & Freedman, 1969), it was found that, although newborn infants of both racial backgrounds had similar levels of central nervous system development at the time of their observation, the Chinese-American infants, in contrast to the Caucasian-American infants, were found to be calm, stable, without too much variation in their responses. Recently, an objective method has been developed by Kagan and Snidman (1991) to investigate infants at the age of four months: a standardized stimulation of language, movement objects, smell, sound, and sudden noise is given according to a specific protocol, and the responses made by the infants are recorded for study. Based on this method, studies have been conducted of infants in Boston (United States), Doublin (Ireland), and Beijing (China). According to Wang, Shen, and Chang (1997), the Chinese baby, in contrast to the American baby or the Irish baby, made fewer movement responses, smiled with less vocalization, and cried less in response to external stimulation during the investigation. This supports the previous reports on subjective observations.

### b. Cultural Variations of Child Development

Based on their fieldwork around the world, many cultural anthropologists have pointed out that existing developmental theories based on people in central Europe and America are biased, and therefore limited from a cultural perspective, and need revision and expansion (Jacobs, 1964, pp. 133–158; Shrier, Hsu, & Yang, 1996). These developmental theories will be elaborated here from a cross-cultural perspective.

*Psychosexual Development.*  The developmental theory originally proposed by Sigmund Freud focused on the psychosexual aspects of individual development. Because it concerns biological instinct, it is regarded as applicable universally. However, owing to the individual's unique developmental course, it is reasonable to speculate that the drive that emerges in each developmental stage may be subject to variations. In particular, scholars have pointed out that the intensity of the triangular parent–child relationship conflict that occurs at the phallic stage, called the Oedipus complex, will depend on the sexual attitudes that exist in the environment. It also will be subject to variations based on the family system and structure within the society.

Anthropologist B. Malinowski (1927), based on his field study of the Trobriand Islands in Melanesia near Australia, reported that in a matrilineal society, where the family lineage is traced from mother to daughter (rather than from father to son as in a patrilineal system), the relationship between the son and the mother's brother (maternal uncle) is more intense than between the son and his own biological father. Also in the matrilineal family system, the bond between brother and sister is an important one. Malinowski reported that in such a society, a boy-child tends to have dream wishes of the death of his brother, his potential rival subject. Thus, based on the family system, the persons involved in the triangular relationship will vary. Based on cross-cultural knowledge, Chinese-American anthropologist Hsu (1972) proposed different primary bonds or dyads within different families, such as the husband-wife dyad in European-American families, the father-son dyad in Asian families, the mother-son dyad in Hindu families, and the brother-sister dyad in matrilineal societies (such as those in Micronesia). Based on the emphasis of different dyads existing within different families, Hsu suggested that different personality patterns may be observed. As an extension of this, it may be speculated that the nature of the triangular conflict may be subject to variation. Echoing this, cultural psychiatrists Abel and Metraux (1974) pointed out that the social structure also will influence the nature of the Oedipus complex.

Furthermore, the cultural impact on the Oedipus complex has been discussed in terms of the solution pattern that may be proposed for it. For instance, the Chinese solution to the conflict, as reflected in opera and fairy tales, sometimes has the son being killed by the father (rather than the father being killed by the son, as in the Western Oedipus story), an appropriate solution for the parent-child triangular conflict in a society that emphasizes parental respect and authority (Tseng & Hsu, 1972). In India, the son was killed by his father as well as reflected in the story of Ganesha complex (Kakar & Ross, 1987). In Japan, the wish for the son to kill his mother (rather than father) was described as the Adjase complex by Japanese psychiatrist Keigo Okonogi (1978). Thus, centering around the parent-child triangular complex, there exist various patterns of conflict and possible solutions described cross-culturally. The Greek model of the Oedipus complex and its solution is but one of them. A broader view is necessary from cross-cultural perspectives.

*Psychosocial Development.*    The psychosocial development theory developed by Erik H. Erikson (1963) deserves cultural adjustment as well. Erikson, as an analyst and child psychiatrist, proposed a theory based on his fieldwork with two Native American tribes, in addition to his clinical experiences with Caucasian child patients. Thus, from a cross-cultural perspective, there are no sufficient and divergent cultural samples, and the theory is subject to expansion and improvement, a need that is even recognized by Erikson himself. Based on the clinical experiences of cultural psychiatrists from divergent cultural backgrounds, it has been realized that the major theme emphasized in each stage of development warrants cross-cultural expansion or revision, and the pace of development from stage to stage needs cross-cultural adjustment and modification.

Concerning the major theme in each stage, there are many suggestions for expansion and revision in this area. Regarding the oral stage, instead of establishing *basic trust,* as described by Erickson, the need for obtaining a sense of *security* is more important for children who are living in societies where people suffer from a lack of adequate basic living conditions and struggle for daily survival. This is the current situation in many societies in Africa, India, and some parts of Asia, as well as for aboriginal people in Australia.

Regarding the muscular-anal stage, it has been pointed out that for many Asian children, a sense of *dependence* and *indulgence* is permitted, while the emphasis on *autonomy* is rather delayed in association with the prolongation of the oral stage. For the majority of Chinese living in rural-agricultural settings, anal discipline through toilet training is less strict, whereas there is greater stress on behavior control through *shame* (Tseng & Hsu, 1969/1970).

During the locomotor-genital stage, *initiative* is not necessarily stressed in many cultures. Instead, *collaterality,* (i.e., how to live with others harmoniously and interdependently, and not "stick out" from others in the group) is the ethos that receives more emphasis. This is exemplified by people living in small island societies with limited resources, such as Micronesia, where mutual dependency and collaterality are vital.

At the stage of latency, *industry* is valued in many societies. However, in addition, in many societies, particularly agricultural or so-called underdeveloped societies, *responsibility* is stressed. For instance, the emphasis is not so much on studying at school, working in a factory (as a junior laborer), or joining the adults working diligently in the field. Rather, the emphasis is on taking full responsibility, almost as an adult substitute, for performing many important tasks, such as taking care of younger siblings, tending the cows or sheep (important sources of food for the family), or even learning to cook for the family. In other words, the youngsters are expected to learn to take responsibility in association with their rapid entry into adult life and to take part in production.

In the stage of puberty and adolescence, the degree of emphasis on gender identity varies cross-culturally. For instance, David D. Glimore (1990) conducted a survey of ideas about manhood in various cultures. He found that in many societies there is an *exaggeration* of masculinity for men, and a good many take this emphasis to the extreme. It was speculated that the emphasis on gender identity (VIZ., emphasis on masculinity), in addition to occurring as a defense against close mother-son ties, may arise as the result of socioeconomic conditions. Thus, the harsher the environment and the scarcer the resources, the more manhood is stressed as an inspiration and a goal. In contrast, in many societies that are conservative in sexual matters, there is a delay and *discouragement* of gender identity among youngsters. Any appearance, behavior, or activities that provoke man-woman relations are greatly inhibited until later. For instance, students are required to wear uniforms at school (with no sexually exhibiting dressing allowed) and any individual man-woman interaction (such as social dating between individual boys and girls) is strongly prohibited.

As an extension of this, during the stage of young adulthood, *intimacy* between man and woman and enjoyment in social life are not greatly stressed in many societies. Particularly in societies that still practice arranged marriages, intimacy between couples is not expected until later in their married lives, sometimes after middle age. Instead, *accountability* in work (economic achievement, domestic work, raising children, etc.) are considered the primary issues for young adults. Also, social isolation is not feared if the society is characterized by strong social bonds.

Generally speaking, *generativity* is important throughout adulthood, and striving for progress in life is critical in many societies, particularly achievement-oriented cultures, so that no stagnation results. However, in many cultures, an *obligation* to work, to support one's family, and to raise children are the basic tasks stressed for adults. Later, in many cultures, instead of aged people being concerned with *ego integrity* and avoiding despair, old age is considered the stage in which a person experiences a sense of *belonging* to family and being cared by his or her children. *Comfort* in life is the essential issue in this final stage of life.

*The Pace of Development from Stage to Stage.*    It is not merely the major theme in each stage of development, but also the pace from stage to stage that is considered from a cross-cultural point of view. For instance, how long a child is permitted to stay in the oral stage may be determined by child-rearing patterns, including the ways in which the infant is viewed and cared for.

In contrast to the contemporary American way of raising children, with a great emphasis on growing up fast, in general, many other societies take a more laid-back attitude toward their babies. Small children are allowed to stay babies, indulged by their parents, grandparents, and siblings, and there is no pressure for them to move into the next stage of development.

However, the pace after that can change rather abruptly. Among the Chinese, it has been pointed out that diligence is stressed for youngsters in the latency period, with the inculcation of the desire to achieve. This is a drastic shift in developmental requirements from earlier stages of indulgence. However, drastic psychological turmoil is not often noticed. This might be because the stage of puberty and adolescence is relatively prolonged and the entry into young adulthood is delayed (Bond, 1991). Related to this, intense relations and bonds with same-sex peers are permitted and maintained during latency, while heterosexual relations are suppressed as long as possible (Tseng, 1994).

Concerning the adolescent stage, Margaret Mead's study of adolescent turmoil outside of Euro-American societies was a landmark investigation. Based on her anthropological fieldwork in Samoa in the South Pacific, Mead (1928) claimed that the psychosocial lives of adolescents there (at the time) were not as tumultuous as those observed in many Western societies, exemplified by contemporary American society. According to her, youngsters in Samoa usually went through a relatively calm transition from childhood to adulthood, without drastic changes in the adolescent period.

Thus, there is a need to consider the cross-cultural adjustment and revision of psychosexual development that were originally proposed by Erikson. The basic concept of development by stages is universally applicable; however, the main themes emphasized in each stage and the pace of the transition from stage to stage are certainly subject to cross-cultural revision, as illustrated by Figure 9.

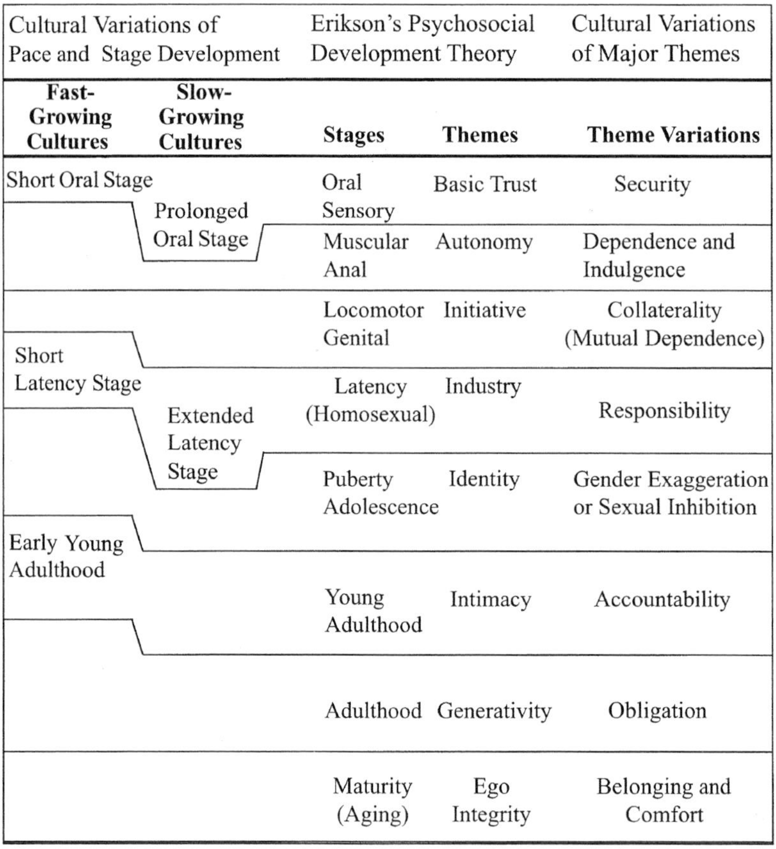

| Cultural Variations of Pace and Stage Development | | Erikson's Psychosocial Development Theory | | Cultural Variations of Major Themes |
|---|---|---|---|---|
| **Fast-Growing Cultures** | **Slow-Growing Cultures** | **Stages** | **Themes** | **Theme Variations** |
| Short Oral Stage | | Oral Sensory | Basic Trust | Security |
| | Prolonged Oral Stage | Muscular Anal | Autonomy | Dependence and Indulgence |
| Short Latency Stage | | Locomotor Genital | Initiative | Collaterality (Mutual Dependence) |
| | Extended Latency Stage | Latency (Homosexual) | Industry | Responsibility |
| | | Puberty Adolescence | Identity | Gender Exaggeration or Sexual Inhibition |
| Early Young Adulthood | | Young Adulthood | Intimacy | Accountability |
| | | Adulthood | Generativity | Obligation |
| | | Maturity (Aging) | Ego Integrity | Belonging and Comfort |

FIGURE 9  Cultural modifications of personality development theory—variations on stages and themes of development.

In addition to the psychosexual and psychosocial developmental theories elaborated so far, there is an increasing awareness among cross-cultural psychologists that the cognitive development theory proposed by Piaget needs sociocultural adjustment as well, at least concerning the rhythms of the stages of development (Segall et al., 1990, pp. 143–159). Concerning ego development, Charles Pinderhughes (1974) offered hypotheses that culture will shape ego attitude, emotional attachments, and cognitive styles in the process of development. He stressed that, although a person, as a human being, will follow certain universal rules of individual development, the pattern of ego development, in terms of the themes emphasized and the process followed, will vary according to the sociocultural environment.

### c. Enculturation

"Enculturation" is a professional term used by anthropologists to refer to the process through which an individual, starting from early childhood, acquires a cultural system through his environment, particularly from his parents, family, neighbors, school, and society at large. The process occurs as an unconscious introjection or as a conscious learning of ways of thinking, attitudes toward things, values, and belief systems. Thus, it is a part of psychological development and growth; however, such a process of enculturation varies from culture to culture in terms of the total cultural system incorporated and integrated.

The process of enculturation is considered to take place as soon as an infant starts to incorporate stimulation from outside. However, the process of enculturation becomes active when a child reaches the age of 4 or 5 and has developed sufficient cognitive ability to think and perceive things differently. This coincides with the stage of socialization associated with the experience of schooling when a child is expected to learn more social matters, including etiquette, rules, and views about the community or society at large. It is also the stage when the parents and schoolteachers actively impart their views and attitudes on the youngster. However, the process of enculturation takes a passive form. It is around the adolescent stage, when the youngster is equipped with the cognitive ability to make subjective criticisms and have preferences about things happening around him, that he or she begins the process of enculturation more or less selectively and actively. (See Fig. 10.)

Clinically, problems of enculturation are observed when a child is faced with incorporating drastically different, or even contradictory, sets of value systems and confusion results. Such confusion occurs when the family provides contradictory value systems, or the surrounding society changes rapidly, so that the value system fluctuates and changes dramatically, making it difficult for the child to follow and integrate it.

FIGURE 10    Encultured behavior patterns. (a) Maori boys in New Zealand practice sticking out their tongues and making sounds with popeyed looks in the belief that such gestures will threaten their enemies and chase away evil. (b) Maori adult males demonstrate the tongue-protruding gesture in the performance of a war dance. (c) These behaviors are portrayed in the image of a protective god, illustrating that culturally patterned behavior is not only practiced during childhood and performed in adulthood but projected into a cultural product. [From *Anthropology: The Study of Man*, by E. A. Hoebel. McGraw-Hill, 1972. Courtesy of the American Museum of Natural History Library.]

## 4. Personality and Ethnic Identity

### a. Culture and Personality

Although anthropologists have long been interested in behavior patterns manifested in various cultural settings, the subject of "culture and personality" has been actively discussed among behavior scientists and psychiatrists since the 1920s. Greatly influenced by psychoanalytic theory, particularly the notion that early childhood experience, through patterns of child rearing by primary caretakers, will shape the mode of behavior in adulthood, many cultural anthropologists engaged in field research. The classic study of culture and personality reached its peak in the 1950s and then gradually faded (for details, see Tseng, 2001, Chapter 5: Personality and Depth Psychology, pp. 79–80).

Ethnic character refers to a common personality configuration that is manifested by the majority of members of an ethnic group and distinguishes them from other ethnic group members. It is based on the notion that every culture has a typical personality that is distinctive and characteristic of that culture and is produced or conditioned by some aspect of the culture. Historically, three theoretical concepts have been proposed regarding ethnic character.

*Ideal Personality or Configurational Personality.*    According to Ruth Benedict (1934), each society has a more or less clear idea of what constitutes the "good man" and "good woman," the kind of person an individual ought to be. Through rewards and punishment, a society is directed toward molding all members in the image of the ideal. Thus, the ideological contours of a culture are impressed upon individuals in terms of an ideal personality type. Consequently, the personalities of the majority in any society are largely reflections of the configurational personality presented by that society's culture.

*Basic Personality Structure.*    Abram Kardiner, a psychoanalyst by training, proposed in 1945 that certain culturally established techniques of child rearing (primary institutional) shape basic attitudes toward life that exist throughout the life of the individual. This nuclear constellation of attitudes and behavior formed by culturally standardized patterns of child rearing in any society is the basic personality structure that is characteristic of that society. The nuclear constellations derived from primary institutions are subsequently reflected in the development of secondary institutions, such as art, folklore, mythology, religion, and social organization. Therefore, an interrelation exists between culture and personality.

*Model Personality Structure.*    Anthropologist Cora DuBois (1944) proposed the concept of the model personality. A wide range of variations of personalities exists within any given society. However, if the range is measured on a common baseline, data will show central tendencies that constitute the model personality for any particular culture. Thus, model personality is based on statistical constructs. Data are most easily gathered by giving psychological tests.

As pointed out by Wallace (1970, p. 153), in terms of basic personality, there was difficulty dealing with questions of frequency, whereas with model personality, there was difficulty dealing with questions of structure and patterns. Clearly, there is no single view of ethnic character that can satisfy both theoretical perspectives and practical applications. Yet, each theory contributes to the understanding of culture and personality in its own way (for details, see Tseng, 2001, Chapter 5: Personality and Depth Psychology, pp. 81–82).

### b. Some National Characters Studied

Instead of studying culture and personality in small, undeveloped societies, as earlier investigators did, after the 1950s, scholars were interested in culture and personality in large, modernized nations. Their efforts were called national character studies. Although it is difficult to generalize about personality in large societies composed of numerous ethnic groups, social classes, or subcultures, these attempts to study character patterns in certain nations deserve to be mentioned.

*American Personality.*    In the early 1940s, when America was about to become involved in World War II in Europe, Margaret Mead examined American culture (Caucasian-Americans) in contrast to European culture, from which these Americans originally came. In her book, *And Keep Your Powder Dry* (Mead, 1942, pp. 193–194), she summarized her view that American people have a certain character, which originated in Europe, but developed in the New World and took a shape all its own. It is a character geared toward success and movement in which aggressiveness is uncertain and undefined and which measures its successes and failures only against near contemporaries and engages in various quantitative devices for reducing every contemporary to its own structure; which sees success as the reward of virtue and failure as the stigma for not being good enough; and which is uninterested in the past, except when ancestry can be used to make points against other people in the game of success; which is oriented toward an unknown future and is ambivalent toward other cultures, which are regarded with a sense of inferiority as more coherent than our own and with a sense of superiority because newcomers in America display the strongest mark of other cultural membership in the form of foreignness.

Recently, after reviewing past observations and surveys regarding the American national character, Alex Inkeles, in his book, *National Character* (1997), summarized the continuity and change of the American national character as reflected in the beliefs, attitudes, and behavior of Americans. According to Inkeles (1997, pp. 167–179), continuity is noticed in relation to several issues. This includes: self-reliance, autonomy, and independence; communal action, voluntarism, and cooperation with neighbors; trust in interpersonal relations; innovations and openness to new experiences; antiauthoritarianism; and equality. Inkeles (1997, pp. 180–185) also described the recent change in American beliefs and attitudes in several areas, namely: an increasing tolerance of diversity; a decreasing of the ethic of hard work, temperance, and frugality; and an erosion of political confidence.

*Japanese Personality.*    During and after World War II, in order to understand America's Japanese enemy, cultural anthropologist Ruth Benedict was ordered to lead a team to study the Japanese and Japanese culture. As it was not possible to carry out fieldwork in Japan during wartime, Benedict's study relied on literature, history, travelers' tales, movies, art, and expatriate interviews. Through this "study at a distance" and the model personality concept, Benedict completed her study of Japanese behavior. As reflected in the title of her book, *The Chrysanthemum and the Sword* (1946), Benedict described contradictory features of Japanese psychology and behavior patterns (1946, p. 2). That is, the Japanese are, to the highest degree, both aggressive and unaggressive, militaristic and aesthetic, insolent and polite, rigid and adaptable, submissive and resentful of being pushed around, loyal and treacherous, brave and timid, and conservative and hospitable to new ways.

Takeo Doi is an analytical psychiatrist in Japan who described the Japanese term *amae* as one of the key concepts in understanding Japanese personality structure (1962, 1973). Doi reported that, in his clinical experience of treating a bilingual Japanese-English woman, the patient used the Japanese word *amaeru* while she was in the middle of complaining in English about her son not intimately relating to her as a child. From such a trivial observation of language discrepancy between Japanese and English, Doi learned that *amaeru* is a unique Japanese word reflecting a special interpersonal relationship for the Japanese. *Amae* (adjective) and *amaeru* (verb) literally mean "sweet," but also imply "indulgence" or "dependence." A child can be indulged and dependent on (*amaeru*) his parent, or indulgent parents may treat their child sweetly (*amaeru*). Such benevolent dependence continues into adult relationships with others, with an expectation of consideration and thoughtfulness between people and lifelong interdependency. If the need of *amae* is not satisfied, then a person, like an unhappy child, can become *hinekureru* (bitter in expressing resentfulness). Doi's work illustrated that cultural behavior or psychology can be reflected in language, and vice versa. Also, most importantly, it indicates the view that interdependency is not necessarily negative, as it is seen in Western society, but is benevolent and positive in many non-Western societies.

*Russian Personality.*  Gorer and Rickman (1949) pointed out that there are marked differences in character between the Russian elite and the masses. After reviewing child-rearing patterns among rural farmers, Gorer proposed the swaddling hypothesis. He reported that rural farmers, in order to allow the mothers to work in the field at a distance, swaddled their young babies in long strips of material, holding their legs straight and their arms down by their sides. The practice was based on the idea that the baby was potentially so strong that if it were not swaddled, it would risk destroying itself or doing itself irreparable harm. Gorer postulated that such restriction on muscular movement in early childhood may contribute to the Russian peasants' character, which is able to endure physical suffering with great stoicism and is indifferent to the physical suffering of others. The peasants also tend to oscillate between unconscious fears of isolation and loneliness and an absence of feelings of individuality, so that the self is, as it were, merged with its peers in a "soul collective." The mass of the population is oppressed (by administrative authority), with diffuse feelings of guilt and hostility, but shows very little anxiety. It tends to oscillate suddenly and unpredictably from one attitude to its contrary, especially from violence to gentleness, from excessive activity to passivity, and from orgiastic indulgence to ascetic abstemiousness (p. 189).

A multidisciplinary group from Columbia University and the American Museum of Natural History Studies had utilized literary, historical, and other published materials, personal documents, folklore, films and photographs, and some interviews with individuals who had been away from the USSR to study the national character of Great Russians. Clyde Kluckhohn (1955) summarized what seemed the most interesting generalizations in several matters. Her findings appeared in her book, *Culture and Behavior* (1962, pp. 214–215). She pointed out that there is a sizable gap between the modal personality type advocated by the Soviet leadership and most characteristics of Great Russians in general. The people are warmly human, tremendously dependent on secure social affiliations, labile, nonrational, strong but undisciplined, and needing to submit to authority. The counteractive Bolshevik ideal demanded stern, ascetic, vigilant, incorruptible, and obedient personalities who would not be deflected from the aims of the Party and the state by family or personal ties and affections. The attitude of the people remains, on the whole, that strong authority is both hateful and essential.

*Chinese Personality.*    In order to study the character traits of the Chinese, a research psychologist from the Chinese Academy of Science in China, Song Weizhen (1985), led a national team in administering the MMPI (Minnesota Multiphasic Personality Inventory) to nearly two thousand Han nationals from six major areas of China. The results indicated that, in contrast to data reported for American subjects, the mean profiles of normal Chinese subjects had a higher normal range for scales of D (depression) and Sc (schizophrenia). This was true for both male and female subjects. Based on these test results, Song interpreted that Chinese, in contrast to Americans, are emotionally more reserved, introverted, fond of tranquility, overly considerate, socially overcautious, and habitually self-restrained.

Concerning cross-cultural validity, a group of Chinese psychologist developed the Chinese Personality Assessment Inventory (CPAI) (Cheung et al., 1996) to measure the personality of the Chinese. It aims for cultural relevancy to capture the important dimensions of the Chinese personality. In addition to including culturally universal constructs, personality characteristics that were considered to be culturally specific to the Chinese culture were identified. Scales were developed for personality constructs that are deemed to be of specific interest to the Chinese culture, such as Harmony, *Ren Qing* (interpersonal favor), Face, Thrift versus Extravagance, Graciousness versus Meanness, Veraciousness versus Slickness, *Ah*-Q Mentality (passive-rationalization defensiveness), Family Orientation, and Somatization. It is explained that the characteristics associated with these personality scales reflect a strong Chinese orientation toward interdependence, instrumental relationship, avoidance of conflict, and adherence to tradition and norms.

### c. Ethnic Identity

*Ethnic Identity Formation.*   Ethnic identity refers to the psychological way in which a person identifies his own ethnic background and how he feels about his own ethnicity. In contrast to an individual or personal identity, ethnic identity is one kind of group identity. American anthropologists De Vos and Romanucci-Ross (1975) clarified ethnic identity by saying that: "It is essentially subjective, a sense of social belonging and ultimate loyalty; is a form of role attribution, both internal and external" (p. 3). Further, they pointed out that "ethnic identity is in essence a past-oriented form of identity, embedded in the cultural heritage of the individual or group" (p. 363). From a psychological perspective, it needs to be pointed out that prejudice plays a big part in how one self-identifies ethnically, as well as in terms of race, nationality, social class, or religious group.

In general, a person has to deal with identities on various levels. These include "personal identity," "family identity," and other "group identities," relating to community, school, occupation, religion, society, or nation. Ethnic identity is one kind of group identity dealing with the psychological function of identification at the "ethnic" level.

Theoretically, the process of ethnic identification and/or racial identity starts to take place at an early age, when cognitive function becomes such that a child is able to perceive, understand, and identify the differences of ethnicity or race that are expressed by the external characteristics of behavior or appearance. Aboud (1987) reported that, based on external appearance, racial differences are recognized by children at the ages of 3 and 4, whereas cognitively conceptualized ethnic differences are not recognized until age 7.

The formation and function of group identity is subject to numerous reality factors, and the process tends to fluctuate. Although group identity formation is an intrapsychic phenomena, it depend greatly on external stimuli. When other distinguishable groups and stimulation for the need to distinguish the differences exist, the sense of group identity is provoked. In other words, as indicated by Devereux (1975), "ethnic identity develops only after an ethnic group recognizes the existence of others who do not belong to the group." For instance, a group of schoolmates will obtain a sense of their "school identity" when their school is in competition with other schools in sports or other activities. The process of identifying with his own school with a sense of loyalty will be stimulated. A citizen will increase his "national identity" and demonstrate loyalty toward his own country when it is in open conflict (such as war) with other countries. If the external stimulation is rather long-standing, such as discrimination against an underprivileged minority, the stimulation for identity formation will become rather continuous. If there has been a long history of conflict and hostile relations between different groups, exemplified with the situation for the Irish Protestants and Irish Catholics in Northern Ireland, the antagonism and conflict continues for centuries. Ethnic identity is also strongly influenced by political factors. Based on the circumstance, ethnic identity may change over time. This is well illustrated in the situation in Russia, where people identified with the former Soviets for many decades, and the country changed overnight to Russia.

Depending on the situation, ethnic or racial identity can be changed over the time. This is well illustrated by the situation of African-Americans in the United States. Numerous studies have reported that African-American children have had a more positive image of themselves as African-Americans recently than they did several decades ago (Fish & Larr, 1972; Ward & Braun, 1972). These findings are interpreted to mean that African-American children are more positively aware and accepting of their racial and ethnic background now than they were before 1960 (Harris, Blue, & Griffith, 1995).

In general, the process of identity development is a dynamic one and will fluctuate with vicissitude depending on the external situation (Devereux, 1975). This is true for the whole life cycle. However, associated with the developmental stage, adolescents tend to be more sensitive to the matter of ethnic identification and may react to related issues with psychological turmoil.

*Functional or Dysfunctional Ethnic Identity.*    The nature of ethnic or racial identity can be discussed in terms of whether it is positive or negative, functional or dysfunctional. Just as personal, family, or other kinds of group identity, a sound and positive ethnic identity is important for an individual's psychological well-being and health. To know one's origins is to have not only a sense of provenance, but also, and perhaps more importantly, a sense of continuity in which one finds to some degree the personal and social meaning of human existence (De Vos & Romanucci-Ross, 1975, p. 364). Thus, developing a healthy ethnic identity is a matter of concern from a mental health point of view.

Needless to say, if an ethnic or racial group is looked down upon by other groups, or by the dominant group, its members will tend to develop an inferior image of their group, forming a negative ethnic or racial identity. Such a negative identity will greatly influence the mental health of the group's members.

Dysfunctional ethnic identity is usually illustrated by extreme ethnocentrism (i.e., taking an extremely ethnic, self-centered view associated with a very negative attitude toward ethnic groups other than one's own). Good examples of such dysfunctional ethnic identity are the Germans in Hitler's era, who believed that Germans were the most superior ethnic group and discriminated against and even tried to exterminate Jewish people; the Japanese in World War II, who believed that they were blessed ethnically by the existence of the Japanese emperor, and used this idea to "rescue" colonized people and start the war in Asia; and the KKK groups in the United States, who believe that minority groups, particularly blacks, should be discriminated against and excluded from the society.

As explained by De Vos and Rommanucci-Ross (1975), how a person maintains a healthy ethnic identity if he is living as a member of a minority group within a pluralistic society becomes a mental health concern. The offspring of interethnic or interracial marriage will face issues of mixed ethnic identity. As pointed out by De Vos and Romanucci-Ross, a dual or combined identity is not denied but encouraged. For instance, the Mestizos in Mexico are a recognized ethnic group whose members are graded according to the degree of their racial mixture and their Spanish or Indian cultural behavior. In the multiethnic society of Hawaii, as a result of mixed marriages among different ethnic groups, the off-spring identify themselves merely as a "mixed" group without psychological problems associated with that identification.

How we identify with self, family, a small group, or a large collective group, including a society, ethnicity, race, or culture, has a direct impact on our psychology and mental health. However, in the past, little effort has been made to understand the process of ethnic identity formation and its relation to mental health (Sue & Sue, 1990). What constitutes normal and healthy ethnic identity versus abnormal or dysfunctional ethnic identity is a subject awaiting further exploration.

---

### CASE 1

A Laotian Man Who Overidentified with America (Shae Locke)

Yang is a young man who was born in Laos during wartime. He has seven brothers and three sisters. In his early years, he recalls being told how the villagers were taken into a cave by the communists and all the men and boys were shot. Apparently his life was spared, as he was suckling and his mother had been able to hide his genitalia with her hand. His father escaped death on this occasion due to prior imprisonment. He recalls his fears during his overnight visits to see his father in prison as he grew up. He was nevertheless a good student and managed to graduate at the top of his class from high school. As was all the villagers' desire, he saw escape from his home country as his best choice. One day, he seized an opportunity and swam across the Mekong to a refugee camp in Thailand. After a year in Thailand, he was transferred to a camp in the Philippines, before emigrating to the United States as a refugee. In the United States, his mental illness manifested under the stresses of a new language and country, in addition to scholastic demands and work. Unfortunately, distant family members in the United States rejected him due to his mental illness, as did subsequently his nuclear family members left in Laos. Facing such rejection, his behavior changed. In his daily life, he routinely wore the American flag and other patriotic paraphernalia. He further insisted he had only ever eaten "American" food and preferred to be called by the name "John Smith." His psychotic decompensations were prominently marked by a fixation on Caucasian overidentification. He pointed to random Caucasian figures in magazines, variously identifying them as members of his nuclear family, often tearing out the pages to hang in his room or to place in scrapbooks.

## 5. Customs, Beliefs, and Rituals

Conceptually, any behavior is subject to cultural impact and is, therefore, more or less related to culture. However, there are special sets of behavior that are deeply rooted in culture and consciously prescribed for members to follow in their daily lives, regulating their behavior within the society. Such customarily observed, culture-rooted behavior may include rituals, customs, etiquette, superstitions belief, taboos, or other culture-regulated behaviors. As a member of a society, a person's behavior, in addition to biological factors, individual psychology, and personality, is always subject to customary regulating factors derived from sociocultural dimensions. These regulating factors are exercised and enforced through rituals, etiquette, customs, taboos, or laws. Let us examine some customary behavior that impacts people's minds and shapes their behavior in daily life.

### a. Rituals

In every society, people traditionally observe and practice certain sets of rites, or prescribed ceremonies, in public situations. This is a formal way of enforcing rules or prescribed customs. In association with the life cycle, there are usually rituals related to birth, ceremonies recognizing puberty (such as initiation rites), formal wedding procedures, and funerals for deaths.

Initiation rites are stressed in some cultures to recognize the growth and maturity of the young people. The intensity of initiation rites for boys is often related to the degree of closeness between mother and son during childhood. Psychologically, initiation rites serve to break these close ties and enable the boy to move into the stage of adulthood.

For Americans, birthday celebrations are emphasized for all age groups, with considerable stress on the birthdays of children. Adults' birthday celebrations are often considered successful if they are in the format of a "surprise" party. In contrast, the Chinese traditionally celebrate the birthdays mainly of parents and the elderly rather than the children. Birthday celebrations, particularly for the elderly, are planned formally and publicly without any secrecy. They are intended to show respect as a part of filial behavior. Children's birthdays were not celebrated annually in the past. In some rural areas, birthdays were not observed until the children reached preschool age. It was feared that announcing the existence of small children by holding birthday celebrations might catch the attention of the god-in-hell, who would come and take away the children's lives. Such precautions were considered necessary in the past, when the mortality rate for children was high.

### b. Etiquette

Etiquette refers to the forms and manners established by convention as acceptable or required social relations in public settings. Many different etiquettes are observed in various cultures. For instance, Westerners once considered it a virtue for gentlemen to open doors for ladies and to escort ladies in public settings. Now, in societies that emphasize women's liberation, to open a door for a woman or to yield a seat for a lady may be regarded as an unwelcome act of male chauvinism. In societies where the superiority of men is traditionally stressed, women are not expected to be treated by men in a polite way. It is considered correct etiquette for the wife to walk in the street, several steps behind, not preceding her husband or walking side by side with him.

In Micronesia, with its matrilineal family system, the brother-sister bond is considered very important. However, in order to protect this culturally prescribed bond, a certain etiquette needs to be observed. If a brother and sister happen to be together in a room, without the presence of other people, one of them has to leave right away. This is true even when they are grown up and married. This etiquette of avoidance serves as a protection against intimacy between them.

At the dinner table, Hawaiian children are told to follow the etiquette of "listening but not talking" (i.e., listening to the adults' conversation and learning from it, not speaking up and disturbing it). In contrast, contemporary Westerners, at least in America, consider it a virtue for family members to carry on conversations that include small children. For them, dinner is considered a precious time of intimate socialization and communication among close family members.

### c. Customs

Customs are habitual ways of behaving carried out by tradition and enforced by social sanctions. For instance, among different cultural groups, different customs are observed with regard to the exposure of body parts. Muslim women cover their faces with veils in the belief that it is not a virtue to expose their facial features to anyone other than their husbands. Westerners do not mind exposing their upper chests, including part of the breasts, but take care not to expose their legs on formal occasions. In contrast, Easterners, such as Chinese, consider it all right to expose women's lower legs when they wear traditional *qipau* clothes, even on public occasions. However, they consider it disgraceful for women to expose their upper chests, particularly in low-necked dresses. Interestingly enough, Japanese women, when they wear traditional *kimono*, while covering almost all parts of their bodies, may expose the backs of their neck to make themselves sexually attractive (see Fig. 11).

Based on their religious thought, Muslim people do not eat pork, and Buddhists avoid eating any meat. Asian farmers customarily do not eat buffalo meat, based on their belief that the buffalo have worked hard for the farmer, and it is not kind to eat their meat after they die. Mormons do not drink alcohol or coffee, believing that such substances will affect their brains, and that it is not right to do so. Even regarding food, there are diversified customs among different cultural groups.

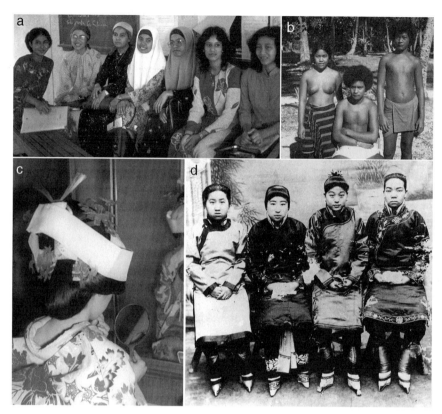

FIGURE 11   Customary behavior in different cultures. (a) Malay ladies, following Islam custom, cover their hair to conceal their sexual attractiveness from the opposite sex. (b) Micronesian ladies in the past were not concerned with exposing the tops of their bodies, but carefully covered the area between the umbilica and the knees. (c) Japanese woman in a traditional *kimono*, exposing the back of her neck as a sign of sexual beauty. (d) Chinese young ladies from affluent families had their feet bound from childhood to show their well-bred backgrounds as well as a sign of beauty for their future husbands.

### d. Taboo

A taboo is a social prohibition or restriction that is derived from convention or tradition. Breaking a taboo is considered socially undesirable, with the belief that certain ill effects might result. Many different taboos are observed in various cultures. Following are some examples. In Micronesia, people traditionally follow a pregnancy taboo (i.e., if a wife becomes pregnant, she returns to her home of origin and avoids any labor). Her husband is allowed to visit her, is expected to bring nutritious food for her, but is not permitted to have intimate relations with her. It is believed that sexual relations with the pregnant wife will have ill effects

FIGURE 12   Pregnancy taboo in Micronesia. Traditionally, a wife who becomes pregnant has to return to her family of origin not only for the period of gestation, but also for the first year of child rearing. This is a custom to ensure the health of the mother and child. The photograph illustrates public showing of the healthy mother and the birth of a lively new child—the most important issues for the island people.

on her as well as on the fetus. Not only during pregnancy, but even after the baby is born, until it is 1 year old, and knows how to dip its head into the water and hold its breath (basic survival skills for island people), the taboo continues and the wife stays in her own home. This may be considered a culturally pre-scribed method of protecting pregnant women and new babies or a measure of population control for the islanders. (See Fig. 12.)

According to Australian cultural psychiatrist John Cawte (1976), the aborig-ines who inhabited the Wellesley Islands of the Gulf of Carpentaria, Australia, observed a sea-land territorial taboo. The people believed there was a mutual antipathy between the land and the sea. A person who entered the sea without washing his hands after handling land food ran the risk of succumbing to *malgri,* a special kind of sickness. According to this taboo, if the precautions were neglected, the totemic spirit that guarded that particular territory was believed to invade the belly "like a bullet." In many cultures, particularly in Africa, a severe form of punishment was believed to occur in the form of voodoo death if a person broke certain taboos prescribed by their culture (See Chapter 3: A, Culture-Related Specific Syndromes).

### e. Superstitious Beliefs and Avoidance

The term "superstitions" refers to a set of beliefs collectively held by a group of people that are considered by people outside of the group to have no basis in reality or that cannot logically be explained by scientific knowledge. Therefore, they are labeled "superstitions" by outsiders. Although they might not be believed by outsiders, the people inside the culture are psychologically influenced by such beliefs, which are manifested in their emotions and behavior. *Superstitious avoidance* is a set of customarily observed avoidance behaviors based on superstitious beliefs. It is closely related to a taboo, yet it differs in that there is no serious punitive action taken when the regulation is broken. It is merely considered undesirable if the avoidance is not observed.

Many Christians, based on historical events described in the Bible, believe that Friday the 13th is an unlucky day. Some Christians avoid going out on that day. There is no 13th floor in some hotels and no bed No. 13 in some hospitals in the strong (superstitious) belief that the number is unlucky. The Japanese do not care about the number 13, but they try to avoid the number four if they can, as the sound of "four" is similar to that of "death." The Chinese favor the number nine, as "nine" sounds the same as "long," implying longevity. In Hong Kong, many people are willing to pay a fortune for a car license plate that includes many nines.

Depending on how you interpret it, some Chinese still strongly believe in *fengshui*, a geographic concept that the position of a mountain, the direction of a subject, plus the natural force of wind and water will affect practical situations in life, bringing bad or good luck. This concept may have originally reflected accumulated experience and knowledge about the effects of the physical environment. However, for some Chinese, it has become such a strong, superstitious belief that they have to consult an "expert" to select the location of a building, the arrangement of furniture, and so on, including which direction their heads should be pointing when they are in bed.

This review of customary behavior helps us to understand that, in our daily lives, particularly in social relations, we are led to behave or think in certain ways without knowing how much our behavior is shaped by our culture. Unless we take the position of an "outsider," we may not be able to comprehend the nature of our ordinary daily behavior objectively. Although only some examples of culture-rooted customary behavior are described, it is hoped that a review of these examples will increase our insight into how culture influences our behavior.

## 6. Adulthood, Aging, and Death

The life cycle after a person has reached adulthood has seldom been explored seriously by scholars in the past, with the general assumption that life is the same once one has grown up and become an adult. Is there a universal pattern for a person in growing up as an adult? Is there any cultural variation to going through adulthood? Associated with the longer lives of contemporary people, is there any change in the latter part of life? Any cultural differences in dealing with the prolonged later life? These issues need to be addressed.

According to Birren and Renner (1977), it is useful to differentiate three aspects of human age and aging: biological, psychological, and social age. The biological age of an individual can be defined as an estimate of the individual's present position with respect to his potential life span; psychological age refers to the adaptive capacities of the individual; and social age refers to the roles and social habits of an individual with respect to other members of a society. From a cultural point of view, we are more concerned with the latter two, particularly social age.

### a. Views and Attitudes About Aging

The views and attitudes toward aged people are rather negative in contemporary American society, and the term "ageism" is even used (K. S. Berger, 1994, p. 586). Ageism is similar in many respects to racism and sexism, in the sense that it is based on subjective, stereotyped, falsified, negative views of a particular group without a base in reality and is harmful to the group against which the prejudiced is directed. The main reason for the strength of ageism in the contemporary United States is the culture's emphasis on youth, strength, and success. The aged person is viewed as a negative or an obstacle in striving toward such a cultural ideal. Thus, as Butler and Lewis (1982) have pointed out, any sign of a person's "beginning to fail" is feared and exaggerated in its seriousness.

Even though "age," and particularly "aging," can be viewed from biological, psychological, and social perspectives, behavior and social scientists tend to take the view that aging represents one of many aspects of reality that is socially defined and that old age is a social category whose properties and problems are constructed within the context of shared expectations particular to specific groups. This is well illustrated by the study by Bengtson, Kasschau, and Ragan (1977). They conducted subjective assessments of age among populations living in southern California. The results revealed that self-categorization of aging varied considerably by ethnic group membership. For example, the Mexican-Americans tend to identify themselves as "old" at age 57; the African-Americans, at age 63; and the Caucasian-Americans, around age 70. It has been pointed out that, in the United States, minority group members perceive themselves as "old" at a considerably earlier chronological age than the majority group because of the repeated hardships they have faced through a lifetime of economic and social disadvantage (Jackson, 1970).

### b. Coping with Some Aging Landmarks

*Menopause.*  It has been noticed that, associated with the improvement of living conditions in modern societies, the onset of puberty among youngsters is occurring several years earlier than in the past, whereas the age of menopause is coming later, increasing the span of reproductive years from a biological standpoint as reflected in chronological age. Strictly speaking, menopause is a physiological change that occurs in women at the end of the reproductive stage. It occurs as the result of hormonal changes associated with a cluster of somatic symptoms, such as flushing and heavy sweating.

Concerning possible influences of race on the onset of menopause, a study has been carried out by Goodman, Grove, and Gilbert (1978) in Hawaii, comparing age at menopause in relation to reproductive history in Japanese-Americans, Caucasian-Americans, Chinese-Americans, and Hawaiian women living in Hawaii. Their results indicated that there were no noticeable differences among them in terms of age of menarche, or age of menopause. There were no interactions of ethnic group with age at menarche, parity, or months spent breast-feeding. Because they were living in more or less similar social settings, the age for menarche and menopause seemed similar among the different ethnic or racial groups.

However, medical investigation has revealed that the severity of menopausal symptoms and complaints varies cross-ethnically. It has been found that this is related mainly to food-intake patterns rather than to psychological factors. For instance, Japanese women were found to have less severe menopausal symptoms, related to their high intake of *tofu* (bean curd), which is rich in "vegetable estrogen," a substance that could reduce the symptoms associated with menopause.

Despite the biological basis for menopause, there still exist cultural factors that influence reactions to its occurrence, with different meanings for the arrival of menopause depending on how people interpret it. It may be seen as the termination of the reproductive stage, with reproduction an important function for women in some cultures, or a signal for relief of the burdens associated with reproduction, including the cyclic occurrence of menstruation. Menstruation is viewed in some cultures as a "dirty" discharge, with many ways developed to avoid its contamination.

*Middle-Age Adjustment.*   The concept of a middle-age crisis is rather popular in Western society, where youth is valued and the signs of aging produce relatively serious psychological reactions. This may not be true in societies where middle age is considered a time for people to enjoy social status and power.

Several factors are involved in the midlife transition. They are bodily changes, changes in time perceptions, changes in marital relationships and relationships with children, and social and financial changes (Colarusso & Nemiroff, 1981, pp. 122–124). Considering marital change, it can be pointed out that, associated with the family system, family structure, and the practices of separation, divorce, and remarriage, different courses of marital relationships will be observed during middle age. For instance, in a society where the production of children is encouraged and divorce is not permitted, adults at middle age will be surrounded by many children and living with a spouse, whether or not the person feels happy. In contrast, in a society where the bearing of children is not valued and divorce is easy, there is a higher chance for a middle-age person to be living alone, without a spouse and with few children. Again, whether or not the person feels gratified with his life, it is certainly a different way to go through the midlife stage and to encounter different natures and degrees of crisis.

From social and financial perspectives, it is easy to understand that, in the individual-oriented capitalist society, a person needs to depend on his own financial achievement in middle age. His source of security is his own individual effort and success. In contrast, in a society where financial achievement is the product of collective effort, and there is a solid public system of support even after people become old, they will have different social and financial experiences in middle age.

*Retirement.*    The system of retirement is a product of industrialized society. For most of human history, no one stopped working until their health failed. This was true in hunting and agricultural societies where no artificial line was drawn to indicate when a person stopped his productive work. Today, however, the vast majority of people in developed societies work for three decades or more and then stop when late adulthood begins, going through the developmental landmark of "retirement" and adjusting to postretirement life. According to Quinn and Burkhouser (1990), in the United States, the majority of retirees leave the workforce because they want to and their employers encourage it. Most retirees not only adjust well to their change in lifestyle but even improve in health and happiness. The exceptions are primarily among those who retire prematurely and involuntarily and are abruptly severed from their major source of status and social support.

### c. Death and Mourning

*Views and Attitudes toward Death.*    Even though death, from a narrow perspective, is primarily a biological phenomenon (i.e., the end of the life of an organism), it is associated greatly with psychological matters. Death can have many meanings: it can be seen merely as a biological event, a rite of passage, an inevitable natural occurrence, or many other things. Needless to day, culture contributes to the perspectives on death and dying (A. Berger et al., 1989; Ross, 1981).

In most African traditions, as pointed out by Opaku (1989), elders take on an important new status through death, joining the ancestors who watch over their own descendants, as well as the entire village. Therefore, everyone in the village participates in a funeral to prepare the deceased's journey to the ancestral realm. The death of the individual becomes an occasion for the affirmation of the entire community, as members jointly celebrate their connection with each other and with their collective past.

In contrast, in many Muslim societies, death affirms their faith in their god, Allah. People are taught that the achievements, problems, and pleasures of this life are transitory and ephemeral, and that everyone should be mindful of, and ready for, death at any time. In Buddhist societies, such as Thailand, based on their religious thoughts of incarnation, the present life is considered part of the whole circulating cycle. Death is simply an entrance to another part of the cycle. In Hindu societies, such as India, helping the dying to relinquish their ties to this world and prepare for the next is a particularly important obligation for the immediate family (Firth, 1989).

From the examples just mentioned, it is clear that attitudes toward death and reactions to the loss of a close person are shaped by religious thought or philosophy of life. However, as Eisenbruch pointed out (1984), when we look at how the individual actually feels and deals with his predicament, the suffering individual is not content with theological thought or philosophical explanation. Further, Eisenbruch stated that, even within any one religious denomination, there can be many different explanations of the meaning of death that are mirrored by that group's characteristic ways of grieving. This is illustrated by the variety that exists within Christian groups.

In the past, throughout most of Western society, death was an accepted, familiar event that usually occurred at home. In 20th-century North America and western Europe, death came to be withdrawn from everyday life. More and more people died alone in hospitals rather than at home among family members (K. S. Berger, 1994, p. 680).

*Grief and Mourning.*    Although the loss of a significant person in life is always an emotional event, there are numerous diverse customs prescribed by different cultures for people to guide their reactions when they experience a close person's death (Rosenblatt, Walsh, & Jackson, 1976).

According to the customs of Orthodox Jews, relatives must remain with a dying family member so that the soul does not leave while the person is alone. Jews do not leave a dead body unattended, as that would be a sign of disrespect (Rabinowicz, 1979). In the Jewish tradition, those who are making condolence visits are advised to enter the house and sit silently unless the mourners show a desire to speak of their loss (Chafetz, 1980).

Who mourns for whom is a basic question that sometimes needs to be addressed because of different family systems. For example, among the Ifaluk people living in Micronesia, a wife was not expected to grieve for her husband. Within that matrilineal society, a woman's emotional ties remained with male members of her maternal family, and she was culturally expected to grieve for her father and her brothers, but not for her husband.

In China in the past, following a custom established in Confucius's time, a different period of time for mourning was expected for different people (e.g., three years for parents, one year for a husband, and one month for children).

Also, it was generally expected that women would show their feelings of sorrow openly in public. It was almost a ritual for a female to cry loudly at the time of the funeral. When a parent(s) died, it was considered the primary job of both the daughter(s) and the daughter(s)-in-law to cry loudly to show how the family missed the deceased parent-in-law.

*Widowhood.*    Losing a lifelong marital partner is a major event affecting development in many adults. The developmental tasks for people in widowhood are to mourn emotionally; to form new life patterns in regard to daily activity and work, if still working; to become reinvolved with others in new ways; and possibly to remarry or to reform intimate relations with a new life partner.

Different experiences of widowhood have been described cross-culturally by Mathison (1970) as follows. India has a strong patrilineal social organization in which women are devalued. The Hindu religion has decreed that a widow shall not remarry, although a widower is urged to remarry as soon as possible. The situation is worsened by another Hindu custom: girls are frequently betrothed while still very young to much older boys or even to men. With the age differential and the death rate in India, it is not uncommon for a girl to become a widow before the marriage is even consummated. Throughout history, the life of a widow in India has been dismal. She can stay with her husband's family, but is then regarded as the most menial of all the other persons in the household. She cannot attend ceremonies of rejoicing, as her presence is considered a bad omen. As pointed out by Mathison (1970), at least part of the rationale behind the dehumanizing treatment of widows lies in the Hindu belief that the husband's death has in some way resulted from the sins the wife has committed in a past life.

In contrast, the fate of widows among the Trobriand Islanders in New Guinea is consistent with matrilineal social organization, in which women occupy a more prestigious position than in other societies. The widow is provided with highly structured rituals to observe during her bereavement. During the several days of funeral rites, the widow is required to mourn ostentatiously and dramatically, shaving her head and howling loudly with grief. After this, she enters a small cage built into her home and remains in the dark for a period of six months to two years. This is said to keep the husband's ghost from finding her. Kinsmen are with her at all times. Once the period of mourning is terminated, she is ceremonially washed and dressed in a gaily decorated grass skirt. She is then considered to be available for remarriage. Because women in this culture control material goods through the matrilineal descent system, and are thus an economic asset to men, remarriage is highly likely (Mathison, 1970).

Examining individual grief and mourning processes across cultures through a review of ethnographic literature, Rosenblatt and associates (1976) found that societies which performed final ceremonies sometime after a person's death lacked prolonged expressions of grief, whereas grief is prolonged (and often disturbed) in societies that lack final postburial ceremonies.

Comparing bereavement in Samoan and American communities, Ablon (1971) brought up the issue that Samoans view death as natural, even in the experiencing of life. In contrast, death in the United States is a subject that is generally hidden, or at least ignored as much as possible.

### d. Euthanasia, or Physician-Assisted Suicide

Associated with the extension of life spans and the increase of deteriorated physical or mental conditions for some aged persons, the possibility of actively ending someone's life has become a consideration, and physician-assisted suicide, or euthanasia, has become a controversial topic in many societies (Coomaraswamy, 1996). There is a need to distinguish between "active" and "passive" euthanasia. In the former, the physician takes an active role in ending a person's life, using medical means to end the life of a person wishing to die. In the latter, the physician withdraws any medical methods of sustaining a person's life so that the person will eventually die.

After reviewing the situations in Germany, Holland, and the United States, Battin (1991) pointed out that, although they are alike in having aging populations that die primarily of deteriorative diseases, the end-of-life dilemmas are handled differently in these three countries. In the United States, up to now, withholding and withdrawing of treatment were the only legally recognized means of aiding dying. In Holland, voluntary active euthanasia is practiced by physicians. In Germany, assisted suicide is a legal option but is usually practiced outside of a medical setting.

Clearly, the way we deal with a person wishing to end his life is a complicated issue that needs to be thought about and decided upon carefully. It involves philosophical, practical, medical, legal, and cultural matters that are awaiting examination and answers in the near future.

## C. HOW DOES CULTURE RELATE TO PATHOLOGY?

In contrast to other fields of medicine, psychiatry is still far from knowing the exact etiological causes for various mental disorders. While medical knowledge has increased remarkably, most explanations of the causes of psychiatric disorders are still at the stage of speculation and hypotheses (Marsella, 1993). Contemporary psychiatrists generally consider that multiple factors, including biological (such as hereditary and organic), psychological (relating to the individual and/or his family), and social-cultural factors, in different combinations and in an integrative, dynamic way, all contribute to the occurrence of mental sickness.

The term "psychopathology" implies a psychological condition that is pathological and different from the normal. It includes psychiatric disorders that are viewed as morbid entities manifesting certain pathological mental conditions. Severe mental symptoms or signs recognized by professionals (such as disorientation, hallucination, delusion, depression, anxiety) are present, leading to the distress or disability of the person concerned. It also includes abnormal behavior that may or may not belong to the category of mental disorders, but certainly deviates from normal behavior and is considered dysfunctional (such as extreme shyness, suspicion, or explosive behavior). Such behavior not merely deviates from social norms but is also intolerable or disturbing from the point of view of the society in which it occurs. From a mental health perspective, clinicians pay attention to emotional or behavior problems in a broad way, encompassing many daily life problems (such as school maladjustment, marital problems, acculturation problems).

As pointed out by Berrios (1994), since the beginning of modern psychiatry, clinicians and scholars have debated on the matter of the "continuity" and "discontinuity" of pathology. According to the continuity model, there exists a continual spectrum from normal (nonpathological) to pathological psychic phenomena. Manifestations of mild degrees of anxiety, fear, or depression fit this model. Intellectual impairment, drinking behavior, or personality problems can exist within the continuity spectrum as well. The discontinuity model holds that there are pathological psychic symptoms that have no counterparts in normal behavior. Bizarre psychotic symptoms or pathognomonic organic mental conditions belong to this model and are explained according to the concept of mental disease rather than viewed merely as exaggerations of normal into abnormal behavior.

Depending on their professional backgrounds and orientations, psychiatrists, as clinicians, prefer to use the term "pathology," implying that the disordered condition is related to the morbid entity of disease; whereas behavioral scientists, such as psychologists, tend to use the term "abnormality," meaning dysfunctional behavior that measurably deviates from the normal range. Here, the term and concept of "psychopathology" are used to refer broadly to any pathological mental condition or abnormal behavior.

## 1. Different Ways Culture Contributes to Pathology

Recognizing that psychopathology is attributed to multiple factors, including biological and psychological ones, we are going to focus primarily on cultural contributions to psychopathology. From a conceptual point of view, there are different ways that culture can contribute to psychopathology, depending on how the impact occurs: in the form of pathogenic, pathoselective, pathoplastic, pathoelaborating, pathofacilitative, pathodiscriminating, and pathoreactive effects. Let us examine how culture impacts psychopathology in these different ways.

### a. Pathogenic Effects

Pathogenic effects refer to situations in which culture is a direct causative factor in forming or "generating" psychopathology. There are several ways that cultural ideas and beliefs can contribute to stress, which, in turn, produces psychopathology (see Section 2A, Culture and Stress). Stress can be created by culturally formed anxiety, culturally demanded performance, and special culturally prescribed roles and duties. In such cases, culture is considered to be a causative factor, as culturally shared specific beliefs or ideas contribute *directly* to the formation of a particular stress, inducing a certain mode of psychopathology. Without such a formal, culturally rooted idea or belief, the psychopathology would not occur.

Since the cultural beliefs that cause psychopathology are often culture-specific, culture-induced psychopathology tends to be unique to the cultures that hold those beliefs. In other words, culture contributes to the development of an entirely unique psychopathology that is observed only in certain cultural environments and cannot phenomenologically be categorized into (or even closely related to) any diagnostic group that exists in current (Western) classification systems. As such disorders are heavily related to culture, the disorders are considered to be culture-related specific psychiatric syndromes, such as *koro* (genital-retraction anxiety disorder), *daht* syndrome (semen-loss anxiety disorder), frigophobia (excessive phobia of catching cold), and *voodoo* death (magic-fear-induced death) (see Section 3A, Culture-Related Specific Syndromes). They comprise only a small number of psychiatric disorders that are recognized in the field of psychiatry, yet the pathogenetic effects of culture are vividly illustrated by these rare and unique clinical conditions.

### b. Pathoselective Effects

At an individual level, we can analyze how a person, influenced by personal factors, such as personality and other psychological conditions, "selects" certain patterns of reaction toward stress, choosing a certain type of psychopathology. At a cultural level, it can be understood that a group of people in society, as a result of cultural influences, tends to select certain reaction patterns, resulting in the manifestation of certain psychopathologies.

Without their knowing it, culture has a powerful influence on the choices people make in reacting to stressful situations and shapes the nature of the psychopathology that occurs as a result of those choices. Running *amok* (indiscriminate mass homocide attacks) or family suicide (parental suicide and child homocide) as a way to cope with desperate situations are some clinical examples (see Section 3A, Culture-Related Specific Syndromes). Of course, this only applies to minor psychiatric disorders, particularly of culture-related specific syndromes, not to major psychiatric disorders. However, it is clearly illustrated in the extreme cases that culture plays a significant role in determining the patterns of our reactions and the manifestations of our psychopathology.

### c. Pathoplastic Effects

Psychopathoplastic effects are the ways in which culture contributes to modeling or "plastering" of the manifestations of psychopathology. This can occur on two different levels: shaping the content of symptoms or modeling the clinical picture as a whole.

Culture can shape symptom manifestation at the level of the content presented. The content of delusions, auditory hallucinations, obsessions, or phobias is subject to the environmental context in which the pathology is manifested. For instance, an individual's grandiose delusions may be characterized by the belief that he is a Russian emperor, Jesus Christ, Buddha, or the president of the United States, depending on which figure is more popular or important in his society. A phobic patient may be preoccupied with the fear of many things. He may be afraid of being contaminated by germs, viruses, placental fluid, menses, bewitched subjects, or nuclear toxins, depending on what subjects are viewed as "dirty" or "dangerous" by the members of his society at a particular time. Fear of passing gas, exposing one's own body smell, or having one's face flush in front of others can be serious, obsessive social phobias if it is believed that such occurrences are embarrassing in social situations.

The effect of cultural factors on psychopathology can be observed at the level of the presence (or exaggeration) or absence of certain symptoms that modify the total manifestation of the clinical picture to some extent. Psychopathology is often shaped by social and cultural factors so that the clinical picture does not necessarily manifest uniformly at the universal level or similarly to the way it manifests in Western populations. For instances, *Taijin-kuofu-sho* (fear of interpersonal relations disorder)—characterized by a pathological concern over not being able to relate to intermediately close friends, classmates, or colleagues, but not to strangers, as observed in Japan as a special form of "social phobia"—or brain fag syndrome—characterized by complaints of intellectual impairment, as well as somatic complaints of pain in the head or neck, as observed in Africa—are two examples.

Depending on the intensity of the plastic effect and the degree of modification of symptomatology, culture will affect the psychopathology in such a way that the disorders could be recognized as "atypical," "subtypes," or "variations" of disorders officially recognized in the current (Western) classification system. Some of them will be included as culture-related specific syndromes, if cultural attention is considered important.

### d. Pathoelaborating Effects

Certain behavior reactions (either normal or pathological) may be universal, but they may become exaggerated to the extreme in some cultures through cultural reinforcement (Simons, 1996). Some mental conditions are not necessarily pathological and fulfill certain needs of the individual as well as the society; others are clearly pathological and are intensely elaborated by the culture.

The concept of pathoelaborating effects is well illustrated by the unique mental phenomenon *latah*, which is mainly observed in Malaysia. The phenomenon is characterized by the sudden onset of a transient dissociative attack induced by startling, and such behavior may be utilized by people for social amusement (see section 3A, Culture-Related Specific Syndromes). At present, many people in the United States are very concerned with body weight in relation to health. Many methods of diet control and equipment for physical exercise have been developed. In addition to health-related concerns, the culture-shaped body image belief that "slim is beautiful" is certainly at the root of body-weight anxiety. Associated with this social emphasis on body weight, it is speculated that anorexia nervosa has become more frequent.

### e. Pathofacilitative Effects

Pathofacilitative imply that although cultural factors do not change the manifestation of the psychopathology too much, (i.e., the clinical picture can still be recognized and categorized without difficulty in the existing classification system, cultural factors do contribute to the frequent occurrence of certain mental disorders in a society. In other words, the disorder potentially exists and is recognized globally; however, due to cultural factors, it becomes prevalent in certain cultures at particular times. Thus, it "facilitates" effects, making it easier for certain psychopathologies to develop and influencing their frequency.

Many psychiatric disorders that are intimately tied to psychological and sociocultural variables in their development tend to have a wider range of variation of prevalence. Suicidal behavior (Kok & Tseng, 1992), alcoholism (Day, 1995), and substance abuse (Anthony & Helzer, 1995) are examples of disorders whose frequency varies among different societies and whose occurrence is significantly influenced by the sociocultural context.

### f. Pathodiscriminating Effects

Sociocultural factors may not influence the occurrence or manifestation of the psychopathology but may determine whether the mental condition or behavior is regarded by society and professionals as "abnormal" or "pathological." There are several different ways to discriminate normal and abnormal. Decision by professional judgment and definition, by means, and by function are some examples, but sociocultural factors are certainly among them (Offer & Sabshin, 1974). Several mental conditions or behaviors, such as personality disorders, sexual deviation, and substance abuse (e.g., smoking or drinking) can be seen as socially acceptable normal behaviors or pathological conditions, depending on discrimination according to cultural factors.

### g. Pathoreactive Effects

These effects indicate that although cultural factors do not directly affect the manifestation or frequency of the mental disorder, they influence people's beliefs and understanding of the disorder and mold their "reaction" toward it. Culture influences how people label a disorder and how they react to it emotionally, and then it guides them in expressing their suffering. Consequently, the clinical picture of the mental disorder is colored by the cultural reaction, at a secondary level, to the extent that the total process of the illness varies.

Studies indicate that the prognosis of schizophrenia may vary in different societies. It tends to have a poor prognosis in highly developed, industrialized, urban societies, and better outcomes in less developed, rural, farming societies. It is considered that the social environment, particularly family and community attitudes toward the patient, determine how well the person suffering from a schizophrenic disorder will rehabilitate into social and family life, thus affecting the prognosis of the disorder. Posttraumatic stress disorder associated with war is another example. How the society perceives the disorder and reacts to the emotional sequel—with a sympathetic attitude, many social welfare benefits, or none—will influence how many people will claim to have such a disorder and how they will describe the severity of their suffering. It is generally observed that the frequency of certain disorders, such as conversion and dissociation disorder, is gradually decreasing. It is speculated that lay people's understanding of and attitude toward such disorders will significantly change their prevalence.

## 2. Cultural Impact on Different Groups of Psychopathology

We have clarified how culture contributes to psychopathology in different ways. Following this, it is important to recognize the different nature of cultural impact, depending on the different groups of disorders or the nature of psychopathology. Generally speaking, psychopathology that is predominantly determined by biological factors is influenced less by cultural factors, and any such influence is secondary or peripheral. In contrast, psychopathology that is predominantly determined by psychological factors is attributed more to cultural factors. This basic distinction is necessary in discussing different levels of cultural impact on various types of psychopathology.

These levels of distinction are illustrated in Figure 13. It shows how culture impacts psychopathology in various ways, namely, genetic, selective, plastic, elaborating, facilitating, discriminating, or reactive ways, for different groups of psychopathology, which vary from predominantly biologically, psychologically, socioculturally determined psychopathology.

It can be said that there is a range of universally uniform psychopathologies versus culture-elaborated specific psychopathologies. The degree of cultural input varies between the extremes of distantly culture-related to closely culture-related psychopathology. These integrated conceptual views will assist in elaborating the subject of "culture and psychopathology" without confusion or ambiguity.

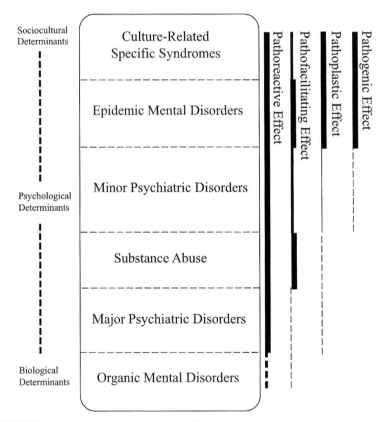

FIGURE 13    Spectrum of psychopathology—different natures of determinants and their cultural impact.

# REFERENCES

## A. What Is Cultural Psychiatry?

American Psychiatric Association (APA). (1969). Position statement on the delineation of transcultural psychiatry as a specialized field of study. *American Journal of Psychiatry, 126*(3), 453–455.

Favazza, A. R., & Oman, M. (1978). Overview: Foundations of cultural psychiatry. *American Journal of Psychiatry, 135,* 293–303.

Mezzich, J. E., Kleinman, A., Fabrega, H., Jr., & Parron, D. L. (Eds.). (1996). *Culture and psychiatric diagnosis: A DSM-IV perspective.* Washington, DC: American Psychiatric Press.

Prince, R. H., Okpaku, S. O., & Merkel, L. (1998). Transcultural psychiatry: A note on origins and definitions. In S. O. Okpaku (Ed.), *Clinical methods in transcultural psychiatry.* Washington, DC: American Psychiatric Press.

Tseng, W.S. (2001). Handbook of cultural psychiatry. San Diego, CA: Academic Press.

## B:1. What Is Culture?

American Anthropological Association. (1999). AAA statement on race. *American Anthropologist, 100*(3), 712–713.

De Vos, G. A. (1975). Ethnic pluralism: Conflict and accommodation. In G. A. De Vos & L. Romanucci-Ross (Eds.), *Ethnicity: Cultural continuities and change* (p. 9). Palo Alto, CA: Mayfield.

Draguns, J. G. (1989). Dilemmas and choice in cross-cultural counseling: The universal versus the culturally distinctive. In P. B. Pedersen, J. G. Draguns, W. J. Lonner, & J. E. Trimble (Eds.), *Counseling across cultures* (pp. 3–21). Honolulu: University Press of Hawaii.

Herskovits, M. J. (1964). *Cultural dynamics.* New York: Alfred A. Knopf Publisher.

Hoebel, E. A. (1972). *Anthropology: The study of man.* New York: McGraw-Hill.

Kottak, C. P. (1994). *Cultural anthropology* (6th ed.). New York: McGraw-Hill.

Nanda, S. (1980). *Cultural anthropology.* New York: D. Van Nostrand.

Vanneman, R., & Cannon, L. W. (1987). *The American perception of class.* Philadelphia: Temple University Press.

Wohlfarth, T., & van den Brink, W. (1998). Social class and substance use disorders: The value of social class as distinct from socioeconomic status. *Social Science and Medicine, 47*(1), 51–58.

## B:2. Marriage and the Family

Bilge, B., & Kaufman, G. (1983). Children of divorce and one-parent families: Cross-cultural perspectives. *Family Relations, 32,* 59–71.

Haviland, W. A. (1978). *Cultural anthropology* (2nd ed.). New York: Holt, Rinehart & Winston.

Hoebel, E. A. (1972). *Anthropology: The study of man.* New York: McGraw-Hill.

Hsu, F. L. K. (1972). Kinship and ways of life: An exploration. In F. L. K. Hsu (Ed.), *Psychological anthropology* (new edition) (pp. 509–567). Cambridge, MA: Schenkman.

Koch-Nielsen, I. (1980). One-parent families in Denmark [Special issue]. *Journal of Comparative Family Studies, 11*(3), 17–29.

Lefaucheur, N. (1980). Single-parenthood and illegitimacy in France [Special issue]. *Journal of Comparative Family Studies, 11*(3), 31–48.

Levine, N., & Sangree, W. H. (1980). Conclusion: Asian and African systems of polyandry [Special issue]. *Journal of Comparative Family Studies, 11*(3), 385–410.

Nanda, S. (1980). *Cultural anthropology*. New York: Van Nostrand.

Tseng, W. S., & Hsu, J. (1991). *Culture and family: Problems and therapy*. New York: Haworth Press.

Visher, J. S., & Visher, E. B. (1982). Stepfamilies and stepparenting. In F. Walsh (Ed.), *Normal family process.* New York: Guilford Press.

## B:3.  Child Development and Enculturation

Abel, T. M., & Metraux, R. (1974). *Culture and Psychotherapy* (p. 127). New Haven, CT: College & University Press.

Bond, M. H. (1991). *Beyond the Chinese face: Insights from psychology*. Hong Kong: Oxford University Press.

Caudill, W., & Weinstein H. (1969). Maternal care and infant behavior in Japan and America. *Psychiatry, 32,* 12–43.

Erikson, E. H. (1963). *Childhood and society* (2nd ed.). New York: Norton.

Freedman, D. G., & Freedman, M. (1969). Behavioral differences between Chinese-American and American newborns. *Nature* (London), *224,* 1227.

Glimore, D. D. (1990). *Manhood in the making: Cultural concepts of masculinity*. New Haven, CT: Yale University Press.

Hsu, F. L. K. (1972). Kinship and ways of life: An exploration. In F. L. K. Hsu (Ed.), *Psychological anthropology* (new edition) (pp. 509–567). Cambridge, MA: schenkman.

Jacobs, M. (1964). *Pattern in cultural anthropology*. Homewood, IL: Dorsey Press.

Kagan, J., & Snidman, N. (1991). Temperamental factors in human development. *American Psychologist, 46,* 856–862.

Kakar, S., & Ross, J. M. (1987). *Tales of love, sex and danger*. London: Unwin Hyman.

Malinowski, B. (1927). *Sex and repression in savage society*. New York: International Library.

Mead, M. (1928). *Coming of age in Samoa*. New York: Morrow.

Mead, M., & Wolfenstein, M. (Eds.), (1955). *Childhood in contemporary cultures.* Chicago: University of Chicago Press.

Okonogi, K. (1978). The Aajase complex of the Japanese (1). *Japan Echo, 5*(4), 88–105.

Pinderhughes, C. A. (1974). Ego development and cultural differences. *American Journal of Psychiatry, 131,* 171–175.

Segall, M. H., Dasen, P. R., Berry, J. W., & Poortinga, Y. H. (1990). *Human behavior in global perspective: An introduction to cross-cultural psychology*. New York: Pergamon.

Shrier, D. K., Hsu, C. C., & Yang, X. L. (1996). Cross-cultural perspective on normal child and adolescent development: Chinese and American. Part I, Introduction, historical overview, normal child and adolescent development, and future directions. In F. Lih Mak & C. C. Nadelson (Eds.), *International Review of Psychiatry, Vol. 2* (pp. 301–334). Washington, DC: American Psychiatry Press.

Tseng W. S. (1994). Psychotherapy for the Chinese: Cultural consideration. In Proceeding for the Second International Conference on Psychotherapy for the Chinese. Hong Kong: Chinese University of Hong Kong.

Tseng, W. S., & Hsu, J. (1969/1970). Chinese culture, personality formation and mental illness. *International Journal of Social Psychiatry, 16*(1), 5–14.

Tseng, W. S., & Hsu, J. (1972). The Chinese attitude toward parental authority as expressed in Chinese children's stories. *Archives of General Psychiatry, 26,* 28–34.

Wang, Y. F., Shen, Y. C., & Chang, J. S. (1997). Characteristics of Chinese children's temperament: A series of studies. In W. S. Tseng (Ed.), *Chinese mind and therapy* (pp. 87–109). Beijing: Beijing University and Xieho University United Press (in Chinese).

Whiting, J. W. M., & Child, I. L. (1953). *Child training and personality*. New Haven, CT: Yale University Press.

Whiting, B. B., & Whiting, J. W. M. (1975). *Children of six cultures: A psycho-cultural analysis.* Cambridge, MA: Harvard University Press.

## B:4. Personality and Ethnic Identity

Aboud, F. E. (1987). The development of ethnic self-identification and attitudes. In J. S. Phinney & M. J. Rotherman (Eds.), *Children's ethnic socialization: Pluralism and development* (pp. 29–51). Newbury Park, CA: Sage.

Benedict, R. (1934). *Patterns of culture.* Boston: Houghton Mifflin.

Benedict, R. (1946). *The chrysanthemum and the sword.* Boston: Houghton Mifflin.

Cheung, F. M., Leung, K., Fan, R. M., Song, W. S., Zhang, J. X., & Zhang, J. P. (1996). Development of the Chinese Personality Assessment Inventory. *Journal of Cross-Cultural Psychology, 27*(2), 181–199.

Devereux, G. (1975). Ethnic identity: Its logical foundations and its dysfunctions. In G. De Vos & L. Romanucci-Ross (Eds.), *Ethnic identity: Cultural continuities and change.* Palo Alto, CA: Mayfield.

De Vos, G., & Romanucci-Ross, L. (Eds.), (1975). *Ethnic identity: Cultural continuities and change.* Palo Alto, CA: Mayfield.

Doi, T. (1962). Amae—A key concept for understanding Japanese personality structure. In R. J. Smith & R. K. Beardsley (Eds.), *Japanese culture: Its development and characteristics.* Chicago: Aldine.

Doi, T. (1973). *The anatomy of dependence.* Tokyo: Kodansha International. (Original work published 1971 in Japanese.)

DuBois, C. (1944). The people of Alor. Minneapolis: University of Minnesota Press.

Fish, J. E., & Larr, C. J. (1972). A decade of change in drawings by black children. *American Journal of Psychiatry, 129*(4), 421–426.

Gorer, G., & Rickman, J. (1949). *The people of Great Russia: A psychological study.* London: Cresset Press.

Harris, H. W., Blue, H. C., & Griffith, E. E. H. (Eds.), (1995). *Racial and ethnic identity: Psychological development and creative expression.* New York: Routledge.

Inkeles, A. (1997). *National character: A psycho-social perspective.* New Brunswick, NJ: Transaction Books.

Kardiner, A. (1945). The concept of basic personality structure as an operational tool in social sciences. In R. Linton (Ed.), *The science of man in the world crisis.* New York: Columbia University Press.

Kluckhohn, C. (1955). Recent studies of the "national character" of Great Russians. Human Development Bulletin, papers presented at the Six Annual Symposium, Chicago. Published as a chapter in C. Kluckhohn (Ed.), (1962), *Culture and behavior.* New York: Free Press.

Mead, M. (1942). *And keep your powder dry: An anthropologist looks at America.* New York: William Morrow and Company.

Song, W. Z. (1985). A preliminary study of the character traits of the Chinese. In W. S. Tseng & D. Y. H. Wu (Eds.), *Chinese culture and mental health.* Orlando: Academic Press.

Sue, D. W., & Sue, D. (1990). Racial/cultural identity development. In D. W. Sue & D. Sue, *Counseling the culturally different: Theory and practice.* New York: Wiley.

Tseng, W. S. (2001). *Handbook of cultural psychiatry.* San Diego, CA: Academic Press.

Wallace, A. F. C. (1970). *Culture and personality* (2nd ed.). New York: Random House.

Ward, S. H., & Braun, J. (1972). Self-esteem and racial preference in black children. *American Journal of Orthopsychiatry, 42*(4), 644–647.

## B:5. Customs, Beliefs, and Rituals

Cawte, J. E. (1976). *Malgri:* A culture-bound syndrome. In W. P. Lebra (Ed.), *Culture-bound syndromes, ethnopsychiatry, and alternate therapies* (pp. 22–31). Honolulu: University Press of Hawaii.

## B:6. Adulthood, Aging, and Death

Ablon, J. (1971). Bereavement in a Samoan community. *British Journal of Medical Psychology*, *44*, 329–337.

Battin, M. P. (1991). Euthanasia: The way we do it, the way they do it [Special issues]. *Journal of Pain and Symptom Management*, *6*(5), 298–305.

Bengtson, V. L., Kasschau, P. O., & Ragan, P. K. (1977). The impact of social structure on the aging individual. In J. Birren & K. W. Schaie (Eds.), *Handbook of the psychology of aging*. New York: Van Nostrand-Reinhold.

Berger, A., Badham, P., Kutscher, A. H., Berger, J., Perry, V. M., & Beloff, J. (Eds.), (1989). *Perspectives on death and dying: Cross-cultural and multi-disciplinary views*. Philadelphia: Charles Press.

Berger, K. S. (1994). *The developing person through the life span* (3rd ed.). New York: Worth.

Birren J. E., & Renner, V. J. (1977). Research on the psychology of aging: Principles and experimentation. In J. E. Birren & K. W. Schaie (Eds.), *Handbook of the psychology of aging*. New York: Van Nostrand-Reinhold.

Butler, R. N., & Lewis, M. I. (1982). *Aging and mental health: Positive psychosocial and biomedical approaches* (3rd ed.). St. Louis: Mosby.

Chafetz, P. (1980). Jewish practices in death and mourning. *Death Education*, *3*(4), 367–369.

Colarusso, C. A., & Nemiroff, R. A. (1981). *Adult development: A new dimension in psychodynamic theory and practice*. New York: Plenum Press.

Coomaraswamy, R. P. (1996). Death, dying, and assisted suicide. In G. J. Kennedy (Ed.), *Suicide and depression in late life: Critical issues in treatment, research, and public policy*. New York: Wiley.

Eisenbruch, M. (1984). Cross-cultural aspects of bereavement. I: A conceptual framework for comparative analysis. *Culture, Medicine and Psychiatry*, *8*(3), 283–309.

Firth, S. (1989). The good death: Approaches to death, dying, and bereavement among British Hindus. In A. Berger et al. (Eds.), *Perspectives on death and dying: Cross-cultural and multi-disciplinary views*. Philadelphia: Charles Press.

Goodman, M., Grove, J. S., & Gilbert, F., Jr. (1978). Age at menopause in relation to reproductive history in Japanese, Caucasian, Chinese and Hawaiian women living in Hawaii. *Journal of Gerontology*, *33*(5), 688–694.

Jackson, J. J. (1970). Aged negroes: Their cultural departures from statistical stereotypes and rural-urban differences. *The Gerontologist*, *10*, 140–145.

Mathison, J. (1970). A cross-cultural view of widowhood. *Omega*, *1*, 201–218.

Opaku, K. A. (1989). African perspectives on death and dying. In A. Berger et al. (Eds.), *Perspectives on death and dying: Cross-cultural and multi-disciplinary views*. Philadelphia: Charles Press.

Quinn, J. F., & Burkhouser, R. V. (1990). Work and retirement. In R. H. Binstock & L. K. George (Eds.), *Handbook of aging and the social sciences* (3rd ed.). San Diego: Academic Press.

Rabinowicz, H. (1979). The Jewish view of death. *Nursing Times*, *75*(18), 757.

Rosenblatt, P. C., Walsh, R. P., & Jackson, D. A. (1976). Grief and mourning. In P. C. Rosenblatt, R. P. Walsh, & D. A. Jackson, *Cross-cultural perspective*. New Haven, CT: HRAF Press.

Ross, H. M. (1981). Societal/cultural views regarding death and dying. *Topics in Clincal Nursing, 3*, 1–16.

## C. How Does Culture Relate to Pathology?

Anthony, J. C., & Helzer, J. E. (1995). Epidemiology of drug dependence. In M. T. Tsuang, M. Tohen, G. E. P. Zahner (Eds.), *Textbook in psychiatric epidemiology* (pp. 361–406). New York: Wiley-Liss.

Berrios, G. E. (1994). The history of descriptive psychopathology. In J. E. Mezzich, M. R. Jorge, & I. M. Salloum (Eds.), *Psychiatric epidemiology: Assessment concepts and method*. Baltimore: Johns Hopkins University Press.

Day, N. L. (1995). Epidemiology of alcohol use, abuse, and dependence. In M. T. Tsuang, M. Tohen, & G. E. P. Zahner (Eds.), *Textbook in psychiatric epidemiology* (pp. 345–360). New York: Wiley-Liss.

Kok, L. P., & Tseng, W. S. (Eds). (1992). *Suicidal behavior in the Asia-Pacific region*. Singapore: Singapore University.

Marsella, A. J. (1993). Sociocultural foundations of psychopathology: An historical overview of concepts, events and pioneers prior to 1970. *Transcultural Psychiatric Research Review 30*(2), 97–142.

Offer, D., & Sabshin, M. (1974). *Normality: Theoretical and clinical concepts of mental health*, (2nd ed.). New York: Basic Books.

Simons, R. C. (1996). *Boo!—Culture, experience, and the startle reflex*. New York: Oxford University Press.

# CHAPTER 2

# Culture, Stress, and Illness Reactions

## A. CULTURE AND STRESS

In this chapter "stress" is used as a generic term for psychological stress, referring to a condition that creates outstanding psychological problems, burdens, pressures, traumas, frustrations, or conflicts to which the subject must react with excessive effort, inducing a considerable disturbance of his emotional state. The term "problem" is used alternatively to refer to a difficulty encountered that requires extra effort to handle. Either stress or problem, by definition, is psychological in nature and therefore subject to cultural influence. From a dynamic perspective, stress is a complicated matter. Stress is influenced by multiple and compound factors, including the occurrence of stress itself, its perception or appraisal by the subject experiencing it, and supporting resources for coping and the strength to cope available to the subject that enable him to face the stress. From a cultural perspective, culture influences stress in various ways.

### 1. Stress Created by Culturally Formed Anxiety

Culture may contribute to the occurrence of stress directly through the beliefs that are held by the members of a society. Numerous examples illustrate this. The folk belief that excessive or inappropriate sexual encounters will cause shrinkage of penis into the abdomen, threatening death, is an example of a culture-induced anxiety resulting in *koro*, a panic attack among some Chinese and Thai people, and people in Bangladesh, sometimes in epidemic form. Similarly, the belief that leaking of the semen through urination, as a result of excessive masturbation, will cause serious illness is another example of culture-derived anxiety (referred to as the *daht* syndrome) among some young people in India. Cross-territorial anxiety relating to the sea and land, observed among aborigines in Australia, causing multiple somatic pains (*malgri*) or *voodoo* death resulting from taboo breaking are also examples of how culture can cause severe anxiety and even panic-related death (see Section 3A, Culture-Related Specific Syndromes, Case 1 and 2). Fear of vampires, the end of the world, a UFO invasion, a heart attack, contamination from nuclear radiation, the hazards of smoking, or the ill-effects of being overweight are other examples of anxiety that may originate from supernatural beliefs, scientific knowledge, or reality. Such group-shared anxieties can escalate or decline according to the attitudes and degrees of concern shared by people in a given time and place.

## 2. Stress Induced by Special Culturally Prescribed Roles and Duties

Some members of a society are prescribed certain roles and duties from a cultural perspective. If the role prescribed is an inferior one and the duties are hard to perform, the person concerned may suffer a stressful life experience. Such situations are exemplified by the following examples.

In China in the past, it was the custom that if a family was poor and had too many children, the parents would give up their youngest daughter for adoption to another family for monetary payment. This "adopted daughter," even though she was still young, was expected to work hard as a domestic maid for the adoptive parents. In other words, she was sold to work as a maid. Until she was grownup and ready for marriage, she had to wake up early and stay up late doing all the chores in the household. She had to obey her adoptive mother and was subjected to harsh discipline if she did not perform well. There are stories describing such miserable "adopted daughters" living their youths with tears in their eyes all the time. This is similar to the situation of African-Americans brought to work as slaves in the United States in the past, who suffered from their underprivileged roles and harsh duties.

In traditional Muslim culture, a husband was allowed to have more than one wife, while it was considered a woman's main function to bear children. If a woman failed to bear children, she faced the breakup of her marriage. This caused stress-induced anxiety that has been described as one kind of culture-bound neurosis (El-Islam, 1975).

---

CASE 1

---

The Muslim Woman with One Foot in the Past
(Abstracted from El-Islam, 2001)

Maryam, a Qatari woman, aged 39, presented for psychiatric attention with an eight-year history of a variety of somatic symptoms, such as tightness in the chest, headache, and difficulty in going to sleep. After repeated physical investigations locally and in Europe failed to find any organic basis for her symptoms, she was referred to a psychiatrist.

Maryam was brought up in a traditional Qatari extended-family household. As the eldest daughter, she had the duty, since reaching puberty, to help her mother with household chores and to look after her youngest siblings. Her parents came from wealthy families that belonged to high-status tribes, and Maryam was thus married by arrangement at the age of 15. Now she had six children and two grand-children. She felt physically run-down by the rapid succession of childbirths and resorted to the use of oral contraceptives *without* informing her husband. She hid this from her husband because it was his "right" in this culture to have as many children as he considered appropriate to his high status and wealth. Needless to say, this has been a constant psychological burden for her, with the fear of what would happen if her husband discovered her secret. According to the culture, she could be divorced by her husband for her behavior.

Further, she was annoyed by the conflict that centered around interparental differences in attitudes toward their children. She leaned toward liberalism in raising their sons, encouraging their independence in choice of friends, television programs, and time for doing homework on school subjects, whereas her husband was much more restrictive and traditional. Conflict between time-honored, traditional codes and parental values that were internalized during childhood and maturation and liberal, modern pursuits often led to interpersonal strife, intercouple tension, and intrapersonal conflict.

---

In India, when a woman became a widow, others subconsciously considered her an "evil" woman who had caused her husband's death. Thus, she was treated as an unfavorable person in the household. This was reinforced by the cultural attitude that, under the patrilineal family system, a woman is nothing but an accessory of a man. The widow was confined to her domestic environment and not permitted to socialize outside of the house. She was given a lifelong sentence of confinement, even if she was still young. Remarriage was out of the question.

## 3. Stress Produced by Culturally Demanding Performance

Although a certain amount of pressure regarding performance is necessary for individuals and society at large, sometimes the demand is so excessive that it may

FIGURE 1   Stress created by culturally demanded performance. Japanese students nervously search for their names on the college bulletin board for the results of the entrance examination; this is the most anxious time in their lives.

cause culture-produced stress in the individuals as well as in the society as a whole.

The American behavioral scientist Vogel (1962), who studied emotional disturbances in Japanese society, has described the psychological pressure encountered by youngsters, particularly relating to school entrance examinations (see Fig. 1). The problem of gaining admission to good academic institutions is not peculiar to Japan; the tension surrounding admission is probably found in every society. However, what is peculiar to Japan, according to Vogel, is the severity and intensity of the problem. He reported that most middle-class Japanese, even if they are short of funds, will struggle to provide their children with desks and other facilities conducive to long hours of study. A tutor is hired for perhaps a year or two to work regularly with the child in preparation for the examination. A high school student may stop various other activities and settle down to many hours of serious study every day after school.

There is a cultural reason for this emphasis on entrance examinations in Japan. Historically, the best way to obtain competent people for government offices was to select them from certain institutions of higher learning. Indeed, as Vogel explained, the educational institution a person attended was the main criterion for employment in government. Furthermore, Japanese firms generally make a life commitment to an employee at the time of hiring. An employee of one company almost never leaves to work at another company. Each firm seeks to obtain men of considerable competence because they will be committed to these men for life. Because the best students will almost invariably try to get into the best universities, the most reliable factor for judging competence is the university attended. Very much determined by the historical and social structural characteristics of Japanese society, Japanese mothers will put considerable pressure on the child for good school performance, starting from kindergarten. The society believes that a good kindergarten leads to a good grade school, a good grade school leads to a good high school and then to a good university, which, in turn, leads to a good company for life.

## 4. Stress Imposed by Cultural Limitations on Behavior Expression

In contrast to the situations just described, in which culture demands certain performance and achievement, are circumstances in which culture limits behavior expression and discourages social performance, contributing to the occurrence of stress among those who are being limited. Such situations can occur in subtle or explicit ways. An illustration of the former is when women are not permitted to pursue higher education and are expected not to perform outside of their domestic environments. The latter is exemplified by American women living in Saudi Arabia. As described by Becker (1991), there is a tendency toward prohibition against women in Muslim societies, such as Saudi Arabia, enforcing the dependency of women on men. This restrictive aspect of Saudi society often creates stress among American women, who are raised in their home cultures to behavior independently from men and to express themselves in social settings. Facing such cultural limitations, many American women feel confined and helpless in this foreign setting. Depression or anger may develop. The anger is often brought into the marital relationship, which is further stressed because of the lack of outside outlets to diffuse tension and conflicts.

Certain cultural systems create tight restrictions on the lives of all members of the society, in comparison with other ethnic or cultural units. The cultural restrictions on the range of behavior may be associated with a religion, military situation, or political condition. Probably the best example is that of the people of the Hutterite religious sect living in certain areas of Canada and the United States. Their dress is prescribed and their duties as farmers, sheepherders, cooks, tailors, and shoemakers are assigned. Their children are not allowed even to ice skate. Their choice of husbands or wives must be approved by the brethren; the request for permission to marry is ritualized. The preparation and eating of food follow traditional sex-segregation etiquette. Contacts with nearby towns are limited to necessity. The Hutterites do not necessarily suffer from their restricted life patterns. However, outsiders who come to live with them may have psychological difficulty following their cultural restrictions.

## 5. Problems Due to Cultural Regulations of Choice

Instead of restrictions on life behavior as a whole, problems may result from cultural regulation of choices in special matters that have a significant impact on life. Choosing a mate, a professional career, or whether to stay in one's own country or migrate to another place, are some examples. If the choices are determined by the culture, through taboo, custom, or cultural regulation, and are outside of an individual's own will, they will affect an individual's mental life significantly.

Even now, many societies still practice marriage by arrangement. Usually the parents find a suitable marriage partner. The parents screen the person for negative factors and consider the favorable conditions for selection of a lifelong marital partner. The parents may or may not consider whether the partners concerned are fond of each other. They may base their choice entirely on other considerations, such as the families on both sides or financial or health factors. Affection between the man and the woman may not be part of the picture. Arranged marriage does not necessarily bring an unhappy end. On the contrary, it works well for many couples. However, being forced to marry someone you dislike simply for the sake of family, financial, or political reasons tends to be associated with emotional unhappiness.

The incest taboo is observed in most societies, but the scope of incestuous relations is defined differently by different cultures. In Chinese and Korean culture, it is considered taboo to marry someone who has the same family name. By definition, a person who has the same family name belongs to the same "family" (clan). He or she may be your cousin or niece if you trace the family clan back for a hundred or a thousand generations and is thus a "relative" by definition. This concept is arbitrarily observed only in paternal family systems, according to which a woman becomes a part of her husband's family when she marries and is excluded from her family of origin. A taboo against marrying a person with the same family name does not cause problems if there are many common family names in a society, as there are in Japan and in Western societies. There is a wide range of choices of people to date. However, it is more difficult when there are only a few family mames, as in China and Korea. There are only several dozen common Chinese family names, such as Chang, Chen, Lin, and Wang. There are even fewer in Korea, such as Kim, Pak, Lee, and Kang. Despite this, there is a strict cultural rule that defines relations between a man and a woman who have the same family name as incestuous. Thus, if two people who are in love have the same family name, they are not permitted to marry. Such cases often end in tragedy, with the lovers committing suicide together. In such cultures, it is important to clarify a person's name before you start dating to avoid serious trouble.

## 6. Problems That Arise from Sociocultural Discrimination

Societies have a dismaying habit of dividing themselves into the accepted and the not accepted, the chosen and the outcast, the favored and the merely tolerated. The majority group looks down on the minority; the superior caste discriminates against the lower castes. Groups such as the Vietnamese "boat people" and Cuban refugees, which were first given sympathy and help by others, soon began to be seen as financial burdens and threats to job-seekers; discrimination against these victims of tragedy grew rapidly.

African-Americans have been liberated politically, but many of them still suffer from less education and employment, poor housing, and long-existing racial discrimination. Jews are still subject to social slights. In Hawaii, where many ethnic groups live without outward discord, disdain continues to find expression. Some Japanese still look down on Okinawans. There are still mutual feelings of inferiority among a few members of different Chinese subethnic groups, such as Bendi (local) people and Hakka (guest) people, or mainland Chinese and Taiwan-Chinese. Discrimination may be between ethnic or subethnic groups, or within a group. Such intergroup discrimination often causes tension, affects interpersonal relations and social involvement in a subtle way, or induces conflicts or riots in an explicit way. It may affect the self-image of a group or individual, influencing mental health (see Section 11B, Minorities).

A unique race-related stress is elaborated by Loo, Singh, Scurfield, and Kilauano (1998) in connection with the experiences of Asian-American soldiers during the Vietnam War. In combat situations in Vietnam, American soldiers were required to respond to ambiguous visual stimuli with split-second decisions for survival, judging whether the Asian-looking people they encountered were threatening or friendly. Negative racial stereotypes of Asians were socially conditioned by the association of fear of the enemy with fear of Asians in general. As a result, simply because of their physical similarity to the "enemy" (Viet Cong), Asian-American soldiers were exposed to various kinds of stress. As a result of combat indoctrination, dehumanization, and racial hatred, they were subjected to hostility and estrangement as the "enemy"; exposed to a greater potential of and actual life threats; and afraid of being suspected of disloyalty to their fellow American soldiers. Consequently, they might have dehumanized Vietnamese civilians in ways that led to later feelings of regret or remorse.

## 7. Problems Induced by Rapid Cultural Change

It is commonly recognized that when a society goes through rapid cultural change within a short period of time, resulting in radical changes in value systems, lifestyles, and behavior norms, psychological problems tend to occur among the people due to difficulties in adjustment. These problems may be illustrated by a wide generational gap, misbehavior of youth, and confusion among adults and will be elaborated in detail later (see Section 11A, Sociocultural Change, Migration, and Refuge).

If a person moves to live, either temporarily (as a visitor) or permanently (as an immigrant), in a society that has a radically different cultural background, he will experience culture shock. According to Mumford (2000), the term "culture shock" was originally coined by anthropologist Kalervo Oberg in 1960 and referred to an occupational disease of people who have been suddenly transplanted abroad. Taft (1977) expanded and elaborated on the transcultural situation in which a person experiences considerable strain due to the effort required to make necessary psychological adaptations to the new culture; a sense of loss and feelings of deprivation regarding the friends, status, profession, and possessions that a person had in the original culture; rejection by and/or rejecting members of the new culture; confusion of roles, role expectations, values, feelings, and self-identity; and feelings of impotence due to the inability to cope with the new environment.

## 8. Problems Related to Cultural Uprooting or Destruction

If the occurrence of cultural change is so great that it almost results in the loss of a society's cultural roots, or the cultural system is almost completely destroyed by others, people will suffer from cultural uprooting. They will encounter emotional pain and psychological suffering, loss of meaning and direction in their lives, and confusion about the way to live. These results of cultural destruction produce what is called a state of anomie by scholars. According to Spencer (2000, p. 8) the sociologist Durkheim claimed that social life is "nomic" (i.e., governed by a set of rules, mostly unwritten, shared by the collective consciousness of a group). Nomie exists when individual interests are subordinated to the common interests, resulting in social stability and mental well-being. However, if there is gross and rapid change in society resulting in cultural uprooting, called anomie," people will suffer from the loss of long-established life patterns with feelings of demoralization and dispossession. These phenomena are observed among indigenous people everywhere who encounter the invasion of a more powerful dominant culture, creating personal conflict and social distress. Unsatisfactory relief is sought through a variety of strategies such as substance use and antisocial behavior. For instance, Spencer (2000) pointed out that the aboriginal people in Australia remained disadvantaged socially, professionally, and educationally for several centuries after the arrival of Western people. Imprisonment rates for aboriginal people exceed by severalfold those of the rest of the population. Infant mortality rates are four to five times greater, and life expectancy is 15 to 20 years shorter. Maternal deaths, alcoholism, obesity, diabetes, smoking, and substance abuse are just some of the many disorders on this very depressing list of high prevalence rates.

## B. CULTURE-SHAPED COPING PATTERNS

Despite the difficulty of categorizing various coping patterns utilized by individuals in different cultures, there are many examples available to illustrate some specific coping patterns or strategies that have been utilized by certain societies in particular eras from a historical point of view.

*Passive-Resistance Coping Method.* It is well-known that Indians, led by Gandhi, successfully eliminated British colonial control through nonviolent passive resistance. Instead of an aggressive, bloody revolution, the Indian people, following their political and philosophical leader, made good use of their cultural heritage of endurance and patience to fight the British administration successfully without a drop of blood.

*Self-Destructive Coping Choice.* Toward the end of the war in the Pacific, when Americans mobilized their forces to take over the island of Okinawa and were ready to land on the Japanese islands proper, the Japanese coped with the critical situation in a desperate way, adopting the strategy of *kamikaze* attacks. Many young pilots were asked to go on self-destructive missions to attack the enemy. This military strategy could take place only in a society whose culture expected complete obedience toward superiors and loyalty to authority (the emperor). It was also based on the belief that it was a duty and an honor for a soldier to sacrifice his individual life to save the country as a whole. Actually, even before the war in the Pacific had started, the Japanese navy had planned and executed minisubmarine suicide attacks on Pearl Harbor, when it was not yet at a point of desperation. Near the end of the war, the collective suicides of Japanese civilians were performed here and there in Manchuria and on Okinawa and Saipan. With the cultural belief that "It is better to be a broken jade rather than to survive as a complete piece of brick," people were indoctrinated to choose death rather than surrender to the enemy. In order to carry out the suicides, for the civilians, cyanide was offered in Manchuria, hand grenades were distributed in Okinawa, and in Saipan, several hundreds or thousands of civilians were ordered by military personnel to jump from a suicide cliff shouting "banzai" (ten-thousand years' life) for the emperor (see Fig. 2).

*Self-Isolation Coping Pattern.* In Russia, during Stalin's era, the country was shut off from the outside for several decades. The "iron curtain" was built so that

FIGURE 2  Culture advocated coping: collective suicide in Saipan. (a) At the end of the Pacific War, by order of the army, many Japanese civilians, ended their lives by jumping from a cliff in Saipan, Micronesia, shouting "banzai." The cliff is now called Banzai Cliff by local people. (b) Three decades after the war ended, the wooden jumping board is still left in the memorial site of the suicide cliff.

people inside did not have access to news from the outside, including how afflu-ent life was in the capitalistic societies in the West. It helped the government control the people and maintain a certain social stability, even though people were suffering under communism and dictatorship. A similar kind of self-isolation was enforced in China, with the so-called bamboo curtain. This was a politically derived coping method utilized to control people's minds and lives. It took a certain cultural mentality for people to accept and comply with such self-isolation.

*Externalizing the Enemy Maneuver.* An historically well-known, politically derived coping moneuver involves identifying an outside enemy in order to maintain a strong cohesion internally and create social or national unity despite the preexistence of fragmentation or instability within the society or nation. By identifying an outside enemy, the people's anger, fear, or resentment is projected outward and gives them an excuse to express their aggression externally. This coping method was best exemplified in the Nazi era in Germany. Greatly stirred up by Hitler and his party, the German people were motivated to wage war against their neighboring countries, fulfill their ambition to unite Europe, and carry out the massive execution of the unwelcome Jewish ethnic group. Beyond a fanatical political leader, a certain national character was also involved, one that was willing to obey authority without question. A similar strategy was utilized by the Japanese army in starting the war in the Pacific as part of World War II. To fulfill its military ambition, the Japanese adopted the political rational of chasing Western imperialism out of Asia for the sake of "coexistence and peace for Asians." The slogan that was never appreciated by any other Asian people during or after the war, but the Japanese firmly believed it.

For the sake of convenience, all the examples just given were operating more or less at the societal level. However, they illustrate indirectly that the choice of coping patterns can be shaped by culture at the individual level as well. Certain kinds of defense mechanisms (such as suppression vs. expression of desire) or culturally sanctioned unique coping mechanisms (such as passive rationalization for accepting reality) may be utilized more by people of one culture than others. It is important for clinicians to recognize and understand the cultural impact on a patient's reaction patterns for coping with stress (Fairbank & Hough, 1981; Ide et al., 1990; Kasl, 1996).

## C. FOLK EXPLANATIONS OF MENTAL PROBLEMS

There is good reason to speculate that mental illness has existed from the beginning of the history of human beings. Folk explanations have been offered by laymen or indigenous healers in the past that may still be believed and utilized by people in various cultures today. It is important for clinicians to be aware of these folk explanations and give proper attention to them during the service of patients. It has been pointed out that folk concepts of illness are not based on simple grounds (Good & Good, 1982). They can be formed according to etiological speculation or descriptive phenomena. It should be noted that folk terms for mental disorders may refer to specific conditions or may be used generically without distinguishing clearly among various kinds of disorders as recognized by contemporary medicine. Further, the explanations provided include supernatural ones that are not found in contemporary medicine.

## 1. Supernatural Explanations

These explanations are based on supernatural beliefs. They attribute the causes of sickness to supernatural powers, which are beyond human understanding and control. Supernatural explanations of illnesses take many forms.

*Object Intrusion.*   In a concrete way, sickness is interpreted as the result of the intrusion of certain undesirable objects, such as tiny bones, bits of leather, coagulated blood, insects, or hairs. All are considered evil and are proven to be the causes of illnesses in a concrete and convincing way by people who believe in this theory. It is based on magical thought, which is different from the nature-orientated pathogenic object theory. According to Clements (1932), this is perhaps one of the most primitive ways of interpreting the causes of sickness.

*Soul Loss.*   "Soul" here refers to the supernatural being of "self," which usually resides in our bodies. This is a view held by many people in preliterate societies. It is believed that for some reason, such as being frightened, hit on the head (where the soul resides), sneezing, or experiencing troubled sleep, the soul will leave the body and be unable to return. It is thought that when a person has lost his individual "soul," he will behave and feel differently and, in extreme conditions, become sick. The *susto* concept held by Latin people is one example. Prayer or a ceremony is required to bring back the lost or wandering soul.

*Spirit Intrusion and Possession.*   This explanation takes the view that sickness is due to the presence in the body of evil spirits. Although the presence of spirits or other supernatural beings does not necessarily cause sickness all the time, the intrusion of malicious spirits does. When a person speaks and talks as if he has been taken over by a supernatural being, he is described as "possessed." This is a special form of spirit intrusion. The disorder of fox possession (*kitsune-tuski*) described in Japan (Eguchi, 1991) is one special example that is commonly recognized and labeled by a layperson. Certain ceremonies can be performed to satisfy the intruding or possessing spirit's demands, asking it to leave the body, or exorcisms can be conducted to chase it away.

*Breach of Taboo.*   This explanation sees sickness as a punishment by the gods for the breach of religious prohibitions or social taboos that have divine sanction. The breach may be unintentional or even unknown to the sufferer, but it is still interpreted as the cause of the illness. Voodoo death is often attributed to breach of taboo. According to this interpretation, there are certain ways to undo the punishment, including confession.

*Sorcery.*   This interpretation considers sickness to be the result of the manipulations of persons skilled in magic or having supernatural powers. It is suspected that illness is induced with malicious intent by the acts of others, through the use of supernatural powers. The mechanism of projection is used to affect others, and interpersonal conflict often exists. However, an underlying belief in supernatural powers is necessary for this to occur. Repairing troubled interpersonal relations is one way to remove the effects of the sorcery; performing counteracting sorcery is another.

## 2. Natural Explanations

Natural explanations stem from the basic assumption that there are underlying principles of the universe that govern all of nature, including man's life, behavior, and health. When physical or mental illness, misfortune, or great unhappiness occur, the causes are thought to be related to natural matters in several ways, as follows.

*Disharmony of Natural Elements.*   It is assumed that certain homeostatic conditions exist in the world of nature by means of the harmonic balancing of various elements. If there is disharmony among these natural elements, illness as an undesirable condition will occur. The humoral view of Greek medicine and the five-element theory of Chinese medicine are both rooted in this basic concept.

*Incompatibility with Natural Principles.*   Closely related to the concept of the correspondence between microcosm and macrocosm, some people believe that misfortune or illness is brought about by incompatibility with natural principles. Astrologers may interpret misfortune as the result of unusual movement of your designated star in the sky. Geometrists (or *feng shui* masters) may explain that you suffer from a chronic illness because your ancestor was buried in a place that does not fit geometric or *feng shui* principles. A fortune-teller may interpret frequent marital problems as the result of the mismatching of the animal natures of the husband and wife. For instance, a man with a horse nature does not fit with a woman with a tiger nature, as a tiger will not be subordinate to and will only threaten a horse. It offers explanations symbolically regarding the concept of harmony versus antagonism, the basic principle elaborated by the yin and yang theory.

*Philosophical Explanations and Acceptance.*   The occurrence of illnesses, particularly malicious or untreatable ones, may be attributed to fate, with the philosophical attitude of accepting and tolerating it. For instance, if a person attempts suicide repeatedly, it may be explained that he has a predetermined fate to end his life early.

*Noxious Factors in the Environment.*   In this view, when any natural element, such as wind or water, is excessive or unnatural, it becomes noxious and is thought to be the cause of mental illness. Cold air is considered to be the cause of "catching cold," even by modern man. Apoplexy was thought to occur as the result of the intrusion of "wind" in Chinese medicine. Thus, the condition was labeled *zhong-feng*, which literally means "attack by wind."

## 3. Somato-Medical Explanations

The somato-medical explanations view sickness as the result of undesirable conditions existing within our own bodies. It considers certain conditions necessary for the organism to function. Any factors that are not favorable to these conditions will result in sickness.

*Physical-Physiognomy Problems.*   In this view, a person faces illness as the result of some physical problem, such as physical appearance or structure. The person is often born with the problem, and it may cause him difficulty in life. For example, a person with a flat nose is considered to lack a strong will and have difficulty carrying out tasks. A person with long ears is considered to have a successful future, with good fortune in both wealth and achievement.

*Distress or Dysfunction of Certain Visceral Organs.*   This explanation is based on the belief that certain visceral organs are closely related to certain emotional or mental functions. Due to distress or other reasons, dysfunction of particular organs may occur, which in turn leads to certain somatoemotional disturbances. The heart distress conceived by Iranian people (Good, 1977); the kidney-deficiency syndrome of the Chinese, based on traditional concepts (Wen, 1995); and neurasthenia, or exhaustion of the nervous system observed by Western psychiatrists at the turn of the 19th century, are some examples.

*Physiological Imbalance or Exhaustion.*   A badly balanced diet, exhaustion, or inappropriate activity, especially sexual, is considered to cause physiological disturbances that result in mental disorders. Loss of energy through excessive sexual activity has been held responsible for psychiatric conditions in both the Eastern and the Western worlds. An elevated fire element in the body, causing an irritated temper and anger (labeled *hwa-byung* by Koreans), is an example.

Based on the Greek humoral concept of pathology, according to which the four bodily fluids or "humors" were characterized by a combination of hot or cold with wetness or dryness, people in Latin America today classify most foods, beverages, herbs, and medicines as "hot" or "cold." By extension, illness is often attributed to an imbalance between heat and cold in the body (Currier, 1966).

*Insufficient Vitality.*   It is believed that a person, as an organism, needs a certain force, vitality, or energy to function. Many terms have been used to describe the concept of such a force or vitality in different societies, such as *mana* for Hawaiians, *Jing* and *qi* for Chinese, *dhat* for Indians, and *genki* for Japanese. No matter what term is used, the basic underlying concept is that it is important to acquire, maintain, and reserve this biological-mental force in order for a person to function effectively. If there is insufficiency or excessive loss of the force, it will often result in sickness, and a resupply of the force will be needed.

*Inborn or Acquired Pathologies.*   This explanation takes the view that mental illness occurs as the result of a physical handicap or vulnerability that was inborn or acquired through infection, trauma, intoxication, or other organic causes. This is an organic view held even by medical professionals.

## 4. Psychological Explanations

Psychological explanations are entirely different from those described previously in that they take the view that the mental sickness is an ill-function of the mental condition that can be induced by an undesirable mental affect. Thus, it is based on the psychogenic theory of mental illness.

*Fright.*   If a person is subjected to excessive and undesirable emotional excitement, such as fright, it may cause a disturbance in his mental balance and result in mental sickness. The conditions causing fright vary. A person may be frightened by lightning, encountering a ghost, or witnessing a horrifying situation, such as murder.

*Overburdening.*   Strongly related to the homeostatic view of organisms, it is held that if a person uses his brain in an excessive way he will exhaust it and cause an overburdened condition. Naturally, mental rest as well as nutritional supplements are considered ways to help the brain recuperate from such an exhausted condition.

*Excessive Discharge of Emotion.*   Based on daily life observation, it is believed that excessive emotional discharge, in the form of anger, sorrow, or even excitement, particularly for long periods of time, will bring ill effects on the body.

Therefore, it is recommended that a person maintain a certain regulation of emotional expression and not be excessively angry, happy, or sad. This is a psychosomatic view of sickness.

## D. TRADITIONAL MEDICINE AND CONCEPTS OF DISORDERS

Any medical systems that are outside of formally recognized, modern medicine are labeled "traditional" medicine. They were established in the past with formal, systematic theories, knowledge, and accumulated experiences of practice that deserve attention. Let us examine some of the most well-established traditional medical systems.

### 1. Chinese Traditional Medicine

Chinese traditional medicine is considered one of the most well-established traditional medical systems in the world. It has a history of several thousand years and is still officially recognized and clinically practiced in contemporary China.

*The Concept of Yin and Yang.*    According to this theory, the human body, like the cosmos, can be divided fundamentally into a positive force (yang) and a negative force (yin), which are complementary to each other. In the cosmos, the sun symbolizes the positive force, whereas the moon is the negative. Among living beings, the male symbolizes yang and the female, yin. Even food is subdivided into two categories. Spicy foods, tonics, and meat are considered "hot," or yang foods; whereas most green vegetables and fruits are "cold," or yin foods.

The concept of positive and negative forces applies not only to physiology, but also to psychopathology and treatments for it. If the two forces are balanced and in harmony, good health is maintained; if not, illness will result. For example, excited insanity is the result of excessive positive force, whereas falling sickness (i.e., epilepsy) or *shuoyang* (literally, shrinkage of the yang instrument, or penis; also *koro*) is caused by excessive negative force. In treatment, reduction of the positive force is considered necessary for excited insanity, whereas supplementing the positive force is needed for falling sickness or *shuoyang* (*koro*) attacks. Yin and yang are thus interpreted as the dual forces operating in nature as well as in human beings; they emphasize the principle of balance.

*The Theory of Five Elements.*    This theory proposes that everything in nature, including human bodies, belongs to one of five categorical elements, represented by *water, wood, fire, earth,* and *metal.* In nature, the five climatic factors of *wind, heat, humidity, dryness,* and *cold* are related to these five elements. In humans, the

TABLE 1    The theory of the five elements in Chinese traditional medicine.

| Element | Water | Wood | Fire | Earth | Metal |
|---|---|---|---|---|---|
| **Climatic factors** | Humidity | Wind | Heat | Dryness | Cold |
| **Visceral organs** | Kidney | Heart | Liver | Spleen | Lung |
| **Emotions** | Fear | Joy | Anger | Worry | Sorrow |

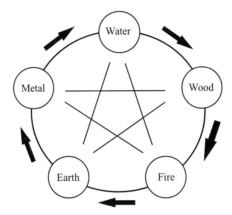

FIGURE 3    Circular relations and paired antagonisms among the five elements.

five primary visceral organs—*liver, heart, spleen, lungs,* and *kidneys*—correspond to the five elements, which in turn are related to the five basic emotions of *anger, joy, worry, sorrow,* and *fear* (see Table 1).

According to this theory, certain orderly relationships exist among the five elements: water creates wood, wood creates fire, fire creates earth, earth creates metal, and metal creates water. Therefore, circular relationships exist among them. At the same time, there is antagonism between water and fire, fire and metal, metal and wood, wood and earth, and earth and water (see Fig. 3).

Because each element as a concept represents many aspects of things, including the structure and functions of the body, the relationships among these aspects are revealed by the relationships among the five elements. The basic idea emphasized by the theory of five elements is the interactional relationship among things, with circular input and paired antagonism. It attempts to explain the complicated relationships that exist in the world, as well as in the body and mind.

*Basic View of the Visceral Organs.*    Without the knowledge and techniques for examining the body physiologically, as is done in modern times, everything occurring in the body and mind was interpreted as an expression of the visceral organs, the parts of the human body existing in the trunk, which could be observed easily. The heart was thought to house the superior mind; the liver, to control the spiritual soul; the lungs, the animal soul; the spleen, ideas and intelligence; and the kidney, vitality and will. When vital air was concentrated on the heart, joy was created; on the lungs, sorrow; on the liver, anger; on the spleen, worry; and on the kidney, fear. Thus, it was considered that various emotions were stirred through the visceral organs. In accordance with this medical knowledge, the common people used in daily life, many organ-related sayings such as "elevated liver fire," "losing spleen spirit," "hasty heart," and "exhausted kidney" to denote becoming angry and irritated, losing one's temper, being anxious, and generally fatigued, respectively.

*The Idea of Correspondence between Microcosm and Macrocosm.*   In this view, human beings are governed by the principles that rule nature. Therefore, the phenomena occurring inside of a person can be understood in terms of the phenomena manifested in nature. In the same way that the four seasons and five climatic elements—wind, heat, humidity, dryness, and cold—manifest changes in nature, changes in the body's five viscera and five spirits are expressed in emotions such as joy, anger, worry, sorrow, and fear. In other words, a person's emotions are viewed as equivalent to the weather in nature (see Fig. 4).

This view sees extraordinary conditions of wind, cold, heat, humidity, and dryness as *external causes*, and extraordinary conditions of joy, anger, worry, sorrow, and fear as *internal causes* of illness. It stresses the critical influences of natural phenomena externally and affection internally. As a whole, this view emphasizes the significance of harmony and stability.

*Three Categories of Etiology for Illness.*   The causes of disorders were subdivided simply into three categories: external, internal, and others, which included those that could not be categorized as either external or internal. Based on the medical knowledge of the time, there was no concept of organism-caused

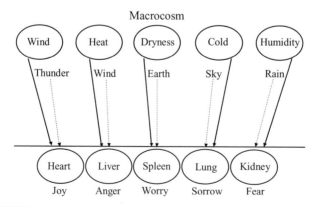

FIGURE 4   The idea of correspondence between microcosm and macrocosm.

infection as one etiology of disorders. External causes referred to any illness factors arising from nature in the form of weather conditions, such as extraordinary wind or humidity or excessive heat or cold, as well as injury. Internal causes referred to factors arising from inside a person (i.e., improper emotional experiences). It was believed that physical disorders would affect the emotions, and that, at the same time, unnatural emotional experiences would result in illness. In other words, a psychogenic view of somatic illness was not only recognized but was also very much emphasized from the beginning of Chinese traditional medicine.

*The Concept of Vital Energy and Vital Air.* Vital energy, called *Jing*, refers to the essence of the life force that exists in the body and regulates the vitality of the organism. When a person is full of vital energy, he functions efficiently both mentally and in bodily productivity. Without sufficient vital energy, illness and even death may occur. Conservation of *Jing* becomes an important practice for the preservation of health. Paralleling *Jing* is vital air, *Qi*, which is considered an abstract energy that gives strength to the body and mind. Proper conservation and an adequate supply of these vital forces or energies are cardinal to maintaining health.

## 2. *Ayurvedic* Medicine

*Ayurveda,* the traditional Indian system of medicine, has its root in *Atharva Veda*, an older, prehistoric, oral medical tradition, which is still active and vibrant today as folk medicine (Kutumbiah, 1962). As pointed out by Kutumbiah, *ayurveda* is an extremely rational, logical, and coherent system of medicine based on the "logicist or rationalist school of Indian philosophy." Rooted in the humoral theories, it has a fundamental similarity with other traditional medical systems. Its emphasis on the listing of names, metonymy, synonymy, and poetic elaboration, linking it to the social and cultural constructions of symbols and relations, is unique.

Conceptually, the basis of the diagnoses, pathology, and therapeutics of *ayurveda* is the doctrine of *tridosa*. It envisages the body as being composed of the elemental ingredients, called *bhutas*, of space, air, fire, water, and earth. These interact and are modified to support the body with *dhatus* formed from ingested food. The waste products of food, *vayu, pitta,* and *kaph* (roughly equivalent to wind, bile, and phlegm, respectively), support the *dhatus* when they are in proper measure and balance. However, they become *dosas* (disease) when they vitiate *dhatus* through imbalance.

It is interesting to note that the great teacher Charaka classifies diseases into three groups: physical, accidental, and mental. Physical disease arises from abnormal conditions of the body. Accidental diseases are from the action of spirits, poisons, wind, fire, and violence done to the body. Mental diseases (*manasa*) are those that arise from nonattainment of objects desired or coveted. Excessive anger, grief, fear, joy, and malice are all part of mental distemper. This exposition is very simplified. However, it is worth noting that the psychological attributes of sickness were well recognized in ancient times.

*Ayurveda* covers every aspect of medicine, from gynecology to dentistry. Surgery developed as a parallel system. Psychiatry, however, should be given a place of pride in *ayurveda*. The world's first tranquilizer, rawlfia serpentina, has been used by it for mental disease since antiquity. *Ayurveda* gives elaborates classifications to mental disorders. It recognizes endogenous causes (imbalances of the humors in the body interacting with the elements or *dhatus*) as well as exogenous causes (bad spirit, magic, and sorcery). Though the latter are discounted in modern times as "superstition," social causation is implicit in them, as treatment of disorders in this group involves the community. Folk medicine, however, is more dominant in this sphere. Apart from treatment with herbs and chemicals, *ayurveda* contains elaborate psychotherapeutic prescriptions for mental diseases. *Ayurveda*'s strongest point is that, being holistic, it equates stability, balance, and equilibrium with health. It considers mental health as an integral part of life. Medicine only helps to maintain a long and healthy life.

## 3. Galenic-Islamic Medicine

The backbone of traditional Galenic-Islamic medicine is the humoral theory, according to which illness arises from an excess or deficiency of the humors, or the basic qualities of life. The heart is perceived as an organ of emotional functioning or the seat of the vital soul, providing "innate heat" and "vital breath" to the body. Consequently, malfunctioning of the heart provides the cultural framework for focusing attention on the heartbeat, establishing causal links between irregularities in heartbeat and specific personal and social conditions. According to Good (1977, p. 32), heart distress clinically ranges along a continuum from mild excitation to chronic sensations of irregularities to fainting and heart attack. Thus, a cluster of emotional disorders is linked to the distress of the "heart" organ. Further, when the possible causes of heart distress were surveyed, Good found a long list of answers offered by laymen. This included feelings of sadness and anxiety; situational difficulties relating to death, debts, poverty, quarrels, and family illness; problems associated with old age, pregnancy, delivery and miscarriage, or usage of contraceptives; or somatic reasons of lack of blood, low blood pressure, too few vitamins, nerve problems, and so on. Through statistical analysis, the two most important fields of symbols and experiences that emerged were "the problematic of female sexuality" and "the oppression of daily life," two of the most common psychological problems encountered by females in that culture.

# E. ILLNESS BEHAVIOR: RECOGNITION AND HELP-SEEKING

The term "illness behavior" is used to describe how a person behaves when he becomes ill. In a broad sense, it covers a set of sequential behaviors, including how the person recognizes, perceives, and interprets the discomfort or suffering and reacts against it; how he seeks help, attention, or treatment from others; how he communicates and presents his problems or illness to his family, healers, and others; how his role changes when he is sick, including how he is cared for by family members, friends, or others; how he reacts to therapy prescribed or treatment offered by healers, including compliance and adherence to it; and how he accepts or reacts to the results of treatment and the prognosis of his disorders. Thus, illness behavior includes several identifiable elements that are involved in the process of illness (Chrisman, 1977).

## 1. Folk and Professional Mental Disorders Recognized

From the review of mental disorders recognized by folk people, including pre-literate people, it becomes obvious that there is a certain degree of difference in the ways laymen and professional therapists conceive the sickness from which a patient is suffering. The scope of mental sickness covered by ordinary people and medical professionals is different. Ordinary people tend to be concerned with sicknesses that are more explicitly recognizable and may bring more gross disturbance to the community; whereas professional therapists tend to focus on sicknesses that are more or less treatable. Ordinary people follow the rules of reality, while therapists follow the dictates of biomedical professional knowledge. Also, as indicated by Eisenbruch (1990), explanations given by common folk tend to be personal; those given by professionals tend to be impersonal.

A comparison of various explanations given by laymen and professionals shows that there are certain differences in the explanations offered by lay people, traditional or folk healers, and contemporary professionals. The different explanations offered by folk people and professionals is illustrated by Table 2.

## 2. Distinction between "Illness" and "Disease"

From the review just given, it is evident that the way laymen perceive and conceptualize their physical disorders or mental problems is not necessarily congruent with the way they are defined and conceived by contemporary physicians. Through their field experience, this difference was pointed out by scholars and clinicians quite some time ago (Clements, 1932; Lipowski, 1969; Mechanic, 1962). However, the need to make a conceptual distinction between "illness" and

TABLE 2    Range of explanations offered by folk people and professionals.

| | | Folk Concept | Professional Concept |
|---|---|---|---|
| Supernatural | Object intrusion | ++ | − |
| Explanations | Soul loss | +++ | − |
| | Spirit possession | +++ | − |
| | Breach of taboo | ++ | − |
| | Sorcery | ++ | − |
| Natural | Disharmony of nature | +++ | ± |
| Explanations | Incompatibility with natural principles | ++ | + |
| | Fate in life | ++ | − |
| | Noxious features in the environment | + | + |
| Somato-Medical | Insufficient vitality | ++ | ± |
| Explanations | Physical-physiognomy problems | ++ | +++ |
| | Dysfunction of visceral organs | +++ | ++ |
| | Physiological imbalance or exhaustion | +++ | +++ |
| | Inborn or acquired pathologies (heredity) | + | +++ |
| Psychological | Fright | ++ | ± |
| Explanations | Excessive discharge of emotion | + | ± |
| | Overburdening or exhaustion | + | ++ |
| | Psychological trauma | ± | +++ |
| Societal | Social disorder or pressure | − | ++ |
| Explanations | Cultural confusion | − | ++ |

In the table, the level of usage of different explanations is indicated by + signs (+++ indicating high usage) and − indicating no usage.

The table shows that supernatural explanations are utilized only by folk healers and believed by some laypeople, but not by contemporary professionals. Natural explanations are applied more in folk concepts than professional concepts. Somato-medical explanations are used by both folk healers and professionals, and psychological explanations more by professionals. Societal explanations are utilized only by contemporary professionals.

"disease" was advocated only recently, beginning with American social psychiatrist Leon Eisenberg (1977). It is suggested that the two terms, "illness" and "disease," be distinguished and used differently. Artificially, "illness" is assigned to the sickness that is experienced and conceived by the patient or his family. It is subjective, experiential, and stems from the folk point of view. It is based on personal knowledge, folk concepts, and the cultural interpretation of how a laymen describes suffering, attributes the cause of his problems, and reacts and copes with the ill condition.

In contrast, "disease" refers to the morbid condition or pathological entity that is defined and conceptualized by modern physicians (and psychiatrists). A certain etiological cause is considered (or speculated, even if it is still unknown). It is assumed that the disease will manifest certain patterns, creating an identifiable

|            | Disease                                                                                       | Illness                                                                          |
|------------|-----------------------------------------------------------------------------------------------|----------------------------------------------------------------------------------|
| Definition | Pathological entity conceptualized by professionals                                           | Morbid condition experienced and conceived by patient and family                 |
| Orientation | Objective observation of disorder                                                            | Subjective experience of suffering                                               |
| Foundation | Biomedical foundation                                                                          | Personal-sociocultural orientation                                               |
| Phenomena  | Manifest certain pattern with identifiable clinical picture and predictable course            | Dysfunctional phenomena with disturbance to self, family, community              |
| Help-Seeking | Visit modern health facilities                                                               | Consult folk healers                                                             |
| Assessment | Diagnosis by objective evidence                                                               | Comprehend by intuition                                                          |
| Explanation | Scientific explanation                                                                        | Folk, supernatural interpretation                                                |
| Remedy     | Specific treatment to be prescribed                                                           | Magic and symbolic maneuver                                                      |
| Therapy    | Direct treatment for etiology                                                                 | Indirect, subtle intervention                                                    |
| Goal       | Cure of disorder Regaining health                                                             | Help the person from suffering or solve the problems                             |

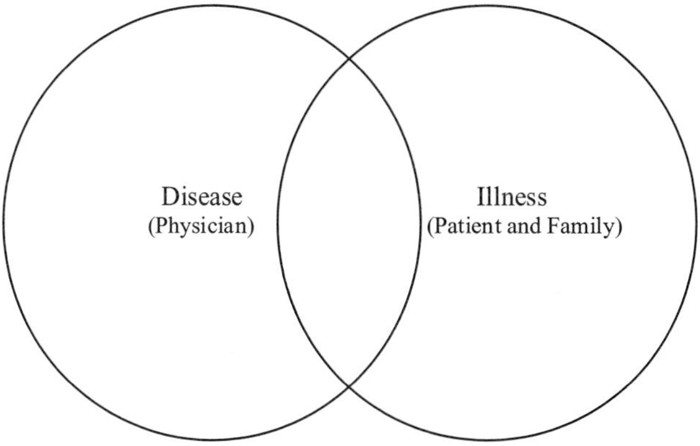

Disease
(Physician)

Illness
(Patient and Family)

FIGURE 5   Conceptual distinction between "disease" and "illness."

clinical picture, and will take a predictable clinical course with a certain prognosis. Also, based on the diagnosis, a specific treatment can be prescribed, if such a remedy is available. Thus, there are two systems operating on the same patient or on the same sickness—"illness" from the patient's perspective and "disease" from the physician's point of view. They may overlap or be incongruent with each other (see Fig. 5).

For example, a person who suffers from headaches and back pain, cannot concentrate at work, loses his temper easily, cannot sleep well at night, and feels tired most of the day may consider himself to be suffering from nervous exhaustion.

He may try an herb medicine or rest and recuperation, hoping that his weakened nervous system will recover and regain strength. If the same person consulted a psychiatrist, he might be diagnosed as suffering from depression and an antidepressant might be prescribed for him. A parent whose child is suffering from irritability, frequent nightmares, poor appetite, and loose stools and is not responding to ordinary available remedies may perceive the problems to be the result of his child losing his soul due to fright. A folk healer may be consulted to call back the lost soul. If the child were brought to see a pediatrician, it might be suggested that he go through a series of laboratory tests to see if he is suffering from some kind of medical disease.

Thus, the physician looks for certain objective evidence to meet the diagnostic criteria that has been established, based on professional knowledge and accumulated experience, and then makes plans for treatment accordingly. The diagnostic criteria may change according to a change in medical knowledge and professional views (as illustrated by the periodical revising of official classification systems). However, physicians hold the view that "disease," as an "entity," exists, and, based on their accumulated professional knowledge, they know how to identify it accurately and treat it effectively. The physician's knowledge is objective, oriented toward scientific logic, and is characterized by a biomedical foundation. This is quite different from the perspective of the patient, who is subjective, even speculative, but, to him, the illness is "actual," subject to individual as well as traditional views and cultural interpretation.

Thus, it is important for the clinician to recognize the potential differences that exist between the way the patient and the therapist perceive and interpret the sickness and conceptualize the problems. It is a clinical art to be able to integrate the realities of illness and disease that are conceived by the patient and the therapist.

### 3. Sick Role and the Reactions of Others

From a sociological point of view, "role" refers to the behavioral expectations of others regarding the individual in question as determined by general cultural norms of proper behavior and the individual's particular social identity (Twaddle, 1972). In each society, a person suffering from illness is delegated a certain "sick role" to play and receives certain reactions and treatments from others. As elaborated by Parsons (1951, p. 436), a sick person is generally exempted from normal social responsibilities. Society generally recognizes that the sick person cannot get well by himself and needs certain kinds of care and help. At the same time, the state of being ill is itself regarded as undesirable and carries with it the obligation to "want to get well." If a person becomes sick, it is generally considered necessary for him to seek technically competent help.

In general, if a person suffers from an acute physical illness with somatic distress, he may be regarded as a "sick" person, receiving comfort and care from others. However, if a person suffers from a chronic disability, is unable to take care of himself, is disturbing others' lives, and is being a burden to family members or staff who offer care, he may be perceived as an undesirable patient and be subjected to neglect or even abuse. Depending on the nature and severity of their disorders, psychiatric patients may be responded to by others in different ways. For instance, charming and hysterical patients, who know how to get attention from others, may receive considerable care from their service deliverers. A hypochondriacal patient may be reacted to positively or negatively by others, depending on whether he is liked or disliked. Strangely behaving psychotic patients, particularly socially disturbing ones, will often be stigmatized or treated in a negative way. Thus, how the patient manifests his problems, and how the people around him react to him, will affect the pathways to treatment, the course of therapy, and the outcome of care.

In Western society, if a person complains that he is "depressed," he will get considerable attention from others. At his workplace, he will be permitted to take a less severe workload, at least temporarily. He will receive care from and the concern of family members or his spouse, if they have a good relationship. At a clinic, he will get attention from the therapist who will ask if he has any suicidal thoughts. It is common medical practice (as well as a medical-legal requirement) for a therapist to do so. If the answer is yes, then the therapist will consider the need for the patient to be hospitalized, to be protected from taking suicidal action, and to receive needed treatment. In contrast, in other cultures, where people are struggling for a living, worrying about food and shelter, if a person mentions that he is "depressed," he will receive a "so what?" kind of reaction. His depression will be viewed as a part of everyday life, nothing to be alarmed about or something about which nothing can be done. In a society where people are expected to work hard and take responsibility for their own lives, others may react to a person's depression as if it were his own fault because he did not have enough will power or a strong enough character to resolve his own problems. He will not receive any special attention or sympathy from others but will be considered a "weak" person. Thus, different patients who are suffering from the same pathology may be reacted to differently by professionals and others and be assigned different "sick" roles.

For instance, in China, a stigma is still strongly attached to psychiatric illness. The patients often find it difficult to get married, particularly females; have trouble finding employment; and are stigmatized by others. As a result, families were still very concerned with having a member who was mentally ill, with more than one-third of them trying to keep it a secret from others (Bunai et al., 1988). In Japan, the stigma toward patients suffering from schizophrenia was so strong that Japanese Psychiatric Association has decided recently to rename the disorder as "integration disbalanced disorder" to reduce a public stigma against schizophrenia.

## 4. Help-Seeking Behavior and Pathways

"Help-seeking behavior" is a part of overall illness behavior. It particularly refers to how the patient (or his family) seeks help for the care of his illness. Help-seeking behavior is determined by multiple factors, including, for instance, how the patient perceives the nature and severity of his illness; how he is motivated to seek help from the health system; how he understands the appropriate health service for his illness and whether he knows such a service is available; how he feels about visiting a care-delivery service; what the sociocultural implications will be of receiving health care; and what the economic effects will be of receiving service delivery. Needless to say, these factors will also be influenced by the availability of the service system that exists in the community. From the standpoint of the community health system, examining a patient's help-seeking behavior is a major issue, as it will reveal the general pattern of how the patient utilizes the health system and whether or not he does so relevantly, adequately, and effectively. From a cultural perspective, it is useful to know the stylized pattern that is adopted by the patient in seeking help in his cultural setting. Such knowledge will offer us an opportunity to alter it if necessary for improvement.

As indicated by Rogler and Cortes (1993), "help-seeking pathways" mean the sequence of contacts made with individuals and organizations by the distressed person and the efforts of his significant others in seeking help, as well as the help that is supplied in response to those efforts. As pointed out by Rogler and Cortes, help-seeking pathways are not random; they are structured by the convergence of psychosocial and cultural factors.

It is a clinical impression that, in many societies, both East and West, patients who have mental illnesses or emotional problems often seek help from folk healers or alternative health systems before they visit psychiatrists (Kleinman, Eisenberg, & Good, 1978; Ness & Wintrob, 1981). Why patients go to see folk healers or psychiatrists is a legitimate question from both clinical and administrative points of view. In some societies, because of the lack of modern psychiatrists, the local people still utilize folk healers as the major source of help in dealing with mental problems. However, in many societies, even though modern psychiatrists are available, patients still utilize folk healers as alternative sources of help. The medical anthropologist Castillo (2001), after examining various forms of alternative therapies, pointed out that there are several reasons for this phenomenon. Cultural congruence, orientation to treating "illness," and familiarity were some of the reasons listed. This does not mean that there were no disadvantages to consulting folk healers. Some negative consequences were mentioned, such as neglect or delaying "proper" treatment, suffering from financial fraud at the hands of greedy, unethical healers, or other malpractice, including improper sexual behavior toward female clients by male healers. Still, many people, particularly those who were not satisfied with modern psychiatric service, sought help from alternative therapists in whom they believed.

## 5. Service Utilization and Compliance

We all know that many social factors significantly affect the pattern of mental health service utilization. Financial factors, including the medical insurance system, the cost of visits, and the availability of service are some of the social factors that have a direct impact on how the services are utilized by a patient. Beyond these factors, there are ethnic, racial, and cultural factors, as well.

Many investigations conducted in the United States have pointed out that, in contrast to the majority group of Caucasian-Americans, many minority groups tend to underutilize the existing (modern) mental health system (K. M. Lin et al., 1982; T. Y. Lin et al., 1978; Sue, 1977) and also tend not to adhere to the service if they do connect with it. For example, Sue and Zane (1987) reported that among ethnic minorities, more than 50 percent dropped psychotherapeutic treatment after their first appointment. Wells, Hough, Golding, Burnam, and Karno (1987) reported that less-acculturated Mexican-Americans tended to use outpatient mental health services less frequently (one-seventh as much) than non-Hispanic Caucasian-Americans in the Los Angeles area.

Many explanations have been offered for these phenomena. For instance, Karno and Edgerton (1969) have pointed out that, due to their perception and definition of mental illness, Mexican-Americans tend to seek treatment for obviously psychiatric disorders from family physicians. The patients' orientation to and understanding and expectation of psychiatric therapy affect their patterns of utilization. Cultural incongruities between the patient and treatment are considered to play a role in the results among Hispanic patients (Miranda, 1976). Language barriers are always cited as major problems. The utilization of interpreters in psychiatric settings, particularly in psychotherapy, tend to disrupt and delay the work, making it difficult. Finally, therapists' cultural insensitivity is another reason that needs to be considered.

Culturally relevant psychiatric care is a crucial need in clinical reality. This subject will be elaborated in further detail in Chapters 5, Culturally Competent Clinical Assessement, and Chapter 6, Culturally Comptent Clinical Care.

## REFERENCES

### A. Culture and Stress

Becker, S. (1991). Treating the American expatriate in Saudi Arabia. *International Journal of Mental Health, 20*(2), 86–93.

El-Islam, M. F. (1975). Culture bound neurosis in Qatari women. *Social Psychiatry, 10,* 25–29.

El-Islam, M. F. (2001). The woman with one foot in the past. In W. S. Tseng & J. Streltzer (Eds.), *Culture and Psychotherapy: A guide to clinical practice* (pp. 27–41). Washington, DC: American Psychiatric Press.

Loo, C. M., Singh, K., Scurfield, R., & Kilauano, B. (1998). Race-related stress among Asian American veterans: A model to enhance diagnosis. *Cultural Diversity and Mental Health, 4*(2), 75–90.

Mumford, D. B. (2000). Culture shock among young British volunteers working abroad: Predictors, risk factors and outcome. *Transcultural Psychiatry, 37*(1), 73–87.

Spencer, D. J. (2000). Anomie and demoralization in transitional cultures: The Australian aboriginal model. *Transcultural Psychiatry, 37*(1), 5–10.

Taft, R. (1977). Coping with unfamiliar cultures. In N. Warren (Ed.), *Studies in cross-cultural psychology* (Vol. 1). London: Academic Press.

Vogel, E. F. (1962). Entrance examination and emotional disturbances in Japan's "new middle-class." In R. J. Smith & R. K. Beardsley (Eds.), *Japanese culture: Its development and characteristics.* Chicago: Aldine.

## B. Culture-Shaped Coping Patterns

Fairbank, D. T., & Hough, R. L. (1981). Cross-cultural differences in perception of life events. In B. S. Dohrenwend & B. P. Dohrenwend (Eds.), *Stressful life events and their contexts.* New York: Prodist.

Ide, B. A., Tobias, C., Kay, M., Monk, J., & de Zapien, J. G. (1990). A comparison of coping strategies used effectively by older Anglo and Mexican-American widows: A longitudinal study. *Health Care for Women International, 11*(3), 237–249.

Kasl, S. V. (1996). Theory of stress and health. In C. L. Cooper (Ed.), *Handbook of stress, medicine, and health.* Boca Raton, FL: CRC Press.

## C. Folk Explanations of Mental Problems

Clements, F. E. (1932). Primitive concepts of disease. University of California Publications in *American Archaeology and Ethnology, 32,* 185–252.

Currier, R. L. (1966). The hot-cold syndrome and symbol balance in Mexican and Spanish-American folk medicine. *Ethnology, 5*(3), 251–263.

Eguchi, S. (1991). Between folk concepts of illness and psychiatric diagnosis: Kitsune-tuski (fox possession) in a mountain village of Western Japan. *Culture, Medicine and Psychiatry, 15,* 421–451.

Good, B. J. (1977). The heart of what's the matter: The semantics of illness in Iran. *Culture, Medicine and Psychiatry, 1*(1), 25–58.

Good, B. J., & Good, M. D. (1982). Toward a meaning-centered analysis of popular illness categories: "Fright-illness" and "heart distress" in Iran. In A. J. Marsella & G. M. White (Eds.), *Cultural conceptions of mental health and therapy* (pp. 141–166). Dordrecht, The Netherlands: Reidel.

Wen, J. K. (1995). Sexual beliefs and problems in contemporary Taiwan. In T. Y. Lin, W. S. Tseng, & E. K. Yeh (Eds.), *Chinese society and mental health* (pp. 219–230). Hong Kong: Oxford University Press.

## D. Traditional Medicine and Concepts of Disorders

Good, B. J. (1977). The heart of what's the matter: The semantics of illness in Iran. *Culture, Medicine and Psychiatry, 1*(1), 25–58.

Kutumbiah, P. (1962). *Ancient Indian medicine.* Calcutta, India: Orient Longmans.

## E. Illness Behavior: Recognition and Help-Seeking

Bunai, S., Asai, K. H., Asai, T., Zheng, Z. P., & Wang, Z. C. (1988). A cross-cultural study of patterns of help-seeking: Schizophrenic patients in Japan and China. *Japanese Journal of Social Psychiatry, 11*(1), 71–81. (In Japanese.)

Castillo, R. J. (2001). Lessons from folk healing. In W. S. Tseng & J. Streltzer (Eds.), *Culture and psychotherapy: A guide for clinical practice* (pp. 81–101). Washington, DC: American Psychiatric Press.

Chrisman, N. J. (1977). The health seeking process: An approach to the natural history of illness. *Culture, Medicine and Psychiatry, 1*(4), 351–377.

Clements, F. E. (1932). Primitive concepts of disease. University of California Publications in *American Archaeology and Ethnology, 32*, 185–252.

Eisenberg, L. (1977). Disease and illness: Distinctions between professional and popular ideas of sickness. *Culture, Medicine and Psychiatry, 1*(1), 9–23.

Eisenbruch, M. (1990). Classification of natural and supernatural causes of mental distress: Development of a mental distress explanatory model questionnaire. *Journal of Nervous and Mental Disease, 178*(11), 712–719.

Karno, M., & Edgerton, R. B. (1969). Perception of mental illness in a Mexican-American community. *Archives of General Psychiatry, 20*, 233–238.

Kleinman, A., Eisenberg, L., & Good, B. (1978). Culture, illness, and care: Clinical lessons from anthroplogic and cross-cultural research. *Annals of Internal Medicine, 88*, 251–258.

Lin, K. M., Inui, T. S., Kleinman, A. M., & Womack, W. M. (1982). Sociocultural determinants of the help-seeking behavior of patients with mental illness. *Journal of Nervous and Mental Disease, 170*, 78–85.

Lin, T. Y., Tardiff, K., Donetz, G., & Goresky, W. (1978). Ethnicity and patterns of help-seeking. *Culture, Medicine and Psychiatry, 2*, 3–14.

Lipowski, Z. J. (1969). Psychological aspect of disease. *Annals of Internal Medicine, 71*(6), 1197–1206.

Mechanic, D. (1962). Some factors in identifying and defining mental illness. *Mental Hygiene, 46*, 66–74.

Miranda, M. R. (1976). *Psychotherapy with the Spanish-speaking: Issues in research and service delivery* [Monograph 3]. Los Angeles: Spanish-Speaking Mental Health Research Center.

Ness, R. C., & Wintrob, R. (1981). Folk, healing: A description and synthesis. *American Journal of Psychiatry, 138*, 1477–1481.

Parsons, T. (1951). *The social system.* Clencoe, IL: Free Press.

Rogler, L., & Cortes, D. E. (1993). Help-seeking pathways: A unifying concept in mental health care. *American Journal of Psychiatry, 150*(4), 554–561.

Sue, S. (1977). Community mental health services to minority groups: Some optimism, some pessimism. *American Psychology, 32*, 616–624.

Sue, S., & Zane, N. (1987). The role of culture and cultural techniques in psychotherapy: A critical reformulation. *American Psychology, 42*, 37–45.

Twaddle, A. C. (1972). The concept of the sick role and illness behavior. *Advancement in Psychosomatic Medicine, 8*, 162–179.

Wells, K. B., Hough, R. L., Golding, J. M., Burnam, M. A., & Karno, M. (1987). Which Mexican-Americans underutilize health services? *American Journal of Psychiatry, 144*, 918–922.

# CHAPTER 3

# Culture and Psychopathology: Specific Phenomena

## A. CULTURE-RELATED SPECIFIC SYNDROMES

### 1. What Are Culture-Related Specific Syndromes?

Culture-related specific psychiatric syndromes, also called culture-bound syndromes (Yap, 1967) or culture-specific disorders (Jilek & Jilek-Aall, 2001), refer to mental conditions or psychiatric syndromes whose occurrence or manifestation is closely related to cultural factors and thus warrant understanding and management primarily from a cultural perspective. Because its presentation is usually unique, with special clinical manifestations, it is called a culture-related specific psychiatric syndrome. From a phenomenological point of view, such a condition is not easily categorized according to existing psychiatric classifications, which are based on clinical experiences of commonly observed psychiatric disorders in Western societies, without adequate orientation toward less frequently encountered psychiatric conditions and diverse cultures worldwide.

Around the turn of the 20th century, during a period of colonization by Western societies, Western ministers, physicians, and others visited faraway countries, where they encountered behaviors and unique psychiatric conditions that they had never experienced at home. Most of these conditions were known to the local people by folk names, such as *latah, amok, koro, and susto*, and were described by Westerners as "exotic," "rare," "uncommon," or "extraordinary" mental disorders (Meth, 1974; Friedmann & Faguet, 1982), mental illnesses "peculiar to certain cultures" (Yap, 1951), or "culture-bound syndromes" (Yap, 1967), implying that such syndromes are "bound" to a particular cultural region.

Recently, however, cultural psychiatrists have realized that such psychiatric manifestations are not necessarily confined to particular ethnic-cultural groups (see Table 1). For instance, epidemic occurrences of *koro* (penis-shrinking panic) occur among Thai or Indian people, not just among the southern Chinese; and sporadic occurrences of *amok* attacks (mass, indiscriminate homicidal acts) are observed in the Philippines, Thailand, and Papua New Guinea (Burton-Bradley, 1975), and epidemic occurrences of *amok* have been seen in many places in South Asia, in addition to Malaysia (Westermeyer, 1973). Terrifying examples of *amok* have recently occurred with frequency on school campuses and in workplaces in the United States.

Thus, the term "culture-bound" does not seem to apply, and it has been suggested that the term "culture-related specific psychiatric syndrome" would be more accurate to describe a syndrome that is closely *related* to certain *cultural traits* or *cultural features* rather than *bound* specifically to any one *cultural system* or *culture region* (Tseng & McDermott, 1981). Accordingly, the definition has been modified to "a collection of signs and symptoms that is restricted to a limited number of cultures, primarily by reason of certain of their psychosocial features" (Prince & Tcheng-Laroche, 1987), even though it is recognized that every psychopathology is influenced by culture to a certain degree.

As discussed previously (see Section 1: C, How Does Culture Relate to Pathology?), cultural influences on psychiatric syndromes can occur in various ways: through pathogenetic, pathoselective, pathoplastic, pathoelaborating, pathodiscriminating, pathofacilitating, or pathoreactive effect. Based on this framework, culture-related specific syndromes can be positioned according to two parameters: the degree and nature of cultural impact and whether or not the manifested syndromes are specific (Fig. 1). This will help us to examine, compare, and understand them.

## 2. Culture-Related Beliefs as Causes of the Occurrence (Pathogenetic Effects)

### a. Koro *(Genital-Retraction Anxiety Disorder)*

*Definition. Koro* is a Malay term of uncertain origin, which means "to shrink." Clinically, it refers to the psychiatric condition in which the patient is morbidly concerned that his penis is shrinking excessively and that dangerous

TABLE 1  Regional distribution of recognized culture-related specific syndromes.

| Regions / Syndrome | Africa | Central America | South America | Arctic | Asia | South Asia | Australia New Zealand | Pacific |
|---|---|---|---|---|---|---|---|---|
| *Koro* | | | | | South China | Indonesia (?) | | |
| (*Koro* Epidemic) | | | | | South China | Singapore Thailand | | |
| *Daht* Syndrome | | | | | | India | | |
| Frigophobia | | | | | Taiwan, China | India | | |
| Voodoo Death | Africa | | South America | | | | Australia New Zealand | Pacific Islands |
| *Malgri* | | | | | | | Wellesly Is. Australia | |
| *Amok* | | | | | | Malay, Laos, Thailand, Phillipines | | Papua New Guinea |
| Family Suicide | | | | | Japan | | | |
| Cargo Cult | | | | | | | | Melanesia |
| *Taijinkyofusho* | | | | | Japan Korea | | | |
| Brain Fag Syndrome | Nigeria, Uganda | | | | | | | |
| Arctic Hysteria | | | | Greenland and other Arctic areas | | | | |
| Malignant Anxiety | Nigeria and others | | | | | | | |
| Ataques de Nervios | | Puerto Rico | Latin America | | | | | |
| *Latah* (Imu) | | | | | Hokkaido, Japan | Malay, Burma Indonesia Thailand Phillipines | | |
| *Huabyung* | | | Latin America | | Korea | | | |
| *Susto* | | | Latin America | | | | | |

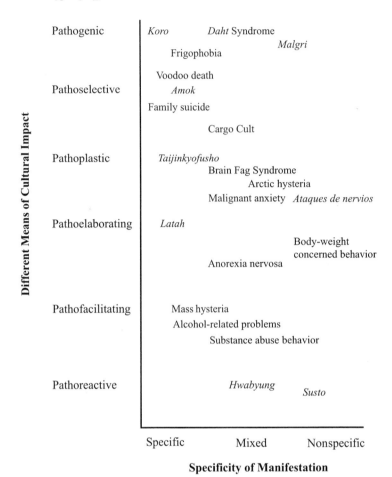

*Type of Effect*

FIGURE 1    Position of culture-related syndromes according to two parameters.

consequences (such as death) might occur. The manifested symptoms may vary from simple excessive concern to obsessive/hypochondriac concern, intense anxiety, or a panic condition related to the "shrinking of the penis." Clinically, this is usually a benign (nonpsychotic) condition that occurs in individual, sporadic cases, but occasionally it may grow to epidemic proportions. The majority of cases are young males who fear that their penises are shrinking. However, the organ concerned may be any protruding part of the body, such as the nose or ear (particularly when patients are prepuberty children) or the nipples or labia (in females). The patient may simply be concerned that his penis is shrinking, with some vague idea that there may be ill results, but some believe specifically that excessive shrinking of the penis into the abdomen may result in death. Therefore, they panic, anxiously seeking life-saving remedies (see Fig. 2). Based on local folk beliefs, different treatments may be undertaken. For example, the patient might drink a hot substance, such as ginger juice or chili pepper jam, to supplement the needed yang element; physically hold or pull the shrinking organ, to avoid the fatal effect; or make noise to chase away the possessing evil, if they believe that the attack is the result of possession by an evil spirit.

---

CASE 1

A Chinese *Koro* Case Reported from Taiwan (abstracted from Rin, 1965)

A 32-year-old single Chinese cook migrated to Taiwan when mainland China was taken over by the communists. He visited a psychiatric clinic with complaints of panic attacks and multiple somatic symptoms. One month prior to his visit, he had seen a traditional Chinese herb doctor, who diagnosed him as suffering from *shenkui* ("kidney deficiency," indicating insufficient vitality) and prescribed the drinking of a young boy's first-morning urine and eating human placenta as a way to supply *qi* (vitality). Around this time, the patient began to notice his penis shrinking and withdrawing into his abdomen, usually a day or two after having sexual intercourse with a prostitute. He became anxious about the condition and ate excessively to relieve intolerable hunger pangs.

The patient's history revealed that he had been brought up in a small town on the Yang-zi River. The eldest of five sons, he was his mother's favorite child. He had little contact with his father, who worked on a junk and was seldom at home. His father died of an unknown disease when the patient was 7. His mother remarried, but the stepfather disliked the patient and frequently abused him physically. Under these circumstances, the patient became an apprentice barber at age 11 and started to learn cooking when he was 16. He was soon able to support himself, but he spent most of his earnings gambling and in brothels, upsetting his mother greatly. At the age of 18, according to the patient, because of excessive masturbation, he became emaciated. He took many kinds of herb medicines, with no relief, until he followed the herb doctor's suggestion and started drinking his own first urine every morning, which cured him in four months.

After he migrated to Taiwan at the age of 22, he worked in a bakery, and once again started gambling and going to brothels when he lost his money. For several years he had sexual intercourse every night to relieve the mounting sexual tension. At age 30, he had his first attack of breathlessness and palpitations. He wandered from one doctor to another for vitamin injections, believing that they supplemented a vital element for him. Later, he consulted the herb doctor and was warned that he was suffering from *shenkui* and would eventually die if he continued going to prostitutes. Almost irresistible sexual desire seized him whenever he felt slightly better; yet he experienced strange "empty" feelings in his abdomen when he had sexual intercourse. He often found his penis shrinking into his abdomen, became very anxious, and held on to his penis in terror.

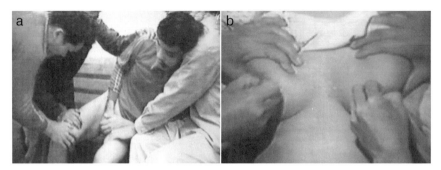

FIGURE 2    *Koro* in Southern China. (a) A Chinese man, during an epidemic in Leizhou Peninsula in 1985, suffered from a *koro* panic attack, shouting for help in the fear that his penis would
shrink into his abdomen and he might die, while his wife and friends tried to "rescue" him. (b) A
Chinese female, suspected to be suffering from *koro*, was "rescued" by her female friends, who held
her and pulled at her "shrinking" nipples [Courtesy of Mo Gan-Ming, M.D.].

*Common Clinical Manifestation.*    Most of the sporadic *koro* cases involve young
male patients, who are mostly single (as illustrated by Case 1). At the core of the
symptoms is the concern that the penis is shrinking or is going to retract into
the abdomen. There may be an accompanying fear of impending death. Based
on the severity of the fear, clinically the patient may manifest anxiety, hypochondriacal concern, or a panic state, with some somatic complaints. In sporadic cases,
the condition may become chronic, but in epidemic cases, it is usually transient,
with full recovery.

Sporadic occurrences of female *koro* cases have never been reported. However,
in *koro* epidemics, a small portion of the victims may be female (Chowdhury,
1994; Tseng et al., 1988). In those cases, the female patients demonstrate slightly
different clinical pictures, mainly focusing on the retraction of the nipples and
some on the labia. The clinical condition is characterized by a more or less hysterical panic, associated with multiple somatic symptoms, a bewitched feeling, or
the misinterpretation or accusation by others of being bewitched, which may
occur during an epidemic.

*Geographic and Ethnic Group Distribution.*    Cultural psychiatrists originally considered *koro* (or *suoyang* in Chinese term) to be a culture-bound disorder related
only to the Chinese (Gwee, 1963, 1968; Rin, 1965; Yap, 1965). Most Chinese
investigators have taken the view that the disorder is related to the Chinese cultural belief in *suoyang* (literally means "shrinkage of yang organ"). Gwee (1963),
Yap (1965), and Tan (1981) speculated further that the occurrence of *koro* among
people in South Asian countries, such as Malay and Indonesia, was the result of
Chinese migrants. However, this cultural-diffusion view is doubted now, since
*koro* epidemics have been reported in Thailand and India, as well, involving non-
Chinese victims.

As a result of the dissemination of knowledge about *koro* as a culture-bound syndrome, there is increased literature reporting so-called *koro* cases from various ethnic groups around the world, such as from the United Kindgom (Ang & Weller, 1984; Barrett, 1978), Canada (Ede, 1976), or Israel (Hes & Nassi, 1977). Chiniwala, Alfonso, Torres, and Lefer (1996) reported that a Muslim West African man, who migrated to New York from Guinea, developed an acute psychotic condition associated with the belief that his penis was retracting into his body. His psychotic onset coincided with the holy month of Ramadan and was an expression of guilt over having had sex with prostitutes. Berrios and Morley (1984) reviewed literature that described *koro*like symptoms in a total of 15 non-Chinese subjects. They pointed out that among the cases reported, all suffered from many psychiatric conditions: affective disorders, schizophrenia, and anxiety disorders, as well as drug abuse and organic brain disorders. They referred to the cases as having "*koro*like symptoms," which is not exactly the same as the "*koro* syndrome." Thus, it is necessary for clinicians to recognize that "*koro*" is referred to on different levels as a symptom, a syndrome, or an epidemic disorder (see Section 3: B, Epidemic or Collective Mental Disorders).

*Theoretical Consideration.*    According to Edwards (1985), as soon as the *koro* case was reported in literature at the end of the 19th century, it engendered psychoanalytic interpretations. Due to its focus on the male genital organ, castration anxiety was one of the natural dynamic speculations made by some clinicians (Kobler, 1948; Rin, 1965). Chinese cultural psychiatrist Wen (1995) pointed out that *suoyang* as a genital-retraction anxiety disorder can be viewed as a part of a cluster of culture-related sexual-somato-anxiety disorders that include brain neurasthenia, kidney-deficiency disorder, and frigophobia, in addition to *suoyang*. These morbid conditions, although manifested symptomatically in different ways, share the common underlying concern with the weakness or vulnerability of a person (lacking vitality or yang deficiency). They can also be considered part of a pathological spectrum including various hidden psychosexual disorders. These concerns are based on two interrelated cultural beliefs: the yin and yang theory, according to which excessive loss of the yang element (through semen discharge) will result in sickness; and the belief that an evil spirit, such as the fox spirit, wanting the yang element, may disguise itself as a pretty young female who seduces a male to obtain his yang element. A man seduced by such an evil spirit will become sick and even die from the excessive loss of his yang element, a common theme that appears frequently in the folk ghost stories of Liao-Zhai (see Fig. 3).

Similarly, Carstairs (1956) has suggested that the *dhat* syndrome (described in India) and *koro* share a common pathology, the former being concerned with the excessive leaking of semen and the latter with the retraction of the genital organ, both vulnerable conditions for a man.

FIGURE 3    Picture from the Chinese folk ghost story of *Liao-Zhai*. This story is about an evil fox spirit disguised as a pretty woman who seduces young men, absorbing their yang element—the core concept associated with *suoyang* (*koro*) problems.

*Clinical Implications.*    Clinicians habitually try to fit pathologies into certain diagnostic categories. Because the patient, based on "misinterpretation" (from an etic point of view), is morbidly preoccupied with the idea that certain ill-effects may occur due to the excessive retraction of his genital organ, the condition may, in a broad sense, be classified as a hypochondriac disorder as defined in DSM-IV. The condition is also similar to a body dysmorphic disorder, as the patient is preoccupied with a culturally induced, imagined defect in his physical condition. If the focus is on how the patient reacts emotionally, how he responds to the culture-genic stress, with fear, anxiety, or a panic state, anxiety disorder may be considered. Although depersonalization was originally proposed by Yap (1965), most cases do not exhibit such altered states of consciousness. However, when we try to categorize culture-related specific syndromes according to the existing nosologically oriented classification system, their meaning and purpose are lost.

As for therapy of sporadic individual cases, assurance may be provided or medical knowledge offered in the form of educational counseling to eliminate the patient's concern about impending death. This supportive therapy may work in many cases, but, for someone who firmly believes the *koro* concept, it may not. In general, a young, unmarried male, who lacks adequate psychosexual knowledge and experience, will respond favorably to therapy. If necessary, it is desirable to work on issues such as the patient's self-image, self-confidence, or masculinity.

### b. Dhat *Syndrome (Semen-Loss Anxiety)*

Very closely related to the genital-retraction anxiety disorder (*koro*) is the semen-loss or semen-leaking anxiety disorder, or spermatorrhea, also known by its Indian folk name, *dhat* syndrome. According to Indian psychiatrists Bhatia and Malik (1991), the word "*dhat*" derives from the Sanskrit *Dhatu*, which refers to the elixir that constitutes the body. Of the seven types of *Dhatus* described, semen is considered the most important. In the Indian system of medicine, *Ayurveda*, it is suggested that disturbances in the *Dhatus* result in an increased susceptibility to physical and mental disease.

The term "*dhat* syndrome" was first used by the Indian psychiatrist N. N. Wig in 1960 and by J. S. Neki in 1973. The syndrome refers to the clinical condition in which the patient is morbidly preoccupied with the excessive loss of semen from an "improper form of leaking," such as nocturnal emissions, masturbation, or urination. The underlying anxiety is based on the cultural belief that excessive semen loss will result in illness. Therefore, it is a pathogenically induced psychological disorder. The medical term "spermatorrhea" is a misnomer, as there is no actual problem of sperm leakage from a urological point of view.

From a clinical point of view, the patients are predominantly young males who present vague, multiple somatic symptoms such as fatigue, weakness, anxiety, loss of appetite, and feelings of guilt (about having indulged in sexual acts such as masturbation or having sex with prostitutes). Some also complain of sexual dysfunction (impotence or premature ejaculation). The chief complaint is often that the urine is opaque, which is attributed to the presence of semen (Paris, 1992). The patient attributes the passing of semen in the urine to his excessive indulgence in masturbation or other socially defined sexual improprieties (Bhatia & Malik, 1991). Clinically, the patient is characterized as anxious or hypochondriacal. As part of the illness behavior, the patient will ask the physician to examine his urine to determine whether there is leaking of semen or not. The patient also always asks for a tonic or other remedy to regain the vitality lost due to excess leakage of semen.

According to Bhatia and Malik (1991), the syndrome is also widespread in Nepal, Sri Lanka (where it is referred to as *prameha* disease), Bangladesh, and Pakistan. In Taiwan, Wen (1995) considers *shenkui* ("kidney deficiency," or insufficient vitality due to excessive loss of semen), prevalent among young Taiwanese men, as the counterpart of the *dhat* syndrome observed among the Chinese. The *shenkui* disorder in traditional medical terminology is often considered equivalent to the neurasthenia referred to by modern Chinese psychiatrists.

Whether it is called *dhat* syndrome in India, *prameha* in Sri Lanka, or *shenkui* in China, there is a common characteristic among these syndromes: They are based on folk beliefs that excessive loss of semen will result in illness. Akhtar (1988) pointed out that, according to the religious scriptures of the Hindus, "Forty meals produce one drop of blood, 40 drops of blood give rise to one drop of bone marrow, and 40 drops of marrow form one drop of semen." Variations on this saying are found in the other cultures where semen-loss anxiety disorder is observed. These cultural beliefs that conservation of vitality is important and loss of semen is harmful to the health create culture-genic stress and contribute to the formation of semen-loss anxiety.

It should be explained that the concept of conserving semen as the main resource of vitality is not specific to Asian culture (Bottéro, 1991). Nocturnal emissions were also considered symptoms of excessive venery in European society during the 19th century. However, as noted by Malhotra and Wig (1975), Asian culture condemns all types of orgasms because they involve semen loss and are therefore "dangerous." In contrast, the Judeo-Christian cultures of the 18th and 19th centuries in Europe considered most types of sexual activities outside marriage to be "sinful."

### c. Frigophobia

Frigophobia, or "morbid fear of catching cold," is a clinical condition described by Chinese psychiatrists as a culture-related syndrome of the Chinese (Rin, 1966). In Chinese (Mandarin) it is called *pa-len* or *wei-han* (literally, fear of cold). Such a morbid condition is not very prevalent. Only sporadic cases have been reported since attention was given to the condition as a culture-bound syndrome (Chang, Rin, & Chen, 1975; Chiu et al., 1994).

This unique disorder is characterized by the patient's excessive concern with and morbid fear of catching cold. According to Chinese traditional theory of yin and yang, an imbalance between yin and yang will result in disorders. Excessive yin, caused by cold air or excessive eating of cold food (such as watermelon), will result in weakness and sickness. The chilling sensation of cold sweat is interpreted as a sign of weakness due to excessive yin. Based on these folk concepts, even ordinary people will avoid cold air, cold rain, and eating too much cold food and will wear belly-bands around their abdomens to protect them from catching cold, particularly in cold weather.

At the extreme of this concern, a patient who develops frigophobia will overdress in warm clothes (even in hot weather), wearing a heavy hat to protect his head, surrounding his neck with a warm neckerchief, and wearing many layers of clothing to keep his body from catching cold. In an extreme case, the patient will wrap himself up with a blanket or heavy quilt and stay in bed, afraid to go outside and be exposed to the cold air (Fig. 4).

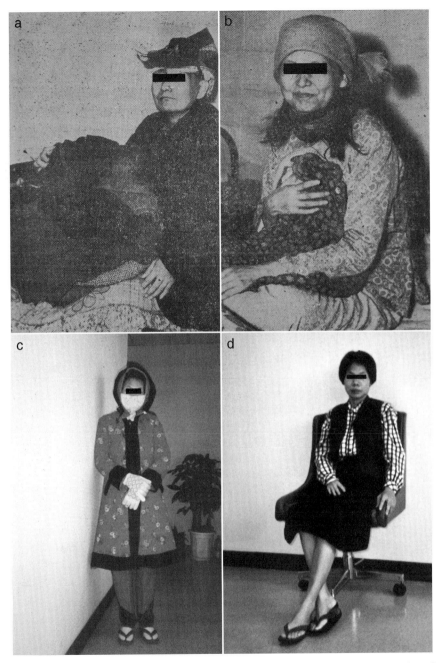

FIGURE 4  Frigophobia reported from Taiwan. (a) A middle-aged Chinese man, after the loss of money and his concubine, wore a wool hat and a cotton-padded overcoat and covered his body with quilts during the hot summer for fear of catching cold. (b) After having a stillbirth, a married women covered her head with a wool scarf, wrapping her neck with a towel, and holding heavy clothes to protect her throat and abdomen from catching cold while ordinary people are wearing short-sleeved summer clothes [From *Bulletin of the Chinese Society of Neurology and Psychiatry*, *1*(2), 1975. Permission from Hai-Gwo Hwu, M.D.]. (c) A divorced woman, after encountering terrifying events, such as being robbed or threatened with a knife by a villain, would develop episodes with fear of catching cold, wearing heavy socks, gloves, a coat, and a face mask to protect herself. (d) Dressed in an ordinary way after recovering from her frigophobia. [(c) and (d) Courtesy of Nien-Mu Chiu, M.D.]

---

CASE 2

---

A Chinese Man Who Suffered from Excessive Fear of Cold
(Abstracted from Tseng & Hsu, 1969/1970)

A 40-year-old Chinese man was born as the eldest and only son of a rich, traditional, extended family. He slept with his grandmother until the age of 11 and was
babied by her. Like every Chinese mother and grandmother, she was concerned
with his bodily health and especially with his warmth. She kept him overdressed
and wearing a belly-band, even in adult life. He was not permitted to leave the bed
at night. Arrangements were made for him to urinate into a chamber pot until he
was 11 years old, as a precaution against catching cold.

When he was grown up, borrowing power from his father, he became a general
when he was only in his early 30s. It was arranged for him to marry a woman older
than himself, whereas it is usual for a Chinese man to marry a younger woman.
His family thought that an older woman would take good care of him. Because of
wealth and social status, he was later able to have several concubines. When the
communists took over mainland China, he fled to Taiwan, taking with him only his
money and one of his concubines.

Several years later, he learned that his father had been persecuted by the communists and his mother had died of sickness after the tragedy. This precipitated
his first attack of frigophobia when he was 35. He presented himself at the hospital in the heat of the summer swathed in many layers of clothing and quilts and
complaining of feeling cold (see Fig. 4a). He did not complain of feelings of sadness,
loneliness, or depression. Similar attacks occurred twice more, each time following a loss. In one instance it was a loss of money; in the other, the loss of his
concubine.

---

As pointed out by Chang and associates (1975), as well as Tseng and Hsu
(1969/1970), there is a common tendency for Chinese patients to manifest their
psychological problems with somatized symptoms. However, in some cases, the
somatization is not manifested merely as a somatic symptom, but as an elaborate
way of being concerned and complaining about a morbid somatic condition.
Fear of catching cold is one such example.

### d. Sorcery Fear and Voodoo Death (Magic-Fear-Induced Death)

The peculiar phenomena of "voodoo death" refers to the sudden occurrence of
death associated with taboo-breaking or curse fear. It is based on the belief in
witchcraft, the putative power to bring about misfortune, disability, and even
death through "spiritual" mechanisms (Hughes, 1996). If someone breaks a taboo,
or is cursed by others, he will be punished by death. A severe fear reaction may
result from such beliefs, which may actually end in death. From a psychosomatic

point of view, it would be psychogenically induced death. From a cultural psychiatric perspective, it is another example of culture-induced morbid fear reaction.

---

CASE 3
_____

An African Man Died after Learning That He Broke a Taboo

A young African man on a journey in the Congo lodged at a friend's house for the night. The friend had prepared a wild hen for their breakfast, a food strictly banned by a local rule that was supposed to be inviolably observed by the young. The young man inquired whether it was indeed a wild hen, and when the host answered, "No," he ate heartily and proceeded on his way. A few years later, when the two met again, the old friend asked the young man if he would eat a wild hen. He answered that he had been solemnly charged by a wizard not to eat that food. Thereupon the host began to laugh and asked him why he refused now after having eaten it at his table before. On hearing this, the young man immediately began to tremble, so greatly was he possessed by fear, and in less than 24 hours he was dead. (According to Cannon, 1957, this case was reported by Merolla on his voyage to the Congo in 1682, and was cited by Pinketon, 1814.)

---

Modern physicians (Engel, 1971) have recognized sudden death related to psychological stress occurring during experiences of acute grief, the threat of the loss of a close person, personal danger, or other stressful situations. Instead of considering these instances of psychogenic death, there has been speculation on the mechanism of death, for instance, the possibility of death resulting from natural causes coincidentally or the possible use of poisons in association with sorcery or witchcraft. Investigating the medical records and interviewing aboriginal medical field workers in Australia, Eastwell (1982) speculated that the victims, secondary to excessive fear reaction, died from dehydration or existing physical illness, particularly the elderly patients. No matter what the direct cause of death, the psychological fear of sorcery by the victim, his family, or other people around him, certainly contributed to the intense emotional fear and fatalistic reactions. Such psychological reactions will in turn contribute to physical ill effects, such as not eating or drinking water, or provoke the aggravation of underlying physical illnesses and become fatal.

### e. Malgri _(Territorial Anxiety Syndrome)_

Another interesting psychiatric syndrome attributed to culture-induced stress is the so-called _malgri_ originally reported by Australian cultural psychiatrist John Cawte (1976). _Malgri_ is a local name for aborigines who inhabit the Wellesley Islands of the Gulf of Carpentaria, Australia. The central theme in _malgri_ is a mutual antipathy between land and sea. The local people believe that a person who enters the sea without washing his hands after handling land food runs the risk of succumbing to *malgri*. If the precautions are neglected, the totemic spirit that guards the particular littoral is believed to invade the belly "like a bullet." The victim grows sick, tired, and drowsy. He suffers from headaches, a distended abdomen, and groans in pain. Clinical symptoms cover a range of Western diagnoses. The local people have special remedies to treat this "sickness of intruders." A grass or hair belt is unraveled to provide a long cord, one end of which is tied to the victim's foot, while the other end is run down to the water, to point the way home for the intruding spirit.

### 3. Culture-Patterned Specific Coping Reactions (Pathoselective Effect)

#### a. Amok *(Indiscriminate Mass Homicide Attacks)*

*The Nature of the Behavior.* "*Amok*" is a Malay term that means "to engage furiously in battle" (Westermeyer, 1973). Cultural psychiatrist P. M. Yap (1951), who brought attention to this phenomenon as one of the mental diseases "peculiar to certain cultures," defined *amok* as "an acute outburst of unrestrained violence associated with (indiscriminate) homicidal attacks, preceded by a period of brooding and ending with exhaustion and amnesia." *Amok* homicides are distinct from other murders: The killer chooses an extremely destructive weapon, a crowded location, and insanely and indiscriminately kills a large number of people (Westermeyer, 1972).

Running *amok* has been noticed in Malay in the past and has even been described in a book (see Fig. 5a). There has been much speculation as to why *amok* behavior tends to occur in Malay society. One explanation is its connection to the religious background of the people. Muslims are not permitted to commit suicide, which is considered a most heinous act in the Mohammedan religion (Ellis, 1893). Amercian cultural psychiatrist Joseph Westermeyer (1982) has reviewed past explanations about the nature of *amok* from multiple perspectives, including biological, psychological, social, and cultural. Aggressive-homicidal behavior influenced by infectious diseases has been considered, along with malaria, dengue, neurosyphilis, epilepsy, and so on, as biological in some cases. From a psychological point of view, an extraordinary sensitivity to hurt and the tendency to blame others for one's own difficulties are considered possible causes for the phenomenon. Loss of social standing by way of insult, loss of employment, or financial loss have been posited as a precipitating event for *amok*.

From a cultural perspective, behavioral scientist J. E. Carr (1978) has done a detailed analysis to explain the relation between *amok* behavior and Malay culture.

FIGURE 5   *Amok* in Malay. (a) A picture from an old book showing a Malay man with a knife in his hand running *amok* and being chased by the villagers with weapons [from *The Real Malay*, by Swettenham, Sir Frank, London: John Lane, 1900]. (b) A specially designed weapon, kept in a police station in Malaysia in the past, for catching dangerous men who had run *amok* [Courtesy of Eng-Seong Tan, M.D.].

According to Carr, there is a great emphasis on being passive, unemotional, nonconfrontational, and obedient in Malay culture. Hence, the people, especially those in traditional rural areas, are inexperienced and unprepared to cope with social stress in the form of interpersonal confrontation, social or economic frustration, and psychological assault. According to social expectations, a person must comply and withdraw until the conditions for exercising traditional options for retaliation (in the form of *amok*) and subsequent social sanctions (explained as "insanity") are fulfilled. As Carr points out, the culture itself, evolved to reduce tensions, may contribute significantly to the stress of its members. Still, the cultural system does provide, in its own way, the means by which threatening phenomena can be defined and explained, corrective measures applied, and favorable outcomes anticipated. In other words, *amok* behavior is a purposive, motivated, and subtly sanctioned coping behavior (Carr & Tan, 1976; Tan & Carr, 1977), by means of pathoselective effects.

Because *amok* is a phenomenon commonly observed in Malay in the past, a special weapon has been designed and placed in all police stations for dealing with *amok* people (see Fig. 5b). It is a tridentlike weapon in the shape of a two-forked prong attached to a long handle, which allows police to press an *amok* runner against a wall and capture him without having to grapple with him.

*Psychiatric Examination of Subjects.* The Chinese-Malay psychiatrist Een-Seong Tan has had the opportunity to carry out psychiatric examinations of surviving *amok* runners. According to Tan (1965), during a three-year period (1962–1965) at Tampoi Mental Hospital in Johore Bahru, Malaya, there were 107 remanded criminal cases. Among them, 15 involved homicidal behavior. Of these, five were recognized as *amok* cases, and all were diagnosed as schizophrenia. As mental health specialists of the South Pacific commission, Schmidt and his colleagues (1977) were able to study 24 cases of *amok* found between 1958 and 1969 in Sarawak, East Malaysia. According to them, all of the subjects warranted psychiatric diagnoses that included paranoid schizophrenia (seven cases); paranoia and endogenous depression (three cases each); chronic schizophrenia, anxiety reaction, and neurosyphilis (two cases each); and paranoid reaction, paranoid personality, involutional melancholia, manic-depression, and epilepsy (one case each). As they pointed out, it is apparent that *amok* behavior does not appear in conjunction with one specific psychiatric disorder. Since many of the people who run *amok* may be killed during their violent behavior, there is no opportunity to examine them. Only those who are caught alive are available for psychiatric assessment. Therefore, there is no way to assess clinically the kind of people *amok* runners are as a whole.

*Amok Behavior in Other Areas.* The outburst of aggressive (mass) homicidal behavior is not necessarily confined to one cultural area but can potentially be observed elsewhere. As the only psychiatrist available in the Territory of Papua and New Guinea, B. G. Burton-Bradley (1968) reported seven cases of *amok* syndrome that he observed over his eight-year service there, between 1960 and 1968. His report challenged the notion that *amok* is culturally bound to Malay society.

In 1972, the American cultural psychiatrist J. Westermeyer, after serving as a consultant to Laos for many years, studied a total of 32 homicidal cases. Among them, 20 were considered *amok* cases. Reviewing the *amok* behavior reported in various societies, including Thailand, the Philippines, Malaysia, Indonesia, plus his own field observations in Laos, Westermeyer (1973) challenged the previous view that *amok* occurs endemically within a particular society. He indicated that *amok* could happen in a fashion by "communicability" and through "transmission" from one population to another. He also pointed out that *amok* homicide tends to wax and wane in epidemic proportions over time. During periods of momentous political, social, and economic upheaval, there could be increased rates of *amok* in a society.

During the past decade in the United States, there have been increasing episodes of massive (and aimless) killing of people in neighborhoods and work-places and of teachers/students in schools by deadly military weapons. The episodes are occurring so frequently, in such a "fashionable" manner, that they have caused anxious concern in many communities. These are American versions of *amok* attacks.

### b. Family Suicide

When adults encounter severe difficulties (such as financial debt or a disgraceful event), there are many ways to deal with such problems. Japanese parents, may decide to commit suicide together with their young children. This stress–coping method is based on the cultural belief that it would be disgraceful to live after a shameful thing had happened, and that the shame would be relieved by ending one's life. This is coupled with the belief that the children, if left as orphans, would be mistreated by others. Therefore, it would be better for them to die with their parents (see Fig. 6). This unique way of solving problems was often

FIGURE 6   Family suicide in Japan. (a) Mr. A, his wife, and their son and daughter died together from their car exhaust fumes because they were unable to pay their debts. (b) Mr. B, his wife, and their two daughters commited suicide together by driving their car over a cliff into the sea. [From Japanese newspapers. Courtesy of Shingo Takahashi, M.D.]

observed in Japan in the past and even continues at present (see Chapter 4: H, Suicide Behavior).

### c. Cargo–Cult Syndromes (Millenniary Delusions)

Numerous social and behavior scientists have noted that, historically, there have been occurrences of "crisis cults" in many different countries. The Taiping (Great Peace) Rebellion in China, Kikuyu maumau in Kenya, and the Ghost Dance of the Plains Indians of North America are some examples. Central to all these cultures are marked feelings of inferiority, conflict, and anxiety among the member-participants after being exposed to other, superior cultures and an attempt to renovate their self-images. Underlying these nonlogical, magic-religious endeavors is a strong wish for resolution of their social, economic, and political problems and for a new and better way of life, such as that of the invading, superior cultures.

One kind of crisis cult is the "cargo cult" that has repeatedly arisen in Melanesia over the past century as a means of obtaining the manufactured articles possessed by European invaders (Lidz, Lidz, & Burton-Bradley, 1973). "Cargo" is a neo-Melanesian or pidgin word that designates all of the manufactured goods, including canned foods and weapons, possessed by the Europeans, which are greatly desired by the indigenous people. Without knowing how the "cargo" was manufactured in the home countries of Europe, based on their own folk beliefs, the local people thought that it was given to the white people by their powerful ancestors through the performance of proper rituals. Accordingly, the local people tried to perform the white people's rituals, in the hopes that their ancestors would send them a lot of cargo and their lives would eventually be full of wealth.

To describe this phenomenon, B. G. Burton-Bradley, a cultural psychiatrist who practiced in Papua New Guinea, presented the term "cargo–cult syndrome" in 1975. Basically, the term referred to people who believed in the cargo cult and were possessed by the magical, grandiose idea that they could communicate with and eventually receive cargo from the gods. Most of the people lived in the highlands (see Fig. 7a) where they saw the "big bird" (airplane) deliver cargo to the airport, the only way to transport material to the area (see Fig. 7b). It was their misinterpretation that if they followed the white people's behavior, they would also receive things that they wanted from the gods. In order to achieve their goal, they practiced various odd rituals, usually imitating white people's behavior, such as building a cross in the back yard for worship (see Fig. 7c), imitating a foreign soldier's march (see Fig. 7d), or clearing their back yards (as if building an airstrip), hoping that the "big bird" would land with cargo for them. Some would perform the traditional ritual of sacrificing a human being to please the gods. This behavior might be individual, or it might involve a group of followers who gave up their normal lives to perform religious rituals, waiting for the arrival of the cargo, not only for several months, but for many years. They would become collectively deluded and led by a cult leader.

FIGURE 7   Cargo cult in Papua New Guinea. (a) People living in the highland area, where the airport is the main place to interact with the outside world. (b) The airport with a "big bird" arriving and delivering cargo. (c) The local people, believing in the cargo cult, built a cross in imitation of the white people's worshiping of the almighty God. (d) Local people marching like U.S. soldiers in imitation of a white people's "ritual." [Source unknown.]

A report from Burton-Bradley's investigation (1975, 1982) indicated that many people involved in cargo cults, particularly the cult leaders, could be considered clinically psychotic cases, suffering from schizophrenia, delusional disorders, or mania. Some manifested their cargo-cult behavior alone, but, often, there were many followers, and the phenomenon needed to be considered a collective mental disorder.

As a culture-related specific syndrome, it may be understood that culture contributed to the stress that was encountered and also shaped the unique, pathological pattern of coping with it, a combination of pathogenic and pathoselective effects. Because there were no further reports of cargo cults after Burton-Bradley's initial report in 1975, it is unclear whether this phenomenon is still observed in Papua New Guinea.

## 4. Culture-Shaped Variations of Psychopathology (Psychoplastic Effect)

This category includes a group of disorders that manifests a clinical picture that is considerably "different" from the "ordinal" symptomatology of identified disorders described in current psychiatric classifications (of Euro-American origin). It is considered that the uniqueness of the symptomatology may be culturally attributed (i.e., to cultural pathoplastic effects). Culture affects not only the content of symptoms but, even more, the total clinical picture by the absence, addition, or variation of symptoms, resulting in considerable change in the manifestations of variations or subtypes of universally recognized psychiatric disorders.

### a. Anthrophobia (Interpersonal Relation Phobia)

*Definition and Nature of the Disorder.* "Anthrophobia" is the English translation for the Japanese term *taijinkyofushio*. In Japanese, *taijin* means interpersonal, *kyofu* means phobic, and *shio* means syndrome or disorder. Therefore, *taijinkyofushio* literally means the disorder with fear of interpersonal relation. (In this sense, the English term anthrophobia, fear of "human subject," is an incorrect translation.) *Taijinkyofushio* as a psychiatric diagnostic term was invented by Japanese psychiatrist Shoma Morita in the 1920s to address a special type of neurosis commonly observed among Japanese patients (Kitanishi & Mori, 1995). *Taijinkyofushio* is said to be prevalent among Japanese and is considered a culture-related psychiatric disorder.

*Major Clinical Picture.* There are several clinical studies reported by Japanese psychiatrists that provide overviews of the clinical picture of the disorder. Yamashita (1977/1993) has reviewed 100 consecutive cases of *taijinkyofushio* under his care at the university clinic. According to the data, the onset of illness was as early as 10–14 years old (18%), mostly between 15 and 19 years (44%), some later at 20–24 years (26%), and a few after 25 years (12%). In his series of cases, there were 76 males and 24 females, showing that the disorder is more prevalent among males, with a ratio of roughly 3:1. The cardinal symptoms manifested by the patients are fear of one's bodily odors (28%), fear of flushing (22%), fear of showing odd attitudes toward others (18%), fear of eye contact with others (15%), concern about others' attitudes toward oneself (9%), and fear of body dysmorphia (5%). In summary, the majority of the patients suffering from *taijinkyofushio* were teenagers or young adults. Males were three times more likely than females to suffer from this disorder.

*Dynamic Interpretation and Culture Formulation.* Morita theory takes the view that *shinkeishitsu* (including *taijinkyofushio*) is caused by the combined factors of temperamental predisposition, hypochnidical tendency, and psychological interactional effects. The term "psychological interactional effects" refers to a person's excessive attention to certain (body) sensations or external stimulation. As a result, the sensations are alerted and, in turn, lead to more attention. Through this vicious interactional cycle of morbid preoccupation and obsession (called *toraware* in Japanese), a person becomes overly sensitive to and fixated on the morbid condition. The main focus of Morita therapy is to disrupt the cycle of overattention by learning to ignore the sensations or stimulation.

Kasahara (1974) brought out an important point: the characteristic of *taijinkyofushio* is that the fear is induced in the presence of classmates, colleagues, or friends, those who are neither particularly close (such as family members) nor totally strange (such as people in the street). In other words, subjects are concerned with how to relate to people of intermediate familiarity. It is toward these people that a person must exercise delicate social etiquette.

Kasahara explained further that Japan is a situationally oriented society, very much concerned with how others see your behavior. Japanese parents often discipline their children by saying, "Neighbors are watching whatever you do." Also, it is considered that the act of staring at the person to whom one is talking is quite extraordinary and considered to be rude. Thus, there are cultural characteristics that cause Japanese to be hypersensitive about "looking at" and "being looked at."

Kimura (1982) pointed out that patients who were suffering from *taijinkyofushio* were not phobic toward human subjects. On the contrary, they were eager to socialize with others. However, because they were concerned with how they were perceived by others, particularly their friends, they became embarrassed and nervous when relating to them. They were not so concerned about strangers or close family members, just semiclose friends. Within Japanese society, there is such a strong demand to be sensitive to interpersonal interactions that sensitivity is heightened.

*Taijinkyofushio* is a psychological disorder of the adolescent. It is closely related to the problems associated with psychological development in the area of socialization. The Japanese child is raised in an atmosphere of indulgence and trust. However, when this protected child enters the wider world of junior high school, he faces multiple tasks: coping with conflict between biological needs and social restrictions, personal identity problems, and an increasing need for acceptance and love by others in social settings. This intensifies a feeling of unworthiness, making him more concerned about others' sensibilities and reactions (Yamashita, 1977/1993).

For many years, Japanese psychiatrists held the view that anthrophobia was a culture-bound disorder especially related to Japanese culture. This view was challenged when Korean psychiatrist S. H. Lee (1987) reported that anthrophobia is found to be prevalent in Korea, as well. Later, a similar view was mentioned by psychiatrists from mainland China (Y. H. Cui, personal communication, 1996). Based on this new information, it may be said that *taijinkyofushio* is not a psychiatric condition "bound" to Japanese society (or culture). It is a psychiatric problem that can be observed in various societies in Asia in which there are certain cultural traits, that is, where there is overconcern about interpersonal relations with intermediately surrounding persons and a child-development pattern that tends to make it difficult for adolescents, who were overprotected in child-hood, to deal with delicate social relations after entering young adulthood.

### b. Brain Fag Syndrome

Brain fag syndrome was described by Canadian cultural psychiatrist Raymond Prince (1960), who worked as a medical officer in Nigeria in the 1950s. According to Prince, a very common minor psychiatric disorder occurring among the students of southern Nigeria is characterized by subjective complaints of intel-lectual impairment, (visual) sensory impairment, and somatic complaints, mostly of pain or a burning sensation in the head and neck. The student-patients often used the term "brain fag" to complain that they were no longer able to read, grasp what they were reading, or recall what they had just read, basically stress-ing their difficulty in mentation. The term "brain fag" syndrome was suggested by Prince (1960) for this distinct clinical mental condition.

According to Prince, the patients were mostly students in secondary school or university, or teachers or government clerks who were studying in their spare time to raise their educational levels. The patients generally attributed their illnesses to fatigue of the brain due to excessive mental work. Actually, most often the symptoms commenced during periods of intensive reading and study prior to or after examinations. In addition to the subjects' faulty study habits, spending long hours poring over their books with little relaxation, Prince explained that the syndrome was in some way related to the imposition of European learning techniques upon the Nigerian personality. European learning techniques emphasize isolated endeavor, individual responsibility, and orderliness, activities and traits that are foreign to the Nigerian by reason of the collectivist society from which he derives, with its heightened "oralness" and per-missiveness. Prince noted that in Nigeria education was often a family affair, in which one of the brighter children was supported financially by family members; the educated member in turn was expected to be responsible for other family members when the need arose. Because of this family aspect of education, the student was burdened by the responsibility of maintaining the family's prestige. Thus, his academic success or failure was associated with great stress. Prince (1990) considered it more relevant to understand this condition as "adjustment disorder."

Two decades after Prince's initial report on this syndrome in 1960, R. O. Jegede (1983), a psychiatrist from Nigeria, claimed that the disorder was not necessarily confined to students and that excessive studying for examinations may be just one of several possible precipitating factors. For instance, some of the patients with these complaints were housewives. Further, Jegede reported that patients who were sophisticated enough to explain their symptoms in more psy-chologically oriented terms were less likely to complain of the somatic symp-toms associated with brain fag. He suggested that brain fag syndrome did not constitute a single disease entity, as the patients were, in a way, suffering from anxiety neurosis or depressive neurosis.

Twenty-five years after he first described this disorder among the Yoruba, Ibo, and other ethnic groups in southern Nigeria, Prince indicated that it was subsequently observed in Uganda, Liberia, the Ivory Coast, and Malawi (Prince, 1990). Based on this, Prince confirmed that brain fag syndrome was a widespread and prevalent stress disorder among students in Africa south of the Sahara. It should be mentioned that, in China, many students and intellectuals who are excessively competitive academically or under great occupational demands develop a similar kind of "brain-exhausted" syndrome, labeled "brain neurasthenia" by the Chinese (Wen, 1995).

### c. Arctic Hysteria (Pibloktoq)

Arctic (or polar) hysteria, also known by the local name *pibloktoq*, refers to a unique hysterical attack observed among the polar Eskimo people living in Arctic areas. According to Gussow (1960/1985), A. A. Brill published in 1913 the first account of the disorder in psychiatric literature, introducing this native Eskimo illness found in Northwestern Greenland.

The clinical condition is characterized by the sudden onset of loss or disturbance of consciousness. During the attack, as summarized by Gussow (1960/1985) and Foulks (1972), the patient may show various abnormal behaviors, such as tearing off his clothing, glossolalia, fleeing (nude or clothed), rolling in the snow, throwing anything handy around, performing mimetic acts, convulsion, or other bizarre behavior (see Fig. 8). This emotional outburst occurs predominantly in women, but occasionally among men.

FIGURE 8  Arctic Hysteria (*Pibloktoq*) in Greenland. (a) An Eskimo woman suffered from a *pibloktoq* attack, falling on the ground and demonstrating a carpo-pedal spasm. (b) No one knew exactly what to do with her. [From *The Arctic Hysterias*, by Edward F. Foulks, M.D., American Anthropological Association, 1972. Courtesy of the American Museum of Natural History Library.]

No specific precipitating causes are noted. It has been speculated that the reaction is a manifestation of the basic Eskimo personality. Because the reaction is prevalent in winter, it is also thought that it may be related to increased threats of starvation or higher accident rates. Generally, it is suspected that the disorder is due to some basic, underlying anxiety, triggered by severe, culturally typical stresses: fear of certain impending situations, fear of loss, or fear of losing emotional support, including the sense of being on safe, solid, familiar ground.

Because a *pibloktoq* attack is usually brief and followed by complete remission, with the subject claiming amnesia, it can be classified as a hysterical attack. In a certain way, it may be understood as a culturally patterned emotional reaction to stress or trauma. The geographic environment of the polar area may contribute to its occurrence.

From an entirely different angle, some scholars entertain the theory that Arctic hysteria may represent behaviors associated with hypoglycemia. Lack of adequate dietary calcium and low levels of vitamin D synthesis during the Arctic winter are among the reasons considered (Foulks, 1972).

### d. Malignant Anxiety

A special, intensified form of anxiety disorder observed in Africa was reported by Nigerian psychiatrist T. Adeoye Lambo (1960, 1962). He described the condition as characterized by intense anxiety, extreme irritability, restlessness, and intense fear and, therefore, named it malignant anxiety. It was referred to as frenzied anxiety as well. Often, the patient claimed that there was a change in his sense of self and reality, but there was no sign of personality deterioration or disintegration and no latent or overt psychotic symptoms. However, patients often suffered from intense feelings of anger that led to homicidal behavior. The condition usually occurred in sporadic cases, but occasionally as an endemic. Lambo (1962) explained that the occurrence of the disorder was situationally related, associated with adaptational problems to new and stressful life situations. Very often the patients were culturally "marginal" persons, who were in the process of renouncing their age-old cultures, but who had failed to assimilate the new.

## 5. Culturally Elaborated Unique Behavior (Psychoelaborating Effect)

### a. Latah *(Startle-Induced Dissociative Reaction)*

*Defining the Condition.* *Latah* is a Malay word referring to the condition in which a person, after being startled by external stimuli, such as being tickled, suddenly experiences an altered consciousness and falls into a transient, dissociated state, exhibiting unusual behavior (such as echolalia, echopraxia, or command automatism), including explosive verbal outbursts, usually of erotic words that are not ordinarily acceptable. The phenomenon has been observed in other places around the world and has been given various folk names: in Burma (where it is called *yaun*), Indonesia, Thailand (*bah-tsche*) (Suwanlert, 1988), the Philippines (*mali-mali*), and indigenous tribes in Siberia, Russia (*myriachit*), as well as among the Ainu in Japan (who call it *imu*). However, this phenomenon has been found more frequently among the people in Malay, and literature reporting the "mental malady of the Malay" (Ellis, 1897) appeared as early as the end of the 19th century.

The *latah* reaction is found predominantly among women, although men may occasionally be involved. Winzeler (1995) carried out fieldwork in the Kelantan state of mainland Malaysia and Sarawak on the island of Borneo. He reported that, in a village of about 800 people he surveyed, 40 were regarded as *latah* by their neighbors. It was found that *latah* tends to run in families. The overwhelming majority of cases were female. The men who had *latah* experiences were not known to be transvestites or in any way distinctly feminine, as had previously been thought.

In the past, it was primarily young women who were involved in *latah*. Most of the subjects found now are beyond middle age. Most cases are found in rural areas. Some develop *latah* reactions insidiously, without any precipitating events, whereas others symptoms occur after they endure psychologically stressful events. The loss of a significant person usually occurs shortly before the first experience of *latah* reaction. Once the reaction is experienced, it becomes habitual, and, thereafter, any sudden stimulation may provoke it. Hearing a sudden noise or being suddenly touched or poked by others may cause *latah*. Throwing a rope or other snakelike object in front of the person or simply shouting "snake!" will sufficiently startle the person to start a *latah* reaction. During the reaction, the subject will imitate the words of other people (echlalia), repeat other people's actions (echopraxia), follow others' commands, such as barking like a dog (autonomic obedience), sing in a euphoric mood, say words that have sexual overtones, or try to touch or hit a man, which is against cultural dictates (see Fig. 9).

The condition may last for several minutes or several hours if the person is continuously provoked. After the dissociative reaction is over, the subject usually claims amnesia and is puzzled about what has happened. Often, the subject is very apologetic and embarrassed for the (socially) "inappropriate" things she may have said (sexually colored, "dirty" words) or done (such as touching men) during the attack.

It should be pointed out that, in contrast to altered states of consciousness (such as those exhibited in meditation or shaman performances) which are induced through the mental mechanisms of monotonous stimulation (such as quiet chanting or simple, repetitive rhymes) and/or intensive concentration (meditation), the dissociated state of *latah* is induced (or conditioned) by sudden stimulation.

FIGURE 9    A Malay woman provoked into having a *Latah* attack. (a) A Malay woman was startled and, with both her hands raised upward, began to fall into a dissociated *latah* attack. (b) During the *latah* condition, the woman tried to hit the man who provoked her. (c) She joyfully imitated her provoker's gestures (echopraxia) as well as repeated whatever he said (echolaria). [From a documentary film made by Ronald Simons, M.D.]

---

CASE 4

Two Latah Cases Found in Kuala Lumpur, Malay

Mrs. A was a 40-year-old woman who had been working at a university cafeteria for many years. She was known among her co-workers as having *latah* attacks. According to her, she married her husband when she was 20 and bore three children. As a wife and mother, she had an ordinary life. However, about ten years earlier, she had learned that her younger brother had been killed in a traffic accident while riding his motorcycle. She was shocked at this bad news and became sad. One day, while she was gazing into the air, thinking about her deceased brother, someone nearby startled her by touching her from behind. She suddenly became dissociated and manifested strange behavior, talking nonsense for a while, imitating others' behavior. The condition lasted for about ten minutes. She felt slightly dizzy after the episode. After that, every time she was startled by others, either by being poked suddenly or hearing a noise, she fell into this *latah* condition. People around her began to notice this and would provoke her once in a while

*(continues)*

for the sake of amusement. She begged her co-workers not to disturb or startle her, as she wanted to keep her job. She had been working at the university cafeteria for almost a decade and was successful in concealing her *latah* from her supervisor (see Fig. 10).

Mrs. B was about 30 years old. She worked at the university cafeteria with Mrs. A. She recalled that one evening several years earlier, her husband had suddenly touched her, inducing a startled reaction. Since then, her husband liked to startle her sometimes at night before they went to bed. He enjoyed having her become dissociated and acting joyfully and freely before they had intimate relations. However, at her workplace, hardly anyone knew that she had a *latah* tendency and no one bothered her (see Fig. 10).

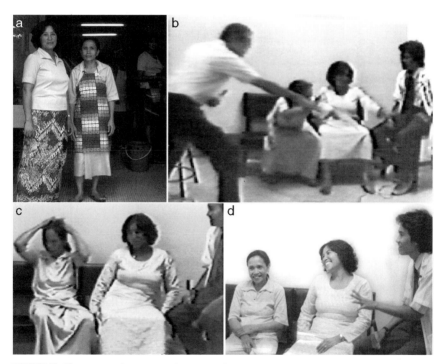

FIGURE 10    Two Malay women demonstrated *Latah*. (a) Two ordinary Malay women (Mrs. A and Mrs. B), who worked in a university cafeteria and were found to have histories of *latah*, agreed to be provoked together in front of a camera and be videotaped. (b) After being startled by a provoker, who pointed toward a nearby man's leg and said it was a "snake," the dissociated woman on the left rushed toward the man, trying to hit his legs (as if it was a snake). (c) In their trance states, they made "monkeylike" gestures, scratching their hair with rhythmic mannerisms and imitating monkey sounds. (d) After they recovered from their attacks and were shown the videotape of their behavior, they felt embarrassed for hitting a man. [Courtesy of Woon Tai-Huang, M.D.]

*The Nature of the Reaction.*    Actually, there is a debate among scholars as to whether the *latah* condition should be regarded as a culture-related "mental disorder" or merely as an "unusual behavior response" found in some cultures. According to Chinese-Malaysian psychiatrist T. H. Woon (1988), who has practiced psychiatry for more than two decades, no patient has ever sought psychiatric help for *latah*; also, among 20 *latah* subjects he investigated in a field study, he found only one subject who had ever sought help from a traditional healer (*bomoh*) for this phenomenon. No healing suggestion was offered by the healer, as the subject was not considered to be suffering from an illness but just exhibiting entertaining behavior. In other words, local people as well as healers do not view this condition as a problem or an "illness." Woon pointed out that it is mainly Western physicians, unused to observing dissociative episodes in daily life, who categorize and report the condition as a "mental disease."

According to Woon (1988), the majority of subjects who experience the *latah* condition are considered "ordinary" people. Except during their *latah* reactions, they function effectively in the community. However, there have been a few cases in which it was difficult to control (or terminate) the dissociated condition of the subjects, and they injured themselves or became aggressive or homicidal toward others. These reactions were labeled "malignant," as opposed to "regular," *latah*.

While subjects are seldom involved in criminal acts during *latah* states, they do occasionally injure others by using nearby weapons in startled reflex actions or at the criminal suggestions of others. Whether or not the person in the *latah* state was criminally responsible in such situations had become a forensic issue as early as the beginning of the century (Fletcher, 1908).

*Etiological Speculations.*    From an etiological point of view, various theories have been proposed. Because most of the examples of *latah* were reported among indigenous groups from south Asia, including aboriginal tribes in Siberia and northern Japan, it has been speculated that race is the essential factor in the etiology.

Anthropologists have tried to understand the *latah* condition from a cultural point of view. Regarding the incidence of *latah* among the Javanese, Geertz (1968) has pointed out that Java culture is characterized by four themes: the value of elegant and polite speech, a concern with social status, sexual prudery, and the dread of being startled. The *latah* reaction is remarkably congruent with the cultural themes emphasized, but in a paradoxical way. Geertz's view was echoed by Kenny (1983), who indicated that the *latah* condition has a profound internal relationship with Malay-Indonesian culture. He stressed the meaning of *latah* as a peculiarly appropriate means of communicating marginality to others. R. L. M. Lee (1981) contended that *latah* subjects are engaging in a "performance," "a role," and "theater," a culture-specific idiom expressing marginality while simultaneously reaffirming normative boundaries. Bartholomew (1994) examined 37 cases of *latah* and reported that 33 belonged to the "habitual" category, a culturally conditioned, cathartic stress response to sudden startling; the remaining four cases belonged to the "performance" category, *latah* as a form of ritualized social gain. He stressed that *latah* was mistakenly labeled in medical terms as "mental illness" because outsiders misunderstood this behavior.

As pointed out by Chiu and colleagues (1972), the traditional polygamous Malay extended family structure is male dominated. Within this cultural system, *latah* is socially accepted as a female attention-seeking response, one of the few permissible overt, excitable, aggressive and/or sexual demonstrations. In other words, *latah* is a culturally sanctioned emotional outlet for females.

American cultural psychiatrist Ronald C. Simons (1980, 1996), after carrying out intensive fieldwork in Malay, hypothesized that most or all human populations contain individuals who can be easily and strongly startled. However, in some cultures, such a hypersensitive startle response is sanctioned and utilized for social purposes. According to Simons, the *latah* reaction is a culture-specific exploitation of a neurophysiologically determined behavioral potential. The condition, similar to fainting, is frequent in populations whose cultures notice, expect, shape, and elaborate on such behavior and rare but not absent in populations that do not pay special attention to it.

*Similar Behavior in Other Areas.*    Numerous conditions that are similar to the *latah* phenomenon have been reported in the literature. *Mali-mali* in the Philippines (Musgrave & Sison, 1910), *young-dah-het* in Burma (Still, 1940), *bahtsche* in Thailand (Simons, 1980), and *myriachit* in Siberia are some examples. The Japanese psychiatrist Uchimura (1956) reported the phenomenon of *imu* among the Ainu, an aboriginal minority ethnic group inhabiting the northern Japanese island of Hokkaido. *Imu* in the Ainu language literally means "possessed." According to the Japanese psychiatrists working in Kokkaido, Daiguji and Shichida (1998), the phenomenon of *imu* among the Ainu has declined and is rarely observed today.

### b. Multiple-Personality Disorder

There are increased reports among Western societies of multiple-personality disorder. Instead of the animal or spirit possession found in developing societies, possession by an "other" self or selves is described in developed societies, where animal or spirit possession is not believed. Whether it is the substitute or variation of dissociation or possession disorder is unclear. Why such a disorder becomes more prevalent, or obtains professional attention in developed societies, is a question we are challenged to answer. Some scholars take the view that such disorders stirred up professional interest among psychiatrists and, as a result, the patients are encouraged to manifest such phenomena. In other words, the disorder is elaborated through professional curiosity.

### c. Body-Weight-Concerned Behavior and Anorexia Nervosa

Excessive concern with being overweight is currently observed in many European and American societies. It is primarily based on health-related concerns, but it is also rooted in the cultural view that "keeping the body in good shape is important." In order to live up to this cultural standard, many diets have been developed to ensure eating the proper low-calorie foods, and many exercise programs have been designed to maintain an ideal body weight. Many diet cookbooks have been published, and the sale of exercise machines has become a good business. In other words, in addition to being healthy, people are under cultural pressure to be slim and beautiful, and they develop elaborate ways to meet these expectations.

Although the causes of eating disorders are still not clear, it is speculated that they may be more likely to happen in some cultures than others. First, in some societies, food is so scarce that people are anxious to obtain it for survival. It is unlikely for people in such a society to not want to eat food. Eating disorders will only be prevalent in societies where food is reasonably abundant. The second observation is crucial: how people perceive the body, particularly the female body. In some cultures, it is considered beautiful to be "fat"—Hawaii, Samoa, and other Pacific Islands, for instance; in some cultures, being fat is considered a sign of being fortunate or blessed. Obviously, there is no concern about being "overweight," and thus there is no reason for suffering from anorexia nervosa.

In contrast, in contemporary European and American societies, there is a tendency to emphasize "slimness" as a sign of beauty or good health. The popular models are usually tall and slim, to the extent that, by other cultures' perceptions and standards, they look "anorexic." Based on this sociocultural factor, anorexia nervosa is considered a culture-related specific syndrome observed mainly in European and American societies (Gordon, 1990; Swartz, 1985). The psychopathological condition is nourished, elaborated, and enforced by the value systems existing in these societies (see Section 4G, Eating Problems).

### 6. Cultural Influence of Prevalent Occurrence of Disorders (Pathofacilitating Effects)

The pathofacilitating effects category includes several conditions that are commonly known as psychiatric disorders. There is nothing particular about them in terms of clinical manifestation (thus, they are not *specific* or *unique* disorders). However, their prevalence is influenced strongly enough by cultural factors that they may be viewed as heavily culture-related syndromes, rather than merely *ordinary* psychiatric disorders. Some examples of pathofacilitating effects are massive hysteria, group suicide, alcohol-related problems, or substance abuse. (Those disorders will be described more in detail in Sections 3B, Epidemic or Collective

Mental Disorders; 4E, Alcohol-Related Problems; and 4F, Other Substance Abuse.)

## 7. Cultural Interpretation of Certain Mental Conditions (Pathoreactive Effect)

### a. Ataques de Nervios *(Attack of Nerves)*

The folk name, *ataques de nervios*, literally meaning attack of nerves, refers to a stress-induced, culturally shaped unique emotional reaction with mixed anxiety-hysterical features (Guarnaccia, Rubio-Stipec, & Canino, 1989; Oquendo, Horwath, & Martines, 1992). This is an illness category used frequently by Hispanic people. Initially observed among Puerto Rican army recruits, it was also labeled "Puerto Rican syndrome" (Fernández-Marian, 1959; Mehlman, 1961).

According to Guarnaccia and associates (1989), this condition typically occurs at funerals, in accidents, or in family conflicts and calls forth family or other social supports. Commonly experienced symptoms include shaking, palpitations, a sense of heat rising to the head, and numbness, symptoms resembling a panic attack (Liebowitz et al., 1994). The individual may shout, swear, and strike out at others, and finally fall to the ground, manifesting convulsionlike movements.

Based on their clinical samples, Salmán and colleagues (1998) reported that most of the patients (about 80 percent) were female. From a clinical, diagnostic point of view, according to DSM-III-R criteria, the condition belongs to many subtypes of disorders, including panic disorder (41.3%), recurrent major depression (19.3%), generalized anxiety disorder (8.3%), nonspecific anxiety disorder (8.3%), and others. Because the clinical picture is of a mixed, rather than a specific, nature, it may be interpreted simply as a folk label for an emotional reaction. Guarnaccia (1993) stressed that *ataques de nervois* refers to an acute episode of social and psychological distress related to upsetting or frightening events in the family sphere. Focusing on symptoms alone misses what is most salient and meaningful about illness categories.

### b. Hwabyung *(Fire Sickness)*

*Hwabyung* in the Korean language literally means "fire (*hwa*) sickness (*byung*)." Based on a traditional Chinese medical concept still prevalent in Korea today wherein an imbalance among the five elements within the body (metal, wood, water, fire, and earth) may cause physical disorders, laypeople in Korea use the folk term "fire sickness" to describe ill conditions. This is a folk idiom of distress characterized by a wide range of somatic and emotional symptoms. According to Korean psychiatrist Si-Hyung Lee (1977), three-fourths of the patients that complained of *hwabyung* were women, who linked their conditions to anger provoked by domestic problems, such as their husbands' extramarital affairs and strained in-law relationships. As pointed out by Pang (1990), the occurrence of *hwabyung* was interpreted when distressed emotions developed in association with intolerable and tragic life situations. Min and Lee (1988) explained that male chauvinism has always been dominant in Korean society, and women tend to suffer from their vulnerable status. When a housewife is mistreated by her husband or is having troubles with her in-laws, according to Korean culture, she has to suppress her emotional reactions so that there will be no disturbance in the stability of the family. As a woman, she is taught to accept defeat, bear frustration, and suppress her hatred. As a result, accumulated "resentment" (*hahn* in Korean) becomes a major issue for some women. Min and Lee interpreted this as the core dynamic for understanding *hwabyung*.

The patients who alleged that they were suffering from *huabyung* usually presented multiple somatopsychological symptoms. Min and Lee (1988) examined Korean patients who claimed that they were suffering from the *hwabyung* condition. Based on the criteria of DSM-III, they claimed that these patients could be diagnosed as having combined depressive and somatization disorders. In addition, general anxiety, panic attacks, and phobias are associated diagnoses. In other words, there is no specific, homogeneous clinical syndrome associated with the claimed condition of *hwabyung*.

It seems that it is better to understand *hwabyung* as a "cultural interpretation" of suffering (through pathoreactive effects). Cultural factors may indirectly contribute to the occurrence of particular psychological problems that are encountered by Korean women, but they do not contribute to the formation of particular psychiatric syndromes (pathogenetically) with unique manifestations (pathoplastically). Almost any emotional reaction was labeled by laymen as an indication of "fire sickness" (*hwabyung*).

From a clinical point of view, particularly among Korean-Americans (as an immigrant population) in the United States, it would be useful for clinicians to know about the folk interpretations of patients so that appropriate psychotherapy could be offered for underlying emotional conflicts (Lin, 1983; Pang, 1990).

### c. Susto *(Soul Loss)*

*Susto* is a Spanish word that literally means "fright." The term is widely used by people in Latin America to refer to the condition of loss of soul (Rubel, 1964 Rubel, O'Nell, & Collado, 1985). It is based on the folk belief that every individual possesses a soul, but, through certain experiences, such as being frightened or startled, a person's soul may depart from the body. As a result, the soul-lost person will manifest certain morbid mental conditions and illness behavior. The remedy for such a condition is to recapture the soul through certain rituals.

George Murdock (1980), based on the study of a world sample from his *Ethnographic Atlas* (Murdock, 1967), identified more than a dozen theories of natural and supernatural causes of illness. Among them, one theory of the cause of sickness was attributed to fright, resulting in soul loss. Thus, it is not surprising that the concept of loss of soul as a cause for sickness is prevalent and that terms similar, or equivalent, to *susto* are found widely distributed across many different cultural groups, such as *el miedo* (fright) in Bolivia (Hollweg, 1997), *lanti* in the Philippines (Hart, 1985), or *mogo laya* in Papua New Guinea (Frankel, 1985).

It should be pointed out that, although the cause is uniformly attributed to spiritual-psychological reasons relating mostly to a frightening experience or misfortune, from a clinical point of view, the manifested syndrome is quite heterogeneous, without a commonly shared syndrome (Gillin, 1948). The victim may manifest loss of appetite, sleep disturbance, reduced strength, absentmindedness, headache, dizziness, or other somatic symptoms, as well as emotional symptoms of depression, anxiety, or irritability. Therefore, strictly speaking, it is not a culture-related specific syndrome derived from psychogenic or psychoplastic effects. It is culture-related *only* in the sense that the morbid condition is interpreted after the fact according to folk concepts of etiology and certain ways of regaining the lost soul, such as rituals, are offered. Therefore, the role of culture is interpretation of and reaction to the illness.

## 8. Other Questionable Conditions

There are almost countless mental disorders labeled by folk names (Simons & Hughes, 1985). This is particularly true in societies in which modern psychiatry is not prevalent and contemporary mental health service is lacking. Therefore, folk names still play an important role in identifying morbid conditions and deciding how to manage them. Whether or not the morbid conditions described by local folk names need to be considered as culture-related specific syndromes depends on the extent to which culture impacts the formation of the condition and the specificity of the psychopathology manifested. There are also several clinical conditions labeled in the past by scholars as culture-bound syndromes. However, whether such disorders should be considered as culture-related specific syndrome is questionable awaiting further elaboration and discussion.

### a. Spirit Possession

Many people in different societies around the world develop the disorder of possession. A person may talk and behave as if possessed by another being and announce that he is possessed; or, it is often family, friends, neighbors, or other onlookers who claim that the person is possessed. The being possessing a person may be a deceased family member, a local god, or even an animal spirit. Based on the local language and the possessing being, numerous terms used in various societies have been reported by clinicians and scholars. For instance, *Phii pob* (spirit possession) has been reported in Thailand (Suwanlert, 1976); *kitsune-tsuski* (fox possession) in Japan (Daiguji, 1993; Eguchi, 1991; Sasaki, 1969); and *shie-bing* (evil sickness) in Taiwan (T. Y. Lin, 1953).

Although spirit possession syndrome is becoming rare in developed European and American societies, it is frequently observed in many other societies, particularly where most people still strongly believe in the possibility of an individual becoming possessed by a supernatural being (Castillo, 1994; Pak, 1996). Pathoreactive effects are clearly observed in such a condition, in terms of how the dissociated/possessed behavior is interpreted, perceived, and responded to and how the possibility of pathoplastic effects should be considered. However, to what further extent the condition is attributed to specific cultural features is awaiting future study.

### b. Windigo Psychosis

One kind of possession disorder is known as *windigo* psychosis. The terms "*windigo*" (Ojibwa) or "*witiko*" (Cree) refer to a folk monster that eats human flesh. It has been speculated that hunters living in the pole area, when they failed at hunting and were starving, may have developed a dissociated state as a result of the desire to eat human flesh, believing they were possessed by the *windigo* monster.

A careful review of the literature has disclosed that this term of disorder was invented based on the fragmented accounts of informants or nonprofessional people. A diagnosis and classification had been made with no observation of an actual case. As pointed out by Marano (1982/1985), there never were any *windigo* psychotics in the sense that cannibalism and murder were committed to satisfy an obsessive craving for human flesh. American cultural psychiatrist Robert Kraus (personal communication, 1996), who worked in the pole area for many years, commented that he never encountered or heard of any *windigo* like clinical case in his field experiences.

### 9. Final Comments

### a. Culture "-Bound" or "-Related" Issues

Although the term "culture-bound syndrome" originally referred to the existence of specific psychiatric syndromes "bound" to particular cultural groups (Yap, 1967), recent studies favor the view that such syndromes are not necessarily bound to particular cultural groups and can be observed among various ethnic groups across different geographic areas. Good examples are the sporadic and epidemic occurrences of mass, nondiscriminatory murderous behavior (*amok*) observed in many south Asia societies (such as Laos, the Philippines, and

Thailand) beyond Malay (Westermeyer, 1973), as well as in developed societies such as the United States. *Koro* epidemics have been noted beyond south China, in India and Thailand (Tseng et al., 1988). The *latah* behavior found in Malay is observed also as *imu* among Ainu in northern Japan (Uchimura, 1956). *Taijinky-ofushio,* considered special to the Japanese, is now claimed to also exist among the Koreans (S. H. Lee, 1987).

Thus, a culture-bound syndrome is not always "bound" to a particular culture unit or system identified in association with ethnicity but can be observed among several different ethnic groups in different geographic areas (Westermyer & Janca, 1997). Such syndromes need to be reformulated as heavily "related" to certain cultural traits that can be found in different geographic areas, or across ethnicity or cultural unit or systems, which share the common cultural view, attitude, or elements attributed to the formation of the specific syndrome. Based on this new understanding, the term should be changed to culture-related specific syndromes to reflect its nature accurately (Tseng & McDermot, 1981).

### b. Diagnosis and Classification Issues

Associated with the increased awareness of the impact of culture on psychiatric classifications, as reflected in the recently published American classification system DSM-IV, there is controversy regarding how to deal with culture-related specific syndromes from a diagnostic point of view (Hughes, 1996, 1998). Some clinicians feel strongly that various known culture-bound syndromes (such as *koro* or *hwabyung*) should be officially recognized and included in the present classification system.

However, it needs to be pointed out that the present DSM classification system is based on the descriptive approach, categorizing psychiatric disorders by certain sets of manifested symptomatology. If we try to fit culture-related specific syndromes into the categories of the existing classification system or try to create new categories of disorders, they will be classified as NOS (not otherwise specified) or, at best, as "variations" of presently recognized disorders. Many culture-related syndromes are ill-defined or manifested by multiple psychiatric conditions that are difficult to categorize (Chowdhury, 1996; Guarnaccia & Rogler, 1999). Most importantly, by squeezing the culture-related specific syndromes into the descriptive-oriented classification system, we will lose the unique meaning of the syndromes from a cultural perspective (Guarnaccia, 1993; Pfeiffer, 1982).

### c. Culture-Related Syndromes in Western Societies

The last point that must be made is that, by definition, culture-related specific syndromes should be able to be discovered everywhere, as every society has its own culture. However, the trend has been to consider that most culture-related specific syndromes (such as *koro, amok,* or *dhat* syndromes) occur in non-Western societies. This is due to two reasons: they were considered "peculiar" phenomena observed in areas previously colonized by Western people, or they simply did not fit the classification system developed for Euro-American populations. This trend is now changing. There is an increased interest among Western cultural psychiatrists (such as Littlewood & Lipsedge, 1986) to recognize syndromes in "our own" Western cultures that are heavily culture-related. Several psychiatric disorders have been suggested by various scholars for consideration as Western culture-related syndromes. These include anorexia nervosa (Littlewood & Lipsedge, 1986; Palazzoli, 1985; Swartz, 1985), obesity (Ritenbaugh, 1982), drug-induced dissociated states, multiple personalities, and even premenstrual syndrome (Johnson, 1987), disorders that are seldom observed or concerned in non-Western societies. Because these conditions are already recognized in the existing Western nosological system, they are, in a sense, not viewed as specific syndromes. However, they can be viewed as culture-related psychiatric conditions that are influenced by the pathoelaborative, pathofacilitative, or pathoplastic effects of Western culture.

## B. EPIDEMIC OR COLLECTIVE MENTAL DISORDERS

### 1. What Is Epidemic Mental Disorder?

"Epidemic mental disorders" or "collective mental disorders" refer to mental disorders or pathological psychological reactions that occur among groups of people in a contagious way within a relatively short period of time in a particular social setting. The mental disorders may involve many subjects collectively through the process of contagion in an endemic or epidemic fashion, and are therefore called contagious or epidemic. Because the mental disorders are transmitted or spread from one person to another, involving tens, hundreds, or thousands of people, the nature of the transmissions is understood to be psychological, closely related to the social atmosphere and community setting at the particular time and the common beliefs or attitudes shared by the group of people involved, and a part of the mechanism of group psychology. The psychiatric symptoms are usually manifested as hysterical conversion reactions (such as fainting, paralysis, or convulsions) or panic states (such as fear of disaster, danger, or death). However, they may also take the form of collective depressive or delusional states or a mixture of various disturbances. From a cultural point of view, next to specific culture-related syndromes, epidemic mental disorders are probably among the most interesting psychopathological conditions. Because their development is closely related to social and cultural factors, they have attracted keen attention from cultural psychiatrists.

## 2. Some Epidemic Episodes

During the past several decades, numerous cases of mental epidemics have been reported in scientific literature in both the East and West. Those that were reported after the 1940s and were well-investigated and described in terms of the dynamics of epidemic occurrence are noted here to illustrate possible correlations between elements of a particular culture and the type of mass behavior that occurred. For the sake of comparison, the epidemics are grouped according to the cardinal symptoms manifested.

### a. *Epidemics of Genital-Retraction Panic* (Koro)

As described in Section 3A, Culture-Related Specific Syndromes, *koro* is a special kind of mental illness characterized by the belief that if the penis shrinks into the abdomen, death will result. This fear can be manifested as anxiety or a state of panic. The condition usually occurs in sporadic cases, but sometimes develops collectively as an endemic or epidemic *koro*. As an epidemic, it is manifested as a panic state rather than an anxiety or obsessive state. According to scientific reports, epidemic *koro* has been observed in several areas in southern Asia and in India (see Fig. 11).

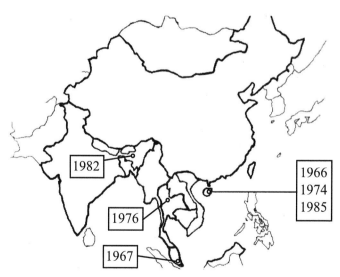

FIGURE 11   Geographic locations of *Koro* epidemics in the past. *Koro* epidemics occurred in 1952, 1962, 1966, 1974, and 1984–1985 in Hainan, China; 1967 in Singapore; 1976 in the northeast of Thailand; and 1982 in West Bengal and Lower Asam in India.

Suoyang *(Koro) Epidemic in Singapore.*   According to Ngui (1969), a collective occurrence of *suoyang*, or *koro*, was observed in Singapore in 1967. Swine fever had broken out, and a program to inoculate pigs was publicized and carried out. Several months later, a case of *suoyang* suddenly appeared. Unfortunately, a rumor that eating inoculated pork could cause *koro* created public panic. Soon the incidence of *koro* assumed epidemic proportions. At the peak of the epidemic, as many as a hundred cases were seen at general hospitals in a single day. It was speculated that nearly a thousand people claimed that they were attacked by *suoyang* during the epidemic, which lasted a couple of months. Although Singapore is a multiracial society, including Chinese, Malays, Indians, and Eurasians, clearly, it was mainly the Chinese ethnic group that contracted *suoyang* (see Fig. 12). It was speculated that some interracial tension may have existed and been aggravated prior to the occurrence of the epidemic, mainly between the Chinese and the Malay groups. It was taboo for the Malay, who were Muslim,

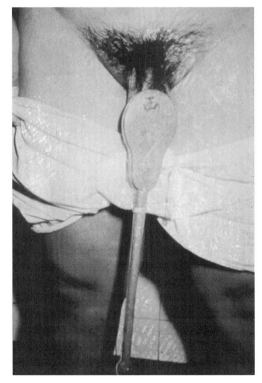

FIGURE 12   *Koro* epidemic in Singapore, 1969. A Chinese-Singaporean using a traditional Chinese weight case to clamp the penis during *a koro* attack [From Koro Study Team—Courtesy of <u>Gwee</u> Ah Leng, M.D., with permission from <u>Kua</u> Ee Heok, M.D.].

to eat pork, an important meat for the Chinese. The rumor that eating infected pork would cause illness might have been related to the racial tension.

*Wartime* Koro *Epidemic in Thailand.*   A *koro* epidemic erupted in northeast Thailand in November 1976, shortly after the war started in Vietnam (Suwanlert & Coates, 1979). During the war, many Cambodian refugees migrated from their country to Thailand. The Thais feared a communist invasion. There was also tension between local Thais and the refugees who disrupted their communities. In this atmosphere of political and military apprehension, a rumor spread that communists had put a certain herb into the food, mainly the rice, that would make Thai males sexually impotent, thus making it easy for the communists to seduce Thai women. Men allegedly suffering from *koro* began to ask for treatment. More than a thousand cases were reported during the epidemic. The government had to form a health team in the region to counteract the rumor and calm the panic.

Koro *Epidemic and Endemic in India.*   Although from an anthropological point of view the people of India are remarkably different from the people of south Asia, with different faiths (mainly Hindu and partly Muslim), they share common concerns about sexual matters. Both believe that it is important for men to conserve semen, and that its excessive discharge may harm their bodies. It is well known that Indian males suffer from *dhat* syndrome (fear of losing semen by leakage), a unique psychosomatic disorder that is based on this sex-related belief. Also reflecting this concern were outbreaks of *koro* epidemics in the eastern part of India in 1982.

According to Dutta, Phookan, and Das (1982) and Chakraborty (1983, 1984), a *koro* epidemic occurred in India in 1982. The epidemic seems to have started in the foothills of the Himalayas and affected West Bengal and four districts in the neighboring state of Assam, rapidly spreading from west to east and to the south, eventually engulfing the suburbs of Calcutta. The affected areas were mostly semitribal and agricultural.

Some people suspected that the initial cases of this epidemic may have been provoked by serious illnesses and deaths that had occurred recently in the areas. However, according to Chakraborty (1983, 1984), the areas hit by the epidemic had recently experienced severe interracial strife. A heavy influx of economically active and industrious Hindu refugees from what is now Bangladesh had changed landownership and created collective anxieties among the local tribal people. Around the time of the *koro* outbreak, the tribesmen had prepared a militant action against the immigrant Bengalis that was aborted by government intervention.

*Recurrent* Suoyang *(Koro) Epidemics in Southern China.*   According to Chinese psychiatrists (Mo, Chen, Li, & Tseng, 1995), recurrent instances of *suoyang*

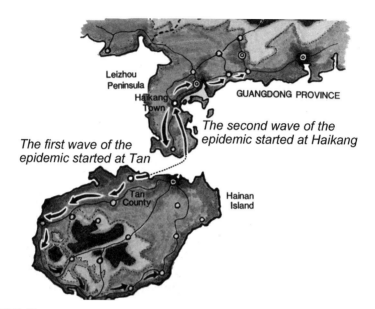

The second wave of the
epidemic started at Haikang

The first wave of the
epidemic started at Tan

FIGURE 13   Epidemic spread of *Koro* in Guangdong, China, in 1984–1985. An epidemic originated in a village near Tan County in Hainan Island, spreading from one village to another southward in the coastal area of the island. The news of the disaster was brought to Haikang Town on
Leizhou Peninsula, where a second wave started, spreading southward and northward on the peninsula. [Revised with permission from W. S. Tseng *et al.*, *American Journal of Psychiatry*, *145*(12), 1539,
1988.]

epidemics had been noted on Hainan Island and the neighboring Leizhou
Peninsula of Guangdong in South China about 130 years before. During the past
half century, five major epidemics were noted in Hainan, in 1952, 1962, 1966,
1974, and 1984 (see Fig. 13). It seems that a specific social tension was related
to the occurrence of each *suoyang* epidemic. Most of the people in the epidemic
areas believed that all social disasters would ultimately result in a *suoyang*
occurrence.

When a *suoyang* case broke out in a village, several to several dozens of
people might be affected (see Fig. 14a). The people in the community usually
became hysterical, particularly when numerous victims were found at the
same time. The villagers would strike drums, gongs, or anything that made
loud noises, or set off firecrackers to scare off the evil ghosts (see Fig. 14b,c).
The men would carry knives, swords, spears, or other weapons and patrol the
streets. They would block the village gate to stop outsiders from entering.
They were afraid that a ghost disguised as a human might infiltrate the village.
As soon as a new case occurred in a neighboring village, the original village was
set free because people believed that the evil ghosts had gone on to the other
village.

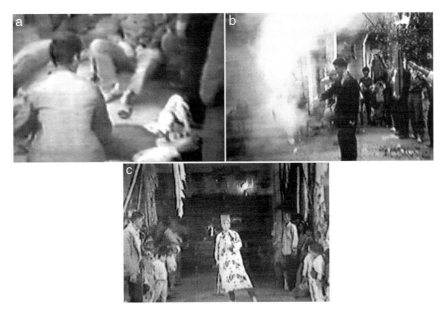

FIGURE 14    *Koro* epidemic in southern China, 1984–1985. (a) Two Chinese men simultaneously suffered from attacks through contagion during the epidemic—one sitting on the street holding his "shrinking" penis, the other lying on the ground shouting for help. (b) Scared villagers set off fire-crackers to scare off the evil ghost, believing that the ghost had infiltrated the village to steal yang element. (c) A Daoist monk performed a ritual to chase away the evil from the village. [From Guang-dong Suoyang Epidemic Research Team; Courtesy of <u>Mo</u> Gan-Ming, M.D.]

### b. Mass Hysteria (or Epidemic Conversion/Dissociation Attacks)

Mass hysteria is one of the most common collective mental disorders observed and reported in scientific literature in both the East and the West. Hysteria is used here in a restrictive sense, referring to the sudden occurrence of conversion reaction (manifested by symptoms of motor dysfunctions, sensational disturbances, fainting, and other converted somatic symptoms) and/or dissociation reaction. From literature, many episodes were noted from East and West both. Examples are nervous twitching epidemic in Baltimore, Maryland, United States (Schuler & Parenton, 1943); hyperventilating attack in Blackburn, England (Moss & McEvedy, 1966); mass hysteria in an Arab culture in the Middle East (Amin, Hamdi, & Eapen, 1997); or endemic hysteria in Malaysia schools (Tan, 1963; Woon, 1976; Teoh, Soewondo, & Sidharta, 1975) (for details, see Tseng, 2001, Chapter 14: Epidemic Mental Disorders, pp. 274–275).

### c. Endemic Anxiety or Fear Reaction

Occurrence of anxiety or panic attack involving a group of people collectively in a community associated with shared reason for anxiety could be observed occasionally. The sudden development of a communitywide fear reaction in the small city of Matton, Illinois, with common fear of a "phantom anesthetist" (Johnson, 1945) is a one example. One evening in September 1944, a woman reported to the police that someone had opened her bedroom window and sprayed her with a sickly sweet-smelling gas that partially paralyzed her legs and made her ill. The police found no sign of an intruder, but the next day the local newspaper carried a front-page story on the "gas attack," with the headline: "Anesthetist Prowler on Loose." The following day, a man reported to the police that he and his wife had had a similar occurrence. This "incident" was also reported in the newspaper. It created an atmosphere of fear and anxiety in the community. Two new attacks were reported after the second news report. Following this, within a period of 12 days, a total of 22 cases were reported of similar attacks by the phantom anesthetist, with victims claiming that they smelled the gas, became sick with various somatic symptoms of nausea, vomiting, palpitations, paralysis of the legs, dryness of the mouth and throat, and so on. After analyzing the records and interviewing most of the victims, Johnson concluded that the case of the "phantom anesthetist" was entirely psychogenic. It was his assessment that the news media, by printing exciting, uncritical stories, created anxiety and a fear reaction that snowballed.

### d. Collective Delusions

The difference between ordinary beliefs and delusions is a matter of degree, with a thin boundary. If a belief is shared by a mass population, in the form of a political, religious, or folk belief, it may become a matter of judgment to decide whether the belief is "normal" or "pathological." When a group of people faces a common enemy or a dangerous situation, collective suspicion is a common reaction. It may take an outsider or a third party to get an objective view of the belief shared by society. It may take time, perhaps one or two decades, to obtain insight into the pathology of a delusion shared collectively by a society. The Nazis' attempt to exterminate the Jewish people in Hitler's era and the Chinese attempt to destroy the established culture and exterminate the intelligent people during the cultural revolution in Mao's era are two examples of political delusions passionately believed by mass populations in recent history.

While individuals, or a family member, may at times lose touch with reality as their culture defines it, whole communities ordinarily do not. However, Medalia and Larsen (1958) reported a communitywide delusional windshield-pitting epidemic that broke out in Seattle, Washington, in the spring of 1954. A Seattle newspaper carried intermittent reports of damage to automobile windshields in a city located to the north of Seattle. Initially, police suspected vandalism, but failed to gather proof. Conjecture as to the cause ranged from meteoric dust to sandflea eggs hatching in the glass, but centered on possible radioactive fallout from the Eniwetok H-bomb tests conducted earlier that year.

Then an epidemic occurred. A total of more than 200 people telephoned the Seattle Police Department reporting damage to over 3000 automobiles. Most commonly, the damage reported consisted of pitting marks that grew into bubbles in the glass of about the size of a thumbnail. Finally, the mayor of Seattle declared the damage was no longer a police matter and made an emergency appeal to the governor and to President Dwight Eisenhower for help. The newspaper mentioned the possibility that the community's collective concern with pitting might have sprung largely from mass hysteria. Three weeks later, calls to police dropped gradually ending this short-lived collective delusional reaction that was stirred up by mass communication, the newspaper.

### e. Contagious Family Mental Disorder (Folie à Famille)

Emotional disorders can spread from person to person. The French term "*folie a deux*" refers to two persons sharing a similar psychopathology through mental contagion. In English, it is called associated psychoses. The people involved are usually members of the same family or emotionally close partners. As extensions of the *folie a deux* (psychoses of two)—*folie a trois* (psychoses of three) or *folie a famile* (psychoses of a family)—may develop. These usually take the form of psychosis, hysteria, or delusion. Although the phenomenon of *folie à famille* is considered rare, sporadic occurrences have been reported in the Philippines (Goduco-Angular & Wintrob, 1964), Malaysia (Woon, 1976), and Taiwan (Tseng, 1969). Woon reported a collective dissociation outburst in a family. The case concerned a Chinese-Malaysian family whose two young adult brothers and one sister simultaneously developed dissociated conditions, creating sensational turmoil in a rural village in Malaysia. The situation occurred after their aged father, a village shaman, suffered a stroke, making it necessary to choose a successor from among his adult children. Affected by intense feelings of competition and unable to handle these emotions, the siblings one after another developed dissociated conditions (see Fig. 15).

Reviewing this contagious family mental disorder, it is apparent that, in addition to the existing premorbid personalities of the family members, a strong emotional bond between them facilitated the occurrence of the condition, particularly when they faced a stressful situation together. Sharing a similar psychiatric condition appeared to be an alternative way for the siblings to deal with the common crisis they encountered. It is speculated that such an unusual contagious reaction tends to be observed in societies where family ties are stressed.

### f. Collective Suicide

It is well known that some individuals or a group of people might collectively commit suicide in wartime. For instance, in medieval times in India, the rite of *Jauhar* was practiced, in which women would commit mass suicide by self-

FIGURE 15   Collective family dissociation outburst in Malaysia. (a) An aged village shaman suffered a stroke in a rural area, necessitating the choice of a successor from among his three children. (b) The outburst started when the daughter fell on the ground in a dissociated state. (c) The younger son soon fell into a dissociated state. (d) He was followed by the elder son, who also fell into a possessed state. (e) While the three of them were sitting in the living room, they all simultaneously fell into dissociated or possessed states. (f) Villagers watched what was happening in this household. [Courtesy of Woon Tai-Huang, M.D.]

immolation to avoid capture and dishonor at the hands of the Muslim invaders (Adityanjee, 1994). According to the rite of *Jauhar*, as a last resort, when defeat threatened and there was no other way, it was better for the men to go out and die in the fields of battle and for the women to burn themselves on a pyre. Death was considered preferable to slavery and degradation. In the 20th century, at the end of World War II, a number of Japanese soldiers and citizens committed group suicide on Saipan and Okinawa (see Section 2:B, Culture-Shaped Coping Patterns). However, collective suicidal actions have also occurred in non-wartime situations in various societies for one reason or another. It is commonly known that psychiatric patients in hospitals might kill themselves in an endemic fashion (Taiminen, Salmenpera, & Lehtinen, 1992). Suggestion and identification were considered the precipitating factors of this suicide endemic.

Religious belief-related, ceremonial, mysterious, group suicidal acts have been heard of occasionally in Europe or Canada among members of the Sun cult. The Japanese psychiatrist Takahashi (1989) reported an incident in which seven female members (between 25 and 67 years of age) of a local religious cult (the Truth Church) committed suicide one after another following the leader's death in Japan in 1986. The collective suicidal action of 914 cult members at Jonestown in 1978 is still fresh in our memories (see Fig. 16). Many explanations have been offered in efforts to understand this rather unusual mass madness. The concept of collective pathological regression within a charismatically led mass movement was suggested by Ulman and Abse (1983). It was speculated that the psychic stability of both the leader and the followers was founded on a pattern of interaction characterized by the leader's sadistic demand for mirrored grandiosity and the followers' masochistic surrender in the hopes of merging with an idealized and omnipotent self-object. The religious vision of death as the ultimate beauty was the base for the group undertaking collective suicide. The occurrence of mass suicide by self-immolation in Waco, Texas, in the United States, is another example of mass suicidal behavior related to a cult movement (Adityanjee, 1994). The recent episode of the Heaven's Gate mass suicide surprised many of us. As Comet Hale-Bopp grew bright, reaching its closest proximity to earth on March 22, 1997, the 39 members of Heaven's Gate committed a planned group suicide, orchestrated by their director. In a rich suburban California mansion, they quietly packed their suitcases with clothes and spiral notebooks, swallowed phenobarbital, and died in waves over the next three days (see Fig. 17). The members followed their leader in what they believed was an ascension to the next level of their lives (*Newsweek*, 1997).

## 3. Overview: Frequency, Mechanisms, and Dynamic

News about the occurrence of epidemic mental disorders may appear in local newspapers, yet such events may or may not always be reported in scientific

FIGURE 16   Mass suicide in Jonestown, Guyana, in 1978. (a) More than 900 American citizens, members of the People's Temple, followed their leader to a jungle settlement in South America, and committed suicide together by swallowing poison, either voluntarily or by threat. [Courtesy of Eagles Roar, Inc.] (b) They died from cyanide that was put into their drinks. [With permission by Time Inc., 1978.]

literature. Thus, information from literature is usually limited, and occurrences are underreported.

Sirois (1974) found 78 episodes of epidemic hysteria outbreaks in literature from around the world during a 100-year period (1872–1972). However, according to Teoh and associates (1975), in Malaysia alone, 29 episodes involving school students were reported in the ten-year period between 1962 and 1971. In a computer search of English literature for the period 1985 to 1996, 30 citations were revealed, with case reports of 23 incidences from Medline, and 19 citations from Clinpsyc. This supports the fact that epidemic mental disorders are frequently elaborated academic topics and that the occurrence of epidemics are not as rare as one may think. It may be said that collective mental disorders are observed around the world, whether the society is developing or developed, in the East or in the West. Such disorders are not that rare; they are a part of our common daily lives.

From a sociological point of view, several mechanisms, including group influence, social isolation, or crowd response, should be considered in group contagion (Kerckhoff & Back, 1965). Today, mass communication by newspaper or

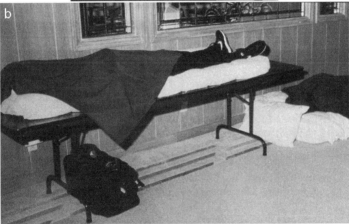

FIGURE 17    Planned group suicide of Heaven's Gate members, 1997. (a) In order to ascend to the next levels of their lives, 39 members of the Heaven's Gate cult journeyed together to their deaths. (b) The members packed their suitcases, covered their bodies with purple cloths, and took poison. [From *Newsweek*, April 1997, with permission from AP/Wide World Photos.]

radio, and especially television, may facilitate the rapid spread of information and help create an atmosphere of excitement, frenzy, or fear. In this way, a whole community may become very quickly and deeply involved (Hefez, 1985; Johnson, 1945).

However, it is important to note that the precipitating ideas, beliefs, or false beliefs (delusions) transmitted or shared by members of the group must seem so true and/or familiar that the group readily accepts or adopts them. In other words, the illness-belief or collective misperception has to be shared by the people in the community. Group members then transform these ideas into conflicts to which they are already vulnerable, or which are latent in them. Conflicts are then expressed as disabling symptoms or as a culturally rational attempt at problem solving (Bartholomew, 1994).

It does not matter whether the information concerns a "scientific" explanation, such as gas intoxication or radiation from H-bomb tests as the cause of "pitting marks" on car windshields (Medalia & Larsen, 1958); a "religious" one, such as believing the end of the world will arrive on a certain day, causing a community's collective panic over the predicted disaster (as observed on many occasions, and recently in Korea in 1995); or a supernatural explanation, such as obeying the spirits of dead ancestors as the cause of agitated behavior (Ebrahim, 1968); or the famous witch hunting that occurred in 1692, in Salem, Massachusetts, in the United States. The important factor is that the reaction is expressed within a social context to which people collectively respond and react. As pointed out by Cheng (1996), it is a social malady maintained by cultural beliefs that affects the whole community.

The epidemic may develop as a "group protest" against authority, as in the case of girl students angered by the rumor that school officials would force them to submit to pregnancy tests to check for sexual promiscuity (Knight, Friedman, & Sulianti, 1965). The epidemic may provide a channel to express a complaint when no other alternative exists (Adomakoh, 1973). However, it may also be merely a collective reaction to the emotional frustration or helplessness of losing a school football game (Levine, 1977). From a dynamic point of view, the occurrence of such epidemics may serve as a coping defense that helps the group deal with problems they are facing.

# REFERENCES

## A. Culture-Related Specific Syndromes

Akhtar, S. (1988). Four culture-bound psychiatric syndromes in India. *International Journal of Social Psychiatry, 34,* 70–74.

Ang, P. C., & Weller, M. P. I. (1984). Koro and psychosis. *British Journal of Psychiatry, 145,* 335.

Barrett, K. (1978). Koro in a Londoner. *Lancet, 8103,* 1319.

Bartholomew, R. E. (1994). Disease, disorder, or deception? Latah as habit in a Malay extended family. *Journal of Nervous and Mental Diseases, 182*(6), 331–338.

Berrios, G. E., & Morley, S. J. (1984). Koro-like symptom in a non-Chinese subject. *British Journal of Psychiatry, 145,* 331–334.

Bhatia, M. S. & Malik, S. C. (1991). Dhat syndrome—A useful diagnostic entity in Indian culture. *British Journal of Psychiatry, 159,* 691–695.

Bottéro, A. (1991). Consumption by semen loss in India and elsewhere. *Culture, Medicine and Psychiatry, 15,* 303–320.

Burton-Bradley, B. G. (1968). The *amok* syndrome in Papua and New Guinea. *Medical Journal of Australia, 1,* 252–256.

Burton-Bradley, B. G. (1975). Cargo cult. In B. G. Burton-Bradley, *Stone age crisis: A psychiatric appraisal* (pp. 10–31). Nashville, TN: Vanderbilt University Press.

Burton-Bradley, B. G. (1982). Cargo cult syndromes. In C. T. H. Friedman & R. A. Faguet (Eds.), *Extraordinary disorders of human behavior.* New York: Plenum Press.

Cannon, W. B. (1957). "Voodoo" death. *Psychosomatic Medicine, 19,* 182–190.

Carr, J. E. (1978). Ethno-behaviorism and the culture-bound syndromes: The case of *amok*. *Culture, Medicine and Psychiatry, 2,* 269–293.

Carr, J. E., & Tan, E. K. (1976). In search of the true *amok: Amok* as viewed within the Malay culture. *American Journal of Psychiatry, 133*(11), 1295–1299.

Carstairs, G. M. (1956). *Hinjra* and *Jiryan:* Two derivatives of Hindu attitudes to sexuality. *British Journal of Medical Psychology, 29,* 128–138.

Castillo, R. J. (1994). Spirit possession in South Asia: Dissociation or hysteria? Part 1. Theoretical background. *Culture, Medicine and Psychiatry, 18*(1), 1–22.

Cawte, J. E. (1976). *Malgri:* A culture-bound syndrome. In W. P. Lebra (Ed.), *Culture-bound syndromes, ethnopsychiatry, and alternate therapies* (pp. 22–31). Honolulu: University Press of Hawaii.

Chang, Y. H., Rin, H., & Chen, C. C. (1975). Frigophobia: A report of five cases. *Bulletin of the Chinese Society of Neurology and Psychiatry, 1*(2), 9–13. [In Chinese.]

Chiniwala, M., Alfonso, C. A., Torres, J. R., & Lefer, J. (1996). Koro in an immigrant from Guinea with brief psychotic disorder. *American Journal of Psychiatry, 153*(5), 736.

Chiu, N. M., Liu, C. Y., Chen, C. C., & Yang, Y. Y. (1994). Frigophobia: Report of two cases. *Chinese Psychiatry, 8*(4), 297–302. [In Chinese.]

Chiu, T. L., Tong, J. E., & Schmidt, K. E. (1972). A clinical and survey study of latah in Sarawak, Malaysia. *Psychological Medicine, 2,* 155–165.

Chowdhury, A. N. (1994). Koro in females: An analysis of 48 cases. *Transcultural Psychiatric Research Review, 31,* 369–380.

Chowdhury, A. N. (1996). The definition and classification of koro. *Culture, Medicine and Psychiatry, 20,* 41–65.

Daiguji, M. (1993). *Psychopathology of possession: Modern clinical study.* Tokyo: Seiwa. [In Japanese.]

Daiguji, M., & Shichida, H. (1998, October). *Imu* phenomena observed among the Ainu people in northern Japan: Past and present. Presented at Second Pan Asia-Pacific Mental Health Conference, Beijing.

Eastwell, D. (1982). Voodoo death and the mechanism for dispatch of the dying in East Arnhem, Australia. *American Anthropologist, 84,* 5–18. (Reviewed by E. A. Gomez in Transcultural Psychiatry Research Review, *21*(1), 66–67 [1984].)

Ede, A. (1976). Koro in an Anglo-Saxon Canadian. *Canadian Psychiatric Association Journal, 21,* 389–392.

Edwards, J. W. (1985). Indigenous koro, a genital retraction syndrome of Insular Southeast Asia: A critical review. In R. C. Simons & C. C. Hughes (Eds.), *The culture-bound syndromes: Folk illness of psychiatric and anthropological interest* (pp. 169–191). Dordrecht, The Netherlands: Reidel.

Eguchi, S. Y. (1991). Between folk concepts of illness and psychiatric diagnosis: Kitsune-tsuki (fox possession) in a mountain village of western Japan. *Culture, Medicine and Psychiatry, 15*(4), 421–452.

Ellis, W. G. (1893). The *amok* of the Malays. *Journal of Mental Science, 39,* 325–338.

Ellis, W. G. (1897). Latah: A mental malady of the Malays. *Journal of Mental Science, 43,* 33–40.

Engel, G. L. (1971). Sudden and rapid death during psychological stress: Folklore or folk wisdom? *Annals of Internal Medicine, 74,* 771–782.

Fernández-Marian, R. (1959). The Puerto Rican syndrome: Its dynamic and cultural determinants. *Psychiatry, 24,* 79–82.

Fletcher, W. (1908). Latah and crime. *Lancet, 2,* 254–255.

Foulks, E. F. (1972). The Arctic hysterias of the North Alaskan Eskimo. In D. H. Maybury-Lewis (Ed.), *Anthropological studies* (No. 10). Washington, DC: American Anthropological Association.

Frankel, S. (1985). *Mogo laya,* a New Guinea fright illness. In R. C. Simons & C. C. Hughes (Eds.), *The culture-bound syndromes* (pp. 399–404). Dordrecht, The Netherlands: Reidel.

Friedmann, C. T. H., & Faguet, R. A. (Eds.). (1982). *Extraordinary disorders of human behavior.* New York: Plenum Press.

Geertz, H. (1968). Latah in Java: A theoretical paradox. *Indonesia, 5,* 93–104.

Gillin, J. (1948). Magical fright. *Psychiatry, 11,* 387–400.

Gordon, R. A. (1990). *Anorexia and bulimia: Anatomy of a social epidemic.* Cambridge, UK: Basil/ Blackwell.

Guarnaccia, P. J. (1993). Ataques de nervios in Puerto Rico: Culture-bound syndrome or popular illness? *Medical Anthropology, 15,* 157–170.

Guarnaccia, P. J., & Rogler, L. H. (1999). Research on culture-bound syndromes: New directions. *American Journal of Psychiatry, 156*(9), 1322–1327.

Guarnaccia, P. J., Rubio-Stipec, M., & Canino, G. J. (1989). *Ataques de nervios* in the Puerto Rican Diagnostic Interview Schedule: The impact of cultural categories on psychiatric epidemiology. *Culture, Medicine and Psychiatry, 13,* 275–295.

Gussow, Z. (1985). Pibloktoq (hysteria) among the Polar Eskimo: An ethnopsychiatric study. In R. C. Simons & C. C. Hughes (Eds.), *The culture-bound syndromes* (pp. 271–287). Dordrecht, The Netherland: Reidel. [Original work published 1960.]

Gwee, A. L. (1963). Koro: A cultural disease. *Singapore Medical Journal, 4,* 119–122.

Gwee, A. L. (1968). Koro: Its origin and nature as a disease entity. *Singapore Medical Journal, 9,* 3–6.

Hart, D. V. (1985). Lanti, illness by fright among Bisayan Filipino. In R. C. Simons & C. C. Hughes (Eds.), *The culture-bound syndromes* (pp. 371–397). Dordrecht, The Netherland: Reidel.

Hes, J. P., & Nassi, G. (1977). Koro in a Yemenite and a Georgian Jewish immigrant. *Confinia Psychiatrica, 20,* 180–184.

Hollweg, M. G. (1997). Main culture bound syndromes in Bolivia. *Curare, 20*(1), 23–28.

Hughes, C. C. (1996). The culture-bound syndromes and psychiatric diagnosis. In J. E. Mezzich, A. Kleinman, H. Fabrega, Jr., & D. L. Parron (Eds.), *Culture and psychiatric diagnosis: A DSM-IV perspective* (pp. 289–307). Washington, DC: American Psychiatric Press.

Hughes, C. C. (1998). The glossary of "culture-bound sydromes" in DSM-IV: A critique. *Transcultural Psychiatry, 35*(3), 413–421.

Jegede, R. O. (1983). Psychiatric illness in African students: "Brain fag" syndrome revisited. *Canadian Journal of Psychiatry, 28,* 188–192.

Jilek, W. G., & Jilek-Aall, L. (2001). Culture-specific mental disorders. In F. Henn, N. Sartorius, H. Helmchen, & H. Lauter (Eds.), *Contemporary psychiatry. Vol. 2, Psychiatry in special situations* (pp. 219–245). Berlin: Springer.

Johnson, T. M. (1987). Premenstrual syndrome as a Western culture-specific disorder. *Culture, Medicine and Psychiatry, 11*(3), 337–356.

Kasahara, Y. (1974). Fear of eye-to-eye confrontation among neurotic patients in Japan. In T. S. Lebra & P. L. Lebra (Eds.), *Japanese culture and behavior* (pp. 396–406). Honolulu: University Press of Hawaii.

Kenny, M. G. (1983). Paradox lost: The latah problem revisited. *Journal of Nervous and Mental Disease, 171*(3), 159–167.

Kimura, S. (1982). *Nihonjin no taijinkyofushio* [Japanese anthrophobia]. Tokyo: Keso Shobo. (In Japanese.)

Kitanishi, K., & Mori, A. (1995). Morita therapy: 1919 to 1995. *Psychiatry and Clinical Neurosciences, 13,* 31–37.

Kobler, F. (1948). Description of an acute castration fear, based on superstition. *Psychoanalytic Review*, *35*, 285–289.

Lambo, T. A. (1960, December 10). Further neuropsychiatric observations in Nigeria: With comments on the need for epidemiological study in Africa. *British Medical Journal*, pp. 1696–1704.

Lambo, T. A. (1962). Malignant anxiety: A syndrome associated with criminal conduct in Africans. *Journal of Mental Science*, *108*, 256–264.

Lee, R. L. M. (1981). Structure and anti-structure in the culture-bound syndromes: The Malay case. *Culture, Medicine and Psychiatry*, *5*, 233–248.

Lee, S. H. (1977). A study on the "*hwabyung*" (anger syndrome). *Journal of the Korean General Hospital*, *1*, 63–69.

Lee, S. H. (1987). Social phobia in Korea. In *Social phobia in Japan and Korea*, Proceedings of the First Cultural Psychiatry Symposium between Japan and Korea. Seoul: The East Asian Academy of Cultural Psychiatry.

Lidz, R. W., Lidz, T., & Burton-Bradley, B. G. (1973). Culture, personality and social structure: Cargo cultism—A psychosocial study of Melanesian millenarianism. *Journal of Nervous and Mental Disease*, *157*(5), 370–388.

Liebowitz, M. R., Salmán, E., Jusino, C. M., Garfinkel, R., Street, L., Cárdenas, D. L., Silvestre, J., Fyer, A. J., Carrasco, J. L., Davies, S., Guarnaccia, P., & Klein, D. F. (1994). Ataque de nervios and panic disorder. *American Journal of Psychiatry*, *151*, 871–875.

Lin, K. M. (1983). *Hwa-byung*: A Korean culture-bound syndrome? *American Journal of Psychiatry*, *140*(1), 105–107.

Lin, T. Y. (1953). An epidemiological study of the incidence of mental disorder in Chinese and other cultures. *Psychiatry*, *16*, 313–336.

Littlewood, R., & Lipsedge, M. (1986). The "culture-bound syndromes" of the dominant culture: Culture, psychopathology and biomedicine. In J. L. Cox (Ed.), *Transcultural psychiatry* (pp. 253–273). London: Croom Helm.

Malhotra, H. K., & Wig, N. N. (1975). Dhat syndrome: A culture-bound sex neurosis of the Orient. *Archives of Sexual Behavior*, *4*(5), 519–528.

Marano L. (1985). Windigo psychosis: The anatomy of an emic-etic confusion. In R. C. Simons & C. C. Hughes (Eds.), *The culture-bound syndromes* (pp. 411–448). Dordrecht, The Netherland: Reidel. [Original work published 1982.]

Mehlman, R. D. (1961). The Puerto Rican syndrome. *American Journal of Psychiatry*, *118*, 328–332.

Meth, J. M. (1974). Exotic psychiatric syndromes. In S. Arieti & E. B. Brody (Eds.), *American handbook of psychiatry: Vol. 3, Adult clinical psychiatry* (pp. 723–739). New York: Basic Books.

Min, S. K., & Lee, H. Y. (1988). *A clinical study on* hwabyung. Presented at the Fourth scientific meeting of the Pacific Rim College of Psychiatry, Hong Kong.

Murdock, G. P. (1967). *Ethnographic atlas*. Pittsburgh: University of Pittsburgh Press.

Murdock, G. P. (1980). *Theories of illness: A world survey*. Pittsburgh: University of Pittsburgh Press.

Musgrave, W. E., & Sison, A. G. (1910). Mali-mali, a mimic psychosis in the Philippine Islands: A plenary report. *Philippine Journal of Science*, *5*, 335–339.

Neki, J. S. (1973). Psychiatry in South-east Asia. *British Journal of Psychiatry*, *123*, 256–269.

Oquendo, M., Horwath, E., & Martines, A. (1992). Ataques de nervios: Proposed diagnostic criteria for a culture specific syndrome. *Culture, Medicine and Psychiatry*, *16*(3), 367–376.

Pak, O. K. (1996). Spirit possession in East Asia. *Transcultural Psychiatric Research Review*, *33*(1), 81–87.

Palazzoli, M. S. (1985). Anorexia nervosa: A syndrome of the affluent society. *Transcultural Psychiatric Research Review*, *22*(3), 199–205.

Pang, K. Y. C. (1990). *Hwabyung*: The construction of a Korean popular illness among Korean elderly immigrant women in the United States. *Culture, Medicine and Psychiatry*, *14*, 495–512.

Paris, J. (1992). Dhat: The semen loss anxiety syndrome. *Transcultural Psychiatric Research Review*, *29*(2), 109–118.

Pfeiffer, W. M. (1982). Culture-bound syndromes. In I. Al-Issa (Ed.), *Culture and psychopathology.* Baltimore: University Park Press.

Prince, R. (1960). The "brain fag" syndrome in Nigerian students. *Journal of Mental Science, 104,* 559–570.

Prince, R. (1990). The brain-fag syndrome. In K. Pelzer & P. O. Ebigbo (Eds.), *A textbook of clinical psychiatry in Africa.* Enugu, Nigeria: Chuka.

Prince, R., & Tcheng-Laroche, F. (1987). Culture-bound syndromes and international disease classifications. *Culture, Medicine and Psychiatry, 11,* 3–19.

Rin, H. (1965). A study of the aetiology of *koro* in respect to the Chinese concept of illness. *International Journal of Social Psychiatry, 11,* 7–13.

Rin, H. (1966). Two forms of vital deficiency syndrome among Chinese male mental patients. *Transcultural Psychiatric Research Review, 3,* 19–21.

Ritenbaugh, C. (1982). Obesity as a culture-bound syndrome. *Culture, Medicine and Psychiatry, 6*(4), 347–361.

Rubel, A. J. (1964). The epidemiology of a folk illness: *Susto* in Hispanic America. *Ethology, 3,* 268–283.

Rubel, A. J., O'Nell, C. W., & Collado, R. (1985). The folk illness called *susto.* In R. C. Simons & C. C. Hughes (Eds.), *The Culture-bound syndromes* (pp. 333–350). Dordrecht, The Netherlands: Reidel.

Salmán, E., Liebowitz, M. R., Guarnaccia, P. J., Jusino, C. M., Garfinkel, R., Street, L., Cárdenas, D. L., Silvestre, J., Fyer, A. J., Carrasco, J. L., Davies, S. O., & Klein, D. (1998). Subtypes of ataques de nervios: The influence of coexisting psychiatric diagnosis. *Culture, Medicine and Psychiatry, 22,* 231–244.

Sasaki, Y. (1969). Psychiatic study of the shaman in Japan. In W. Caudil & T. Y. Lin (Eds.), *Mental health research in Asia and the Pacific* (pp. 223–241). Honolulu: East-West Center Press.

Schmidt, K., Hill, L., & Guthrie, G. (1977). Running amok. *International Journal of Psychiatry, 23*(4), 264–274.

Simons, R. C. (1980). The resolution of the latah paradox. *Journal of Nervous and Mental Disease, 168*(4), 195–206.

Simons, R. C. (1996). *Boo!—Culture, experience, and the startle reflex.* New York: Oxford University Press.

Simons, R. C., & Hughes, C. C. (1985). *The culture-bound syndromes: Folk illnesses of psychiatric and anthropological interest.* Dordrecht, The Netherlands: Reidel.

Still, R. M. (1940). Remarks on the aetiology and symptoms of young-dah-het with a report on four cases and its medical-legal significance. *Indian Medical Gazette, 75,* 88–91.

Suwanlert, S. (1976). *Phii pob:* Spirit possession in rural Thailand. In W. P. Lebra (Ed.), *Culture-bound syndromes, ethnopsychiatry, and alternate therapies.* Honolulu: University Press of Hawaii.

Suwanlert, S. (1988). A study of *latah* in Thailand. *Journal of the Psychiatric Association of Thailand, 33*(3), 129–133.

Swartz, L. (1985). Anorexia nervosa as a culture bound syndrome. *Transcultural Psychiatric Research Review, 22*(3), 205–207.

Tan, E. S. (1965). *Amok:* A diagnostic consideration. Proceedings of the Second Malaysian Congress of Medicine, pp. 22–25.

Tan, E. S. (1981). Culture-bound syndromes among overseas Chinese. In A. Kleinman & T. Y. Lin (Eds.), *Normal and abnormal behavior in Chinese culture* (pp. 371–386). Dordrecht, The Netherlands: Reidel.

Tan, E. S., & Carr, J. E. (1977). Psychiatric sequelae of amok. *Culture, Medicine and Psychiatry, 1*(1), 59–67.

Tseng, W. S., & Hsu, J. (1969/1970). Chinese culture, personality formation and mental illness. *International Journal of Social Psychiatry, 16*(1), 5–14.

Tseng, W. S., & McDermott, J. F., Jr. (1981). *Culture, mind and therapy: An introduction to cultural psychiatry.* New York: Brunner/Mazel.

Tseng, W. S., Mo, G. M., Hsu, J., Li, L. S., Ou, L. W., Chen, G. Q., & Jiang, D. W. (1988). A socio-cultural study of koro epidemics in Guandong, China. *American Journal of Psychiatry, 145*(12), 1538–1543.

Uchimura, V. Y. (1956). Imu, eine psychoracktive Erscheinung der ainu-Frauen [*Imu*, a psychoactive pnenomenon of *ainu*-women]. *Nervenarzt, 12*, 535–540. [In German.]

Wen, J. K. (1995). Sexual beliefs and problems in contemporary Taiwan. In T. Y. Lin, W. S. Tseng, & E. K. Yeh (Eds.), *Chinese societies and mental health* (pp. 219–230). Hong Kong: Oxford University Press.

Westermeyer, J. (1972). A comparison of *amok* and other homicide in Laos. *American Journal of Psychiatry, 129*(6), 703–709.

Westermeyer, J. (1973). On the epidemicy of *amok* violence. *Archives of General Psychiatry, 28*, 873–876.

Westermeyer, J. (1982). *Amok*. In C. T. H. Friedmann & R. T. Faguet (Eds.), *Extraordinary disorders of human behavior*. New York: Plenum Press.

Westermeyer, J., & Janca, A. (1997). Language, culture and psychopathology: Conceptual and methodological issues. *Transcultural Psychiatry, 34*(3), 291–311.

Wig, N. N. (1960). Problem of mental health in India. *Journal of Clinical and Social Psychiatry* (College of Lucknow, India), *17*(2), 48–53.

Winzeler, R. L. (1995). *Latah in Southeast Asia: The ethnography and history of a culture-bound syndrome*. Cambridge, UK: Cambridge University Press. (Reviewed by M. G. Kenny in *Transcultural Psychiatry Research Review, 33*, 43–54 [1996].)

Woon, T. H. (1988). The latah phenomena. Presented at the annual meeting of Pacific Rim College of Psychiatry, Hong Kong.

Yamashita, I. (1993). *Taijin-kyofu or delusional social phobia*. Sapporo: Hokkaido University Press. [English translation of Japanese book originally published in 1977, Tokyo: Kanehara.] (Reviewed by S. C. Chang in *Transcultural Psychiatry Research Review, 2*, 283–288 [1984].)

Yap, P. M. (1951). Mental diseases peculiar to certain cultures: A survey of comparative psychiatry. *Journal of Mental Science, 97*, 313–327.

Yap, P. M. (1965). Koro—A culture-bound depersonalization syndrome. *British Journal of Psychiatry, 111*, 43–50.

Yap, P. M. (1967). Classification of the culture-bound reactive syndromes. *Australia and New Zealand Journal of Psychiatry, 1*, 172–179.

## B. Epidemic or Collective Mental Disorders

Adityanjee (1994). Mass suicide by self-immolation in Waco, Texas. *Journal of Nervous and Mental Disease, 182*(12), 727–728.

Adomakoh, C. G. (1973). The pattern of epidemic hysteria in a girls' school in Ghana. *Ghana Medical Journal, 12*, 407–411.

Amin, Y., Hamdi, E., & Eapen, V. (1997). Mass hysteria in an Arab culture. *International Journal of Social Psychiatry, 43*(4), 303–306.

Bartholomew, R. E. (1994). Tarantism, dancing mania and demonopathy: The anthro-political aspects of "mass psychogenic illness." *Psychological Medicine, 24*(2), 281–306.

Chakraborty, A. (1983, December). *Koro* makes an epidemic appearance in India. *Transcultural Psychiatric Newsletter*, Vol. 3 (3 and 4).

Chakraborty, A. (1984). An epidemic of koro in West Bengal (India). *Transcultural Psychiatric Research Review, 21*(1), 59–61. [Abstracted by W. G. Jilek.]

Cheng, S. T. (1996). A critical review of Chinese *koro*. *Culture, Medicine and Psychiatry, 20*, 67–82.

Dutta, D., Phookan, H. R., & Das, P. D. (1982). The *koro* epidemic in Lower Assam. *Indian Journal of Psychiatry, 24*(4), 370–374. (Reviewed in *Traanscultural Psychiatry Research Review, 21*(1), 59–61 [1984].)

Ebrahim, G. J. (1968). Mass hysteria in schoolchildren: Notes on three outbreaks in East Africa. *Clinical Pediatrics, 7,* 437–448.

Goduco-Angular, C., & Wintrob, R. (1964). *Folie à famille* in the Philippines. *Psychiatric Quarterly, 38,* 278–291.

Hefez, A. (1985). The role of the press and the medical community in the epidemic of "mysterious gas poisoning' in the Jordan West Bank. *American Journal of Psychiatry, 142*(7), 833–837.

Johnson, D. M. (1945). The "phantom anesthetist" of Mattoon: A field study of mass hysteria. *Journal of Abnormal and Social Psychology, 40,* 175–186.

Kerckhoff, A. C., & Back, K. W. (1965). Sociometric patterns in hysterial contagion. *Sociometry, 28,* 2–15.

Knight, J. A., Friedman, T. I., & Sulianti, J. (1965). Epidemic hysteria. A field study. *American Journal of Public Health, 55,* 858–865.

Levine, R. J. (1977). Epidemic faintness and syncope in a school marching band. *Journal of American Medical Association, 238,* 2373–2378.

Medalia, N. Z., & Larsen, O. N. (1958). Diffusion and belief in a collective delusion: The Seattle windshield pitting epidemic. *American Sociology Review, 23,* 180–186.

Mo, G. M., Chen, G. Q., Li, L. X., & Tseng, W. S. (1995). *Koro* epidemic in Southern China. In T. Y. Lin, W. S. Tseng, & E. K. Yeh (Eds.), *Chinese societies and mental health* (pp. 231–243). Hong Kong: Oxford University Press.

Moss, P. D. & McEvedy, C. P. (1966). An epidemic of overbreathing among school girls. *British Medical Journal, 2,* 1295–1300.

Newsweek (1997, April 7). Web of death pp. 26–49. Special report: UFO's, comets and cult—'Follow me': Inside the Heaven's Gate mass suicide.

Ngui, P. W. (1969). The koro epidemic in Singapore. *Australian New Zealand Journal of Psychiatry,* Special Issue II, on Anxiety, *3,* 263–266.

Schuler, E. A., & Parenton, V. J. (1943). A recent epidemic of hysteria in a Louisiana high school. *Journal of Social Psychology, 17,* 221–235.

Sirois, F. (1974). Epidemic hysteria. *Acta Psychiatrica Scandinavica, Supplementum, 252,* 1–46.

Suwanlert, S., & Coates, D. (1979). Epidemic koro in Thailand—Clinical and social aspects. *Transcultural Psychiatric Research Review, 15,* 64–66.

Taiminen, T., Salmenpera, T., & Lehtinen, K. (1992). A suicide epidemic in a psychiatric hospital. *Suicide and Life-Threatening Behavior, 22*(3), 350–363.

Takahashi, Y. (1989). Mass suicide by members of the Japanese friend of Truth Church. *Suicide and Life-Threatening Behavior, 19*(3), 289–296.

Tan, E. S. (1963). Epidemic hysteria. *Medical Journal of Malaya, 18,* 72–76.

Teoh, J. I., Soewondo, S., & Sidharta, M. (1975). Epidemic hysteria in Malaysian schools: An illustrative episode. *Psychiatry, 38,* 258–268.

Tseng, W. S. (1969). A paranoid family in Taiwan: A dynamic study of *folie à famille*. *Archives of General Psychiatry, 21,* 55–65.

Tseng, W. S. (2001). *Handbook of Cultural Psychiatry.* San Diego, CA: Academic Press.

Ulman, R.B., & Abse, D. W. (1983). The group psychology of mass madness, Jonestown. *Political Psychology, 4*(4), 637–661.

Woon, T. H. (1976). Epidemic hysteria in a Malaysian Chinese extended family. *Medical Journal of Malaysia, 31,* 108–112.

# CHAPTER 4

# Culture and Psychopathology: General Disorders

In contrast to the previous chapter, which focused on psychopathologies of a special nature, this chapter will review pathologies of a general nature. Most of them are recognized by official, contemporary, psychiatric diagnostic systems and are observed in various societies and cultural settings around the world. Nevertheless, their prevalence, clinical pictures, and prognoses may vary from culture to culture. Therefore, this discussion will be based primarily on cross-cultural research and epidemiological data. It should be remembered, however, that the information obtained from cross-cultural epidemiological studies needs to be carefully interpreted, as there are often inherent methodological problems involved.

One of the most critical problems involved with epidemiological data in cross-cultural comparisons is that investigations carried out in different social or cultural settings are often conducted by different investigators using different methods for gathering data and different ways to analyze the collected information. This makes forming direct cross-comparisons and meaningful interpretations difficult. Any findings that illustrate a substantial difference in certain kinds of psychopathologies between, or among, subjects of different ethnic, racial, or cultural backgrounds should not be immediately attributed to "ethnic" or "cultural" factors. Many other factors, including biological and social, should first be considered. From a cultural perspective, another common problem found in psychiatric epidemiological studies in the past was that most did not include the study of cultural information. Even when the data were compared with data from different cultural settings, in an attempt at a "cross-cultural" comparison, most investigations focused on social or demographic data, which are not the same as cultural variables. Ethnic or racial background, social class, economic level, and religious background may indirectly reflect the attitudes, beliefs, or values of the subjects, but they are not a direct reflection of the culture. They only allow us to make some inferential interpretations. (For details, read Tseng, 2001, Chapter 12: Culture and Psychiatric Epidemiology.)

Finally, no matter how sophisticated the methodology, there are still many issues that need to be considered from a cultural perspective in order to obtain culturally relevant epidemiological data. These include language, examination setting, style of interviewing, the cultural pattern of the subject's reaction to the interview and questionnaire survey, confidentiality, the choice and revision of the questionnaires to be used, and the analysis and interpretation of the data obtained. (For details, read Tseng, 2001, Chapter 48: Cross-Cultural Research.)

## A. ANXIETY DISORDERS

"Anxiety disorders" is used here as a generic term referring to various subgroup of disorders. It includes general anxiety disorders, specific phobias, social phobias, panic disorders, obsessive-compulsive disorders (OCD), and posttraumatic stress disorders (PTSD). Those disorders share the common core problem of "anxiety," even though they may manifest distinctly different or mixed clinical pictures of anxiety-rooted problems.

The diagnostic criteria of minor psychiatric disorders are so subjectively defined and loosely constructed that they tend to vary according to practitioners' patterns of diagnostic work. The nature of minor psychiatric disorders is closely related to a person's cognitive conceptions, emotional reactions, and life experiences and therefore varies widely, depending on individual as well as environmental factors including culture.

### 1. Diagnostic Distribution of Anxiety Disorders

#### a. Data from General Health Care

A large-scale international, multisite comparative investigation was carried out by the World Health Organization (WHO), the Collaborative Study of Psychological Problems in General Health Care (Üstün & Sartorius, 1995), involving 14 countries around the world. The investigation focused on (medical) patients visiting general healthcare facilities. It examined the prevalence of minor psychiatric disorders as well as other clinical issues.

The mental disorders investigated in this WHO study included general anxiety disorder, panic disorder, agoraphobia, depression, dysthymia, somatization disorder, hypochondriasis, and neurasthenia, as defined by ICD-10. The results showed that, as illustrated in Table 1, there are certain degrees of variation in terms of the prevalence of these disorders. For example, the prevalence of general anxiety disorder is relatively high in South America: 22.6% in Rio de Janirio (Brazil) and 18.7% in Santigo de Chile (Chile). In contrast, it is only 0.9% in Ankara (Turkey) and 1.9% in Shanghai (China), paralleling the trend that patients visiting general-health facilities there seldom present psychological problems. Given the information obtained from this study, it is unclear what cardinal factors influence these results.

### b. Reports from Community Surveys

It is useful to have cross-cultural information about the nature and pattern of problems presented by patients attending general healthcare facilities; however, such data are limited because it is not clear to what extent it reflects the actual situation in the community. Several community survey studies have shed some light for us, even though their data are difficult to compare with data obtained from different cultural areas because no standardized methodology was applied.

*(1) China—Twelve-Region Epidemiological Study of Neuroses.*   To comprehend the prevalence of various neuroses in the community, China undertook a national survey in 1982, involving 12 geographic areas around the country, both rural and urban (Cooper & Sartorius, 1996; Psychiatric Epidemiological Collaboration Team, 1986). The results revealed that the prevalence rate of neurotic disorders was 22.21 per 1000 population investigated.

As for different categories of neurotic disorders, as a whole, the total prevalence rates per 1000 population, in declining order, were 13.0 for neurasthenia, 3.55 for hysteria, 3.11 for neurotic depression, 1.48 for anxiety disorder, 0.59 for phobic disorder, 0.30 for obsessive-compulsive disorder, and 0.15 for hypochondriasis. It should be noted that neurasthenia was the most frequently diagnosed category, with a prevalence rate of 13.0, far higher than any other kind of neurosis disorder. Anxiety disorders, including phobic and obsessive-compulsive disorders, had a prevalence rate of only 2.37 altogether.

*(2) United States: Catchment Area Study.*   The Epidemiological Catchment Area (ECA) Study carried out in the United States in the 1980s was not primarily designed as a cross-cultural study. Still, cross-ethnic comparison was made among three ethnic groups: Caucasian-American, African-American, and

TABLE 1  Psychological Problems Presented in General Health Care: WHO's International Study.

| Study Centers | Ankara, Turkey | Athens, Greece | Bangalore, India | Berlin, Germany | Groninge, Netherlands | Ibadan, Nigeria | Mainz, Germany | Manchester, United Kingdom | Nagasaki, Japan | Paris, France | Rio de Janeiro, Brazil | Santiago de Chile, Chile | Seattle, United States | Shanghai, China | Verona, Italy |
|---|---|---|---|---|---|---|---|---|---|---|---|---|---|---|---|
| **Presenting Complaints**[a] | | | | | | | | | | | | | | | |
| Psychological | 2.6 | 2.2 | 1.3 | 3.7 | 12.8 | 2.3 | 3.6 | 9.4 | 1.3 | 11.0 | 7.6 | 13.2 | 2.6 | 0.2 | 6.4 |
| Fatigue/sleep | 5.6 | 5.1 | 8.0 | 5.2 | 5.7 | 9.0 | 0.6 | 13.4 | 9.5 | 8.4 | 5.1 | 3.6 | 1.6 | 13.3 | 3.7 |
| Pain | 80.5 | 21.9 | 35.1 | 32.3 | 28.2 | 51.4 | 28.0 | 24.8 | 21.3 | 25.3 | 42.1 | 17.4 | 17.0 | 26.2 | 25.9 |
| Other somatic | 44.4 | 33.5 | 17.7 | 36.0 | 37.0 | 31.0 | 33.5 | 38.2 | 22.8 | 39.6 | 16.9 | 31.6 | 15.8 | 52.9 | 25.6 |
| **ICD Diagnoses** | | | | | | | | | | | | | | | |
| Alcohol dependence | 1.0 | 1.0 | 1.4 | 5.3 | 3.4 | 0.4 | 7.2 | 2.2 | 3.7 | 4.3 | 4.1 | 2.5 | 1.5 | 1.1 | 0.5 |
| Harmful use of alcohol | 0.8 | 3.5 | 0.6 | 4.0 | 5.5 | 0.8 | 3.0 | 1.4 | 2.5 | 5.0 | 1.7 | 10.0 | 8.6 | 1.6 | 2.6 |
| Current depression | 11.6 | 6.4 | 9.1 | 6.1 | 15.9 | 4.2 | 11.2 | 16.9 | 2.6 | 13.7 | 15.8 | 29.5 | 6.3 | 4.0 | 4.7 |
| Dysthymia | 0.9 | 1.4 | 9.8 | 0.5 | 1.8 | 1.3 | 0.9 | 2.0 | 0.4 | 3.6 | 2.4 | 4.2 | 0.3 | 0.6 | 2.0 |
| Agoraphobia | 1.2 | 0.9 | 0.1 | 1.5 | 2.7 | 0.1 | 1.6 | 3.8 | 0.0 | 2.2 | 2.7 | 3.9 | 1.3 | 0.1 | 0.6 |
| Panic disorder | 0.2 | 0.7 | 1.0 | 0.9 | 1.5 | 0.7 | 1.7 | 3.5 | 0.2 | 1.7 | 0.0 | 0.6 | 1.9 | 0.2 | 1.5 |
| Generalized anxiety disorder | 0.9 | 14.9 | 8.5 | 9.0 | 6.4 | 2.9 | 7.9 | 7.1 | 5.0 | 11.9 | 22.6 | 18.7 | 2.1 | 1.9 | 3.7 |
| Somatization disorder | 1.9 | 1.3 | 1.8 | 1.3 | 2.8 | 0.4 | 3.0 | 0.4 | 0.1 | 1.7 | 8.5 | 17.7 | 1.7 | 1.5 | 0.1 |
| Hypochondriasis | 0.2 | 0.2 | 0.2 | 0.4 | 1.0 | 1.9 | 1.2 | 0.5 | 0.4 | 0.1 | 1.1 | 3.8 | 0.6 | 0.4 | 0.3 |
| Neurasthenia | 4.1 | 4.6 | 2.7 | 7.4 | 10.5 | 1.1 | 7.7 | 9.7 | 3.4 | 9.3 | 4.5 | 10.5 | 2.1 | 2.0 | 2.1 |
| One or more mental disorders | 17.6 | 22.1 | 23.9 | 25.2 | 29.0 | 10.4 | 30.6 | 26.2 | 14.8 | 31.2 | 38.0 | 53.5 | 20.4 | 9.7 | 12.4 |
| All patients (%) | 100.0 | 100.0 | 100.0 | 100.0 | 100.0 | 100.0 | 100.0 | 100.0 | 100.0 | 100.0 | 100.0 | 100.0 | 100.0 | 100.0 | 100.0 |
| ICD-10 disorders[b] | 8.2 | 11.6 | 16.2 | 32.5 | 27.0 | 27.9 | 33.0 | 28.1 | 4.8 | 30.3 | 20.4 | 58.5 | 19.7 | 5.4 | 47.3 |

[a]Number by percentage.

[b]ICD-10 disorder recognized by treating physicians as a psychological case.

Modified from *Mental illness in general health care: An international study*. T. B. Üstün and N. Sartorius (Eds.) 1995. Copyright © John Wiley & Sons Limited. Reproduced with permission.

Hispanic-American, depending on the number of subjects in the selected catchment area who were available for statistical comparison.

Regarding anxiety disorders, there were several findings concerning these three ethnic groups. The lifetime prevalence of panic disorder was found to be 1.62, 1.31, and 0.87%, respectively, in the three ethnic groups. Caucasian-Americans had a relatively higher prevalence, Hispanic-Americans were lower, while African-Americans were in between (Eaton, Dryman, & Weissman, 1991, p. 159). The one-year prevalence rates of general anxiety disorder were 1.64, 2.74, and 0.86%, respectively, for the three groups, with African-Americans being relatively higher and Hispanic-Americans lower (Blazer et al., 1991, p. 187). Regarding obsessive-compulsive disorder, the lifetime prevalence was 2.63, 2.31, and 1.82%, respectively, with Caucasian-Americans relatively higher and Hispanic-Americans lower (Karno & Golding, 1991, p. 211). Thus, there were variations among the three ethnic groups examined for each category of anxiety disorder surveyed.

## 2. Cultural Aspects of Various Types of Anxiety Disorders

### a. (Simple) Anxiety Disorders

The adjective "simple" is added here to the term "anxiety disorder" to imply that, unlike a general anxiety disorder (as defined by DSM-IV), it can occur as a brief episode, in reaction to external distress or intrapsychic conflict, and may be manifested primarily as an anxiety picture. The DSM-IV included in the definition of a general anxiety disorder the arbitrary requirement that the anxiety state lasts more than six months. However, anxiety disorders observed in other cultures do not necessarily have such a chronic quality.

As already elaborated (see Section 2A, Culture and Stress), in addition to individual factors, the source and nature of stress are subjected greatly to the sociocultural environment. Briefly, culture itself produces stress, influences the perception of stress, shapes the way people cope with the distress encountered, and affects supporting resources for managing stress. Anxiety can be created by cultural beliefs, such as penis shrinkage anxiety (*koro* cases), semen leakage anxiety (*daht* and *shenkui* syndromes), or taboo-breaking anxiety (causing *voodoo* death or *malgri* attacks) (see Section 3A, Culture-Related Specific Syndromes). Anxiety can also be produced by cultural demands. Bearing a son to succeed the family line, academic achievement, the regulated choice of a mate, or the restricted life of a widow are some examples. Family conflicts associated with widening generational gaps among immigrants, severe discrimination by a majority group, rapid change and confusion of value systems, and family separation due to war or social disaster are additional examples of sources of anxiety that are closely related to sociocultural situations. In many societies, cultural dictates on how to secure food, how to find money to pay debts or mortgages, and how to obtain medicine for sicknesses are some causes of anxiety that tend to occur in daily life.

From a clinical point of view, it should be mentioned that the reaction to distress does not necessarily take the "pure" or "typical" form of an anxiety state. The reaction often manifests as a mixture of anxiety, depression, and various somatic symptoms.

### b. Social Phobia

The diagnostic consideration of social phobia has increased considerably in the United States in the past decade. Whether this is due to an increase in such cases (doubtful) or an increase in diagnostic attention by clinicians (likely) deserves examination. It should be pointed out that the diagnostic category of social phobia was not listed among international classification systems previously until it recently appeared in ICD-10 (1992). In the American system of DSM, there was no such category in the past either; it did not appear until 1980, when the DSM-III was revised. In contrast, Japanese psychiatrists coined the diagnostic term *taijinkyofusho* (disorder of fear of interpersonal relations, also translated as "anthrophobia" in English) at the turn of the 20th century, and it has been used widely since (see Section 3A, Culture-Related Specific Syndromes). A study revealed that Japanese psychiatrists are familiar with this disorder clinically and diagnose it easily (Tseng et al., 1992). A special mode of therapy (i.e., Morita therapy) has even been invented for treating this disorder.

Although Western psychiatrists are eager to include *taijinkyofusho* as social phobia in a broad sense, Japanese psychiatrists insist that the disorder is different from Western social phobias. They have pointed out that Japanese patients with *taijinkyofusho* are more concerned with self (in others' views), associated with feelings of embarrassment, and many dysmorphobic concerns (Kasahara, 1974; Kimura, 1982). The patients are eager to socialize with others and have no problems relating with strangers, but they are concerned with how to relate properly to friends, colleagues, or superiors (to make a good impression on them). As indicated by Kimura (1982) and Uchinuma (1990), if social relations are divided into three groups, namely, intimate (family, close friends), intermediately familiar or acquainted with (neighbors, classmates, or co-workers), and strangers (nonacquainted persons), Japanese *taijinkyofusho* patients have difficulty mainly with the intermediately familiar group in semiprivate/public circumstances. Western social phobic patients defined by DSM-IV, on the other hand, are those who have problems mostly with strangers in open public settings.

### c. Obsessive-Compulsive Disorders

Although OCDs have relatively clear and unique clinical manifestations and are easy to diagnose, only a handful of works address their cultural aspects. In the

United States, based on discharge diagnostic data collected from the McLean Hospital from 1969 to 1990, Stoll, Tohen, and Baldessarini (1992) reported that the proportion of patients discharged with this diagnosis increased almost four-fold. They speculated that the increase was associated with advances in the clinical study and treatment of these disorders. There is no comparable information from other countries. However, by reviewing epidemiological literature, Staley and Wand (1995) reported that OCD is generally similar in prevalence, sociodemographic characteristics, and clinical features in adult populations in Western and non-Western societies. Associated with improvements in the psychopharmacological treatment of this disorder, biological causes for this disorder are becoming more prevalent among psychiatrists at the present time.

### d. Posttraumatic Stress Disorders

It is common knowledge, even among laypeople, that humans will react mentally to severe stress, including acute trauma, severe disaster, sexual or violent assault, and chronic, intense tension. This includes war situations in which people encounter extreme danger with the possibility of death. It has been pointed out that cultural factors will influence the perception and interpretation of trauma and modify the core process of trauma reaction and the expression of trauma symptoms (Chemtob, 1996; Marsella et al., 1996).

Historically, the different diagnostic labels that have been used for war-related stress disorders in different wars include "nostalgia" during the American Civil War, "shell shock" in World War I, "combat neuroses" in World War II, and "combat exhaustion" in the Korean War (Davidson et al., 1990). It has been the practice of Army psychiatrists to manage psychiatric casualties in a war zone according to the three basic principles of immediacy, proximity, and expectancy (Block, 1969).

PTSD have been frequently diagnosed disorders in the United States, particularly among Vietnam War veterans, during the last several decades. In contrast to the traditional wars of the past, the Vietnam War was different for American soldiers in many respects. There was no clear distinction between civilians and the "enemy." The battles often took place in the jungle. There was no clear front, or combat zone, or base to which to retreat. The goal of the war was unclear. Many civilians were killed by the soldiers, and many soldiers were severely tortured when captured by the enemy. In other words, it was a "terrible" war. After losing the war, the returning veterans were not welcomed by their fellow Americans. Those were the primarily different experiences of Vietnam veterans. However, most interesting is that, after the so-called posttraumatic stress disorder was "discovered," identified, and labeled, and a welfare system was established to deal with it, the number of patients claiming this disorder increased rapidly. It was estimated that, among the veterans, the prevalence of this disorder ranged from 20 to 60% (Friedman, 1981). This may be because, after official recognition of the disorder and the establishment of a treatment program for it, many patients became more comfortable with admitting their suffering and seeking help.

This speculation is provoked by available information from other countries. Relatively few reports of war-related PTSD appeared in literature. There were some reports from Israel (Solomon, 1989) and a few from Europe (Bell et al., 1988) but almost no reports from Japan, relating to World War II, or from China, relating to the four-year China-Japan War, followed by another four years fighting World War II and the civil war between the communist and the nationalist governments. Was it that the war-related traumatic disorders did not occur, or that they did occur, but never caught the attention of clinicians and the government? This is an interesting question awaiting future investigation and clarification.

It is clear that anxiety and other minor psychiatric disorders are greatly subject to sociocultural factors and cannot be understood or approached without cultural considerations. This includes understanding the nature of the problem, making a clinical assessment and diagnosis, and offering treatment for the patient. From a cultural point of view, it would be more interesting to focus on the dynamic interaction of the pathogenic, pathoplastic, pathoreactive effects of anxiety disorders rather than the frequency of such disorders (through pathofacilitating effects).

## B. DEPRESSION DISORDERS

### 1. Introduction and Clarification

The cultural aspects of depression have created keen interest among cultural psychiatrists since the 1960s. This coincided with the availability of antidepressants for treatment but was motivated by the discovery that, in spite of a sharply increasing clinical trend in Euro-American societies of diagnosing depression, there was a low prevalence of it in non-Western societies. Instead of investigating why there were fewer depressive cases observed in non-Western societies, many Western clinicians and investigators turned their attention to the examination and exploration of the possibility that depression might be "masked" in its manifestation (as an emotional expression of depression) in non-Western societies.

With an increase in clinical knowledge, psychiatrists now take the view that depression, particularly of a severe or endogenous type, is closely related to biological factors. However, as pointed out by Marsella et al. (1985), even if some types of depression are shown to have primary biological causes, cultural factors could still modify the behavioral expression of the biological factors (pathoplastic effects) and interpret the abnormal experiences and respond to the social reactions to that behavior differently (pathoreactive effects).

### a. Questions about Different Qualities of Depression

There is a great breadth of issues raised by a cross-cultural study of depression, including: Do all people, regardless of their cultures, experience emotions in similar ways? Does the description of the experience of an emotion change from culture to culture, or is it the same? To explore cross-cultural variations in the meaning and subjective experience of depression, Tanaka-Matsumi and Marsella (1976) asked Japanese, Japanese-American, and Caucasian-American college students to associate a word with "depression." As a results, they revealed that Japanese do not experience (mild or ordinary) depression in the same way as Americans, nor do they express feelings in the same way. For the Japanese, concrete images from nature allow personal emotions to be expressed impersonally. Because this particular study utilized normal college students as subjects, a basic question still remained: Are the tendencies revealed applicable to clinically depressed groups?

### b. About the Masking of Depression

Another clinical concept used by psychiatrists in the past was *masked depression*, which takes the view that certain individuals, in reacting to loss or frustration, instead of manifesting the emotional reaction of depression, show other clinical pictures, such as somatization or behavior problems. This view is founded on the basic assumption that when a person encounters the psychological trauma of loss or frustration, he responds primarily with the mood disorder of depression. If, for some reason, the person is not able to respond with depression, and the trauma is manifested by another mental condition, it is considered to be masked depression. This clinical assumption is not useful, and is even misleading, in cross-cultural applications. It assumes that human beings are allowed to react emotionally only in a defined way, ignoring that there are rich variations in the emotional and behavioral reactions of human beings in different cultural environments. It is biased in identifying one reaction as primary and others as "masked."

### c. Depression and Somatic Symptoms

From a cultural perspective, it is more useful to understand the problem-presentation styles (or patterns) manifested by patients. The information and problems presented by patients to physicians are subject to various factors, including patient-therapist relations, culturally molded patterns of making complaints, and the clinical setting in which the interactions take place. This also applies to depression. The meaning of complaining about depression versus somatic symptoms deserves careful evaluation and consideration. Simon et al. (1999) used data from the World Health Organization study of psychological problems in general healthcare to examine the relation between somatic symptoms and depression. They found that, among patients studied at 15 primary care centers in 14 countries on 5 continents, about 10% who presented somatic symptoms to the primary caretaker met the criteria for major depression. Further, they revealed that a somatic presentation was more common at centers where patients lacked an ongoing relationship with a primary care physician than at centers where most patients had a personal physician. This supports indirectly the view that the nature of complaints made by the patients is closely related to patient-doctor relations.

## 2. Variations in Clinical Pictures

### a. Variations of Depression as a Clinical Condition

*(1) Individual Scholars' Reports.*    Even focusing merely on clinically recognized conditions of "depression," cultural variations are recognized. In the late 1970s, German cultural psychiatrist Wolfgang Pfeiffer (1968) reviewed many works on depression in non-European cultures. He pointed out that, the "core" symptoms of depression (i.e., change of mood, disruption of physiological functions such as sleep and appetite, and hypochondriacal symptoms) in these cultures were the same as in Europe. However, other symptoms, such as feelings of guilt and suicidal tendencies, showed variations of frequency and intensity among cultures. This view was later supported by other investigators (Binitie, 1975; Sartorius, 1975).

Many clinical reports back up the view just given. For instance, based on clinical observation of depressive illness in Afghanistan, Waziri (1973) reported that the majority of depressed patients expressed "death wishes" instead of suicidal intentions or thoughts. In Afghanistan, with their Muslim religious backgrounds, people believe suicide is a sin. Waziri said that the depressed patients who were asked how they viewed life answered that they "wished they were dead" or that they had "prayed to God to take their life away." Actually, the suicide rate among the general population is very low, namely 0.25 per 100,000 population (Gobar, 1970). This illustrates that even though a suicidal tendency is associated with depression, cultural attitudes either sanctioning or forbidding self-destruction can modify the expression of suicidal ideas.

The presence or absence of self-depreciation, self-blame in the form of feeling ashamed or guilty, is another aspect that has gained attention and been debated from cross-cultural perspectives. According to Prince (1968), in Africa, mental-emotional self-castigation is rare or absent in the early stages of depressed patients. Earlier, Murphy, Wittkower, and Chance (1967) proposed that the higher incidence of guilt feelings in Western cultures was perhaps due to the influence of the Christian religion. However, after examining depressed Christian and Muslim patients in Cairo, El-Islam (1969) reported that the presence or absence of guilt feelings was often associated with the level of education or literacy and the degree of depression and not to religious background. He concluded that guilt and Christianity are not necessarily closely linked.

*(2) WHO's International Survey of Depressive Symptomatology.* The possibility of cultural variations of depressive symptomatology was investigated systematically by WHO, using standardized methods, beginning in 1972 (Sartorius et al., 1983). Five study centers in four countries were involved: Basel (Switzerland), Montreal (Canada), Nagasaki (Japan), Teheran (Iran), and Tokyo (Japan). The WHO Schedule for Standardized Assessment of Depressive Disorders (SADD) was used for clinical assessment by trained clinicians in each study center. Specified diagnostic criteria of the International Statistical Classification of Diseases and Related Health Problems, 9th Version (ICD-9), was included in the study of depressive patients. A total of 573 patients from the five centers were examined. Results revealed similar patterns of depressive disorders in all settings. Patients in all the sites were found to have high frequencies of sadness, joylessness, anxiety, tension, lack of energy, loss of interest, concentration difficulties, and feelings of inadequacy, but there were also considerable variations in the frequencies with which certain symptoms appeared across the study centers. For example, guilt feelings were present in 68% of the Swiss patients, but in only 32% of the Iranian patients; somatic symptoms were present in 57% of the Iranian patients, but in only 27% of the Canadian patients. Suicidal ideas were present in 70% of the Canadian patients, but in only 40% of the Japanese patients. There were different levels of severity of depression in the different study centers, patients in Nagasaki, Montreal, and Basel were more anergic and retarded than patients in Tokyo and Teheran. It is not clear whether the differences in frequencies of certain symptoms were due to the levels of severity of depression or to ethnocultural variations.

### b. Mixed Anxiety-Depression-Somatic State

As we have discussed, clinicians must be aware that the clearly defined and sharply distinguished depressive state is not necessarily a rule. Rather, it is often mixed with anxiety and a somatic state. This is true for patients from our society (i.e., America) and, even more so, from societies with different cultures. The disorders of depression include various clinical conditions on a spectrum that ranges from primarily biologically determined depressive "disorders" (exemplified by endogenous, periodically occurring depression) to predominantly psychologically related depressive "reactions." The human mind does not respond to an internal or external situation purely according to a defined "disorder." This is particularly true when a person is reacting to psychological distress. The response is often a combination of anxiety, depression, anger, a feeling of frustration, and many concomitant physiological symptoms. This is very important for cross-cultural applications. Diagnostically mixed types of disorders can be more the rule than the exception. Sometimes, when a classification system that originated from one culture is applied to another, an "atypical" type is a more typical occurrence, while a "typical" type is more atypical.

## 3. Cultural Contribution to Causes of Depression

Perhaps, from a cultural psychiatric point of view, one of the most useful areas of study is the psychological causes of depression from a cross-cultural perspective because it offers a rich resource of examples of how human beings experience psychological trauma or distress and react to loss or frustration in various ways. Of course, it would need to focus on the study of "reactive" rather than "endogenous" depression. Dynamic psychiatrists view depression as a reaction to loss, deprivation, frustration, injury to self-esteem, or conflict over the aggressive drive or as a threat to a personality structure marked by narcissism or dependency. In addition to these clinical theories, the psychological causes for depression can also include social-cultural determinants.

Many clinicians speculate that childhood separation produces a vulnerability to depression that can be triggered by separation in adult life. A parent's death during one's childhood can precipitate later depression, just as separation, divorce, or prolonged absence of parents may cause the same delayed result. It is not always the loss itself that plants the seed of later depression. The circumstances of the original loss and the provision or lack of alternative relationships or supportive figures also influence the emotional impact of the initial trauma. From a sociocultural viewpoint, family structure (such as the nuclear or extended family), child-rearing practices (e.g., child rearing with or without care), and the presence or absence of parental substitutes (e.g., grandparents or aunts who live nearby) all must be considered as causes or deterrents to later depression.

How a community views death and ritualizes mourning may also affect the occurrence of depression. In Samoa, death is seen as a natural event in life experience. Behavior patterns in the Samoan family and community provide effective support when someone dies (Ablon, 1971). In Fiji, Indian people still hold the traditional view that when a woman's husband passes away, she is no longer allowed to participate in any social activities or to have any social contact with men other than her father-in-law and brothers-in-law. Remarriage is unthinkable, even if she is still young. She is expected to devote herself to the care of her own children and to observe her widowhood for the rest of her life. Consequently, many widows suffer from depression. This phenomenon is not observed among the Fijian women living on the same island, as the indigenous Fijians have no such views of or practices for widows.

A socially, occupationally, or economically deprived status can also help weave the fabric of depression. In fact, the minority status of an ethnic group may outweigh ethnic characteristics as a contributing cause of depressive illness. Fernando (1975) compared Jewish and Protestant depressive patients in the East End of London. He studied familial and social factors and found that increasing paternal inadequacy and weakening ethnic links and religious faith were related to depressive ills among Jews, but not among Protestants. He suggested that mental stress arose from the marginal position of Jews in British society rather than from specific traits or customs within Jewish culture.

As a summary, it is suggested that, instead of studying "depressive disorders" broadly or inclusively, attention should be focused on psychologically induced depression, which is more culturally related. There is clearly room for meaningful examination of the causes of depression.

## C. DISSOCIATION, POSSESSION DISORDERS, AND HYSTERIA

Among all mental phenomena and psychopathology, the related mental states of trance, dissociation, possession, and altered personality have fascinated clinicians and scholars for a long time (Bourguignon, 1973; Prince, 1968; Ward, 1989). These unique mental conditions are characterized by their dramatic, puzzling, and mysterious nature. The description and understanding of the phenomena have changed a great deal along the developmental path of psychiatry. They have caught the interest of scholars from the perspectives of medical history and cultural anthropology. Because various impacts of culture on mental conditions can be studied explicitly by examining this particular set of mental phenomena, it has also attracted great attention among cultural psychiatrists.

### 1. Introduction and Clarification

#### a. The Core of the Phenomena: Altered Consciousness State

Although trance, dissociation, possession, and altered personality states differ in certain ways, they share several common characteristics. As mental conditions, they are related to some extent to the basic mechanism of the alteration of the state of consciousness and the awareness of self-identification. They are related to the verification of mental integration and involve change of personality and awareness and identity of selfness. Based on these mental mechanisms, different mental conditions emerge that may occur as normal life conditions, on special daily life occasions, or as morbid states. Thus, they are found on a spectrum ranging between the normal and the pathological (Fig. 1). Another unique feature of these mental conditions is that they can be induced by the self, can occur rather suddenly, and the individual experiencing them can return to his original

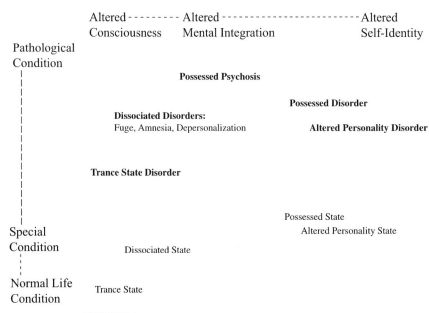

FIGURE 1    Spectrum of various altered consciousness states.

state within a certain time. These conditions can occur in ordinary daily life situations, such as meditation and daydreaming, or as part of a religious or healing ceremony or professional practice, such as hypnosis. They can also occur in reaction to emotional stress. If they occur as pathological disorders, psychological therapy becomes the main approach for treatment.

### b. Phenomenological Distinction

Even though most psychiatrists working with Euro-American patients encounter less dissociated disorder or possession disorder, and they less familiar with such clinical conditions, these disorders are still prevalently observed among people from various societies, and it is important for clinicians to be familiar with these various kinds of unique psychopathologies. A conceptual distinction among these related but different mental conditions is in order. These conditions include trance state, dissociated state, altered personality state, and possessed state. (For more details, see Tseng, 2001, Chapter 17: Dissociation, Possession Disorders and Hysteria, pp. 318–320.)

Concerning the trance and possession state, as observed in the ordinary life of society, cultural anthropologist Erika Bourguignon (1973) carried out statistical studies by drawing a worldwide sample from Murdock's *Ethnographic Atlas*. She reported that there is a relationship between types of altered states manifested by the members of society and societal characteristics reflecting variations in complexity. She pointed out that the less complex a society is, the more likely it is to have only a trance state; whereas a more complex society is more likely to have possession trance. Bourguignon (1976) interpreted trance as an intrapersonal psychic event. In contrast, possession involves the impersonation of another being on an occasion when there are witnesses. As such, it is an interpersonal event because the witnesses and the audience play crucial roles in the event. In other words, a possession state, in contrast to a simple trance state, involves a much more complex psychic function.

## 2. Various Types of Disorders

### a. Dissociation Disorder

Dissociation as a morbid condition is still frequently observed in many societies, particularly from developing countries. The rigid sociocultural regulation necessitating dissociation as one of the coping pattern for encountered problems is speculated as the frequent occurrence of such condition. Lack of psychiatric knowledge is another factor allowing such a coping pattern to exist. In contrast to this, in developed societies, where psychiatric knowledge among people is common, dissociation disorder tends to occur less frequently or is seldom observed.

---

CASE 1

An African-American Women Who Has Frequent "Blackouts" (Sonia Patel)

A middle-aged African-American, separated, unemployed female, sought treatment at a psychiatric clinic with the chief compliant of "I need help." Patient revealed that over the last few years she had suffered episodes of depression and "blackouts." She described having no memory of what happened during the blackouts. After the blackouts, she found herself in different locations, found things in her house rearranged, and noticed that time had lapsed. She had no explanation for how those things happened. People told her that during the blackouts she crawled under furniture, cried, and became aggressive if people tried to touch her. She was not sure what triggered the events and speculated that it might be related to the miscarriage many years ago with her second husband.

Family history revealed that her father left her mother before the patient was born. As a child and adolescent, the patient was raped frequently by her uncle and several older male family friends. Regarding the rape, the patient was most disturbed by her mother not doing anything to protect her from the frequent rapes; the patient was reluctant to explore more concerning that issue. The patient had

*(continues)*

been through two marriages. Her first marriage was as a teenager; this marriage resulted in one child. Her second marriage during her middle thirties. During this marriage, she had a miscarriage and her husband did not visit her during or after her hospitalization. Thus, the marriage ended. She had sought treatment from psychiatrists in the past and, at one time, was suspected of having "epilepsy." However, after being observed during a psychiatric hospitalization, a diagnosis of dissociation disorder was given.

### b. Possession Disorder

Possession disorders may occur as morbid conditions to people without relation to healing practices or other social functions but merely as a reaction to emotional stress to others. Possession disorders are believed to occur in many parts of the world. Possession and possession disorder tend to be reported more in psychiatric literature from Asian regions. This may reflect that such phenomena are still prevalent there and have therefore caught the interest of cultural psychiatrists for investigation and report.

In Japan, besides the orthodox religion of *Sin-do*, Japanese are traditionally pantheists, believing animals (such as foxes, raccoons, dogs, snakes), trees, mountains, stones, and other subjects are all associated with spirits. In Japanese folk legend, animal spirits, particularly the fox spirit, are commonly described. The spirit of the cunning fox can disguise itself into any human form, often a young lady, and play tricks on people. The Japanese commonly say *kitsune-ni-bakasareru*, literally meaning to be fooled by the spirit of a fox (*kitsune*). Perhaps related to this, when a person is possessed, people tend to interpret him as being possessed by an animal spirit, mostly a fox, and occasionally a dog or a cat. According to Kitanish (1993), the spirit of the animal that tends to possess people is believed to stay in certain households. The household with *tsukinomo-suji* (spirit lineage) tends to be looked down upon by others and is kept at a distance socially. It is speculated that such households may have originally been those of migrated families that wandered into the established village. Another explanation is that the possessing spirit was brought by a shaman to inhabit the designated household. It is generally believed that such animal spirits will be transmitted through marriage and kept within a family.

In Thailand, although most possessing beings are the spirits of animals or deceased persons, as elsewhere, there is a unique phenomenon by which a person can be possessed by the spirit of a living person. According to a cultural psychiatrist from Thailand, Sangun Suwanlert (1976), Thai people believe that *phii pob* is the soul of a living person that may come and go among people. When *phii pob* possesses a person, it takes the role of that person. Such possession of a living person's soul is observed mainly in northern Thailand.

---

CASE 2
_____

A Thai Girl Scolded Stepfather during Her Possessed State
(from Suwanlert, 1976)

A 16-year-old girl in Thailand was sent to live with her grandmother at age 2, when her father died. Many years later, when her mother remarried, she came back to live with her mother and her stepfather. One day, when she witnessed her drunken stepfather slap her mother during an argument, she suddenly acted differently, as if she was one of her stepfather's male friends who lived in the next village. It was clear to others that she was possessed by _phii pob_. In a male voice, she warned her stepfather that if he did not behave, the ancestor's spirit would punish him by breaking his neck. After the stepfather, in front of relatives, promised that he would behave, the _phii pob_, the soul of the stepfather's friend, departed via the patient's mouth.

---

The case illustrates beautifully how a young girl, faced with a fearful situation, and without knowing how to deal with her drunken, abusive stepfather, turned herself (via a possession state) into a socially more powerful person and borrowed the authority of an ancestor to control her stepfather.

In the south of Taiwan, cultural psychiatrist Jung-Kuang Wen (1996) conducted a community survey of a selected area and estimated that the people who had possession experiences (both ordinary and morbid conditions) were not less than 1% of the adult population. He pointed out that the traditional belief of pantheism and ancestor worship, belief in close relations and interaction with deceased ancestors, serves as the common ground for the frequent occurrence of possessed states. However, it is speculated that, in contrast to Japan, the belief in the possibility of interference from an ancestor spirit is more intense for people in Taiwan.

As for mainland China, according to the available literature, possession disorders are reported more frequently in the northeastern region of China, including the areas previously called Manchuria and internal Mongolia. These areas are geographically close to Siberia, where anthropologists believe the practice of shamanism (in a narrow sense) originated.

According to Zhang (1992), a psychiatrist from Liaoning Province Mental Hospital, located in the northeastern region of China, there were altogether a total of 4714 forensic cases brought to the hospital for psychiatric evaluation in the past. Of those cases, 52 (1.1%) had committed murder under possession disorders. Interestingly, among them, there were six sets of group patients (with more than four people in each group) who carried out murder together. Most of them were family members or relatives who had developed a collective trance state or a "shared" possession state. In these conditions, they killed their victims with the conviction that the person was possessed by an evil that needed to be exorcized.

---

CASE 3

---

In an Altered Conscious State, a Chinese Family Jointly Killed a Son (from Zhang, 1992)

Mr. and Mrs. Wang were a middle-aged couple in their fifties. They had two sons. Mrs. Wang had a history of possessed episodes, claiming that she was often possessed by the spirit of her deceased mother-in-law. Their 24-year-old eldest son, after illegally cohabiting with his girlfriend, began to behave seclusively and strangely, claiming that he was a "headless evil" and intended to kill all his family members. One night, hearing a noise on the roof, the mother suddenly fell into a possessed state, claiming that she was possessed by a shaman who had come to expel the headless evil from her son. She induced her husband, Mr. Wang, and her 18-year-old son, to fall into trance states. In these states, together they pounded 43 nails into the eldest son's body and stabbed his abdomen with a knife. As a result, the eldest son died. After the event, Mrs. Wang remained in a trance state for ten days, claiming that she had expelled and killed the dangerous headless evil. After she recovered from her trance state and learned that she had killed her son, she began to cry loudly.

---

Dynamically, a tempting interpretation is that the mother who psychologically lost her son to his girlfriend reacted with the belief that her son was evil. Her possessed state gave her an excuse to act out her wish to punish the unfilial (or emotionally betraying) son. Clinically, it is a case of associated or collective mental disorders, which take place among the members of a family. The common belief in the possibility of a person being possessed by evil and the need to conduct an exorcism was the basis for this family group of psychiatric disorders.

From the case just described, it becomes immediately clear that the distinction between possession disorder (of a hysterical nature) and possession psychoses is not merely a clinical matter, but also a forensic challenge, if the patient is involved in a crime (see Section 6G: Forensic Psychiatric Service).

### c. Possession Psychoses

"Possession psychoses" refers to a psychotic condition characterized by the delusion of being possessed, in addition to other psychotic pictures, including hallucination, bizarre behavior, and thought disorder. This condition, even though manifested as a possession state, is different from possession disorder of a hysterical nature in that its onset is not necessarily sudden or in reaction to external stress, it may last a relatively long time, more than several weeks or months, and it does not respond favorably to any psychological treatment for underlying psychological stress. For this type of possession psychoses, the term "invocation psychosis" is still used by psychiatrists in some societies, including Japan. From a forensic point of view, the patient suffering from this condition is considered less responsible for criminal acts that he may commit.

### d. Altered Personality Disorder

Characteristically different from possession disorder is the altered personality disorder. In the latter there is no interpretation by either the patient or other people that the patient is possessed by "others." It is understood that the person alternates between (or among) different personalities either in a trance state or without it. In other words, there is a psychological and not a supernatural interpretation of the phenomena. Therefore, it is observed mainly in "modernized" societies where folk beliefs of a supernatural nature have more or less diminished. It is a common notion among psychiatrists that, in traditional societies, where trance and possession states are more frequent, the phenomena of altered personality and multiple personality disorders are seldom found. In contrast, in modern societies, possessed disorders are rare or diminishing, and double or multiple personality disorders are becoming more prevalent.

According to Ross (1991), the frequency of diagnosed multiple personality disorder in clinical populations increased exponentially during the 1980s. Reviewing the entire world literature, Greaves (1980) pointed out that not more than a couple of hundred cases (mainly in Western societies) have been reported since the beginning of this century. However, according to Ross, P. Coons in 1986 estimated that 6000 cases of multiple personality disorders had been diagnosed in North America. In contrast to this, Adityanjee, Raju, and Khandelwal (1989) in India reported that only two cases of multiple personality disorder had been reported in India in the past. They claimed that there was a frequent diagnosis of possession disorder, but that the diagnosis of multiple personality disorder was rare. A similar situation has been observed in Japan (Takahashi, 1990).

Beyond the influence of diagnostic practice patterns in different societies, there is good reason to speculate that, in association with the level of modernization or the degree of belief about folk supernatural powers, there is a trend away from the possessed state to the altered personality state. If we think carefully, we will realize that the possession state and the altered personality state are similar, except that the former is interpreted as the takeover of the self by an "external (supernatural) being," whereas the latter is the taking over of the self by an "internal (psychological) being," or another part of the self. Both offer mechanisms for avoiding taking responsibility for one's actions, but in different ways, based on the common beliefs shared by the people in the society.

## 3. Hysteria

Associated with the descriptive orientation of DSM system, the diagnostic nosology of hysteria no longer exists in the DSM system. However, because hysteria of dissociate type clinically contains the manifestations of trance, dissociation, possession, or altered personalization, a discussion of hysteria as recognized in the past is relevant. As pointed out by medical historian Ilza Vieth (1965), hysteria has undergone many and radical changes historically in terms of the concept of its nature, its manifestation, and its management. Thus, of all mental disorders, hysteria has occupied the most interest among scholars for illustrating how time and knowledge shape and modify the view and understanding of disease. (For more details, see Tseng, 2001, Chapter 17: Dissociation, Possession, and Hysteria, pp. 321–323.)

### a. Frequency of Hysterical Disorders

Despite the revision in formal classification, eliminating the nosological category of hysteria, in practice, in many parts of the world, the concept and term of "hysteria" are still used prevalently for diagnosis and to guide clinicians in treating this unique disorder. This nosology is also retained for epidemiological study.

A large-scale psychiatric epidemic study of minor psychiatric disorders was carried out in China in 1982, involving 12 geographic areas and nearly 7000 people. From this study, it was reported (Epidemic Survey Collaboratory Teams, 1986) that the overall prevalence rate for hysteria was 3.55 per 1000 population of adults between the ages of 15 and 59. Among all neurotic disorders, hysteria was second only to neurasthenia; thus, it was a commonly observed minor psychiatric disorder. In rural areas, the rate was 5.00; whereas in urban areas, it was 2.09, indicating that the disorder was much more prevalent in rural areas. The disorder occurred much more frequently among females than males.

In India, a report was made by Dube (1970) based on an epidemiological study carried out by home visits in a census survey in the Agra region of Uttar Pradesh, northern India. Among 29,468 residents, they found 261 cases of conversion symptoms in the form of hysterical fits, with a prevalence rate of 8.9 per 1000 population. They reported that females (mostly ages 15 to 24) constituted 96.1% of all cases. The roles of caste, marital status, and educational level were found to be associated with the occurrence of hysteria.

### b. Waning of the Disorder?

In addition to the fact that the prevalence of hysteria differs remarkably among various societies, being more prevalent in traditional and culturally restricted societies and less so in culturally liberal and modernized societies, there is another trend that has been noticed by clinicians. That is, based on historical observation and clinical impression, the occurrence of hysteria is waning around the world in both traditional and modern societies. There was one follow-up epidemiological study carried out in rural areas of India supporting the declining trend of hysteria there.

Indian psychiatrists Nandi et al. (1992) reported data that derived from their follow-up epidemiological studies carried out in two rural communities, Gambhirgachi and Paharpur, in West Bengal. The former was surveyed in 1972 and, 10 years later, in 1982; the latter was studied in 1972 and, 15 years later, in 1987. The results of the surveys indicated that the prevalence of hysteria declined considerably in these two villages, from 16.9 to 4.6 per 1000 population and 32.3 to 2.05 per 1000 population in Gambhirgachi and Paharpur, respectively. It is interesting that, associated with this remarkable decline in the prevalence of hysteria, there was a moderate increase in depression: from 37.7 to 53.3 per 1000 population and 61.9 to 77.2 per 1000 population in the two villages, respectively. Nandi and his associates reported that, between these two surveys, besides the increase in population, there was a clearly visible change in the quality of life of the people. They attribute the improvement in social status of women to the fall of the prevalence of hysteria.

Hysteria is a psychological disorder very much bound by cultural settings. The vicissitude of the disorder is directly determined by the views, attitudes, and reactions shared by the culture toward the phenomenon. Hysterical episodes offer patients a socially acceptable relief from stress and a culturally relevant outlet from repression. It gives a social signal to family, friends, and others that the person concerned is on the verge of a breakdown and needs special attention. Because the patient himself does not exhibit the (abnormal) behavior during the episode of altered consciousness and/or personality, whatever he says, complains about, or requests is attributed to others. Thus, a hysterical attack serves as a safety valve for a less protected individual living in strict, traditional societies. When a society becomes more liberal, the need to rely on hysterical attacks to express personal desire will diminish.

## D. SOMATOFORM DISORDERS, INCLUDING NEURASTHENIA

### 1. Introduction and Clarification

#### a. Historical Path of Concept and Definition

Along with the evolution of professional knowledge, as well as the viscidity of psychiatric disorders relating to sociocultural change, the formal classification systems for certain psychiatric disorders have been revised extensively. This is particularly true regarding the nosology of conversion, neurasthenia, chronic fatigue syndrome, and somatoform disorders, a cluster of medical terms centering around the clinical condition manifested primarily by somatic symptoms or characterized by somatic complaints. The terms "somatization" and "somatic complaint syndrome" (Prince, 1990), "functional somatic syndrome" (Canino et al., 1992), and "somatoform disorders" have been proposed by various scholars to deal with patients who tend to present somatic symptoms associated with psychological problems. (For details, see Tseng, 2001, Chapter 16: Somatoform Disorders, Including Neurasthenia, pp. 303–304.)

As pointed out by Kirmayer (1984, 1988), *somatization* (as well as *somatoform disorders*) is a concept born of Western mind-body dualism. Even though the concept of psychological impact on the health of the body is clearly recognized in many traditional medical systems, such as the Chinese or Ayurveda medicine (practiced in India), there is no sharp dichotomization between mind and body, and a psychological orientation to problems is not considered "superior" to, or more "developed," from an evolutionary perspective, than a somatic one.

### b. Cultural Impact on Somatic Presentation

How cultural factors will shape patients' illness-behavior and guide them to make somatic presentations during their visits to a psychiatric clinic is well elaborated by several scholars. Racy (1980), an American-trained, Arabic-speaking psychiatrist, observed that during his consultantship to Saudi Arabia, the women patients would often make predictable and stereotyped complaints to the psychiatrists, mainly of a somatic nature. When a woman failed to bear a male child, it caused her almost as much difficulty as if she were sterile. With polygamy still practiced, the common concern for married women was being neglected or rejected by their husbands in favor of a younger and prettier wife. In such a cultural setting, negative feelings, unhappiness, and conflicts within herself, and between her and members of her family, readily translate into somatic terms, as physical symptoms in such a culture are safe, morally acceptable, and generally lead to some form of help seeking. In other words, as Racy pointed out, for women in strictly controlled, socially inferior positions, somatic complaints can express emotional problems that have no other outlets.

In Taiwan, Tseng (1975) examined psychiatric patients who visited psychiatric clinics. In their initial visits, more than 80% of them presented somatic problems initially. However, if skillfully guided in the process of evaluation, they were ready to describe the psychological problems that brought them to see the psychiatrists. Tseng pointed out that making a somatic presentation initially is merely a culturally sanctioned "prologue" for the occasion. Thus, the nature of somatic presentation needs to be understood and grasped dynamically, rather than merely given the label of somatization or somatoform disorders.

In a clinical study in Montreal, Canada, Kirmayer and Robbins (1996) reported that patients who "somatize" in primary care can be divided into three groups—initial, facultative, and true somatizers—based on their willingness to offer or endorse a psychosocial cause for their symptoms. Initial somatizers readily acknowledge their psychological distress, in spite of their initial somatic presentation; true somatizers tend to reject psychosocial explanations; facultative somatizers are in between. Kirmayer and Robbins pointed out that patients with somatic symptoms exist heterogeneously in the spectrum, acknowledging a range of degrees a psychosocial contribution to their distress.

Among Hispanic groups, Koss (1990) pointed out that the process of somatization could have three meanings—the use of the body as a channel of communication; the result of attention focused on the body; and an idiom of distress or a way of making sense out of suffering. She indicated that somatic complaint syndromes are not necessarily indicative of severe psychological distress or psychiatric disorder. Furthermore, she pointed out that although Western culture values the mind (and person) who dominates and controls his body and distances himself from body feelings, popular Hispanic cultural priorities lie on opposite sides of the objective/subjective, rational/irrational, monistic/holistic continuum.

## 2. Cultural Perspectives of Some Forms of Disorders

### a. Conversion Disorder

From an epidemiological perspective, conversion disorder as a pathological condition disappeared almost, if not completely, from many developed societies. However, it is still commonly observed in many other societies. It is thought to occur primarily in societies with relatively strict social systems in which people cannot express their feelings or desires toward others directly, particularly when they encounter conflict or distress. The society is still required to observe traditional ways of life, and many behaviors, including sexual ones, cannot be manifested freely. Temporary somatic dysfunction is one mode of communication available to people, particularly for a suppressed gender or less-privileged group of people. Furthermore, people in the society tend to give considerable attention to the dramatic occurrence of such phenomena so that the clinical condition serves certain social functions for patients who develop such disorders.

However, once people become more psychologically minded and begin to understand such morbid conditions as emotional disorders, with rather negative attitudes toward them, the disorders tend to fade away. This is rather similar to the fate of "fainting," which was often "practiced" by females in Western societies in the past.

---

CASE 4

---

A Filipino Woman Who Became Paralyzed Shortly after Giving Birth
(Eileen Ha)

A Catholic, 30-year-old, Filipino female moved to Hawaii from the Philippines to work as a nanny. She had kept the fact that she was five months pregnant a secret from her family in the Philippines, as well as from her employer in Hawaii. She was afraid her mother would not approve of her having a child out of wedlock and also knew that abortion was not an option. In Hawaii, she tried to hide her pregnancy for as long as she could and sought no prenatal care for this reason. Once it became apparent that she was pregnant, the family she worked for felt betrayed and cheated because they would not have intentionally hired a pregnant nanny. After much consideration, the family informed her that she could stay in Hawaii and that they would help her through her pregnancy. She still did not tell her mother. She gave birth to a healthy baby boy without any complications. On her third day in the hospital, just before discharge, she began to complain of numbness and weakness in her legs, which made it difficult for her to walk. A full medical and neurological evaluation revealed no organic basis for her weakness. A psychiatric consultation was requested to evaluate her for conversion disorder. Before the consulting team arrived, a Filipino chaplain visited the patient and discovered her anxieties and fears about how her mother would react to the news of her new baby. She also felt like a burden to her employer in Hawaii. Without her knowledge, her employer had contacted her mother in the Philippines and informed her about the birth of her grandson. Her employer relayed to the patient that her mother was very excited about the baby and forgave her for keeping this secret. She was reassured that she could stay with them until she went back home. With this news, the patient felt relief and suddenly her weakness subsided. She was discharged that same day.

---

### b. Neurasthenia

The term "neurasthenia" was originally applied in 1869 by an American neuropsychiatrist, George M. Beard, to describe a clinical syndrome with core symptoms of mental fatigue, associated with poor memory, poor concentration, irritability, headaches, tinnitus, insomnia, and other vague somatic complaints. Beard believed that the disorder derived from an exhaustion of the victim's nervous system. It was interpreted that the condition occurred as the result of overstimulation and the sufferer's mind refusing to take on new stresses. According to Gabbard (1995, p. 453). In an early stage of his career, Sigmund Freud (1894) categorized neurasthenia together with anxiety neuroses and hypochondriasis "actual neurosis," conceptualizing that such a disorder has a neurological base in the nervous system (therefore, "actual"); in contrast to hysteria, phobia, and obsessional neuroses, which are psychological in nature and regarded as "psychoneuroses" (implying that they originated from a "psychic" cause).

It is important to point out that, according to Üstün and Sartorius (1995), a worldwide epidemiological study of ICD-10 defined psychological studies, including neurasthenia, revealed that the estimated prevalence of neurasthenia syndrome was frequently seen (though not always recognized) both in economically advantaged and less-advantaged countries. According to the study, the prevalence of neurasthenia was 10.5% in both Groningen (Netherlands) and Santiago (Chile); 9.7% in Manchester (United Kingdom); 9.3% in Paris (France); 7.7% in Mainz and 7.4% in Berlin (Germany); 4.6% in Athens (Greece); 4.1% in Ankara (Turkey); 3.4% in Nagasaki (Japan); 2.1% in Verona (Italy); and 2.0% in Shanghai (China). It is surprising to note that the prevalence of the disorder, according to this study, is relatively low in Shanghai, China. In a separate study (Zheng et al., 1997), it was revealed that the prevalence of neurasthenia was 6.4% among Chinese-Americans in Los Angeles, California.

Recently, in Euro-American societies, patients with complaints primarily of tiredness have been given the diagnosis of chronic fatigue syndrome, a disorder characterized by fatigue lasting months to years (Ware & Kleinman, 1992; Wessely, 1994). According to Goldberg and Huxley (1980), investigation has shown that complaints of fatigue and irritability commonly accompany anxiety and mild depression. Thus, many factors may contribute to the occurrence, labeling, and official usage of diagnostic terms relating to neurasthenia. This issue deserves further investigation and clarification.

### c. Hypochondriasis

As pointed out by Barsky and Klerman (1983), hypochondriasis can be conceptualized in different ways. These views include clinically, as a unique psychiatric syndrome composed of "functional" somatic symptoms, bodily preoccupation, fear of disease, and the persistent pursuit of medical care; psychodynamically, as a derivative of aggressive or oral drives, defending against psychological problems; psychologically, characterized by a perceptual amplification of bodily sensations and their cognitive misinterpretation; and socioculturally, as a learned illness behavior eliciting interpersonal rewards for attention and care from others. Based on the last view, it is reasonable to speculate that hypochondriacal behavior is closely related socioculturally to illness behavior.

Cross-cultural differences among people of different cultural groups have been commented on by numerous scholars. For instance, regarding clinical study, a Jewish psychiatrist from Jerusalem (Hes, 1958) did a comparative study of Jewish immigrants to Israel. Based on clinical data, he reported that, in comparison to an Occidental group (from west, central, or east Europe), Oriental Jewish immigrants (from Iraq, North Africa, Yemen, etc.) showed a greater incidence of hypochondriacal symptoms.

### d. Pain Disorder

As pointed out by Streltzer (1997), relief of pain has been a critical part of the practice of medicine throughout history; however, the pain disorder as a diagnostic nosology has not been clearly held by psychiatrists until very recently. The complaint of pain is a subjective experience for which there is no objective measurement. There is a good reason to suspect that pain-related experience, including complaining behavior and care for it, is subject to cultural influences.

The most well-known and earliest study relating culture to pain was carried out by Zborowski (1952) in New York. He studied veterans with chronic pain and divided them into ethnic groups. He reported that the patients with white Anglo-Saxon Protestant backgrounds were characterized as stoic in response to pain, in marked contrast to two other ethnic groups studied: Jewish people and Italians. Both groups did not hesitate to complain about pain, being quite expressive and emotional. However, they were different from each other in certain ways: The Italians were eager for pain relief, whereas the Jewish people were fearful of medication that would take away their pain.

A more objective study on experimental pain with a larger number of subjects was carried out by Woodrow and co-workers in 1972, through the Kaiser Foundation Health Plan in California. As a test, a certain apparatus was used to give pressure to the Achilles tendon to evaluate the threshold for pain. It was found out that Caucasians tolerated more pain than African-Americans, who in turn tolerated more pain than Asians.

Streltzer and Wade (1981) carried out a comparative study of acute clinical pain in the multiethnic society of Hawaii. Surgery patients receiving elective gall bladder removal were examined in terms of the medication received for pain at the stage of postoperative care in the hosptial. It was found that Caucasian patients received the most pain medication. Filipinos, Japanese, and Chinese received the least, while Hawaiians were intermediate.

These findings are related to the study of the pain experience or pain management rather than the disorders themselves. However, they give us a glance at how ethnic factors may influence the pain experience in either experimental or clinical situations.

### e. Body Dysmorphic Disorder

From a cross-cultural perspective, there are few studies about body dysmorphic disorder. It is commonly known that Japanese patients diagnosed with *taijinky-ofusho* often presented symptoms concerning their dysmorphic condition; however, they were not diagnosed primarily with body dsymorphic disorder. It is known from social experience that some Asian women receive cosmetic surgery to create double eyelids so that they look like Westerners. But not as many Asian women receive cosmetic surgery for their breasts as women in European-American societies. This suggests that, based on cultural attitudes, there are different parts of body with which people are not satisfied, leading them to want surgical "improvement." It also suggests that there are culturally different emphases on body parts for self-image and beauty, as well as for sexual attraction. To what extent the differences in emphasis on various parts of the body may relate to dysmorphobic concern is a question awaiting future investigation.

In summary, it can be said that, a cross-cultural study supports the view that there is a spectrum of symptoms and complaints between the "psychological" and "somatic" dimensions. The extent to which somatic symptoms will be focused on and presented varies among patients of different sociocultural backgrounds and is subject to cultural orientations toward the distinction between body and mind, as well as other factors. As pointed out by Kirmayer and Young (1998), historically the tendency of somatization among psychiatric patients was regarded by cultural psychiatrists as a culture-related specific clinical feature of some ethnic groups (including many Asian and Hispanic ethnic groups). Associated with the increase of cross-cultural information and knowledge, it is no longer viewed as an ethnic-related unique clinical feature. While the prevalence and specific features of somatic complaining syndromes vary considerably across cultures, clinically presenting somatic distress is universal, and somatic symptoms are probably the most common clinical expressions of emotional distress worldwide (Isaac, Janca, & Orley, 1996).

# E. ALCOHOL-RELATED PROBLEMS

Abuse and dependence on alcohol or other chemical substances, including drugs, are biologically related phenomena as far as the clinical conditions of intoxication, dependence, and withdrawal are concerned. However, psychological factors are associated with the indulgence in and control of substance abuse. Furthermore, sociocultural factors contribute to the prevalence and viscidity of alcohol problems or substance abuse. Thus, basically, the three dimensions of biology, psychology, and socioculture need to be considered simultaneously; none of them can be ignored.

Many substances are abused by people and lead to intoxication or dependence. Alcohol has been used by humans for many centuries and is accepted as a part of daily life in many societies. Also, differences in attitude toward drinking associated with religious, ethnic, and cultural background are obvious.

## 1. Factors and Problems Related to Drinking

### a. Attitudes toward Drinking

People learned to use alcohol even in prehistoric times (Westermeyer, 1988). It is easy to produce alcohol by simply fermenting fruits, rice, wheat, or other plant products. In many societies, it has been a part of daily drinking or has been used for special celebrations, or only for religious ceremonies. However, distinctly different attitudes toward drinking have developed in different societies. An anthropologist distinguishes four different types of attitudes represented in various cultural groups that seem to have different effects on the rate of alcoholism (Bales, 1949). They are complete abstinence (drinking alcohol is not allowed for any purpose), a ritual attitude (alcoholic beverages are used only as part of religious ceremonies), a convivial attitude (drinking is a "social" ritual), and a utilitarian attitude (drinking for medicinal reasons and for self-interest or personal satisfaction).

### b. Variations of Drinking Patterns

Besides the attitude toward drinking, the pattern of drinking also varies among different societies. For instance, in the wine-drinking society of France, people drink wine as part of their daily lives, at lunch and/or dinner. Although they consume a large amount, they carefully regulate the manner of their drinking. Among the Chinese, if anyone drinks daily, he is looked down on as a "drinking person" by family members or others in the society. On special occasions, however, such as weddings, birthdays, or festivals, people are expected to drink during a banquet. In China, Japan, and Korea, as well as Lao, he who could drink more was considered more "manly." In Japan, women were traditionally sanctioned from drinking. However, recently, the alcohol consumption of women has increased tremendously. Liberated young women drink in bars and other public places with others, but middle-age women, still under the influence of traditional views, drink within their private households by themselves, even in the daytime, and are described by the Japanese as "kitchen drunks."

In Micronesia, drinking was strictly prohibited by the previous rulers (Germans and Japanese). The Micronesians were forbidden to drink, for the reason that "savage people will become wild after drinking." However, after World War II, when Micronesia became an American Trust Territory, the people were relieved of this prohibition. They started to drink American-imported beer daily, almost in the same way as drinking Coca Cola, Seven Up, or other kinds of soft drinks. Even children, in the company of adults, drink beer without any prohibition (see Fig. 2). Further, as with most Pacific Islanders, whenever alcohol is available, groups of friends tend to drink excessively on weekends and holidays until they become drunk or all the drink is gone. There is no concept or habit of regulating the amount of drink. Among teenagers, such drinking often results in violent behavior, involving fighting and injuring others (see Fig. 3). Thus, there are different patterns of drinking among different cultures.

### c. Alcohol Consumption in Various Societies

Closely associated with the attitude toward drinking is the amount of alcohol consumed, which varies remarkably among different societies. As shown in Table

FIGURE 2    Culturally patterned drinking behavior in Micronesia. (a) When the drinking prohibitions of the past were removed after World War II, small children learned how to drink beer like
their parents. (b) Beer cans were piled up in the front yard of almost every household, showing off
how much beer had been consumed. [Courtesy of Boyd Slomoff, M.D.]

2 (based on data prior to 1992, gathered by Mackay, 1993), regarding the annual
consumption of alcohol as defined by the total amount of alcohol (liter by 100%
alcohol) consumed by a person per year, there is a very wide range: from 16.2
liters in France (or 18.3 liters in Luxembourg) to 0.1 liter in Libya and Egypt
(or even less than 0.1 liter in India). If the drinking is arbitrarily subdivided into
high (above 6 liters), moderate (between 1 to 6 liters), and low (less than 1 liter)
consumption, it can be said that most of the high consumption is observed among
Euro-American societies, with the exception of Japan and South Korea. Most
societies in Asia and some in northern Europe and South America have moderate to low consumption. Obviously, societies with Muslim backgrounds all have
low consumption.

In general, religious beliefs and attitudes toward drinking affect the amount
of consumption. This is particularly true for Muslim societies, in which drinking is strictly prohibited. This applies also to Orthodox Jewish people in Israel
and, even more so, in Ethiopia. However, this does not apply to people of
Christian religions in European or North American societies. As for the
Buddhists, despite the fact that monks are inhibited from drinking, no explicit
rule applies to the ordinary people so the pattern of drinking varies greatly
among Buddhist societies, as illustrated by South Korea and Japan being high and
Thailand low.

### d. Boundary between Socially Normal and Pathological Drinking

Bennett et al. (1993) reported the Cross-Cultural Application Research (CAR)
study carried out in 1991. This worldwide study resulted in valuable knowledge,
namely, that wide cross-cultural differences exist in how people describe the
amount of alcohol they consume, how they defined heavy drinkers, and the signs

FIGURE 3   Alcohol-Related Youth Problems in Micronesia—(a) Adolescent boys drinking liquor in the bush in Truk, Micronesia; (b) The same group of adolescents, after getting drunk, started fighting in the street, damaging a passing car and injuring others.

of alcohol effects on them. Gureje et al. (1997) pointed out that a number of core concepts underpinning diagnosis of disorders relating to the use of alcohol have no equivalence in the local languages of the various cultures, whereas some others lacked cultural applicability because of their relative "distance" from cultural and ethnic norms of drinking. This distance often relates to the difficulties of adapting descriptions of drinking norms in a "wet" culture to one that is decidedly "dry." Overall, the study suggests that the boundaries between "socially normal" and "socially abnormal" drinking need to be defined carefully for cross-cultural application.

TABLE 2    Annual Alcohol Consumption around the World (unit by liter).

| High consumption | | Moderate consumption | | Low consumption | |
|---|---|---|---|---|---|
| France | 16.2 | Ireland | 6.0 | Thailand | 0.9 |
| Argentina | 12.6 | South Africa | 5.9 | Turkey | 0.9 |
| Italy | 12.6 | Sweden | 5.6 | Angola | 0.8 |
| Spain | 11.9 | Norway | 4.2 | Ethiopia | 0.8 |
| Germany | 11.6 | North Korea | 3.7 | Albania | 0.6 |
| Portugal | 11.6 | Nigeria | 3.6 | Cambodia | 0.6 |
| Belgium | 11.3 | Iceland | 3.3 | Iraq | 0.4 |
| Switzerland | 11.0 | Panama | 3.1 | Indonesia | 0.4 |
| Czechoslovakia | 10.3 | Israel | 2.9 | Vietnam | 0.4 |
| Australia | 10.1 | Bolivia | 2.9 | Iran | 0.3 |
| Austria | 9.7 | Philippines | 2.8 | Jordan | 0.3 |
| Denmark | 9.7 | Colombia | 2.7 | Nepal | 0.2 |
| New Zealand | 9.1 | Congo | 2.7 | Libya | 0.1 |
| Netherlands | 8.9 | Brazil | 2.6 | Egypt | 0.1 |
| United States | 8.4 | Mexico | 2.6 | India | 0.1 |
| South Korea | 8.1 | Peru | 2.4 | | |
| Poland | 7.4 | Cuba | 2.3 | | |
| Greece | 7.3 | Hong Kong | 2.2 | | |
| United Kingdom | 6.9 | Singapore | 1.6 | | |
| Japan | 6.8 | Kenya | 1.6 | | |
| Chile | 6.7 | China | 1.2 | | |

## 2. Drinking and Problems in Various Societies

### a. East Asia

The ethnic Chinese have been understood to have a traditionally low prevalence of alcoholism. In mainland China, in 1982, an epidemiological study of psychiatric disorders was undertaken that involved 12 geographic areas and a total of 38,136 Han nationals. The study revealed that the morbidity rate for alcoholism was very low, only 0.19 per 1000 population (Shen, 1987). In Taiwan, an epidemiological survey carried out in 1948 which disclosed the prevalence of alcoholism was merely 0.1 per 1,000 population (Lin, 1953). However, a more recent epidemiological survey, carried out in 1990 from the selected sample areas of a metropolitan city, a small town, and a rural village, revealed lifetime prevalence rates for alcohol abuse of 3.4, 8.0, and 6.3% and for alcohol dependence of 1.5, 1.8, and 1.2%, respectively (Hwu, Chen, & Yeh, 1995). Hwu and associates concluded that there had been a significant increase in alcohol problems in Taiwan during the past three decades.

In Japan, a small bottle of *sake* has long accompanied the festivity of weddings and the gravity of mourning. Social drinking is a Japanese tradition, but drinking as a real problem is a post–World War II development. Before the war, per capita consumption was 2.3 liters of alcohol (Yamamuro, 1973). However, according to the Ministry of Health and Welfare (1996), it had increased to 5.9 liters in 1965 and 8.9 liters in 1990. Surprisingly, the increase in consumption was attributed mainly to the increase in drinking by women. The amount of consumption by females increased almost seven times after the war. Alcoholism was estimated roughly at 3% of the population in 1963 by Moore (1964).

The situation in South Korea is similar to that in Japan, but it is worse in terms of the amount consumed annually. As pointed out by Kim (1990, 1993), most Korean psychiatrists had the impression that there was no serious alcoholic problem in Korea because of an extremely low admission rate of alcoholics to hospitals, and they attributed it to racial sensitivity to alcohol. However, epidemiological surveys indicated that the occurrence of alcoholic disorder was very high. According to the Ministry of Health and Welfare (1997) in Seoul, the alcohol consumption rate was only 1.0 liter in 1960, but it increased rapidly to 8.3 liters in 1975 and reached a peak of 11.0 liters in 1995, the highest consumption among Asian societies. Associated with rapid economic development and improvement of the quality of life, the habit of drinking has increased among the people in South Korea (Kim, 1990). This is quite a contrast to North Korea; with much different economic conditions and style of life due to the political system, the alcohol consumption was only 3.7 liters in 1990 (Mackay, 1993). This shows that, even the same group of people, divided politically into north and south, and living in remarkably different social systems, have very different patterns of alcohol consumption.

### b. North America

A comprehensive review of the trends of alcohol problems in the United States has been made by M. C. Defour (1995) and the Group for the Advancement of Psychiatry (GAP, 1996). Concerning the historical trend, Defour reported that after Prohibition, when alcohol was illegal (1925–1933), the per capita alcohol consumption of Americans increased through the 1960s (about 9.5 liters) and 1970s (about 11.5 liters), peaking in 1980 (about 12.5 liters). According to the Statistical Abstract of the United States (1997), the annual consumption, after the peak in 1980, gradually declined to 9.5 liters in 1995.

As for ethnic group differences, based on data from the Epidemiological Catchment Area study, Helzer, Burnam, and McEvoy (1991, pp. 87–89) summarized that the ethnic groups show strikingly different patterns of age-related lifetime rates of alcoholism. When the age groups are subdivided into young adults (18–29), adults (30–44), middle-age adults (45–64), and aged adults (65+), it was found that the lifetime rates (by percentage) for the Caucasian-American male are high for young adults, but gradually decrease with age. In contrast, African-American males show a relatively low rate for young adults, increasing remarkably among adults and middle-age adults, with rates higher than the other two groups at middle age. As for Hispanic-American males, the rate starts high for young adults, reaching a peak at the adult level, and then declining with age. Female are generally lower than males. Regarding lifetime rates, in general, the ratios are lower when they are younger, but increase in the older groups. This is particularly true for aged Hispanic-American adults who are still under the influence of past tradition.

Although there is a general impression that alcohol has a disruptive effect on North American Indians, there are no systematic data to indicate the nature and extent of the problem. There is only some indirect information. For instance, Brod (1975) cited studies documenting several phenomena. For Native Americans, the alcohol-related arrest rate is 12 times the national average; the alcoholism-related death rate is 4.3 to 5.5 times the U.S. rate for all races. It is generally considered that the rates of alcohol problems differs among different tribes, and overall generalization should be avoided.

### c. South America

South America is a large continent composed of 12 countries and two geo-political units. In each country, the population is composed of different proportions of indigenous people and outside migrants (mostly Latin American). By and large, Latin American drinking customs are highly liberal. Alcoholic beverages can be obtained easily in all kinds of stores and public places. Cultural pressure toward drinking is particularly high for males. In some areas, a heavy drinking habit is considered a manifestation of virility, and men who exhibit an ability to "hold their liquor" carry a fair amount of social prestige (Negrete, 1976).

Caetano and Carlini-Cotrim (1993) reviewed the alcohol epidemiology in South America. They reported that the annual consumption by liter per capita was 7.5 for Argentina, 6.4 for Uruguay and Chile, 3.4 for Brazil, 3.3 for Venezuela, 3.0 for Colombia, 1.4 for Peru, and 1.2 for Paraguay. These figures indicated that most of the consumption in South American countries was in the moderate range and was lower than in the United States. In general, the social norms in South America governing alcohol consumption were less restrictive for men than for women.

Regarding the prevalence of alcoholism among men varied from 5% in Argentina to 10% in Colombia (Caetano & Carlini-Cotrim, 1993). As for alcohol-related problems, the range was from 12% in Chile to 28% in Argentina (Caetano, 1984). There was also considerable variation within countries, especially in large countries such as Brazil, where rates of alcohol abuse and dependence in three metropolitan areas ranged from 7.5 to 9.2% (Almeida Filho et al., 1992).

### d. Europe

In Italy, drinking wine with meals is taken for granted. The average Italian may drink a significant amount of alcohol every day, yet he is not often, or seriously, drunk. Even the Italian who, at times, may show signs of intoxication is not considered to be an alcoholic. Drinking is, and always has been, a part of Italian culture. Acceptance of the wine-with-food kind of drinking is complete. Attitudes are also tolerant toward alcoholism, a condition recognized in Rome before the time of Christ. However, Bonfiglio, Falli, and Pacini (1977) found that this traditional Mediterranean wine drinking is now being overshadowed by alcoholism of the northern European and Anglo-Saxon type. Drinking wine is supplemented or replaced by drinking hard liquor. Between 1941 and 1972, Italy's wine consumption increased almost 100%, beer consumption increased by more than 600%, and drinking spirits jumped by approximately 700%. During this same period, deaths from cirrhosis of the liver increased from 9.32 to 29.90 per 100,000 population. The government has used mass media to try to reduce per capita intake.

In France, which is similar to Italy, drinking patterns have also changed in recent years. In the 1960s, alcoholic intake was 95% wine. In the 1980s, wine accounted for only 6% of the total consumption; whiskey, vodka, and gin consumption have doubled in a decade, and beer drinking has risen. Today, *la défonce du samedi soir*, "the Saturday night bender," drinking oneself into a stupor on hard liquor, has entered the French way of life.

As described by Dorman and Towle (1991), official concerns about alcohol consumption in Russia have been evident since at least the beginning of the century, when the Czarist regime implemented prohibition in 1914. Prohibition was imposed by Stalin in the late 1920s, by Khrushchev in 1958, and by Brezhnev in 1972 and 1979. The campaigns against drinking were seen as fragmented and ineffective, and heavy drinking and alcohol-related problems continued to increase into the early 1980s. It was reported that, between 1960 and 1980, annual consumption had doubled from 3.9 liters to 8.7 liters even by a conservative estimate. However, it needs to be noted that alcohol consumption patterns differed according to region and ethnicity. According to Dorman and Towle (1991), *The Economist* in 1989 reported that a decrease in life expectancy for Soviet males, from 66 years in 1965 to 62 years in 1984, was largely attributed to heavy alcohol consumption. Studies from the West suggested that alcoholism was the third leading cause of death in the former Soviet Union, after heart disease and cancer.

### e. Africa

It has been described that traditionally alcohol played a very important social function in sub-Saharan, non-Muslim African cultures. Alcohol was always present in meetings when elders settled disputes, after a successful hunt or harvest, and when marriages were arranged. In contrast to other parts of the world, as stressed by Haworth (1993), one of the most important patterns in Africa was the high rate of consumption of homemade, often illegal, alcoholic beverages; home brews were assumed to have a high alcohol content and to be potentially toxic.

A psychiatrist from Nairobi, Kenya, Acuda (1985) has reviewed past research and publications on alcohol consumption and problems from east Africa. For instance, the first Western psychiatrist to work in Kenya, Carothers, reported that of the total 558 patients admitted to the hospital in Nairobi between 1939 and 1943, only 4 cases (0.7%) were admitted with alcohol psychosis, despite the heavy consumption of drinks with a high alcohol content by the Africans in the reserves. In contrast, concerning Uganda, alcohol psychoses was an important cause of admission to the mental hospital in Butabiak during the 1960s, constituting 13% of all admissions.

It can be summarized that the differences regarding the attitudes toward drinking, patterns of drinking, and amounts consumed all indicate the strong sociocultural impact on drinking behavior, which, in turn, coupled with biological predisposition and psychological vulnerability, contribute to the development of physiologically related psychopathology. The sociocultural input into this disorder is evidenced by the wide range of the prevalence of alcohol problems among societies with different cultures, and the obvious fluctuation of the prevalence of the disorder observed even within the same society in association with changes occurring in the society.

Alcoholism serves as one of the social indexes of mental health conditions. There is also the potential of regulating drinking problems through social and cultural approaches. Among the trends observed around the world, there are two common threads. First, among culturally uprooted, economically unprivileged minority groups, drinking problems tend to be prevalent. This suggests that, when people are trapped in a situation characterized by chronic frustration, without hope for the future, they tend to indulge in drinking as one way to cope with the stress. The second thread is that, associated with the improvement of economic conditions, drinking tends to increase as well. It has been observed that drinking and related problems, after reaching their peak, tend to level off in some developed societies; yet, in many developing societies, drinking is increasing, and complications from drinking are becoming serious, calling for urgent attention.

## F. OTHER SUBSTANCE ABUSE

### 1. Introduction

After examining alcohol problems in the previous section, the abuse of substances other than alcohol will be elaborated in this section. It will focus mainly on drug abuse, even though many nondrug chemical substances, such as paint, can be abused. Substance abuse is characterized, on the one hand, as strongly related to biological factors in its occurrence and manifestation and, on the other, as heavily influenced by psychological and sociocultural factors in its development and spread. It is a particular kind of psychiatric disorder that shows remarkable vicissitude subject to social and cultural factors.

The usage of psychoactive substances by human beings started in prehistory. The people of Africa, Asia, and Europe, in addition to preparing alcohol, also grew opium, cannabis, and some stimulant plant compounds (Westermeyer, 1999). The chemical substances that have been abused have varied in different societies and at different times in the same societies. Abuse depends on the availability of a substance, as well as economic aspects, social control, and cultural fashions. Proscribed or taboo use of certain chemical substances exists in many societies. Some substances are totally forbidden under any circumstances. Alcohol in Saudi Arabia, coffee among Mormons, and heroin in the United States are examples (Westermeyer, 1987). Substances take on symbolic meaning, in some instances, representing certain values, attitudes, and identities related to ethnicity. For instance, alcoholism or drunkenness is considered by many Jewish people as non-Jewish behavior, and many Muslims see it as being sinful. In China, as a result of the Opium War, opium was regarded as a substance of national shame.

## 2. Historical Episodes or Unique Situations in Some Societies

It is almost impossible to describe in detail the phenomena of substance abuse around the world on a cross-cultural comparative base. However, there were some historical episodes or unique situations observed in some societies illustrating the social and cultural contributions to the phenomena.

*Postwar Epidemic of Amphetamines in Japan.*    Immediately after World War II, the Japanese were faced with grave problems of social reconstruction. Most of the cities or manufacturers were severely damaged from the bombing. Everyone was forced to work long and hard for food, clothing, and housing and to rebuild the industries. During this period, the central nervous stimulant amphetamine appeared on the market. Amphetamines were widely used by the Army during World War II to promote a fighting spirit among soldiers (Kato, 1990). Later, many Japanese learned that the *kamikaze* pilots had used the drugs in their suicide attacks. Now, it was being sold commercially with advertising that advised, "Get rid of slumber and be full of energy." At first, only night workers, such as waitresses, bartenders, and entertainers took amphetamines. Later, use of the drug spread to the general population. College students used it for late night study; laborers, for extended work hours. Very soon society reacted against the mass abuse of the drug, and restrictions to control it went into effect. Soon, use of the drug virtually ceased; only runaways and juvenile delinquents took amphetamines (Hemmi, 1974). Thus, the phenomenon was a transient one that started in 1945 and ended around 1956, reflecting the social atmosphere at the time.

*Radical Eradication of Opium Abuse in China.*    Toward the end of the Chin dynasty, when China was under the influence of Western imperialism, opium addiction had become a serious social problem in China. For economic benefit, the British East India Company imported and sold opium to China. This provoked the Chinese-British Opium War when the Chinese people tried to burn the imported "poison" at the harbor of Guangzhou. The Chinese lost the war, and the British government was allowed to conduct its opium business for many decades. It was estimated that, by the turn of the 20th century, many millions of Chinese were addicted to opium (Fields & Tararin, 1970; Lowinger, 1973). When the communists took over China in 1949, the new government immediately tried to eradicate the problem through political action. A massive campaign was undertaken, labeling opium abuse as an offense against the country. The major thrust was to change the ideology of the young and prevent new addicts, whereas those already addicted were treated medically and socially for rehabilitation. Associated with the distribution of the land from landlords to peasants, all poppy fields were replaced by food crops. As the country's door toward the outside was closed, there was no way to sneak the "poison" into the country again. Local communist cadres serving each household in the neighborhood were used to detect any person abusing opium. Heavy penalties, including execution, were imposed for those responsible for growing, manufacturing, and selling opium. Thus, almost a century of opium abuse had been relegated to history within just three years.

*Post-Vietnam War Epidemic in the United States.*    Most Americans witnessed the rapid rise of substance abuse around the era of the Vietnam War. Associated with the Hippie movement, as a cultural reaction against the establishment and conservative tradition, many young people lived lifestyles characterized by informality. Marijuana was widely used. When the Vietnam War started, many young people were concerned about the purpose of the war and were afraid of being drafted and involved in it. An antigovernment and antiwar movement arose, which contributed to the tension within the society. It accelerated drug abuse, as well. In the meantime, soldiers fighting in Vietnam, under severe stress, began to indulge in substance abuse. When they returned to American soil, many continued abuse of various kinds. As a result, there was a substance-abuse epidemic in the United States for more than a decade (Trimble, Bolek, & Niemcryk, 1992).

*Unique Situation Observed in Laos.*    The opium use among the Meo people of Laos is rather unique. As described by the American cultural psychiatrist Joseph Westermeyer (1971, 1974), who did fieldwork there for many years, for most of these tribal people, the primary value of opium was economic; nearly every household grew opium to trade for silver and iron. Although some Meo smoked opium occasionally and some were addicted, the majority did not abuse it. Westermeyer found that most addicts were farmers living in rural areas, women addicts far outnumbered men, and addiction was not associated with criminality or

FIGURE 4    Laotian Hill Tribe's traditional opium-detox treatment. (a) A sacrificial offering to the opium goddess; (b) Taking a sacred vow to abstain in front of a model of the palace of the opium goddess. [Courtesy of Wolfgang Jilek, M.D.]

related to decreasing social competency. This was very different from other places, where opium addiction was primarily a city phenomenon associated with criminality and low social competency. Because the Meo raised their own opium, no one was driven to crime or violence to obtain it. Addiction was not considered socially desirable, but no great social opprobrium descended on the addicted person (see Fig. 4).

## 3. Epidemiological Findings from Various Societies

When substance abuse is illegal, it is difficult to conduct formal community surveys because abusers tend to deny abusive behavior. Therefore, it is extremely difficult to obtain epidemiological data (Anthony & Helzer, 1995). At best, studies rely on indirect information, such as number of people arrested by police. However, even such data are subject to the nature of the law and the way it is carried out. An alternative way to collect data is to examine the rate of treatment service utilization. However, because most of abusers may not utilize treatment services, the data are incomplete.

In order to help countries seeking to implement prevention programs, a World Health Organization project was established: the Development of Strategies and Guidelines for the Prevention of Drug-Related Problems. Smart, Murray, and Arif (1988) reviewed the reports that countries around the world prepared for this WHO project. They pointed out that while the pattern and degree of drug abuse varied from country to country, some general findings were noticed. Clearly the typical abuser of most illegal drugs was a young male, unemployed, relatively unskilled, and living in lower-class circumstances.

### a. Some Findings from Asian Societies

There are considerable data available from most Asian societies for cross-societal comparison and longitudinal comparison within the same society (Tseng et al., 2001). Data are the recorded number of people arrested for substance abuse, mainly for defined illegal substances. It needs to be cautioned that such figures are heavily influenced by political attitudes toward abusive behavior and the pattern of law enforcement. Thus, there are limitations for direct cross-societal comparisons based on the number of people arrested for abuse. However, comparisons made within the same society are relatively meaningful from a chronological standpoint.

It is clear that the figures may fluctuate greatly in different societies even within a decade. For instance, in terms of the number of arrest cases per 100,000, it was high in Japan in the 1980s (e.g., 20.1 in 1982; 20.4 in 1984) and became lower in the 1990s (e.g., 12.4 in 1992; 12.0 in 1994). In contrast, in South Korea, the rate increased steadily from the 1980s (e.g., 1.8 in 1984) to the 1990s (e.g., 5.3 in 1994). The increase in Taiwan was much more remarkable (from 1.1 in 1984 to 41.7 in 1994). Beginning in the mid-1970s, heroin abuse in Malaysia became such a rampant problem that, in 1984 (with the rate of 66.5), it was declared "public enemy No. 1" by the prime minister. In 1996 the rate had declined almost half (35.0) (Tseng et al., 2001).

### b. Data from the United States

In the early 1960s, the number of opiate addicts in the United States started to rise, reaching a peak in the late 1970s. According to Kaplan (1983), the estimated number of heroin addicts ranged between 387,000 and 453,000 at the peak of usage. Meanwhile, other drugs became popular, and drug problems became more widespread. According to the U.S. Department of Health and Human Services (USDHHS) (1991), over one-fifth of adolescents (ages 12 to 17) and over half of young adults (ages 18 to 25) reported trying illicit drugs by 1974. The lifetime rate of marijuana use among college students doubled between 1970 and 1984; whereas cocaine use increased tenfold in that same period, from 2.7 to 30% (Rouse, 1991).

Data available from the Drug Abuse Warning Network in 1993 showed different patterns among three ethnic groups compared in the manner of drug-related deaths (National Institute on Drug Abuse, 1995, p. 85). It was revealed that the percentage of deaths associated with accident or suicide was 62.9% vs. 7.8% among African-Americans (with a ratio of 8.1/1), 80.5% vs. 11.1% for Hispanic-Americans (with a ratio of 7.3/1), and 51.8% vs. 26.7% for Caucasian-Americans (with a ratio of 1.9/1). In other words, African-American and Hispanic-American drug abusers tended to end their lives through drug-related accidents; Caucasian-Americans, by suicide.

It is interesting to note that, in the United States, recent data available from the USDHHS (1997) concerning the percentage of users in a community show a national trend of steady decline for all substances from the 1980s to the 1990s. This is true for marijuana, cocaine, and cigarettes, respectively. This indicates that, associated with an increased concern for health, as well as changes in the social situation, there has been considerable improvement from the peak of substance abuse observed in the post-Vietnam era. Associated with the recent increased awareness of the health hazards of smoking, cigarette use has been declining slowly but significantly over the past two decades.

### c. Some Information from Europe

From Italy, Davoli and associates (1997) reported that there was a persistent rise in mortality among injection drug users in Rome between 1980 and 1992. They reviewed a total of 4200 injection drug users attending the three largest drug treatment centers in Rome between 1980 and 1988. The cohort of subjects was followed up in December 1992. Results revealed that the age-adjusted mortality rate of this cohort reached a minimum of 7.8/1000 persons/year in 1985/86 and rose steadily to 27.7/1000 in 1991/92. The major cause of death was overdose in 1987/88; thereafter, AIDS became the first cause of death.

### d. Fragmented Information from Africa

Comprehensive epidemiological information about substance abuse in Africa is scarce. Abiodun (1991) reviewed drug abuse with special reference to Nigeria. He pointed out that, in addition to alcohol, other substances were being abused and had become a major public health problem in Nigeria.

Among all substances, cannabis was the most widely abused illicit drug in the country. It was introduced into the country and other parts of west Africa during and after World War II by soldiers and sailors returning from the Middle East, the Far East, and north Africa. Bensodiazepines are the most widely abused therapeutic agents. The widespread use of this group of drugs results partly from the overprescribing habits of medical practitioners and the freedom of patients to purchase drugs without prescription from chemists' shops and medicine stores. These drugs were found to be more abused by females and older persons. Psychostimulants, such as proplus (a caffeine concentrate) and amphetamines, were mainly abused by students, long-distance drivers, and soldiers. Stimulants are taken not for their pleasurable effects but to improve intellectual performance and to postpone inattentiveness and sleepiness. Organic solvents and hallucinogens remain uncommon, but hard drugs, such as cocaine and heroin, appear to be on the increase in big cities.

It is clear that substance abuse needs to be understood as a pathology attributed to different biological, psychological, and sociocultural factors. Cultural factors, functioning closely with social ones, contribute to the basic attitudes toward the abuse of substances, the choice of chemical indulgence as a coping mechanism for stress, and efforts to deal with social problems. There is a general tendency, when a society as a whole is facing certain stresses, whether socio-economic crisis, social instability, or cultural disintegration, for the problems of substance abuse and other associated social pathologies (such as suicidal, violent, or criminal behavior) to rise. The emergence of substance abuse, in turn, accelerates the process of social and cultural disintegration in a vicious way. Thus, substance abuse serves as one of the indexes for social stability.

## G. EATING PROBLEMS

### 1. Introduction and Clarification

Eating disorders, such as anorexia nervosa, bulimia nervosa, and other eating-related behavior problems, have become a new concern recently, particularly among societies in Western Europe and North America, due to the relative increase in their prevalence in the past several decades. Associated with the increased sociocultural emphasis on slimness in Western societies, eating disorders are considered closely related to such cultural concerns over body weight and image. Some cultural psychiatrists have even speculated that eating disorders are Western culture-related specific psychiatric syndromes (DiNichola, 1990; Littlewood & Lipsedge, 1987).

#### a. Ethnic Differences Concerning Body Image and Eating Habits

It is obvious that, as with body height, there are considerable differences in the (average or mean) body weight of people of different racial or ethnic groups. For instance, people in Polynesia, such as Hawaiians and Samoans, are well known for their relatively heavy body weight. There is no shortage of examples of people weighing over 300 pounds, and 600 or 700 pounds in some extreme cases. In contrast, Asian people, particularly Filipinos, Vietnamese, Thais, and Indians are commonly known for their light body weights, usually not much above 100 pounds, even among adults.

Although many reasons have been considered for overweight, biological elements are major predisposing factors that cannot be denied. Attitudes toward a certain body image are psychological phenomena that can contribute to body weight from a cultural point of view. Hawaiians and Samoans both hold the cultural attitude that heavy men and women are beautiful, healthy, and desirable for mates. People in Asia used to consider "being fat" as a sign of wealth and fortune. A "skinny" person is interpreted as possibly suffering from poverty or being sick. To the Asian eye, a tall, skinny contemporary (Western) fashion model is "terribly" skinny. Thus, there are clearly culture-biased perceptions, definitions, and attitudes toward "desirable" body weight and body image.

### b. Intensified Eating Concerns or Clinical Eating Disorders

To what extent culture-related eating behaviors are related to clinically identified, morbid eating disorders, such as anorexia nervous and bulimia nervosa, is not yet clarified. From cultural and clinical perspectives, it seems necessary to distinguish eating-related behavior at three levels: "ordinary" eating-related attitudes and behavior, observed in daily life as anxiety-free life patterns, subject to cultural variations, which tend to last for life and may be transmitted through generations; "intensified" (or "alerted") eating-concerned attitudes or behavior, manifesting extra concern with diet, being overcareful in choices of food and calorie intake, or engaging in excessive physical exercise to control body weight, and a conscious concern with body image; and "morbid" eating behavior, which is clinically identified and categorized as anorexia nervosa or bulimia nervosa, has a recognized onset, and runs a certain clinical course. It is very clear that cultural factors will have a direct impact on the former two conditions. However, there is no substantial evidence to date to support the notion that culture has a direct impact (as an etiological factor through "pathogenetic effects") on the occurrence of clinically identified "morbid" eating disorders. Culture might indirectly promote (through "pathofacilitative effects") the occurrence of such disorders, at most (see Section 1C: How Does Culture Relate to Psychopathology?).

### c. Problems of Cross-Cultural Study of Eating Disorders

There are several methodological problems at present that limit relevant cross-cultural comparisons of eating disorders and the study of eating disorders from cultural dimensions. First, eating disorders, as clinical entities, are new concerns among clinicians mainly in western Europe and North America, and most of the literature is derived from those geographic areas, with relevance to Caucasian groups. There is scarce clinical information from other ethnic and racial groups in other geographic regions, limiting meaningful cross-cultural comparisons (Habermas, 1991). Second, many of the reports, particularly from other geographic regions, are clinical case reports, which are often colored by subjective interpretations. When quantitative investigations were performed by questionnaire surveys, there were some basic problems. If the investigators used their own idiomatic questionnaires, it made cross-comparisons almost impossible. If Western-derived questionnaires were used, there were problems of content equivalence, since the eating-related behavior could be heavily subject to cultural factors (King & Bhugra, 1989). Third, there are problems with the criteria used in defining eating disorders. Although clinically recognized morbid eating disorders (anorexia nervosa and bulimic nervosa) are characterized by rather homogenous clinical manifestations (in contrast to other psychiatric disorders), some investigators tend to use their own criteria in defining cases, making comparisons with data from other investigations limited.

## 2. Information from Different Sociocultural Settings

### a. The United States

Although traditionally it was believed by clinicians and researchers that eating disturbances were confined primarily to white, upper-middle-class, college-age women, J. E. Smith and Krejci (1991) investigated high school minority populations and obtained unpredicted findings. They used the Eating Disorder Inventory (EDI, by Garner, Olmsted, & Polivy, 1983) and the Bulimia Test (BULT, by Smith & Thelen, 1984) for questionnaire surveys of three public high schools in the southeast United States. The student-subjects were composed of 60% Hispanics, 23.7% Native Americans, and 16.3% (non-Hispanic) Caucasians. The results revealed that the Native Americans consistently scored highest on each of seven items representing disturbed eating behaviors and attitudes. From these results, the researchers felt it was safe to conclude that the rates of disturbed eating patterns among Native Americans and Hispanic youth were at least comparable to those of Caucasian adolescents.

### b. Switzerland

Willi and Grossman (1983) conducted a retrospective study of the anorexia nervosa cases admitted to hospitals in the industrialized canton of Zurich during three randomly selected sampling periods between 1956 and 1975. They found that the incidence of first-time admitted cases per 100,000 population increased significantly from 0.38 in 1956–1958 to 0.55 in 1963–1965 to 1.12 in 1973–1975. They explained that this increase reflected that anorexic patients were now being hospitalized for less severe illnesses. Later, Willi, Giacometti, and Limacher (1990) did a follow-up study for the period 1983–1985. They reported that the incidence of anorexia nervosa did not increase from the previously studied period of 1973–1975. However, they commented that there was more frequent use of vomiting and abuse of laxatives in 1983–1985, which may have indicated an increase in cases with mixed features of anorexia and bulimia.

### c. India

In order to test the general clinical impression that the prevalence of eating disorders was very low in Third World populations, psychiatrists from London, King and Bhugra (1989), carried out a field survey in India. Schoolgirls, living in a small northern Indian industrial town, were screened, using the Eating Attitudes Test (EAT). EAT is a 26-item questionnaire that was developed for the evaluation of abnormal eating attitudes (Garner, Olmsted, & Polivy, 1983) and has been used widely in Western societies as a screening inventory for eating disorders. Surprisingly, the results revealed that, almost one-third of the schoolgirls studied scored above the recommended cutoff for the EAT, opposite findings from what had been believed on the basis of clinical impressions. However, conclusion should not be made in hurry. To solve this puzzle, a detailed study was made of the responding pattern. The investigators disclosed that there were consistent patterns of response for the whole population on five items, which appeared to have been due to sociocultural influences. The items to which the Indian girls often responded "always," contributing to the high total scores, were statements such as "Cut my food into small pieces" and "Display self-control around food," both of which addressed culturally desirable behaviors for Indians; therefore, many of the girls answered affirmatively. Other statements such as "Eat diet foods" and "Engaged in dieting behavior" were related to Hindu religious fasting concepts, while the statement "Feel that food controls my life" appeared to have been interpreted literally by the girls.

If examined carefully, these questions are not "specific" (or "pathognomic") to eating disorders and are very much subject to cultural situations. For instance, cutting food into small pieces is a regular way of preparing food in societies where the fingers (India) or chopsticks (most of Asia) are used for eating; this is different from societies that use a knife and fork. In many societies where food is often potentially scarce, it is common to value food, feeling that "food controls one's life." The investigators revealed that, in contrast to these culture-biased questions, other questions concerning "core" characteristics of abnormal eating attitudes, such as "Find myself preoccupied with food," "Have gone on eating binges when I felt that I may not be able to stop," and "Think about burning up calories whenever I exercise," were answered affirmatively only by small number of subjects. This information indicated that the number of subjects with abnormal eating attitudes was low.

Indian psychiatrists Khandelwal, Sharan, and Saxena (1995), after intensive review of the literature, presented their Indian perspective of eating disorders. They pointed out that Indian cases did not show the overactivity or disturbances in body image characteristically seen in (Western) anorexia nervosa, thus, their Indian cases tended to be "atypical" in terms of Western criteria. According to them, possible reasons for the seeming rarity of anorexia nervosa in India were lack of sensitivity about the diagnosis among clinicians; the use of Western diagnostic criteria, which possibly missed the diagnosis of "atypical" cases commonly seen in India; and the absence of pressure on a majority of young women to be thin or to restrain their eating, which may have protected vulnerable individuals from the principal route of entry into a clinically morbid condition.

### d. Egypt

Nasser (1986) investigated matched samples of Arab female college students attending Cairo University in Cairo and several colleges in London universities, as well as independent colleges in London. He applied the Eating Attitude Test to the two groups of subjects—the Cairo group and the London group. Using the cutoff score of 30 on the EAT (as originally designed and validated on Canadian subjects by Garner & Garfinkel, 1979), Nasser reported that 22% of the London sample scored as positive cases, compared to only 12% of the Cairo sample. Furthermore, Nasser conducted clinical interviews of the high scorers in both groups and reported that, in the London group, 6 out of 11 EAT-positive cases fulfilled the diagnostic criteria of bulimia nervosa and none, for anorexia nervosa. In contrast, no cases of anorexia or bulimia nervosa were identified in the Cairo group.

Regarding the differences found between the Arab female colleges students in Cairo and those in London, Nasser felt that because the latter group went to London as family members, selective factors associated with migration were unlikely. He interpreted the differences as related to the degree of exposure and contact with the Western style of life. The Arab students in London were similar to European students in dress and social behavior, whereas the Cairo students were generally more traditional in their dress, some of them still even wearing veils so that they were less concerned about exposing their body figure in public.

### e. China

Questionnaire surveys were administered to 509 college freshman (males and females) in two cities, Chongqing and Shanghai, in China by Zhang and colleagues (1992). The 100-item questionnaire, designed by the investigators, was used to elicit attitudes about weight and food, weight control behavior, and information needed to diagnosis anorexia and bulimia nervosa according to the criteria of the Chinese classification system and DSM-III-R. They reported that 1.1% of the students investigated (1.1% of females) met both Chinese classification and DSM-III-R criteria for bulimia; however, none were binge eating and purging on a regular basis. None met the diagnostic criteria for anorexia nervosa.

Although Lee, Ho, and Hsu (1993) reported that 58.6% of the anorexic patients reviewed in Hong Kong did not exhibit any fear of fatness through their course of illness and were thus labeled as "non-fat phobic anorexia," the finding was not the same in Beijing. Psychiatrists from Beijing, Song and Fang (1990), reported nine anorexic patients who had visited the Institute of Mental Health of Beijing Medical University between 1982 and 1988. They reported that all of these patients were female, aged 13 to 25, most were concerned about "being fat," and they started diet control after their friends commented that they were overweight.

An interesting report was given by psychiatrists from the Fujien area regarding child anorexia cases. Chen, Cheng, and Wang (1993) reported 200 cases of children, who were brought by their parents to visit a children's eating disorder clinic from 1988 to 1990. Surprisingly, among these 200 cases, 112 cases were boys and 88 were girls. They explained that, associated with the single-child family-planning policy, many single children were spoiled by their parents and allowed to pick at their food, have an unbalanced diet, or develop unhealthy eating habits, which contributed to their underweight.

## 3. Integration and Comments

*Increased Prevalence.*   It is commonly noted by clinicians in various parts of the world that there has been an increased prevalence of eating disorders in Western societies recently, which is simply attributed to the influence of Western culture (Iancu et al., 1994). Szmukler (1985), after examining the investigations that have been carried out in the past regarding the epidemiology of anorexia nervosa, commented that there were basic methodological problems regarding the definition as well as the detection of cases. Apparently, different times and settings, different methods of investigation, and the use of the same or different investigators led to different conclusions about the increase of anorexia nervosa among western European and North American societies.

It is not only in western European and North American societies that eating disorders are considered prevalent at present. There is also the notion that eating disorders are rising in some non-Western regions and that the increased prevalence is beginning to attract attention. For instance, Nogami and Yabana (1977) mentioned that eating disorders, particularly bulimia, were seldom diagnosed by Japanese psychiatrists until the early 1980s, when Nogami published a paper about bulimia and aroused attention among his Japanese colleagues. Similar comments have been made in India (Khandelwal, Sharan, & Saxena, 1995), Hong Kong (Hsu & Lee, 1993), and Pakistan (Mumford, Whitehouse, & Choudry, 1992).

*Typical and Atypical.*   Several investigators, based on their clinical experiences with different ethnic populations, have pointed out that eating disorders have an "atypical" clinical syndrome complex compared with "typical" diagnostic criteria set up in American classification criteria. More specifically, Hsu and Lee (1993) raised the question of whether weight phobia was necessary for a diagnosis of anorexia nervosa. Their experiences with ethnic Chinese anorexic patients in Hong Kong indicated that nearly half seldom showed a concern with being overweight. Khandelwal, Sharan, and Saxena (1995) also claimed that the eating disorder cases in India lacked a fear of becoming fat, body-image distortion.

These views raised the question: What do we mean by typical cases and atypical cases or "variations"? As mentioned previously, Walsh (1997, p. 1202) pointed out that (even among American patients) atypical eating disorders outnumbered typical eating disorders. There seems to be a need to clarify and reexamine the diagnostic categories of eating disorders, particularly from cross-cultural perspectives. According to Hsu and Sobkiewicz (1991), the general assumption that perceptual body width distortion was pathognomic for eating disorders deserves reexamination and clarification.

## H. SUICIDE BEHAVIOR

Suicidal behavior is relatively more suited to cross-cultural comparative study than any other kind of psychopathology. This is because it is a well-defined behavior about which official data are often available. Further, suicidal behavior is predominantly related to psychological factors and can therefore be analyzed and understood as an emotion-related disturbance whose sociocultural aspects can be examined (Farberow, 1975; Kok & Tseng, 1992; Tseng et al., 2001).

However, there are some problems inherent in the cross-cultural study of suicide. Strictly speaking, from the standpoint of cause, suicide is not a homogeneous clinical phenomenon. Some suicide behaviors occur as complications of severe psychiatric disorders, such as delusion or hallucination, or are associated with major depression. They may occur as a secondary reaction to stigmatized mental disorders that are chronic or untreatable. Suicide is often associated with substance abuse or dependence. Thus, some suicide behaviors are directly related to psychiatric disorders. Many other suicide behaviors occur as daily life reactions to emotional turmoil or frustration and, as psychologically related, very much reflect the distress that exists in a society or cultural system. The different natures of suicide behavior are generally not distinguished in statistical data of suicide, but are lumped together, which influences the interpretation of the information from a sociocultural perspective. Depending on their religious backgrounds, social attitudes toward suicide vary greatly in different societies and may affect medical and official willingness to report suicide occurrences. These factors need to be taken into consideration in cross-cultural comparisons of epidemiological data.

Finally, the distinction between "committed suicide" or "completed suicide" (normally referred to simply as "suicide") and "suicidal attempt" (or "parasuicide," in the British system) is arbitrary and depends on whether the suicidal behavior is successful. However, clinicians generally believe that the two have some different features. The age of the population, male/female ratio, motivation for action, and associated psychiatric disorders, for instance, are relatively different in committed and attempted suicides. Following professional custom, the two will be reviewed separately here.

## 1. Committed Suicide

### a. Comparison of Frequencies of Suicide

*Total Suicide Rate.*   Based on the World Health Organization's special report on suicide (1973) for the period between 1950 and 1969 and official annual data from the World Health Statistics Annuals (WHO, 1976–1996), available for the period of 1970–1994, supplemented by information from individual investigators (mostly from underdeveloped and developing countries), the total suicide rates (per 100,000 population) of different countries (or societies) in different world regions are compiled in Table 3. Although in most of the countries there were considerable differences in rates between males and females, for the sake of convenience, they are combined as total suicide rates.

There are several findings regarding the total suicide rates of various countries. First, there is a rather wide range of rates among the different countries. This range of differences in rates is in very wide contrast to other psychiatric disorders, such as schizophrenia, which has a difference of merely several times. There are no particular geographic distribution patterns noted among the groups. Actually, considerable differences have been found among neighboring countries, such as Denmark, Sweden, and Norway in Scandinavia, a phenomenon that has attracted the interest and speculation of scholars. Many of the very low rate countries are Muslim or Catholic societies that have prohibitive religious attitudes toward self-killing.

Another valuable finding is that the suicide rates for many countries are generally stable even over several decades. However, if there is dramatic sociocultural change or political turmoil, there are relatively obvious vicissitudes of suicide rates. In terms of socioeconomic development, some scholars have indicated that the rate of suicide is generally low in less-developed cultural areas. For example, Asuni (1962) estimated that the suicide rate in Western Nigeria (from 1957 to 1960) was extremely low, less than 1 per 100,000 population. Fallers and Fallers (1960) reported that the suicide rate for Busoga in Uganda (from 1952 to 1954) was 7.0 per 100,000 population.

*Age Distribution of Suicide.*   Even within the same society, suicide behavior is subject to different variables, such as age and gender, which provide valuable information regarding the nature of suicide behavior in the society concerned. The perception and experience of stress and reactions to distress are not necessarily the same among different age groups, even within the same society. As a result, the frequency of suicide among different age groups differs, manifesting different age-related suicide curves. Based on information available regarding age distribution of suicide rates, WHO (Ruzicka, 1976) has recognized three types of suicide curves, the "Czechoslovakian," "Finnish," and "Japanese." The "Micronesian" type was added by Tseng and Kok (1992) to describe the particular pattern

TABLE 3    Worldwide Suicide Rates: Chronological Trends from 1950 to 1994.

| Countries | Period of years | | | | | | | | |
|---|---|---|---|---|---|---|---|---|---|
| | 50–54 | 55–59 | 60–64 | 65–69 | 70–74 | 75–79 | 80–84 | 85–89 | 90–94 |
| Hungary | | | | | 36.9 | 38.4 | | 41.9 | 36.2 |
| Finland | | | | | 24.0 | 25.1 | 21.8 | 28.2 | 27.2 |
| Denmark | | 22.0 | 19.2 | 19.2 | 23.9 | 24.1 | 23.9 | 28.0 | 22.6 |
| S. Korea[a] | | | | 29.8 | 27.0 | 31.9 | 26.0 | 21.0 | 17.0 |
| Austria | | | | | 23.4 | 24.1 | 22.5 | 25.0 | 23.1 |
| Switzerland | 22.1 | 20.9 | 18.0 | 17.8 | 19.5 | 20.6 | | 22.7 | 21.6 |
| Czechoslovakia | | | | | 24.6 | | 18.5 | 19.2 | 18.8 |
| Japan | 20.0 | 24.5 | 18.0 | | 16.8 | 18.0 | 14.5 | 18.9 | 17.0 |
| France | | 16.6 | 15.5 | 15.4 | 16.1 | 15.6 | 15.5 | 22.1 | 21.6 |
| Belgium | | 14.2 | 14.2 | 15.0 | 15.4 | 14.9 | 17.1 | 22.5 | 18.0 |
| Sweden | | | | | 20.3 | 19.4 | 15.5 | 18.5 | 15.2 |
| Germany | | 18.8 | 19.1 | 20.6 | 19.9 | 21.0 | | 17.9 | 15.8 |
| Australia | 10.2 | 11.3 | 13.4 | 13.7 | | 11.7 | 10.3 | 13.8 | 11.6 |
| USA | | | 10.7 | 10.9 | 11.5 | 12.1 | 10.4 | 12.9 | 12.4 |
| Taiwan, China[b] | 10.0 | 14.0 | 16.0 | 19.0 | 13.0 | 10.0 | 11.0 | 12.0 | |
| Canada | 7.4 | 7.4 | 7.6 | 9.4 | 12.2 | 12.9 | 12.9 | 12.3 | 12.8 |
| Poland | | | | | 12.0 | 11.3 | | 12.4 | 14.9 |
| Singapore[c] | 13.1 | 12.2 | 10.4 | 9.4 | 9.8 | 10.9 | 10.7 | 9.9 | 12.7 |
| Norway | | | 7.3 | 7.6 | 9.0 | 10.4 | 14.5 | 15.6 | 14.5 |
| New Zealand | 9.6 | 9.2 | 8.8 | 9.6 | 8.8 | 9.0 | 10.3 | 11.0 | 12.9 |
| UK | 10.5 | 11.6 | 11.7 | 9.8 | 7.7 | 7.9 | 8.7 | 10.3 | 7.6 |
| Netherlands | 6.1 | 6.4 | 6.5 | 6.8 | 8.2 | 8.9 | 9.0 | 11.4 | 10.5 |
| Italy | | | 5.5 | 5.3 | 5.8 | 5.4 | 5.7 | 8.3 | 8.1 |
| Israel | | | | | 7.5 | 5.5 | | 7.8 | 7.1 |
| Spain | | | | | 4.4 | 4.0 | 4.5 | 6.6 | 7.9 |
| Chile | | | | | 5.5 | 5.5 | 6.3 | 5.4 | 5.8 |
| Greece | | | | | 27 | | 2.9 | | 3.5 |
| Mexico | | | | | 0.7 | 2.1 | | 2.2 | 3.0 |
| Malaysia[d] | | | | | | 0.6 | 1.5 | 1.6 | |
| Philippines | | | | | 0.6 | 1.2 | | | |

[a]The Bureau of Statistics (1998) Annual Statistics of Death and Its Cause, 1998, Seoul, Korea.
[b]Chong et al. (1992).
[c]Kok (1992).
[d]Ong and Leng (1992).
Based on World Health Statistics (WHO, 1976–1996) and other sources.

observed in Micronesia, Hawaii, and other island societies in the Pacific. These are illustrated in Figure 5. (For details of each type, see Tseng, 2001, Chapter 22: Suicidal Behavior, pp. 378–381.) The age-related suicide pattern in Japan three decades ago was characteristically of Japanese type. However, the suicide curve in contemporary Japan has change. With the lives of young people becoming more favorable after the World War II, the peak that originally existed in the 20-

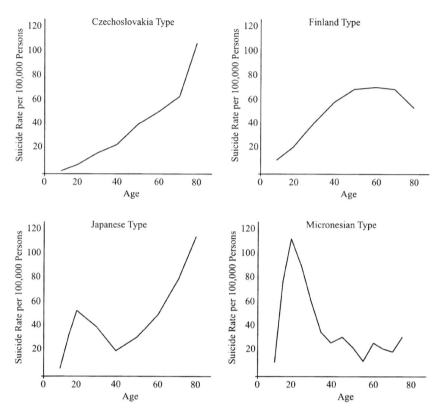

FIGURE 5    Various types of age-related suicide curves. [From WHO, 1976; and W. S. Tseng and L. P. Kok, in *Suicidal Behavior in the Asia-Pacific Region*. By permission of Singapore University Press, Singapore, 1992.

to 30-year-old age group disappeared. As a result, the total suicidal curve for the Japanese gradually changed into the Czechoslovakian type over the past three decades (see Fig. 6).

*Male/Female Suicide Ratios.*    In contrast to suicide attempts, which are more prevalent among female subjects, the rate of committed suicide is generally higher for males than females in most countries around the world. The male/female ratios vary considerably. Data from WHO (1993) showed that the rate (or ratio) of male/female was 19.9/4.8 (4.15/1) for the United States; 20.4/5.2 (3.92/1) for Canada; 34.6/11.6 (2.98/1) for Austria; and 30.0/15.1 (1.99/1) for Denmark. Thus, disregarding the actual rates, the number of completed suicides is always higher for male than for females (Canetto & Lester, 1998). Scholars in the past have interpreted owing to the fact that male subjects use more lethal methods than female subjects, ending more often in successful suicides. However, this view needs to be revised. Newly available data from mainland China, which comprises more than one-fifth of the world's population, have shown that the committed suicide rate is considerably higher for females than males, with a male/female ratio of 0.77/1 (Pritchard, 1996). This is particularly true in rural areas and among young females. For the 15- to 24-year age group, the male/female ratio is 0.52/1 for the whole country, meaning that the rate for young females is almost twice that of young males (Pritchard, 1996). This reflects that, as in the past, the role of women is still less favorable than that of men, especially in rural traditional society, and that the lives of young females—as unmarried women, young wives, or daughters-in-law—are still more full of distress. Ending their own lives remains one of the choices available to them for dealing with the difficulties they encounter.

*Vicissitude of Suicide Rates within the Same Society.*    As mentioned previously, although the total suicide rate for a society may tend to be stable over many decades, a considerable fluctuation may be noticed in association with dramatic social changes occurring within a decade or so. For instance, according to Yoshimatsu (1992), the total suicide rate for the Japanese was rather consistent from 1890 to 1935, mostly in the range of 15 to 20 per 100,000 population. However, after 1935, when Japan went to war with China and later was involved in the war in the Pacific with America and its allies, the suicide rate declined considerably, reaching a bottom of 12 in 1943, shortly before World War II ended. After the war, while the Japanese were trying to reconstruct their country, the suicide rate increased gradually but steadily, reaching a peak of 25 around 1958, when reconstruction was completed and people started to enjoy affluent lives again. After this, the rate declined and returned almost to its previous baseline (see Fig. 7). This supports the view that suicide tends to decline when a society is at war with an external enemy. Yoshimatsu pointed out that the increase in the suicide rate between 1955 and 1960 was attributed to the increase in suicide among the elderly. He called this a cohort phenomenon, explaining that this cohort of the population went through hard times as children and teenagers during the war, worked very hard for socioeconomic recovery during adulthood, but lost their life goals and had difficulty adjusting to the cultural changes in their society when they reached old age.

Vicissitudes in the total suicide rates associated with rapid sociocultural change have been reported in Taiwan as well (Chong, Yeh, & Wen, 1992; Yeh, 1985). The total suicide rate was around 10 per 100,000 population in 1948, rising sharply and reaching a peak of 18 in 1963, then declining gradually to a level of 10 after 1975 (see Fig. 8). The change in suicide rates was associated with the rapid sociocultural change that occurred in Taiwan during that period of time. After

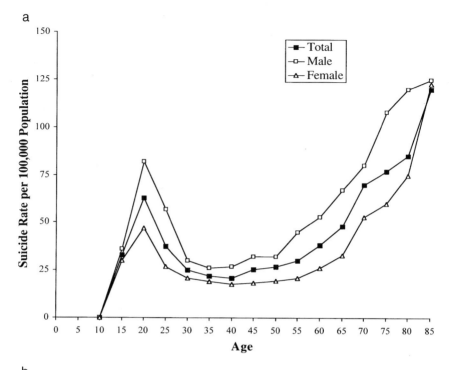

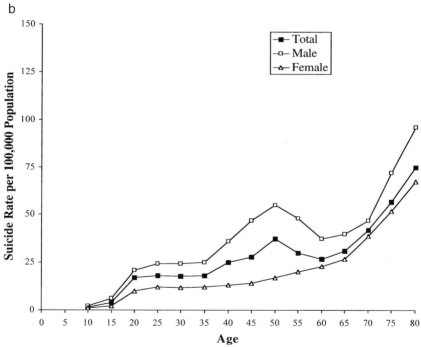

FIGURE 6  Conversion of age-related suicide curves in Japan from 1955 to 1986 (a) 1955; (b) 1986. [From K. Yoshimatsu, in *Suicidal Behavior in the Asia-Pacific Region*, Singapore: Singapore University Press, 1992, with permission.]

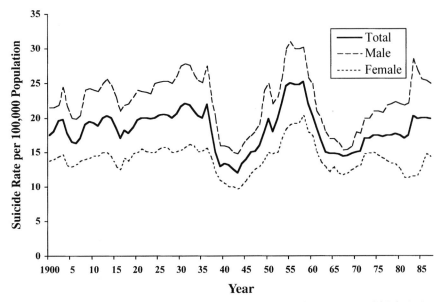

FIGURE 7   Suicide rates in Japan from 1890 to 1987 [From K. Yoshimatsu, in *Suicidal Behavior in the Asia-Pacific Region*, Singapore: Singapore University Press, 1992, with permission.]

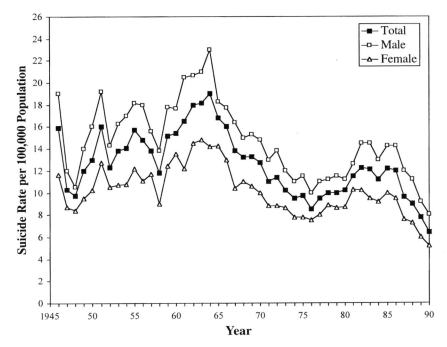

FIGURE 8   Suicide rates in Taiwan between 1946 and 1990. [From M. Y. Chong & T. A. Cheng, in *Chinese Societies and Mental Health*, Hong Kong: Oxford University Press (China) Ltd., 1995, with permission.]

mainland China was taken over by the communists in 1948, the Nationalist government retreated to Taiwan with a couple of million soldiers and civilians. This massive internal migration, along with the military tension that remained in the China Strait, produced dramatic social, political, and cultural changes. After two decades, when the society was stabilized, the total suicide rate returned to its original level.

### b. Comparison of Suicidal Behavior

*Method of Suicide.* Cross-ethnic comparisons of methods used to commit suicide reveal considerable differences. After members of the same ethnic group have moved to a different social environment and associated with the length of time they have been there, their method of suicide will change. In general, this illustrates that availability of method is a major determining factor in the one that is chosen for suicide, while familiarity of method also contributes to the choice. Mostly, there is no strong belief or attitude attached to the method of ending one's life.

*Motives for Suicide.* Because information on possible motives for suicide is often the result of speculation by family members or others after the occurrence of the event, it is not adequate or reliable. However, available information can be used to discuss general trends and to illustrate that cultural factors may contribute strongly to the motives for suicide. Some characteristic trends are revealed. In a society where mental illness still carries a strong stigma, a relatively high percentage of people may commit suicide owing to mental illness. Suffering from a serious physical illness is another cause of suicide, particularly for males in cultures where men are considered the key financial support of the family. Suicide is often attributed to family conflict in societies in which family relationships are highly valued and there is still a strong emphasis on hierarchy within the family system. Hidden tensions or open conflicts exist in such family systems, often between in-laws, and suicide becomes one of the choices for resolving the conflict when few alternatives are available. Relationship problems are common reasons for suicide in societies in which romantic relations are highly valued and the man-woman relationship is a predominant axis in interpersonal relations. A failure in man-woman relations can cause serious emotional frustration and become a cause for ending one's life. This is often observed in many Western societies. Poverty, financial debt, or unemployment as causes for killing oneself are relatively rare in economically developed societies; however, financial difficulty can be a serious life threat, and, as a motive for suicide, it is still common in undeveloped or developing societies. It is obvious that many different reasons can lead to the same phenomenon of self-killing. Culture has a strong impact on people's perception and experience of and reaction to stress.

## 2. Suicide Attempts

As mentioned previously, suicide attempts (also called parasuicides by the British) are arbitrarily distinguished from successful suicides. The distinction depends on whether a serious method of suicide was used or if the person attempting suicide was found and rescued in time. From the standpoint of frequency, in contrast to suicides, attempted suicides are often underestimated. This is because the former generally require medical-legal attention, so figures are closer to reality; whereas figures for the latter depend on the extent to which those who attempted suicide are referred for medical attention. If there is a negative attitude toward suicide in the society, such as in India, where, until recently, suicidal behavior was regarded as "a punishable legal offense" (Latha, Bhat, & D'Souza, 1996), suicide attempts tend to be concealed by the community.

Despite the limited data on suicide attempts available internationally, some trends have been observed through cross-cultural comparisons among various countries. In contrast to the relatively stable rate for committed suicide, there was a marked increase in the rates of suicide attempts. This was particularly noted by Weissman (1974) in many Western societies, with an almost twofold increase in Great Britain, Australia, and the United States in the decade between 1960 and 1971. Regardless of place or time, there is no exception to the observation that suicide attempts tend to be among the young, between the ages of 20 and 30 years, with the peak from 20 to 24. In terms of gender, the preponderance of female over male attempters was noted in all countries in the time period studied—most of the studies reported a ratio of about 2:1. Weissman (1974) speculated that the increase in suicide attempts worldwide reflected the problems of the youth culture. The strong family life and religion that at one time served to integrate the person within a social group were no longer effective resources for young people. The changing roles of women may also have had an impact—with young women facing the conflicts and challenges of traditional and contemporary lifestyles.

## 3. Clinical Implications

A certain "personal profile" has been identified clinically for individuals who are considered to be potentially at high risk for committing suicide, such as aged widowers with physical illnesses or drinking problems who are living alone (among male Caucasians, for instance). However, knowledge of such a personal profile is not useful in dealing with an individual patient in a clinical setting. Each person needs to be assessed and dealt with according to his own individual situation. This is also true of a "cultural profile" for suicide that has been recognized in an ethnic or cultural group. Even knowing about the cultural profile, including the ethnic or cultural group's shared attitudes toward death or the likelihood of its members choosing suicide as a way of solving life problems, will not give us a concrete guide on how to deal with an individual patient of that ethnic-cultural background. Although suicidal behavior as a whole is very much colored by sociocultural factors, each person needs to be evaluated and approached clinically on an individual basis, considering many variables.

However, from a cultural point of view, several issues can be recommended for consideration in clinical situations. First, it should be kept in mind that there are different cultural attitudes toward the communication of suicidal ideas. People in some cultures consider having suicidal ideas very disgraceful or a private matter that should not be readily revealed to others, including physicians or psychiatrists. Even when asked directly, they tend to deny having them. In contrast, people in other cultures may feel comfortable disclosing such ideas. In some societies, people have even learned that expressing suicidal ideas is a powerful way of getting professional attention and care, even if, in reality, they are not seriously occupied with such depressive thoughts. In other words, there are cultural differences in the disclosure of suicidal ideas.

It is necessary to recognize that culture influences people's consideration of self-killing as one of their choices in dealing with their problems. In cultures, such as the Muslim, with strong religious beliefs that the body should not be damaged intentionally, self-injury is less likely. Societies with statistically relatively low suicide rates belong to this category. In ethnic groups where self-killing is a traditionally accepted way of dealing with distress, suicide is a relatively easier action to undertake. People with statistically relatively high suicide rates belong to this category.

Finally, it is useful to be aware of common causes of suicide among different ethnic groups so that suitable management can be given accordingly. For instance, a person from a group with a strong stigma toward mental illness, when diagnosed with a mental disorder with a poor prognosis, has a relatively high chance of choosing to end his life. When a man who culturally believes that it is important to be physically healthy and support his family discovers that he has a serious physical illness and cannot fulfill his culture's image of a man, he might become vulnerable to suicide. When a young woman in a traditional family with close relationships suffers from frequent conflicts with in-laws, her chances of committing suicide may be higher than someone from a different family system.

## I. PERSONALITY DISORDERS

### 1. General Debates about Personality Disorders

Of the various kinds of psychopathologies, personality disorders have been the least subject to empirical research. There have been many debates among clinicians regarding the nature, diagnosis, and categorization of personality disorders. Further, knowledge about how to treat such disorders is still very scant. From a cross-cultural point of view, although the relation between culture and personality stirred up keen interest among scholars several decades ago (see Section 1B,4 Personality and Ethnic Identity), attention to disorders of the personality has only been recent (Alarcón, Foulks, & Vakkur, 1998). Cross-cultural information about personality disorders is nearly vacant, awaiting further investigation.

There is a basic debate among clinicians about the nature of personality disorders. One group takes the spectrum view and regards personality disorders as the extreme of normal personality (Paris, 1997). Others maintain that personality disorders belong to a distinct category of disorders. For instance, as pointed out by Haslam (1997), substantial evidence shows that antisocial, schizotypal, and probably borderline personality disorders correspond to discrete categories rather than continua.

## 2. Cultural Influence on Personality Disorders

*Diagnosing the Disorder.*   The identification of personality disorders is based on the general diagnostic criteria of "an enduring pattern of inner experience and behavior that deviates markedly from the expectations of the individual's *culture*" and "the enduring pattern leads to clinically significant distress or impairment in *social*, occupational, or other important areas of functioning" (DSM-IV). This means that the diagnostic decision relies on how the society views and tolerates the behavior concerned. It is subjective, relative, and culturally defined. Naturally, there is ample room for cross-cultural bias and differences in making diagnoses and identifying the disorders. As stressed by Foulks (1996), different cultures have tended to emphasize different traits of personality as ideal. From a cultural perspective, defining or labeling deviancies from "normal personality" is clearly a culture-relative exercise, and its boundaries are reflective of the specific values, ideas, worldview, resources, and social structure of the society.

*Examining the Frequency of Disorder.*   The frequency of a personality disorder is relatively difficult to study through epidemiological surveys because they are one-time studies and do not examine a person's life thoroughly or objectively enough to make it possible to diagnose a "personality disorder." Unless a survey was carried out with intensive psychological assessment, most kinds of personality disorders would be difficult to diagnose. Of all the recognized personality disorders, antisocial personality disorder is the most relatively possible to identify owing to its nature.

## 3. Specific Categories of Personality Disorders

*Antisocial Personality Disorder.*   Based on the findings obtained from the ECA study, Robins, Tipp and Pryzbeck (1991) reported that there were no racial differences whatever in the prevalence of antisocial personality in the United States. However, at the same time, it was also commonly known that the percentage of racial distribution among inmates in prisons was remarkably influenced by racial factors. Kosson, Smith, and Newman (1990) reported that 45% of the prisoners in the United States were African-American (while their percentage in the general population was less than 13%). Lopez (1989) suggested that there was an overpathologizing bias toward African-Americans and lower-class individuals relative to Caucasian-American and female subjects in the diagnosis of antisocial personality disorder. Alarcón and Foulks (1995) pointed out that as many as half of inner-city youth may have this diagnosis misapplied, as the criteria are inappropriate for settings in which value systems and behavioral rules make learning to be violent a protective and survival strategy.

*Histrionic Personality Disorder.*   It is a well-known trend that clinically the diagnosis of hysterical personality disorder is especially prone to gender bias from the point of view of the examiner: more females than males are diagnosed with this disorder by (male) clinicians. A male might be labeled as antisocial, instead. This shows that the diagnosis of histrionic personality disorder relies heavily on the view of the examiner and is subjective. In transcultural practice, if there is a wide gap between the patient and the clinician in terms of how they express emotion, owing to cultural factors, there is a high possibility of a misdiagnosis in the category of personality disorder. This is particularly true if the clinician, according to his cultural background, emphasizes the control of emotional expression, whereas the patient, following his cultural experience, values the free and dramatic expression of emotion.

*Borderline Personality Disorder.*   The frequency of clinical diagnoses of borderline personality disorder has increased significantly in North America during the past three decades, associated with the clarification of the concept of nosology and the increased awareness of such a disorder among clinicians. In contrast, in many other societies, particularly in Asia, while attention to the disorder is increasing, the number of cases actually diagnosed is not necessarily rising accordingly. To what extent the increased prevalence of the disorder is related to diagnostic patterns or to the actual increase of such cases is not clear.

An unstable early childhood, increased history of abuse, unstable family environment, and other life factors have been hypothesized as the precipitating factors for developing borderline personality disorder when the youngster reaches adulthood. Thus, there is good reason to speculate that such a disorder may be less prevalent in certain societies where people go through a relatively less traumatic early childhood and live in a stable family environment. Examining those who had developed borderline disorder after migrating to developed societies, Paris (1996) considered that the social protective factors (that existed in traditional societies) may have suppressed the development of the borderline traits into diagnosable personality disorders. Certainly, this speculation is awaiting cross-ethnic or cross-cultural validation.

There is little literature from other societies regarding borderline personality disorder. The validity of the borderline concept is still challenged (Kroll, Carley, & Sines, 1982). From Japan, Moriya and Colleagues (1993) have reported that, comparing their data with data obtained from literature on American patients, Japanese borderline patients tended to show fewer symptoms of substance abuse, but had higher scores for depersonalization and derealization. Japanese patients were more likely to have intense masochistic-dependent relationships, were less likely to be socially isolated, and were more likely to be living at home rather than being homeless.

*Avoidant Personality Disorder.* If a society stresses the importance of social interaction in daily life, avoiding such relations may be recognized as avoidant. In a society that has a high tolerance for withdrawn behavior, people (such as hermits) may be considered "saints" for periodically going on long retreats for the purposes of self-training. No one in those social circumstances would label such people as having "avoidant" or "schizotypal" personality disorders. As pointed out by Foulks (1996), many individuals in severely oppressed, minority groups are reluctant to participate in social situations because of a fear of saying something inappropriate; they show anxiety in front of others, are unwilling to get involved with people, and avoid social activities involving oppressive majority groups. These characteristics are related to acculturation problems and are not to be labeled as avoidant behavior.

In summary, there is no argument that in each society there are a certain number of people who manifest enduring patterns of behavior that "deviate markedly from the expectations of their culture" and result in a disturbance in social functioning. However, there is a need to clarify the threshold for such deviation and impairment according to each society. It is most likely that, depending on its culture, each society tends to show a different tolerance for different kinds of behavior deviation. Therefore, the identification and labeling of personality disorders are very much subject to cultural definition and social recognition.

## J. SEXUAL DISORDERS

Sexual behavior and sexual disorders are private personal matters for most people, and they are relatively difficult to investigate systematically and formally. Therefore, literature relating to the cross-cultural examination of sexual behavior and disorders is limited. However, there are sufficient ethological studies among primate societies and anthropological reports of tribal human societies indicating how sexual behavior vary among different societies.

## 1. Ethology and Anthropological View of Sexual Behavior

By ethological study it is revealed that among primate societies various types of social organization in term of male/female relations are found that, in turn, shape sexual behavior (Castillo, 1997, pp. 14–119). Regarding human societies, anthropology studies have disclosed that all human societies have elaborate rules concerning sexual behavior, especially the sexual behavior of women and post-pubescent females. Similar to primate societies, the higher the degree of male dominance, the more complete the control over female sexuality.

Attitudes toward sex vary greatly among different human societies. Anthropologists give examples of two extremes. In a small island off the coast of Ireland, Inis Beag, studied by Messenger (1993) in the 1950s and 1960s, sexual renunciation was identified with moral and religious virtue (of Roman Catholics). Anything related to sex was highly controlled and socially suppressed. Courtship was almost nonexistent, and late marriage and celibacy were prevalent. A "good" woman was considered to be one who did not like sex and did not disrupt social relations between a man and his male comrades. People believed that sex is a "duty" that a wife must "endure." Ignorance of sexual practices was profound in this society, along with a lack of sexual variation.

In contrast to this, the island of Mangaia in the South Pacific presented different pattern as studies by Marshall (1993) in the 1950s and 1960s. In this Polynesian society, females have achieved a great degree of sexual freedom. Post-pubescent daughters could receive and make love to varied suitors nightly. Young men receive instruction in sex, being educated how to please a woman. Sex for pleasure was a major concern of their culture.

## 2. Cultural Aspects of Sexual Disorders

When the subject is turned into sexual disorders, cross-cultural clinical investigations on this subject become scared. Medical anthropologist, R. Castillo (1997, pp. 124–134), by examining various types of paraphilias defined in DSM-IV, pointed out that there is a need for caution in recognizing and defining various kinds of sexual disorders. For instance, concerning exhibitionism, it was indicated that this pathological behavior (for a man to exhibit his penis to females for sexual excitement) has meaning only in societies where the genitals are normally covered in public. In many tribal societies in tropical areas, no clothing is traditionally worn. Consequently, exposure of the genitals to a stranger of the opposite sex is not considered to be a sexual act as it is in other societies, such as Western societies, where the genitals are always kept covered in public.

Regarding transexualism there are some literatures in the past from Southeast Asian societies (Heiman & Le, 1975; Tsoi, Kok, & Long, 1977). From Singapore,

Tsoi and Kok (1995) reported that the number of transsexuals appearing in the medical setting increased significantly with the availability and publicity of sex-change operations in Singapore in 1970s, correcting the myth held previously that such sexual disorders were rare among the Chinese. As a part of the pre-operation psychiatric screening, Tsoi and Kok examined male transsexuals seeking surgical treatment. They reported that among the Chinese, Malay, and Indian ethnic groups in Singapore, there is no difference regarding their personal background or history of psychosexual development. They presented their view that if ethnic or cultural factor have any impact on the development of this disorder, it is a minor and peripheral one.

Medical professionals from European and American societies have revised radically their view about homosexuality during the past several decades by no longer regarding homosexuality as a disorder. However, social recognition and cultural attitude toward such sexual orientation varies greatly among different culture. Some are very liberal, while many remain still very negative. Ho (1995) from Hong Kong tried to explore the social and psychological forces that influence the identity of a man who has come to describe himself as a "homosexual." Ho pointed out that homosexual identity arises not so much from homosexual behavior per se but from the stigma and heterosexual beliefs that encompass it. For the Chinese in Hong Kong, the acquisition of homosexual identity is largely a response to the cultural definition of marriage and family, gender, and sex roles. It is relatively difficult for the male homosexual to getting access to emotional and sexual fulfillment in an environment that prohibits it. Up to recently, in mainland China, those who demonstrated homosexual behavior in public could face legal punishment for the reason of "disturbing the social mode." As a result, no patients dared to complain about homosexuality, even to mental health professionals, and families tended to hide such disgraceful problems from others.

---

CASE 5

A Homosexual Chinese Male Who Presented a Problem of Anxiety

A 19-year-old male college freshman was brought by his father to visit a university-affiliated psychiatric clinic in China for a thorough consultation for his chief complaint of anxiety. He said that he had suffered from nervousness, tension, and difficulty sleeping for almost one year after he started to live in a dormitory. He had been treated at the school mental health clinic for anxiety, but it had not solved his problem. During the examination, the psychiatrist skillfully inquired into the content of his dreams at night. It was revealed that he dreamed about intimacy with men. Thus, it was revealed that his problem was homosexuality and living with male classmates in a dormitory was the main cause of his anxiety. He admitted

*(continues)*

that, knowing how people and society would react to his homosexuality, he was scared to tell anybody about his problem, even the mental health counselor he was seeing at school for many months. When his problem was revealed to his father, who accompanied him to see the expert, it was a surprise to the psychiatrist that the father did not show any emotional reaction. It was not clear what the father's understanding of being a gay was, but he simply stated that, as long as his son would marry eventually and bear a grandchild for him, he did not care whether he was gay or not. The father seemed only to have a cultural concern about the continuation of the family clan and refused to face the problems his son had about his sexual orientation.

Despite the shortage of formal and systematic cross-cultural studies of sexual disorders, overall, it can be said that it is the general view of scholars and clinicians that not only does sexual behavior vary as a result of social and cultural configuration, but sexual disorders are also subject to cultural influences. Culture shapes the definition of the disorder (pathodiscriminating effect), its impact possibly on the prevalence of disorders (pathofacilitating effect), and most obviously the reaction to the disorders (pathoreactive effect).

## K. SCHIZOPHRENIC DISORDER

Among all major psychiatric disorders, schizophrenia has been of greatest concern to clinicians and scholars since the very beginning of the history of psychiatry because it is one of the most severe and prevalent mental disorders of humankind. Many approaches have been taken in the past to understand the nature of this disorder, including social and cultural investigations. Although most scholars now view schizophrenia as predominantly attributed to biological, including hereditary, factors, past attempts to investigate the disorder from social and cultural perspectives have made certain contributions that deserve to be reviewed here.

### 1. Concerning Clinical Manifestation

It is well known that Emil Kraepelin, the founder of modern (descriptive) psychiatry, established a classification system for psychiatric disorders in the late 19th century. He was curious as to how his classification system, which was based on the clinical observation of patients in Germany, could be applied to patients in other societies with diverse cultures. He traveled to Southeast Asia, including Indonesia, in the 1890s to make field observations and to test his classification system. He was relieved to learn that schizophrenia of a basically similar clinical picture was found in other cultures, such as Indonesia. If there was any difference, it was in the variation of subtypes (e.g., catatonic cases were found more in Indonesia than in Germany).

Later, American anthropologist and sociologist Marvin K. Opler (1959) carried out a cross-ethnic comparison of the symptomatology of schizophrenia between Italian- and Irish-American patients. Examining hospitalized schizophrenic patients of different ethnic backgrounds in New York City, he reported that there were more Italian patients than Irish patients manifesting overt homosexual tendencies during psychotic conditions, behavior problems, and attitudes of rejecting authority. In contrast, more Irish patients than Italian patients were preoccupied with sin and guilt ideation, manifested chronic alcoholism, and had fixed delusional thoughts. Opler's study opened the door to the study of schizophrenic symptomatology cross-ethnically. However, it was later criticized by scholars that the findings revealed ethnic personality differences rather than differences in the schizophrenic disorders themselves. In other words, the differences had nothing to do with the core of the schizophrenic condition but merely represented secondary symptoms or behavior problems associated with such psychotic conditions.

More than a decade later, a systematic study on a larger scale was launched by the World Health Organization, the International Pilot Study of Schizophrenia (IPSS), involving nine study centers around the world: Aarhus (Denmark), Agra (India), Cali (Colombia), Ibadan (Nigeria), London (United Kingdom), Moscow (U.S.S.R.), Prague (Chechoslovakia), Taipei (Taiwan, China), and Washington (United States) (World Health Organization, 1973). It was the first formal comparative study that involved multiple culture sites and used standardized methods to collect information and to compare the clinical picture of schizophrenia from different societies of divergent ethnic/culture backgrounds.

The results revealed first that the average percentage scores were very similar across all the centers. All had high scores on lack of insight, predelusional signs, flatness of affect, auditory hallucinations (except the Washington center), and experiences of control. This indicated that schizophrenic patients from diverse cultural settings share basically similar symptomatology. It was also revealed that, among all the patients studied from all the centers, the largest distribution of subtype was paranoid schizophrenia (39.8%), followed the schizo-affective (13.2%). There were only few cases of the catatonic subtype (6.7%) from Agra (India), Cali (Colombia), and Ibadan (Nigeria). This shows that the distribution of the catatonic subtype was rather uneven among the nine study centers, found mainly in three centers in developing societies. These findings support the clinical impression held by clinicians that catatonic schizophrenia is diminishing and paranoid schizophrenia is rising in developed societies.

## 2. Regarding Causative Social Variables

In the past, many investigations have been carried out around the world regarding the nature of schizophrenia with the intent to reveal the possible social variables that may contribute to the occurrence of such disorders.

Numerous investigations have been based on the early clinical impression that more immigrants than others in a community were hospitalized (as schizophrenic patients) in mental hospitals. It was even speculated that life stress associated with transcultural immigration caused or, at least, provoked the occurrence of severe mental disorders. An alternative speculation was that people with psychotic tendencies were already not stable in their lives and might more often choose to migrate to foreign societies. Later, however, scholars pointed out that the process of migration is a complex phenomenon, and there is no simple relation between it and the occurrence of severe mental disorders such as schizophrenia.

There have been several investigations on the possible effects of social class on the occurrence of mental disorders, including severe disorders such as schizophrenia. For instance, Hollingshead and Redlich (1958) carried out an epidemiological investigation in the Great New Haven area in the United States in the late 1950s. The subjects were grouped into five classes according to the ecological area of residence, occupation, and education. Results revealed that the patients diagnosed as psychotic (mainly with schizophrenia) were found more in the lower social classes. This has generated several hypotheses regarding this phenomena, namely, social drifting or social attraction. Subsequent studies support the speculation that severe mental patients, owing to the general deterioration of their lives, tend to drift into social settings characterized as lower class.

Only a few studies have involved longitudinal follow-up investigations of the prevalence of mental disorders. The 15-year follow-up study by Lin et al. (1969) in Taiwan was one such investigation. The study of the prevalence of mental disorders was carried out in three selected communities originally in 1946–1948. Fifteen years later, after significant socioeconomic-cultural changes in the society, the same chief investigators conducted a follow-up survey using similar methods. It was revealed that, although the prevalence rate of neurotic disorders increased remarkably (almost seven times), the rate of psychoses had not changed. This indicated that rapid sociocultural change occurring in the community over one and a half decades did not affect the prevalence of psychotic disorders (mainly schizophrenia).

## 3. Studying Frequency of Disorder

Stimulated by the success of the IPSS international study of the clinical picture of schizophrenia, described earlier, several years later, in the late 1970s, the World Health Organization launched another multisociety investigation, the WHO Collaborative Study on the Determinants of Outcomes of Severe Mental Disorders (DOS) (Jablensky et al., 1991). This time, 12 study centers were selected: Asrhus (Denmark), Agra and Chandigarh (India), Cali (Columbia), Dublin (Ireland), Honolulu and Rochester (United States), Ibadan (Nigeria), Moscow (U.S.S.R.), Nagasaki (Japan), Nottingham (United Kingdom), and Prague (Czechoslovakia).

The results revealed that (Jablensky et al., 1991, pp. 45–52), if a broad definition of schizophrenia was used, incident rates were different in the different
centers investigated. However, the annual incidence rates ranged merely from 1.5
to 4.2 per 10,000 population at risk, ages 15–54. If a stricter research definition
of schizophrenia was used, the incidence rates did not differ among the centers
with a range of 0.7 to 1.4 per 10,000 population aged 15–54.

In the 1980s, an intensive epidemiological study organized by the National
Institute of Mental Health, the Epidemiological Catchment Area Study, was carried
out in the United States (Regier et al., 1984). This study involved several catchment areas in the nation and produced much useful information about the prevalence of mental disorders in the United States. Because of the limitation of sample
selection, only African-Americans, Hispanic-Americans, and Caucasian-Americans
were compared for prevalence of any disorders in their ethnic groups (Regier &
Kaelber, 1995, pp. 142–143). Based on the ECA data obtained from the Los Angeles
site, Karno and colleagues (1987) were able to compare the lifetime prevalence of
specific psychiatric disorders among Mexian-Americans and non-Hispanic whites
in Los Angeles, the only site where there was a sufficient sample size to compare
these two ethnic groups. The analysis showed that the overall rates for any diagnosed disorder were similar for the two groups. There was a significant difference
for only two disorders: drug abuse/dependence and major depression, which were
more prevalent among non-Hispanic whites. As for schizophrenia, the lifetime
prevalence rate per 10,000 population was 0.4 for Mexican-Americans and 0.8 for
non-Hispanice whites, not a significant difference.

## 4. Examining Clinical Prognosis

As the second phase of WHO's International Pilot Study of Schizophrenia, a two-
year follow-up study was carried out to examine the outcomes of the schizophrenic patients in the different sites investigated (Sartorius, Jablensky & Shapiro,
1977). Surprisingly, results revealed that the level of social development has a
certain relation to the short-term prognosis of schizophrenia (i.e., cases in developing societies), in contrast to more developed societies, which have more favorable outcomes. It has been speculated that the family, social, and cultural factors
may have psychopathoreactive effects on functional psychoses, such as schizophrenia, resulting in different prognoses. An accommodating community, supportive family, and relatively simple lifestyle may favor the recovery of the
psychotic condition (Sartorius, Jablensky, & Shapiro, 1978). Later, a five-year
follow-up of the patients initially included in the IPSS was conducted in eight
of the nine centers (Leff, Sartorius, Jablensky, Korten, & Ernberg,1992). Results
indicated that both clinical and social outcomes were significantly better for
patients in Agra (India) and Ibandan (Nigeria) than for those in the centers in
developed countries.

In order to validate the reverse relation between the level of social development and the prognosis for schizophrenia found in the IPSS, a few years later, the World Health Organization undertook a second study, the Determinants of Outcomes of Severe Mental Disorders. In addition to the frequency of occurrence, this study focused more sharply than the IPSS on the natural history of schizophrenic illness and the factors associated with differences in course and outcome.

A two-year follow-up study was carried out among schizophrenic patients in the 12 study sites, which had different levels of social development. The outcomes of the disorder were defined in terms of the frequency of relapse and the length of remission. Results reconfirmed the previous findings that the outcomes of schizophrenic patients were better in developing societies than in developed ones. It was also revealed that the difference could not be fully explained by the higher frequency of acute onsets among the developing countries, a speculation that had been made after the IPSS (Sartorius et al., 1986).

Although much more social and family information was collected in this study than in the IPSS, no fundamentally different findings emerged to clarify the kind of factors that contributed to the favorable prognosis of the disorder. A long-term follow-up study (15 and 25 years after initial examination) of schizophrenia by WHO in 16 countries is currently under way to gather even more information in addition to the short-term follow-up studies that have been conducted so far (Sartorius et al., 1996).

Based heavily on their clinical experiences and on the results of the surveys on the prognoses of schizophrenia in different settings, scholars have proposed that the course of schizophrenia is highly influenced by the family atmosphere (Vaughn & Leff, 1976a). Based on the concept of expressed emotion (EE), studies have been conducted to explore the attitudes of close relatives toward a mentally ill family member, especially measuring critical and hostile comments and evidence of emotional overinvolvement, such as exaggerated affect and overly self-sacrificing behavior (Karno et al., 1987; Vaughn & Leff, 1976b, Vaughn et al., 1992). Most of the studies have indicated that patients who returned from the hospital to live with relatives who reacted with high expressed emotions toward them relapsed more often than patients whose relatives did not express negative attitudes (Hooley, 1987; Weisman et al., 1993). It was illustrated further that family intervention in the form of family psychoeducation and/or behavioral family therapy was highly effective in reducing families' expressed emotions and improving patients' relapse rates and outcomes (Penn & Mueser, 1996). All this information led to the speculation that cultural factors (through pathoreactive effect) possibly contributed to the outcomes of severe mental patients, such as schizophrenics, based on the attitudes toward mental patients and the reactions toward patients in home settings.

In summary, it may be said that for various psychiatric disorders, culture factors have various ways of contributing to the disorders, through pathogenetic, pathoplastic, pathodiscriminating, pathofacilitating, pathoelaborating, or pathoreactive effects (see Section 1C, How Does Culture Relate to Psychopathology?). In this chapter, various commonly recognized psychiatric disorders are examined primarily from cultural perspectives. Many psychiatric disorders are heavily related to culture factors, while others are less. Among those disorders in the spectrum, major psychiatric disorder as well as organic mental disorder have relatively little direct impact from cultural factors, while culture-related specific syndromes, by definition, have more significant impact from culture.

# REFERENCES

Tseng, W. S. (2001). Culture and psychiatric epidemiology. In W. S. Tseng, *Handbook of cultural psychiatry* (pp. 195–209). San Diego, CA: Academic Press.

Tseng, W. S. (2001). Cross-cultural research. In W. S. Tseng, *Handbook of cultural psychiatry* (pp. 763–777). San Diego, CA: Academic Press.

## A. Anxiety Disorders

Bell, P., Kee, M., Loughrey, G. C., Roddy, R. J., & Curran, P. S. (1988). Posttraumatic stress in Northern Ireland. *Acta Psychiatrica Scandinavica, 77*, 166–169.

Blazer, D. G., Hughes, D., George, L. K., Swartz, M., & Boyer, R. (1991). General anxiety disorder. In L. N. Robins & D. A. Regier (Eds.), *Psychiatric disorder in America: The Epidemiologic Catchment Area Study*. New York: Fress Press.

Block, H. S. (1969). Army clinical psychiatry in the combat zone—1967–1968. *American Journal of Psychiatry, 126*(3), 289–298.

Chemtob, C. M. (1996). Posttraumatic stress disorder, trauma, and culture. In F. Lih Mak & C. C. Nadelson (Eds.), *International review of psychiatry*, Vol. 2, Washington, DC: American Psychiatric Press.

Cooper, J. E., & Sartorius, N. (Eds.). (1996). *Mental disorders in China*. London: Gaskell.

Davidson, J. R. T., Kudler, H. S., Saunders, W. B., & Smith, R. D. (1990). Symptom and comorbidity patterns in World War II and Vietnam veterans with posttraumatic stress disorder. *Comprehensive Psychiatry, 31*(2), 162–170.

Eaton, W. W., Dryman, A., & Weissman, M. M. (1991). Panic and phobia. In L. N. Robins & D. A. Regier (Eds.), *Psychiatric disorder in America: The Epidemiologic Catchment Area Study*. New York: Free Press.

Friedman, M. J. (1981). Post-Vietnam syndrome: Recognition and management. *Psychosomatics, 22*(11), 931–943.

Karno, M., & Golding, J. M. (1991). Obsessive compulsive disorder. In L. N. Robins & D. A. Regier (Eds.), *Psychiatric disorder in America: The Epidemiologic Catchment Area Study*. New York: Free Press.

Kasahara, Y. (1974). Fear of eye-to-eye confrontation among neurotic patients in Japan. In T. S. Lebra & W. P. Lebra (Eds.), *Japanese culture and behavior: Selected readings* (pp. 396–406). Honolulu: University Press of Hawaii.

Kimura, S. (1982). *Nihonjin-no taijinkuofu [Japanese anthrophobia]*. Tokyo: Keiso Book Co. (In Japanese.)

Marsella, A. J., Friedman, M. J., Gerrity, E. T., & Scurfield, R. M. (1996). Ethnocultural aspects of PTSD: Some closing thoughts. In A. J. Marsella, M. J. Friedman, E. T. Gerrity, & R. M. Scurfield

(Eds.), *Ethnocultural aspects of posttraumatic stress disorder: Issues, research, and clinical applications.* Washington, DC: American Psychological Association.

Psychiatric Epidemiological Collaboration Team (1986). Epidemiological survey of neuroses in 12 geographic regions. *Chinese Neuropsychiatric Journal, 19*(2), 87–91. (In Chinese.)

Solomon, Z. (1989). Psychological sequelae of war: A 3-year perspective study of Israeli combat stress reaction casualties. *Journal of Nervous and Mental Disease, 177*(6), 342–346.

Staley, D., & Wand, R. R. (1995). Obsessive-compulsive disorder: A review of the cross-cultural epidemiological literature. *Transcultural Psychiatric Research Review, 32*(2), 103–136.

Stoll, A. L., Tohen, M., & Baldessarini, R. J. (1992). Increasing frequency of the diagnosis of obsessive-compulsive disorder. *American Journal of Psychiatry, 149*(5), 638–640.

Tseng, W. S., Asai, M. H., Kitanish, K. J., McLaughlin, D., & Kyomen, H. (1992). Diagnostic pattern of social phobia: Comparison in Tokyo and Hawaii. *Journal of Nervous and Mental Diseases, 180,* 380–385.

Uchinuma, Y. (1990). *Taijinkyofusho [Disorder of interpersonal relations fear].* Tokyo: Kodansha. (In Japanese.)

Üstün, T. B., & Sartorius, N. (Eds.). (1995). *Mental illness in general health care: An international study.* Chichester: Wiley (on behalf of WHO).

## B. Depression Disorders

Ablon, J. (1971). Bereavement in a Samoan community. *British Journal of Psychology, 44,* 329–337.

Binitie, A. (1975). A factor-analytical study of depression across cultures (African and European). *British Journal of Psychiatry, 127,* 559–563.

El-Islam, M. F. (1969). Depression and guilt: A study at an Arab psychiatric clinic. *Social Psychiatry, 4,* 56–58.

Fernando, S. J. M. (1975). A cross-cultural study of some familial and social factors in depressive illness. *British Journal of Psychiatry, 127,* 46–53.

Gobar, A. H. (1970). Suicide in Afghanistan. *British Journal of Psychiatry, 116,* 493–496.

Marsella, A. J., Sartorius, N., Jablensky, A., & Fenton, F. R. (1985). Cross-cultural studies of depressive disorders: An overview. In A. Kleinman & B. Good (Eds.), *Culture and depression: Studies in the anthropology and cross-cultural psychiatry of affect and disorder* (pp. 299–324). Berkeley: University of California Press.

Murphy, H. B. M., Wittkower, E. D., & Chance, N. (1967). Crosscultural inquiry into the symptomatology of depression: A preliminary report. *International Journal of Psychiatry, 3*(1), 6–22.

Pfeiffer, W. (1968). The symptomatology of depression viewed transculturally. *Transcultural Psychiatric Research Review, 5,* 121–124.

Prince, R. (1968). The changing picture of depressive syndromes in Africa: Is it fact or diagnostic fashion? *Canadian Journal of African Studies, 1,* 177–192.

Sartorius, N. (1975). Epidemiology of depression. *WHO Chronicle, 29,* 423–427.

Sartorius, N., Davidian, H., Ernberg, G., Fenton, F. R., Jujii, I., Gastpar, M., Guibinat, W., Jablensky, A., Kielholz, P., Lehmann, H. E., Naraghi, M., Shimizu, M., Shinfuku, N., & Takahashi, R. (1983). *Depressive disorders in different cultures: Report on the WHO collaborative study on standardized assessment of depressive disorders.* Geneva: World Health Organization.

Simon, G. E., von Korff, M., Piccinelli, M., Fullerton, C., & Ormel, J. (1999). An international study of the relation between somatic symptoms and depression. *New England Journal of Medicine, 341*(18), 1329–1335.

Tanaka-Matsumi, J., & Marsella, A. J. (1976). Cross-cultural variations in the phenomenological experiences of depression: I. Word association studies. *Journal of Cross-Cultural Psychology, 7,* 379–396.

Waziri, R. (1973). Symptomatology of depressive illness in Afghanistan. *American Journal of Psychiatry, 130,* 213–217.

## C. Dissociation, Possession Disorders, and Hysteria

Adityanjee Raju, G. S. P., & Khandelwal, S. K. (1989). Current status of multiple personality disorder in India. *American Journal of Psychiatry, 146*(12), 1607–1610.

Bourguignon, E. (Ed.). (1973). *Religion, altered states of consciousness, and social change.* Columbus: Ohio State University Press.

Bourguignon, E. (1976). Possession and trance in cross-cultural studies of mental health. In W. P. Lebra (Ed.), *Culture-bound syndromes, ethnopsychiatry, and alternate therapies.* Honolulu: University Press of Hawaii.

Dube, K. C. (1970). A study of prevalence and biosocial variables in mental illness in a rural and an urban community in Uttar Pradesh, India. *Acta Psychiatrica Scandinavica, 46,* 327–359.

Epidemic Survey Collaboratory Teams (1986). Epidemic survey of neurotic disorders in 12 geographic areas. *Chinese Neuropsychiatric Journal, 19,* 87–91.

Greaves, G. B. (1980). Multiple personality disorder: 165 years after Mary Reynolds. *Journal of Nervous and Mental Disease, 168,* 577–596.

Kitanish, K. (1993). Possession phenomena in Japan. In *Possession phenomena in East Asia.* Proceedings of the Fourth Cultural Psychiatry Symposium. Seoul: East Asian Academy of Cultural Psychiatry.

Nandi, D. N., Banerjee, G., Nadi, S., & Nandi, P. (1992). Is hysteria on the wane? *British Journal of Psychiatry, 160,* 87–91.

Prince, R. (Ed.). (1968). Trance and possession states. Proceedings of Second Annual Conference. Montreal: R.M. Bucke Memorial Society.

Ross, C. A. (1991). Epidemiology of multiple personality disorder and dissociation. *Psychiatric Clinics of North America, 14*(3), 503–517.

Suwanlert, S. (1976). *Phii pob*: Spirit possession in rural Thailand. In W. P. Lebra (Ed.), *Culture-bound syndromes, ethnopsychiatry, and alternate therapies* (pp. 68–87). Honolulu: University Press of Hawaii.

Takahashi, Y. (1990). Is multiple personality really rare in Japan? *Dissociation, 3*(2), 57–59.

Tseng, W. S. (2001). Dissociation, possession, and hysteria. In W. S. Tseng, *Handbook of cultural psychiatry* (pp. 317–334). San Diego: Academic Press.

Vieth, I. (1965). *Hysteria: The history of a disease.* Chicago: University of Chicago Press.

Ward, C. A. (Ed.). (1989). *Culture and altered states of consciousness.* Beverly Hills, CA: Sage.

Wen, J. K. (1996). Possession phenomena and psychothreapy. In W. S. Tseng (Ed.), *Chinese mind and therapy* (pp. 295–330). Taipei: Laureate Publisher. (In Chinese.)

Zhang, X. F. (1992). A report of 32 cases with hysteria involved in homicide. *Chinese Mental Health Journal, 6*(4), 175–176. (In Chinese.)

## D. Somatoform Disorders, Including Neurasthenia

Barsky, A. J., & Klerman, G. L. (1983). Overview: Hypochondriasis, bodily complaints, and somatic styles. *American Journal of Psychiatry, 140*(3), 273–283.

Beard, G. M. (1880). *A practical treatise on nervous exhaustion (neurasthenia), its symptoms, nature, sequences, treatment.* New York: William Wood.

Canino, I. A., Rubio-Stipec, M., Canino, G., & Escobar, J. I. (1992). Functional somatic symptoms: A cross-ethnic comparison. *American Journal of Orthopsychiatry, 62,* 605–612.

Gabbard, G. O. (1995). Psychoanalysis. In H. I. Kaplan & B. J. Sadock (Eds.), *Comprehensive textbook of psychiatry/VI,* (Vol.1). Baltimore: Williams & Wilkins.

Goldberg, D., & Huxley, P. (1980). *Mental illness in community.* London: Tavistock.

Hes, J. P. (1958). Hypochondriasis in Oriental Jewish immigrants: A preliminary report. *International Journal of Social Psychiatry, 44,* 18–23.

Isaac, M., Janca, A., & Orley, J. (1996). Somatization—A culture-bound or universal syndrome? *Journal of Mental Health, 5*, 219–222.

Kirmayer, L. J. (1984). Culture, affect and somatization. *Transcultural Psychiatric Research Review, 21,* 159–188.

Kirmayer, L. J. (1988). Mind and body as metaphors: Hidden values in biomedicine. In M. Lock & D. R. Gordon (Eds.), *Biomedicine examined.* Boston: Kluwer Academic Publishers.

Kirmayer, L. J., & Robbins, J. M. (1996). Patients who somatize in primary care: A longitudinal study of cognitive and social characteristics. *Psychological Medicine, 26,* 937–951.

Koss, J. D. (1990). Somatization and somatic complaint syndromes among Hispanics: Overview and ethnopsychological perspectives. *Transcultural Psychiatric Research Review, 27*(1), 5–29.

Prince, R. (1990). Somatic complaint syndromes and depression: The problems of cultural effects on symptomatology. Paper presented to the spring convention of the Korean Neuropsychiatric Association, Seoul, Korea, 1989. (Reviewed in *Transcultural Psychiatric Research Review, 27*(1), 31–36, 1990).

Racy, J. (1980). Somatization in Saudi women: A therapeutic challenge. *British Journal of Psychiatry, 137,* 212–216.

Streltzer, J. (1997). Pain. In W. S. Tseng & J. Streltzer (Eds.), *Culture and psychopathology* (pp. 87–100). New York: Brunner/Mazel.

Streltzer, J., & Wade, T. C. (1981). The influence of cultural group in the undertreatment of postoperative pain. *Psychosomatic Medicine, 43,* 397–403.

Tseng, W. S. (1975). The nature of somatic complaints among psychiatric patients: The Chinese case. *Comprehensive Psychiatry, 16*(3), 237–245.

Üstün, T. B., & Sartorius, N. (Eds.). (1995). *Mental illness in general health care: An international study.* Chichester: Wiley (on behalf of WHO).

Ware, N. C., & Kleinman, A. (1992). Culture and somatic experience: The social course of illness in neurasthenia and chronic fatigue syndrome. *Psychosomatic Medicine, 54*(5), 546–560.

Wessely, S. (1994). Neurasthenia and chronic fatigue: Theory and practice in Britain and America. *Transcultural Psychiatric Research Review, 31*(2), 173–209.

Woodrow, K. M., Friedman, G. D., Siegelaub, A. B., & Collen, M. F. (1972). Pain tolerance: Differences according to age, sex and race. *Psychosomatic Medicine, 34*(6), 548–556.

Zborowski, M. (1952). Cultural components in responses to pain. *Journal of Social Issues, 8,* 16–30.

Zheng, Y. P., Lin, K. M., Takeuchi, D., Kurasaki, K. S., Wang, Y., & Cheung, F. (1997). An epidemiological study of neurasthenia in Chinese-American in Los Angeles. *Comprehensive Psychiatry, 38*(5), 249–259.

# E. Alcohol-Related Problems

Acuda, S. W. (1985). International review series: Alcohol and alcohol problem research. I: East Africa. *British Journal of Addiction, 80*(2), 121–126.

Almeida Filho, N., Mari, J. J., Coutinho, E., Franca, F. F., Fernandes, J. G., Andreoli, S. B., & Busnello, E. D. (1992). Estudo muticentrico de morbidade Psyquiátrica em areas Unbans brasiliaras (Brasilia, Sâo Paulo, Porto Alegre). *Revista de ABP-APAL, 14,* 93–104.

Bales, R. F. (1949). Cultural differences in rates of alcoholism. *Quarterly Journal of Studies on Alcohol, 6,* 480–499.

Bennett, L. A., Janca, A., Grant, B. F., & Sartorius, N. (1993). Boundaries between normal and pathological drinking: A cross-cultural comparison. *Alcohol Health & Research World, 17*(3), 190–195.

Bonfiglio, G., Falli, S., & Pacini, A. (1977). Alcoholism in Italy: An outline highlighting some special features. *British Journal of Addiction, 72,* 3–12.

Brod, T. M. (1975). Alcoholism as a mental health problem of Native Americans: A review of the literature. *Archives of General Psychiatry, 32,* 1385–1391.

Caetano, R. (1984). Manifestations of alcohol problems in Latin America: A review. *Bulletin of the Pan American Health Organization, 18*(3), 258–280.

Caetano, R., & Carlini-Cotrim, B. (1993). Perspectives on alcohol epidemiology research in South America. *Alcohol Health & Research World, 17*(3), 244–250.

Defour, M. C. (1995). Twenty-five years of alcohol epidemiology: Trends, technique, and transitions. *Alcohol Health & Research World, 19*(1), 77–84.

Dorman, N. D., & Towle, L. (1991). Initiatives to curb alcohol abuse and alcoholism in the former Soviet Union. *Alcohol Health & Research World, 15*(4), 303–306.

Group for the Advancement of Psychiatry (GAP) (1996). *Alcoholism in the United States.* (Formulated by the Committee on Cultural Psychiatry) Report No. 141. Washington, DC: American Psychiatric Association.

Gureje, O., Mavreas, V., Vazquez-Barquero, J. L., & Janca, A. (1997). Problems related to alcohol use: A cross-cultural perspective. *Culture, Medicine and Psychiatry, 21*, 199–211.

Haworth, A. (1993). A perspective on alcohol studies in Africa. *Alcohol Health & Research World, 17*(3), 242–243.

Helzer, J. E., Burnam, A., & McEvoy, L. T. (1991). Alcohol abuse and dependence. In L. N. Robins & D. A. Regier (Eds.), *Psychiatric disorders in America: The Epidemiologic Catchment Area Study.* New York: Free Press.

Hwu, H. G., Chen, C. C., & Yeh, E. K. (1995). Alcoholism in Taiwan: The Chinese and aborigines. In T. Y. Lin, W. S. Tseng & E. K. Yeh (Eds.), *Chinese societies and mental health* (pp. 181–196). Hong Kong: Oxford University Press.

Kim, K. I. (1990). Alcoholic disorder in Korea. *Mental Health Research, 9*, 131–147.

Kim. K. I. (1993). Drinking behavior in Korea. In *Culture and alcoholism.* Proceeding of the Seminar on the Prevention and Treatment of Alcoholism. Seoul, Korea: Yonsei University and World Health Organization, Department of Psychiatry.

Lin, T. Y. (1953). An epidemiological study of the incidence of mental disorder in Chinese and other cultures. *Psychiatry, 16*, 313–336.

Mackay, J. (1993). *The state of health atlas.* New York: Simon & Schuster.

Ministry of Health and Welfare (1996). *Annual report of mental health.* Tokyo: Ministry of Health and Welfare.

Ministry of Health and Welfare (1997). *Annual statistics of health and welfare,* Seoul: Ministry of Health and Welfare.

Moore, R. A. (1964). Alcoholism in Japan. *Quarterly Journal of Studies on Alcohol. 25*, 142–150.

Negrete, J. C. (1976). Alcoholism in Latin America. *Annuals of the New York Academy of Sciences, 273*, 9–23.

Shen, Y. C. (1987). Recent epidemiological data of alcoholism in China. *Chinese Mental Health Journal, 6*, 251–256. (in Chinese).

Statistical Abstract of the United States (1997). Washington, DC: Bureau of the Census.

Westermeyer, J. (1988). The pursuit of intoxication: Our 100 century-old romance with psychoactive substances. *American Journal of Drug and Alcohol Abuse, 14*, 175–187.

Yamamuro, B. (1973). Alcoholism in Tokyo. *Quaterly Journal of Studies on Alcohol, 34*, 950–954.

## F. Other Substance Abuse

Abiodun, O. A. (1991). Drug abuse and its clinical implications with reference to Nigeria. *Central African Journal of Medicine, 37*, 24–30.

Anthony, J. C., & Helzer, J. E. (1995). Epidemiology of drug dependence. In M. T. Tsuang, M. Tohen, & G. E. P. Zahner (Eds.), *Textbook in psychiatric epidemiology* (pp. 361–406). New York: Wiley-Liss.

Davoli, M., Perucci, C. A., Rapiti E., Bargagli, A. M., D'lppoliti, D., Forastiere, F., & Abeni, D. (1997). A persistent rise in mortality among injection drug users in Rome, 1980 through 1992. *American Journal of Public Health, 87*, 851–853.

Fields, A., & Tararin, P. A. (1970). Opium in China. *British Journal of Addiction. 64*, 371–382.

Hemmi, T. (1974). Sociopsychiatric study of drug abuse in Japan. In Proceedings of the Fifth World Congress of Psychiatry. Mexico, D.F.: World Pasychiatric Association.

Kaplan, J. (1983). *The hardest drug: Heroin and public policy*. Chicago: University of Chicago Press.

Kato, M. (1990). Brief history of control, prevention and treatment of drug dependence in Japan. *Drug and Alcohol Dependence, 25*, 213–214.

Lowinger, P. (1973). How the People's Republic of China solve the drug abuse problem. *American Journal of Chinese Medicine, 1*(2), 275–282.

National Institute on Drug Abuse (1995). *Drug use among racial/ethnic minorities*. Rockville, MD: National Institute of Health.

Rouse, B. A. (1991). Trends in cocaine use in the general population. In S. Schober & C. Schade (Eds.), *The epidemiology of cocaine use and abuse*. NIDA Research Monograph 110 (DHHS Publication No. ADM 91-1787). Rockville, MD: U.S. Department of Health and Human Service.

Smart, R., Murray, G. F., & Arif, A. (1988). Drug abuse and prevention programs in 29 countries. *International Journal of the Addictions, 23*, 1–17.

Trimble, J. E., Bolek, C. S., & Niemcryk, S. J. (Eds.). (1992). *Ethnic and multicultural drug abuse: Perspective on current research*. New York: Harrington Park Press.

Tseng, W. S., Ebata, K., Kim, K. I., Krahl, W., Kua, E. K., Lu, Q. Y., Shen, Y. C., Tan, E. S., & Yang, M. J. (2001). Mental health in Asia: Social improvement and challenges. *International Journal of Social Psychiatry, 47*(1), 8–23.

U.S. Department of Health and Human Services (USDHHS). (1991). *Drug abuse and drug abuse research*. The third triennial report to Congress from the Secretary, Department of Health and Human Service (DHHS Publication No. ADM 91-1704). Rockville, MD: USDHHS.

U.S. Department of Health and Human Services (USDHHS). (1997). *National household survey on drug abuse: Main findings 1995*. Washington, DC: USDHHS.

Westermeyer, J. (1971). Use of alcohol and opium by the Meo of Laos. *American Journal of Psychiatry, 127*, 1019–1023.

Westermeyer, J. (1974). Opium smoking in Laos: A survey of 40 addicts. *American Journal of Psychiatry, 131*, 165–170.

Westermeyer, J. (1987). Cultural patterns of drug and alcohol use: An analysis of host and agent in the cultural environment. *United Nations Bulletin of Narcotics, 39*, 11–27.

Westermeyer, J. (1999). Cross-cultural aspects of substance abuse. In M. Galanter & H. D. Kleber (Eds.), *Textbook of substance abuse treatment* (pp. 75–85). Washington, DC: American Psychiatric Press, Inc.

## G. Eating Problems

Chen, D. G., Cheng, X. F., & Wang, L. L. (1993). Clinical analysis of 200 cases of child anorexia. *Chinese Mental Health Journal, 7*(1), 5–6. (In Chinese.)

DiNichola, V. F. (1990). Anorexia multiform: Self-starvation in historical and cultural context, Part II: Anorexia nervosa as a culture-reactive syndrome. *Transcultural Psychiatric Research Review, 27*, 245–286.

Garner, D. M., & Garfinkel, P. E. (1979). The eating attitude test: An index of the symptoms of anorexia nervosa. *Psychological Medicine, 9*, 273–279.

Garner, D. M., Olmsted, M. P., & Polivy, J. (1983). Development and validation of a multidimensional eating disorder inventory for anorexia nervosa and bulimia. *International Journal of Eating Disorders, 2*, 15–34.

Habermas, T. (1991). The role of psychiatric and medical traditions in the discovery and description of anorexia nervosa in France, Germany, and Italy, 1873–1918. *Journal of Nervous and Mental Disease, 179*(6), 360–365.

Hsu, L. K. G., & Lee, S. (1993). Is weight phobia always necessary for a diagnosis of anorexia nervosa? *American Journal of Psychiatry, 150*(10), 1466–1471.

Hsu, L. K. G., & Sobkiewicz, T. A. (1991). Body image disturbance: Time to abandon the concept for eating disorder? *International Journal of Eating Disorders, 10*(1), 15–30.

Iancu, I., Spivak, B., Ratzoni, G., Apter, A., & Weizman, A. (1994). The sociocultural theory in the development of anorexia nervosa. *Psychopathology, 27*, 29–36.

Khandelwal, S. K., Sharan, P., & Saxena, S. (1995). Eating disorders: An Indian perspective. *International Journal of Social Psychiatry, 41*(2), 132–146.

King, M. B., & Bhugra, D. (1989). Eating disorders: Lessons from a cross-cultural study. *Psychological Medicine, 19*, 955–958.

Lee, S., Ho, T. P., and Hsu, L. K. G. (1993). Fat phobic and non-fat phobic anorexia nervosa—A comparative study of 70 Chinese patients in Hong Kong. *Psychological Medicine, 23*, 999–1017.

Littlewood, R., & Lipsedge, M. (1987). The butterfly and the serpent: Culture, psychopathology and biomedicine. *Culture, Medicine, and Psychiatry, 11*(3), 289–335.

Mumford, D. B., Whitehouse, A. M., & Choudry, I. Y. (1992). Survey of eating disorders in English-medium schools in Lahore, Pakistan. *International Journal of Eating Disorders, 11*(2), 173–184.

Nasser, M. (1986). Comparative study of the prevalence of abnormal eating attitudes among Arab female students of both London and Cairo Universities. *Psychological Medicine, 16*, 621–625.

Nogami, Y., & Yabana, F. (1977). On *kibarashi-gui* (binge eating). *Folia Psychiatrica et Neurologica Japonica, 31*(2), 159–166.

Smith, J. E., & Krejci, J. (1991). Minorities join the majority: Eating disturbances among Hispanic and native American youth. *International Journal of Eating Disorders, 10*(2), 179–186.

Smith, M., & Thelen, M. H. (1984). Development and validation of a test for bulimia. *Journal of Consulting and Clinical Psychology, 52*, 863–872.

Song, Y. H., & Fang, Y. Q. (1990). Clinical report on nine anorexia nervosa cases. *Chinese Mental Health Journal, 4*(1), 24–25. (In Chinese.)

Szmukler, G. I. (1985). The epidemiology of anorexia nervosa and bulimia. *Journal of Psychiatric Research, 19*, 143–153.

Walsh, B. T. (1997). Eating disorders. In A. Tasman, J. Kay, & J. A. Lieberman (Eds.), *Psychiatry (Vol. 2)* (pp. 1202–1290). Philadelphia: Saunders.

Willi, J., Giacometti, G., & Limacher, B. (1990). Update on the epidemiology of anorexia nervousa in a defined region of Switzerland. *American Journal of Psychiatry, 147*(11), 1514–1517.

Willi, J., & Grossman, S. (1983). Epidemiology of anorexia nervosa in a defined region of Switzerland. *American Journal of Psychiatry, 140*, 564–567.

Zhang, F. C., Mitchell, J. E., Kuang, L., Wang, M. Y., Yang, D. L., Zheng, J., Zhau, Y. R., Zhang, Z. H., Filice, G. A., Pomeroy, C., & Pyle, R. L. (1992). The prevalence of anorexia nervosa and bulimia nervosa among freshman medical college students in China. *International Journal of Eating Disorders, 12*(2), 209–214.

# H. Suicide Behavior

Asuni, T. (1962). Suicide in Western Nigeria. *British Medical Journal, 2*, 1091–1097.

The Bureau of Statistics (1998). *Annual Statistics of Death and Its Cause 1998*. Seoul, Korea.

Canetto, S. S., & Lester, D. (1998). Gender, culture, and suicidal behavior. *Transcultural Psychiatry, 35*(2), 163–190.

Chong, M.Y., & Cheng, T. A. (1995). Suicidal behavior deserved in Taiwan: Trends over four decades. In T.Y. Lin, W. S. Tseng, E. K.Yeh (Eds.), Chinese societies and mental health (pp. 209–218). Hong Kong: Oxford University Press.

Chong, M. Y., Yeh, E. K., & Wen, J. K. (1992) Suicidal behaviour in Taiwan. In L. P. Kok & W. S. Tseng (Eds.), Suicidal behavior in the Asia-Pacific region (pp. 69–82). Singapore: Singapore University.

Fallers, L. A., & Fallers, M. C. (1960). Homicide and suicide in Busoga. In P. Bohannan (Ed.), African homicide and suicide. Princeton, NJ: Princeton University Press.

Farberow, N. L. (Ed.). (1975). Suicide in different cultures. Baltimore: University Park Press.

Kok, L. P. (1992). Suicidal behavior in Singapore. In L. P. Kok & W. S. Tseng (Eds.), Suicidal behavior in the Asia-Pacific region (pp. 176–198). Singapore: Singapore University

Kok, L. P., & Tseng, W. S. (Eds.). (1992). Suicidal behavior in the Asia-Pacific region. Singapore: Singapore University.

Latha, K. S., Bhat, S. M., & D'Souza, P. (1996). Suicide attempters in a general hospital unit in India: Their socio-demographic and clinical profile—emphasis on cross-cultural aspects. Acta Psychiatrica Scandinavica, 94, 26–30.

Ong, S., & Leng, Y. K. (1992). Suicidal behavior in Kuala Lumpur, Malaysia. In L. P. Kok & W. S. Tseng (Eds.). Suicidal behavior in the Asia-Pacific Region (pp. 144–175). Singapore: Singapore University.

Pritchard, C. (1996). Suicide in the People's Republic of China categorized by age and gender: Evidence of the influence of culture on suicide. Acta Psychiatrica Scandinavica, 93, 362–367.

Ruzicka, L. T. (1976). II. Special subject: Suicide, 1950 to 1971. World Health Statistic Report, 29(7), 396–413.

Tseng, W. S. (2001). Suicidal behavior. In W. S. Tseng, Handbook of cultural psychiatry (pp. 375–396). San Diego: Academic Press.

Tseng, W. S., Ebata, K., Kim, K. I., Karahl, W., Kua, E. H., Lu, Q. Y., Shen, Y. C., Tan, E. S., & Yang, M. J. (2001). Mental health in Asia: Social improvement and challenges. International Journal of Social Psychiatry, 47(1), 8–23.

Tseng, W. S., & Kok, L. P. (1992). Conclusion: Comparison of reports from Asia and the Pacific. In L. P. Kok & W. S. Tseng (Eds.), Suicidal behavior in the Asia-Pacific region (pp. 249–265). Singapore: Singapore University Press.

Weissman, M. M. (1974). The epidemiology of suicide attempts 1960 to 1971. Archives of General Psychiatry, 30, 737–746.

World Health Organization (WHO). (1973). Epidemiological and vital statistics report: Mortality from suicide 1950–1969. Genè: WHO.

World Health Organization (WHO). (1976). World Health Statistics Report: II. Special Subject: Suicide, 1950 to 1971 (p. 404). Vol. 29, No. 7. Geneva: WHO.

World Health Organization (WHO). (1993). 1992 World Health Statistics Annual. Geneva: WHO.

Yeh, E. K. (1985). Sociocultural changes and prevalence of mental disorders in Taiwan. In W. S. Tseng & D. Y. H. Wu (Eds.), Chinese culture and mental health (pp. 265–286). Orlando, FL: Academic Press.

Yoshimatsu, K. (1992). Suicidal behaviour in Japan. In L. P. Kok & W. S. Tseng, (Eds.). Suicidal behavior in the Asia-Pacific region (pp. 15–40). Singapore: Singapore University Press.

## I. Personality Disorders

Alarcón, R. D., Foulks, E. F., & Vakkur, M. (1998). Personality disorders and culture: Clinical and conceptual interactions. New York: Wiley.

Alarcón, R., & Foulks, E. (1995). Personality disorders and culture: Contemporary clinical views, Part A. Cultural Diversity and Mental Health, 1, 3–17.

Foulks, E. F. (1996). Culture and personality disorders. In J. E. Mezzich, A. Kleinman, H. Fabrega, Jr., & D. L. Parron (Eds.). *Culture and psychiatric diagnosis: A DSM-IV perspective.* Washington, DC: American Psychiatric Press, Inc.

Haslam, N. (1997). Personality disorders as social categories. *Transcultural Psychiatry, 34*(4), 473–479.

Kosson, D. S., Smith, S. S., & Newman, J. P. (1990). Evaluating the construct validity of psychopathy in Black and White male inmates: Three preliminary studies. *Journal of Abnormal Psychology, 99*(3), 250–259.

Kroll, J., Carley, K., & Sines, L. (1982). Are there borderlines in Britain? *Archives of General Psychiatry, 39,* 60–63.

Lopez, S. R. (1989). Patient variable biases in clinical judgement: Conceptual overview and methodological considerations. *Psychological Bulletin, 106,* 184–203.

Moriya, N., Miyake, Y., Minakawa, K., Ikuta, N., & Nishizono-Maher, A. (1993). Diagnosis and clinical features of borderline personality disorder in the East and West: A preliminary report. *Comprehensive Psychiatry, 34,* 418–423.

Paris, J. (1996). Cultural factors in the emergence of borderline pathology. *Psychiatry, 59,* 185–192.

Paris, J. (1997). Social factors in personality disorders. *Transcultural Psychiatry, 34*(4), 421–452.

Robins, L. N., Tipp, J., & Pryzbeck, T. (1991). Antisocial personality. In L. N. Robins & D. A. Rogers (Eds.), *Psychiatric disorders in America: The Epidemiologic Catchment Area Study.* New York: Free Press.

## J. Sexual Disorders

Castillo, R. J. (1997). Sexual and gender identity disorders. In: *Culture and mental illness: A client-centered approach* (pp. 113–147). Pacific Grove, CA: Brooks/Cole.

Heiman, E. M., & Le, C. V. (1975). Transsexualism in Vietnam. *Archives of Sexual Behavior. 4*(1), 89–95.

Ho, P. S. (1995). Male homosexual identity in Hong Kong: A social construction. *Journal of Homosexuality, 29*(1), 71–88.

Marshall, D. S. (1993). Sexual aspects of the life cycle. In D. N. Suggs & A. W. Miracle (Eds.), *Culture and human sexuality* (pp. 240–261). Pacific Grove, CA: Brooks/Cole.

Messenger, J. C. (1993). Sex and repression in an Irish folk community. In D. N. Suggs & A. W. Miracle (Eds.), *Culture and human sexuality* (pp. 240–261). Pacific Grove, CA: Brooks/Cole.

Tsoi, Y. F., & Kok, L. P. (1995). Mental disorders in Singapore. In T. Y. Lin, W. S. Tseng, & E. K. Yeh (Eds.), *Chinese societies and mental health* (pp. 266–278). Hong Kong: Oxford University Press.

Tsoi, Y. F., Kok, L. P., & Long, F. Y. (1977). Male transsexualism in Singapore: A description of 56 cases. *British Journal of Psychiatry, 131*: 405–409.

## K. Schizophrenic Disorder

Hollingshead, A. B., & Redlich, F. C. (1958). *Social class and mental illness: A community study.* New York: Wiley.

Hooley, J. M. (1987). The nature and origins of expressed emotion. In K. Hahlweg & M. Goldstein (Eds.), *Understanding major mental disorder: The contribution of family interaction research.* New York: Family Process.

Leff, J., Sartorius, N., Jablensky, A., Korten, A., & Ernberg, G. (1992). The International Pilot Study of Schizophrenia: Five-year follow-up findings. *Psychological Medicine, 22,* 131–145.

Lin, T. Y., Rin, H., Yeh, E. K., Hsu, C. C., & Chu, H. M. (1969). Mental disorders in Taiwan, fifteen years later: A preliminary report. In W. Caudil & T. Y. Lin (Eds.), *Mental health research in Asia and the Pacific* (pp. 66–91). Honolulu: East-West Center Press.

Jablensky, A., Sartorius, N., Ernberg, G., Anker, M., Korten, A., Cooper, J. E., Day, R., & Bertelsen, A. (1991). *Schizophrenia: Manifestations, incidence and course in different cultures: A World Health Organization ten-country study*. (Psychological Medicine, Monograph Supplement No. 20). Cambridge: Cambridge University Press.

Karno, M., Jenkins, J. H., De La Selva, A., Santana, F., Telles, C., Lopes, S., & Mintz, J. (1987). Expressed emotion and schizophrenia outcome among Mexican-American families. *Journal of Nervous and Mental Disease, 175*(3), 143–151.

Opler, M. K. (1959). Cultural differences in mental disorders: An Italian and Irish contrast in the schizophrenia—U.S.A. In M. K. Opler (Ed.), *Culture and mental health: Cross-cultural studies* (pp. 425–442). New York: Macmillan Company.

Penn, D. L., & Mueser, K. T. (1996). Research update on the psychosocial treatment of schizophrenia. *American Journal of Psychiatry, 153*(5), 607–617.

Regier, D. A., & Kaelber, C. T. (1995). The Epidemiologic Catchment Area (ECA) Program: Studying the prevalence and incidence of psychopathology. In M. T. Tsung, M. Tohen, & G. E. P. Zahner (Eds.), *Textbook in psychiatric epidemiology* (pp. 135–155). New York: Wiley.

Regier, D. A., Myers, J. K., Kramer, M., Robins, L. N., Blazer, D. G., Hough, R. L., Eaton, W. W., & Locke, B. Z. (1984). The NIMH Epidemiologic Catchment Area Program: Historical context, major objectives, and study population characteristics. *Archives of General Psychiatry, 41*, 934–941.

Sartorius, N., Gulbinat, W., Harrison, G., Laska, E., & Siegel, C. (1996). Long-term follow-up of schizophrenia in 16 countries: A description of the International Study of Schizophrenia conducted by the World Health Organization. *Social Psychiatry and Psychiatric Epidemiology, 31*, 249–258.

Sartorius, N., Jablensky, A., Korten, A., Ernberg, G., Anker, M., Cooper, J. E., & Day, R. (1986). Early manifestation and first-contact incidence of schizophrenia in different cultures: A preliminary report on the initial evaluation phase of the WHO Collaborative Study on Determinants of Outcome of Severe Mental Disorders. *Psychological Medicine, 16*, 909–928.

Sartorius, N., Jablensky, A., & Shapiro, R. (1977). Two-year follow-up of the patients included in the WHO International Pilot Study of Schizophrenia. *Psychological Medicine, 7*, 529–541.

Sartorius, N., Jablensky, A., & Shapiro, R. (1978). Cross-cultural differences in the short-term prognosis of schizophrenic psychoses. *Schizophrenia Bulletin, 4*, 102–113.

Vaughn, C., Doyle, M., McConaghy, N., Blaszczynski, A., Fox, A., & Tarrier, N. (1992). The relationship between relatives' expressed emotion and schizophrenic relapse: An Australian replication. *Social Psychiatry and Psychiatric Epidemiology, 27*, 10–15.

Vaughn, C. E., & Leff, J. P. (1976a). The influence of family and social factors on the course of psychiatric illness. *British Journal of Psychiatry, 129*, 125–137.

Vaughn, C. E., & Leff, J. P. (1976b). The measurement of expressed emotion in the families of psychiatric patients. *British Journal of Social and Clinical Psychology, 15*, 157–165.

Weisman, A., Lópes, S. R., Karno, M., & Jenkins, J. (1993). An attributional analysis of expressed emotion in Mexican-American families with schizophrenia. *Journal of Abnormal Psychology, 102*(4), 601–606.

World Health Organization (WHO). (1973). *The international study of schizophrenia*. Geneva: WHO.

# CHAPTER 5

# Culturally Competent Clinical Assessment

## A. THE NEED FOR CULTURAL COMPETENCE

It is becoming common opinion that beyond being "clinically competent," every clinician needs to be "culturally competent." In other words, a psychiatrist needs to be competent in biological psychiatry, psychological psychiatry, and cultural psychiatry to ensure that the whole spectrum of psychiatry is covered in effective clinical work. Cultural competency has recently been suggested as a basic requirement. It is particularly important when clinicians are working in multiple ethnic-cultural societies, providing care for patients of diverse backgrounds. Even in mono-ethnic-cultural societies (such as Japan and Korea in the East or Finland and Poland in the West), when closely examined, there is no difficulty finding many subgroups based on social class differences and geographic differences, minority groups created by social or psychological factors (rather than by ethnicity or race), or the presence of foreigners associated with education, business, diplomatic work, or transient travelers who may need mental health care at one time or another. Associated with the improvement of transportation and increase of migration, many societies are becoming multiethnic. The United States is one example. The diversified populations in society require certainly training in cultural psychiatry for clinicians.

Several basic qualities are required to become a culturally competent clinician, for which training must aim (Foulks, 1980; Lu, Lim & Mezzich, 1995; Moffic, Kendrick, & Reid, 1988; Tseng & Streltzer, 2001; Westermeyer, 1989; Yutrzenka, 1995). These qualities include cultural sensitivity, cultural knowledge, cultural empathy, culture-relevant relations and interaction, and the ability to provide cultural guidance and will be elaborated next.

## 1. Sharpening of Cultural Sensitivity

The clinician needs to have the clinical quality of cultural sensitivity. This is fundamental to being able to appreciate the existence of various lifestyles among human beings, diverse views and attitudes toward patterns of living, different natures of stress encountered, and dissimilar or unique coping patterns utilized for adaptation. Actual experience encountering cultures other than one's own can facilitate and stimulate the development of cultural awareness and sensitivity.

Beyond such awareness, the clinician needs to be perceptive enough to be able to sense cultural differences among people and know how to appreciate them without ignorance, bias, prejudice, or stereotyping. For instance, if a patient complains that his "heart is vacant," another that she is "feeling cold on her back," another that he has "butterflies in the stomach," and another that he has "lost his soul," the clinician needs to develop a cultural curiosity about what the patients are trying to communicate through such sayings. If a mother scratches her baby's body with a coin, causing scars (to deal with sickness), or if a patient wears cloth rings on her wrist (to deal with evil), a culturally sensitive clinician would try to find out whether these actions reflect the patients' own idiosyncratic style or are culturally common and accepted ways of coping with crises. The clinician would further try to find out whether there is any symbolic meaning behind the patients' symptoms and behavior.

The clinician or therapist needs to be willing to communicate and to learn as much as necessary from his patients and their families about their beliefs, attitudes, values systems, and their ways of dealing with problems. It is not merely a matter of sensitive perception but also an attitude of wanting to learn others' lifestyles rather than being trapped in one's own subjective perception and interpretation of others' behavior. Sometimes, we are ignorant in the sense of not knowing that we do not know something. In cultural matters, this is referred to as cultural blindness, not knowing the existence of certain cultural areas and not even being aware of our ignorance. This is common when we encounter very divergent, unfamiliar, foreign cultural systems. If we are culturally sensitive, such cultural ignorance or so-called cultural scotoma is minimized. Being sensitive in our perceptions, maintaining curiosity about differences, being willing to learn and understand the nature of uniqueness, and having an understanding attitude that appreciates cultural differences are all qualities of cultural sensitivity.

## 2. Acquiring Cultural Knowledge

Beyond sensitivity, a clinician needs to have a certain base of cultural knowledge about humankind as a whole and of the particular patient and family concerned. It is difficult even for well-trained professional anthropologists to know about every cultural system. They tend to choose certain cultural areas for their field studies and become knowledgeable about certain cultural systems. Clinicians are not anthropologists and, therefore, it is impossible to expect them to know about all the cultural systems that exist. It is, however, desirable for them to have some basic anthropological knowledge about how human beings vary in their habits, customs, beliefs, value systems, and illness-behavior, in particular. They should know more about the cultural systems of their patients so that culture-relevant assessment and care can be delivered. For instance, it is important to know that Asian people scratch the skin of babies to create scar tissue is an attempt to stir up the yong (fire) element to resist (or counteract) sickness; that a concern with feeling cold is based on the cold-hot theory of sickness, according to which feeling cold on the trunk of the body is a serious sign of losing the yang element; that butterflies in the stomach is an Anglo-Saxon symbol for irritated anxiety; that the loss of soul is a Latin American expression describing an absent mind, loss of will, or emotional instability; and that cloth rings worn around the wrist are Micronesians charms against sickness evil. Such knowledge will help the clinician distinguish between the normality and pathology of behavior from a cultural perspective, extremely useful cultural knowledge in relation to illness behavior.

Reading books and other literature is one way to obtain such cultural information. Consulting with medical anthropologists on general issues or experts on a particular cultural system is another approach. If such material or consultation is not easily available, the patient and his family or friends of the same ethnic-cultural background may be used as resources, even though careful judgment is needed in determining their accuracy or relevance.

## 3. Enhancement of Cultural Empathy

Cognitive information about a patient's culture alone is not sufficient to reach the patient transculturally. There is another quality needed, namely, being able to feel and to understand at an emotional level from the patient's own cultural perspective. Otherwise, a gap in understanding will remain still, and the therapist will be unable to participate in the emotional experience of the patient, an ability that is important to the quality of therapy (Pinderhughes, 1984). This ability is known as cultural empathy, the ability to have empathy in therapeutic situations, with an emphasis on the cultural level.

For example, knowing cognitively that a patient's concern with "feeling cold on her back" or "fearing his penis is shrinking into his abdomen" is related to a hot-cold folk theory is not sufficient. The clinician needs to be able to sense, to feel, and to share the patient's anxiety about his bodily symptoms as matters of life or death, based on the patient's folk beliefs. The symptoms are not merely somatic symptoms derived from folk medical concepts but also critical signs of impending death (from the patient's cultural perspective), as much as if a person were having a heart attack (from the physician's medical perspective). The clinician must show concern, provide comfort, and offer assurance to the patient, as if he were treating a serious condition.

If a parent becomes extremely upset about someone hitting his young child on the head, it is necessary to understand cognitively that the parent is so upset because, according to his folk belief, the head is where the soul is located. A physical examination to rule out the possibility of any head injury is not enough. The clinician also needs to comprehend, feel, and share the parent's fear that the child may lose his soul, a very serious possibility (according to the parent's belief system), much more serious than a severe concussion, in the physician's medical view. Assurance that the soul is intact is the central issue in the care of the parent. Being able to demonstrate empathy for the patient from a cultural perspective is an important quality for the clinician.

## 4. Adjustment of Culturally Relevant Relations and Interactions

In a clinical setting, particularly in a psychotherapeutic situation, the therapist is greatly concerned with maintaining a proper professional relationship with the patient. The aim is to achieve therapeutic effects and minimize any complications or ill effects. The age, gender, and personality of the patient, the nature and severity of the psychopathology, and the purpose of therapy are some of the elements to consider in adjusting patient-therapist relations. As an extension of this, there is a need to incorporate cultural attributes. That is, the relation and interaction between the therapist and the patient need to take into consideration the cultural background of the patient, the therapist, and the setting in which the therapy takes place.

More specifically, it is always necessary to consider the proper relation between an authoritative and a subservient figure and persons of different genders, and whether it is a professional or a social occasion. Such cultural knowledge, in addition to clinical judgment, will lead to a proper therapist-patient relationship and interaction, aimed at both cultural relevancy and therapeutic effect.

Involved here are not only the nature of the relationship between therapist and patient, in terms of role, status, and level of intimacy, but also issues of inter-action, including communication, understanding, and giving and receiving between therapist and patient. A practical example is determining the proper and therapeutic way for a male therapist to relate to a female patient from a culture in which a submissive role and passive behavior is the norm for females. Shall the therapist expect and encourage the female patient to have "good" eye contact with the male therapist, or would that violate the cultural norms of the patient? Is it possible for the therapist to give a "wrong" message to the patient by asking her to maintain direct eye contact with the therapist, or would it serve as a "ther-apeutic" maneuver, encouraging the female patient to be more assertive and relate to males on an equal basis?

What does it mean when a patient keeps saying, "Yes, yes, doctor" to the therapist? Is it the culturally patterned behavior toward an authority figure (the therapist) of a patient from a culture that emphasizes hierarchy? Does saying "yes" merely acknowledge "I am listening" rather than express agreement? For therapeutic purposes, should the therapist encourage the patient to feel comfortable negotiating or even disagreeing with the therapist? These are issues that need careful consideration before action is taken.

The ability to detect, comprehend, and manage ethnic or race-related trans-ference and countertransference is also needed in dealing with patients of dis-tinctly different ethnic or racial backgrounds. This is particularly true when negative and even hostile relations preexist between the ethnicity or racial back-grounds of the patient and the therapist. The same applies to the association of a minority group member and a majority group member when discrimination and an imbalanced power preexist between them. These are issues that signifi-cantly influence the process of therapy. The willingness of the therapist to give careful consideration to these issues, in order to properly manage and make appropriate adjustments to therapy, is important for cultural competence.

Further, it is necessary to pay attention to the ethical aspects of clinical prac-tice, a cultural perspective beyond general clinical consideration. Although the basic principles of medical ethics apply universally and cross-culturally, certain cultural modifications or variations are necessary to adapt to the culture of the patient and the environment in which the clinical care takes place.

## 5. Establishment of Ability for Cultural Guidance

It is important for the therapist to be able to select clinically suitable and cul-turally relevant ways of treatment that will work best for the patient. It is becoming clear among cultural psychiatrists that there are no specific treatment models for particular ethnic groups. There are so many kinds of problems even within one ethnic group that there is a need to apply different therapeutic approaches accordingly. However, a certain therapeutic approach may be better suited to a certain ethnic group depending on that group's understanding of psychiatric service, style of relating to the therapist, and pattern of working on psychological problems. For instance, directive, educational, cognitive therapy is suited better for ethnic people who welcome such an approach, in contrast to an emotion-oriented, analytic approach. Besides, even within the same ethnic group, there are various subgroups that deserve careful evaluation when selecting a therapeutic approach. However, accumulated clinical knowledge on the basic rules and principles needs consideration in the proper selection of a treatment approach to match cultural style as well as therapeutic effect. This is a part of the cultural competence necessary for successful clinical care by every clinician.

Moreover, a clinician needs to be able to make proper judgments on the extent to which and in what way the patient's problems are related to cultural factors and to comprehend dynamically how to provide culturally relevant advice for patients in dealing with their problems. This may involve choice of coping style, ways of dealing with problems, and the ultimate goal of resolving the conflict. Culturally determined norms, values, and goals may need to be challenged and adjusted to treat problems or resolve conflicts. Culturally sanctioned coping mechanisms may need reinforcement, or, if ineffective, to be confronted. Alternatives to culturally defined solutions may need to be proposed. It takes not only clinical judgment but also cultural insight to find relevant and optimal solutions (Tseng & Streltzer, 2001).

For instance, if a young patient is facing the dilemma of establishing his independence to meet contemporary cultural emphasis on the one hand and complying with filial obedience to his parents and following traditional cultural expectations on the other, finding a suitable way to deal delicately with this complicated situation is a challenge in cultural guidance. Another example is finding a way for a woman to strive for self-reliance, either personally or professionally, and still maintain a subordinate status toward her husband to fulfill cultural demands of the husband–wife roles, a delicate matter needing sensitive and proper guidance. It is the task of the clinician to comprehend the whole situation within the biological, medical, psychological, social, and cultural spectrum.

Finally, it is vital to know that psychiatric treatment, particularly psychotherapy, involves the interaction of two value systems, the patient's and the therapist's. Therapeutic interaction provides opportunities for exposure, exchange, and incorporation of differing cultural elements between therapist and patient (Tseng & Hsu, 1979). Cultural insight allows regulation of this core interaction and the overall therapeutic process in a culturally competent manner.

In summary, the basic professional qualities of cultural sensitivity, cultural knowledge, cultural empathy, culturally relevant relations and interaction, and cultural guidance are essential for performing culturally competent clinical work. These qualities are expected in every modern clinician.

## B. CULTURALLY RELEVANT ASSESSMENT AND DIAGNOSIS

In contrast to medical practice, psychiatric work relies heavily on clinical skill to solicit information from the patient for assessment and diagnosis. Soliciting information involves interaction between the clinician and the patient. This interaction is subject to personal factors of the patient (gender, personality, sociocultural background as well as motivation for making complaints, understanding of problems, style of problem presentation) and the psychopathology involved (such as its severity and nature). It is subject also to factors of the therapist (including personality, sociocultural background as well as professional orientation, conceptualization of disorders, perception of pathology, and clinical skill). This interaction is influenced by the clinician–patient relationship itself, which is subject to various factors (such as status assignment, power structure between them), includ-

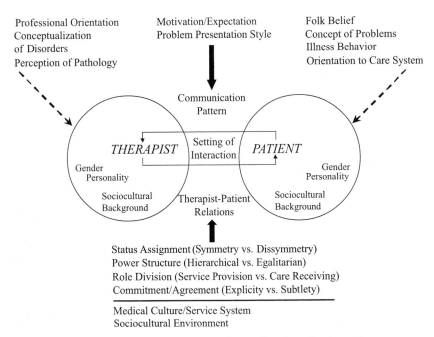

FIGURE 1   Cultural factors that influence therapist-patient interaction.

ing the medical culture and service system in which the interaction takes place (See Figure 1). Naturally, the whole process of clinical assessment is subject to cultural impact (Fabrega, 1987; Rogler, 1993).

## 1. Therapist–Patient Relations

From a clinical point of view, it is crucial to understand and pay attention to the therapist-patient relationship, since it represents the requisite condition for rendering effective healthcare (Fisher & Leigh, 1989). This is particularly true in psychiatric practice, which relies heavily on the face-to-face interaction and relationship between the therapist and the patient. The relationship is itself a therapeutic tool and the outcome of treatment may vary significantly depending on the quality of the relationship. This is particularly true and requires special attention and adjustment when a therapist is going to offer services to a patient with a different cultural background because the relationship between healer and client may vary according to various factors, including cultural attributes.

### a. Cultural Differences in Relations

Reviewing the cultural aspects of the physician-patient relationship, Nilchaikovit, Hill, and Holland (1993) explained the possible differences that may be observed among Asians and Americans. They pointed out that, in America, the predominant form of physician-patient relationship is egalitarian, based on a contractual agreement between the two, influenced heavily by an ideological emphasis on individualism, autonomy, and consumerism. In contrast, in many Asian cultures, the relationship is modeled after the ideal form of hierarchical relationship. The physician is seen as an authority figure who is endowed with knowledge and experience. An ideal doctor should have great virtue and be concerned, caring, and conscientiously responsible for the patient's welfare. In return, the patient must show respect and deference for the physician's authority and suggestions.

Although their comments refer to idealized situations with some overgeneralizations, for the sake of reference, it is useful for clinicians to be aware that such differences exist. As pointed out by Nilchaikovit and colleagues, when an Asian patient is seen by an American physician, some intercultural problems may occur. Particularly when expectations are not fulfilled, the patient does not usually express his feelings and communicate his frustrations. In return, the patient is seen as passive-aggressive and noncompliant by the physician. The treatment is often terminated prematurely and the patient goes "doctor shopping."

---

CASE 1

---

A Filipino Patient Who Kept Replying, "Yes, Doctor!" (Streltzer, 1998)

Filipino patients, following the traditional concept of the "powerful" physician as an almost "almighty" authority figure, tend to relate to physicians, including psychiatrists and psychotherapists, in a subordinate way, demonstrating obedience and shying away from any disagreement. "Yes, doctor!" is the common response given to physicians and psychotherapists. A middle-age Filipino man suffered from hypertension. He came to visit his American internist faithfully for several months, as he was instructed. Medication for hypertension was prescribed and an explanation was given on how to take it. The patient replied, "Yes, doctor!" When there was no response to the medication, the dose was increased, but still there was no favorable response. When the physician asked the patient whether he was taking the medication as prescribed, the patient replied, "Yes, doctor." As the increased dose did not have any effect, another kind of medication was prescribed. After taking the patient's blood pressure, the doctor informed him that there was still no response. The patient replied, "I am sorry, doctor!" Finally, the physician checked with the patient's spouse and found that the patient never took any of the medication that was prescribed. When the patient experienced undesirable side effects, he stopped taking the medication right away, believing that medicine that causes side effects is not good. However, he never mentioned his mistrust of the drug prescribed or any disagreement toward the physician, continuing to give his patterned response of "Yes, doctor!"

---

### b. Therapist-Patient Matching

There is considerably increased concern among mental health workers about the need for therapist-patient matching by ethnicity, race, and cultural background. This concern is very much stimulated by the human rights movement. Although the matching of therapist and patient by ethnicity, race, or cultural background sounds reasonable and desirable, it is not a simple matter. Such matching not only may be impractical, but may also not necessarily guarantee successful therapy clinically, which relies on professional competence reflected in knowledge and experience. It also depends on the therapist's personal ability to establish a positive relationship with and show empathy toward the patient. In other words, while the matching of ethnic or cultural background might be beneficial, without clinical competence, it will not necessarily bring about desirable therapy outcomes. In addition, therapists with the same ethnic or racial backgrounds as their patients may sometimes bring about ill effects. This is particularly true if the patient does not want to reveal his personal background to a therapist with the same background or the therapist does not offer a proper figure for ethnic identification. Ethnic and cultural transference and countertransference need to be considered as well. (These issues will be elaborated further in Section 7A: Intercultural Psychotherapy: Challenges and Competency.)

## 2. Interview and Communication

Psychiatric interview is one of the basic clinical approaches by which a psychiatrist obtains needed information from the patient for the purpose of making diagnosis, understanding the patient's problems, and providing relevant therapy. Thus, communication is one of the major aspects of therapist-patient interaction. How the patient presents complaints and informs the therapist of his problems and how the therapist, reciprocally, listens and provides relevant explanations to the patient are key areas of patient-therapist communication that closely relate to the achievement of meaningful, satisfactory, and effective therapy (Francis, Korsch, & Morris, 1969).

### a. Style of Clinical Interview

(1) **Direct versus Open Style of Inquiry.**    From the standpoint of an ordinary clinical interview for the purpose of assessment and therapy, the clinician is aware that the interview can be carried out in one of two formats (i.e., direct or open style). In the direct style of interview, the interviewer takes a relatively active role, asking certain questions to solicit needed information. The advantage of this style is that it allow the clinician to go through certain areas that need to be covered and obtain information needed for assessment. The downside of this style is that the clinician may miss areas with which the patient is particularly concerned or the patient may present material from a conscious level, with less possibility of exploring the psychic sphere in depth. In contrast, in the open style, the interviewer encourages the patient to present freely any material that he may want to communicate. This allows the interviewer to observe and examine the patient's thinking style and content of thought and concern. The shortcoming of this style is that it is time-consuming and sometimes makes the patient feel uncomfortable, not knowing what is expected. These two basic approach to interviews can be applied alternatively at each session or in different stages in the course of treatment. Generally speaking, a skillful interviewer will know how to apply the direct style at the beginning of a session, allowing time to shift to the open style later in the session.

From a cultural point of view, it is suggested that the interviewer make proper judgments as to what extent the patient is familiar with the psychiatric examination procedure, to provide necessary explanations and assistance, particularly for those who feel unfamiliar with the psychiatric system. The interviewer should utilize an active style in the beginning to obtain basic information needed for assessment of the "disease" but make sure that the patient is given the opportunity to communicate his concerns and problems from the perspective of "illness" (see Section 2E: Illness Behavior: Recognition and Help Seeking). The ability to skillfully adopt these two interview styles is an indication of competence from a clinical as well as a cultural perspective.

(2) **With Family or without Family.**    Another issue that will challenge clinicians, particularly in Western societies, is whether family should be involved in the process of psychiatric examination, assessment, and treatment. In many Eastern societies, based on their cultures, it is considered "natural" to involve the family from the beginning to the end of psychiatric work. It is almost impossible to exclude the family in societies that are very family-oriented (rather than individually oriented). Based on clinical experiences, we know that involvement of the family in an interview sessions has both advantages and disadvantages. Among the advantages are that, as advocated by family therapists, it will relieve the family's anxiety and enable the clinician to obtain needed collateral information right away to assist in the process of assessment, provide an opportunity for the interviewer to observe how the patient and his family interact, and validate what is presented on both sides, making it easier to produce a more accurate assessment and diagnosis. It will definitely increase the quality of care and support from the family in helping the patient recover. Disadvantages are that it may discourage the patient from expressing his personal concerns or communicating individual, private problems in front of the family. This is also true in reverse, making family members hesitant to express their concerns about the patient in front of the patient. Therefore, it is necessary to approach the patient and family separately at some time during the interview process if it is deemed necessary.

From a cultural point of view, it cannot be emphasized too much how important it is to involve the family in the process of assessment and therapy. The family will serve not only as a resource for collateral information but also as a base from which to check cultural reality. Unless a family is suffering from joint or contagious mental disorders (or family psychoses), the interviewer can obtain from the family members (culturally) objective information that indicates to what extent the thoughts and behaviors manifested by the patient are normal, unusual, or deviated from the sociocultural norm. The interviewer also can gain (culturally) useful knowledge or suggestions from the family as to relevant (cultural) choices of coping from which the patient can chose to resolve his problems.

### b. The Patient's Mode of Presenting Initial Complaints

In psychiatric practice, which is similar to medical practice, it is generally expected that the patient will present his (chief) complaint(s) to the therapist.

How a patient presents his cardinal complaints in his initial encounter with the therapist is an interesting subject that deserves attention. The symptoms or problems presented initially may not be the patient's major concerns. They may be merely excuses for the presentation of problems that is expected as part of the initial meeting, or the patient may simply be following a certain custom (or fashion) of complaint presentation. In other words, this may be a socioculturally patterned or stylized presentation of complaints.

Tseng (1975) has elaborated this point with regard to the nature of somatic complaints among Chinese psychiatric patients. Even though nearly 70 percent of the neurotic psychiatric outpatients presented somatic complaints to their psychiatrists during their first visits, careful clinical examination revealed several explanations for this, namely, the influence of the patient's knowledge and concepts about "problems"; the socially recognized and accepted signs of illness; reluctance and resistance to explore emotional problems; and, finally, a hypochondriacal cultural trait among the Chinese. Thus, the patient's mode of complaint presentation needs careful evaluation and understanding, including from a cultural perspective.

### c. Concern Needed for Acquiring Information from the Patient

Although it is desirable for a patient to communicate freely his personal background, history of illness, and other related information to the therapist, this is not always true in clinical situations. The patient's ability to describe things and willingness to communicate are often influenced by his clinical condition, his motivation, and his understanding of the purpose of doing so. In addition, there is a cultural impact on the process of problem communication.

Emotional problems and personal feelings are generally considered highly private matters. As pointed out by Nilchaikovit and colleagues (1993), for people in many cultures, talking about one's inner feelings is about as discreet and commendable as parading nude in public. Family conflicts are often regarded as "inside" problems that should not be revealed to an outsider (Hsu, 1983).

Sex life and sexual problems are often difficult areas to explore. For instance, with the Chinese, the anatomical terms for "penis" or "vagina" should be avoided. They should instead be referred to indirectly as the "yang part" and the "yin part." The Japanese refer to them as "private parts" or "shameful parts" of the body. It is considered blunt to refer explicitly to sexual intercourse between husband and wife. Depending on the culture, many different terms, such as "intimacy between a couple," "business in the (bed)room," and "making a baby," are used by physicians as delicate and sophisticated ways of inferring sexual intercourse.

Further, clinicians should be aware that in some cultures, it is "taboo" to reveal certain things to others. Inquiring about a lady's age may be socially impolite in Western society, as it is considered embarrassing for a lady to disclose her age, while asking about the cause of a parent's death is a breach of a taboo in Micronesia that will invite fear of punishment.

It may be all right for a friend to ask an Asian person how much it cost him to buy a new house or a new car, how much he spent for his children's wedding, and so on, but for Westerners, in general, these are considered private matters. Even when asked by a close friend, such questions would be viewed as impolite intrusions into a person's confidential matters.

### d. Communication through Interpreters

The problems of communication between therapist and patient are highlighted when the therapist and the patient do not share the same language and have to rely on the assistance of interpreters to communicate. Who serves as the interpreter, whether a close family member, a friend, a member of the same ethnic group, or a trained interpreter with mental health knowledge and experience, will affect significantly the process and quality of interpretation. There will be problems of how to translate properly, relevantly, and meaningfully for clinical purposes. The deletion or omission of information, distortion of meaning, exaggeration or addtion of information are some of the problems encountered through interpretation, which needs to be minimized as much as possible (Lee, 1997).

How to select a proper interpreter and utilize the interpreter for the goal of communication with the patient during a psychiatric assessment is a matter of clinical skill and art (Kinzie, 1985; Marcos, 1979; Paniagua, 1998). In general, it is desirable to have an interpreter who has knowledge and experience in mental health work. The interpreter needs orientation, and perhaps training, for the work that is to be done. Basically, there are several different ways to use an interpreter: word-for-word translation is needed, for areas that are delicate and significant; summary translation, for areas that require abstract interpretation; and meaning interpretation, for areas that need elaboration and explanation in addition to translation. By coaching the interpreter in these different styles of interpretation, the process will be more efficient and useful (Westermeyer, 1990) (see Section 7A: Intercultural Psychotherapy: Challenges and Competency).

### e. Issues Relating to Mental Status Examination

**(1) Proper Preparation and Orientation.**    As a part of the initial diagnostic interview, it is expected that a clinician will carry out formal mental status examination (i.e., to examine the patient's state of mind by going through various aspects of mental function including orientation, cognition, perception, affection, intellectual function, etc.). The examination is often carried out in a format that allows a clinical judgment to be achieved by the responses given. However, such a stylized way of examining the status of the mind warrants cultural concern. Patient who are not familiar with such psychiatric mental status examinations will often be confused and puzzled and will react in an unusual way, which may mislead the diagnosis. Careful explanation and guidance are always helpful.

How questions are asked to elicit correct responses is very important. For example, the patient may not understand the question "Do you hear any voices?" as an inquiry into the presence of auditory hallucinations. Instead, he may answer that his hearing ability is intact. This caution is needed for all patients, particularly those who are unfamiliar with psychiatric terms and concepts, and especially those whose cultural backgrounds include few experiences with psychiatric jargon. "How do you feel?" and "Are you depressed?" are other examples that sound so simple in daily English but can be very confusing from the language and conceptual perspectives of those who use language without referring to "feeling" or states of "depression." "Do you feel tired?", "No energy for daily work?", "Lost appetite to eat?", or "No interest in living every day?" may be more suitable questions to ask.

**(2) Cultural Modification of the Examination.**    As a part of the mental status examination, clinicians often ask questions such as "Who is the president of the United States?" to examine the patient's level of social information. This is a proper question to ask if the patient is a citizen of the United States, currently living in the country, with adequate contact with the social environment through news media. However, such a question is irrelevant when it is addressed to a foreigner or someone who hardly ever has access to social media.

Another example is the interpretation of proverbs. In order to examine the patient's thinking process, the clinician routinely asks about his interpretations of certain proverbs. For instance, it is usually asked what people mean when they say "A rolling stone gathers no moss" or "The grass is greener on the other side of the fence." However, it needs to be pointed out that these standardized proverbs have their roots in British language and culture but can be foreign to many non-Westerners who may know more about their own proverbs, such as "Even *kappa* [a legendary animal good at swimming] would drown in the river" (by Japanese) or " After three years, even a dog in school will learn how to bark poems" (by Korean, implying the virtues of persistence and diligence), but be entirely unfamiliar with British proverbs. In other words, proverbs are cultural products and are often difficult to understand across cultures. Some proverbs have the same basic meaning but are expressed in different ways. Proper selection of proverbs to suit the individual patient is very important for a culturally relevant mental status examination.

## 3. Assessment and Diagnosis

To understand the impact of culture on clinical assessment, several basic issues need to be clarified and understood. The clinician needs to comprehend how

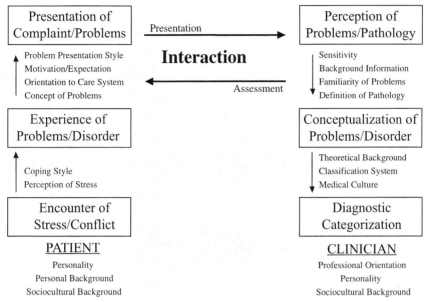

FIGURE 2   Dynamic process of clinical assessment. [From W. S. Tseng, in *Culture and Psychopathology*, New York: Brunner/Mazel, 1997.]

the process of clinical assessment takes place in clinical situations with dynamic natures and how culture play its role in such dynamic process of clinical assessment.

### a. The Dynamic Nature of Psychiatric Evaluation

Psychiatric assessment results from a dynamic process that involves multiple levels of interaction between the patient (and sometimes the patient's family) and the clinician (Tseng, 1997). This process involves a series of steps, as illustrated in Figure 2. It starts with the distress or problems experienced and perceived by the patient and proceeds to the presentation of complaints made by the patient to the clinician. These are perceived and understood as specific types of problems by the clinician. Finally, an assessment, which includes categorization and diagnosis, is made by the clinician of the disorder in question. Thus, it is a process involving different steps or compartments.

**(1) Experience of Problems or Distress (by the Patient).**   This refers to the distress the patient experiences inside of himself. A person experiences "pain" when he is hit; feels "anxious" if he is worried about something, becomes "paranoid" if he suspects that he is being persecuted by others, or has the feeling of going "downhill" if he has lost something significant to him. All these reactions to distress, which may be manifested as symptoms or signs, are subjective, experiential phenomena. They cannot be precisely measured from the outside. It is thus impossible to know to what extent the actual "experience" of distress is influenced by cultural factors.

However, it is clear that sociocultural factors can have an impact on the forerunner of the distress, namely, the stress itself. Stress can be produced by culture in numerous ways. For instance, stress can be generated by culturally demanded performance, cultural restrictions of behavior, or sociocultural discrimination, all of which may provoke distress in the individual (see Section 2A: Culture and Stress).

**(2) Perception of Problems or Disorders by the Patient.**    Following the experience of distress and symptom manifestation, the next step is for the patient to perceive and interpret his distressful experience. How he does this is a psychological phenomenon that is subject to the influence of cultural factors, in addition to other variables, such as the patient's personality, knowledge, and psychological needs.

Based on how the problem is understood and perceived by the patient, he will show a secondary process of various reactions to the distress. For instance, if a person interprets the chest pain he is having as nothing but a chest pain, he will react to it lightly; if he perceives and interprets it as a sign of an impending heart attack, he may become very anxious and even panic, further complicating the primary symptom of the chest pain. In a similar way, if a person believes that shrinking of the penis into the abdomen is fatal, he will react severely to any sign of penis shrinkage, even if his penis never shrinks into his abdomen. If a person does not adhere to such beliefs, he will be impervious to normal changes in his body. In other words, the patient's perception of and reaction to the primary symptoms will add secondary symptoms that compound the clinical picture. The process of forming secondary symptoms is usually subject to cultural influences.

**(3) Presentation of Complaints or Illness by the Patient or His Family.**    The next step is the presentation of the complaints or illness by the patient to others: the process and art of "complaining." Analysis of this process has shown that the way the problem, symptom, or illness is presented or communicated to the clinician is based on the patient's (or his family's) orientation to illness, the meaning of the symptoms, the motivation for help-seeking, and the culturally expected or sanctioned "problem-presenting style." A combination of the results of these factors affects the process of complaining. However, culture definitely plays a clear role in this complaining process.

For instance, patients of certain ethnic groups tend to make somatic complaints to their clinicians in their initial sessions at mental health clinics. This tendency needs careful understanding. There may be several alternative implications, namely, that a physical condition is the patient's primary concern, that somatic symptoms are being used as socially recognized signals of illness, that a culturally sanctioned symptoms are prelude to revealing psychological problems, or that a reflection of hypochondriacal traits are shared by the group (Tseng, 1975). Thus, the nature of the somatic complaint needs to be carefully evaluated and understood rather than simply dealt with or labeled a somatoform disorder.

In the reverse of this situation, a patient from another ethnic background may present many psychological problems to the therapist in the initial session, complaining that, as a small child, he was abused by some adult, never adequately loved by his parents, and is now confused about his own identity, unclear about the meaning of life, and so on. It is necessary for the clinician to determine how much of this psychologized complaint may merely reflect the patient's learned behavior from public communication about patienthood and how much of it is really his primary concern. That is, the performance of complaining or problem presentation is an art that does not directly reflect the distress or problem from which the patient is suffering. A dynamic interpretation and understanding are very necessary (Westermeyer, 1985).

### (4) Perception and Understanding of the Disorder by the Clinician.

A clinician, as a human being, a cultural person, and a professional has his own ways of perceiving and understanding the complaints that are presented by his patients. His psychological sensitivity, cultural awareness, and professional orientation and experience, as well as medical competence, will all act together to influence his assessment of the problems a patient has presented. The cultural background of the clinician is a significant factor and deserves special attention, particularly when he is examining a patient with a different cultural background or one with which the clinician is unfamiliar.

How the clinician's own cultural background affects the clinical assessment was shown in a study of the assessment of parent-child behavior by Japanese and American psychiatrists (Tseng et al., 1982). A series of videotaped family interaction patterns was shown to child psychiatrists in Tokyo and Honolulu. The clinicians in the two cultures reached remarkably different assessment conclusions. In one videotape, a father did not interact with his daughter, leaving this role to his wife. Japanese child psychiatrists tended to view this as "adequate" and "all right" parenting behavior, whereas their American counterparts viewed it as "not involved" and "inadequate" parenting behavior. The main reason for these different assessments was the clinicians' cultural expectations of a father's behavior. For Americans, it is culturally expected that the father, like the mother, interact and be involved with all of his children, whereas the Japanese consider it the mother's job to interact and be involved with the children and not appropriate for the father to engage in this behavior. If a father interacts directly and too much with his daughter, it is considered "inappropriate behavior" in

Japanese culture. This clearly demonstrates that a clinician's value system and cultural beliefs affect his way of making assessments.

It is well recognized that the clinician's style of interviewing, perception of and sensitivity toward pathology, and familiarity with the disorder under examination all influence the interaction between the patient and the clinician, which, in turn, influences the outcome of the clinician's understanding of the disorder. For example, an Asian patient's elaborate idiomatic complaints of suffering due to "weakness of the kidney" (psychosexual problem), "elevated fire in the body or liver" (anger or anxiousness), "loss of soul" (depression or dissociated behavior), "disturbance from a deceased aunt's spirit," and so on may not be fully comprehended with cultural empathy by an American clinician; and the problems of polysubstance abuse or psychosexual problems presented by an American patient may be unfamiliar to an Asian clinician, who is at a loss as to how to relevantly explore and understand the problems.

A clinical study supports the idea that how familiar a clinician is with a patient's pathology will shape the result of his clinical assessment. A group of case vignettes of social phobia was presented to clinicians in Tokyo and Honolulu, for their clinical diagnosis. More than 90% of the Japanese psychiatrists recognized the diagnosis of social phobia, compared to only a small percentage of the American psychiatrists. This illustrates that Japanese psychiatrists, who commonly see social phobia in their clinical work, will give congruent diagnoses of social phobia when such cases are presented to them; whereas American psychiatrists, who are relatively unfamiliar with this condition, will not—they tend to give diagnoses of anxiety disorder, avoidant personality disorder, or others (Tseng et al., 1992).

**(5) Diagnosis and Categorization of the Disorder by the Clinician.** The final step in the process of evaluation is making a clinical diagnosis. Finding the appropriate clinical category for diagnosis is influenced by the professional orientation of the clinician, the classification system used, and the purpose of making the diagnosis (Cooper et al., 1969; Tseng et al., 1992). In many societies, a clinician needs to take into consideration the social impact of diagnostic labeling on the patient and his family when making a clinical diagnosis.

To understand why most of the psychotic inpatients in the United States were diagnosed with schizophrenia, while a much higher percentage of those in the United Kingdom were diagnosed with affective disorders, a clinical investigation was conducted. A videotaped record of a group of (psychotic) patients was presented to psychiatrists in both New York and London. Despite equivalent recognition of symptoms by both British and American psychiatrists, their diagnoses were different. British psychiatrists tended to diagnose affective psychoses in the same patients that American psychiatrists diagnosed schizophrenia (Cooper et al., 1972). At the time of the investigation, American psychiatrists had a broad concept of schizophrenia, whereas British psychiatrists had a more restrictive view.

In sum, making a clinical assessment and diagnosis is a complex matter involving a dynamic process between the help seeker and the help provider. This assessment and diagnostic process is influenced in a variety of ways by the cultural background of the *patient*, as well as that of the *clinician*. The clinician should be aware of how cultural factors will affect each step in the process of interaction between him and the patient.

As emphasized by Mezzich, Kleinman, Fabrega, and Parron (1996b), culture is involved in psychiatric assessment in different ways, including shaping the phenomenology of clinical manifestations; providing the matrix for the interpersonal situation of the diagnostic interview, which involves the transcultural process between clinicians and patient; influencing diagnostic rationales and practices regarding group symptoms; and impacting the overall conceptualization of the diagnostic system.

### b. Definition of Normality and Pathology

To assess the influence of culture on psychopathology, one must take into account the operating definition of normality versus pathology, as the distinction between normal and abnormal where certain psychopathologies are concerned may vary greatly in different cultures. Clinically, as pointed out by Offer and Sabshin (1974), there are four ways to distinguish normality from pathology. They are by professional definition, deviation from the mean, assessment of function, and social definition.

**(1) By Professional Definition.**    This approach takes the view that normality or pathology can be differentiated clearly by the nature of the phenomenon itself and a judgment can be made on it by professionals. In medicine, bleeding or a bone fracture, by its nature, is judged without doubt to be pathological and requiring medical care. In psychiatry, if a person talks to nonexistent people, claims to hear the voice of a spaceman, or eats his own feces, he will be professionally considered to be suffering from a pathological mental condition. This approach maintains that certain conditions (manifested as signs or symptoms) are absolutely pathological in nature. A diagnosis that is applicable universally, beyond cultural boundaries, can be made on such conditions. Gross organic brain disorders, such as severe dementia, a delirious state, or a severe psychotic condition with pathological thought disorders or disorganized behavior, tend to be easily and without too much doubt diagnosed by experts, even cross-culturally.

**(2) By Deviation from the Mean.**    This approach relies on mathematical measurement and uses a range of deviations from the mean to distinguish between normal and abnormal. For example, hypertension and underweight are medical conditions defined as normal according to certain scales and measurements; a pathological condition is diagnosed when the measurement goes beyond the average range. In psychiatry, the measurement of IQ serves to distinguish normal or subnormal intelligence. The concept of mean is universal, yet the range of mean often needs to be adjusted for different populations. This is true when personality is assessed by questionnaires cross-culturally. The cutting point for defining behavior disorders as measured by questionnaires is another area that requires careful cross-cultural adjustment. Determining what amount of drinking is excessive requires biological, social, and cultural adjustments.

**(3) By Assessment of Function.** This approach considers the effect of thoughts, feelings, or behavior on function. Whether the condition provides (healthy) function or (unhealthy) dysfunction in the individual is the basis for the judgment. Memory disturbance is determined by the extent to which a person can retain information and reproduce it through recollection. If a person living in an urban setting cannot recall the street number of his house or the name of the street where he lives, and, thus, does not know how to return home, he is clearly suffering from memory dysfunction. In contrast, if a person living in a remote rural area, where a street number is not significant, does not recall it, he may not be considered "dysfunctional" unless he forgets where his village is located, how it looks, and loses his way returning to it. Thus, it is the purpose and function of memory that needs to be considered, rather than the information that needs to be recollected (Thompson, Donegand, & Lavond, 1986). Regarding outward behavior, generally, openly aggressive behavior that frequently disturbs family, neighbors, or society will be perceived by the family or community as dysfunctional and, therefore, pathological. On the other hand, quiet, seclusive, and asocial behavior, if it does not cause any problems to other people, may not be considered dysfunctional and, thus, may not be labeled pathological. Studies have shown that clinicians' evaluations of hyperactive children vary greatly in different cultures (Mann et al., 1992). In other words, behavior tends to be judged primarily by its impact on the individual, others, and the environment, from a functional point of view.

**(4) By Social Definition.** This approach utilizes social and cultural judgment in deciding if behavior is normal or pathological. The decision is subject to the social knowledge and cultural attitudes found among the members of a society. Thus, the conclusion is subjective and collectively made. For instance, walking half-naked in a public area may be considered "normal" behavior in one situation (such as on Waikiki Beach in Honolulu), "unusual" in another (such as on Fifth Avenue in New York), and "obscene" in a third (such as at the Meiji Shrine in Tokyo), depending on how each society defines such behavior and its cultural tolerance of it. When a man continues to live with his parents after age 25 he may be considered "dependent" in America but "ordinary" in Filipino society. Speaking out against authority figures (such as parents, teachers, or the police) may be regarded as "brave" behavior in a democratic society but "anti-social" in an autocratic one. The judgments made by a society may vary greatly, depending on its customs, beliefs, and values. In general, social behavior tends to be assessed and defined by sociocultural judgment.

It is important for a clinician to be aware of which of these approaches is being utilized in making a clinical judgment, to recognize the limitations of each, and to make whatever adjustments are necessary in making the final assessment.

### c. Some Conceptual Issues Relating to Assessment

**(1) Distinction between "Disease" and "Illness."**   As elaborated previously (Section 2E: Illness Behavior: Recognition and Help Seeking), in medical anthropology, a conceptual distinction is made between the concepts of disease and illness (Eisenberg, 1977). The term "disease" refers to the pathological or malfunctioning condition that is diagnosed by a doctor or folk healer. It is the clinician's conceptualization of the patient's problem, which derives from the paradigm of disease in which the clinician was trained. For example, a biomedically oriented psychiatrist is trained to diagnose brain disease; a psychoanalyst is trained to diagnose psychodynamic problems; and a folk healer might be trained to conceptualize and interpret such things as spirit possession or sorcery. For a medically oriented psychiatrist, a mental "disease" is used to describe a pathological condition that can be grasped and comprehended from a medical point of view, providing an objective and professional perspective on how the sickness may occur, how it is manifested, how it progresses, and how it ends.

In contrast, the term "illness" refers to the sickness that is experienced and perceived by the patient, his subjective perception, experience, and interpretation of his suffering. Although the terms "disease" and "illness" are linguistically almost synonymous, they are purposely used differently to refer to two separate conditions. It is intended to illustrate that disease as perceived by the healer or doctor may or may not be similar to illness as perceived and experienced by the person in suffering. This artificial distinction is useful from a cultural perspective because it illustrates a potential gap between the healer (or doctor) and the help seeker (or patient) in viewing the problems. Although the biomedically oriented physician tends to assume that "disease" is a universal and medical entity, from a medical anthropological point of view, all clinicians' diagnoses, as well as patients' illness experiences, are cognitive constructions based on cultural schema.

The potential gap between disease and illness is an area that deserves the clinician's attention and management in making the clinical assessment meaningful and useful, particularly in a cross-cultural situation.

**(2) Range of the Phenomenology of Psychopathology.**   Language reflects the concerns of the cultural group. For example, Eskimo people, who are surrounded by snow year-round, recognize many different kinds of snow, which they refer to with different words. Likewise, Micronesian people living on small islands in the middle of the ocean have different terms to distinguish many types of clouds, rather than referring simply to clouds in general. This helps them to predict weather conditions for survival in sailing. Asian people use many different terms to express their concern with the delicate hierarchy of relations among family members. For instance, the Chinese use two terms, *gege* and *didi*, to address elder brother and younger brother, respectively, rather than simply referring to them both as "brothers" as in English. In contrast, the Chinese are familiar with only one or two kinds of wine (mostly rice wine), whereas Westerners are familiar with endless varieties. In the Japanese language, many vocabulary words exist to refer to the intimate dependency that exists in an interpersonal relationship, such as *amai*, *amaeru*, and *amanzuru*. These linguistic phenomena reflect a characteristic of the Japanese people and their culture, in which dependence is valued, permitted, elaborated, and expected (Doi, 1973).

All these examples indicate that, beyond a universal base, there are variations in human thought or concern, which are reflected in a peoples' use of language. In a similar way, it can be expected that human beings experience or manifest different spectrums, fields, or ranges of mental conditions, based on their life context or sociocultural background, with certain areas greatly elaborated, and others less defined. Further, it may be speculated that this phenomenon applies to pathological mental conditions. In addition to the basic, core, or universal pathologies, people with different cultural backgrounds will experience and manifest different ranges of psychopathology. This is particularly true in the case of minor psychiatric disorders, which are more predominantly influenced by psychological and social factors (see Section 1C: How Does Culture Relate to Pathology?).

**(3) The "Netting Effect" in Assessment.**    Closely related to the concepts of variation of range of psychic expression and the different nature of cultural impact on psychopathology as previously described is the concept of the "netting effect" on collecting psychic expression. The netting effect is best illustrated by fishing with a net. The results of fishing will be very different, depending on what *kind* of fishing net (e.g., the size or shape of the mesh) is used to catch the fish and *where* the fishing net is cast, as different kinds of fish exist in different areas. These factors will determine the size and kind of fish that will be caught.

Related to this analogy, we need to understand that clinicians in their practices use different "fishing nets" to catch (or gather) information about their patients, and the symptoms or signs manifested. The net used by a clinician is comprised of his professional knowledge, experience, laboratory instruments, or diagnostic classification system. Based on his professional training, experience, or orientation, a clinician learns to use different ways (or nets) to gather, organize, and interpret information. The outcome of the clinical assessment is influenced by the process and method of this netting. In a cross-cultural setting, the clinician should be aware that his clinical evaluation is very much influenced by the netting effect, depending on how perceptive and sensitive he is, and what method and criteria he uses to analyze and categorize the data.

**(4) Etic or Emic Approach.**    Finally, one more important matter that needs attention is whether to use an etic or emic approach in making clinical assessments. The terms "etic" and "emic" were originally derived from the linguistic terms "phonetic" (sound for universal language) and "phonemic" (sound for a specific language). *Etic* is used to address things that are considered universal (or culture-common), while *emic* is culture-specific (Brislin, 2000). In the field of research, the etic strategy holds that investigation can take place anywhere in the world, because the characteristics to be studied are universal; the emic approach takes the position that the characteristics are indigenous and distinctive, and only applicable to certain cultural groups (Draguns, 1989). At another level, the etic approach implies that research is conducted by an *outsider*; the emic approach, by an *insider*. Each approach has its own inherent advantages and shortcomings.

Applied to the clinical task of assessment, from a cultural perspective, *etic* evaluation is performed by a clinician who is from outside of the patient's cultural system. An *etic* evaluation may have the advantage of the outsider's fresh and objective perspective, but it may also be handicapped by the loss of meaning in interpreting the phenomena observed. In contrast, an *emic* evaluation is carried out by a clinician of the same cultural group as the patient. The advantage is that meaningful interpretation may be obtained with cultural insight, but it may be biased by subjectivity. In doing clinical assessment, it is pertinent for the clinician to be aware of his position, whether it is *etic* or *emic*, in making his clinical assessment and interpretation, and to recognize the advantages as well as the shortcomings of his situation.

### d. Different Classification Systems Used in Various Societies

It is important for clinicians to be aware that, in different societies, different classification systems have been adopted and used in the field of psychiatry. This is still true, even though efforts have been made to unify the classification system at an international level, through the work of the World Health Organization, which suggests the use of the International Classification of Disease (ICD) system. The expanding influence of the American psychiatric classification system, the Diagnostic and Statistical Manual (DSM) system, beyond national boundaries is noticeable. Also, a collaborative effort to reduce the discongruence between ICD and DSM has been undertaken. Still, there are considerable differences in the formal classification systems adopted and practiced among various societies around the world. Also, as pointed out by Westermeyer (1985), certain specific psychiatric disorders have been identified in some countries that have been carried over from the past. For instance, French psychiatrists still use the diagnostic term "*bouffees delirantes*" to refer to a type of acute psychosis; Spanish and German psychiatrists still use the diagnostic term "involutional paraphrenia" to refer to a delusional disorder that occurs in mid-life; Scandinavian psychiatrists continue to prefer the diagnostic concept of reactive psychosis, as distinct from schizophrenia. These and other specific diagnostic nosologies used in some countries, but not in others, illustrate that the diagnostic categories are rather unique.

### e. Cross-Cultural Investigation of Making Diagnosis

Some cross-cultural studies on diagnosis have shed light for us on how culture affects the process and results of making diagnoses. For instance, the U.S.-U.K. study of diagnostic patterns of schizophrenia (Cooper et al., 1972) revealed that psychiatrists in the two nations (United States and United Kingdom) tended to observe and describe the patients' psychopathology similarly but made different clinical diagnoses pending how they categorized the disorders. From the study of diagnostic patterns of neuroses in China, Japan, and America, Tseng et al. (1986) found that, among various kinds of minor psychiatric disorders, in cases with well-distinguished clinical pictures, the diagnoses tended to be congruent in the three countries. Diagnostic disagreement occurred in cases involving symptoms of a decline in mental function, which were overwhelmingly diagnosed as neurasthenia by Chinese clinicians, whereas cases involving situational stress tended to be diagnosed as adjustment reaction by the Americans. The study supported the view that different professional concepts and classification systems are used in different countries that explain, at least partially, the different diagnostic distributions noted in the clinical survey in these three countries.

### f. Practical Considerations in Clinical Assessment and Diagnosis

In actual practice, the clinician must overcome several challenges in order to conduct an appropriate cross-cultural assessment and diagnosis with a patient of different cultural background.

**(1) Overcoming the Language Barrier.** The first problem the clinician needs to solve is overcoming any language barrier that may exist with the patient. Clearly, a language problem will affect communication and limit the process and results of the clinician's evaluation. If there is no common language used between the clinician and the patient, an interpreter is needed. There is a skill involved in using an interpreter during a psychiatric assessment (for details, see Section 5B2: Interview and Communication). A caution is needed when there is a common language between the clinician and the patient, so that communication is possible, but the common language is not the clinician's primary language.

There may be a symbolic cultural meaning behind a word or a phrase that is beyond semantic understanding. Many subtle misunderstandings may occur without the clinician even being aware of them (Hsu & Tseng, 1972).

**(2) Obtaining Cultural Background Information.**   Because a mental health worker is unlikely to be a trained anthropologist, it is unreasonable to expect that he will have extensive knowledge about people of various cultural backgrounds. However, in clinical practice, it is very important to have a basic knowledge of the cultural background of a patient in order to have a meaningful understanding of the patient's behavior. A clinician may read an anthropological book or consult with an anthropologist to gain the necessary information, or he may consult with people from the same cultural background as the patient. One practical approach is to ask the patient or a member of his family to assist the clinician in understanding his cultural background. "How do your friends or the people in your community normally behave, think, and react in such a situation?" and "What is their interpretation of such behavior?" are the types of questions to be asked. The aim is to learn the common behavior collectively shared in the patient's society in order to distinguish it from an individual idiosyncratic response.

A caution is needed in how to refer to cultural matters. Sometimes, everything is attributed to ethnic or cultural matters, whereas at other times, the existence of cultural impact is completely denied (Lopez & Hernandez, 1987). The appropriate and objective utilization of cultural matters in interpreting the nature of behavior is in need of careful evaluation. Either overinterpretation or underinterpretation of cultural impact will miss the point.

**(3) Becoming Culturally Sensitive and Empathetic.**   Although, practically speaking, it is impossible to expect all clinicians to receive training as cultural psychiatrists or mental health workers, it should be the aim of every clinician or mental health worker to learn to be culturally sensitive. As long as clinicians are aware of the possible effect of culture on psychopathology and mental health practice, they will be more likely to search for and understand human behavior from a cultural dimension, in addition to other dimensions that impact our behavior and psychopathology. This cultural sensitivity should be a basic expectation for every mental health worker. Beyond cultural sensitivity, another desirable quality is the ability for cultural empathy. This refers to the mental ability to understand emotionally and experientially another's perception, experience, and feeling from a cultural point of view. What does it mean to a person to have his infidelity made public, Why does he attempt suicide when such a personal matter is exposed to the community, or Why does a person become angry enough to try to kill his fellow villagers when he is teased for his unmanly behavior? These are examples of things a clinician needs to know in order to understand what a person is experiencing and feeling in his own cultural environment.

**(4) Dealing Carefully with Certain Diagnostic Dilemmas.** Experience has indicated that diagnostic dilemmas in dealing with patients of diversified ethnic or cultural backgrounds occur in certain areas. Following are some of the areas that cause problems in making clinical assessments and diagnoses.

*Judging Distortion from Reality.* It is often difficult for clinicians to make diagnostic judgments when there is a question as to what extent the patient has lost his sense of reality or his behavior is distorted from reality. This is mainly because the clinician lacks a clear sense of the patient's reality, according to the patient's background, which is necessary in making such a judgment. For instance, if a former inmate complained that he was maltreated by his guards, who forced him to sleep naked on a cement floor, even during the cold winter, how could the clinician tell if his story was true or if he was merely exaggerating or presenting confabulation? If a teenager who stole a car tire and was arrested by police and sent to a clinician for psychiatric assessment told the clinician that the majority of his schoolmates also stole car tires, how would the clinician know whether he was simply behaving like other kids in his (poor and undisciplined) community or was a juvenile delinquent trying to minimize his antisocial behavior? Not having background information with which to verify the reality is, indeed, a dilemma that a clinician must face. Applying this situation cross-culturally, if a person from a faraway foreign country, where the clinician has never been, claimed that he had a half-dozen wives and nearly a hundred children, how would the clinician know if he was describing an actual situation or expressing his own grandiose delusions? If a woman who lost her son recently said that she talked to her deceased son often, how would the clinician know if she was manifesting culturally acceptable behavior or demonstrating psychotic self-talking? Delusion or psychotic thought needs to be verified in reality. The clinician needs to gather information about the patient's "reality" in order to make an accurate clinical assessment, something that is always challenging and difficult. Information from the patient's family or friends is often useful, unless they are members of an insane collective sharing the same delusions.

*Assessing Unfamiliar Mental Phenomena.* Another area that is often problematic for clinicians is encountering mental phenomena or behavior with which they are unfamiliar, making a clinical judgment difficult. If the clinician is practicing in a modern, Western urban setting, without experience in the behavior of possession, he may have difficultly distinguishing between "normal" possession manifested by ordinary people or a professional person (such as a shaman) and "pathological" possession experienced by a decompensated patient. It will also be difficult to judge between a hermit and a deteriorated schizophrenic patient who does not pay attention to personal hygiene. In contrast, a clinician practicing in a society where homosexuality is strictly prohibited would have difficultly in assessing a person who openly shows intimacy with his homosexual partner in public, as such behavior is uncommon in the prevailing social environment.

*Distinguishing Pathological from Cultural Behavior.* Another area that often becomes controversial is that of distinguishing between culturally accepted coping patterns and pathological behavior. Again, referring to the woman mentioned earlier, who recently lost her teenage son in a tragic accident, as a part of her grief reaction, she prepared her son's favorite food daily and offered it to him at the family altar, slept on her son's bed at night, and talked to him, comforting him. Such behavior should not be viewed as that of a psychotic mother who is behaving strangely because of the shock of losing her son. Her family and relatives will share with the clinician that she is exhibiting culturally acceptable behavior that is part of the mourning process, and that there is no need for alarm. Similarly, if the clinician has never heard of the traditional medical practice of an adult drinking a little boy's early morning urine as a way of treating "kidney deficient disorder," he may, without hesitation, interpret such behavior as "strange" and suspect that the person is psychotic.

These are examples of issues that always challenge the clinician in making assessments and diagnoses. A rule of thumb is not to make a clinical judgment on the basis of a single manifestation. A competent clinician will review all the information gathered and base his assessment on the total picture. If possible, he should obtain information from the patient's family and friends, and consult with people from the same ethnic-cultural background. Consultation with a cultural expert is always a good idea.

### g. DSM-IV Cultural Formulation

A considerable improvement has been noted concerning cultural orientation in the official classification system DSM-IV that has been revised in the United States (APA, 1994). It is suggested that the clinician assess the patient systematically in the following areas:

Cultural identity of the individual;
Cultural explanation of the individual's illness;
Cultural factors related to the psychosocial environment and functioning;
Cultural elements of the relationship between the individual and the clinician;
Overall cultural assessment for diagnosis and care.

It has been advocated recently (Lu, Lim, & Mezzich, 1995; Mezzich et al., 1996a) that, from a practical point of view, a systematic evaluation of the cultural background of a patient needs to be performed through such suggested "cultural formulation" (Committee on Cultural Psychiatry, 2002).

### h. Diagnostic Issues Relating to Culture-Bound Syndromes

Closely related to the cultural concern of diagnositic classification as reflected in DSM-IV, it is almost impossible not to discuss culture-related specific psychiatric syndromes from the perspective of diagnostic classification. Associated with the minority movement, some cultural psychiatrists take the strong position that it is important to make room in the classification system for so-called culture-bound syndromes recognized in many foreign countries outside of developed societies, or among minority groups within Western societies. However, this idea is not supported by the majority of cultural psychiatrists, as it would defeat the purpose of recognizing special syndromes that are closely related to cultural dimensions (see Section 3A: Culture-Related Specific Syndromes). Because DSM is phenomenologically based, but not etiologically oriented, there is no room to include psychopathogenetically conceived syndromes.

### i. Sociocultural Implications of Diagnostic Nosology

Finally, as a clinician, it is important to raise the questions: What are the clinical implications for making a certain diagnosis and what are the social and cultural implications of the diagnosis? The labeling of a disorder can bring a certain social stigma on the patient and his family. Leprosy is a medical disease that is still seen negatively in many societies. Similarly, schizophrenia, a psychosis, is regarded as a terrible disease in many cultural areas. Many efforts are applied to avoid such labeling. Suicide is a negative category in many societies with strong Muslim or Catholic backgrounds. Many alternative labels might be used instead.

In contrast, certain mental disorders give a legitimate excuse for a person to be relieved from social responsibility. This is particularly true if such a disorder is considered to be caused by either internal or external factors and is not the patient's own fault. Chinese prefer the diagnosis of neurasthenia, as it is attributed to the weakness or exhaustion of the nervous system, rather than the patient's emotional vulnerability. In contrast, American patients prefer the label of adjustment disorder, as it is attributed to a noxious external situation. Labels that suggest a person has an inherent vulnerability, such as a weak nervous system, are not welcome.

Thus, a clinician needs to pay attention to the implications for the patient, his family, his friends, and the society when certain diagnostic labeling is given. This consideration is needed not only from a personal level but also from social and cultural levels.

## C. CULTURALLY ADJUSTED PSYCHOLOGICAL MEASUREMENT

In clinical and research work, psychological testing is often conducted to evaluate a patient's psychological status, personality, psychopathology, stress encountered, and patterns of adjustment and coping. This provides supplemental objective data in addition to subjective clinical information that will lead to a comprehensive understanding, assessment, and diagnosis of the patient.

Most of the tools of psychological measurement have been designed by Euro-American behavior scientists or clinicians for respondents of Euro-American backgrounds. This raises questions of reliability and usefulness when the tools are applied to respondents of different ethnic-cultural backgrounds living in Euro-American societies; or when, after translation and perhaps some modifications, they are applied to respondents or patients in non-Western societies. There is a growing recognition that cultural factors cannot be ignored in cross-cultural testing and assessment and transcultural applicability deserve careful attention (Brislin, 2000; Lonner, 1990; Lonner & Berry, 1986; Ratner, 1997; Segall et al., 1990).

## 1. Basic Considerations: Methodological Issues

### a. Area and Scope of Measurement

Numerous basic issues need to be addressed in testing and assessment in different cultural settings. The first is whether the method and instrument are applied appropriately and adequately cover the scope of the examination: intelligence, personality, psychopathology, or other subjects to be investigated. The fundamental issue is that, even though we are all human beings, our intelligence does not performs in the same way, our behavior patterns are not necessarily demonstrated within the same categories, and our pathological mental conditions are not manifested within the same scope of abnormality. Following the concept of "netting effect" described earlier, there is always a need to design culturally specific instrument that will investigate different areas or scope of mental function to be investigated.

### b. Problems of Administration

In the administration of psychological tests in cross-cultural situations, it is important to question the familiarity of the people with testing. As pointed out by Lonner (1990, pp. 58–59), probably no other country can match the United States in test usage. Most current tests were developed here and are based on the assumptions that individuals can order or rank stimuli along linearly constructed stimuli, can readily produce judgments about social and psychological stimuli; and are capable of self-assessment and self-refection (Trimble, Lonner, & Boucher, 1983). Clearly, such assumptions do not apply to people in many other cultures, even psychologized ones, not to mention those in which people have never heard of, or experienced, testing.

Closely related to this are people's attitudes and reactions to testing, how they feel about revealing to strangers (test administrators), their private selves, their attitudes toward authority (represented by the examiners), and the meaning of being tested. It is common knowledge that people may respond to testing in certain ways, such as agreeing with just about everything (acquiescence), responding in socially approved directions (social desirability), or responding in the middle (positional). Such response styles, in addition to personality, are often shaped by cultural factors and greatly affect the results of measurement.

### c. Problems of Sampling

In any study, it is essential to consider how the sample to be studied is selected and to what extent the subjects reflect the targeted group as a whole. This is particularly true when the study involves cross-cultural comparison. It must be asked to what extent the subjects are comparable in their backgrounds and are representative of the cultural group to be studied. Most pen-and-paper instruments involve writing, which is a problem if the study is to be carried out in populations that have different literacy rates. Also, there will be an imbalance in volunteer sampling if some members of a society tend to shy away from taking tests, while others do not. For the sake of convenience, many psychological tests are administered to college students. This creates problems in cross-cultural comparisons. College students hardly represent all the members of a society. Also, the status of college students may differ from one culture to another. The sampling needs to take into account not only the range but also the representativeness of the culture and behavior (Berry, 1980).

### d. Equivalency of Meaning

If cultures are to be meaningfully compared, several kinds of equivalency need to be met. Berry (1980) named functional, conceptual, and metric equivalence; Brislin (2000) indicated translation, conceptual, and metric equivalence; while Flaherty and his colleagues (1988) were concerned with content, semantic, technical, criterion, and conceptual equivalence.

*Functional Equivalence.*    This concerns whether two or more behaviors (in two or more cultural systems) are related to "functionally" similar problems. For example, generosity toward others in one culture might be measured by how much money one donates to a church; in another, by how much food one gives to other clan members.

*Conceptual Equivalence.*    This demonstrates that our tests and concepts have identical meaning in the cultures being examined. The researchers must find out the local meaning of concepts within the cognitive systems of the people and groups being compared. Only if a common meaning is discovered can comparison legitimately take place (Berry, 1980, p. 9). Therefore, it is a precondition of comparison.

*Semantic or Translation Equivalence.*    When an instrument designed in one language is to be translated into another for transcultural application, semantic translation becomes an important issue from the standpoint of conceptual equivalence. The use of forward and back translation of words has been suggested (Brislin, 1970, 1976, 2000). This involves an initial translation into a target language by one bilingual person. Then the translated item is translated back into the original language by another bilingual person. For instance, when the English words "I had problems with the police this morning" are translated into another language and translated back as "I committed a crime this morning," this illustrates a conceptual gap in the understanding of "had problems with the police" in the two cultures. Any discrepancies will indicate conceptual nonequivalence. Through back translation, translation equivalence can be assured. To operationalize conceptual equivalence, semantic differential analysis should be carried out (Osgood, 1965).

*Technical Equivalence.*    The key issue in technical equivalence is whether the method of data collection affects the results differently in different cultures studied (Flaherty et al., 1988). Certain cultures may be uncomfortable and unfamiliar with the technical aspects of testing and data collection methods that are not problems in other cultures.

*Metric Equivalence.*    Metric equivalence centers on the analysis of the same concepts across cultures, and its analysis assumes that the same scale (after proper translation procedures) can be used to measure the concept everywhere (Brislin, 2000, p. 103). This is important when mean scores between cultures are to be compared. To demonstrate metric equivalence in any two cultures, it is necessary to establish that the statistical behavior of the items in each culture is the same (Kline, 1983). Therefore, a score in one culture can be directly compared with a score in another.

### e. Validity of the Measurement

Validity concerns whether or not a test, questionnaire, or set of observations measures what it is supposed to measure. In the cross-cultural application of testing, the most critical matter is the validity of the measurement. What is the value of the results obtained from the testing ? Do the results really represent the issues being measured? How do we know that the bases of comparison are equivalent across cultures? These are questions that need to be raised and answered (Rogler, 1999).

It has been challenged that, unless the investigators are very familiar with the culture of the respondents, they may have difficulty interpreting the data obtained in cross-cultural settings. Without such knowledge, the data cannot be interpreted correctly and meaningfully. Generally speaking, it would be desirable to have a collaboration of investigators from both inside and outside of the culture so that more meaningful and relevant interpretation of the obtained data, both subjectively and objectively, could be made.

## 2. Instruments and Cross-Cultural Applications

Numerous psychological tests have been developed and used by behavior scientists and clinicians for research and clinical application. Some of the more commonly used measurements are discussed here from the perspective of their transcultural applications.

### a. Personality Assessment

**(1) Minnesota Multiphasic Personality Inventory (MMPI).** Perhaps this is one of the most widely used questionnaires for the objective assessment of personality as well as psychopathology. It was originally developed in 1937 by a psychologist, Starke R. Hathaway, and a neurologist and psychiatrist, John C. McKinley. The norm was based on the data collected from normal samples (mostly patients' relatives and other visitors to a university hospital) from Minnesota (Hathaway & McKinley, 1940).

However, as pointed out by Colligan and Offord (1985), the MMPI has aged. Since its inception in the 1940s, remarkable changes have taken place in American society. Besides the improvement of living standards, increased levels of education, the impact of the feminist movement, and the liberalizing of religious and moral views, there have been changes in family structure in our technological society. There is a need for revitalization of the MMPI. Based on this, Colligan and Offord carried out a project to develop contemporary norms. From the same geographic area of Minnesota, through random sampling of household residents, they systematically included normal subjects in the survey. They disclosed that MMPI response patterns among normal people have changed. Analysis of data yielded scores and profiles higher than those obtained from the original standardization group in the 1940s. The differences were more apparent for men than for women. The investigators speculated that the response pattern changes were probably due more to changes in social attitudes and perceptions than to a change in mental health status. This illustrates that, even within the same society, and the same (Caucasian-American) ethnic group, the norm of this instrument needs adjustment to reflect changes that have occurred during the past four decades.

There have been several reports on the application of the MMPI to minority ethnic groups in America. Early in the 1970s, Gynther (1972) reported that African-American respondents generally obtain higher scores than Caucasian-American respondents on Scale *F* (Infrequency scale), 8 (Schizophrenia), and 9

(Hypomania). He interpreted these differences as representing differences in values, perceptions, and expectations rather than levels of adjustment.

Pollack and Shore (1980) reported that Native American respondents from various Pacific Northwest tribes all had similar MMPI profiles and, compared to the norm of Caucasian respondents, had significant elevations in Scales $Sc$ (Schizophrenia), $Pd$ (Psychopathic deviance), and $Pa$ (Paranoia). The authors believe that the similarity of all subgroup profiles demonstrates a significant cultural influence on the results of the MMPI in the Native American population investigated.

When the MMPI was applied to Chinese in China, Song (1985) reported that, for both male and female normal respondents, the scores for $D$ (Depression) and $Sc$ (Schizophrenia) were elevated in contrast to the norms of American respondents. Song interpreted that the Chinese people have some character traits that are utterly different from those of Americans. The Chinese are emotionally more reserved, introverted, fond of tranquility, overly considerate, socially overcautious, and habitually self-restrained, as manifested in the test results. This indicates the need to use modified norms for the Chinese in measuring personality traits. In other words, if the Chinese norms were applied in the measurement of American respondents, the scores for $D$ and $Sc$ would be degraded, meaning that, from the Chinese perspective, Americans are more extroverted, freely express emotion, are less considerate in interpersonal relations, and are socially less cautious. This reflects that things are relative, depending on the perspective from which the data are measured and interpreted. It also points to the need for adjustment in the transcultural application of the MMPI in terms of scoring for norms. Based on these findings, Cheung and Song designed a Chinese version of objective personality measurement, including special items for the Chinese, and labeled the instrument the Chinese Personality Assessment Inventory (CPAI) (Cheung et al., 1996). Japanese psychologists also indicated elevations of the scales on $Sc$ (Schizophrenia) and $D$ (Depression) when the inventory of MMPI was applied to Japanese respondents.

**(2) Rorschach Test.**    Although many projective tests rely less on written language than objective tests, it is the general opinion that projective testing is subject to problems in cross-cultural application. This is because the mode of testing itself has poor evidence for reliability and validity and is greatly influenced by the variables of attitude and the personal background of the tester, including ethnic or racial background (Holtzman, 1980). Furthermore, there are basic problems regarding the stimulus properties of the items and their cultural relativity.

The Rorschach test is considered one of the classic projective assessments. The respondents are simply shown a series of arbitrarily designed ink blocks. The respondents are expected to give responses to these figures. Thus, it is considered rather culture-free, as there is no language involved and no formalized figures are presented as stimulants. However, even such a supposedly culture-free test is not immune to cultural influences.

It has been pointed out that the large number of scoring categories for the Rorschach, as with other projective tests, leads to the possibility of many different permutations. Even 20 binary indices will yield more than a million types. Thus, an impressive amount of uniformity will have to be present in order to be noticed or else categories defined in more general terms will have to be the focus of the research (Wallace, 1961).

**(3) Thematic Apperception Test.**    Another commonly used projective test is the Thematic Apperception Test (TAT). Because human figures are used, even though they, as well as the background settings, are intentionally kept ambiguous, it is greatly subject to sociocultural influences, in contrast to the Rorschach test. Children are given the Children Apperception Test (CAT), which substitutes animated figures for ink blocks. However, even the animals are culture-bound. Various kinds of animals have different cultural significance. For instance, pigs raise considerable problems in Muslim or Jewish groups.

Beside such problems, there are several advantages for cross-cultural application. The responses to the TAT are typically more profuse and varied, thus permitting a wider range of inquiries from the same test administration. Further, as pointed out by Spain (1972), the tradition of storytelling is virtually universal, and the user of the TAT can take advantage of this in his fieldwork.

There are few culturally adjusted TATs that are used for people in non-Western societies. The Japanese version of the TAT is one, designed by American cultural anthropologist W. Caudell for study in Japan. According to Kline (1983), S. G. Lee, in 1953, attempted to produce an African TAT, but it proved to be suitable for very few ethnic groups in Africa because the life situation there was so different from that in the West.

### b. Intellectual Assessment

The presently widely used Binet's Intelligence Quotient (IQ) test was designed by French psychologist Binet. At the request of the board of education of Paris, which felt that the city could not afford to send every child to school, Binet sought to detect in advance the children who were unlikely to succeed in the school system. Thus, while Binet's IQ test was developed as a scholastic aptitude test, it is now believed to be an instrument to measure the inborn intellectual capacity of individuals or even whole groups, a false academic assumption, often with dangerous political implications (Segall et al., 1990, p. 59).

### c. Psychiatric Assessment of Psychopathology

**(1) Diagnostic Scales for Epidemiological Study.**    There are several kinds of clinical diagnostic questionnaires designed for epidemiological study.

Diagnostic Interview Schedule (DIS) is one that has been chosen in the United States for an Epidemiologic Catchment Area (ECA) Study and has been applied in other studies relating to different ethnic groups, so that there are more comments from cross-cultural perspectives.

For instance, concerning content validity, Manson, Shore, and Bloom (1985), in their study of Hopi Indians, discovered during pretesting that the concepts of guilt, shame, and sinfulness, which the DIS treated as synonyms, had to be considered as separate concepts. Guarnaccia and colleagues (1992), in their survey of Puerto Ricans, had to modify interpretations of items concerning psychotic experiences. Many features of Puerto Rican culture, because of a proclivity to believe in spirits, such as visions, presentiments, and hearing voices, had to be incorporated into mental health assessments to correct for exaggerated attributions of psychotic symptoms. When Egeland, Hostetter, and Eshelman (1983) were investigating the Amish people for their bipolar disorders, they found that the operationalization of manic symptoms, such as buying sprees, sexual promiscuity, and reckless driving, was not applicable to the Old Order Amish. Flaherty and co-investigators (1988) studied Andean-Indian who migrated from their village to Lima, the capital of Peru. They used the Spanish-language version of DIS, but the team eliminated all of the antisocial items, such as: "Have you had at least four traffic tickets in your life for speeding or running lights?" as none of the migrants studied had ever driven cars. They pointed out that all antisocial items attempt to measure behavior that did not conform to the usual values of society, but that such usual values vary from society to society.

**(2) Scales for Specific Clinical Syndromes.**    Psychiatric epidemiologist Mollica and co-workers (1987) in Boston used the Hopkins Symptom Checklist-25 as a screening instrument for the psychiatric care of refugees from Southeast Asia. They claimed that, after careful translation of the instrument for content equivalence, the brief, simple, and reliable instrument was well received by refugee patients, and offered an effective screening method for the symptoms of anxiety and depression.

In contrast, American cultural psychiatrist J. D. Kinzie and a team of colleagues who had been working with Vietnamese refugees in Oregon for many years found it difficult to use the existing depression scales, such as Zung's (1969), for the assessment of Vietnamese patients under their care. Therefore, they developed a depressive scale in the Vietnamese language that contained culturally consistent items describing the thoughts, feelings, and behaviors of depressed individuals and items describing common clinical characteristics of depressed Vietnamese patients (Kinzie et al., 1982). They claimed that such a specially developed, culturally relevant depressive scale was much more useful for clinical application for this particular group of people.

Zheng and Lin (1991) developed the Chinese Depression Inventory (CDI) for the clinical assessment of depression. They used a sample of 329 currently depressed patients from 24 hospitals across China. They claimed that the CDI was a more culturally sensitive and cross-culturally useful self-report scale for measuring the severity of depression in Chinese than the Beck Depression Inventory designed for Americans in the United States. The inventory was constructed according to culture and verbal styles related to the expression of emotional and physical experiences. For instance, they explained that the words "suicide," "sexual drive," and "sense of failure" were replaced by more euphemistic expressions, namely: "being alive is not interesting," "not interested in the opposite sex," and "a weak person in life." Instead of "depression," the words "being uncomfortable in one's heart" were used. Because suicide is a "bad" behavior and regarded as a shameful thing to talk about in Chinese society; therefore, a more culturally appropriate inquiry was considered.

## 3. Possible Resolution for Transcultural Application

It would be more correct to assume that there are always problems and limitations in the transcultural application of psychological measurement rather than to search for culture-free or universally applicable measurement methods. It would be more useful to examine and disclose in what ways the measurement will be influenced by the cultural factors and how to resolve the problems of transcultural application.

*Adjustment of Norm or Cutting Point.*    When the instrument is designed to distinguish between normality and abnormality by a score, the cutting point may need adjustment when the subjects being investigated are from other cultural backgrounds. Clinical validation is needed for such an adjustment. Alternatively, culturally modified mean scores may be obtained by applying to a large population from the societies in concern in order to establish a new set of norms.

*Making Special Efforts in Translation.*    If the instrument is going to be used in a setting in which the subject uses a language other than that used in the original instrument, extra effort and caution are needed in translating the instrument. Problems not merely of language equivalency but of conceptual equivalency as well need to be resolved.

*Modification of the Test.*    When items included in the instrument are not relevant or valid for transcultural application, they need to be removed, modified, or substituted by new items that are more relevant to the culture. If certain areas are not included in the instrument, causing "netting effect" problems, additional items need to be added. Based on these revisions or additions, new factors will be developed for application, even though the basic conceptual structure of the instrument will be maintained.

*Reconstruction of the Tool.*   When the existing inventory is found unsuitable for transcultural application in the investigation of a particular cultural group, one final solution is to construct a new, culturally appropriate and valid inventory. This is done with the inclusion of items for the areas and scope that need to be evaluated and with consideration of the implications of the obtained data. Clinical validation is needed when a new tool is developed.

Finally, a distinction needs to be drawn between culture-free and culture-fair measurement. As pointed out by Segall (1979, p. 52), the culture-free label would be applied to an instrument that actually measures some inherent quality of human capacity equally well in all cultures. Obviously, there can be no such thing as a culture-free test, so defined. Culture-fair instruments aim to contain the same amount of test items with familiarity to the subject of different cultural backgrounds so that it will be fair in making an assessment. Clearly that modification is needed for applications to any cultural group.

# REFERENCES

## A. The Need for Cultural Competence

Foulks, E. (1980). The concept of culture in psychiatric residency education. *American Journal of Psychiatry, 137*, 811–816.

Lu, F., Lim, R., & Mezzich, J. (1995). Issues in the assessment and diagnosis of culturally diverse individuals. In P. Ruitz (Ed.), *Annual Review of Psychiatry.* Washington, DC: American Psychiatric Press.

Moffic M. S., Kendrick, E. A., & Reid, K. (1988). Cultural psychiatry education during psychiatric residency. *Journal of Psychiatric Education, 12*, 90–101.

Pinderhughes, E. (1984). Teaching empathy: Ethnicity, race, and power at the cross-cultural treatment interface. *American Journal of Social Psychiatry, 4*, 5–12.

Tseng, W. S., & Hsu, J. (1979). Culture and psychotherapy. In A. J. Marsella, R. G. Tharp, & T. J. Ciborowski (Eds.), *Perspectives on cross-cultural psychology* (pp. 333–345). New York: Academic Press.

Tseng, W. S., & Streltzer, J. (2001). Integration and conclusion. In W. S. Tseng & J. Streltzer (Eds.), *Culture and psychotherapy: A guide for clinical practice* (pp. 265–278). Washington, DC: American Psychiatric Press.

Westermeyer, J. (1989). *The psychiatric care of migrants: A clinical guide.* Washington, DC: American Psychiatric Press.

Yutrzenka, B. A. (1995). Making a case for training in ethnic and cultural diversity in increasing treatment efficacy. *Journal of Consulting and Clinical Psychology, 63*(2), 197–206.

## B. Culturally Relevant Assessment and Diagnosis

American Psychiatric Association (APA). (1994). *Diagnostic and statistical manual of mental disorders* (4th ed.). Washington, DC: APA.

Brislin, R. W. (2000). Some methodological concerns in intercultural and cross-cultural research. In R. W. Brislin, *Understanding culture's influence on behavior* (2nd ed.). Fort Worth, TX: Harcourt.

Committee on Cultural Psychiatry (2002). *Cultural assessment in clinical psychiatry* (Group for the Advancement of Psychiatry, Report No. 145). Washington, DC: American Psychiatric Publishing, Inc.

Cooper, J. E., Kendall, R. E., Gurland, B. J., Sartorius, N., & Farkas, T. (1969). Cross-national study of diagnosis of the mental disorders: Some results from the first comparative investigation. *American Journal of Psychiatry, 125* (Suppl.), 21–29.

Cooper, J. E., Kendell, R. E., Gurland, B. J., Sharpe, L., Copeland, J. R. M., & Simon, R. (1972). *Psychiatric diagnosis in New York and London.* London: Oxford University Press.

Doi, T. (1973). *The anatomy of dependence* (pp. 28–32). Tokyo: Kodansha International.

Draguns, J. G. (1989). Dilemmas and choices in cross-cultural counseling: The universal versus the culturally distinctive. In P. B. Pedersen, J. G. Draguns, W. J. Lonner, & J. E. Trimble (Eds.), *Counseling across cultures* (pp. 3–21). Honolulu: University of Hawaii Press.

Eisenberg, L. (1977). Disease and illness: Distinctions between professional and popular ideas of sickness. *Culture, Medicine and Psychiatry, 1*(1), 9–23.

Fabrega, H. (1987). Psychiatric diagnosis: A cultural perspective. *Journal of Nervous and Mental Disease, 175,* 383–394.

Fisher, F. D., & Leigh, H. (1989). Models of the doctor-patient relationship. In R. Michels (Ed.), *Psychiatry* (Vol. 2). Philadelphia: JB Lippincott.

Francis, V., Korsch, B. M., & Morris, M. J. (1969). Gaps in doctor-patient communication. *New England Journal of Medicine, 280*(10), 535–540.

Hsu, J. (1983). Asian family interaction patterns and their therapeutic implications. *International Journal of Family Psychiatry, 4*(4), 307–320.

Hsu, J., & Tseng, W. S. (1972). Intercultural psychotherapy. *Archives of General Psychiatry, 26,* 700–705.

Kinzie, D. (1985). Cultural aspects of psychiatric treatment with Indochinese refugees. *American Journal of Social Psychiatry, 5*(1), 47–53.

Lee, E. (1997). Cross-cultural communication: Therapeutic use of interpreters. In E. Lee (Ed.), *Working with Asian Americans: A guide for clinicians* (pp. 477–489). New York: Guiford.

Lopez, S., & Hernandez, R. (1987). When culture is considered in the evaluation and treatment of Hispanic patients. *Psychotherapy, 24,* 120–126.

Lu, F. G., Lim, R. F., & Mezzich, J. E. (1995). Issues in the assessment and diagnosis of culturally diverse individuals. In J. M. Oldham & M. B. Riba (Eds.), *American psychiatric press review of psychiatry* (Vol. 14). Washington, DC: American Psychiatric Press.

Mann, E. M., Ikeda, Y., Mueller, C. W., Takahashi, A. H., Tao, K. T., Humris, E., Li, B. L., & Chin, D. (1992). Cross-cultural differences in rating hyperactive-disruptive behaviors in children. *American Journal of Psychiatry, 149*(11), 1539–1542.

Marcos, L. R. (1979). Effects of interpreters on the evaluation of psychopathology in non-English-speaking patients. *American Journal of Psychiatry, 136,* 171–174.

Mezzich, J. E., Kleinman, A., Fabrega, J., & Parron, D. L. (Eds.). (1996a). *Culture and psychiatric diagnosis: A DSM-IV perspective.* Washington, DC: American Psychiatric Press.

Mezzich, J. E., Kleinman, A., Fabrega, J., & Parron, D. L. (1996b). In J. E. Mezzich, A. Kleinman, J. Fabrega, & D. L. Parron (Eds.), *Culture and psychiatric diagnosis: A DSM-IV perspective* (pp. xvii–xviii, Introduction). Washington, DC: American Psychiatric Press.

Nilchaikovit, T., Hill, J. M., & Holland, J. C. (1993). The effects of culture on illness behavior and medical care: Asian and American differences. *General Hospital Psychiatry, 15,* 41–50.

Offer, D., & Sabshin, M. (1974). *Normality: Theoretical and clinical concepts of mental health.* (2nd ed.). New York: Basic Books.

Paniagua, F. D. (1998). General guidelines for the assessment and treatment of multicultural groups. In F. D. Paniagua, *Assessing and treating cultural diverse clients: A practical guide* (2nd ed.) (pp. 5–19). Thousand Oaks, CA: Sage.

Rogler, L. H. (1993). Culture in psychiatric diagnosis: An issues of scientific accuracy. *Psychiatry, 56,* 324–327.

Streltzer, J. (1998). Cultural impact on consultation-interaction liaison psychiatric services. Presented at the American Psychiatric Association annual meeting workshop on Cultural Influence on Medical Practice, Toronto, Canada.

Thompson, R. F., Donegan, N. H., & Lavond, D. G. (1986). The psychobiology of learning and memory. In R. C. Atkinson, R. J. Herrnstein, G. Lindzey, & R. D. Luce (Eds.), *Steven's handbook of experimental psychology* (2nd ed.). New York: Wiley.

Tseng, W. S. (1975). The nature of somatic complaints among psychiatric patients: The Chinese case. *Comprehensive Psychiatry, 16,* 237–245.

Tseng, W. S. (1997). Overview: Culture and psychopathology. In W. S. Tseng & J. Streltzer (Eds.), *Culture and psychopathology: A guide to clinical assessment* (pp. 1–27). New York: Brunner/Mazel.

Tseng, W. S., Asai, M. H., Kitanishi, K. J., McLaughlin, D., & Kyomen, H. (1992). Diagnostic pattern of social phobia: Comparison in Tokyo and Hawaii. *Journal of Nerve and Mental Disorders, 180,* 380–385.

Tseng, W. S., McDermott, J. F., Jr., Ogino, K., & Ebata, K. (1982). Cross-cultural differences in parent-child assessment: U.S.A. and Japan. *International Journal of Social Psychiatry, 28,* 305–317.

Tseng, W. S., Xu, D., Ebata, K., Hsu, J., & Cui, J. (1986). Diagnostic pattern for neuroses in China, Japan and America. *American Journal of Psychiatry, 143,* 1010–1014.

Westermeyer, J. (1985). Psychiatric diagnosis across cultural boundaries. *American Journal of Psychiatry, 142,* 798–805.

Westermeyer, J. (1990). Working with an interpreter in psychiatric assessment and treatment. *Journal of Nervous and Mental Disease, 178,* 745–749.

## C. Culturally Adjusted Psychological Measurement

Berry, J. W. (1980). Introduction to methodology. In H. C. Triandis & J. W. Berry (Eds.). *Handbook of cross-cultural psychology: Vol. 2. Methodology* (pp. 1–28). Boston: Allyn & Bacon.

Brislin, R. (1970). Back translation for cross-cultural research. *Journal of Cross-Cultural Psychology, 1,* 185–216.

Brislin, R. (1976). *Translation: Applications and research.* New York: Wiley-Halsted.

Brislin, R. W. (2000). Some methodological concerns in intercultural and cross-cultural research. In R. W. Brislin, *Understanding culture's influence on behavior* (2nd ed.). Fort Worth, TX: Harcourt.

Cheung, F. M., Leung, K., Fan, R. M., Song, W. S., Zhang, J. X., & Zhang, J. P. (1996). Development of the Chinese Personality Assessment Inventory. *Journal of Cross-Cultural Psychology 27*(2), 181–199.

Colligan, R. C., & Offord, K. P. (1985). Revitalizing the MMPI: The development of contemporary norms. *Psychiatric Annals, 15*(9), 558–568.

Egeland, J. A., Hostetter, A. M., & Eshleman, S. K. (1983). Amish study, III: The impact of cultural factors on diagnosis of bipolar illness. *American Journal of Psychiatry, 140,* 67–71.

Flaherty, J. A., Gaviria, M., Pathak, D., Mitchell, T., Wintrob, R., Richman, J., & Birz, S. (1988). Developing instruments for cross-cultural psychiatric research. *Journal of Nervous and Mental Disease, 176*(5), 257–263.

Guarnaccia, P. J., Guevara-Ramos, L. M., Gonzales, G., Canino, G. J., & Bird, H. (1992). Cross-cultural aspects of psychotic symptoms in Puerto Rico. *Research in Community and Mental Health, 7,* 99–110.

Gynther, M. D. (1972). White norms and Black MMPIs: A prescription for discrimination? *Psychological Bulletin, 78*(5), 386–402.

Hathaway, S. R., & McKinley, J. C. (1940). A multiphase personality schedule (Minnesota): I. Construction of the schedule. *Journal of Psychology, 10,* 249–254.

Holtzman, W. H. (1980). Projective techniques. In H. C. Triandis & J. W. Berry (Eds.), *Handbook of cross-cultural psychology: Vol. 2: Methodology* (pp. 245–278). Boston: Allyn & Bacon.

Kinzie, J. D., Manson, S. M., Vinh, D. T., Tolan, N. T., Anh, B., & Pho, T. N. (1982). Development and validation of a Vietnamese-Language Depression Rating Scale. *American Journal of Psychiatry, 139*(10), 1276–1281.

Kline, P. (1983). The cross-cultural use of personality tests. In S. H. Irvin & J. W. Berry (Eds.), *Human assessment and cultural factors*. New York: Plenum Press.

Lonner, W. J. (1990). An overview of cross-cultural testing and assessment. In R. W. Brislin (Ed.), *Applied cross-cultural psychology* (pp. 56–76). Newbury Park, CA: Sage.

Lonner, W. J., & Berry, J. W. (Eds). (1986). *Field methods in cross-cultural research*. Newbury Park, CA: Sage.

Manson, S. M., Shore, J. H., & Bloom, J. D. (1985). The depressive experience in American Indian communities: A challenge for psychiatric theory and diagnosis. In A. Kleinman & B. Good (Eds.), *Culture and depression* (pp. 331–368) Berkeley: University of California Press.

Mollica, R. F., Wyshak, G., de Marneffe, D., Khuon, F., & Lavelle, J. (1987). Indochinese version of the Hopkins Symptom Checklist-25: A screening instrument for the psychiatric care of refugees. *American Journal of Psychiatry, 144*(4), 497–500.

Osgood, C. (1965). Cross-cultural comparability in attitude measurement via multilingual semantic differentials. In I. Steiner & M. Fishbein (Eds.), *Current studies in social psychology*. Chicago: Holt, Rinehart & Winston.

Pollack, D., & Shore, J. H. (1980). Validity of the MMPI with Native Americans. *American Journal of Psychiatry, 137*(8), 946–950.

Ratner, C. (1997). *Cultural psychology and qualitative methodology: Theoretical and empirical considerations.* New York: Plenum Press.

Rogler, L. H. (1999). Implementing cultural sensitivity in mental health reserach: Covergence and new directions. Part I: I. Content validity in the development of instruments from concepts. II. Translation of instrument. *Psychline, 3*(1), 5–11.

Segall, M. H. (1979). *Cross-cultural psychology: Human behavior in global perspective.* Monterey, CA: Brooks/Cole.

Segall, M. H., Dasen, P. R., Berry, J. W., & Poortinga, Y. H. (1990). Human behavior in global perspective: An introduction to cross-cultural psychology. New York: Pergamon Press.

Song, W. Z. (1985). A preliminary study of the character traits of the Chinese. In W. S. Tseng & D. Y. H. Wu (Eds.), *Chinese culture and mental health* (pp. 47–55). Orlando, FL: Academic Press.

Spain, D. H. (1972). On the use of projective tests for research in psychological anthropology. In F. L. K. Hsu (Ed.), *Psychological anthropology* (pp. 267–308). Cambridge, MA: Schenkman.

Trimble, J. E., Lonner, W. J., & Boucher, J. (1983). Stalking the wily emic: Alternatives to cross-cultural measurement. In S. Irving & J. W. Berry (Eds.), *Human assessment and cultural factors*. New York: Plenum Press.

Wallace, A. F. C. (1961). The psychic unity of human groups. In B. Kaplan (Ed.), *Studying personality cross-culturally*. Evanston, IL: Harper & Row.

Zheng, Y. P., & Lin, K. M. (1991). Comparison of the Chinese Depression Inventory and the Chinese version of the Beck Depression Inventory. *Acta Psychiatrica Scandinavica, 84*, 531–536.

Zung, W. (1969). A cross-cultural survey of symptoms in depression. *American Journal of Psychiatry, 126*, 116–121.

# CHAPTER 6

# Culturally Competent
# Clinical Care

Not only has cultural psychiatry made progress advocating for cultural sensitivity and awareness, but it has also come to the point of challenging the way in which culturally relevant and competent care by various professional disciplines should be carried out. In this chapter, the cultural aspects of clinical care in various clinical services will be elaborated, including inpatient and outpatient psychiatric care, emergency services, liaison-consultation services, psychiatric nursing care, mental health social work, and forensic psychiatric service. The general issues regarding clinical care, including therapist-patient relations, communication, and clinical assessment, have been examined earlier (see Section 5B: Culturally Relevant Assessment and Diagnosis). Here, only issues relating to particular clinical services or settings will be discussed. The cultural aspects of care for special subpopulation such as children, adolescents, aged persons, women, couples, or families will be elaborated in Chapter 9: Culture and Therapy with Special Subgroups.

## A. INPATIENT PSYCHIATRIC CARE

### 1. General Concerns

It is a general trend for the most severe psychiatric cases to be cared for in inpatient settings. Most severe cases are now considered to be predominantly attributed to biological factors. However, this does not mean that there is no need to be concerned with cultural aspects in providing care for patients suffering from major psychiatric disorders. On the contrary, there is a great need to pay attention to the way in which service should be provided, not only from a professional perspective, to fit the medical needs of the patients, but also from an ethnic or a cultural perspective, to suit the socioeconomic and cultural backgrounds of the patients. This may involve simply how to set up treatment facilities, including bed arrangements, hygiene facilities, food provided, and even the uniforms worn by patients and staff.

*Design of Treatment Setting.*    The design of the physical environment for inpatient care needs to consider not only the perspective of medical treatment, socioeconomic factors, and environmental issues but also the cultural system. For instance, in Bali, according to Castillo (2001), when Balinese psychiatrist D. Thong (1993) took over the psychiatric hospital built during the Dutch occupation, he found that it did not suit the local people, as it was built in a Western style. As the new administrator, Thong ordered that all beds in the hospital be rearranged, with their heads facing toward the north, where the mountain was located. The people in Bali believe that the mountain is a sacred place, where the spirit resides, and people have to sleep with their heads toward it. In Africa, when T. A. Lambo (1966), the first Nigerian psychiatrist trained abroad in the United Kingdom, returned to his home country, he built a villagelike hospital so that families could live together with patients in the "village." This fits the situation in Nigeria, where psychiatric hospitals are available only near the city, and families and patients have to travel far to obtain psychiatric care.

*Facilities and Services.*    Both the design of the treatment structure and the facilities and services provided within it are important. In Japan, some hospitals, following people's daily custom, built Japanese-style *furo* (bathtub) and toilet for patients' use. In Xinjiang, an autonomic area in the western region of China, where the minority Uygur nationals and the Han nationals cohabitate, in order to comply with their food intake patterns (i.e., Uygur nationals, as Muslim, consider it taboo to eat pork, while pork is considered the main meat for the Han nationals), two kitchens were built in the psychiatric hospital to avoid food "contamination" and two kinds of meals were offered to patients, depending on their religious backgrounds. In a multiethnic society such as Hawaii, various kinds of ethnic foods are provided in rotation to meet patients' tastes. A religious room is designed so that it can be converted for ceremonies of various religions, to suit the multifaith patient population. The major thrust is a cultural concern for the environment and the institutional system in which the patients are to be cared for.

*Different Quality of Service.*   Directly influenced by socioeconomic factors, including payment and the patient's financial condition, and the stigma and attitude toward severe mental illness, the quality of inpatient care varies greatly among different societies and may be different even within the same society. Some facilities are very reasonable, even at the luxury level, while some are terrible from a humanistic point of view. How to set up conditions in the hospital in a way that is suitable for medical treatment and also maintains the quality of living of the community, so that there is no big gap between them (i.e., too luxurious or too poor), is very important. If the conditions are too poor, patients will be reluctant to be hospitalized, but, if they are too luxurious, patients will be reluctant to be discharged back into the community.

## 2. Special Issues

*Involuntary Admission and Physical Confinement.*   Based on different social customs, medical practices, and legal systems, how psychiatric patients are admitted to hospitals for inpatient care varies greatly among different societies. Specifically, are patients voluntarily or involuntarily admitted? In many societies, based on the psychiatrist's professional judgment, a law officer's request, or a family member's suggestion, a psychiatric patient will be hospitalized even without his consent. In contrast, in most European and American societies, the patient's consent is required for admission. Unless there is evidence that the patient has the potential to injure himself or others, even if he is psychotic and needs clinical treatment, patients cannot be admitted involuntarily. This follows the basic concern with human rights in those societies. However, this pattern of practice, even though intended to protect patients, may deprive some patients of proper treatment in the times of such need (if the patient is seriously ill mentally, but not dangerous to himself or others). Because every patient and his family may not understand the practice of psychiatry regarding how the patient can or will be hospitalized, a proper explanation is always necessary. Closely related to this is physical confinement. Because of his violent behavior or suicidal tendencies, a patient may be temporarily physically restrained for protection. However, the patient and his family need to have this protective maneuver carefully explained. Otherwise, it may cause misunderstandings, as physical restraint means different things to people from various cultures.

*Implications of Psychiatric Hospitalization.* Depending on how the patient and his family view mental disorders and the quality of the hospital, the patient will have different attitudes and reactions to psychiatric hospitalization. People from societies that still severely stigmatize mental disorders would regard psychiatric hospitalization as the worst thing that could happen, feeling that they were dumped into a hospital and labeled a terrible "mental" patient. This would be particularly true if the quality of the hospital environment was very poor and filled with many very sick mental patients. On the other hand, if a patient does not have such a strong bias against mental disorders, and the quality of the psychiatric ward was better than the patient's own living conditions, the patient might be pleased to be hospitalized and enjoy the better food and facilities. The different reactions to psychiatric hospitalization by patients of diverse cultural backgrounds need attention for relevant clinical care.

---

CASE 1

An Elderly Asian Male Patient Committed Suicide after Admission to a Psychiatric Hospital (Lillian Jones)

A 60-year-old male Asian patient was admitted for the first time to a psychiatric hospital for problems of depression. He was very reluctant about being admitted to and treated in a mental hospital because he held the strong view that a mental disorder was a terrible sickness, and he was concerned about the reputation he would get among his friends for being treated as a psychiatric patient. He mentioned to his family that he would rather die than be put into a place full of crazy people. However, following the psychiatrist's recommendation, he was finally convinced by his family to be hospitalized and receive treatment. After admission, he become more depressed, refusing to eat and reluctant to talk to the staff. The next morning, he was found dead by hanging himself. Apparently, at midnight, he tore his hospital clothes, making a rope and hanging himself from the top of the bathroom door. He had reacted extremely to being hospitalized in the "psychiatric" ward and the stigma of being a "mental patient."

---

*Staff-Patient Relations.* It is common for inpatient care to be carried out by a group of staff members of different disciplines. In addition to a psychiatrist, a psychologist, and a nurse, the team may include a social worker, an occupational therapist, a recreational therapist, and so on. How they work together as a team, and how the patient and his family relate to them, may be subject to social, medical, and culture variables (see Section 5B1: Therapist-Patient Relations). The patients' and their families' knowledge and understanding of the team, as well as their attitudes toward and relations with these staff, deserve careful attention and management so that they can work well with the multidisciplinary staff team.

*Communication and Translation.*   How to conduct interviews and how to communicate with patients was elaborated earlier in Section 5B2: Interview and Communication. Here, we need only to emphasize again how communication affects the process and results of the clinical assessment and diagnosis of psychotic patients. How to solicit the necessary clinical history and clarify the symptoms depend on communication in psychiatric practice. For instance, when inquiring into the presence or absence of auditory hallucinations, to ask, "Do you hear any 'voices'?" may be sufficient for patients who know what it means to hear "voices" (auditory hallucinations), but it may be easily misunderstood as inquiring into the hearing ability of a patient who is not familiar with the way psychiatrists ask for information. The judgment about delusion is based on the presence of "false" belief not endorsed or shared by other people. However, what is true and false, needs careful assessment based on the social reality. If there is a problems in communication, without proper background information and clarification, such a symptom has difficulty for evaluation. If there is language obstacle, translation is needed. How to obtain professionally correct translation and culturally relevant interpretation is a matter of skill that deserve special attention.

*Assessment and Diagnosis.*   As mentioned previously, from a cultural perspective, clinical assessment and diagnosis are difficult to make for the psychotic symptoms of hallucination, delusion, and orientation. Further, it is generally difficult to make an assessment as to whether or not a thought is "bizarre," behavior is "strange," or affection is "inappropriate," as such judgments need to be based on "reality." However, reality is difficult to grasp if the examiner is unfamiliar with the "reality" in which the patient is living. Collateral information from family or friends can be utilized for making such judgments. Clinical diagnosis is often difficult for clinicians if they are unfamiliar or not experienced with certain groups of disorders. For instance, European–American psychiatrists are less experienced with dissociated or possessed disorders, whereas Asian psychiatrists are less familiar with multiple personality disorders or various kinds of substance abuse or sexual disorders, as such cases rarely appear in psychiatric facilities for care. Clinical experiences and familiarity with disorders will certainly influence clinical competence in making a proper diagnosis. This is particularly true for psychotic patients in an inpatient setting.

*Medication.*   For psychotic inpatients, biological treatment in the form of medication is a main approach of therapy. How ethnic factors will influence the psychopharmacological response, which, in turn, shapes the therapeutic dose and severity of side effects, is a subject that deserves careful attention. It is becoming common knowledge that, due to pharmacokinetic differences, therapeutic doses need to be adjusted (i.e., reduced almost by half) for some ethnic groups, such as Asian people, in contrast to Caucasian groups, for which the official recommendation for dosages were established (see Chapter 8: Ethnicity, Culture, and

Drug Therapy). In addition, the psychological effects of prescribing and receiving medication need full attention. Even to the same medication prescribed by different therapists who have different ways of giving medication, patients will respond differently with different results of adherence.

*Therapeutic Activities.*    In addition to drug treatment, various kinds of therapeutic programs are often provided in the psychiatric ward. These may include occupational therapy, recreational therapy, and group therapy. Based on their knowledge and previous behavior patterns, patients of various ethnic or cultural backgrounds may respond differently to these different therapeutic activities. For example, patients from a society where people are not used to expressing their feelings or examining their minds in front of others may not appreciate ward meetings or group therapy with their peer patients, but prefer activity-oriented occupational therapy. This may apply to various modes of psychotherapy offered (see Section 7C: Cultural Considerations in Various Modes of Therapy).

*Family Visits and Discharge.*    Depending on the social customs and the nature of medical practice, how the family participates in the care of a psychiatric patient in a ward setting varies from society to society. In some, the family is allowed to live with the patient day and night, working with the staff to care for the patient; in others, citing that visitors will interfere with the treatment program, friends or family are allowed to visit a patient only at certain times under strict rules. Consequently, the degree and the nature of the involvement of the family in the care of the patient varies greatly. It also indirectly affects the prognosis of the patient after he is discharged from the hospital and staying with his family.

## B. OUTPATIENT PSYCHIATRIC CARE

### 1. Overall Issues

In general, after discharge from the hospital, severely ill psychiatric patients are continuously cared for in outpatient settings. Patients with minor psychiatric disorders are mostly treated as outpatients, as well. Depending on the social and medical system, particularly the availability of facilities, method of payment of fees, and cultural attitudes mental illness, the pattern of outpatient service may vary from society to society. Outpatient care may be offered as a public or private service. The number of patients to be cared for in the outpatient setting will vary greatly based on the nature of service delivered, availability of services and clinicians, and other factors, including payment system. All these factors will directly and indirectly shape the nature and the level of sophistication of the care for outpatients (Well et al., 1987).

*Amount of Patients To Be Served.*    The total number of patients to be treated within a period of time varies tremendously in different societies. In some, the patients are so overcrowded that a psychiatrist has to deal with several dozen patients in a half-day. As a result, the therapist has only a few minutes for each patient, barely enough time to inquire into the patient's chief complaints and, at the same time, prescribe medication for the initial complaint. It becomes a luxury to explore emotional problems and conduct psychological therapy. This is true not only in most underdeveloped and developing societies but also in developed societies, where public health insurance has been adopted (Lefley & Bestman, 1991). In contrast, in some clinics, particularly private ones in developed societies, only a limited number of patients are served at one time, often by an appointment system, so that more psychological treatment can be provided. This certainly shapes the nature and quality of outpatient services provided.

*Nature of the Patient Population to Be Cared for.*    Very closely related to the number of patients to be cared for is the matter of the kind of patient population to be served. It ranges from predominantly chronic psychotic patients in most public settings in many societies to predominantly minor psychiatric disorders or situational adjustment problems in most private clinics in developed societies. This definitely determines the nature of care delivered in outpatient clinics.

## 2. Special Matters

*Appointment System.*    From a cultural perspective, the first issue that deserves mention is that of the appointment system. In contemporary medical systems, the patient comes to visit the physician at a predetermined time, rather than any time the patient wants to drop by. However, such a system is not necessarily familiar to a patient from a different cultural background. This is influenced further by geographic distance and means of transportation available. It is further shaped by the nature of the psychopathology from which the patient is suffering. Due to these factors, it would be a mistake to simply interpret that patients do not adhere to treatment programs if they do not keep to an appointment schedule. In order to accommodate a patient who may not show up on time for treatment, the clinician needs to be flexible in carrying out practice, allowing a patient to show up at any time. In remote or rural areas, when a patient needs to take several days to reach an available clinic, it is often necessary to give immediate service whenever the patient drops in and to prescribe medication for several months, if possible, with the assumption that the patient will probably not return to the clinic for any follow-up service.

*Psychological or Drug Therapy.*    The next issue that needs to be considered is whether or not to provide simply psychological therapy or simply drug therapy, or to do both in combination. Many patients, who are used to visiting a physician, receiving medication, and making payments for them, will feel that they are not receiving any "treatment" merely by talking to the therapist. The clinician needs to make a judgment regarding the kind of therapy that will not only meet the medical needs of the patient but will also satisfy the patient's expectations.

*Involvement of Family.*    In most European-American societies, the patients visit clinics by themselves, with the basic assumption that it is their responsibility to take care of themselves. It is also a matter of confidentiality that grown-up patients prefer to see their therapists by themselves and are seldom accompanied by their families. However, this is not true in other societies or for many ethnic minority groups. For them, it is considered a family matter, and family members often accompany the patients on their visits to the clinic. They are not concerned about confidentiality and are interested in seeing the therapist together with the patient. It is a natural opportunity to view the situation and to conduct a family session at the same time. It useful to be able to make use of the support resources of the family.

*Outreach Program.*    Although the concept of an outreach program has been stressed in association with the community psychiatric service movement, in practice, this approach has not been widely applied. However, from a sociocultural point of view, it is very important for mental health workers to go outside of the clinic and try to reach and provide care for patients and their families. This would resolve the problems related to geographically remote rural and remote areas, but it also would reduce significantly the difficulty encountered by patients of minority ethnic groups who are not used to visiting mental health facilities and are reluctant to see psychiatrists (Wilson, 1980).

*Payment System.*    To ask patient to make payments to the clinician or to the clinic for the care rendered is understood by patient from many societies. However, it may be perceived as "unnatural" for patients from some cultures, in which a physician's care is considered, as that of a religious person, as a "service" for people who are suffering. A voluntary donation with appreciation may be considered, but feel awkward to make a commercialized fee payment. In such societies, it would be helpful to the clinician as well as to the patient to provide a careful explanation of the medical payment system. Related to this is the custom of giving gift to the therapist. This behavior needs to be understood, whether it is merely following cultural custom to express appreciation to the healer or there is any unusual motivation and meaning involved in doing so.

*Adherence and Utilization.*    The final issue that calls for attention is that of adherence to and utilization of service. In the modern psychiatric system, it is assumed that therapy will continue and the patient needs to adhere to treatment until termination is suggested by the therapist. However, this concept and practice are not necessarily applicable to patients from certain other cultures. For them, the patient decides whether or not to continue treatment. Often, when the problems subside, they will terminate their visits to the therapist. It is quite all right to visit several therapists or healers simultaneously, without feeling wrong about doing so. If they are not satisfied with the care they receive, it is their decision to discontinue it. Adherence to service needs to be understood in this cultural context, rather than believing that the patient is not motivated for treatment. The situation depends on how the service is initially conceived and how the rules of therapy are explained.

## C. PSYCHIATRIC EMERGENCY SERVICE

### 1. General Problems

*Immediate Care with Limited Information.*    Although it is the nature of psychiatric emergency service that a clinician needs to make a quick assessment and tentative diagnosis for immediate care, even with limited medical information, this nature of the problem becomes more difficult if the patient is of a different ethnic, racial, or cultural background from the clinician or if there are language differences. It is necessary that a clinician has sufficient clinical experience to enable him to make a clinical judgment and offer care in such emergency situations.

*Dealing with More Certain Psychiatric Problems.*    It is also the nature of emergency service to deal with certain psychiatric disorders (e.g., acute psychoses, delirious states, suicidal attempts, or violent behavior), as such disorders often need emergency care. However, beyond that, certain different psychiatric problems are encountered in different societies associated with social and cultural background. For instance, in contemporary Euro-American societies, many patients will make more emergency visits for substance abuse associated with either intoxication or withdrawal problems. This is because such psychiatric problems are currently prevalent in these societies. A familiarity with the clinical manifestation of various kinds of substance abuse and treatment is necessary for clinicians in these settings. This may be not necessarily be true in other societies, where substance abuse is less frequently observed. In contrast, hysterical disorders, either in the form of conversion disorders or dissociation, may be encountered in emergency service. Literature indicates that this is at least true in China (Luo & Zhou, 1984), India (Dube, 1970), and Saudi Arabia (Al-Habeeb et al.,

1999) and among Ethiopian immigrants to Israel (Grisaru, Budowski, & Witztum, 1997). Under such circumstances, properly distinguishing conversion disorders from organic conditions, including epilepsy, becomes an important clinical task. In other words, in emergency clinics in different sociocultural settings, the clinician has to learn to encounter and deal with different kinds of psychiatric disorders.

## 2. Special Challenge

*Minimizing Diagnostic Error.*   It is the art of emergency service to make proper diagnoses as soon as possible for immediate care. This relies on required medical history and laboratory examination. In order to solicit needed clinical information, it is important to lead the interview actively and to coach the patient and family in providing relevant information in a limited time. Many patients and family members are not familiar with medical situations and are not experienced in presenting their problems. This is particularly true if the patients and families are from different social and cultural backgrounds and do not have a medically oriented "illness" concept. For instance, the patient's family may, based on their beliefs and interpretation, present the story that the patient panicked or became crazy after being frightened by thunder or possessed by an ancestor's spirit. A psychiatrist may be interested in whether the patient had taken any street drug or had had a head injury prior to the onset of the psychotic manifestation. Working through the gap in the knowledge and conceptual differences regarding the "problems" is a task that needs to be accomplished within a limited time, not to mention how to deal with a language barrier if one exists. When there is a language problem between the patient and the psychiatrist, it can be a serious challenge in an emergency setting. The availability of culturally experienced professional translators becomes a crucial factor.

*Adequate Involvement of Family Members.*   In many Western societies, medical practice is oriented to focus on the patient himself and tends not to involve family members immediately in the process of evaluation. Even if the patient is brought to the emergency clinic by his family, in the "patient-focused" medical system, the family is often asked to sit outside in the waiting room while the clinician examines the patient. This pattern of medical practice may be all right in outpatient service, but in an emergency clinic, it makes more sense to involve the family from the very beginning. It will certainly help the clinician to obtain needed collateral information about the patient and will prompt the process of immediate evaluation and diagnosis. This is particularly true for patients from cultural backgrounds with which the clinician is unfamiliar. It will help the clinician to verify the "reality" and to assess to what extent the patient's psychopathology is far from the reality. The diagnosis of certain psychopathologies relies heavily on an assessment against reality, to determine such symptoms as delusion, particularly of a religious nature, or other "strange" behavior. Collateral information and validation from family members becomes very useful. Participation of family members from the beginning will certainly reduce their tension and anxiety. It will also help the clinician to assess whether the patient is ready to be discharged from the clinic and return home.

*Proper Clinical Decision for Care and Disposition.*   One of the main tasks of the clinician in psychiatric emergency service is to decide whether or not to discharge the patient from the emergency clinic after certain management and care has been delivered or to refer the patient to inpatient care. It has been indicated by numerous studies that race tends to play a significant role not only in giving patients more serious diagnoses, shaping the quality of clinical care, but also in hospitalizing patients involuntarily (Kinkenberg & Calsyn, 1997; Segal, Bola, & Watson, 1996; Strakowski et al., 1995). Clinicians have to learn how to make proper clinical judgments in cases without being biased by the racial background of the patients. This is particularly true when the clinician has to make a quick decision and provide care in emergency circumstances.

*Maximally Utilize Available Resources.*   Psychiatric emergency services are supposed not only to make diagnoses and provide care but also to channel the patient to resources for care and support after discharge. This is particularly true for patients and families who are unfamiliar with psychiatric and mental health facilities in the community, such as ethnic minorities and immigrants. Adequate social work becomes important in such circumstances in emergency service.

## D. CONSULTATION-LIAISON SERVICE

### 1. Medical Issues That Need to Be Dealt with

Liaison-consultation services not only provide psychiatric care for medical patients in hospital setting but also often offer consultation services to the physicians who care for those patients. Knowing how to work with physicians, medical staff, and patients and their families becomes a major concern and clinical task. For this reason, in order to carry out culturally competent liaison-consultation services, a psychiatrist needs to first comprehend the culture-related medical issues that he needs to be aware of and how to deal with them from a cultural perspectives (Collins, Dimsdale, & Wilkins, 1992; Luke, 1996; Qureshi, 1994).

*Informing the Patient or Family of the Medical Diagnosis.*   In Western Europe or North America, following contemporary medical practice, a physician will openly and frankly inform the patient of his diagnosis of the disorder from which the patient is suffering. Otherwise, he would be subject to a malpractice suit. However, in contrast, following the cultures of some societies, exemplified by Japan, it is still expected that a physician will conceal the actual diagnosis from the patient, particularly of a serious or fatal illness, to protect the "vulnerable" patient (Elwyn et al., 2002). The actual diagnosis is told only to the family. If the physician were to reveal the actual diagnosis (such as cancer or some other serious or fatal sickness) to the patient without the family's consent, he may be subject to resentment from the family. This is a complicated matter in which the physician needs to act according to proper medical ethics as well as the culture of the society (Beyene, 1992; Krauss-Mars & Lachman, 1994).

*Prescribing and Receiving Medication.*    Western medicine is based on a pharmacotechnology that prepares drugs in pure abstract forms to perform specific pharmacological functions. Modern physicians usually prescribe a single medication for a specific purpose, and for multiple problems they may prescribe multiple medications. However, they usually try to prescribe as few drugs as possible, to avoid drug interactions. In contrast, herbal medicines used in traditional medical practice are thought to work by combining multiple remedies in their raw forms. Multiple herbs are always prescribed, as there is not too much concern over compounding medications. In general, in societies where traditional medicine is still used, Western medicine is considered "strong" and useful for combating the specific etiology of a disorder, but there are usually unwelcome side effects. Traditional herbal medicine is viewed as "harmonious," with fewer side effects, and will "strengthen" the body so that it can overcome the disorder.

Another interesting belief that may be held by laypeople in non-Western societies is that medication by injection is much more powerful than oral medication. An injection, even a shot of vitamins, is perceived as a "powerful" remedy. An intravenous medication is considered even more effective than an intramuscular injection. Thus, physicians may give intravenous injections of normal saline or glucose plus vitamins to induce a placebo effect or simply to satisfy a patient's request.

Modern Western physicians make no secret about the name and nature of prescriptions and often make it a goal to explain to the patient the drug mechanism as well as potential side effects. Traditional physicians, on the other hand, sometimes keep prescriptions "secret" and in some Asian countries, such as Japan, China, and Korea, the patient may not expect the physician to give a full explanation (see Chapter 8: Ethnicity, Culture, and Drug Therapy).

Associated with this is the tendency of patients to feel that there is no need to follow the physician's orders in taking the medication. If the medicine works immediately (within a day or so), the patient will take it. If the symptoms subside, the patient may decide to discontinue the medication, even against the physician's directions. Kandakai and colleagues (1996) examined the use of antibiotics among African-Americans based on gender. Women were more likely to report completing the prescribed trial of antibiotics, while older men were more likely to use antibiotics only until the problem stopped. A significant percentage of men (23%) and women (18%) reported sharing their antibiotics with another person.

*Laboratory Testing.* In modern medical practice, it is common to perform various kinds of laboratory testing to assist in making a diagnosis. Various specimens may be needed for testing. However, due to cultural beliefs regarding the body, certain reactions and preferences may be encountered among different cultural groups. People who believe that blood is one of the major fluids in the body, essential for "vitality," may be reluctant to have blood drawn for testing. They will be extremely concerned with how much is taken. The same applies to spinal tapping when spinal fluid, the essence of the "spirit," is drawn for testing. In contrast, providing urine, feces, or sputum for testing is not a problem, since they are considered "wastes."

*Management of Medical Pain.* The examination of a pain disorder, particularly psychologically based pain, has been elaborated in Section 4D: Somatoform Disorders, Including Neurasthenia). In addition to pain related to somatoform disorders, there can also be medical pain associated with childbirth, cancer, or surgery. Naturally, there is also room for cultural impact on various factors of pain, such as the patient's perception of pain, interaction between the patient and the care-giver, and general expectations and attitudes about pain-killing medicines.

*Issues Relating to Surgical Operations.* Most people now appreciate that surgery can be effective in treating certain medical conditions, such as appendicitis, and may even be needed to save one's life. However, based on unique cultural beliefs, some patients may have special psychological reactions to certain surgeries, such as those that result in the loss of a part of the body. To lose a part of one's own body may be interpreted as a loss of one's integrity. Influenced by such a belief, a diabetic patient may refuse amputation of a leg necrotic from ulcers, or a woman with breast cancer may choose chemotherapy rather than surgical removal of her breast, even though it may result in a lower possibility of cure.

Blood transfusions are also sometimes a necessary part of surgery. While it is common for people to be concerned about how much blood will be lost during an operation, in some cultures, blood is considered a vital body fluid and there might be a strong wish to conserve it as much as possible. In such a case, there might be less opposition toward receiving blood transfusions to gain the needed vital body fluid. In contrast, certain religious beliefs, such as those of Jehovah's Witnesses, might lead its members to refuse to accept blood transfusions, even as life-saving treatments.

*Legal Definition of Death.*   The professional medical and legal definition of "death" is not uniform around the world. In the United States, "brain death," as verified by EEG (Electronic Encephalography) is sufficient to determine death legally. In contrast, Japan is more conservative, defining "death" as the complete stopping of the heartbeat. These different ways of defining "legal" death have a direct impact on organ donation. For instance, only one heart transplant has ever been performed in Japan, and that was 30 years ago. In 1997, *The Honolulu Advertiser* reported a story by E. Talmadge (1997) about an 8-year-old Japanese girl who received $600,000 in donations in Japan for a badly needed heart transplant but had to come to the United States for the operation. It was two years later, after many years' struggle between the professional and legal systems, that Japan finally passed a rule that brain death would be accepted as the criterion for death to facilitate organ donation.

*Organ Donation and Transplantation.*   In spite of the remarkable medical technology that now exists for organ transplantations, not many people are interested in donating their organs after death. Often even physicians who understand the life-saving benefits of organ donation have great difficulty in suggesting such a concept to the patient or his family.

It has been noticed that donor authorizations tend to be especially low among African-Americans and other minority and ethnic groups in the United States. Rubens (1996) carried out a questionnaire survey of the beliefs and attitudes toward organ transplantation and rates of participation regarding organ donation among a sampling of racially and ethnically mixed university students at a state-assisted university in the Midwest. He reported that African-American students differed significantly from Caucasian students in their attitudes and beliefs toward organ donation. However, a greater percentage of African-American students granted permission for organ donation than African-Americans in the general population.

Among the various reasons that people are reluctant about organ donation is the cultural view that it is very important to keep the body intact, even for burial or cremation. Ross (1981) pointed out that in the Islamic religion, a Muslim does not own his body but holds it in a "trust from God." Consequently, a Muslim cannot donate or receive organ transplants, and blood transfusions are permissible only if recommended by a physician who is Muslim for the purpose of saving that person from death. Similarly, traditionally American-Indians view the dead body as a seed that is placed in the ground. As a seed is planted whole, so the body should be buried intact. An amputated limb or excised organ may be claimed for storage in a freezer and retrieved for burial with the body.

*Autopsy.*   In accordance with the belief of keeping the body intact after death, it is relatively difficult to convince surviving family members to agree to an autopsy of the deceased. In many cultures, it is almost impossible to obtain permission for an autopsy, unless it is legally required, such as for forensic purposes. The autopsy rate in Arab countries is extremely low, and cadavers are not permitted for use in teaching or for research purposes. This is also true in many Asian countries, where the family is not keen on the idea of an autopsy, and cadavers for medical teaching often come only from homeless people who die without any families.

*Death, Grief, and Mourning.* Although it is a universal desire for a person to live as long as possible and to find ways to prolong life, attitudes toward death are subject to cultural influences. Prolonging life through intensive care or by mechanical means may not be appreciated in many cultures. In some, it is considered a natural phenomenon to die after a certain age, and death may be treated as a happy occasion rather than a sad one.

In many cultures, it is considered desirable for people to die in their own homes surrounded by their immediate family members. When this is the custom, the family will ask the physician about the patient's medical prognosis. If the patient is considered to have no hope for recovery, it is the physician's responsibility to inform the family of the appropriate time for the patient to be discharged from the hospital so that his last days may be spent at home.

## 2. Culturally Stigmatized Medical Diseases

Because of their poor prognoses and historically limited effectiveness of treatment, the diagnoses of certain medical diseases still carry a substantial stigma despite an improvement in medical management. Leprosy, pulmonary tuberculosis, epilepsy, and veneral disease are some examples of diseases that are are still associated with strong negative views as a result of cultural beliefs, which intensely influence patients' emotional lives as well as their illness behavior. The patient's and his family's medical knowledge definitely has an impact on their attitude toward various kinds of disease (Carpenter & Colwell, 1995; Dancy, 1996; Matsumoto et al., 1995).

As a new, spreading medical disorder, AIDS is viewed as an awful disease because of its undesirable outcome, its association with drug abuse or homosexual behavior, and the possibility of contagion, either homosexually (in most Euro-American societies) or heterosexually (in Africa or Asian societies). Even physicians and dentists have been reluctant to come in contact with and provide care for patients with this disorder. Following a survey of Asian vs. Caucasian dentists practicing in New York City, Raphael and associates (1996) reported that Asian dentists expressed significantly more negative attitudes toward and unwillingness to treat HIV-positive patients than did Caucasian dentists.

## 3. Sex-Related Medical Conditions or Issues

*Breast Cancer.*    The varying degrees to which female breasts have a sexual role in different cultures may influence the patient's understanding of the causes of breast cancer. Chavez and associates (1995) interviewed Salvadoran and Mexican immigrants, Chicanas, and Anglo-Americans in California concerning attitudes toward risk factors for breast cancer. They found two broad cultural models. The Anglo-American model emphasized family history and age as risk factors. The Latin model associated breast trauma and "bad" behaviors (such as alcohol and illegal drug use) as risk factors for breast cancer. A subsequent investigation by Hubbell and his colleagues (1996) in California found that Latinas were more likely than Anglo-American women to believe that factors such as breast trauma (71% vs. 39%) and breast fondling (27% vs. 6%) increased the risk of breast cancer. The investigators concluded that Latinas' beliefs about breast cancer may reflect the moral framework within which they interpret diseases.

*Pregnancy, Pre- and Postnatal Care, and Childbirth.*    Pregnancy and giving birth not only are major events in the parents' lives but also have substantial cultural significance and are impacted by cultural beliefs. Woollet and colleagues (1995) compared the ideas and experiences of pregnancy and childbirth of Asian and non-Asian women in east London. Although Asian women demonstrated a strong commitment to Western maternity care, they continued to follow traditional cultural practices such as observing a special diet in pregnancy and following restrictions on certain activities in the postpartum period. Asian women tended to want their partners present at delivery and to express a greater concern with the gender of the child.

In some ethnic groups, great attention is paid to postpartum care. In traditional Chinese belief, a woman is expected to observe one month of confinement after giving birth. She is not allowed to go outside of her house, to take "cold" foods (such as fruits), or to bath or even wash her hair. A woman is supposed to eat a lot of "hot" foods (such as chicken cooked with sesame oil and ginger). These customs were observed in the past, perhaps to prevent postpartum infection, and are still faithfully observed by some traditional women. In Micronesia, a traditional "pregnancy taboo" requires the wife to return to her family of origin once she discovers she is pregnant. She does not return to her husband's house until her child is old enough to hold his breath under water or to jump across a ditch, activities that ensure a greater likelihood of survival.

Breast-feeding is a very natural way to feed a newborn baby. However, despite the widely acknowledged evidence supporting the benefits of breast-feeding (fewer childhood infections and allergies), the prevalence of breast-feeding in Western countries remains low. This may be due to the development of baby formula or time demands on a working mother. However, Rodriguez-Garcia and Frazier (1995) point out that the cultural notion of the female breast as a primarily sexual object places the act of breast-feeding in a controversial light and can be one of the most influential factors in a woman's decision not to breast-feed.

*Hysterectomy.*    In many cultures, reproduction is considered one of the major functions of women, and losing the uterus is considered to be losing the power of being a woman. Many women fear that their sexual desire will change after a hysterectomy, and that their husbands will not want them because they are "incomplete" women. As a result, they might refuse to have their uteruses removed or develop anxiety and depression after a hysterectomy.

*Menopause.*    Although menopause is a biological phenomenon, the intensity of menopausal symptoms varies among ethnic or racial groups. This may be due partially to diet, with a recent study revealing that Asian women may experience fewer hot flashes because of estrogen derived from soybean products in their meals. To what extent sexual attitudes contribute to emotional adjustment or attitudes toward menopause is a subject that requires future investigation.

## 4. Culturally and Ethically Controversial Medical Practices

*Abortion.*    Abortion is the subject of an intense emotional, political, and ethical debate in many countries. In the United States, there is no foreseeable resolution to the conflict, which has involved radical acts such as the bombing of abortion clinics and the shooting of physicians who perform abortions. However, in many countries, abortion is an accepted part of family planning. This is particularly true in societies where there is societal acceptance of the concept of population control. Thus, abortion is not merely a medical choice but also a social, cultural, and political matter.

*Sterilization.*    From a medical point of view, sterilization is a simple surgical operation and a way of family planning. However, there may be a significant psychological impact depending on how such the procedure is seen by the patient's culture. In some cultures, particularly those that strongly emphasize the need for many children, sterilization can be seen as a very unwelcome procedure. In such cases, sterilization for men may be considered almost equal to castration, even though medically it is not.

*Euthanasia.* Whether physicians are allowed to offer active assistance for patients to end their lives is a controversial subject in many societies. In Holland, euthanasia is actively practiced by physicians (Battin, 1991). In Germany, assisted suicide is a legal option but is usually practiced outside of the medical setting. In the United States, withdrawing from or refusing treatment is the only means currently permitted by law, and then only with legal documentation from the patient or his family.

## 5. Key Areas for Clinical Attention

*Body and Mind Relations.* Several issues need clinical attention in order to provide successful liaison-consultation services. Among them is the matter of the relationship between "body" and "mind," which need to be understood from a cultural perspective. This is strongly influenced by the dualistic concept of Western physicians, who tend to view the body and the mind as separate, dichotomized beings. Closely associated with this epistemological view is the notion that problems expressed through psychological complaints are superior or more mature than somatic complaints. Eastern physicians do not necessarily hold the same view. By viewing body and mind as integrated parts of the whole thing, they do not distinguish distinctly between them and do not try to view psychological or somatic manifestations in a hierarchical way.

*Disease and Illness.* Cultural anthropologists and cultural psychiatrists propose using the terms "disease" and "illness" to denote different semantic concepts. Disease refers to the medical definition of sickness and is explained from the perspective of biological and physiological etiology, manifestation, course, and outcome. Disease is considered objective and universal in nature. Illness implies a patient's psychological construct of the perception, experience, and understanding of suffering. Illness is subjective and open to cultural impact (see Section 2E: Illness Behavior: Recognition and Help-Seeking).

*Psychiatrist and Relations with the Physician.* Associated with the level of medical development and the nature of psychiatric disorders, mental health problems and the role and status of psychiatrists may be viewed differently by physicians and lay people in different societies. In some societies, psychiatric disorders still carry a strong stigma, and seeing a psychiatrist is to be avoided. In contrast, it may be seen as important to seek psychiatric service to work on emotional problems. These attitudes are observed not only among laypeople but also among physicians. They greatly influence psychiatric referrals and the nature of liaison-consultation services. How the psychiatric consultation is requested and how the psychiatrist and the physician should work together are essential factors that will directly and indirectly determine the success of liaison-consultation services.

CASE 2

A Samoan Woman Who Tied a String around Her Neck (Streltzer, 1998)

An old Samoan woman with multiple somatic disorders, including diabetes, hypertension, and kidney problems, was admitted to the hospital at her physician's advice. Emergency psychiatric consultation was requested, as she was found tying a string from the bedside light around her neck, and suicidal intentions were suspected by the medical staff. After a skillful interview by the Caucasian consulting psychiatrist, who established a rapport first by praising the patient on how she was a successful woman, raising a large family by herself after her husband's death, the patient began to open up and reveal her frustrations. She described how she had been very reluctant to stay in the hospital to begin with. It was her family doctor who promised that she needed to stay only for several days for a workup. She had been confined to the hospital for more than 2 weeks and was still not allowed to return home. She became resentful and tied the rope around her neck, wanting not to kill herself but to show her anger toward her physician for his being untruthful and unable to keep his promise. This sensitive therapist, who knew how to engage a patient of a different ethnic background, established a rapport by "talking story" about her family and showed cultural empathy so that the patient eventually was willing to share her inner feelings and allow the consultant to work on her problems. Otherwise, the patient might have been simply treated as a person with suicidal tendencies and transferred to a psychiatric ward with a diagnosis of major depression.

## E. PSYCHIATRIC NURSING CARE

Psychiatric nurses play very significant roles in psychiatric care, particularly in inpatient settings. However, their function may vary in different societies, illustrating how medical and social factors influence their roles and functions as well as how cultural factors need to be considered in providing nursing services. The cultural aspects of psychiatric nursing have been gaining more attention recently, as illustrated by the appearance of publications on this subject (Davis, 1981; Leininger, 1991, 1995; Lipson & Steiger, 1996).

### 1. General Issues

*The Role and Status of Psychiatric Nurses.*    Very much influenced by sociomedical and cultural systems, the role, status, and function of nurses varies in different societies. They are basically shaped by the medical culture operated in a given society at a particular time. For example, in many Asian societies, physicians have the ultimate authority in administrating inpatient services, and nurses have only subordinate status and supplementary roles in providing nursing care; whereas in many European-American societies, nurses play major roles in administrating services in the inpatient unit, while physicians only provide medical treatment.

*Relations with Physicians.*    Traditionally, physicians are male, and nurses are female. As a result, physician-nurse relations are subject to the male-female gender relations defined in the society. For example, in Japan, where in general man has a higher status than woman, even now, nurses are expected to bow to physicians when they meet them. Nurses are expected to play only supplementary and subordinate roles under physicians (Long, 1984). However, in the United States, this hierarchy is less obvious, and nurses and physicians relate to each other more or less in a spirit of equality and democracy.

*Relations with Patients.*    In general, nurses have more direct contact with patients, providing care and maintaining close relations. This is particularly true in a society at where physicians play rather authoritative roles in their relations with patients. Physicians' interactions with patients are minimal, and professional distance is maintained. In this situation, patients feel that nurses are the staff with whom they can communicate and to whom they can relate. Any questions or concerns they have are addressed to the nurses, rather than the physicians. Nurses play the role of intermediator between physicians and patients (and their families).

*Relations with Families.*    Depending on different social, medical, and cultural systems, there are different ways in which the family is involved in the service setting. In some societies, the family is allowed to be present in the ward around the clock, participating in the care of the patient, while in other societies they are permitted only to visit at defined, limited times. The difference in the way families are allowed to contact patients certainly modifies the relations between nurses and family members of the patient, not only in terms of amount but also in nature. In any case, nurses have ample opportunity to interact with family members, not only for observation but also for involvement in care delivery. From a cultural perspective, it is important that nurses understand the family system, structure, interpersonal relations, and functions from a cross-cultural perspective so that proper relationships can be established with the family and beside family counseling offered if necessary.

## 2. Special Issues Relating to Nursing Care

*Spatial Distance and Physical Contact with Patients.*    Nursing care involves maintaining a spatial distance from and physical contact with patients. Spatial distance from and physical contact with others is often defined by social and cultural habit. This is particularly true in the case of persons of different genders. The proper distance between persons (particularly man and woman), the extent to which they are allowed to have physical contact, or the parts of the body with which they are allowed to have physical contact are potentially sensitive issues influenced by different cultures. A culturally sensitive care deliverer needs to be aware of the individual, professional, and sociocultural implications of such body contact. The need for special concern over this matter is illustrated in Micronesia. In the Pacific Islands of Micronesia, women from the outer islands may still practice the custom of going topless (exposing their breasts) in the tropical weather. However, the parts of the body between the umbilicus and the knees are considered very private, and need to be covered. For health reasons, if any male physician or nurse needs to examine the patient's body between the umbilicus and the knees, it is required to have the mother present, if the patient is not married yet, or the husband, if she is.

*Assessment and Judgment of the Patient's Behavior.*   In addition to general medical professional competency, nurses, in the same way as physicians, need to develop cultural competency in their care of psychiatric patients. This includes learning how to observe and understand the patients' as well as their families' behavior from a cultural standpoint so that proper assessment can be made and relevant care can be provided. For instance, if parents try to scratch their child's body and make a mark on the skin of the extremities, trunk, or neck, they are following a folk medical concept and practice to stimulate the discharge of excessive "heat" from the body, to help cure the heat-induced health problems. It should not be misinterpreted as physical abuse by the parents. If a patient needs to kneel down and bow in a certain direction to pray several times a day, he is merely following Muslim religious practice, rather than manifesting "bizarre" behavior. In the same way, if a person who just lost a beloved one keeps talking to the deceased person, he is only manifesting a "normal" grief reaction and not strange or psychotic behavior. It is important to understand and assess a patient's behavior within the total cultural context rather than merely from a single behavioral manifestation.

*Matters Related to Nurturing and Independence.*   Even though it is the professional job of healthcare deliverers to offer nurturing care for ill patients, particularly for those who are very sick, or disabled patients, in contemporary medicine, careful consideration and debate needs to be given to what nurturing care means and to what extent care needs to be provided for patients. It is considered that patients need to be encouraged to care for themselves for the sake of quickening the process of rehabilitation. Professional persons should be careful not to deprive patients from the opportunity of self-healing and self-recovery. This is a particularly important area of study in the field of psychiatry, which deals not so much with physical as with psychological aspects. However, "proper" nurturing care is a matter of not only professional but also sociocultural judgment and definition. A competent nurse will sensitively reveal what is expected by the patients and their families and provide suitable explanation and education, so that proper care is provided.

## F. MENTAL HEALTH SOCIAL WORK

The primary work of the mental health social worker is to assist the family in determining how to provide care for the patient and to help the patient and family utilize the resources of support existing in the community or social system. It focuses on the maintenance of mental health care needed for the patient and the family during hospitalization; after discharge, it promotes the process of improvement, rehabilitation, and prevention of recurrence of mental health problems. In general, the social worker performs the service as an adjunct to psychiatrist or other mental health workers or independently. In another word, the service is heavily focused on the family, community, and social system at large.

### 1. Common Issues

*Working with Family.*   It is common practice for a pediatrician to involve the parents when he is treating a small child or for a geriatrician to include adult children or a spouse when he is treating an elderly person. However, when treating ordinary adults, modern therapists with Western backgrounds seldom consider the need to involve family members. This stems from the Western therapist's basic philosophical attitude that a person should handle his own problems.

However, this is not necessarily true from a cultural perspective. For many cultures, family ties and interpersonal relationships are so tight that an individual seldom exists by himself. If a person becomes sick, he may be accompanied by his parents, spouse, and children and visited by a group of relatives or friends. This is a culture-derived custom. A mental health worker should take the opportunity to involve family members whenever they are available and to offer family-oriented therapy (Tseng & Hsu, 1991).

It needs to be recognized that family members, whether parent(s), spouses, sibling(s), or children can play different roles when one member becomes sick. A family member can play the role of spokesperson, making statements for the patient as well as the rest of the family. He can play the role of negotiator, trying to communicate with the therapist through indirect channels and to advocate on the patient's behalf. He can provide important assistance to the patient, offering a resource for support, or assist the therapist in supervising the patient's behavior to ensure that the patient complies with the prescribed therapy. Conversely, a family member can become oppositional, resisting the treatment and becoming a major obstacle to improvement.

Thus, recognizing the role played by family member(s) and managing the family for the sake of the patient's therapy and improvement are among the skills a competent therapist must master. This is especially true when a social worker is dealing with a patient who, according to his culture, is very closely related to his family. Knowing how to deal with the patient alone, without knowing how to relate to his family, is not enough for a therapist, at least not from a cultural perspective.

Working with the family, from a cultural perspectives, is necessary to comprehend the cultural aspects of the family, including the family system, structure, relations, and functions, so that proper family-focused care can be provided (Tseng & Hsu, 1991). In multiethnic societies, such as the United States, it is necessary for the social workers to be acquainted with the diverse ethnic backgrounds of families (Allen-Meares & Burman, 1995; Ewalt & Mokuau, 1995; Gross, 1995; McGoldrick, Giordano, & Pearce, 1996) so that proper care and therapy can be offered.

*Working with the Community.*   Every community is different more or less in terms of its socioeconomic condition, medical facilities and system, and ethnic and cultural backgrounds of its members. In order to utilize maximally the support resources available in the community, or society at large, it is necessary for the social worker to be familiar with the nature, structure, and system of the community and society. In addition, it is also important to know the patient's and the family's knowledge, attitudes, and ability to utilize existing social support systems, including social welfare and other services. This is particularly true for foreigners or new immigrants, who are unfamiliar with the host society, which may be quite different from their home societies. It is useful to know that the patients or their families have very different attitudes toward public support systems, such as welfare. Some do not hesitate to accept social welfare, while others tend to avoid such assistance, considering it shameful to rely on such a public system.

## 2. Special Functions and Services

Social workers at large in a community are often involved directly or indirectly in various mental-health-related services. These may include services relating to child protection, custody decisions, or adoption. If these services involve clients of diverse ethnic or racial backgrounds, particularly with communication problems due to language or conceptual issues, special care is warranted. For example, taking small children away from their parents and placing them in foster homes for the purpose of "protection" is an entirely Western concept and practice that has never been heard of or practiced in many Eastern societies, where the togetherness of the family is very valued and respected. To what extent parents are allowed to carry out physical discipline of their children varies greatly among different cultures. To what extent parents can acceptably have physical contact with their small children is different in various societies. Therefore, workers involved with the assessment of child abuse, either physical or sexual, need to be very careful, culturally relevant, and professionally correct in their considerations.

There is no shortage of examples in which misunderstandings between the patient, family members, and mental-health-related workers have occurred as a result of patients and their families who have problems comprehending the socially available mental-health-related system or mental health workers who misjudge the patient's or the family's behavior due to language obstacles and ethnic or cultural ignorance. Following are some case vignettes illustrating such problems in the extreme.

---

CASE 3

The Father Who Called the Wrong Mental Health Service (Eileen Ha)

A couple with small children had recently immigrated from Southeast Asia to the United States. Their English ability was limited, but the husband managed to find a job working outside day and night. The wife became suspicious of her husband's behavior and, wondering if he might be having an extramarital affair, she followed him when he left home for work. The husband, annoyed by his wife's suspicious behavior, was told by his co-worker that psychiatric medication could help. The man looked in the phone book, intending to make a psychiatric appointment for his wife. By mistake, he called a child protection service. In response to the call, a worker visited the home. Due to the language limitations, there were problems in communication. The upset wife started to yell at her husband, and a quarrel occurred between them. This upset the small children, who started to cry. In the middle of this turmoil, the worker made the judgment that the children were being "abused" by the parents and removed them from the home for their "protection." The wife became depressed and agitated because she did not understand why her children had been taken away from her. She was sent to a hospital emergency room by the worker. Subsequently, the wife was admitted to a hospital with the diagnosis of depression, while her husband was puzzled as to what had happened to his wife and their children.

---

CASE 4

Tragedy of a Father Who Was Suspected of Being a "Sexual Abuser"

A couple with a 5-year-old daughter migrated from Asia. Their English were very limited, but the wife was able to find a job outside of the house, leaving the husband to take care of the home. Their daughter developed a skin rash around her private parts and was given some ointment by her doctor for local application. The father, who thought that it was his job to help the daughter apply the ointment, kindly did, without thinking that it might be wrong to do so. At the daughter's kindergarten, as part of a routine exercise, the teacher gave a picture to all the students,

*(continues)*

inquiring if any person had touched their private place. The teacher was surprised when this particular girl replied that her father touched her private place every day. The alarmed teacher reported this to the child protection service, and the worker went to the house, intending to remove the girl for her "protection." Without knowing what was going on, the father panicked and tried to stop his daughter from being taken away. He physically struggled with the police. In the middle of the physical conflict, the policeman drew his gun, perhaps trying to stop the father's desperate, violent behavior, but, by mistake, he shot the father. The mother came back from work and was shocked to discover her daughter in a state of panic and her husband dead.

Attention to the cultural dimensions of social work has increased gradually, as reflected by the publications on the subject (Cheetham, 1982; Ewalt et al. 1996; Triseliotis, 1986). However, there is still a great deal of effort needed to promote more specific considerations and practical applications regarding the cultural aspects of mental health work in general in the future.

## G. FORENSIC PSYCHIATRIC SERVICE

### 1. General Issues

Forensic psychiatry is a special branch of psychiatry that interfaces between psychiatry and the law. It provides psychiatric services for the juridical system in a society. In a practical sense, it involves psychiatric assessment to assist in making a judgment of whether or not a suspect is sane enough to stand for trial, to determine his or her mental status at the time of crime, and to provide a psychiatric opinion for custodial treatment, evaluation of abuse, involuntary admission for treatment, and so on.

To perform culturally relevant forensic psychiatric services, the first require-ment is adequate familiarity with and proper orientation toward the judicial system and the process of practicing law in the society concerned. The legal system is not determined by professional knowledge and experiences but is often shaped by the social and cultural systems. For instance, the legal system in Muslim societies will be no doubt be influenced by Islamic philosophy and values when it comes to the concepts of wrongness and punishment (Chaleby, 1996). In the same way, the legal systems in Buddhist societies will be influenced by Buddhistic thoughts and philosophy. Needless to say, the legal system and practices vary among societies with different cultural backgrounds.

Similarly, the next issue that deserves attention is the basic concern with individual rights and responsibilities from a cultural perspective. Socially observed laws determine to what extent individual rights should be respected and emphasized and in what ways an individual needs to take personal responsibility for his behavior. Based on philosophical, cultural, and political factors, these issues are not necessarily the same in different societies.

## 2. Cultural Issues

*Concepts of Right and Wrong.*    It is the task of forensic psychiatrists to provide consultation to the legal system in deciding whether the defender or the criminal was aware of right and wrong in his behavior. However, it is important to know that the concept of so-called right or wrong is not only defined by the legal system but also shaped by the culture. It is not absolute and may vary from society to society, depending on the intentions and meaning of a person's behavior, the implications of its consequences, and how it is perceived by others in the society. For instance, stealing bread for a starving nephew (described in the French story, *Les Miserables*) may be considered wrong behavior deserving of severe punishment or a minor error that does not require prison and being treated badly for many years. Right and wrong is often judged by social standards, which vary across societies and cultures.

*Lying, Manipulation, or Malingering.*    In order to defend one's behavior, a person may deny, distort, or rationalize the situation relating to the behavior. It may be interpreted and regarded by others as lies, manipulating, or even malingering. Based on the cultural background, such behavior may be considered "bad" and the person as having no creditability no matter what excuse is given. In some cultures, it is understood and tolerated as more or less "acceptable" and is not considered so bad. This is a very important cross-cultural issue that needs particular attention in transcultural examinations of forensic cases. As a survival skill, a person coming from a society where authority is very severe and punishment can be very cruel may learn from childhood how to use denial or distortion as a defense in dealing with situations. A person coming from a society where "honesty" is a virtue—exemplified by George Washington, as a child, admitting that he had cut down the cherry tree—not being honest is considered unreliable and very disgraceful. Such situations need to be understood and evaluated against cultural norms. Making a proper assessment and judgment as to whether or not a person is lying or malingering is a clinical challenge (Bunnting et al., 1996).

*Concept of Responsibility.*    Who should take responsibility is another matter that deserves careful judgment from a cultural perspective. An individual is the sole person who needs to take legal responsibility in an individually oriented society, so that when a crime is committed, no one asks the criminal's parents, spouse, or children to share the responsibility of his wrong behavior. However, in a family-oriented society, the responsibility does not necessarily end with the individual. A person's legal or financial debts need to be payed off by his parents, spouse, or children. An extreme of this situation in the past was when all immediate family members, as well as other close relatives, were decapitated if a person committed a serious offense, such as offending an emperor. The responsibility did not stop at the boundaries of the individual who committed the offense.

*Definition of Insanity.*    The definition of "mental insanity" is not simply decided by a psychiatrist's professional judgment in the legal system. It is subject to everybody's common-sense perceptions and reactions. This is true where juries are concerned, and even attorneys and judges have a direct impact on the perception and judgment of whether or not a person is mentally crazy. Even psychiatrists, as experts, will often debate on how to define mental insanity for the sake of the legal system. It has no direct relation to the diagnostic category defined in the official psychiatric classification system. How to regard a dissociated state, how to deal with borderline disorders, and how to perceive and interpret multiple personality disorders in terms of legal responsibility are some clinical examples that show the gray area that is open for debate among the professionals in the court.

## 3. Clinical Matters

*Method of Evaluation and Assessment.*    Carrying out proper psychiatric assessment and diagnosis in forensic psychiatric work is not different from doing so in ordinary psychiatric clinical work. It needs only to be carried out in a special way to be "nonsuggestive" and "objective," so that it can stand up to challenges in court. If it involves a defendant from an ethnic or cultural background different from that of the examiner, caution is needed and transcultural assessment would apply (see Section 5B: Culturally Relevant Assessment and Diagnosis). How to establish a proper relationship with the defendant and how to maintain a rapport and encourage the defendant to provide accurate background information are essential elements for successful assessment. How to overcome language barriers and interpret the nature of the behavior and symptoms relevantly and correctly are crucial to a valid assessment and diagnosis. A special effort is needed for those defendants who are unfamiliar with both the juridical system and psychiatric assessment.

These concerns also apply to psychological measurement. Whether or not the instruments for testing are cross-culturally applicable and valid deserves careful consideration and checking. This is particularly true in interpreting data obtained for a final report (see Section 5C: Culturally Adjusted Psychological Measurement).

*Judgment of Normality vs. Abnormality.*    True for the transcultural assessment of any patient, but particularly crucial in forensic psychiatry, is judging whether or not the behavior reported or manifested by the defendant is normal or pathological, usual or abnormal. This is especially difficult with certain kinds of psychopathologies, such as delusion (Levy, 1996). It is useful, as with any transcultural examinations, to obtain objective information from family, friends, or a person of the same ethnic or cultural background in the community. However, seeking a consultation from a cultural psychiatrist who is familiar with the language and culture of the defendant and has psychiatric knowledge and experience of his society of origin is always very valuable.

*Voluntary or Involuntary Hospitalization.*    The frequency of compulsory (or involuntary) admissions to psychiatric hospitals varies considerably among countries (Riecher-Rössler & Rössler, 1993). It is closely related to different legislation and administrative regulations in different societies. The rate of compulsory admission will vary even among patients of different ethnic backgrounds living in the same society (Thomas et al., 1993).

*Condition for Release from Institution.*    Deciding whether or not a person should be discharged from a hospital or released from prison requires careful evaluation. In addition to the person's medical condition, forensic psychiatrist need to consider the social safety and reactions of the people in the community. Whether the person concerned will be accepted by his family and into his community, whether he can secure a job and settle down to a regular life, and how he will relate to others are among the factors that need to be considered and evaluated. Therefore, the decision will vary from society to society, depending on the social conditions and cultural attitudes.

## 4. Comments and Suggestions

Forensic psychiatry is a new division of general psychiatry that has recently been getting more professional attention worldwide. It requires the combined knowledge and experience of various professional disciplines and various dimensions, including clinical psychiatry, law, ethics, and community-oriented public mental health. It definitely needs to include cultural psychiatry because the matters of responsibility, judgment of wrongness, and assessment of mental condition and criminal behavior need to be examined from various perspectives, including the social and cultural. The ethnic and cultural backgrounds of forensic psychiatrists will also shape the nature of their service (Griffith, 1998). The cultural aspects of forensic psychiatry is a relatively new area that is awaiting more attention and future development.

# REFERENCES

## A. Inpatient Psychiatric Care

Castillo, R. J. (2001). Lesson from folk healing. In W. S. Tseng & J. Streltzer (Eds.), *Culture and psychotherapy: A guide to clinical practice* (pp. 81–101). Washington, DC: American Psychiatric Press.

Lambo, T. A. (1966). The village of Aro. In M. King (Ed.), *Medical care in developing countries. A symposium from MaKerere.* London: Oxford University Press.

Thong, D. (1993). *A psychiatrist in paradise: Treating mental illness in Bali.* Bankok: White Lotus.

## B. Outpatient Psychiatric Care

Lefley, H. P., & Bestman, E. W. (1991). Public-academic linkages for culturally sensitive community mental health. *Community Mental Health Journal, 27*(6), 473–487.

Well, K., Hough, R. L., Golding, J. M., Burnam, M. A., & Karno, M. (1987). Which Mexican-Americans underutilize health services? *American Journal of Psychiatry, 144*(7), 918–922.

Wilson, L. G. (1980). The clinical home visit in cultural psychiatry. *Journal of Operational Psychiatry, 11*(1), 27–33.

## C. Psychiatric Emergency Service

Al-Habeeb, T. A., Abdulgani, Y. I., Al-Ghamdi, M. S., & Al-Jundi, M. T. (1999). The sociodemographic and clinical pattern of hysteria in Saudi Arabia. *Arab Journal of Psychiatry, 10*(2), 99–109.

Dube, K. C. (1970). A study of prevalence and biosocial variables in mental illness in a rural and an urban community in Uttar Pradesh, India. *Acta Psychiatrica Scandinavia, 46,* 327–359.

Grisaru, N.; Budowski, D., & Witztum, E. (1997). Possession by the "Zar" among Ethiopian immigrants to Israel: Psychopathology or culture-bound syndrome? *Psychopathology, 30*(4), 223–233.

Kinkenberg, W. D., & Calsyn, R. J. (1997). Race as a moderator of the prediction of receipt of after care and psychiatric hospitalization. *International Journal of Social Psychiatry, 43*(4), 276–284.

Luo, H. C., & Zhou, C. S. (1984). Clinical analysis of 1,622 psychiatric emergency cases. *Chinese Neuropsychiatric Journal, 17*(3), 137–138.

Segal, S. P., Bola, J. R., & Watson, M. A. (1996). Race, quality of care, and antipsychotic prescribing practices in psychiatric emergency services. *Psychiatric Services, 47*(3), 282–286.

Strakowski, S. M., Lonczak, H. S., Sax, K. W., West, S. A., Crist, A., Mehta, R., & Thienhaus, O. J. (1995). The effects of race on diagnosis and disposition from a psychiatric emergency service. *Journal of Clinical Psychiatry, 56*(3), 101–107.

## D. Consultation-Liaison Service

Battin, M. P. (1991). Euthanasia: The way we do it, the way they do it. In Special Issues: Medical Ethics: Physician-assisted suicide and euthanasia. *Journal of Pain & Symptom Management, 6*(5), 298–305.

Beyene, Y. (1992). Medical disclosure and refugees. Telling bad news to Ethiopian patients. *Western Journal of Medicine, 157*(3), 328–332.

Carpenter, V., & Colwell, B. (1995). Cancer knowledge, self-efficacy, and cancer screening behaviors among Mexican-American women. *Journal of Cancer Education, 10*(4), 217–222.

Chavez, L. R., Hubbell, F. A., McMullin, J. M., Martinez, R. G., & Mishra, S. I. (1995). Understanding knowledge and attitudes about breast cancer. A cultural analysis. *Archives of Family Medicine, 4*(2), 145–152.

Collins, D., Dimsdale, J. E., & Wilkins, D. (1992). Consultation-liaison psychiatric utilization patterns in different cultural groups. *Psychosomatic Medicine, 54*(2), 240–245.

Dancy, B. (1996). What African-American women know, do, and feel about AIDS: A function of age and education. *AIDS Education and Prevention, 8*(1), 26–36.

Elwyn, T. S., Fetterss, M. D., Sasaki, H., & Tsuda, T. (2002). Responsibility and cancer disclosure in Japan. *Social Science & Medicine, 54,* 281–293.

Hubbell, F. A., Chavez, L. R., Mishra, S. I., & Valdez, R. B. (1996). Differing beliefs about breast cancer among Latinas and Anglo women. *Western Journal of Medicine, 164*(5), 405–409.

Kandakai, T. L., Price, J. H., Telljohann, S. K., & Holiday-Goodman, M. (1996). Knowledge, beliefs, and use of prescribed antibiotic medications among low-socioeconomic African Americans. *Journal of the National Medical Association, 88*(5), 289–294.

Krauss-Mars, A. H., & Lachman, P. (1994). Breaking bad news to parents with disabled children—A cross-cultural study. *Child: Care, Health and Development, 20*(2), 101–113.

Luke, K. (1996). Cervical cancer screening: Meeting the needs of minority ethnic women. *British Journal of Cancer, 74 Supplement 129,* S47–50.

Matsumoto, D., Pun, K. K., Nakatani, M., Kadowaki, D., Weissman, M., McCarter, L., Fletcher, D., & Takeuchi, S. (1995). Cultural differences in attitudes, values and beliefs about osteoporosis in first and second generation Japanese-American women. *Women Health, 23*(4), 39–56.

Qureshi, B. (1994). *Transcultural medicine: Dealing with patients from different cultures* (2nd ed.). Dordrecht: Kluwer Academic Publishers.

Raphael, K. G., Kunzel, C., & Sadowsky, D. (1996). Differences between Asian-American and white American dentists in attitudes toward treatment of HIV-positive patients. *AIDS Education and Prevention, 8*(2), 155–164.

Rodriguez-Garcia, R., & Frazier, L. (1995). Cultural paradoxes relating to sexuality and breast-feeding. *Journal of Human Lactation, 11*(2), 71–74.

Ross, H. M. (1981). Social/cultural views regarding death and dying. *Topics in Clinical Nursing, 3,* 1–16.

Rubens, A. J. (1996). Racial and ethnic differences in students' attitudes and behavior toward organ donation. *Journal of the National Medical Association, 88*(7), 417–421.

Stein, H. F. (1993). *American medicine as culture.* Boulder, CO: Westview Press.

Streltzer, J. (1998). Cultural impact on consultation-liaison psychiatric services. Presented at the American Psychiatric Association annual meeting workshop on Cultural Influence on Medical Practice, at Toronto, Canada.

Talmadge, E. (1997). Girl's need for transplant hindered by Japanese laws. *The Advertiser,* Honolulu: March 27, 1997, p. A3.

Woollet, A., Dosanjh, N., Nicolson, P., Marshall, H., Djhanbakhch, O., & Hadlow, J. (1995). The ideas and experiences of pregnancy and childbirth of Asian and non-Asian women in east London. *British Journal of Medical Psychology, 68*(1), 65–84.

## E. Psychiatric Nursing Care

Davis, B. D. (1981). Culture and psychiatric nursing: Implications for training. In J. Cox (Ed.), *Transcultural psychiatry* (pp. 218–233). London: Croom Helm.

Leininger, M. M. (Ed.). (1991). *Culture care diversity and universality: A theory of nursing.* New York: National League for Nursing Press.

Leininger, M. (1995). *Transcultural nursing: Concepts, theories, research and practices* (2nd ed). New York: McGraw-Hill.

Lipson, J. G., & Steiger, N. J. (1996). *Self-care nursing in a multicultural context.* Thousand Oaks, CA: Sage.

Long, S. O. (1984). The sociocultural context of nursing in Japan. *Culture, Medicine and Psychiatry, 8*(2), 141–163.

## F. Mental Health Social Work

Allen-Meares, P., & Burman, S. (1995). The endangerment of African American men: An appeal for social work action. *Social Work, 40*(3), 268–274.

Cheetham, J. (Ed.). (1982). *Social work and ethnicity.* London: Allen & Unwin.

Ewalt, P. L., Freeman, E. M., Kirk, S. A., & Poole, D. L. (Eds.). (1996). *Multicultural issues in social work.* Washington, DC: NASW (National Association of Social Workers) Press.

Ewalt, P. L., & Mokuau, N. (1995). Self-determination from a Pacific perspective. *Social Work, 40*(3), 168–175.

Gross, E. R. (1995). Deconstructing politically correct practice literature: The American Indian case. *Social Work, 40*(3), 206–213.

McGoldrick, M., Giordano, J., & Pearce, J. K. (Eds.) (1996). *Ethnicity and family therapy (2nd ed.).* New York: Guilford Press.

Triseliotis, J. (1986). Transcultural social work. In J. Cox (Ed.), *Transcultural psychiatry* (pp. 196–217). London: Croom Helm.

Tseng, W. S., & Hsu, J. (1991). *Culture and family: Problems and therapy.* New York: The Haworth Press.

## G. Forensic Psychiatric Service

Bunnting, B. G., Wessels, W. H., Lasich, A. J., & Pillay, B. (1996). The distinction of malingering and mental illness in black forensic cases. *Medicine and Law, 15*(2), 241–247.

Chaleby, K. S. (1996). Issues in forensic psychiatry in Islamic jurisprudence. *Bulletin of the American Academy of Psychiatry and the Law, 24*(1), 117–124.

Griffith, E. E. (1998). Ethics in forensic psychiatry: A cultural response to Stone and Appelbaum. *Journal of the American Academy of Psychiatry and the Law, 26*(2), 171–184.

Levy, A. (1996). Forensic implications of the difficulties of defining delusions. *Medicine and Law, 15*(2), 257–260.

Riecher-Rössler, A., & Rössler, W. (1993). Compulsory admission of psychiatric patients: An international comparison. *Acta Psychiatrica Scandinavica, 87*: 231–236.

Thomas, C. S., Stone, K., Osborn, M., Thomas, P. F., & Fisher, M. (1993). Psychiatric morbidity and compulsory admission among UK-born Europeans, Afro-Caribbeans and Asians in Central Manchester. *British Journal of Psychiatry, 163*: 91–99.

# CHAPTER 7

# Culturally Competent Psychotherapy

## A. INTERCULTURAL PSYCHOTHERAPY: CHALLENGES AND COMPETENCE

Intercultural psychotherapy refers to therapy that is delivered to patients with ethnic or cultural backgrounds considerably different from that of the therapist. With significant differences or gaps between the culture of the therapist and that of the patient, the bilateral *interaction* of cultural components is, either consciously or unconsciously, heavily involved in and significantly influenced by the process of psychotherapy. Thus, it is called intercultural therapy (Hsu & Tseng, 1972) in contrast to intracultural therapy, which takes place between a therapist and patient with basically the same cultural backgrounds. As there is a need to transcend cultural barriers between the therapist and the patient, it is also called transcultural psychotherapy. Intercultural psychotherapy helps clinicians realize and examine the cultural dimensions that are involved in the practice of psychotherapy. Such "extreme" situations make us aware that culture cannot be ignored even in "regular" or "intracultural" psychotherapy, whether the clinician is dealing with a patient of the same cultural background or treating a member of the majority group in a society. There are always challenges for the clinician, even one who shares the same cultural system as the client but has a different socioeconomic, geographic, or subcultural background.

Associated with clinical experiences working with patients in foreign societies, or with minority groups, literature concerning intercultural psychotherapy began to appear in the 1960s. In addition to the term "intercultural" psychotherapy, "cross-cultural" psychotherapy, psychotherapy "across cultures," or "transcultural" psychotherapy have been used by different scholars.

Closely related to the emerging human rights movement in the United States, as well as the increased migration of non-European minority groups into European countries, there was increased concern in the 1970s and 1980s with how to deliver mental health counseling for minorities, migrants, refugees, sojourns, and foreign students. Numerous publications have appeared recently that focus on intercultural therapy among particular groups, such as immigrants, refugees, and minorities, indicating increased awareness of and experience in this area.

Numerous specific issues have been brought up in the clinical experience of intercultural psychotherapy, such as the need for examining the congruence and incongruence of cultural backgrounds between therapist and patient; how to communicate with patients on verbal as well as nonverbal levels; how racism may affect interracial counseling; the problem of ethnic or cultural identification with the therapist; the management of cultural transference and countertransference; how to deal with a therapist's cultural rigidity or cultural blindness; and how to provide culture-fair, -matched, -sensitive, -relevant, or -reactive therapy (Tseng & Streltzer, 2001). In here, the various issues that need considerations in intercultural psychotherapy will be examined.

## 1. Orientation to Psychotherapy

### a. Familiarity and Orientation

The first thing that needs attention in the practice of intercultural psychotherapy is the matter of the patient's familiarity with psychotherapy and his expectations of it. This is particularly true if the patient comes from a place where psychotherapy is not a common professional practice or there are certain biases against it as a healing practice. In many societies, due to tradition and orientation, people value medically oriented service, which includes prescriptions, injections, or operations. They see medical practices as effective and valuable. In contrast, "talking" therapy to them is nothing but talk and is not going to solve their sleeping problems or stomach tension. They may never have seen a movie or read a book describing the psychotherapeutic method of lying on a couch in order to associate freely about "whatever comes to their minds." They may not understand why a father needs to see the therapist when his son has problems relating to his classmates at school, or why a husband and wife both need to talk to the therapist when the wife is the one complaining of frequent tension headaches. They may be puzzled as to why the therapist wants the patient to recall and describe his childhood experiences when he is having a nervous attack at work that relates to his boss. The therapist must first explain the nature of therapy, to orient and prepare the client for it, and not assume that he is familiar with its procedures. This is particularly crucial in situations of intercultural therapy, in which patients are not familiar with psychotherapy.

### b. Expectation, Rules, and Agreement

Closely related to the understanding of psychotherapy is the need to find out and clarify what the patient expects of it and what he assumes to be his role as patient. The roles of the patient and the therapist, who reflects cultural concepts of authority and healer, can be perceived and defined differently in various cultures.

For professional reasons, based on past clinical experience, contemporary psychotherapists have set up certain rules and agreements with which patients must comply. For instance, in order to carry out successful psychotherapy, modern therapists feel strongly that it is essential for the patient to be on time for his appointments and follow his agreement to see the therapist regularly for a determined period of time. These rules are made partly for clinical reasons, but they also reflect the habits demanded by modern industrialized society. These practices are seldom evaluated carefully for their clinical relevance and cultural implications. Many people have no custom of keeping preset appointments. They have no concept of treatment requiring regular visits, even after the initial problems have been resolved or cardinal symptoms have subsided. Further, if people live in a place where there is no convenient transportation, it is rather difficult to see a therapist regularly. When a person lives in a rural area and has to climb a mountain, cross a river, or walk a long way to reach a clinic, it is not easy to show up on time for a session. When a person rides a bus, there is always the possibility of missing it and having to wait for another, and taking several hours to reach a destination. The demand for regular visits should be evaluated from the standpoint of such practical matters, in addition to culture-patterned habits of being on time. It would be culturally careless and a great mistake to interpret a no-show or delayed appointment simply as "resistance" to therapy.

As part of their agreement, patients are expected to pay the therapist for their visits. However, how and how much to pay are not merely technical issues, but also cultural matters. According to traditional custom, people in nonindustrialized societies seldom make cash payments to healers; only voluntary donations are made, in the form of gifts of appreciation. Being asked to make cash payments according to a preset agreement makes the therapy seem like a "commercial business," rather than the charitable work done by folk healers. Making a payment agreement is a delicate and sensitive matter that needs to be handled carefully in intercultural therapy with patients who are not used to businesslike payment systems.

## 2. Communication in Therapy

Communication between the therapist and patient is considered by psychotherapists to be a core element of therapy. Determining how to achieve informative, comprehensive, meaningful, and therapeutic communication is necessary for effective results. In intercultural psychotherapy, many issues in the area of communication need attention.

### a. Spectrum of Words in Language

Human beings around the world use different languages for communication. Chinese, English, or Spanish are some of the main languages used by different ethnic groups. The natures of different languages, including their words, grammar, and communication patterns, vary greatly. For instance, differences in gender among subjects are noted in some languages, such as English, Russian, French, or Spanish, but not in Japanese or Chinese. This is related to the basic structure of the language, but it may also reflect the cognitive style and perceptional and conceptional aspects of the people who use it. For instance, for the hierarchically concerned Japanese, the vocabulary and grammar of their language changes depending on who you are speaking to. The word for "self" changes depending on the gender of the speaker and his relationship with the person being spoken to. It is *boku* when a man refers to himself to his friends; *watakushi* when he is talking to his superior; and *watashi* when a woman addresses herself. The word reflects the concern for gender and social status in Japanese culture. It would be a mistake, and cause confusion, if a woman addressed herself as *boku*, or if a man addressed himself as *watashi*.

The more differentiated a word, or the richness of variations of certain words, often indicates the level of concern for the subject in the culture. For instance, Eskimo people have many different words for "snow," reflecting the reality of their lives in the snow, while in English there is only one word for it. People living in an island society in the Pacific, out of necessity, have developed numerous words for "cloud" to help them predict and adjust to weather changes in the middle of the ocean. Westerners use different words to describe various kinds of wine or liquor, whereas the Chinese have only one inclusive word, "wine." In contrast, the Chinese use several different terms to address uncles or aunts, distinguishing paternal from maternal relatives, as well as age hierarchy. This illustrates the importance to the Chinese of discriminating among different relatives and ages.

It was the Japanese psychiatrist Takeo Doi (1962) who, through clinical experience, realized that, in the Japanese language, in contrast to English or other languages, numerous words are used to refer to the nature of human relationships, or *amae* (benevolent dependence), such as "*amaeru*" and "*amayakasu.*" Doi proposed that the richness of the Japanese word centering on *amae* reflects that Japanese values allow benevolent dependence in interpersonal relationships, a unique aspect of Japanese behavior.

### b. Meaning of Words for Communication

In the process of psychotherapy, it is important to grasp the meaning of words expressed explicitly, subtly, or in a symbolic way. Transculturally, it is difficult to comprehend the subtle or symbolic meaning of words. The meaning needs to be understood through cultural context and with cultural knowledge. For instance, there is no problem understanding what the word "like" means in the English language. However, it would be difficult to comprehend accurately what it really means when an Asian girl says, "I like you." You need to know that conservative Asian men and women never say, "I love you," to each other. At most, they may say, "I like you." Thus, when a traditional Asian girl uses the word "like," it does not merely indicate a positive feeling toward another (equivalent to "fond of"), but could be equivalent to serious and intense affection toward a person of the opposite sex (equivalent to "love" for Occidentals). This illustrates that the issue is not simply understanding a word, but comprehending the cultural meaning beyond it (Hsu & Tseng, 1972).

From a cultural point of view, there are numerous words, phrases, or idioms commonly used by certain cultural groups to convey specific, but subtle, meanings. For instance, if someone says, "My house is far away," it means that you are not welcome to visit it. If someone asks you whether you already ate or not, it does not mean that he is concerned about your meal or interested in offering you a meal, it is simply a social greeting, like asking, "How are you?"

As an extension of this, it is important to know that, in the field of psychiatry, clinicians and patients use some psychiatric terms in their communication, such as "depression" and "hypochondriacal," which deserve careful elaboration and clarification to understand their actual meaning. Even when a patient reveals a wish to kill himself, it should not be taken literally; instead, his statement requires a clinical judgment about the patient, his psychopathology, and his possible motivation for such a revelation. In addition, a cultural judgment is necessary to understand the general custom of people in the patient's culture of revealing a wish to end their lives, its common implication, and the possible message that the person wants to communicate. For example, if a Muslim person, whose faith forbids self-killing, says that he wishes he were dead, this suicidal idea must be interpreted and reacted to in a delicate manner.

In the practice of psychoanalysis, primary thinking material is often analyzed through the interpretation of dreams, fantasies, or slips of the tongue. Interpretation of symbolism becomes important in the process of analysis. It is already recognized that things are associated with different symbolic meanings, depending on universal rules and personal factors, as well as social and cultural interpretations. The same subject can be an opposite symbol in different cultures. For instance, a snake is generally considered a symbol for a male (due to its physical similarity with the male sex organ). However, for the Chinese, the snake usually symbolizes a female (due to its seductive physical movements). A dragon is interpreted as a symbol of evil by Westerners due to past legends (such as the fairy-tale about a young man killing a dragon). However, for the Chinese, a dragon is a symbol of nobility, power, and benign authority. Thus, it is used to represent an emperor or a rain god, who brings the rain needed by the farmers. Thus, the interpretation of symbolism needs to be carried out subjectively, based on the patient's personal and cultural orientation.

### c. Culture-Shaped Communication Patterns

Beyond the words and language used for communication, cultural factors influence how a person communicates with others, which has an impact on the clinical setting. The best example is derived from Micronesia. According to Micronesian tradition, woman are not permitted to talk directly to a stranger, even to a physician. If a stranger wants to talk to her, she is permitted to communicate only through her husband (if she is married) or through her mother (if not yet married). Imagine yourself, as an outside psychiatrist, interviewing a Micronesian couple. Whatever question you ask the wife, she will only reply in her native language to her husband and her husband will translate what she said. This applies even when the wife understands and can speak English. With the conversation going through her husband, it is difficult for you to know to what extent the communication has been screened or distorted by him. This highlights a culture-shaped communication pattern that becomes a challenge in intercultural psychotherapy.

It is also well known that the Japanese tend to respond by saying, "*Hai*! *Hai*!" when you are talking to them. Although *hai* in Japanese literally means "yes," it does not mean that the person is saying "yes" to you or responding affirmatively to whatever is said. It simply indicates that he is listening to what you are saying (even though he may disagree with you). The therapist needs to be aware of this to avoid any misunderstanding.

### d. Nonverbal Communication

Difficulties occur in the area of nonverbal communication as well, including facial expressions, gestures, or behavior. Even though human beings share certain universal nonverbal communication, such as nodding their heads to indicate affirmation, shaking their heads to express denial or disagreement, and using certain facial expressions to demonstrate emotions of pleasure and displeasure, certain nonverbal communication is culture-patterned in specific ways. Without knowing this, a person's message may be missed or misunderstood.

For instance, one Egyptian patient made a sound, "che, che," whenever the therapist said something. This puzzled the therapist until he finally asked the patient what he meant by this. He learned that, in Egypt, such a sound indicates agreement (Hsu & Tseng, 1972). An outside psychiatrist was very much frustrated at his first encounter with a Micronesian patient. No matter what the therapist said to the patient, the latter never made any response, either verbal or nonverbal. After the therapist raised this issue to the patient, almost in an accusing way, the patient protested that he was acknowledging the therapist the whole time in his (cultural) way, raising his eyebrows. Instead of saying "yes," people in Micronesia raise their eyebrows. A Japanese psychiatrist was upset by a Chinese patient who stuck out his tongue in response to certain subjects in the middle of conversation. The therapist was upset because, for the Japanese, sticking out the tongue toward another is an insult. Fortunately, the therapist consulted his Chinese colleagues and learned that, for the Chinese, this is a customary way to indicate astonishment. These examples show that many nonverbal expressions, body gestures, or behavior are specifically culture-patterned, with particular meanings. Once the therapist observes such expressions, he should inquire into and clarify them to avoid any miscommunication.

### e. Styles of Problem Presentation

As a physician, particularly a psychiatrist, and more so as a psychotherapist, it is important to recognize that there are culturally molded styles of problem presentation. A good example is that a patient may make a somatic complaint, not because he actually suffers from a somatic problem, but simply because it is a culture-patterned behavior to present somatic problems (initially) to a physician, or even to a psychiatrist. After proper inquiry or guidance, it will be easy for the patient to reveal any emotional problems that he may have (Tseng, 1975). In contrast, the patient may present a psychologized complaint, such as how much he hates his father, a trauma he encountered in his early childhood, and so on, at his first session with the therapist, as if he were very much psychologically minded and aware of his psychological problems. However, as the therapy goes on, it may be shown that the patient learned to present such "psychoanalytical" material from mass media or from his friends, while he actually knew nothing about his own psychological problems.

If you interviewed Japanese patients diagnosed with *taijinkyofusho* (a special form of social phobia), you would be very surprised to learn that they tend to present their complaints at the initial session in a certain style. They will use the

Japanese *sekimen-kyofu* (erythrophobia), *shisen-kyofu* (fear of eye contact), or *taishiu-kyofu* (fear of having a bad body smell that bothers others) or other profession-alized terms to describe their symptoms, and even mention that they are suffering from *taijinkyofusho*, a medical diagnostic term for interpersonal relationship phobia (equivalent to social phobia). This is because the concept of *taijinkyofusho* has become popular in Japan and even laypeople use the medical term that describes this morbid condition (Tseng et al., 1992).

This illustrates that, without knowing it, patients learn a culturally patterned way of presenting their complaints, particularly in the initial stage of therapy. A therapist needs to know about such culturally stylized problem presentation and how to deal with it. When a young male patient (either from India or China), concerned about the leaking of his semen, asks for a urine examination, or requests a tonic to nourish his kidneys, a therapist should understand that he is presenting his problem according to the folk concept of *daht* syndrome (in the case of an Indian) or *senkui* syndrome (in the case of a Chinese).

### f. Disclosure of Private Matters or Taboo Subjects

In general, a therapist would like to have his patient disclose as much personal information about himself as possible, so that a proper, in-depth understanding of the patient can be achieved. Based on a comprehensive and dynamic under-standing of the patient, proper therapy can be performed. However, to what extent a therapist should encourage a patient to reveal private matters and how much a patient should open his mind and share very personal issues with an out-sider are rather delicate clinical matters. This is particularly true when a thera-pist is dealing with a patient of a different cultural background. From a cultural point of view, there are many customs regarding how much internal informa-tion a person should reveal to an outsider, and what issues are the taboo.

For instance, in Micronesia, it is taboo to mention the death of an ancestor. Even a physician, as an outsider, should not ask his patient about how his parents or grandparents died, although it is desirable for the physician to know about the medical history of the family. The physician may hint to his patient that it is important to know the family's medical history so that a proper diagnosis can be made of the patient's present illness. Nevertheless, the physician should not blatantly ask: "When did your father die?" or " What was the cause of your grand-mother's death?" For the patient to reply to these questions is culturally forbid-den, and the physician would be asking him to break his taboos.

For people in many cultures, including Asians, it is taboo to discuss death in the future. Even if a person is suffering from a terminal disease and death is imminent, it is preferred that the possibility of death not be mentioned. In such a circumstance, breaking the social taboo and helping the person to face reality and prepare for the end of his life, including making a living will and making plans for a funeral, for instance, has to be dealt with delicately and subtly and cannot be discussed openly and liberally. Otherwise, the patient will misinterpret the therapist as wishing him to die soon.

In a less serious way, people from many cultures do not feel comfortable revealing certain family secrets. To reveal that some family member suffered from tuberculosis, indulged in gambling, had an extramarital affair, and so on is considered a shameful thing. "Not to reveal ugly family matters to the outside" is a common saying observed by the Chinese and people of many other cultures. How to take proper personal and family histories and how to deal with "cultural resistence" to information needed for dynamic case formulation become challenging matters in intercultural therapy. They become compound matters beyond the simple concerns and management of "resistence" understood by psychoanalysts.

### g. The Matter of Confidentiality

Closely related to revealing private matters is how confidentiality is conceived and practiced in various cultural settings. If, in the patient's social setting, the rights of the individual are more or less emphasized and personal boundaries are relatively well established, confidentiality can be observed and maintained in the clinical situation. However, in a society where the group (or family) is emphasized, and the boundaries between individual members are not so restrictively stressed, the matter of confidentiality needs to be interpreted and observed in a slightly different way. For example, a conversation with an adolescent child is expected to be shared with his parents in a society where parents have a strong position of authority. If a therapist refuses to share information about adolescent children with their parents, under the concept of confidentially as conceived by the therapist according to his professional and cultural background, his behavior may be interpreted by the parents as offending parental authority. A similar situation may occur in a society where a husband's status is superior to his wife's. The husband may become angry if he finds that the therapist is withholding information about his wife. Thus, if confidentiality is not interpreted and carried out according to the patient's cultural background, it may cause unexpected trouble.

### 3. The Art of Using an Interpreter

For intercultural psychotherapy, language can be a major obstacle, requiring an interpreter in the process of therapy. Depending on who serves as the interpreter, a close family member, a friend, a member of the same ethnic group, or a professionally trained interpreter with mental health knowledge and experience, the process and quality of interpretation will be affected. It is necessary to have translator who can translate properly, relevantly, and meaningfully for clinical purposes.

Furthermore, it is necessary for the clinician to be aware that there are three different ways for interpreters to function in a therapeutic situation, depending on how the interpreter performs his role and what modes of interpretation are undertaken (Westermeyer, 1990).

## a. Different Ways for an Interpreter to Function

*Simple Translation.*    This refers to the situation in which the interpreter performs straightforward, semantic translation. The interpreter can be instructed to perform slightly differently, according to the nature of the interview. For instance, if the interview focuses on a very crucial area or a delicate emotional matter, the interpreter should be asked to carry out "word-by-word" translation so that the therapist will not miss the details of the content or flow of the patient's thoughts. If it is to gather information on a certain subject, such as family history, marital history, or medical history, the interpreter may be instructed to offer a condensed or reintegrated summary of what has been described by the patient on that particular subject. In this way, time can be saved. Interviews conducted through interpreters usually take more time, more than double that of ordinary interviews. Saving time becomes an important matter.

This type of interpretation is required when the therapist has no background knowledge of the patient's language. When the interview takes place, the therapist and the patient are encouraged to face each other, as if they were talking to each other. This will help the therapist establish a relationship with the patient (rather than establishing a relationship between the interpreter and the patient). Also, nonverbal responses can be transmitted between the therapist and the patient to increase the level of mutual understanding. This will make up, to some extent, for the disadvantages of conducting the interview through an interpreter.

For this type of interpretation, the interpreter does not necessarily need a scholarly or comprehensive knowledge of the language in question. Any layperson, including family members or friends, can do it, providing that the interviewer can command a flow of conversational small-talk.

*Cultural Interpretation.*    Cultural interpretation takes place when, in addition to the function just described, the interpreter is asked to give his interpretation of a word, a segment of information, or the whole matter communicated from a cultural perspective. This may take place bilaterally, in interpretation for the therapist as well as for the patient. Thus, the interpreter serves as a culture broker, so to speak. Needless to say, there is no way to guarantee that the cultural interpretation made will be objective and accurate rather than subjective and biased. The therapist should check into it for its accuracy or offer instruction and suggestions on how to do such interpretation without distortion. This level of work requires the to have a certain level of knowledge, ability, and skill.

*Adjunct Therapy.*    Another function that some interpreters may perform is as an assistant to the therapist in carrying out his therapeutic work. For this, the interpreter needs certain training and experience. It would be preferable if the interpreter had training in mental health counseling. In this circumstance, the therapist and the interpreter (or adjunct therapist) act as cotherapists. As a team, they need to practice and constantly review their performance to ensure that their approach is congruent, complementary, and without conflict.

### b. Issues Needing Consideration

Among numerous factors needing consideration, one that deserves particular attention is, if there is a choice, whether to use an interpreter from the same ethnic group as the patient (ingroup) or someone outside the patient's ethnic group (outgroup). Clearly, an ingroup interpreter will possess more knowledge of the patient's culture and greater language efficiency, which will increase the cultural accuracy of the interpretation. However, clinical experience has pointed out that some potential problems exist in using interpreters from the same ethnic group as the patient. The interpreter will explicitly or implicitly identify with a patient of his own ethnic group. He may feel ashamed to reveal the "ugly" information about a person who shares his ethnicity or project his own ethnic views and feelings in the process of interpreting. Furthermore, the patient may hesitate to reveal his personal life to the therapist through an interpreter of the same ethnicity, with the concern, or even fear, that his or her secret may become known to his ethnic fellows in the community. This is particularly true when the ethnic fellows congregate in a small community.

Beyond the matter of interpreting, it is necessary to consider the role of the interpreter, particularly his (social) relation to the patient, and how he feels and identifies with the patient and the patient's culture. For example, if a family member is used as an interpreter, he may not only be functioning as a translator, but also attempting to convey the needs of the patient and/or the family. If social class or caste is still distinctly observed in a society, how such a hierarchical background will affect the clinical work needs special attention. For instance, if the interpreter comes from a lower caste and the patient from a higher caste, the therapy will most likely not work well, as the patient will not be willing to reveal his own personal matters to a person of lower status. The patient will disclose private issues only to the respected therapist. This and other factors need proper attention and management, as they all will significantly affect the process and results of the interpretation.

It cannot be denied that if there is a language barrier between the therapist and the patient, extra effort is required to work through it. When an interpreter is used, there will often be the problems of how the translation is carried out properly, relevantly, and meaningfully for clinical purposes. There will be the problems of deletion or omission of information, distortion of meaning, and exaggeration or adding of information which needs to be minimized as much as possible (Lee, 1997). It is always time-consuming. There are always considerable limitations in communication in therapeutic work. However, such circumstances are not entirely negative. Language barriers provide a legitimate excuse for the therapist to ask the patient to clarify an obscure word or concept, so that new light is thrown on the subject, a process that is highly valued in dynamic therapy (Carstairs, 1961).

## 4. Therapist-Patient Relationship

### a. Culture-Shaped Therapist-Patient Relationship

The therapist-patient relationship usually plays a significant role in the process of psychotherapy and is therefore often closely examined and regulated by the therapist. As clinicians know, the nature of the therapist-patient relationship is subject to numerous factors, including the personalities of the therapist and patient, their gender and age, the nature of the psychopathology and process of therapy. Beyond these factors, the therapist should comprehend and manage the aspects of the therapist-patient relationship that are culturally molded. Attitudes toward and relationships with authority vary widely among different cultural groups. Patients who come from backgrounds where authority tends to be autocratic will expect the therapist to be active, instructive, and responsible, while the patient plays a submissive role and hesitates to make any responses that may be considered disobedient. In contrast, patients who are used to relating with authority in a more democratic way will prefer a more equal relationship and will expect the therapist not to manipulate them.

The relationship between patient and therapist will be affected by the cultural view of man-woman relations. If there is a strong cultural view about the role and status of men and women, such as the man being superior and the woman inferior, it can become problematic if a male patient is treated by a female therapist. This may be true in Muslim societies or in some Asian societies, where the role and status of man and woman are clearly defined and strikingly differentiated. Such a situation will occur not only in intracultural situations but also in intercultural situations across country boundaries. A clinical situation has been reported by Bishop and Winokur (1956) concerning a Japanese man-patient treated by an American woman-therapist. They described that, influenced by traditional attitudes about gender, the patient had difficulty accepting help from a woman (therapist). He tended to show excessive and impeccable Asian courtesy with minimal emotional coloring, particularly in the early part of the treatment sessions.

### b. Ethnic/Cultural Transference and Countertransference Issues

The ethnic and cultural transference and countertransference that are observed in interethnic or intercultural psychotherapy have attracted attention among therapists for some time (Hsu & Tseng, 1972; Schachter & Butts, 1968). Ethnic or cultural transference occurs when a patient develops a certain relationship, feeling, or attitude toward the therapist because of the ethnic/cultural background of the therapist. Ethnic or cultural countertransference is the reverse phenomenon and occurs when a therapist develops a certain relationship with the patient mainly because of the patient's ethnic/cultural background. Transference and countertransference are based primarily on the previous knowledge, impression, bias, or experience of a therapist or a patient in relation to a particular ethnic group or people of a certain cultural system. Since it is easier to identify and react to ethnicity and race, this phenomenon occurs, in fact, as ethnic/racial transference or countertransference. In the same way as personal transference or countertransference, ethnic or racial transference or countertransference can be positive or negative, severely influencing the process of therapy and, therefore, needing prompt attention and management.

Concerning ethnocultural transference, which may be observed in a clinical situation, Comas-Díaz & Jacobsen (1991) indicated that the transference may be manifested as denial of ethnicity and culture; mistrust, suspicion, and hostility; ambivalence toward the therapist; or overcompliance and friendliness. Likewise, countertransference can be shown as denial of ethnocultural differences; being overly curious about the patient's ethnocultural background and developing a clinical anthropological syndrome; or demonstrating excessive feelings of guilt, anger, or ambivalence toward the patient.

### c. Impact of Racism on Intercultural Therapy

The possible negative impact or obstacle of racism on psychotherapy has attracted a great deal of attention (Carter, 1995). This is quite true if negative, or even hostile, relations preexist between the two racial groups concerned. The difficulty of psychotherapy involving racial factors has been demonstrated by extreme circumstances. For example, in South Africa, as pointed out by Lambley and Cooper (1975), individual contact between a white therapist and a black client contained elements of the overall relationship between blacks and whites in apartheid society, and these elements severely affected the therapeutic relationship. The black patient had difficulty trusting the white therapist. The therapist always had difficulty handling the black patient's anger and hatred toward whites in general, which tended to project onto the therapist. Furthermore, if the therapist was genuinely concerned for a black patient, and demonstrated too much sympathy for him, the therapist ran the risk of being arrested by the government under the circumstances of apartheid. It was a political reality.

The psychotherapy of an Arab patient by a Jewish therapist in Israel during the Intifada, an exacerbation of a historical political conflict, as described by Bizi-Nathaniel, Granek, and Golomb (1991), is another example of how political reality may intrude into interracial psychotherapy and interfere with the therapist-patient relationship. Being open with patients at an early stage of therapy about the possible effects of race and ethnic differences on therapy is encouraged (Brantley, 1983), and working on a suitable therapeutic relationship is suggested to minimize the ill effects that are always associated with such negative interracial relations.

### d. Matching of Therapist and Patient

Griffith (1977) addressed different issues that are of concern in certain racial matches between therapist and patients. He pointed out, for instance, that the main issue in the white therapist-black client relationship is "trust"; in the black therapist-black client relationship, "identity"; and in the black therapist-white client relationship, "status contradiction." Resolving these special issues in each different racial match becomes a challenge.

Probably influenced by the minority and human rights movements, some groups have stressed the importance of having ethnic/culture-matched therapy. They assume that, in order to obtain effective therapy, every client is better treated by a therapist of the same ethnic-cultural background and by applying certain culture-relevant models of therapy (Sue & Morishima, 1982).

There is no doubt that the congruence of ethnic-cultural background between the therapist and the patient would definitely benefit the therapy process, particularly during the initial stage, making engagement and meaningful communication relatively easier. However, from a clinical point of view, it has been shown that the congruence of ethnic-cultural background alone is not sufficient (Carlton, 2001). In fact, as pointed out by Kareem and Littlewood (1992), ethnic matching of the client and therapist is not the solution to improving intercultural therapy, as it imprisons the professional and the client in their own racial and cultural identities and diminishes the human element.

Relating to the matter of matching of therapist and patient, Chinese-American psychologists Sue and Zane (1987), based on their clinical work, have pointed out that, in intercultural psychotherapy, it is not enough for the therapist to merely have a cultural sensitivity to and knowledge of the cultural background of the client. Additional factors are needed. Cultural knowledge and culture-consistent strategies need to be linked to two basic processes, credibility and giving, to make the therapy successful.

It is seldom pointed out in literature that there are several negative factors associated with the treatment of minority patients by therapists of the same minority background. The matter of confidentiality becomes a real concern if the minority population is relatively small in the community. Patients of a minority background may prefer to be treated by a therapist from outside of their own group. Negative ethnic transference may also occur. The patient may not trust a therapist of his own kind, with a minority or disadvantaged background, and may prefer to be treated by a therapist from a majority group. Identification with a therapist with an advantaged background may operate in such circumstances.

Regarding the situation in Israel, in spite of the racial problems that exist between people of Arab and Jewish backgrounds, interestingly enough, as pointed out by Bizi-Nathaniel, Granek, and Golomb (1991), many Arab patients in Israel prefer Jewish rather than Arab therapists. Possible explanations offered by Bizi-Nathaniel and colleagues are self-hatred, "identification with the aggressor," higher evaluation of therapists' skills, and confidentiality from their own ethnic group.

### e. Reverse Matching of Therapist and Patient

Reverse matching of therapist and patient has seldom been elaborated and examined in the past. Reverse matching refers to the situation in which a patient of a majority background with social privilege is treated by a therapist from a minority background who is socially disadvantaged. Thus, it is a reverse of the common situation in which a minority patient is treated by a majority therapist. What happens in the matter of identification with the therapist? What about ethnic transference and countertransference? Do they tend to become negative? How does the therapist of a minority background affect the process of therapy from the point of view of value systems? These are questions waiting to be answered. In an interesting way, Cheng and Lo (1991) pointed out the advantages of intercultural psychotherapy with the minority therapist-mainstream patient dyad. They pointed out that, in this reversed intercultural therapy situation, the therapist, as an outsider, may provide cultural objectivity and neutrality for the patient in coping with the stresses of life.

## 5. Assessment and Understanding of Problems

As a part of medical practice, psychotherapy follows the medical model and procedure of making a clinical assessment and establishing a diagnosis, based on which therapeutic work can proceed. The only difference is that, in psychotherapy, the nature of the assessment or diagnosis is not entirely focused on biological or physical aspects but predominantly addresses the psychological perspective. It is not descriptive but dynamic. Understanding the nature of the problems and comprehending the causal factors in the occurrence of emotional problems are crucial parts of assessment in psychotherapeutic work. Assessment is not carried out merely at the initial stage of therapy but is continued throughout the process of treatment, in an accumulative and progressive way (see Section 5B: Culturally Relevant Assessment and Diagnosis).

From a cultural point of view, it is crucial for the therapist to understand accurately the nature of the patient's behavior, emotional reactions, psychological problems, and coping patterns, which are all subject to cultural influence. The therapist not only needs basic knowledge of the patient's culture, but also "culture empathy" (i.e., the ability to comprehend the patient's psychology and behavior at an emotional level in a culturally relevant and accurate way). This is a challenging task for any therapist performing intercultural psychotherapy.

## 6. Interpretation and Giving Advice

It is common knowledge among clinicians that a therapist needs to know how to provide interpretation or advice at the proper time in a suitable way. It is a matter of clinical judgment, depending on the therapeutic process and numerous other factors, including the patient's psychopathological condition, ego strength, readiness for explanation, and level of psychological sophistication. Intercultural psychotherapy needs to consider further how to make interpretations that are culturally suitable, proper, meaningful, and effective. The best language and concepts are those familiar to the patient so that he can receive the explanations with ease and find them meaningful.

For instance, an American psychiatrist was treating a young male hypochondriacal Korean patient and his parents in a family session in Korea when he was visiting there as a consultant. The therapist observed that the patient, an only son, had been using multiple somatic symptoms as excuses to stay close to his mother, even sleeping in the same bedroom with her despite being an adolescent. This analytically oriented family therapist, with professional intentions and deliberately chosen strategies, made a direct comment to the young patient in his broken Korean: "You want to kill your father and marry your mother?!" This may have been all right for an (American) patient and his parents if they were familiar with the psychoanalytic concept of the Oedipus wish. Such a direct comment would certainly point out the core of the problem and wake up their conscious awareness of the unresolved parent-child relationship. However, for the Korean patient and his parents, without any preparation, it was a shocking comment that was difficult for them to understand, accept, and react to. Actually, from a cultural point of view, it was extremely inappropriate to make such an interpretative comment to them. Within a conservative, family-oriented society like traditional Korea, it was almost taboo to stir up conflicts within a family. It might have been a psychoanalytically correct understanding (from a theoretical, conceptual point of view), but it was a premature dynamic interpretation (from a clinical perspective) and an inappropriate therapeutic attempt (on a cultural level). Even though the therapist conceptualized the patient and the family pathology in such a way, practically he should simply have encouraged the patient to grow up and learn how to become a man like his father. There was no need to sexualize the situation and stimulate conflict within the parent-child triangular relationship, the last thing that was desirable within such a cultural system.

In many societies, there are numerous proverbs hinting at how a person should lead his life. "A rolling stone never gathers moss," "the grass is greener on the other side of the fence," and "don't put all your eggs in one basket" are some

Western examples. "A protruding nail will be hit by a hammer" (do not speak up too loudly or you will invite a punitive reaction), "a leaf will fall and return to the root of the tree" (a person in crisis will seek support from his family, or an aged person will seek to return to his home in later life), and "a *samurai* will use a toothpick even if he is hungry" (pretending he just had a meal, not showing his weakness in case of any unexpected fighting) are some Eastern examples. These proverbs reflect the cultural wisdom accumulated from life experiences in the past. It is useful in therapy if the proper sayings or proverbs are selected for particular purposes. They will especially make it easier for the patient to understand and obtain insight. Naturally, it will be desirable for the therapist to know some of the sayings that exist in the patient's culture so that he will be able to utilize them when they are needed.

Contemporary Western psychotherapists are trained not to offer any advice to their patients, particularly relating to major life matters, such as decisions about adoption, separation, divorce, or remarriage. This is based on the belief that patients should be respected for making their own decisions. This reflects a cultural belief in basic human rights, and a professional orientation rooted in the psychoanalytic approach. However, it cannot be denied that no matter how the therapist pretends he is not making any decisions for the patient, the patient is always looking for clues given by the therapist, and the therapist *does* send messages to the patient regarding choices that he should make, with or without knowing that he is doing so through verbal or nonverbal communication.

Many patients suffer from dilemmas that they encounter in their daily lives. Therefore, they need to see psychiatrists for guidance: how to relate to parental authority; the proper role of a wife; whether to decide situations for the sake of the individual self or for the family; whether to have premarital sexual relations, an abortion, or extramarital affairs; whether to separate, divorce, remarry, or continue in the present unhappy marriage. Those are common psychological problems encountered by patients, and the choices they make are subject to personal as well as cultural considerations. Offering advice on these daily life matters is a challenge for the therapist, one that cannot be avoided in intercultural psychotherapy. A culturally relevant therapist should actively explore with the patient the implications of each choice the patient has and elaborate on the implications of difference decisions that the patient is going to make, from the different levels of the personal self, the family, and the group, as well as in terms of social and cultural perspectives.

## 7. Goals of Psychotherapy

The final issue that needs attention in intercultural psychotherapy is the matter of the goals of therapy. Defining a normal, healthy, or mature person is subject to cultural influence. What route should be taken to resolve problems and which coping mechanisms should be utilized are subject to cultural determination.

The process of psychotherapy can be viewed as a communication and exchange of values between two partners: the therapist and the patient. It has been said that patients who have shown greater clinical improvement have displayed a significantly greater change in moral values in the direction of their therapists' values. This is the situation in intracultural psychotherapy. To what extent this is true in intercultural psychotherapy is waiting for validation. If a therapist is working with a patient with a different value system, he needs to assess his values carefully. Questions such as, "Shall a wife show her resentfulness toward her husband more openly?" or "Shall a woman learn to express her sexual desire more directly in a public setting?" should be examined carefully and constantly in terms of the patient's culture. It is important that the therapist not impose values and goals that, although appropriate in the therapist's culture, may not be suitable for the patient.

At the philosophical level, many things have to be elaborated carefully. Encouraging a patient to accept suffering or advising him to deal with obstacles are philosophical matters that deserve assessment from a cultural perspective. For an ordinary contemporary American, it may be ideal to be self-directed and independent, to emphasize work and socialization, and to have a problem-solving approach to life's conflicts. For many Eastern people, it may be better to be dependent, to learn rational control over emotions and desire, and to be harmonious with others and with nature. Therefore, it is very important for the therapist to consider the patient's prior life, his patterns of enculturation, and the kind of cultural environment he is going to live in (in his home community or in a new place) and then to elaborate and discover with the patient which direction he should take to improve his life. The therapist may lend his value system to the patient for the latter's reference, but it is the patient who, under the therapist's guidance, should develop goals for improvement.

It is a fact that the practice of psychotherapy is complex. The therapist needs to pay attention to various factors, including the nature of psychopathology and psychological problems from which the patient suffers, the ego strength of the patient, the coping mechanisms customarily utilized by the patient, the patient's motivation for therapy, the therapist-patient relationship, the strategies to be used in therapy, the process and stages of treatment, the defined goals of therapy, and the socioeconomic condition of the patient, including medical insurance to pay for therapy. Beyond such general clinical and social factors, cultural aspects deserve special attention, and an effort is needed to make the therapy culturally relevant and meaningful for the patient. Numerous obstacles may be encountered and many challenges need to be resolved when a therapist is treating a patients with a diversely different cultural background. A competent intercultural psychotherapy is needed.

As a summary, it needs to be pointed out that, it is a fundamental requirement that the therapist needs to be clinically competent. This includes being sensitive, caring, equipped with clinical knowledge and theories of human behavior, and experienced in clinical work. To be successful in conducting culturally relevant clinical work, particularly for intercultural psychotherapy, many additional qualities are desired. These include cultural sensitivity, knowledge, empathy, proper interaction and relations between therapist and patient, and ability to offer relevant cultural guidance to the patient (see Section 5A: The Need for Cultural Competence).

## B. CULTURAL ADJUSTMENTS OF PSYCHOTHERAPY

It is apparent that the practice of psychotherapy should always be carried out in a way that is relevant to the patient and to the social setting where the practice takes place, including political background, social class, economical situation, ethnic and racial factors, and cultural diversity. Cultural influence on the practice of psychotherapy should be examined actively and dealt with by the therapist (Koss-Chioino & Vargas, 1992). In order to carry out culture-relevant and -competent psychotherapy, there is a need to make adjustments at the technical, theoretical, and philosophical levels (Tseng, Lu, & Yin, 1995).

*Technical Adjustments.* Technical adjustments in psychotherapy refer to the need for the therapist to make proper choices of skills or techniques in therapy to fit the background of the patient. It is commonly known by clinicians that the practice of therapy needs to be adjusted in accordance with various factors, including the patient's age, gender, personality, level of cognitive sophistication, and style of psychological orientation, as well as the nature and severity of the psychopathology. Such technical adjustments are needed, furthermore, to fit the cultural background of the patient.

Generally speaking, from a cultural point of view, there are numerous areas that need technical adjustment. Descriptions of many technical adjustments needed for psychotherapy across culture have been presented in detail in Section 7A: Intercultural Psychotherapy: Challenges and Competence. These areas of adjustment usually concern adequate preparation for starting therapy, suitable adjustment of the therapist-patient relationship, performance culturally relevant communication and interpretation, careful management of ethnic/cultural transference and countertransference, proper selection of modes of therapy, and relevant choice of the goals of therapy.

*Theoretical Modifications.* Beyond technical adjustments, it is also necessary to make conceptual or theoretical modifications relating to therapy to fit the patient's cultural background. Ethnicity and culture are to be recognized as significant parameters in understanding psychological processes (American Psychological Association, 1993). At present, several theories, particularly psychoanalytic ones, are utilized by therapists to understand the patient's personality and behavior. However, these theories are subject to cross-cultural modifications if they are to be used for people living in different sociocultural settings. Some of the examples are concepts of self and ego boundaries (Hsu, 1985; Kirmayer, 1989; Marsella, DeVos, & Hsu, 1985; Roland, 1991), interpersonal relations (Doi, 1962), theories of personality development, theories of defense mechanisms (Vaillant, 1971, 1986), or therapeutic mechanisms concerning expression or suppression (Dwairy, 1997). (For details, see Tseng, 2001a, Chapter 49: Culture and Psychiatric Theories.)

Consider, for example, the theoretical concept of the "self" that needs to be dealt with in psychotherapy. The structural theory of the self (dividing the psychology of the self into the id, ego, and superego), derived from analytical concepts, is useful for understanding human psychology. The theory concerns primarily the intrapsychic sphere and is based on the assumption that there is a clear boundary between self and others. However, it is challenged in terms of cross-cultural expansion. From a cultural perspective, F. L. K. Hsu (1973) indicated that the boundary of the "self" does not end with the superego but extends and merges into the surrounding environment of *society* in a concrete sense (including interrelation and interaction with people such as immediate family, friends, neighbors, or members of society at large) and of *culture* in abstract terms (including ways of thinking, attitudes, and value systems). Thus, as illustrated by Figure 1, the structure of "self" could be expanded into sociocultural layers and the boundary of the self as an individual could become blurred for persons from various cultures.

*Philosophical Considerations.*   In the practice of intercultural psychotherapy, the therapist needs to take into consideration the patient's (as well as the therapist's) philosophical orientation. A patient's basic view of and attitude toward human beings, society, and life, closely related to concepts of normality, maturity, and health, will have an obvious impact on the patient in his search for improvement. Furthermore, the philosophical understanding of suffering and problems as well as the cultural choice of the route for resolution for problems will shape the course and goals of therapy (Hoch, 1990; Varma, 1982). In addition, the therapist's own values system and philosophical attitude toward life and problems will explicitly or implicitly guide the direction of therapy, particularly regarding how to encourage the patient to resolve the problems and how to set up the goals of treatment. (For details, see Tseng, 2001b, Chapter 37: Culture-Relevant Psychotherapy.)

a
## Self In Individual-Oriented Society

7 unconscious
6 preconscious
5 unexpressible conscious
4 expressible conscious

3 intimate society and culture
2 operative society and culture
1 wider society and culture
0 outer world

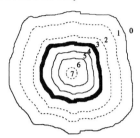

b
## Self In Situation-Oriented Society

7 unconscious
6 preconscious
5 unexpressible conscious
4 expressible conscious

3 intimate society and culture
2 operative society and culture
1 wider society and culture
0 outer world

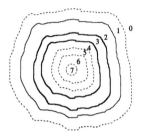

FIGURE 1    Psychosociogram of man in different societies. (a) Ego boundaries are distinctly defined in individual-oriented societies. (b) Ego boundaries are relatively blurred and extend to include the surroundings in situation-oriented societies. [Revised from F. H. L. Hsu, presented at APA annual meeting, Honolulu, 1971.]

# C. CULTURAL CONSIDERATIONS IN VARIOUS MODES OF THERAPY

## 1. Individual Psychotherapy

When therapy is carried out with an individual patient with a format in which the treatment is focused primarily on the patient regarding intrapsychic conflict, personal psychological problems, or issues relating to relations with others, it is called individual psychotherapy. Based on its basic orientation, it is categorized and referred as supportive, analytic, cognitive-behavior therapy. The cultural considerations needed to carry out those individual therapies are summarized briefly.

### a. Supportive Psychotherapy

For any kind of psychotherapy, particularly psychotherapy that is to be carried out as a short-term or time-limited supportive psychotherapy, it is desirable for the therapist to examine carefully the indications and contraindications. These will include considerations of socioeconomic and cultural influences on the understanding and expectation of brief therapy and patterns of adherence to therapy.

To carry out culturally relevant supportive psychotherapy, a therapist needs to know that the patient–therapist relationship is of paramount importance, and that the relationship will be influenced by various individual factors, including personality, gender, and psychopathology as well as the socioculturally defined role and relationship between the therapist and the patient. From a cultural perspective, the therapist needs to examine carefully the proper therapist–patient relationship in terms of the roles to be played and the level and nature of intimacy to be maintained throughout the therapy. This is particularly true concerning the gender and age of the therapist and the patient. It is important to establish and maintain a therapeutic alliance that is not only therapeutic but also socioculturally appropriate.

The concept and expectation of therapy needs to be checked out initially and clarified continuously to avoid any misunderstandings or misleading expectations. The range and nature of support needs to be evaluated against cultural understanding so that the meaning and purpose of therapy will be clear and relevant. The matter of payment and gift giving and receiving should be clarified carefully throughout the course of treatment. They have different meanings within different cultures. The therapist needs to recognize and to utilize maximally the strengths of the patient and the sources of support from the family as well as the sociomedical system and cultural environment to facilitate the patient's improvement.

### b. Analytic Psychotherapy

From a theoretical standpoint, it is important for the therapist to understand that sociocultural factors will shape the structure of self, metaphor and symbolic meaning, the process of personality development, the utilization of various types of defense mechanisms, manifestations of resistence, and ethnic/cultural transference.

From a practical perspective, it is necessary to evaluate the capacity of the patient to engage in and utilize psychodynamic psychotherapy based on factors such as indiviudal personality, psychopathology, and socioeconomic and cultural background. The patient's level of understanding of dynamic concepts needs to be discovered, and proper interpretation of unconscious material should be applied accordingly. Metaphors and symbolic meanings must always be checked against cultural understanding and belief. The interpretation of personal transference deserves careful consideration, depending on how the therapist-patient relationship is viewed and the cultural expectations of that professional relationship. Personalized professional relationships can be very uncomfortable for those who come from a cultural background that strongly emphasizes respect under a hierarchical system. It is important for the therapist to provide culturally relevant interpretation, and to be able to recognize any cultural variations for the manifestation of resistence phenomena. It is crucial for the therapist to manage properly for any personal transference and countertransference as well as ethnic/racial transference and countertransference that may occur and interfere with the process of therapy. The therapeutic maneuver of uncovering vs. suppression of unconscious affect, drive, or conflict deserves careful consideration and proper choice, depending on the patient's cultural background and culturally defined maturity.

### c. Cognitive-Behavior Therapy

To carry out cognitive-behavior therapy, the therapist needs to understand comprehensively the basic principles of the cognitive model including the relationship of thoughts to emotion, behavior, and physiology; the concept of automatic thoughts and cognitive distortion; common cognitive errors; the significance and origin of core beliefs; and the relationship of schemas to dysfunctional thoughts and assumptions, behavioral strategies, and psychopathology. Furthermore, from a cultural perspective, the therapist needs to understand that thought and cognitive "distortion," "errors," or "dysfunctional" behavior need careful evaluation and clarification based on various factors, including sociocultural concept, definition, and judgment.

Careful explanation and orientation of the therapeutic program is always needed initially as many patients are unfamiliar with programmed therapeutic procedures. The concepts and values related to certain issues to be identified and targeted for therapy deserve cultural assessment and consideration. The preference to work on problems at the level of cognition, behavior, or emotion needs to be elaborated and clarified. The therapist needs to clarify the sociocultural implications of positive and negative enforcement utilized for behavioral change. In other words, the cultural implications of the rewards and punishments involved in learning need cultural clarification to avoid any misunderstandings.

### 2. Interpersonal Psychotherapy

### a. Marital Therapy

In marital therapy, the therapist usually works on several different areas, including the partners' expectations of and commitment to marriage, the division of roles between husband and wife, ways of rearing children, relationships with families of origin, communication and sharing between partners, and methods of coping when problems arise. Obviously, all of these issues are subject to cultural factors. Thus, there is a great need for cultural consideration in marital therapy.

In practice, the marital therapist needs to pay attention to the culturally defined roles of man and woman, husband and wife, and father and mother. These roles vary greatly in different cultural groups. For instance, even in trivial matters, which partner should be encouraged or allowed to start the conversation or make the complaint is important from the first session. In a culture that places great emphasis on the dominant role of the man, husband, or father, it is very important to follow the cultural pattern and respect the male participant and allow him to open the conversation or lead in the revealing of problems. Otherwise, there may be an unfavorable outcome, including the discontinuation of therapy by the male for not respecting him as the "boss" in man–woman, husband–wife, or father–mother relations.

One of the basic rules in couple therapy is to avoid alienating one partner and neglecting the other. Taking sides with one of the partners can occur for a number of reasons, including gender or age factors. The similarity or dissimilarity of personal, ethnic, or cultural backgrounds is an additional factor that may affect the therapist-client relationship and needs careful attention.

The acceptable and effective ways of dealing with marital problems vary from culture to culture. For instance, openly acknowledging and facing problems and actively, even aggressively, dealing with problems to resolve them are coping patterns favored in some cultures, whereas passively enduring and concealing problems to maintain harmony may be considered virtues in other cultures. It is the therapist's job to check with his partner-clients to learn the nature and direction of their cultural coping patterns. The goals and outcomes of therapy need to be clarified with the clients from the beginning and throughout the course of treatment.

In general, cultural issues will become more explicit if therapy is undertaken for problems related to intercultural marriage (for details, see Tseng, 2001, Chapter 46, Intercultural marriage: Problems and Therapy). In therapy for intercultural marriage-related problems, the therapeutic maneuvers should focus on the promotion of awareness and understanding of differences in values between the partners; clarifying cultural influences vs. personal factors; encouragement of negotiation and compromise in the resolution of differences; allowing time for the gradual change of culture-related emotions; and permitting a cultural holiday for both partners as needed (Hsu, 2001).

### b. Family Therapy

A family is the basic social unit in life. The cultural aspects of family therapy have been discussed from several perspectives. Regarding the applicability of family therapy, the question has been raised whether ethnic-cultural groups that give greater importance to the family (such as Italian, Portuguese, or Chinese) are better suited for family therapy. Based on clinical experience, it has been pointed out that an emphasis on close family interrelations does not necessarily favor the family therapy approach. For instance, Moitoza (1982) pointed out that Portuguese families' closed family system prevents them from actively seeking family therapy; instead, they attempt to solve their problems via their own family resources and support systems. Chinese families are concerned that "internal disgrace not be known by outsiders"; thus, until a family trusts a therapist, it is relatively difficult to work on their family "secrets" (Hsu, 1983, 1995). Also, it usually takes considerable effort to help a family with culturally fixed, preexisting behavior patterns to unlearn its way of dealing with problems (Tseng & Hsu, 1991).

Concerning the therapist-family relationship, it has been pointed out that it is desirable for the therapist to respect and utilize the culturally defined and sanctioned family hierarchy and relations and constantly evaluate the cultural transference that could occur in family therapy. For instance, McGoldrick and Pearce (1981) pointed out that the Irish cultural attitude toward authority figures will often lead members of an Irish family to show extreme loyalty and willingness to follow through on therapeutic suggestions. In Chinese families, Hsu (1983) suggested that, based on the concept of extended family social relationships, members may feel more comfortable if they are allowed to address the therapist with a pseudokin term (e.g., if the therapist is a woman close to the mother's age, she may be referred to as "auntie").

Numerous points are made by various clinicians concerning cultural aspects directly related to therapeutic strategies. In working with Japanese families, it is necessary to deal with family matters according to cultural priorities is to work on parent-child relations before beginning work on husband-wife issues, according to the Japanese cultural priority of the dyad within a family (Suzuki, 1987). Working with Chicano families, several clinicians (Falicov, 1982; Minuchin et al., 1967) have proposed that it is better to use a structural family therapy approach to satisfy the cultural emphasis on hierarchies within families. McGoldrick and Pearce (1981) have pointed out that Irish families are apt to be threatened by therapy directed at uncovering hostile or erotic feelings and may respond better to a positive reframing of the strategic therapy model. Regarding Jewish families, Herz and Rosen (1982) have mentioned that, closely related to their cultural tendency to treasure suffering as a shared value, the verbal expression of feelings in family therapy may be emphasized.

In sum, a family therapist needs to be familiar with cultural variations of family systems, structures, and interactional patterns, including role playing, communication, and value systems that are emphasized. The therapist also needs to know how to select culturally suitable intervention techniques so that culturally relevant family therapies can be applied for families with different cultural backgrounds (Tseng & Hsu, 1991). If the therapist is working with ethnic minorities, as stressed by Ho (1987), his role is to serve as a "culture broker" rather than an intruder; to facilitate negotiations between systems; and, usually, to work closely with the more acculturated members to promote change within the whole family, facilitating its adjustment to the host society. A similar view has been raised by Jalali (1988), who pointed out that, in treating ethnic families, the therapist is often confronted with a clash of two cultures, two generations, and problems in acculturation. The therapist, at the time of the conflict, explains and teaches the values and norms of both sides and acts as a cultural mediator, encouraging all to become multicultural, or to have a foot in both cultures. Thus, it is clearly indicated that family therapy is focused on cultural adjustment within the family or among family members.

### c. Group Therapy

By definition, group therapy involves working with a group in therapeutic activities. Naturally, it involves group formation, interaction, and many other aspects of group processes and phenomena. In addition to the basic factors relating to group composition, including age, gender, personality, and the psychopathology of the group members, the group transactions will obviously be influenced by the ethnic and cultural backgrounds of the members and the therapist.

A psychiatrist from Nigeria, Asuni (1967), reported that due to the extreme shortage of therapists for standardized individual psychotherapy, an attempt has been made to develop group therapy mainly for hospitalized patients. As for the style of therapy, a nondirective, nonformal procedure was adopted for open group therapy for selected inpatients to fit their local situation and cultural background.

Working with Greek immigrants in group therapy, Dunkas and Nikelly (1975) commented that a Greek was more attuned to group goals than to individual fulfillment. He did what the group approved of and expected, receiving cues through its tacit or obvious approval. Instead of self-actualization and personal happiness, the Greek pursued love, esteem, and admiration from members of his group. The group members tended to maintain an attitude of servility and passivity; they looked up to the therapist and expected him to do the work. Such ethnic-related personality attributes were clearly manifested in transactions of the group during therapy.

Based on his working experience with Orthodox Jewish patients in New York, an Orthodox Jewish therapist, Shapiro (1996), raised issues that are pertinent to treating such a population in group therapy. For instance, due to the small and close ethnic population in the community, individual anonymity was almost impossible to maintain. The mixture of gender in the group was quite untraditional and culturally unfamiliar and resulted in heightened resistance to therapy. Because verbal propriety is a cultural requirement, group members were self-restricting in their language and verbal style and the topics they were willing to discuss.

Leading group therapy for Chicanos in Texas, Martinez (1977) pointed out that there was a Mexican tradition of close-mouthedness and not opening up to others (*no te rajes*). This worked against communication and expression of feelings in group situations. Also, there was a built-in formality in interpersonal relations among Spanish-speaking people, as reflected in their language usage. This greater formality made it difficult for group members to relate to one another candidly as equals and inhibited the voicing of negative feelings toward the therapist.

Based on group therapy experiences with Chinese clients in Canada, Chen (1995) noted that the Chinese tended to expect the therapist to maintain the image of an authority figure with expertise, to educate the group members, and to provide structure for the group process. It was also better for the therapist to define rules and boundaries for the members to follow.

All of the points just raised indicate that the behavior of group members is greatly influenced by their cultural backgrounds in the areas of communication style, relational patterns, and interaction with the therapist, all of which, in turn, impact the process of group therapy. In contrast to individual psychotherapy, which focuses mainly on the psychopathology of an individual, interpersonal psychotherapy deals primarily with problems related to interpersonal issues; thus, there is more of a need to consider and understand cultural impact on interactional human behavior.

When a group is composed of multiethnic members, the situation is much more complicated from a cultural perspective. Through her work with multiethnic groups, Matsukawa (2001) has pointed out that there is a great need for attention to several issues, namely, encouraging the explanation and exploration of ethnically derived values in order to help the members understand the interpersonal behavior that is the result of these values, helping the members observe and understand nonverbal and symbolic forms of communication, exploring the dynamics underlying the cultural transferences arising from group members, examining cultural transferences occurring within the therapist(s), and, finally, helping the members examine their ethnic or racial prejudices in a safe environment that can contain the strong affects that arise.

## D. CULTURAL APPLICATION AND SUPERVISION OF PSYCHOTHERAPY

Although the impact of culture on the practice of psychotherapy has been intensively examined through intercultural psychotherapy in this chapter, it is important for clinicians to realize that attention to culture is needed in various ways in different situations and for different reasons. The culture is not to be focused on *simply* because the patient has a different ethnic or cultural background than that of the therapist, or *merely* because the patient belongs to a minority group or is a foreigner. The impact of culture on an individual or a family varies in different ways according to various circumstances. Therefore, an appropriate "cultural differential diagnosis of a case" is necessary in clinical application (Tseng & McDermott, 1981). Appropriate distinguishing and understanding is needed case by case. The different roles cultural issues play in clinical cases are analyzed and distinguished next.

## 1. Various Situations in Which Culture Plays a Role in Clinical Cases

### a. Psychiatric Cases Directly Imbedded in Cultural Matters

Psychiatric cases that are directly imbedded in cultural matters are those in which the clinically presented problems are related closely to culture-induced stress or problems. Thus, how to solve the culture-related conflict or dilemma is the primary focus of the case.

---

CASE 1

---

A Japanese Physician Is Not Given Approval to Marry His Girlfriend

A young physician was considering double suicide with his girlfriend in a traditional, conservative Japanese society because their love relationship was not accepted or approved by either their parents or their society. His girlfriend was a nurse, but unfortunately she was a widow with a young son. Her husband had died in an accident. In their society, it was unthinkable for a socially respectable man to marry a woman who was married before, particularly with children from the previous marriage. The situation became worse, as this young physician was expected to succeed his father as superintendent of the hospital. It was considered absolutely impossible for him to marry such a "disgraceful" woman and a nurse in the hospital. In traditional Japan, where hierarchy was emphasized, a nurse was considered subordinate to a physician, and not a suitable candidate for the wife of the hospital's superintendent-to-be. There was no way out of this culturally entangled problem.

---

### b. Psychiatric Cases Related Only Indirectly to Cultural Issues

In some cases, the problem is indirectly related to cultural matters, or cultural factors play only a secondary role in the total problem.

---

CASE 2

---

A Filipino–American Wife Who Attempted Suicide

Marital therapy was arranged for a Filipino-American wife after she attempted suicide. She had migrated from the Philippines to the United States several years before, and married a Caucasian man. After she became pregnant, her husband was so happy that he invited his parents to visit them at their new house. His mother had suffered a minor stroke and was not able to attend their wedding. He thought that it was a good time for his parents to meet his wife and become close as a family. However, things went the opposite way. The wife suffered from severe morning sickness and was very much annoyed that her husband spent more time with his parents than with her when she was in need of attention. Despite her warnings, he continued to spend considerable time showing his parents around, hoping that they would have a good time. With his mother physically disabled now, he thought that it might be his only chance to be close to her and be nice to her. However, his wife, not having her own parents nearby (they were far away in the Philippines), was terribly lonely and felt that she was not being treated tenderly enough by her husband at a time when she needed his support. She became emotionally hysterical, overdosed, and ended up being sent to a hospital emergency room.

Her history revealed that this was not the first time the wife had suffered emotional turmoil. Shortly after their marriage, the husband's sister had come to visit them. The wife had a serious quarrel with her husband when he prepared the bed for his sister rather than let his wife, as hostess, do it. Furthermore, it upset her very much when the three of them went out in the car. The husband drove the car as usual, but asked his sister to sit next to him, letting his wife sit in the back seat. He explained that because it was the first time his sister had come to this new place, letting her sit in the front seat would allow her to sightsee better. However, the wife became very upset, feeling that her husband cared more for his sister than he did for his own wife. She cried, caused a scene at home, and her sister-in-law left the uncomfortable situation.

In this case, multiple factors contributed to the problems. The interracial marriage might have contributed indirectly, in matters such as the roles of husband, brother, and son in different circumstances as perceived in different cultures. A certain attitude and reaction may be expected from a husband when his wife is pregnant and experiencing morning sickness. There is a need to explore those issues from a Filipino as well as an American point of view. However, personality and interpersonal relationship patterns certainly played a part for the husband and the wife, at both the individual and marital levels, which are outside of cultural issues. Thus, a comprehensive understanding is needed.

## c. Psychiatric Cases in Which Culture Is a Disguise for Psychiatric Problems

In some cases, the problems presented appear to have originated from or be related directly to ethnic or cultural issues. However, after careful analysis, it is revealed that the problems lie in the psychology of the individual, and that ethnic or cultural factors are merely used as excuses for the occurrence of problems. This phenomenon tends to be observed in cases relating to ethnic minorities or interracial marriages.

---

CASE 3

An Irish-American Woman Suffered from Recurrent Asthma

An Irish-American women in her 40s was referred by her family doctor for psychiatric treatment because she suffered from asthma that was difficult to control by medication. Besides, the doctor suspected that she had some kind of marital displeasure that needed psychiatric attention. This woman had married an African-American man several years before. After the marriage, she discovered that her husband tended to ignore her at home. For instance, in the morning, while both of them were having breakfast, her husband would concentrate on reading the newspaper, hiding his face from her. Unable to tolerate being ignored, she would push the newspaper away from her husband's face and try to talk, but their conversation would only last for a couple of minutes. Then he would sink into the newspaper again. Finally, she would start to cry, provoking an asthma attack, which would finally get his attention, and he would take her to see the doctor. Thus, their marital problems contributed indirectly to her repeated asthma attacks. She blamed her mistake in getting into a mixed marriage as the cause of her problems.

Her history revealed that she had had feelings of inferiority since she was young. She had always felt that she was not good enough as a woman and had difficultly maintaining a meaningful relationship with a man. To cope with this chronic feeling of inferiority, she decided to marry a black man, because she viewed African-Americans as an "inferior" group. She thought that marrying such an inferior man might balance her psychological problems. Her husband married her for the opposite reason. He used to despise white people for their superiority. He thought that marrying a white woman would give him satisfaction by counteracting his fear of being inferior to white people. Thus, subconsciously, he despised his white wife and used her for his own psychological gratification, until she became sick, then he would take care of her out of pity. Because of their racially mixed marriage, they had difficulty establishing and maintaining a social network with either whites or blacks, as they were not accepted by either. Based on this social isolation, the wife felt a greater need to rely on her husband for emotional support. However, in return, what she received was intentional ignoring and despising that aggravated her feelings of rejection.

In this case, intermarriage associated with racial issues seemed to be the core problem. However, a case analysis revealed that race was merely used as an excuse to solve their individual, preexisting, internal psychological problems. Race was merely a disguise for the major problem.

### d. Psychiatric Cases in Which Culture Is Not a Clinical Issue

Psychiatric problems may not be related to cultural matters at all in many cases, even though the patient may belong to a minority or a foreign ethnic group or be part of an interethnic marriage. The psychiatric problems may be primarily of a biological nature, such as dementia, mental subnormality, autism, or organic mental disorder induced by trauma, intoxication, infection, or metabolic or vascular disturbance. Even with major psychoses, such as schizophrenia and bipolar disorders, there is little room for cultural influence except in a secondary way. Race, ethnicity, or culture should not be easily considered the direct or primary cause for this group of psychiatric disorders.

---

CASE 4

A Laotian Woman Tried to Take Away a Stranger's Daughter

A young woman of Laotian origin was brought by police to a psychiatric hospital after she entered a woman's house and physically assaulted her, trying to take away the woman's daughter. She claimed that the daughter was her own. Even though the police were called in and it was explained to her that the girl was the other woman's daughter, the Laotian woman did not want to listen. After being admitted to the hospital, it was revealed that she and her husband had come to the United States as war refugees from her home country. Her husband had been killed in a traffic accident the year before. In reaction to this tragic loss, she developed the idea that the communists in Laos were still trying to persecute them. She interpreted her husband's death not as accidental, but as an assassination because he was anticommunist. After this incident, she began to suspect that someone was following her when she walked on the street and watching her from outside of her house when she returned home. When she began to deteriorate in her daily life, becoming unable to take care of her young daughter, a social worker had to remove the daughter from her house and place the daughter in a foster home not known to the patient. The woman missed her daughter very much and wandered the street day and night, looking for her. One day, she found a girl who looked like her daughter and insisted on bringing back "her own daughter!"

---

In this case, it is quite a temptation to see the woman as a victim of war in her home country, someone who became vulnerable in the host society, especially after her husband's tragic death. The role of ethnicity and culture may be entertained, and hysterical psychosis rather than paranoid psychosis may be considered as a clinical diagnosis. Actually, in this case, when the patient was treated by a dynamically oriented psychiatrist, intensive psychotherapy was given for a month without any improvement. After consultation with a cultural psychiatrist, the attending psychiatrist reluctantly revised his diagnosis, accepting the suggestion of prescribing antipsychotics for the patient, which later improved her psychotic condition considerably.

Sometimes, clinicians will overemphasize ethnic or cultural factors in case formulations and overinterpret culture as the cause of the problems. This is illustrated in the psychotic case just given. Even in the case of minor psychiatric disorders, and common psychological problems, unless there is sufficient solid evidence that culture played a significant role in the cause and formation of the disorders, a clinician should not loosely entertain cultural considerations as psychogenic factors. A proper clinical differential diagnosis, including cultural dimensions, is necessary for proper management and treatment.

Finally, it needs to be said that a clinician should pay attention to social factors, particularly economic condition and social class, either explicitly or implicitly existing within a society; different educational levels; and geographic differences associated with subcultures. Such "social" factors, paralleling "cultural" factors (manifested mostly in attitudes and beliefs), are going to affect the process, style, and effectiveness of psychotherapy and deserve more exploration and understanding (Acosta, Yamamoto, & Evans, 1982; Prince, 1987).

## 2. Various Circumstances That Warrant Attention to Cultural Matters

Although conceptually culture is an important issue that needs to be addressed, strictly speaking, it is not necessary to focus primarily on cultural factors all the time in all clinical situations. Attention to culture is needed for different reasons under different circumstances, and perhaps with different kinds of attention and clinical management. For the sake of simplicity, several circumstances will be listed and elaborated here.

### a. Working on Culture-Related Particular Issues in Therapy

In clinical settings, the primary focus of therapy needs to be on different areas or dimensions, depending on the nature of the problems presented by the patient or perceived by the therapist. If the problems are closely culture-related, then there is a great need to address them in therapy. For instance, when a patient's clinical problems are associated with adjustment problems due to transcultural migration, related to the matter of ethnic or cultural identity confusion, or connected to intercultural marital problems, all will be considered as primarily related to cultural issues. There is a need for specific therapeutic considerations and strategies to work on such issues.

For the problems encountered by minority groups with ethnic identity confusion, Chin, De La Cancela, and Jenkins (1993) suggested that ethnic identity needs to be viewed as bicultural rather than as moving along a linear continuum of acculturation. Many factors that will contribute to the success or failure of transcultural adjustment after migration to a foreign society have been identified. The personality of the migrant, the motivation for migration, the attitude toward the hosting society, and acceptance by the hosting society are all issues that need to be considered for therapy. In general, based on recently accumulated professional knowledge and experience, clinicians are gaining more insight into culture-related psychological problems and how to work on them, opening new clinical areas for exploration in culture and psychotherapy.

### b. Working in Situations of "Intercultural Psychotherapy"

Cultural impact on psychotherapy needs special and active attention in situations of interethnic and/or intercultural psychotherapy, even though the primary clinical problems are not related directly to cultural issues. Because cultural factors have a direct impact on every aspect of the therapeutic process, including communication, therapist-patient relations, and so on, as elaborated in Section 7A: Intercultural Psychotherapy: Challenges and Competency, there is a need for special attention and management by the therapist. This is always more important if the cultural gap is more diverse, a language barrier exists, and the therapist is relatively unfamiliar with the patient's cultural background.

### c. Working with "Special" or "Minority" Populations Needing Cultural Consideration

When a therapist is working with a patient from a special population, such as a different gender (particularly women), sexual orientation, physical condition (handicapped or disabled), age (children or aged persons), or social class (underprivileged lower class), he needs to make an extra effort to consider cultural perspectives, even if the patient belongs to the same ethnic group as he does. These special populations have grown up with different personal experiences than those of the therapist, have different views of the world and life, and retain different value systems. They usually have different kinds of psychological issues and problems that require special understanding and approaches in treating them.

The differences among these special groups will be compounded if they are of different ethnic, racial, or sociopolitical backgrounds. Thus, they provide new areas for clinical exploration beyond the experience and knowledge of working with the ordinary, mainstream adult population. These issues, which are getting more recognition among clinicians and are addressed more in writings (Pedersen, Draguns, & Lonner, 1976; Pederson et al., 1996; Sue & Sue, 1999), include how to work with children of minority groups (Powell, 1983; Vargas &

Koss-Chioino, 1992), ethnic elders (Baker & Lightfoot, 1993), and gay men and lesbians (Krajeski, 1993).

### d. Working with "Common" or "Majority" Populations in Therapy

Finally, from a cultural perspective, the impact of culture on the process of psychotherapy cannot be ignored, even if the therapist is treating a patient of the same cultural background as the general population. There is always a communication problem to overcome, even if the therapist and the patient speak the same language. A metaphor might be different from one person to another. There is always some degree of value differences at the individual level, there are broad differences in attitudes toward birth control, abortion, or divorce, for example, even among Christian groups. There are always different personal views, to some extent, between two individuals that need to be faced, adjusted, or resolved in ordinary daily life as well as in therapeutic situations. This is the dilemma that the psychotherapist has to manage with any kind of patient.

Thus, as pointed out by Wohl (1989), all psychotherapy is "intercultural" in that no two people have internalized identical constructions of their cultural worlds. Cultural issues tend to be noticed only when cultural differences among the patient and therapist are clearly evident. There is no sharp difference between intracultural and intercultural psychotherapy. They are merely different situations on a continuum.

## 3. Transcultural Supervision in Psychotherapy

One area that tends to be neglected or ignored is that of transcultural (or cross-cultural) supervision in psychotherapy. To master the knowledge and skill of psychotherapy, trainees are required to receive individual guidance from supervisors on how to carry out psychotherapy. There is always the possibility that the patient, the supervisee, and the supervisor will not share the same ethnic or cultural background. This will be more complicated if the patient under treatment belongs to an ethnic or cultural background that is neither that of the supervisee or the supervisor. Therefore, the need for transcultural supervision in therapy will occur. For instance, a Caucasian supervisor may supervise an Asian supervisee in treating an African-American or Hispanic patient. This situation involves the ethnic or cultural issues relating to the three partners: the supervisor, the supervisee, and the patient. In addition to the ordinary clinical concern with how to provide supervision relating to common clinical issues, including making an assessment, formulating the nature of the problem, and selecting the choice of therapeutic strategies, there is the matter of how to deal with or overcome the incongruence of ethnic or cultural factors among the three partners involved. This is a challenging issue that has seldom been examined in detail. If it is colored by racism, then how to deal with privilege, power, trust, and communication among partners of different racial backgrounds as well as ethnic/racial transference and countertransference all become essential issues that need to be carefully worked out (Fong & Lease, 1997; Katsnelson, 1998).

The supervisor's ability and competence relating to cultural sensitivity, cultural knowledge, cultural empathy, and cultural guidance all become critical matters. Certainly there is an urgent need to explore this subject in order to improve culturally relevant supervision. Without a doubt, it is not only the therapist in training who needs cultural psychiatry training; the supervisor must also be educated to increase the sensitivity, knowledge, and experience needed to carry out culturally competent psychotherapy.

Finally, it can be said that although the awareness of the need for culturally relevant and competent psychotherapy is becoming more prevalent among clinicians, the next step is to accumulate more comprehensive clinical experience and knowledge on how to provide psychotherapy for patients with diverse cultural backgrounds. This includes trying modified or radically alternative therapy models for patients of different ethnic-cultural backgrounds, coupled with comprehensive evaluation and assessment of these various therapeutic approaches. Based on such systematic clinical exploration, we can obtain better insight into the subject of culture and psychotherapy.

## E. COMPARISON OF FOLK, UNIQUE, AND COMMON THERAPIES

Finally, in order to expand our insight into the cultural aspects of psychotherapy, let us briefly examine various modes of psychological treatment that exist around the world among people of various cultural backgrounds. Using a broad definition of psychotherapy, through an overview of various modes of therapy, either culture-embedded indigenous healing practices, culture-influenced unique psychotherapies, or culture-related common psychotherapies, we can comprehend the cultural implications of psychotherapys. (For details, see Tseng, 2001a, Chapter 32, 33, and 34, respectively, in Section F: Culture and Psychological Therapy.) Further, it is useful for the contemporary therapist to be aware of the various forms of folk or unique therapies that exist because they are utilized often by people, even in modern society.

### 1. Culture-Embedded Indigenous Healing Practices

Folk healing practices are nonorthodox therapeutic practices based on indigenous cultural traditions and operating outside official healthcare systems. The practices are often validated by experience, but are not founded on logico-experimental science (Jilek, 1993, 1994). Indigenous healing practices are observed in various societies, particularly so-called "primitive" or "pre-industrialized" societies, but they can be observed in modern or developed societies as well. These healing practices are intensely embedded in the cultural systems in which they developed and in which they are practiced; therefore, they are often difficult to transplant to entirely different cultural settings, where they are viewed differently.

### a. Spirit Mediumship (Trance-Based Healing System)

Spirit mediumship broadly refers to a situation in which a healer or a client, or both, experience altered states of consciousness, in the form of dissociation or possession, at the time of the healing ritual.

*Shamanism.* It is speculated that the geographic heartland of shamanism is central and northern Eurasia, with widespread diffusion to Southeast Asia and the Americas. Through a religious ceremony, a shaman can work himself into a trance state in which he is "possessed" by a god. Rhythmic singing, dancing, or praying seems to assist the self-induction of the trance state. Among native healers in North and South America, a psychedelic substance (such as cactus) is frequently used to induce an altered state of consciousness. Whether substance- or self-induced, the shaman enters into an ecstatic trance in a healing ceremony. In

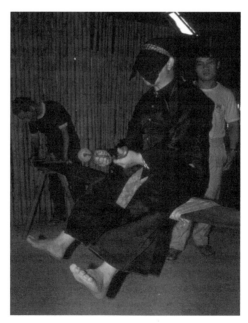

FIGURE 2    Hmong shaman in Laos. Traveling ("riding" a horse) to the spirit world to retrieve a client's lost soul. [Courtesy of Wolfgang Jilek, M.D.]

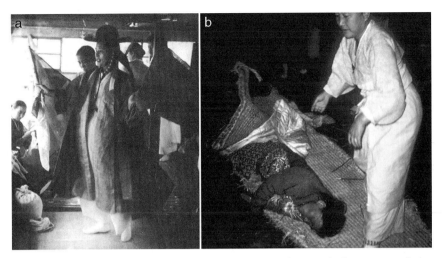

FIGURE 3   Woman shaman in Korea. (a) A woman shaman performing a healing ceremony during a trance state [From *Six Korean Shamans*, by Y. S. Kim Harvey. Honolulu: University of Hawaii Press, 1979]. (b) Conducting a "funeral" ceremony as (counterphobic) therapy for a woman patient preoccupied with the fear that she might die. [Courtesy of Laurel Kendall, Ph.D.]

some cultures, this is not defined as being "possessed" by a supernatural entity; it is merely believed that the shaman is able to link up with the supernatural and work through its powers (see Fig. 2). The client can then consult the supernatural through the shaman for instructions on dealing with his problems.

The causes of problems are usually interpreted according to folk concepts of the culture, involving such things as loss of the soul, sorcery, spirit intrusion, violation of taboos, or disharmony with nature (see Section 2C: Folk Explanations of Mental Problems). Coping methods suggested are usually magical in nature, including prayer, the use of charms, and the performance of extraction, exorcism, or other therapeutic ritual ceremonies (see Figs. 3 and 4). The goal of the healing practice is to resolve the client's problems. Utilizing supernatural powers, acting as an authority figure, making suggestions, and providing hope are among the main healing mechanisms provided by the shaman.

*Zar Ceremonies.*   The term "*zar*" refers to a ceremony as well as a class of spirits. *Zar* rituals are observed primarily in Muslim societies in the Mideast, including Ethiopia, Egypt, Iraq, Kuwait, Sudan, Somaliland, and Iran. *Zar* ritual is different from shamanism in that, in addition to the healer, during the ceremony the client also experiences the dissociated or possessed state.

The ceremony is essentially a means of dealing with the demonic power of evil (*zar* spirit) that may cause an illness. The local people believe that a demon can indeed cause a disorder, and the patient becomes inextricably associated with that particular spirit for the rest of his life. Accordingly, the patient has the respon-

FIGURE 4    Chinese indigenous healers in Taiwan. (a) A male shaman performing a healing practice in front of a family altar for many hours while in a trance state [From *God, Ghosts, and Ancestors,* by David K. Jordan, 1972, with permission]. (b) A shaman hitting his body with a needled–club,
showing he is blessed because he comes to no harm [Courtesy of Jung-Kwang Wen, M.D.]. (c) A
Daoist priest-healer performing a ceremony by climbing up a specially designed "knife ladder,"
showing he is blessed by not being injured when he steps on the sharp knife blades, which serve as
rungs on the ladder. (d) Sitting on top of a four-story-high "knife ladder" the priest is requesting
the blessing of the god in the heaven. (c) and (d) [from *Chinese Time Post*—photos taken by a reporter,
Mr. Gong-Yi Lin. Courtesy of Jung-Kwang Wen, M.D.]

sibility of satisfying the *zar* spirit with a special performance at least once a year
and is obligated to attend the *zar* ceremonies of others.

The *zar* ceremony is primarily a female activity. All of those attending wear
new or clean clothing to please the spirits. The main patient usually wears a
white gown as much gold jewelry as possible and is heavily perfumed. The ceremony master begins the ceremony with a song and drumming. When a spirit
associated with some person in the audience is called, that person begins to shake
in her seat, dancing and trembling until she falls, exhausted, to the floor. Before
the spirit consents to leave, it usually demands special favors, such as jewelry, new

clothing, or expensive foods. It is the duty of the relatives and friends to gather around the prostrate woman and pacify the spirit. The whole tone of the ceremony is one of propitiation and persuasion rather than coercion. The ceremony ends with an animal sacrifice and a feast.

### b. Religious Healing Ceremonies

There are various kinds of religious healing ceremonies observed in different societies that are considered by mental health workers to serve a therapeutic function for their participants. Leighton and Leighton (1941) studied a religious healing ceremony practiced by the Navahos, the largest Indian tribe in the United States, and pointed out that assurance and suggestions are among the therapeutic mechanisms operating in the ceremony.

Concerning specific healing rituals, Jilek (1974, 1982) reported on Salish-speaking Indians of the Pacific Coast of North America who practice a unique spirit dancing ceremony. In the initiation process to the spirit dance, the novice is expected to experience his symbolic death and rebirth into a healthier, culture-congenial life. Physiological and psychological means are utilized to induce altered states of consciousness and achieve personality depatterning and subsequent resynthesis and reorientation.

Cultural psychiatrist Sangun Suwanlert (1997) from Thailand described the *phan yak* chanting treatment for the purpose of *sa dor kro* (to let go of bad things). Based on the concept that evil spirits cause any kind of mental disturbances, religious healing ceremonies are occasionally held in temples for exorcism and purification (see Fig. 5 in Section 11D: Religion).

It is important to know that religious healing ceremonies are not only observed in primitive societies or among uncivilized populations but are quite common in many industrialized societies as well (Pattison & Wintrob, 1981). As

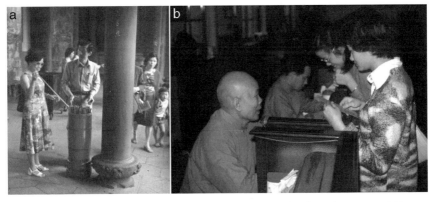

FIGURE 5   Chinese fortune-telling (*chien*-drawing) in Taiwan. (a) After a sincere pray, picking up a bamboo stick (*chien*) for divine instruction. (b) An elderly person in the temple interpreting the fortune and acting as a folk counselor. [Courtesy of Jing Hsu, M.D.]

pointed out by Hufford (1977), religion-related healing systems are increasing rapidly in popularity in the United States. In Christian religious healing, there is a broad spectrum of beliefs and activities, ranging from Christian Science to the fundamentalism of healers such as Oral Roberts to the Roman Catholic rite of anointing of the sick. In reviewing Christian religious rituals, Griffith and Young (1988) pointed out that special styles of prayer, testimony, and spirit possession are integral parts of the services in the black church in the United States. These practices serve as a cohesive force binding blacks together. This form of service is particularly effective when conducted by a charismatic black pastor and allows an oppressed minority to externalize its woes and obtain succor from a righteous God.

Thus, in various forms of religious healing ceremonies, the therapeutic operation is carried out through the ritual of prayer, testimony, sacrifice, reliving experience, or even spirit possession. Assurance, suggestions, and the generation of conviction are some of the healing mechanisms utilized in the practices. The aims of therapy are to heal the patient's problems and give a certain perspective to his life (see Section 11D: Religion).

### c. Divination

Divination refers to the act or practice of trying to foretell the future or the unknown by occult means. It relies on mysterious, magic, or religious methods. The system of reference shifts from the supernatural to the natural in the practice of fortune-telling. Based on the concepts of microcosm and macrocosm, fortune-telling is oriented to the basic belief that human life and behavior are parts of the universe. The nature of the problems is usually explained in terms of an imbalance of vital forces or disharmony with the natural principles that rule the universe. The objective of the practice is to help the client find out how to live compatibly with nature and adjust to the environment more harmoniously.

Although the basic assumption underlying fortune-telling is that every person has a predetermined course in life, this "fate" is not absolutely unchangeable—it may be subject to modification. Thus, it is not a completely passive acceptance of "fate," but allows room for adjustment. Finding a way to adjust your own fortune is the purpose of fortune-telling. Because the interpretation of divine instruction is usually provided by the diviner himself, or an interpreter, the interaction between the diviner/interpreter and the client becomes an important variable (see Fig. 5.)

### 2. Culture-Influenced Unique Psychotherapies

Culture-influenced unique psychotherapies are therapeutic modes that are very culturally flavored and characteristically "unique," different from the "common" or "mainstream" modes of psychotherapy that are currently practiced in

Euro-American societies. Although theoretically any form of psychotherapy is more or less influenced by culture, the adjective term of "culture-influenced" is used here to indicate therapies that are strongly colored by the philosophical concepts or value systems of the societies in which they were created. Therefore, such therapies may be difficult to transplant to other cultures, or to practice in the same society in another era, if significant cultural change has occurred since they were developed. There are seemingly endless numbers of culture-influenced unique psychotherapies that can be identified around the globe. Only some of them have been selected for review and discussion here.

### a. Mesmerism

Mesmerism was invented in the late 18th century by the Austrian physician Franz Anton Mesmer, and became popular in Paris. Mesmer, as a physician, subscribed to the theory that planets influence the physiological and psychological phenomena of human beings. He hypothesized that man was endowed with a special magnetic, animal force that, when liberated, could produce amazing healing effects. Based on this assumption, he developed a method for magnetizing neurotic patients to heal them. In treatment sessions, a group of patients was asked to hold hands in a circle around a *baquet*, a tub filled with "magnetized" water. Mesmer, as the therapist, physically touched the patients, or simply gestured with his hands, with the intention of transmitting a magnetic force from his body to the patients, healing them. Thus, conceptually, the therapy was based on the somatic theory of the transmission and supplementing of animal magnetic force. However, in practice, it was the psychological force (i.e., suggestions) produced by the charismatic therapist that affected the patients.

### b. Rest Therapy

Rest therapy was designed by a neurologist, Silas Weir Mitchell, in the late 19th century in the United States (Schneck, 1975). It was based on the assumption that a neurotic patient's mental illness was caused by exhaustion of the nervous system, or "anemia of the brain." Thus, rest and recuperation were prescribed for the patient, a logical outgrowth of the concept of neurasthenia, developed by George Beard then. The therapy consisted of rest, proper food, and isolation. The patient was prohibited contact with relatives and was separated completely from the setting in which his illness developed. Mitchell considered rest therapy particularly beneficial in the treatment of neurotic women. It reflects the medical knowledge as well as cultural concepts of neurasthenia prevailed then.

### c. Naikan Therapy

Naikan therapy was developed by a Japanese Buddhists-civilian, Ishin Yoshimoto, in Japan five decades ago for the purpose of treating juvenile delinquency and

FIGURE 6   Naikan therapy invented in Japan. (a) The Japanese layperson Ishin Yoshimato, who invented the therapy. (b) The Buddhist temple where Naikan therapy originated. (c) The therapist comes to visit and examine the patient, who is sitting in a corner of a room behind a screen for self-examination. [Courtesy of Ryuzo Kawahara, M.D.]

other problems (see Fig. 6a). *Naikan* in Japanese literally means intra-inspection. Any person intending to participate in the therapy, which originally took place in a temple (see Fig. 6b), needs to vow to respect the master's guidance and discipline. The core of the Naikan practice is the client's self-inspection. Sitting in a corner of a room, facing toward the wall to conduct a self-examination of his own life in the past, with a particular focus on the kind of relationships he has had with significant persons, usually his parents (see Fig. 6c). The client is instructed to review the kinds of things his parents did for him, and what he did in return. Through the process of self-inspection, the client may obtain insight about his attitudes and learn not to complain and cause trouble for others, but to repay others with appreciation and a joyful heart. The change in the patient's attitude toward others and his view of life are the core of the therapy (Murase, 1976).

### d. Erhard Seminars Training

Founded by Werner Erhard, a layperson whose formal education only included high school, Erhard Seminars Training (est) was fashionable among well-educated adults in the United States during the 1970s. It consisted of a structured, two weekend (60-hour) program for self-improvement. The program was organized with certain rules, including a strict 7 hours between bathroom breaks, thus it was nicknamed "no-piss training." As a program, est is concerned primarily with a philosophy of life and self. The seminar is conducted in such a way as to stimulate enlightenment about life. The participants might be humiliated by the seminar leader by being called "assholes," "machines," and so on, but the key point is to help them recognize that life is only what it is, not the way it used to be, ought to be, or might be. Life does not work. There is nothing one can do to make it work, so stop trying. There is nothing to do in life except to live

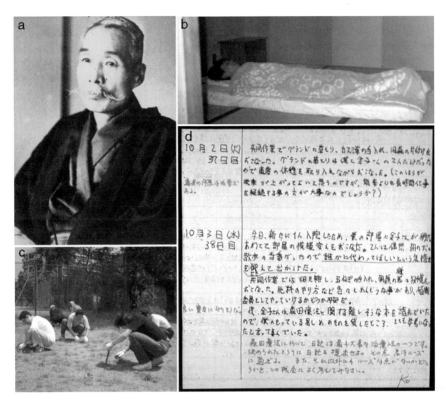

FIGURE 7    Morita therapy originated in Japan. (a) A Japanese psychiatrist, Shoma Morita, founded the experiential therapy, which was later named after him. (b) A young male suffering from *taijinky-ofusho* resting in bed during the first stage of therapy. (c) A group of male patients doing yard work in the second stage of therapy. (d) A patient's diary with comments by his therapist in red pen as a part of the therapeutic activities. [Courtesy of Kenji Kitanishi, M.D.]

it. As recognized by the founder, the training has philosophical views similar to Zen's attitude toward life.

From a cultural perspective, est appealed to well-educated adults during the 1970s because it provided a philosophy of life that was radically different from the beliefs of the contemporary society. In Torrey's interpretation (1986), est tends to affect the participant through the "superman syndrome" (i.e., making a person believe that he has the power to handle his own life).

### e. Morita Therapy

Morita therapy was originally founded by a Japanese psychiatrist, Shoma Morita (see Fig. 7a), in 1919, about the same time that Sigmund Freud developed psychoanalysis in Austria. Morita developed his therapy primarily for the treatment of anthrophobia (*taijinkyofusho* in Japanese) or neurathenia, common minor psychiatric disorders recognized in Japan at the time (Iwai & Reynolds, 1970; A. Kondo, 1953; K. Kondo, 1976). After attempting a variety of treatment methods, he created a new therapy of his own, which he called "experiential therapy."

In experiential therapy, Morita treated patients through different stages of experience, including rest, life renormalization, and life rehabilitation. In the first stage, the patients were asked to take bed rest for 1 or 2 weeks. No talking or reading was allowed through this stage, so that sensory and social activity deprivation would occur, often making patients eager to reenter normal life (see Fig. 7b). Then patients were permitted to wake up, starting to engage in simple life with light chore work, often experiencing appreciation of life around them rather than obsessing about their mental symptoms as they had done before (see Fig. 7c). Starting this second stage, the patients were asked to write a diary which would be commented on by the therapist, with an emphasis on how to establish a new attitude about life (i.e., to accept reality, including symptoms or suffering) as it was (Ohara & Ohara, 1993) (see Fig. 7d).

## 3. Culture-Related Common Psychotherapies

As pointed out previously, psychotherapeutic activities, as cultural products of humankind, are connected to and shaped by culture in their theory and practice to some degree. The influence of cultural factors varies in degree: much more in culturally embedded folk healing practices or culturally influenced unique therapies and less in common psychotherapies. Common psychotherapies refer to the ordinary, mainstream therapies that are recognized by contemporary professionals in European-American societies. It needs to be recognized that the distinction between so-called common or mainstream therapies and unique, alternative, or folk therapies is arbitrary and artificially determined, depending on who is viewing the phenomena and defining the terms.

Because common psychotherapies tend to be viewed as "scientific" medical practices and are assumed to be "universally" applicable, they are seldom studied from cultural perspectives. However, if one takes the view that these "common" or "regular" therapies are cultural products, then there is room to evaluate them in their cultural dimensions. Because it would be impossible to examine every kind of regular psychotherapy that exists, only those that have appeared in literature on the ways in which therapies are culture-related will be reviewed here.

### a. Psychoanalysis

Even though many psychoanalysts take the view that psychoanalysis deals with the basic aspects of the human mind and is universally applicable, some clinicians do not agree. Some scholars have pointed out that the theory and practice of psychoanalysis are very culturally influenced, by the ethnic cultural background of their founder, Sigmund Freud, and the sociocultural environment of Vienna, where they originated.

For example, Meadow and Vetter (1959) indicated how the Judaic cultural value system influenced the Freudian theory of psychotherapy. In contrast to Christianity, Judaism maintains that the ultimate goal of human happiness is attainable in the real world (not in heaven), and that any unhappiness in the real world is evil and needs to be fixed. This is the basic attitude reflected in psychoanalytic theory, and the purpose of therapy. While psychoanalytic therapy views heterosexual relationships as a *sine qua non* for happiness, it is the aim of psychoanalysis to aid the individual in establishing rational control over his sexual drive. This affirmation of rational control is consistent with a major emphasis in the Jewish cultural pattern. The Freudian concept of family relations and the development of the Oedipus complex are closely related to the typical family pattern in Jewish culture: the mother-son relationship is more intense and complete than the relationship between husband and wife, and the ideal marital relationship is one in which the wife treats her husband as a child. From a cultural point of view, it can be explained that most psychoanalysts have Jewish backgrounds, and most of the patients who seek psychoanalysis are also Jewish. At least, this is true in New York, where there is a high percentage of Jewish people.

### b. Client-Centered Psychotherapy

Client-Centered Psychotherapy was developed in the 1940s by Carl R. Rogers, a psychologist with a Freudian background. His method of counseling was originally called "nondirective," and, later, "client-centered." In drastic contrast to the orientations of classic psychoanalysis that were most influential at the time in the United States, Rogers developed a unique mode of counseling with several emphases. The cornerstones of his method were the basic knowableness and trustworthiness of an individual's own inner awareness and his ability to symbolize these inner data accurately and use them to reorganize and make choices (Wexler & Rice, 1974). The fundamental assumption of the therapy was a person's basic motivation toward growth and differentiation. Thus, the therapy focused on the enormous potential of the individual and freeing the client for normal growth and development (Rogers, 1974).

It is interesting to note that Meadow (1964) made cultural comments about client-centered therapy and its relation to the basic American ethos. He pointed out that client-centered therapy is an expression of the fundamental individual "distrust of the expert" theme in American culture. Reflecting the tendency of American culture to deemphasize the past, client-centered therapy places greater stress upon the immediate situation. Most important is that client-centered therapy gives particular attention to the client's need for autonomy or independence. It is closely related to the American ethos: the American not only seeks independence for himself but feels it is his moral duty to make others independent. No wonder such a therapeutic approach is not particularly welcomed by clients in cultural settings where dependence on authority is expected and personal autonomy is less emphasized.

## 4. Comparison and Synthesis

By comparison of various kinds of psychotherapy broadly defined a panoramic view of the nature of "psychotherapy" can be obtained from different perspectives (Tseng, 1999). The most distinguishable variables among the indigenous, unique, and regular psychotherapies is a shift in orientation from the supernatural to the natural, to the physical person, to the philosophical-psychological, and finally to the psychological. The nature of the psychological healing process may have developed historically in this sequence. It is also apparent that psychologically oriented modern psychotherapies may miss other dimensions, namely, the supernatural, the natural, the physical, and the philosophical, that should be addressed in the healing process to meet the needs of the patient from a cultural perspective.

The healing mechanisms utilized in these different modes of therapy cover a broad spectrum. Among the supernaturally oriented healing practices (such as shamanism or divination), belief in a supernatural power itself is an important healing mechanism. Associated with this, magical counteracting or generation of conviction often works in such healing systems. In addition, basic, supportive therapeutic mechanisms, such as emotional catharsis, assurance, suggestion, "naming" effect, or gratification of unfulfilled wishes, are operating. Among socioreligious or philosophical-psychological therapies, many healing mechanisms of psychological natures are operating. Confession, group support, reappraisal of interpersonal relationships (Naikan therapy), creating new life experience (Morita therapy), or reexamination of self (est) are some of the examples. Psychologically focused therapies focus on and utilize certain specifically conceptualized psychological mechanisms, such as transference or insight (psychoanalysis), relearning of behavior (behavior therapy), and learning and restoring relations (family or group therapy) in their therapeutic work.

When the aims of therapy, or the goals of practice, are examined, considerable differences are found among different therapeutic modes. In the supernaturally oriented healing practice, the final goal of healing is to comply with the divine power. Based on this, an attempt is made to find a way to resolve problems and to restore life. In a nature-oriented system, the goal of therapy is also to find a way to comply with the rules of nature. The primary effort is to seek a way to harmonize with nature or to restore natural conditions. When the orientation shifts to a philosophical and psychological one, the aim of therapy becomes accepting the self (as it is), restoring family or group relations (as they

FIGURE 8   Pschotherapy in different cultures. (a) A group study of Mao's teachings in China during the Great Forward Movement era, utilizing political ideology for the improvement of life [Source unknown]. (b) Chinese child psychiatrists counseling parents at the roadside to promote child mental health in Nanjing. Privacy and confidentiality are not concerns in this public situation. [Courtesy of Tao Kuo-Tai, M.D.] (c) Medical officers in Truk, Micronesia, providing counseling to a patient with his family members around—a natural setting for family-involved therapy. (d) A psychiatrist visiting a home in the island society of Samoa to study the mental health of the family members. [(d) Courtesy of Gail Ingram, M.D.]

should be, according to sociocultural definition), or resuming the social role of the self (as politically demanded). The main purpose of this kind of therapy is to find a proper way to perform externally defined roles and to be accepted as a member of the family, group, or society. Finally, when the therapy is psychologically oriented, the emphasis is on "improving" the self, becoming a "mature" person and a "functional" family member or "healthy" group member. Whether such goals are practical and attainable is not the question here. We are merely pointing out that the aims of therapy become increasingly demanding for patients in philosophically and psychologically oriented therapies.

## 5. Integration: Cultural Implications of Psychotherapy

Despite of the differences in major orientations, therapeutic operations, and healing mechanisms among various forms of psychotherapy, there are common cultural implications of therapeutic activities. They are (for details, see Tseng, 2001b, Chapter 37,B: Cultural Implication of Psychotherapy. pp. 602–604]:

a. Provision of culturally permitted channels for fulfilling wishes or desires,
b. Reinforcement of culturally sanctioned coping patterns,
c. Affirmation of central cultural values,
d. Permission for cultural "time out,"
e. Exploration of alternative cultural approaches to resolution,
f. Elaboration and incorporation of "new" cultural systems.

In summary, it can be said that the art of psychological treatment needs to be defined broadly from cultural perspective and various forms of healing practices, whether folk, unique, or modern therapies have been observed around the world. Through different orientation, approach, and mechanism, such various forms of psychological treatment have provide mental healthcare for people in different societies (see Fig. 8). To carry out cultural competent psychotherapy, a clinician needs to know not only how cultural factors influence the process of the treatment undertaken, but, at another level, what the implication of therapeutic work performed by the therapist for the patient is.

## REFERENCES

### A. Intercultural Psychotherapy: Challenges and Competence

Bishop, M. M., & Winokur, G. (1956). Cross-cultural psychotherapy. *Journal of Nervous and Mental Disease, 123*, 369–375.

Bizi-Nathaniel, S., Granek, M., & Golomb, M. (1991). Psychotherapy of an Arab patient by a Jewish therapist in Israel during the Intifada. *American Journal of Psychotherapy, 45*, 594–603.

Brantley, T. (1983). Racism and its impact on psychotherapy. *American Journal of Psychiatry, 140*, 1605–1608.

Carlton, B. (2001). One patient, three therapists. In W. S. Tseng & J. Streltzer (Eds.): *Culture and psychotherapy: A guide for clinical practice* (pp. 67–78). Washington, DC: American Psychiatric Press.

Carstairs, G. M. (1961). Cross-cultural psychiatric interviewing. In B. Kaplan (Ed.), *Studying personality cross-culturally* (pp. 532–548). New York: Harper & Row.

Carter, R. T. (1995). *The influence of race and racial identity in psychotherapy: Toward a racially inclusive model.* New York: Wiley-Interscience.

Cheng, L., & Lo, H. (1991). On the advantages of cross-cultural psychotherapy: The minority therapist/mainstream patient dyad. *Psychiatry, 54*, 386–396.

Comas-Díaz, L., & Jacobsen, F. M. (1991). Ethno cultural transference and countertransference in the therapeutic dyad. *American Journal of Orthopsychiatry, 61*, 392–402.

Doi, T. (1962). Amae—A key concept for understanding Japanese personality structure. In R. J. Smith & R. K. Beardsley (Eds.), *Japanese culture: Its development and characteristics.* Chicago: Aldine.

Griffith, M. S. (1977). The influences of race on the psychotherapeutic relationship. *Psychiatry, 40*, 27–40.

Hsu, J., & Tseng, W. S. (1972). Intercultural psychotherapy. *Archives of General Psychiatry, 27,* 700–705.

Kareem, J., & Littlewood, R. (Eds.). (1992). *Intercultural therapy: Themes, interpretations and practice.* Oxford: Blackwell.

Lambley, P., & Cooper, P. (1975). Psychotherapy and race: Interracial therapy under apartheid. *American Journal of Psychotherapy, 29,* 179–184.

Lee, E. (1997). Cross-cultural communication: Therapeutic use of interpreters. In E. Lee (Ed.), *Working with Asian Americans: A guide for clinicians* (pp. 477–489). New York: Guiford.

Schachter, J. S., & Butts, H. F. (1968). Transference and contertransference in interracial analysis. *Journal of the American Psychoanalytic Association, 16,* 792–808.

Sue, S., & Morishima, J. K. (Eds.). ( 1982). *The mental health of Asian Americans.* San Francisco: Jossey-Bass.

Sue, S., & Zane, N. (1987). The role of culture and cultural techniques in psychotherapy: A critique and reformulation. *American Psychologist, 42,* 37–45.

Tseng, W. S. (1975). The nature of somatic complaints among psychiatric patients: The Chinese case. *Comprehensive Psychiatry, 16,* 237–245.

Tseng, W. S., Asai, M. H., Kitanishi, K. J., McLaughlin, D., & Kyomen, H. (1992). Diagnostic pattern of social phobia: Comparison in Tokyo and Hawaii. *Journal of Nervous and Mental Disease, 180,* 380–385.

Tseng, W. S., & Streltzer, J. (2001). *Culture and psychotherapy: A guide for clinical practice.* Washington, DC.: American Psychiatric Press.

Westermeyer, J. (1990). Working with an interpreter in psychiatric assessment and treatment. *Journal of Nervous and Mental Disease, 178,* 745–749.

## B. Cultural Adjustments of Psychotherapy

American Psychological Association (1993). Guidelines for providers of psychological services to ethnic, linguistic, and culturally diverse populations. *American Psychologist, 48*(1), 45–48.

Doi, T. (1962). *Amae*—A key concept for understanding Japanese personality structure. In R. J. Smith & R. K. Beardsley (Eds.), *Japanese culture: Its development and characteristics.* Chicago: Aldine.

Dwairy, M. (1997). Addressing the repressed needs of the Arabic client. *Cultural Diversity and Mental Health, 3*(1), 1–12.

Hoch, E. M. (1990). Experiences with psychotherapy training in India. *Psychotherapy and Psychosomatics, 53,* 14–20.

Hsu, F. L. K. (1973, May 7). *Psychosocial homeostasis (PSH): A sociocentric model of man.* Presented as William P. Menninger Memorial Lecture at the annual meeting of the American Psychiatric Association, Honolulu.

Hsu, F. L. K. (1985). The self in cross-cultural perspective. In A. Marsella, G. DeVos, & F. L. K. Hsu (Eds.), *Culture and self.* New York: Tavistock.

Kirmayer, L. J. (1989). Psychotherapy and the culture concept of the person. *Sante, Culture, Health, 6*(3), 241–270.

Koss-Chioino, J. D., & Vargas, L. A. (1992). Through the culture looking glass: A model for understanding culturally responsive psychotherapies. In A. Vargas & J. D. Koss-Chioino (Eds.), *Working with culture: Psychotherapeutic interventions with ethnic minority children and adolescents.* San Francisco: Jossey-Bass.

Marsella, A., DeVos, G., & Hsu, F. L. K. (Eds.). (1985). *Culture and self.* New York: Tavistock.

Roland, A. (1991). Psychoanalysis in India and Japan: Toward a comparative psychoanalysis. *American Journal of Psychoanalysis, 51*(1), 1–10.

Tseng, W. S. (2001a). Culture and psychiatric theories. In W. S. Tseng, *Handbook of cultural psychiatry* (pp. 779–794). San Diego, CA: Academic Press.

Tseng, W. S. (2001b). Culture-relevant psychotherapy. In W. S. Tseng, *Handbook of cultural psychiatry* (pp. 595–610). San Diego, CA: Academic Press.

Tseng, W. S., Lu, Q. Y., & Yin, P. Y. (1995). Psychotherapy for the Chinese: Cultural considerations. In T. Y. Lin, W. S. Tseng, and E. K. Yeh (Eds.), *Chinese societies and mental health (pp.* 281–294). Hong Kong: Oxford University Press.

Vaillant, G. E. (1971). Theoretical hierarchy of adaptive ego mechanisms. *Archives of General Psychiatry, 24,* 107–118.

Vaillant, G. E. (1986). *Empirical studies of ego mechanism of defense.* Washington, DC: American Psychiatric Press.

Varma, V. K. (1982). Present state of psychotherapy in India. *Indian Journal of Psychiatry, 24,* 209–226. (Reviewed in *Transcultural Psychiatric Research Review, 21*(4), 291–291[1984].)

## C. Cultural Considerations in Various Modes of Therapy

Asuni, T. (1967). Nigerian experiment in group psychotherapy. *American Journal of Psychotherapy, 12,* 95–104.

Chen, C. P. (1995). Group counseling in a different cultural context: Several primary issues in dealing with Chinese clients. *Group, 19*(1), 45–55.

Dunkas, N., & Nikelly, A. G. (1975). Group psychotherapy with Greek immigrants. *International Journal of Group Psychotherapy, 25,* 402–409.

Falicov, C. J. (1982). Mexican families. In M. McGoldrick, J. K. Pearce, & J. Giordano (Eds.), *Ethnicity and family therapy* (pp. 134–163). New York: Guilford Press.

Herz, F. M., & Rosen, E. J. (1982). Jewish families. In M. McGoldrick, J. K. Pearce, & J. Giordano, (Eds.), *Ethnicity and family therapy* (364–392). New York: Guilford Press.

Ho, M. K. (1987). *Family therapy with ethnic minorities.* Newbury Park, CA: Sage.

Hsu, J. (1983). Asian family interaction patterns and their therapeutic implication. *International Journal of Family Psychiatry, 4,* 307–320.

Hsu, J. (1995). Family therapy for the Chinese: Problems and strategies. In T. Y. Lin, W. S. Tseng, & E. K. Yeh (Eds.), *Chinese societies and mental health* (pp. 295–307). Hong Kong: Oxford University Press.

Hsu, J. (2001). Marital therapy for intercultural couples. In W. S. Tseng, & J. Streltzer (Eds.), *Culture and psychotherapy: A guide to clinical practice* (225–242). Washington DC: American Psychiatric Press.

Jalali, B. (1988). Ethnicity, cultural adjustment, and behavior: Implications for family therapy. In L. Comas-Díaz & E. E. H. Griffith (Eds.), *Clinical guidelines in cross-cultural mental health.* New York: Wiley.

Martinez, C. (1977). Group process and the Chicano: Clinical issues. *International Journal of Group Psychotherapy, 27,* 225–231.

Matsukawa, L. A. (2001). Group therapy with multiethnic members. In W. S. Tseng & J. Streltzer (Eds.), *Culture and psychotherapy: A guide to clinical practice* (243–262). Washington DC: American Psychiatric Press.

McGoldrick, M., & Pearce, J. K. (1981). Family therapy with Irish-Americans. *Family Process, 20,* 223–244.

Minuchin, S., Montalvo, B., Guerney, B. G., Rosman, B. L., & Schumer, G. G. (1967). *Families of the slums.* New York: Basic Books.

Moitoza, E. (1982). Portuguese families. In M. McGoldrick, J. K. Pearce, & J. Giordano, (Eds.), *Ethnicity and family therapy* (412–437). New York: Guilford Press.

Shapiro, R. Y. (1996). Group psychotherapy with Orthodox Jewish patients. Presented in Symposium: Psychiatric Treatment of Orthodox Jews. American Psychiatric Association Meeting, New York, May.

Suzuki, K. (1987). Family therapy in Japan. *AFTA Newsletter*, *27*, 15–18.

Tseng, W. S. (2001). Intercultural marriage: Problems and therapy. In W. S. Tseng, *Handbook of cultural psychiatry* (pp. 729–746). San Diego, CA: Academic press.

Tseng, W. S., & Hsu, J. (1991). *Culture and family: Problems and therapy.* New York: Haworth Press.

## D. Cultural Application and Supervision of Psychotherapy

Acosta, F. X., Yamamoto, J., & Evans, L. A. (1982). *Effective psychotherapy for low income and minority patients.* New York: Plenum.

Baker, F. M., & Lightfoot, O. B. (1993). Psychiatric care of ethnic elders. In A. C. Gaw (Ed.), *Culture, ethnicity, and mental illness* (pp. 517–552). Washington, DC: American Psychiatric Press.

Chin, J. L., De La Cancela, V., & Jenkins, Y. M. (1993). *The politics of race, ethnicity, and gender.* Westport, CT: Praeger.

Fong, M. L., & Lease, S. H. (1997). Crosscultural supervision: Issues for the white supervisor. In D. B. Pope-Davis & H. L. K. Coleman (Eds.), *Multicultural counseling competencies: Assessment, education and training, and supervision.* Thousand Oaks, CA: Sage.

Katsnelson, N. (1998). Transference and countertransference in cross-cultural supervision. Presented at the annual meeting of the Society for the Study of Psychiatry and Culture, Portland, Oregon.

Krajeski, J. P. (1993). Cultural considerations in the psychiatric care of gay men and lesbians. In A. C. Gaw (Ed.), *Culture, ethnicity, and mental illness* (553–572). Washington, DC: American Psychiatric Press.

Pedersen, P., Lonner, W. J., & Draguns, J. G. (Eds.). (1976). *Counseling across cultures.* Honolulu: University Press of Hawaii.

Pedersen, P. B., Draguns, J. G., Lonner, W. J., & Trimble, J. E. (Eds.). (1996). *Counseling across cultures* (4th ed.). Thousand Oaks, CA: Sage.

Powell, G. J. (Ed.). (1983). *The psychosocial development of minority group children.* New York: Brunner/Mazel.

Prince, R. (1987). Alexithymia and verbal psychotherapies in cultural context. *Transcultural Psychiatric Research Review*, *24*(2), 107–118.

Sue, D. W., & Sue, D. (1999). *Counseling the culturally different: Theory and practice* (3rd ed.). New York: Wiley.

Tseng, W. S., & McDermott, J. F., Jr.(1981). *Culture, mind and therapy: An introduction to cultural psychiatry.* New York: Brunner/ Mazel.

Vargas, L. A., & Koss-Chioino, J. D. (1992). *Working with culture: Psychotherapeutic interventions with ethnic minority children and adolescents.* San Francisco: Jossey-Bass.

Wohl, J. (1989). Integration of cultural awareness into psychotherapy. *American Journal of Psychotherapy*, *43*, 343–355.

## E. Comparison of Folk, Unique, and Common Therapies

Griffith, E. E. H., & Young, J. L. (1988). A cross-cultural introduction to the therapeutic aspects of Christian religious ritual. In L. Comas-Díaz & E. E. H. Griffith, (Eds.), *Clinical guidelines in cross-cultural mental health* (69–89). New York: Wiley.

Hufford, D. (1977). Christian religious healing. *Journal of Operational Psychiatry*, *8*(2), 22–27.

Iwai, H., & Reynolds, D. K. (1970). Morita psychotherapy: The views from the West. *American Journal of Psychiatry*, *126*(7), 1031–1036.

Jilek, W. (1974). *Salish Indian mental health and cultural change.* Toronto: Holt, Rinehart & Winston.

Jilek, W. (1982). *Indian healing: Shamanic ceremonialism in the Pacific Northwest today.* Surrey, BC, Canada: Hancock House.

Jilek, W. (1993). Traditional medicine relevant to psychiatry. In N. Sartorius, G. De Girolamo, G. Andrews, & G. A. German (Eds.), *Treatment of mental disorders: A review of effectiveness.* Washington, DC: American Psychiatric Press.

Jilek, W. (1994). Traditional healing in the prevention and treatment of alcohol and drug abuse. *Transcultural Psychiatric Research Review, 31*(3), 219–258.

Leighton, A. H., & Leighton, D. C. (1941). Elements of psychotherapy in Navajo religion. *Psychiatry, 4,* 515–523.

Kondo, A. (1953), Morita therapy—A Japanese therapy for neurosis. *American Journal of Psychoanalysis, 13,* 31–37.

Kondo, K. (1976). The origin of Morita therapy. In W. P. Lebra (Ed.), *Culture-bound syndromes, ethnopsychiatry, and alternate therapies.* Honolulu: University Press of Hawaii.

Meadow, A. (1964). Client-centered therapy and the American ethos. *International Journal of Social Psychiatry, 10*(4), 246–259.

Meadow, A., & Vetter, H. J. (1959). Freudian theory and the Judaic value system. *International Journal of Social Psychiatry, 5*(3), 197–207.

Murase, T. (1976). Naikan therapy. In W. P. Lebra (Ed.), *Culture-bound syndromes, ethnopsychiatry, and alternate therapies* (pp. 259–269). Honolulu: University Press of Hawaii.

Ohara, K., & Ohara, K. I. (1993). *Morita therapy and neo-Morita therapy.* Tokyo: Nihon Bunka Kagakusha [In Japanese.]

Pattison, E. M., & Wintrob, R. M. (1981). Possession and exorcism in contemporary America. *Journal of Operational Psychiatry, 12,* 12–30.

Rogers, C. R. (1974). Remarks on the future of client-centered therapy. In D. A. Wexler & L. N. Rice (Eds.), *Innovations in client-centered therapy.* New York: Wiley.

Schneck, J. M. (1975). United States of America. In J. G. Howells (Ed.), *World history of psychiatry* (pp. 432–475). New York: Brunner/Mazel.

Suwanlert, S. (1997, October 7–10). Phan yak *traditional chanting treats mental disorders.* Poster display at the regional meeting of World Psychiatric Association. Beijing, China.

Torrey, E. F. (1986). *Witchdoctors and psychiatrists: The common roots of psychotherapy and its future.* New York: Harper & Row.

Tseng, W. S. (1999). Culture and psychotherapy: Review and practical guidelines. *Transcultrual Psychiatry, 36*(2), 131–179.

Tseng, W. S. (2001a). Culture and psychological therapy. In W. S. Tseng, *Handbook of cultural psychiatry* (pp. 515–561). San Diego, CA: Academic Press.

Tseng, W. S. (2001b). Cultural implication of psychotherapy. In W. S. Tseng, *Handbook of cultural psychiatry* (602–604). San Diego, CA: Academic Press.

Wexler, D. A., & Rice, L. N. (1974). *Innovations in client-centered therapy* (pp. 1–6). New York: Wiley.

## Suggested Further Readings

Tseng, W. S., & Streltzer, J. (Eds.). (2001). *Culture and Psychotherapy: A guide to clinical practice.* Washington DC: American Psychiatric Press.

# CHAPTER 8

# Ethnicity, Culture, and Drug Therapy

While drug therapy for mental disorders involves pharmacology, it also includes the psychology of prescribing and receiving medication. The two aspects exist side by side. The former is seen primarily from a biological perspective, potentially related to race or ethnicity in terms of genetic or biological factors. In contrast, the latter is mainly associated with psychological variables, involving the understanding, attitudes, expectations, and psychological reactions toward medication. It is therefore influenced by customs, beliefs, and values related to taking drugs, with much room for cultural impact. These two aspects are reviewed in this chapter.

## A. WHAT DO WE KNOW ABOUT ETHNICITY AND PSYCHOPHARMACOLOGY?

For some time, clinicians who have treated patients in multiethnic societies or in different countries have noticed that patients respond to psychotropics differently than the "formal" recommendations described for Caucasian patients. There has been speculation on the effect of race on drug treatment (Kalow, 1989;

Murphy, 1969). This includes the therapeutic dose needed and the severity of side effects manifested by patients. However, it was only a little more than a decade ago that clinicians and researchers began empirical investigations on how people of different ethnic or racial backgrounds may respond differently to psychotropics. There have been remarkable findings revealed on this subject to support clinical experience. One of the pioneers in this field, American cultural psychiatrist K. M. Lin and colleagues (Lin & Poland, & 1995; Lin, Poland, & Anderson, 1995; Lin & Smith, 2000) have made several comprehensive reviews of psychopharmacotherapy in the context of culture and ethnicity that are very useful for updates on this matter.

In most of the literature that has appeared on this subject, the terms "ethnicity" and "race" have often been used interchangeably, and, customarily, "ethnicity" has been used more frequently. Because most of the studies dealt with interracial comparison (such as Caucasian vs. Asian, or "White" vs. "Black"), the term "race" was more appropriate, particularly regarding effects related to biological or genetic issues (see Section 1 B1: What Is Culture?). However, following the literature, and for the sake of simplicity, the term "ethnicity" will be used here.

## 1. Basic Concepts: Pharmacokinetics and Pharmacodynamics

Pharmacokinetics concern factors relating to absorption, distribution, metabolism, and excretion of the medicine administered. These factors together determine the process, fate, and disposition of drugs. Pharmacodynamics refer to how medicines work on target organ receptors to produce pharmacological effects. Through variations in both pharmacokinetics and pharmacodynamics, different drug reactions occur in different persons (interindividual variations) as well as among peoples of different ethnic or racial backgrounds (cross-ethnic/racial variations).

## 2. Genetic-Related Factors

It is becoming clearer to scholars that, in the majority of genes, polymorphism is the rule rather than the exception. It assures the survival of any species and promotes its adaptation to the environment through biodiversity. Further, the frequency and distribution of alleles responsible for polymorphism often vary substantially across ethnic groups. Extensive polymorphism exists in genes governing pharmacokinetics and pharmacodynamics. Therefore, genetic factors may explain not only the interindividual variations but also the cross-ethnic variations in drug responses to a large extent (Lin, Poland, & Nakasaki, 1993).

Most of the drugs are metabolized via phase I and II enzymes. In phase I, mediated by one or more of the cytochrome P450 enzymes (CYPs), oxidation of the substrate takes place. In phase II, mediated by one of the transferases, conjugation occurs. The pharmacokinetics of most psychotropics depend on one or more of the CYP enzymes. The activity of CYP enzymes influences the tissue concentration of drugs significantly. Thus, it determines dose requirements and side effects of their substrates.

Significant genetic polymorphism exists in most of the CYPs, leading to extremely large variations in the activity of these enzymes in any given population as well as across populations of different ethnicities or races (Lin & Poland, 1995). The enzyme CYP2D6, for example, has more than 20 mutations that inactivate, impair, or accelerate its function; most of these mutant alleles are, to a large extent, ethnically specific.

For instance, allele *CYP2D6*4*, which leads to the production of defective proteins, is found in approximately 25% of Caucasians but is rarely identified in other ethnic groups. This mutation is mainly responsible for the high rate of poor metabolizers in 5 to 9% of Caucasians, who are extremely sensitive to drugs metabolized by CYP2D6 (Lin & Smith, 2000). Enzyme *CYP2D6*17* is found in extremely high frequencies among people of African origin, and enzyme *CYP2D6*10*, among those of Asian origin. Both of these alleles are associated with lower enzyme activities and slower metabolism of CYP2D6 substrates. It is speculated that this is in part responsible for slower pharmacokinetic profiles and lower therapeutic dose ranges observed in African-Americans regarding tricyclic antidepressants and in Asians regarding both antipsychotics and tricyclic antidepressants (Lin & Poland, 1995).

Another example is enzyme CYP2C19, which involves the metabolism of diazepam, tertiary tricyclic antidepressants, and citalopram, the new antidepressant. This enzyme also represents obvious cross-ethnic variations in addition to interindividual variations in drug metabolism. It has been demonstrated that up to 20% of East Asians (Chinese, Japanese, and Koreans) are poor metabolizers, compared to only 3 to 5% of Caucasians. It has been found that two unique mutations are responsible for the enzyme deficiency: *CYP2C19*2* and *CYP2C19*3*. The former can be found in all ethnic groups, but the latter appears to be specific to those with eastern Asian origins. The presence of mutation *3, together with a higher rate of *2, is explained as the cause for the higher rate of poor metabolizers among the eastern Asians (Goldstein et al., 1997).

Thus, from recent studies, it has become clear to clinicians that genetic factors, associated with individual and ethnic background, contribute greatly to responses to medications. The variations exist as interindividual variations among the same ethnic group and also as variations among different ethnic groups. These two kinds of variations overlap, resulting in the total picture of variations. This is well illustrated by data obtained by Lin et al. (1988) regarding the variability of haloperidol concentrations in normal volunteers after the administration of

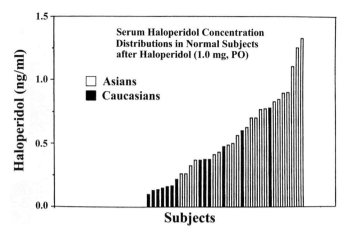

FIGURE 1    Ethnic comparison of serum haloperidol concentration. [From K. M. Lin et al., *Transcultural Psychiatric Research Review*, *32*(1), 1995, with permission.]

haloperidol (0.5 mg, im) to Caucasian and Asian subjects. As shown on Figure 1, the graph indicates (1) substantial interindividual variability within each of the ethnic groups studied and, at the same time, (2) dramatic differences in the pharmacokinetics of haloperidol between the two ethnic groups examined, illustrating the overall overlap of the pharmacokinetics between the two groups.

## 3. Nongenetic Biological Factors

It is important to know that numerous nongenetic biological factors significantly influence the expression of genes in the process of drug metabolization. For example, the activity of most cytochrome P450 enzymes declines significantly in the elderly, who are also likely to suffer from a progressive loss of neuron cells and receptors targeted by psychotropics (Salzman, 1984). Thus, the aged person becomes more sensitive to the effects of medication. Steroid hormones, including sex hormones, are known to be the substrates of some of the cytochrome P450 enzymes and have the capacity to alter the activity of these enzymes through competitive inhibition. Thus, gender is another biological factor that affects the pharmacodynamics of psychotropics.

Smoking, intake of certain foods, such as grapefruit juice, or high-protein and high-carbohydrate diets are all known to affect the activities of cytochrome P450 enzymes. Coupled with this is the interaction with herb medicines. Many herbs are natural substrates for the drug-metabolizing enzymes. Herb-drug interactions often exert significant impact on drug effects, which brings about clinically significant consequences, frequently unsuspected (Lin & Smith, 2000).

It is important to recognize that among the nongenetic factors, even though they are biological in nature, many are indirectly influenced by lifestyle, which, in turn, is closely related to social and cultural factors. This is particularly true regarding smoking, diet intake, or usage of herb medicines.

## B. HOW DOES CULTURE AFFECT GIVING AND TAKING MEDICATION?

Although the prescribing and intake of medicine seems primarily a psychopharmacological matter, and can be grasped from a biological perspective, it is actually a combination of biosociocultural phenomena, which is greatly influenced by social and cultural dimensions (Smith, Lin, & Mendoza, 1993). This can be elaborated from several perspectives.

### 1. Medicine Taking as a Part of Illness Behavior

"Illness behavior" simply means how a person reacts and behaves when he becomes ill. More specifically, it includes how the person recognizes and interprets the discomfort and reacts against suffering when illness occurs; how he seeks help, care, or treatment from others; and how he reacts to the therapy prescribed or treatment offered by healers, including compliance and adherence to therapy (see Section 2E: Illness Behavior: Recognition and Help-Seeking). Several factors contribute to a patient's illness behavior regarding medicine taking.

#### a. General Understanding and Customary Behavior of Seeing Doctors

It is common in some societies, such as America, for a person who becomes sick to go to see his "family doctor" first, and, unless he is referred to a specialist(s), he continues to see him. There is an unspoken understanding (or even agreement) that a patient sticks to one doctor and takes the medicine prescribed by him. If there is some concern about the medicine prescribed, the patient asks and negotiates with the doctor. In many other societies this is not necessarily the case. It is the patient's choice to shop around among doctors and change doctors if he is not satisfied with one; a patient often may see several doctors, either alternatively or simultaneously. In that case, he will receive medicine prescribed by these different doctors. It is a patient's own choice which medications he will take. There is no concept of only one doctor and drugs prescribed only by him. Neither is there any custom of faithfully taking whatever medicine the doctor prescribes.

### b. General Medical Knowledge

Coupled with the choice of seeing multiple therapists and making one's own decisions regarding which medicines to take is the patient's medical knowledge (of his sickness) and the function and purpose of the medicine he is prescribed. Clearly there are different levels of sophistication in medical knowledge and "understanding" of illness that will shape the pattern of medicine taking. Taking a course of antibiotics to radically treat an infectious agent, or a mood stabilizer to prevent the occurrence of bipolar disorder, is a rather unfamiliar medical concept to people who tend to follow the practical rule of taking medicine only for suffering and to discontinue it when the suffering disappears.

The etiological conceptions of illness vary greatly in different cultures and include supernatural, natural, biological, and psychological dimensions. The greater the disparity between contemporary scientific concepts of disease and the patient's folk medical beliefs about illness, the greater the likelihood of non-compliance (Ahmed, 2001).

### c. Traditional Medicine Concepts and Beliefs

The layperson's medical knowledge is often influenced by traditional medical concepts and beliefs. This is particularly true if a society has a relatively well-established traditional medical system with a long history. If the traditional medicine holds the hot-cold theory of disease, for example, a layperson will be concerned with whether his sickness is due to an excess of heat or cold, and, accordingly, the medicine prescribed will be hot or cold in nature. The patient would certainly be reluctant to take medicine that is not compatible with his folk medical beliefs. Based on his traditional medical knowledge, if the patient interprets his sickness as derived from a loss of vitality and believes he needs a tonic or nutritious substance to correct his energy deficiency, he will not welcome medicine that has the side effect of making him feel "weak" rather than "strong" (see Section 2C: Folk Explanations of Mental Problems).

## 2. Medicine and Mode of Administration

For various reasons, a patient may hold certain views about the medicine itself and the mode of administering it that it will greatly influence his medicine-taking behavior.

### a. Medicine Itself

The physical character of medicine, such as its appearance (tablet, capsule, or liquid), color, size, amount, or taste often have different implications to different people concerning its potency or power. For instance, concerning color, white capsules are viewed by Caucasians as analgesics and by African-American as stimulants. However, black capsules are viewed by Caucasians as stimulants and by African-Americans as analgesics (Buckalew & Caulfied, 1982).

Even the source of medicine, whether it is derived from plants, animals, or is synthetic, can have a psychological impact on a patient's response to it. For example, Muslims may not use alcohol-containing liquid medications; and Muslims and orthodox Jews may not use medications containing porcine products because of their religious proscriptions (Ahmed, 2001).

Associated with past historical experience, in India, "English" medicines may be viewed as being more potent than traditional Ayurvedic ones; therefore, "English" medicines are often used by laymen only to a limited extent with the very young and the very old, who are considered too weak to tolerate the potent "English" medicines (Ahmed, 2001). The same phenomenon is observed among many Chinese who believe that "Western" medicine is strong but has too many harmful side effects and should only be used for a short time for very serious illnesses, and that traditional herb medicine is milder but safe for long-term use.

### b. Mode of Administration

In many societies, it is generally viewed that injectable agents, in contrast to oral, are more potent and have more immediate effects. For patients who need the assurance of immediate effects, injections are the mode of choice. Many hysterical patients respond well to the injection of just vitamins, particularly if a hot sensation occurs immediately after the injection. Fluid therapy satisfies patients and their families who believe that the body is weak and in need of "good" stuff.

## 3. Meaning of Medication

The giving and receiving of medications is to be understood not simply as a biological event but as a psychological interaction between the physician and the patient, with significant psychological meaning and implications. This can be elaborated from several perspectives.

### a. From the Physician's Perspective

Beyond the simple reasons for treating a patient with medication, there are often psychological reasons that physicians prescribe medicine. Some of them are subtle, or unconscious, but some occur at the conscious level. Giving medicine usually represents concretely the physician's power to heal a sick person. It can also be the only remedy the physician can use symbolically when there is no alternative or more proper way to help the patient. This is also true when physicians are very much medically and biologically oriented and are not comfortable approaching, or are unable to approach, the patient regarding psychological aspects even when there is a need for such help. Quite commonly, when a physician is not sure of a patient's problem, but feels it is necessary to offer some kind of treatment, medication is the choice of action.

As indicated by Littlewood (1992) from his clinical experience in England and Lopez (1989) in America, African-American psychiatric patients tend to be diagnosed with more severe disorders (such as schizophrenia) compared to their Caucasian counterparts, and, as the clinical picture is often not "comprehensible" to the psychiatrist, more antipsychotics are prescribed. Closely associated with this, when the therapist has negative countertransference toward the patient under treatment, he may, subconsciously or even consciously, prescribe medication (or refuse to prescribe medication) for the patient as a way of expressing his negative feelings. This is particularly observed in cases of substance-abusing patients.

### b. From the Patient's Perspective

There are many different psychological implications from the standpoint of the patient. Receiving medication may imply receiving "care" and "concern" from the therapist. It symbolizes love and attention from the caregiver, even though the patient may not actually take it. Sometimes, even when the medicine is stored in the medicine cabinet and never taken, the patient continues to demand a prescription from the physician, simply to assure himself that he is being given care and love. This is often observed in hypochondriacal patients or lonely elderly patients.

In other words, the giving and receiving of medication often has many psychological implications that are part of the physician-patient interaction. From this perspective, it needs particularly careful analysis and insightful understanding.

### c. From the Health System's Perspective

The situation is often complicated further by the healthcare system, including service delivery patterns and payment systems. In many societies, there is no appointment system for psychiatric visits. Also, there is often a shortage of psychiatrists for the many patients who visit the clinics daily. In order to deal with many patients that need to be seen within a limited time in the outpatient clinic, sometimes giving only several minutes per patient is the only practical solution. Under such conditions, prescribing medication rather than offering talk therapy becomes the only choice for the psychiatrists. Even before the patient sits down and starts making any complaints, the psychiatrist is already filling out a prescription. This is not an unusual situation in developing societies (Nunley, 1996).

Closely related is the existing payment system. In many societies, medical regulation as well as customary expectation is that the physician (or hospital or clinic) may charge the patient for medicine, but not for the time the physician spends talking to the patient. Such a system encourages psychiatrists to prescribe medicine rather than to spend time listening and talking to the patient. This certainly affects the pattern of medical practice, particularly regarding the giving and receiving of medication in psychiatric work.

In summary, it has been elaborated that in psychiatric practice, the giving and receiving of medication involves various factors, including biological (either genetic- or nongenetic-related) and psychological ones. These factors together affect the total process and function of medication. It has been described that, even with genetically related biological factors, there are multiple variations at the interpersonal as well as the interethnic/racial level. Clearly there are distinct differences among people of different ethnic and/or racial backgrounds, but such diversity has superimposed on it interindividual diversity. This is also true of the psychological aspects of medication. Therefore, as pointed out by Lin and Smith (2000), "stereotypical interpretations of culture and ethnic differences in either psychological or biological characteristics are not only misleading but also potentially divisive and dangerous."

## REFERENCES

Ahmed, I. (2001). Psychological aspects of giving and receiving medications. In W. S. Tseng & J. Streltzer (Eds.), *Culture and psychotherapy: A guide for clinical practice* (pp. 123–134). Washington, DC: Amercian Psychiatric Press.

Buckalew, L. W., & Caulfied, K. E. (1982). Drug expectations associated with perceptual characteristics: Ethnic factors. *Perceptual and Motor Skills, 55,* 915–918.

Goldstein, J. A., Ishizaki, T., Chiba, K., de Morais, S. M., Bell, D., Krahn, P., & Evans, D. A. (1997). Frequencies of the defective CYP2C19 alleles responsible for themephenyton poor metabolizer phenotype in various Oriental, Caucasian, Saudi Arabian and American black populations. *Pharmacogenetics, 7,* 59–64.

Kalow, W. (1989). Race and therapeutic drug response. *New England Journal of Medicine, 320,* 588–589.

Lin, K. M., & Poland, R. E. (1995). Ethnicity, culture, and psychopharmacology. In F. E. Bloom & D. I. Kupfer (Eds.), *Psychopharmacology: The fourth generation of progress.* New York: Raven Press.

Lin, K. M., Poland, R. E., & Anderson, D. (1995). Psychopharmacology, ethnicity and culture. *Transcultural Psychiatric Research Review, 32,* 3–40.

Lin, K. M., Poland, R. E., Lau, E. K., & Rubin, R. T. (1988). Haloperidol and prolactin concentrations in Asians and Caucasians. *Journal of Clinical Psychopharmacology, 8,* 195–201.

Lin, K. M., Poland, R. E., & Nakasaki, G. (Eds.). (1993). *Psychopharmacology and psychobiology of ethnicity.* Washington, DC: American Psychiatric Press.

Lin, K. M., & Smith, M. W. (2000). Psychopharmacotherapy in the context of culture and ethnicity. In P. Ruitz (Ed.), *Ethnicity and psychopharmacotherapy* (American Psychiatric Press Review of Psychiatry, Vol. 19) (pp. 1–36). Washington, DC: Amercian Psychiatric Press.

Littlewood, R. (1992). Psychiatric diagnosis and racial bias: Empirical and interpretative approaches. *Social Science and Medicine, 34,* 141–149.

Lopez, S. R. (1989). Patient variable biases in clinical judgement: Conceptual overview and methodological considerations. *Psychological Bulletin, 106,* 184–203.

Murphy, H. B. M. (1969). Ethnic variations in drug responses. *Transcultural Psychiatric Research Review, 6,* 6–23.

Nunley, M. (1996). Why psychiatrists in India prescribe so many drugs. *Culture, Medicine and Psychiatry, 20*(2), 165–197.

Salzman, C. (1984). *Clinical geriatric psychopharmacology.* New York: McGraw-Hill.

Smith, M., Lin, K. M., & Mendoza, R. (1993). "Nonbiological" issues affecting psychopharmacotherapy: Cultural considerations. In K. M. Lin, R. E. Poland, & G. Nakasaki, (Eds.). *Psychopharmacology and psychobiology of ethnicity* (pp. 37–58). Washington, DC: American Psychiatric Press.

# CHAPTER 9

# Culture and Therapy with
# Special Subgroups

This chapter will focus on subgroups of the population served in psychiatric practice by age (i.e., children, adolescents, or aged people—as opposed to ordinary adults); by gender (i.e., women—as opposed to men); as well as the social units of a couple or family—as opposed to an individual. All of the subgroups will be discussed from the standpoint of the cultural aspects of common psychological issues, related psychiatric disorders, and clinical suggestions for care. Thus, in a way, the chapter addresses the cultural aspects of child and adolescent psychiatry, geriatric psychiatry, women's psychiatry, and marital and family therapy.

## A. CHILDREN

### 1. Cultural Aspects of Development and Psychology

Due to their level of mental development, children need special consideration in therapy. From a cultural perspective, several issues need particular attention. This includes variations of pace in processing developmental stages, as well as variation of themes emphasized at different stages of development (see Section 1B3: Child Development and Enculturation). The importance of the family in the lives of children and adolescents cannot be denied. It is necessary to recognize that there are cultural variations of family systems and structure (see Section 1B2: Marriage and the Family).

Beyond the family, children's lives are influenced directly or indirectly by the actual environment in which they are living. If society's conditions are undesirable in terms of health and economics, the children's lives will be subject to greater risk. For instance, the mortality of children in some underdeveloped countries is so high that nearly half of them do not survive beyond childhood, a terrifying contrast to the situation in developed societies. Malnutrition, sickness, and neglect are the major issues for children living in undesirable social conditions. It is assumed in developed societies that every child will go to school to receive a formal education and experience socialization, but this is not necessarily true in underdeveloped societies. It is common in some of these countries for children to help their parents with chores, take care of younger siblings, and even join their parents in working for a living rather than reading books, taking physical exercise classes, playing various sports, and indulging in TV games. Thus, children's lives and patterns of growth are widely diversified.

A child encounters numerous tasks in the process of development. From a cultural perspective, development also involves the process of enculturation. Identification is a part of personal psychology. It involves multiple levels, such as self identification, gender identification, family identification, group identification, and ethnic/racial identification. Ethnic or racial identity starts early, in childhood, it does not wait for adolescence or young adulthood (see Section 1B4: Personality and Ethnic Identity).

## 2. Culture-Related Special Issues

### a. Minority Status and Child Development

"Minority" refers to a relatively smaller group identified against the majority group in the society. A minority tends to be discriminated against by the majority and to suffer from underprivileged and disadvantageous social, political, economic, and cultural conditions. The minority group also suffers from unfavorable psychological conditions that will directly or indirectly influence the psychology of the minority people, their families, and their children, including the psychological development of the children (Greenfield & Cocking, 1994; Powell, 1983).

These disadvantages are derived not only from the phenomenon of discrimination but also from the cultural gap existing between minority and majority groups. For instance, as pointed out by J. R. Joe (1994, p. 112), many Native

American tribes have questioned and/or resisted the dominant (American) society's emphasis on temporal rather than spiritual values, the individual rather than the community, change rather than stability, and what seems like chaos instead of harmony. As indicated by Uribe, Levine, and Levine (1994, p. 52) traditionally, Mexican-Americans, in contrast to Euro-Americans, show more hierarchy by age and gender, more emphasis on respect and obedience, less emphasis on independence and separation during childhood, less social distance between the generation of adults in the family, and greater maintenance of kinship ties throughout life. There clearly is a discongruence of cultural values with the dominant group. Such differences make it difficult for the minority people to adjust to the society at large. This in turn not only affects the psychological adjustment of the adults but also the process of development of their children. Greenfield (1994, p. 30) pointed out that, based on contemporary industrialized culture, we have assumed that encouragement of individual independence and school-based cognitive development are the universal goals of development. We fail to realize that, from a cross-cultural perspective, the opposite poles of interdependence and subsistence skills are stressed in other cultures.

Child development is affected not only by the cultural gap but also the (inferior) group identity, which either originated within the group or was given to it by the dominant group, and psychological discrimination by the majority, both of which have a significant negative impact on the development of minority children (see Section 11B6: Social Discrimination).

Minority status may be closely related to migration. With the improvement of transportation, the ease of moving far distances, the need for sociopolitical refuge, and a search for better economic or educational opportunities, there is an increase in migration in many parts of the world. The recent increase of migrants from eastern Europe, the Mideast, and Africa to Western Europe is causing new social tensions between the migrating minorities and the host majorities. This has certainly raised mental health concerns (Littlewood & Lipsedge, 1989). The problems are not just centered around the adult migrants but also often extend into and are magnified in the next generation, calling for special attention to younger migrants (Powell, 1983; Vargas & Koss-Chioino, 1992).

### b. Impact of Race on Child Development

As explained previously (see Section 1A: What Is Culture?), scholars have now taken the view that races are socially and culturally constructed categories that may have little to do with actual biological differences. However, laypeople still believe that race is characterized by certain physical features, such as color of skin, eyes, and hair, facial or body features, or physical size, that distinguish it from other groups. It is believed that the racial background of an individual is obvious even from the time of birth. Therefore, any physical difference thought to relate to race will strongly impact the psychological development of a child.

The influence of "race" on child development is illustrated in two situations: the mixed-race child and the cross-racial adopted child.

*The Mixed-Race Child.* Clearly, a child becomes "mixed race" as the product of an interracial marriage. The best example is the black–white race-mixed child born to parents with African and Caucasian backgrounds or the Eurasian, a product of a European and an Asian parent. Associated with the increase in travel, international migration, and greater acceptance of interracial unions or marriages, there is an increase in mixed-race children.

The impact of racial mixture on child development is several fold. How the parents and surrounding people perceive and react to racially hybrid children is one thing, how the interracially married parents are going to raise the child from a bicultural perspective is another. The interracially married couple is potentially interculturally married (i.e, they hold different cultural views, including how to raise their children). Raising and disciplining a child is a challenge for parents who have distinctively different value systems. How a child is going to see and identify himself from a racial point of view is another matter. As the child grows, he may have more than the usual problems achieving self-identification, or knowing who he is. This is particularly true in an interracial marriage where physical appearances are markedly different, for example, when an Asian-Caucasian child has long, black hair and a high nose.

In the United States in the 1960s, Stevenson and Stewart (1958) studied children's ethnic identification patterns. They found that both white and black preferred the physical characteristics of white children and had more negative attitudes toward black ones. There has been a shift in more recent years to a more positive self-esteem among African-American children in their drawings (Fish & Larr, 1972), but questions still remain. The children's identification with their parents centered on certain overvalued and ill-understood body parts, capacities, and physical characteristics. Thus, in racially mixed marriages, does the girl identify with her mother and the boy with his father, or does the white identify with the white and the black with the black? Or does the black identify or seek identification with the white? How much does physical similarity influence identification, in addition to the factors of gender and interpersonal relations? These are questions awaiting further study.

*Cross-Racial Adoption.* Cross-racial or heteroracial adoption refers to the situation in which a parent(s) adopts a child or children who has a different racial heritage from that of his adoptive parent(s). This in contrast to the more usual homoracial adoption.

There is an increasing trend among many Caucasian people in Western societies to adopt children of different racial backgrounds, either African, Asian, or other. This is mainly because the parents cannot bear children of their own and there are not enough Caucasian children for adoption. It has become a choice to adopt African-American or Asian children. Sometimes parents, even though they already have their own children, still want to adopt children of other races for different reasons. Helping deserted orphans is one; wanting "different" kinds of children is another.

Due to the racial factor, there is a distinctly noticeable difference in the physical appearances between the adoptive parent(s) and the adopted child(ren) that are recognizable from the very beginning, so that the racial issue affects the process of child rearing in certain ways. Because the color of the skin or hair or other physical features is so different, the racial identity issue is a practical one that needs special attention and management. The most common example is when a white parent(s) adopts a black or Asian child(ren). In the process of growing up, the child(ren) will react to the differences in physical appearance, as will the adoptive parent(s) and the people surrounding them. Of particular importance will be the views and attitudes of the adoptive parent(s) toward the race of the adopted child. Hill and Peltzer (1982) suggested that if parents are concerned about raising their heteroracially adopted children, they should examine their own self-esteem and self-concepts, identify their personal racism, and understand the individual and institutional racism in their society and how they will affect their lives.

Concerning white parents adopting black children, there is major concern related to several matters: the community's reaction to black-white transracial adoption (based on feelings associated with the preexisting relations between the majority and the minority), the parents' motivation in adopting a child of a different racial background (particularly children distinctly identified with minority racial backgrounds), and the psychological and cultural impact on the process of enculturation (Griffith, 1995b). General claims made by some professionals as well as lay persons (with African-American backgrounds) are that "only Black families can teach Black culture to their children" and "African-American parents have a unique ability to pass along to their children the coping skills needed for a minority person to manage in American society."

African-American psychiatrist Ezra Griffith (1995a, 1995b), who has a special concern for this phenomenon, has extensively reviewed the subject from the literature available (Griffith & Silverman, 1995). Some empirical studies have been conducted, which indicated that, despite the concern of some experts, black children adopted by white parents are in general adjusting well. There are no problems of self-esteem. Ethnic and racial identity issues often depend on how the white parents view the black children they adopted. If they openly recognize and feel comfortable about their race, their adopted black children seem to have a sound identity development regarding their racial background.

A burning question that always arises is what will happen to the transracially adopted children when they reach adolescence or adulthood? Based on a 20-year longitudinal follow-up study of transracially adopted children who were now adults, Simon (1993) reported that, as adults, the transracial adoptees were aware of and comfortable with their racial identity. It seems that strong opposition expressed (by people of African-American backgrounds) in the past regarding the potential ill-effects of black–white transracial adoption was not supported by empirical studies.

## 3. Some Mental Health Problems

### a. Child Abuse

It is generally considered that child abuse and neglect are worldwide problems (Korbin, 1981; Krugman, 1996). Regarding the situation in Sub-Saharan Africa, LeVine and LeVine (1981) reported that "marginal" children, the residue of casual unions or of marital breakups, constituted a rapidly increasing high-risk population for abuse or neglect because they tended to receive inferior care. LeVine and LeVine commented that the use of child labor, like many other aspects of African child-rearing practices that have evolved in response to the exigencies of an agricultural economy, might seem harsh or neglectful by Western standards.

Johnson (1981) found that despite a wide range of caretaking practices observed in most areas of lowland South America, it was widely acknowledged that throughout Amazonia, mothers attended to infants with scrupulous care, nursing them on demand and providing close physical contact. It was only when a child reached the crawling or walking stages that parents in some cultures became indifferent to its needs. Children were left for long periods of time without food and were denied emotional reassurance. Johnson went further to explain that, similarly to other societies, undesirable social and economic conditions, such as insecure resources, social isolation, and lack of support, tended to be associated with the occurrence of child neglect. Mothers lacking support from their husbands and extended kinsmen were more likely to find their children frustrating, were less inclined to consider their needs, and were more harsh and punitive with them.

Concerning child-rearing practices in rural areas of India, Poffenberger (1981) reported the differential treatment of boys and girls within this cultural framework. Young girls had to be obedient and learn to conform both in their own homes and in the homes of their in-laws. Because the difficulty in adjusting to a new family required strength of personality, the kind of emotional dependence on the mother that was desirable in sons was not encouraged in daughters. Poffenberger described discipline as common in India, but not battering abuse and neglect. He commented that the very social structure in India that required conformity provided parents with a support system of other adults and older children. The presence of others in the household restrained parental temper and reduced the likelihood that frustration would lead to uncontrolled violence toward young children.

Different forms of child abuse observed in Japan were reported by Wagatsuma (1981). He described the phenomenon of child abandonment, leaving an infant in a hospital, a clinic, or another public place, such as a railway station or a department store. The reasons for deserting infants were unwed pregnancy, financial problems, or family conflict. In Japan, to give one's baby to an orphanage was associated with feelings of shame, as it was necessary to publicly expose the parents' identity. The secret abandonment of their babies became the choice for young mothers who had difficulty keeping them. The causes of abandonment or infanticide were mostly related to the mothers being unwed or having serious marital problems with the possibility of divorce. In Japan, to be an unwed mother and to have an illegitimate child was considered very shameful. Therefore, it was cultural attitudes toward the status and the fates of these women that led to child abandonment. Another form of child abuse pointed out by Wagatsuma was associated with the unique phenomenon of children-murder/parents-suicide acts known as "family suicide." When parents decided to commit joint suicide, they involved their children in their journey to death. The children were killed before their parents killed themselves, or they were forced to commit suicide together with their parents by taking poison or other methods (see Section 3A: Culture-Related Specific Syndromes).

Chinese-American anthropologist David Y. H. Wu (1981) indicated that, in Taiwan, filial piety was one of the oldest moral codes. Extensions of traditional filial piety toward parents are certain extraordinary expectations of children, as described in old books or classic children's stories. These have many themes, such as sacrificing a child's life for the parents' sake, a child accomplishing an impossible task or suffering self-inflicted pain to fulfill a parent's wishes or demands, or a child supporting his parents despite difficult circumstances or self-sacrifice (Tseng & Hsu, 1972). Wu pointed out that such filial concepts and codes express fundamental values in parent-child relations and that child abuse-like behavior is practiced within this cultural context. Institutionalized child abuse against adopted daughters was mentioned by Wu as well. In the past, when a poor family had difficulty supporting itself, one solution was to sell its young daughters to an affluent family. They were called adopted daughters, but, in fact, the girls served as young live-in maids. Very often, these "adopted daughters" were subjected to harsh treatment by their masters or "foster parents."

Based on the cross-cultural information available, Korbin (1981, pp. 1–12, 205–210) remarked on the cultural aspects of child abuse. He indicated that certain facts in the cultural context can act either to increase the incidence of child abuse and neglect or to diminish the likelihood of their occurrence. The factors were the cultural value of children (whether children were viewed as valuable for future generations), beliefs about the categories of children (whether children were considered inadequate or unacceptable categories by cultural standards), beliefs about child capabilities and developmental stages of children (expecting children to behave in certain ways at certain ages in terms of competence and humanness), embeddedness of child rearing in kin and community networks (the existence of a network of concerned individuals beyond the biological parents, a crucial element in the etiology of child abuse). Finally, Korbin pointed out that while children in general might be highly valued by a cultural group, there were categories of children that were more vulnerable to maltreatment. These included illegitimate, adopted, deformed, retarded, high birth order, and female children. Vulnerability depended to a large degree on the cultural context. In summary, child abuse as a childhood-related problem is shown to be subject to various cultural influences in the nature of pathoplastic, pathoselective, and pathofacilitating effects (see Section 1C: How Does Culture Relate to Pathology?).

From a clinical point of view, Maitra (1996) raised the question about a universal diagnostic category for child abuse. Based on his work with south Asian families in Britain, Maitra pointed out that based on cultural beliefs about the self, subjective experience and interpersonal connections, and child-rearing patterns, child abuse could be viewed and defined differently in different societies. Special caution and careful assessment are thus necessary in transcultural practice.

### b. Sexual Abuse

It is not easy to obtain epidemiological data from communities regarding the prevalence of sexual abuse for cross-cultural comparison. This is primarily because the actual occurrence of abuse is often concealed. Instead, many studies rely on retrospective data, examining childhood histories of the sexual abuse of adult subjects, particularly college students, even though they often represent a special subpopulation from an epidemiological perspective.

LeVine and Levine (1981) described the situation in sub-Saharan Africa, where the sexual molestation of girls is a known phenomenon. For instance, they encountered cases of rape of prepubescent girls by adult Gusii men, who, in many instances, were closely related to members of their victims' parents' generation. Actual father-daughter incest occurred occasionally. In addition, the seduction of pubescent girls by male schoolteachers was the occasion for recurrent scandals in Nigeria and Kenya.

Meston and associates from Austin, Texas (1999) examined university students of Asian and European ancestry regarding their histories of childhood abuse. The results showed that male and female students of Asian ancestry reported higher levels of physical and emotional abuse and neglect than their European counterparts. However, female students of European ancestry reported a higher incidence of sexual abuse than female students of Asian ancestry.

Moghal, Nota, and Hobbs (1995) from the United Kingdom also carried out a retrospective study concerning Asian ethnic minority populations. They pointed out that, in the United Kingdom, both professionals and laypeople tended to deny the existence of the sexual abuse of children among Asian ethnic minority populations based on assumptions about the Asian family structure, its culture, and its religion. However, they commented that Asian family members were less likely to initiate concerns and that professionals need to be more open to the possibility of sexual abuse.

### c. Child Indulgence Problems

Regarding contemporary mainland China, Korbin (1981) commented that there were very few cases of child abuse or neglect acknowledged officially. There is good reason to believe that this more or less reflects the actual situation. Associated with the national family policy of "one child per couple" to prevent a potential population explosion, most young couples in urban settings have only one child, whereas nearly half of young parents in rural areas have a second child. A child is viewed as a "treasure" of the parents and is often indulged by the grandparents. Thus, instead of abuse or neglect, child psychiatrists have witnessed problems associated with child indulgence syndrome. Children were more protected by their parents and prevented from having adequate socialization experiences.

### d. Conduct Disorders

Canino and colleagues (1998) pointed out that, of all childhood psychiatric disorders, conduct disorders are perhaps the most highly influenced by cultural and other contextual variables. In clinical diagnosis, it is recommended in DSM-IV (American Psychiatric Association, 1994, p. 88) that conduct disorder be applied only when the behavior in question is symptomatic of an underlying dysfunction within the individual and not simply a reaction to the immediate social context.

Cross-cultural comparison of children's behavior disorders is difficult because the identification of behavior disorders is subject to sociocultural definition. There is no universal standard for defining such disorders. Furthermore, unless a community survey is carried out, clinical data are subject to the influence factor of illness behavior, depending on the reasons and mechanisms for seeking professional help.

### e. Child Obesity

Excessive body weight is attributed to multiple factors, including genetic predisposition, food intake patterns, physical exercise, and attitudes toward excessive body weight. It covers a wide spectrum of factors—biological, psychological, and cultural. There has been an increase in child obesity in Asian societies, such as mainland China, Hong Kong, Japan, Korea, Singapore, and Taiwan. People in these societies, including children, tend to have slim physiques. However, along with economic improvement and sociocultural changes after World War II, the number of overweight children has increased so remarkably that clinics for over-weight children have been set up, a phenomenon that was unheard of in those societies in the past.

Several factors contribute to the new phenomenon of child obesity problems in these societies. Associated with economic improvements, there have been remarkable changes in food intake. More nutritious food has become available and more meat is consumed than before. This has resulted in a higher calorie intake. This is in contrast to the lives of children before and during the war, when they often suffered from malnutrition due to a shortage of food.

In contrast, physical exercise among children has decreased markedly. Associ-ated with improvements in transportation, children seldom walk to school, as they did in the past, often for many miles. Now, school buses and private cars are so available that children hardly ever walk to school. After school, children used to participate in sports and outdoor games, or join their parents in doing house-hold chores. Now, children watch TV, engage in electronic games, or study for school assignments, because of heavy educational pressure. They hardly move their bodies or exhaust their energy. It is becoming common to see obese children. Overweight clinics and body-weight control programs are being advocated. Things have changed greatly from several decades ago, and parents are facing new problems associated with changes in the lifestyles of their children.

### f. Hyperactive Behavior

From a clinical point of view, hyperactive disorder, or attention deficit disorder, is basically understood as a mental disorder that occurs as the result of minor (and multiple) lesions in the brain. It may be attributed to brain injury, intoxi-cation, or other organic, biological causes during early childhood. However, the behavior problems associated with the disorder may be perceived, tolerated, and reacted to differently in different cultures, demonstrating a "pathoreactive effect" (see Section 1C: How Does Culture Relate to Pathology?).

In order to study how a child is perceived and assessed as "hyperactive," Mann and his colleagues (1992) carried out a cross-cultural study involving mental health professionals from China, Japan, Indonesia, and the United States. Chil-dren considered hyperactive by clinicians in their own countries were videotaped in individual and group activities. Videotaped vignettes of four cases were edited and shown to the child mental health professionals. They were asked to rate the degree of hyperactivity based on rating scales. Results showed that Chinese and Indonesian clinicians gave significantly higher scores for hyperactive-disruptive behavior than did their Japanese and American counterparts. This study demon-strated clearly that the perception of socially tolerated hyperactive behavior varied greatly among different cultures and that the boundaries between normal and hyperactive behavior were defined differently by specialists in different societies. In other words, the recognition and diagnosis of hyperactive behavior among children were not absolute. They were relative, depending on the attitudes and tolerance of such behavior in the sociocultural context.

### g. Reading Disability

Originally, some child psychiatrists (such as Makita, 1968) claimed that Japanese and Chinese children who were trained to use the logographic system of writing (Chinese characters) from childhood tended to have a lower possibility of developing a reading disability than European and American children who were taught to use the alphabet. It was speculated that Chinese characters were graphic in nature, and left-right reverse seldom occurred. However, Chinese child psychiatrists in Taiwan, Hsu and colleagues (1995), carried out an intensive study of Chinese children, reporting that reading disabilities did exist among children who learned to read in the Chinese logographic system, and that the prevalence rates were by no means lower than those among children who learned alphabetic writing systems. The pattern of reading disabilities was not manifested by mirror writing (as shown in children reading alphabetic writing systems) but were also associated with Chinese writing, illustrated by the displacement, rotation, or addition or substitution of a basic unit in the Chinese character. In other words, while the manifestation of reading disabilities may vary in association with the writing system, the prevalence was similar cross-racially, supporting the biological-neurological nature of such a disorder.

## 4. Therapeutic Considerations

### a. Basic Strategies: Work on the Family as a Unit

It is a general rule that the family, particularly the parents, needs to be involved in the care of the children. The family is defined broadly to include any person who has an impact on the lives of the children, whether living in the same household or not. In many cultures, grandparents play a significant role in child rearing, so they need to be involved, too. The ways of working with families need careful adjustment, based on different family systems, structures, and functions (Canino & Spurlock, 1994, pp. 138–139; Hsu, 1983). For instance, in cultures where parental figures are highly respected, caution is needed to respect them (particularly the father, as the master of the household) in family sessions. Any comments toward parents are better not made in the presence of the children, so that the parents do not feel offended. When a culture does not encourage open expression of opinions and demonstrating emotion, it is wise not to provoke family members (particularly of the younger generation) to speak out against the older generation. For people who are used to identifying an individual (particularly an identified youngster) as the person having problems, parents often believe that the therapist should fix the child's problems for them. Using family therapy to work on family problems would sound awkward to these parents. When families have such an orientation, it is suggested that the parents be invited to come to the session "to help the therapist decide how to treat the youngster-patient," not to treat (or even work on) family problems.

### b. Cultural Issues Needing Special Consideration

*Attachment and Dependency.*    Among variables themes that are encountered in child development, the issue of independence vs. dependence is viewed very differently by different cultures, particularly between the East and the West. Take the concrete example of when it is the appropriate time for a child to sleep separately from his parents, as a sign of independence. Most contemporary European or American parents will arrange for their newborn baby to sleep in a cradle in a separate room as soon as several days or weeks, at most, after the baby is born. Most Asian parents, however, will let their baby sleep with them in the same bed or, at least, in the same room in the baby's own small bed for many years. It is not unusual to let young children sleep in their parents' room until the children reach school age, or even after that. Besides the reality that there is a shortage of rooms in the household, there is no concept of "separating" the children from the parents as soon as possible.

Besides sleeping arrangements, physical contact between parents and young children varies greatly among different cultures as well. In contemporary times, many Western parents use baby carriers to hold their babies, whereas Eastern mothers carry their babies on their backs or hold them in their arms. When the children reach the age when they can walk, their parents still hold them when walking in the street, or at least hold the child's hand. It is surprising to Eastern parents to see Western parents walking their children on leashes, as if they were walking their dogs.

These examples of child-rearing practices reflect how autonomy and independence are encouraged in one culture and attachment and dependence, in another. In working with children, this is just one area that needs careful evaluation in making clinical judgments and offering therapy.

*Physical Discipline vs. Child Abuse.*    Another area that is easily confused and even mistaken by clinicians is the matter of physical discipline versus physical abuse practiced by parents on children. In many cultures, parents use physical punishment to discipline their children. Even schoolteachers in the past were sometimes allowed to discipline physically students who did not behave well in school, although this is strictly prohibited now in most cultures. Clinically it becomes a challenge to distinguish between corporal discipline and physical abuse inflicted by parents. It is a gray area, but certain rules apply. If the physical punishment is given with the clear intention of disciplining a child's wrong behavior; it is given by parents in a relatively calm way, without emotional upset; the degree of severity is relatively mild; and the part of the body chosen for punishment is selected to avoid causing severe damage, such behavior may be considered "discipline." In contrast, if the physical attack occurs as the result of a parent's emotional upset, an instrument (such as a stick or a club) is used rather than the hand, or the discipline is carried out in an "unusual" way, such as pouring hot water on the child or burning him with a heated iron bar, the damage is obviously severe, causing physical injury, and the action occurs repeatedly, then it is definitely abusive in nature. Detailed information and careful assessment will help clinicians make a judgment.

In various cultures, people distinguish between discipline and abuse according to their social judgments and cultural criteria. For instance, Pacific Islanders consider the head to be where the soul resides. If anybody, including his own parents, hits a child's head, it is considered abuse. It is a cultural custom to hit the child's buttocks, legs, or arms, but not the head, for discipline. Thus, culture-based, proper differential diagnosis is necessary for relevant clinical intervention.

## B. ADOLESCENTS

### 1. Psychological Development

After a person goes through childhood development and reaches puberty, he is more or less ready to enter adulthood. From childhood to adolescence, youngsters continue growing physically and psychologically. Thus, most of the issues raised earlier regarding children also apply to adolescents. The age for entering adulthood varies considerably in different societies. In general, in primitive or simple societies, a person is recognized as an adult as soon as he demonstrates the signs of puberty. In contrast, in more developed, modern, or industrialized societies, there is a tendency to delay the landmarks for entering adulthood.

In many primitive societies, certain rituals, such as puberty initiations, are performed to recognize a youngster's entrance into adulthood. In industrialized societies, there are no clear-cut rituals performed. However, there are some occurrences that indirectly imply the step toward adulthood. The stages set up in the educational system—from junior high to senior high, then to college and post-college—are concrete stages through which the youngsters may progress.

### 2. Common Psychological Challenges

Depending on the pace and theme emphasized in development, adolescents may face several different issues during the stage of adolescence. The emotional turmoil and psychological difficulty associated with adolescence vary cross-culturally. As pointed out by Mead in 1928, in the era of her investigation, the adolescent in Samoa grew into yong adulthood gradually and smoothly and did not experience psychological turmoil as the adolescent encountered in Western societies by abruptly jumping into young adulthood. In many societies, adolescents encounter a second stage of resistance. Associated with their cognitive improvement and ability of abstract thinking and ethnical judgment, they tend to criticize parents' thoughts and behavior and tend to act rebelliously toward authority in the family and society. This is particularly true in societies where authority is valued and stressed, creating generational conflicts.

Adolescents are generally sensitive toward and vulnerable to rapid sociocultural change or unstable social conditions. Coupled with their own developmental emotional turmoil, they tend to manifest various kinds of mental health problem, mostly of an acting-out nature, such as substance abuse, traffic accidents associated with drinking, suicide attempts, violent or even antisocial behavior. These phenomena are more easily observed in a society facing cultural uprooting.

Self-identity and ethnic identity are other issues of concern in adolescence. The nature of problems associated with identification may vary due to the nature of society, minority status, and other factors. Clinically the adolescent's problems of ethnic identity can be more easily observed among immigrants who tend to either overidentify with or reject entirely the ethnicity of the host society. Overidentification as a defense again loss can be manifested at an ethnic level (see Case 1: A Laotian Man Who Overidentified with America, in Section 1B4: Personality and Ethnic Identity).

## 3. Unique Psychological Problems

Associated with the nature of society and the characteristics of culture, several unique psychological problems may be encountered among youngsters beginning in adolescence. Following are some of the examples.

*Narrow-Gate Syndrome.*    This is a culture-related specific mental health problem observed in some societies, particularly east Asian, that places great emphasis on the importance of education and academic study, creating mental health stress for youngsters. This phenomenon is typically observed in Japan, where the educational system is closely related to career development. In order to be hired by a good company (usually for lifelong employment), it is critical to enter and graduate from universities from which companies recruit future employees. In order to enter these prestigious universities, it is important to go to prestigious high schools and junior high schools that prepare students to pass the college entrance examinations. To be successful, it is essential to go to good grade schools, and even good kindergartens. In other words, there are preset stages of education that must be completed to ensure a future career. This creates the narrow-gate syndrome, meaning that opportunities are limited and competition is very high. This sense of competition and success is stressed from kindergarten on, contributing to various culture-related mental health problems. This so-called narrow-gate syndrome is observed in many east Asian societies suchas Korea, Taiwan, and mainland China as well, where children's education is highly valued and academic achievement is stressed (see Fig. 1 in Section 2A: Culture and Stress).

*Parent-Abuse Syndrome.*    A unique form of adolescent psychopathology is observed in some Asian societies, including Japan and mainland China. It is called parent-abuse syndrome and refers to the physical violence of an older child or adolescent toward his parents, mostly his mother. It has been the opinion of Japanese psychiatrists that this problem occurs as the result of overindulgence of the child. When he was small, he was overindulged by his mother for various reasons, mostly because his father was busy at work and not involved in domestic matters, leaving the emotionally lonely mother to cling to her children (particularly her son). A boy growing up in such a situation, overprotected and

---

CASE 1

A Japanese Adolescent Who Hit Her Mother (Todd Elwyn)

A Japanese teenage girl living in Hawaii with her family was brought to the hospital after her mother called police to intervene in her violent outburst at home. The patient became very upset, broke furniture, threw dishes, cut her wrists with the broken pieces, and hit her mother when she was told that she could not use the telephone for a week as punishment for overusing it.

The patient was born in Japan. When she was very young her father disappeared, taking all the family's savings with him. It was suspected that he had abandoned the family to live with another woman. To deal with this crisis, the patient and her sister were sent to live with their maternal grandparents, who felt sorry for the children and gave them extra attention. In particular, the grandfather spoiled the patient. When the patient reached her teens, the mother married a Japanese man working in international trade with America. The mother moved to Hawaii with her two daughters to join her husband. The patient had trouble relating to her stepfather, whom she viewed as stern and rigid, but adjusted reasonably well to life in Hawaii. She became interested in a boy at school and would often talk to him on the phone for many hours, even into the early morning. This behavior annoyed her stepfather, who demanded that the mother set limits on the patient's use of the phone. The mother's disciplinary action triggered the patient's emotional and violent outburst.

exposed infrequently to a father figure for needed discipline, tended to become bullying, if not tyrannical. When he reached adolescence, he tended to exhibit violent behavior toward his parents if his needs were not satisfied, or when his parents tried to set limits on his behavior. Being physically strong at that age, he could hurt or even injure his parents rather seriously when he became violent. Thus, this phenomenon is referred to as parent-abuse syndrome, the opposite of child abuse. This unique problem may be understood from a developmental perspective as part of the rebelliousness of adolescence, when a child wants to distance himself from his parents, only it is manifested in a pathological way.

In traditional Japanese culture, children are expected to behave well and be obedient to their parents. Here, the mother's attempt to set strict limits after overindulgence by the grandparents was difficult for the patient to accept. The parents had trouble adjusting their expectations and their way of disciplining the patient to the new culture in the host society. The task of raising and disciplining children reaching puberty in this new family proved difficult. Regardless of the underlying causes, the turmoil of this experience was difficult for all members of the family.

*School Massacre.* Recently, there has been an alarming increase in *amok*like massive homicidal behavior observed among school students in America as well as European societies. Easy access to dangerous weapons, a social atmosphere that sanctions violence (on TV or in movies), lack of discipline by family and social authorities for internal control of one's own behavior, plus the psychology of imitation, are some of the reasons contributing to the phenomena of school massacres. It is becoming almost a fashion in Western societies for youngsters frustrated in school to undertake mass homicidal behavior to express their anger.

## 4. Some Mental Disorders Commonly Related to Adolescents

*Substance Abuse.* Although it was pointed out that substance abusers worldwide are generally young males (Smart, Murray, & Arif, 1988), it was not clarified to what extent their problems were shared by the youngsters of different societies or ethnic groups. Data from the National Institute on Drug Abuse (1995, pp. 46–49) concerning students in the United States from 1977 to 1994 showed that there were considerable differences in prevalence and the substance abused among the three ethnic groups surveyed (i.e., African-Americans, Caucasian-Americans, and Hispanic-Americans). Economic factors and availability of substances, as well as fashions among them, appeared to work together to shape the pattern of abuse. Abuse of paint inhalants by youngsters in developing societies was clearly determined by such factors. It needs to be pointed out that the trend of substance abuse among adolescents changes often, depending on the time and circumstance (see Section 4F: Other Substance Abuse). Therefore, there is a need to upgrade information frequently.

*Suicide Attempts.* It is well known that, in contrast to committed suicide, attempted suicide is more commonly observed among youngsters, starting from adolescence. It is one coping method available to young people when they encounter difficult emotional problems. In general, it is more prevalent among females than males (see Section 4H: Suicide Behavior).

## 5. Fundamental Therapeutic Considerations

*Privacy and Confidentiality.* One of the characteristics of the psychology of adolescence is the need for keeping personal matters secret from parents. This brings up the issue of how to respect the adolescent's privacy in therapy and observe confidentiality between the adolescent and his parents, as there are different views and practices in different cultures regarding privacy among family members. This is particularly true regarding how much the parents have the right to know about their youngsters. In cultures that stress parental authority, it is a basic assumption of parents that they have the right to know everything about their offspring. To propose confidentiality between parents and children would be unthinkable and would offend the parents. In contrast, in cultures where individuality is the ethos, it is considered that after children reach a certain age, they have the right to keep their personal matters confidential from their parents. This creates a dilemma for therapists regarding the extent to which they should keep information about their adolescent patients confidential from their parents. There is a need for clarification from the very beginning, and adjustments should be made in each case according to cultural considerations.

*The Mode of Therapy.* It is the judgment call of the therapist which mode of therapy to adopt, whether to work primarily with the adolescent patient or the whole family together or to try peer-group therapy. Depending on the extent to which individuality, mutuality, and collectiveness are emphasized in daily life, the therapist could decide to match such cultural norms in the therapeutic process. For instance, if an individual is not used to expressing his personal opinions or feelings in his culture-shaped daily life, peer-group therapy sessions may be more comfortable than one-to-one sessions. If the parents are closely related to their children and eager to know everything about them, it may be a good idea to have individual sessions with the adolescent, family sessions, and sessions with the parents alternated in the course of therapy to enhance the adolescent's individualization and, at the same time, gratify the parents' wishes and involve them properly in the therapeutic work.

*The Matching of the Therapist.*   Associated with cognitive development, the adolescent is more explicitly aware of ethnic or racial differences. Thus, matching the therapist and the adolescent patient becomes more of an issue where ethnicity or racial background are concerned, in addition to gender and age factors. The general rule is that if the adolescent patient is matched with a therapist of the same ethnic or racial background, it will be easier to start a relationship, avoiding potential negative ethnic or racial transference. During the course of treatment, it helps the patient to identify with the therapist, not only on a personal level but also at ethnic or racial levels, an important treatment mechanism for an adolescent patient in therapy. If the therapist happens to be different from the adolescent patient in ethnic or racial background, these issues should be dealt with continuously throughout the course of treatment. Cultural knowledge should be obtained and cultural empathy exercised to make up for the differences that exist in such transcultural interethnic or interracial therapy (see Section 7A: Intercultural Psychotherapy: Challenges and Competency).

## 6. Common Issues to Be Addressed in Therapy

*Autonomy and Independence.*   It is a common desire for the adolescent to be separated from his parents as he is searching for individuality. This is often manifested by the need for privacy, setting personal boundaries from the parents, and being sensitive about intrusion of the parents. However, parents of different cultural backgrounds often react to this developmental need differently. Parents who strongly believe that their children are their possessions and that children should be filial to their parents and obey them often consider their parental right to oversee their children's personal lives and inspect their personal belongings, such as reading their letters and diaries and inquiring into their private matters, for example, what happens on dates. There is less of a sense that the adolescent needs to be respected as a growing-up individual, and that his privacy and desire for individuality should be considered. In such cases, there is a need to help the parents redefine their roles and adjust the extent to which they should respect their children's personal lives. This is not so much a problem for parents whose culture recognizes that every person should be treated as an individual, even youngsters.

*Cultural Gap with Their Parents.*   The generational gap between parents and youngsters is often one of the issues that needs to be focused on in therapy for the adolescence. The cultural gap between generations is often widened when there is rapid cultural change or when the family immigrates to a foreign country.

It becomes the therapist's job to deal with the generational gap by helping the parents and youngsters to communicate, exchange views, and make compromises between them, if possible. It is important to stress to parents and children both that there is no "wrong or right," but that things are viewed "differently" according to different life experiences and cultural beliefs in different times and circumstances. How to work out differences between generations is the main issue. In addition to clinical skill, the therapist needs to have a comprehensive and proper understanding of the cultural aspects of the lives of both the parents and the youngsters so that proper advice and suggestions can be made to narrow the gap between them, making compromises, or at least understanding and feeling comfortable with the existence of differences between the generations.

*Psychosexual Development.*    Among the cultural variables that need special consideration in adolescent therapy are psychosexual issues. Because views and attitudes toward sexual matters vary greatly among different cultures, so also do the problems experienced by adolescents in this area. In conservative societies, the issues faced by adolescents are often related to inhibiting their sexual interests, avoiding masturbation (as it is considered undesirable in folk belief), or controlling their sexual desires; whereas in sexually liberated societies, the matters concerning adolescents are how they appear to friends or the opposite sex, how to date boy- or girlfriends, how to be popular among their peers of the opposite sex, and so on. What is normal psychosexual development as measured by their sexual interest, knowledge, and experience needs careful consideration from a cultural perspective. How to adjust their sexual development within their cultural context is challenging.

*Ethnic or Racial Identity Issues.*    Adolescence is the stage in which ethnic or racial identity becomes a major issue in psychological development. The sense of self-identity is heightened at this stage of development, as does ethnic or racial identity. In addition to asking, "What kind of person am I?", "Do others like me or not?" and "Which group do I belong to?" there are similar questions about what kind of ethnic or racial group I belong to, how others see me as part of a particular ethnic or racial group, and with which ethnic or racial group I should identify. Thus, the issues of identity become more complicated. If the youngsters are surrounded by people of different ethnic or racial groups in their living environment, their ethnic or racial identity will be stimulated early in their development and can become an issue when they reach adolescence. This is particularly so if they belong to an ethnic minority and experience ethnic or racial discrimination. Depending on their actual experiences in life, their ethnic- or race-related identity can be either positive or negative, affecting their psychology accordingly. Sometimes, they are unclear or confused about their ethnic or racial identity, which can influence their mental health and require professional help.

## 7. Some Groups Needing Special Attention

*Socioculturally Deprived Minority Youth.* Sociocultural deprivation refers to a person experiencing less than desirable conditions from social and cultural perspectives. In a concrete sense, the person suffers from poor economic conditions and less opportunity for education or employment, tends to be exposed to confused values systems (as traditional cultural systems are uprooted) and to experience unfair treatment from others, and suffers from negative group or ethnic/racial identification. This is often observed among indigenous minorities whose sociocultural system is destroyed by (invading) outsiders or due to exposure to rapid social and cultural change associated with "modernization."

The youngsters of such backgrounds often experience undesirable mental health conditions manifested by a prevalence of drinking problems; substance abuse; behavior problems, including juvenile delinquency; and self-destructive behavior, such as suicide. These are rather universally observed phenomena among young people who are members of a minority growing up in a socioculturally deprived environment. They are reactions to and products of such circumstances.

Clinical experience has suggested that ethnic and cultural issues need to be dealt with actively in therapeutic intervention (Vargas & Koss-Chioino, 1992). Furtheremore, for youngsters with these kinds of mental health problems, group and social-activity approaches are more meaningful and useful than traditional, individual therapy. In other words, the whole community needs to be focused and worked on, rather than merely the single person. It is quite a challenge for the clinician, as it takes a lot of energy, effort, and time.

*The Immigrant Youngster.* When people migrate from one society to another, the growing process of the youngsters is often disrupted in terms of language, ways of behavior, education, and socialization. The youngsters have to adjust to changes in their personal lives, family situations, and society at large. If the youngsters have difficulty going through this migration-related adjustment, many mental health problems may occur, the same as those for socioculturally deprived minority groups. However, if they learn the new language and new ways of life, make good use of the educational system, and are successful in adjusting their family life and socialization with others, they can adjust well and become successful in their later lives. Even though they are vulnerable because of migration, there is a chance for their adjustment and improvement (Nguyen & Williams, 1989).

In therapy, they need to be encouraged to improve in their new language, to learn the ways of behaving and doing things in the host society, and to activate their socialization. If the youngsters receive sufficient attention from their teachers at school and proper care at home and are welcomed by their peers, there is always a good chance for their successful adjustment to the hosting society. The role of the therapist is to facilitate these issues in all dimensions.

*Traumatized Refugee Youngsters.*    Refugee children are generally considered to be at high risk for mental health problems because of the extreme stressors they experienced in the past. From a therapeutic standpoint, a debate often occurs over the question of whether to break the silence surrounding the war and repression that have become part of family and social relationships. According to Rousseau (1995) who reviewed the available literature, most Latin American authors considered social silence to be a consequence desired by oppressive political regimes. Given this situation, some clinicians, such as Becker and colleagues (1990), suggest that group therapy creates a space to hold past experiences and all their associated emotions, allowing symbolization to begin. Giving testimony is in itself therapeutic, providing an instrument of struggle and protest against the aggressor and an act of recognition of the emotional hurt. Otherwise, children may become "unintentional transmitters of undiscussable traumatic life events" (Bar-On, 1993). For some clinicians, intervention in the form of community or school programs has been applied. In general, it is considered that mental health intervention for refugee children cannot be confined to a psychiatric approach centered on psychopatholpogy. Cultural, social, political, and even historical dimensions must be incorporated.

*The Mixed-Race Youngster.*    Associated with the increase in interracial or interethnic marriage, there is an increase in the number of mixed-race or mixed-ethnic youngsters. The common concerns related to mixed-race adolescents are the matters of social marginality, sexual identity, and racial identity (Gibbs, 1987). When parents are joined together in interethnic or interracial marriages, they often encounter certain issues in their marital lives. One issue is how to raise their children, who are the products of their intermarriage.

If parents know how to care for their mixed children with affection, basically there will be no problems for the youngsters. However, if there are problems between the parents, that the youngsters are mixed could aggravate triangular relationship problems with the parents. For instance, in a black (husband)–white (wife) interracial marriage, if the son happens to have more white features, the black father may see him as the wife's son rather than theirs (unconsciously or consciously) and treat him with certain negative feelings, or hate and resent him, in the worst case. It could obstruct the father-son identification and intensify the triangular conflict if the white mother tended to take a sympathetic and protective attitude toward the son. It needs to be clarified that the racial appearance of the youngster alone does not create such conflict and problems; rather, the preexisting problems between the husband and wife are provoked or aggravated by the racial appearance of the child. The same situation could occur with a daughter depending on her racial appearance. Because each child would be different, different situations could occur for different children.

It is not only racial appearance that can provoke conflict between the parents and induce family problems, but also the different value systems held by the parents, widened by the intercultural marriage situation. Again, if the marital adjustment is successful, the problems of racially or ethnically mixed youngsters will not occur, or will be minor issues.

## C. AGED PERSONS

### 1. Psychological Problems Encountered

Aged persons are vulnerable to certain mental health problems and psychiatric disorders. Some of them, such as dementia, are predominantly related to biological factors, whereas others, such as feelings of insecurity due to aging, prolonged grief reaction after the loss of a spouse, and frustrations associated with deteriorating physical conditions, are attributed mainly to psychological factors. The problems that are psychological in nature are usually colored by cultural elements. The discussion here will be regarding cultural aspects of psychological problems that may be encountered by the elderly of diverse cultural backgrounds.

#### a. Negative Views and Attitudes about Aging

Negative views and attitudes about aging are fundamental issues related to the psychological problems of aged persons. As elaborated previously, an individual's views and attitudes toward aging will be shaped by cultural attitudes and values toward aged persons (see Section 1B6: Adulthood, Aging, and Death). If aging is viewed as negative, aging will become an undesirable stage of life. If getting older is seen as a positive experience, then approaching the later stages of life can be enjoyable and met with optimism (Butler, 1974).

In many societies, particularly traditional agricultural societies, the wisdom of past experience is often valued for the improvement of production as well as the regulation of social interaction. Becoming old is equivalent to being experienced in life. In order to maintain social order, the status of the elderly is emphasized. Thus, the elderly are associated with respect and authority. They are often given certain roles in daily life and contribute to the functioning of the family as a whole. Therefore, there is a basic security and dignity associated with the process of aging. It is relatively free from the fear of being alone, neglected, and abandoned.

In contrast, modern, industrial, urban societies, such as those in contemporary Europe and America, are as a whole characterized by an emphasis on youth. When you are young, you can enjoy the opportunities, prospects, beauty, and attractions in life. However, when wrinkles appear on your face and your hair turns gray, this is perceived as the end of the glorious stage of life. Becoming old is considered the beginning of despair and hopelessness. An effort is made to hide age, to pretend that you are still young, and there is an unspoken fear of being alone, ignored, and disabled. This general attitude toward aging in a society will negatively color the life of the elderly.

### b. Unprepared Psychologically for the Late Stage of Life

Associated with improvements in social and health conditions, the human life span has increased tremendously during the past several decades. Instead of dying at the age of 40 or 50 at the most, as was the case a mere half century ago, it is now common to live on average until 70 or 80 in most developed societies. However, as this is still a new experience for human beings, many people are not well prepared to live to such a late stage in life, many decades after their retirement from work. This phenomenon is quite true in many societies, such as those in Japan, Korea, and Singapore in Asia, and in other areas around the world, where there have been rapid and remarkable social, economic, and health improvements and life expectancy has suddenly increased by 20 years or so.

### c. Difficult Widowhood after the Loss of Marital Partner

Associated with the process of getting old, sooner or later, one spouse in a married couple is going to lose a marital partner and become a widow or widower. Even though this is an unavoidable and often very sad event in a person's life, the experience of losing a spouse varies among individuals in different societies. From a cultural perspective, the experience varies according to many factors. Most importantly, it depends on how much the marital relationship means to an individual person. In a society in which the spouse is the primary axis in family life, where, in contrast to parent-child or sibling relationships, or other family dyads, the husband-wife dyad has more weight in their lives, and has been the sole resource of emotional support, the loss of the primary partner will have a significant impact on the life of the widow or widower. In contrast, if the spousal relation is embedded in other dyads of the family system, the loss of the spouse will not make as desperate a difference in the life of the person, who will still be surrounded by other family members.

In addition, the fate of the widow or widower will be shaped by cultural expectations and regulations (see Section 1B6: Adulthood, Aging, and Death). Based on cultural views and practices, the quality of life of the widows after the loss of their spouses will vary. Also, depending on the culture-defined role divisions between husband and wife, the life of a widower will vary greatly after the loss of his wife. For instance, husbands in Japan or Korea are seldom involved in domestic chores. For a man to enter the kitchen is culturally almost taboo. Most men never learned how to cook rice or make tea, not to mention how to cook daily meals or do the laundry. If a man's wife dies and he is living by himself, without children, a phenomenon occurring more often in urban settings, he is sure to encounter practical problems of daily survival. This is not necessarily true for Chinese men, who do not have such cultural rules and most of whom know how to work in the kitchen if they have to. Thus, the nature and severity of the same experience of losing their spouses are shaped by varying cultural factors.

### d. Problems of Relationships with Adult Children

When a person becomes old, the nature of the relationships with his adult children will change. This is a part of the change associated with an individual's life cycle as well as that of the family. The new generation of adult children begin to have their own life experiences, attitudes toward things, and philosophical views, which may be considerably different from those of their aged parents. This is particularly true if relatively rapid sociocultural change has occurred in the society. Within a family, the locus of power will shift gradually from the aged parents to the adult children. Thus, psychologically, there may be a struggle associated with the reversed parent-child relationship.

This reversed parent-child relationship becomes more severe for immigrants who have migrated to culturally different host societies. In contrast to their young-adult children, the aged parents often become vulnerable. They become underprivileged in terms of learning the new language, knowledge, and experiences necessary for adjustment to the host society. Their wisdom and experience from their society of origin become useless or even obstacles to their adapting to their new lives. If the host society's language is foreign to them, their problems in communication and catching up on knowledge will become severe. They will have to depend heavily on their adult children for social life outside of the household. If they have grandchildren, they often speak the new language of the host society, but not the native language of the grandparents, while the grandparents speak very little of the new language; thus, severe communications obstacles will exist between them.

If the migration is to a society that puts less emphasis and respect on aged persons, the loss for the migrated aged person is doubled if he came originally from a society in which aged persons have a certain status and value. It is difficult for aged persons to follow the family and migrate transculturally, often to a more advanced and developed society. It is often too late for them to learn to drive a car or to learn a new language, and they are shut off from the opportunities of gaining new knowledge and adapting to the new lifestyle. They also have to become humble in their relations with their culturally more privileged adult children, as well as their grandchildren.

### e. Unable to Utilize Social Support Systems

In general, in addition to family life and domestic systems, there are public life and societal systems for networking and support. According to their cultures, some societies concentrate more heavily on the former and less on the latter, whereas others emphasis both. In culturally conservative societies, when a person becomes old, sick, or disabled, he may still prefer living with his family in a personal setting rather than in a public institution, such as a nursing home. The resistance to living in a nursing home is rather strong in many societies, including Asian. It is considered a "disgrace" to be separated from your family and "dumped" with strangers in a nursing home. It is not only the aged themselves who do not like it, but often their adult children as well. They feel that they will be criticized by their friends or relatives for allowing their aged parents to live in such a "miserable" place. This is in great contrast to other societies, which consider it a natural alternative to live in an institutional setting if it becomes difficult to live in a family environment. Views on being placed in a nursing home in these societies are only minimally negative.

## 2. Psychotherapy for the Elderly

### a. Exercise Practically Oriented, Brief Psychotherapy

It is a general rule among geriatric psychiatrists that it is better to focus on practical aspects of life and realistic problems in therapy for elderly persons (Niederehe, 1994). This is particularly true when the therapist is dealing with elderly patients who are unfamiliar with the nature and procedures of psychotherapy. Many—especially those from home societies where psychiatry is still not a popular specialty, psychological therapy is not a commonly practiced mental health service, and the concept of analytic psychotherapy is unheard of among most laypeople—will often be confused when they are asked to review their psychological lives, to reveal their intrapsychic material, or even to discuss emotional matters (Baker & Takeshita, 2001). Regarding ethnic minority elderly, Grant (1995) pointed out that therapists must recognize the diversity within ethnic groups and often must be broad based, multilevel, and direct therapy at the multiple conditions contributing to the presenting problems. He supported the view that, although ethnic minority elderly tend to be unfamiliar with the practice of psychotherapy, it still can be very effective, especially when dealing with depression and anxiety associated with psychological problems.

### b. Attention to Therapist–Patient Relations and Countertransference

It is a common rule that therapist-patient relations should be geared toward the ethnic-cultural background of the patient so that the relations can be more relevant, meaningful, and effective in therapy. This is especially true when dealing with elderly persons. Based on their cultural backgrounds, they have certain views and expectations regarding authority-subordinate relations in various interpersonal situations, including how the elderly should be treated by younger persons.

Generally, therapists for elderly patients are younger than their patients. Even though the therapists may be respected by the patients as "physicians" or "healers," at the same time, they are considered "younger" and of a "lower" social status compared to the aged patients. How to show culturally expected respect toward the aged persons and their life-experience authority is one of the issues that needs careful attention. This may not be so important in a society where people are educated to treat each other "equally," disregarding age differences. However, it can be a crucial matter for people who come from societies where, culturally, aged persons are expected to be respected.

Along the same it is important to examine and handle the countertransference that the therapist might have toward the elderly person. This is particularly true when the therapist is dealing with a patient from another culture that has different views and attitudes toward the aging process. The therapist's negative attitudes toward aging may reflect on the way the aged patient is handled and the way therapy is directed.

### c. Application of Cultural Knowledge and Empathy

In any situation involving transcultural therapy, it is necessary for the therapist to have a basic knowledge of the cultural background of the patient under care so that proper cultural empathy can occur in the therapeutic process. This is particularly true when the patient has a cultural background that is different from that of the therapist. When a therapist is working with an elderly patient from another sociocultural background, there is often not only a potential "cultural gap" between them, but a wide "time (or era) gap," as well. For example, when a patient talks about his World War II experiences in the Pacific, it will sound almost like a historical story to a younger therapist who was born after the war. A woman patient's experiences of traditional life characterized by strict rules about marriage and sexual life (i.e., premarital sex and adultery viewed as social sins), without the availability of birth control (in a time when it was common for married women to bear more than half-a-dozen children) but with the possibility of losing many children in infancy due to health conditions, and so on, might sound unthinkable to a young, contemporary therapist. Transcending the double gap of "culture" and "era" for needed empathy is a technical challenge that therapists have to deal with when they are treating much older patients from other cultures.

### d. Reasonable Encouragement to "Talk Story"

"Talk story" means to talk freely about any social or personal matter for the sake of social interaction. As part of the process of aging, the time orientation for a person will shift from the future in youth, to the present in adults, and to the past in the aged. These are changes observed in psychological orientations to time throughout a person's life span. Seeing less opportunities in the future, perhaps, elderly persons shift their focus to recollections of the past. By utilizing this psychological characteristic, the skillful psychotherapist will encourage elderly patients to talk about their personal lives in the past as a way of stimulating their interest in interaction with the therapist. "Talking story" about their past, without saying it, will indirectly help them to examine the present and to prepare for the future. This is not a waste of time in therapy; rather it may serve as the main part of the therapeutic interaction if it is handled skillfully and utilized properly. To let the patient talk story in therapy sessions is particularly pertinent for elderly patients who have different cultural backgrounds from the therapist. It offers a splendid opportunity to help the therapist learn about not only the patient's personal history, but also his cultural background, significantly promoting cultural empathy. Talking story is a format that makes elderly patients feel comfortable about engaging with the therapist in therapy sessions, as it is a more "natural" way for them to examine and reveal their lives than a formal psychiatric examination or analytic process.

### e. Sensitive Avoidance of Mental Illness Stigma

Based on the background and history of development of psychiatry within their societies, many people around the world still hold rather negative views about psychiatric disorders and are very sensitive about being labeled mentally ill. This is particularly true for elderly persons who were brought up in an era in which there was no optimistic way of treating the mentally ill and many severely disordered mental patients had to be confined to institutional care. This attitude is also present if the elderly are from home countries where the practice of psychiatry is still rather backward.

With this in mind, in therapy, the therapist is advised to avoid labeling the patient as "mentally ill" as much as possible. Mental problems can always be reframed as medical problems that need medical attention by examinations, checkups, and medications. The medicalization rather than psychologicalization of problems is more suitable and acceptable to elderly patients. Mental illness is often associated with being "crazy" and having emotional problems is viewed as a personality weakness or failure to "tough it out."

Psychotherapy, or so-called talk therapy, is better conducted as part of a "medical" treatment than as (pure) "psychological" therapy. Taking the patient's blood pressure and using a stethoscope, familiar physicians' medical maneuvers, without hesitation as a part of the session activities, in addition to talking to the patient, or letting the patient talk, will put the patient more at ease with the therapist. In other words, from a practical perspective, the dichotomy of medicalization and psychologicalization should be minimized. Conceptually the distinction between somatic and psychology needs to be reduced as well. The wholistic approach is much more relevant and appreciated in working with elderly persons, who tend to view the body and mind together without distinction or dichotomatization.

### f. Balanced Acceptance of Folk Healing

It is not surprising that many modern people utilize folk or alternative healing services besides modern professional therapies. This is especially true for elderly persons, who feel more at home with folk ways of healing and traditional remedies. This is simply a refection of their time of life, views, and experiences. Based on this understanding, the modern therapist is advised to maintain a rather wholistic view of treatment, a balanced attitude toward alternative therapies, and even to take an active interest with patients in nonorthodox approaches. This will help the therapist develop closer therapeutic relations with the patient. Through such a joining with the patient, the therapist will be in a better position to make more meaningful and powerful therapeutic suggestions.

### g. Psycho-Education for the Elderly and Their Families

Technically, psychotherapy with elderly patients, like that with children or adolescents, may take the format of "psycho-education," with a primary focus on how to deal with actual daily life. This may include how to overcome the emotional issues of going out shopping, taking care of family chores, or relating to neighbors or their families.

---

CASE 2

A Korean Widow Who Was Afraid to Die Alone

An elderly Korean widow suffered from an anxiety attack after she experienced vertigo episodes. Her condition was aggravated by the thought of what would happen if she fainted and died suddenly. According to her cultural beliefs, it would be a terrible thing for a person to die without being cared for by immediate family members. She had been living alone in her apartment since her husband died several years earlier. Her grown-up daughter, married to a Caucasian husband, with three children, was living only one block away from the patient. The patient demanded that her daughter call her by phone at least twice a day to make sure that she was alive and all right. She thought that, according to her culture, it was a simple task for a filial daughter to perform for her widowed mother. However, this arrangement did not last long. The daughter was working outside the home, and it was difficult to call her mother during working hours. After work, she was concerned with her husband's feelings, also. She was afraid that he would not understand and appreciate her "overconcerned" behavior and being "over

*(continues)*

bonded" to her mother, even after marriage. After a family session, the therapist explained to the patient that there was no danger to her life, and that for her daughter to call her once a day, in the evening, should be enough. Also, it was suggested that the teenage granddaughters could help their mother by taking turns calling their grandmother, so that it was not too great a burden on their mother. These were simple, practical suggestions, but they worked for the elderly patient and her family. This is often what is involved in working with elderly patients, helping them deal with daily life problems.

Working with elderly patients cannot exclude working with their families. This is particularly true when there is conflict between the elderly patients and their adult children, or between or among adult children with regard to their elderly parents. This is especially so in a society where, culturally, close ties between parents and children are stressed in daily life. When parents become old, preexisting conflicts among children that are rooted in their early childhoods might surface and disturb them again, even though they have become adults.

### h. Working on Various Issues Relating to Aging

Numerous issues need to be worked on when therapists are caring for aged patients. Sometimes it is necessary to arrange for elderly parents to live in institutional settings, such as nursing homes, if the parents become disabled, either mentally or physically. Many aged persons could easily be "dumped" into such public institutions by their careless children; however, this is not always the case. The situation can also be the opposite. This could potentially cause psychological problems for the adult children, who were raised with the belief that children should be filial to their parents and take good care of them when they become old. Making arrangements for their parents to live in a nursing home could provoke strong guilt feelings.

Although the ending of life by death is a natural phenomenon, the subject of death is not easily faced or discussed in many societies. In some cultures, it is even considered taboo to mention death, to discuss openly the possibility of death and how to prepare for it. In such a cultural milieu, the death of elderly persons is a subject that is avoided by immediate family members and ignored by the elderly persons themselves. In such circumstances, it can become the therapist's role to include the subject in the process of therapy with the patient as well as with family members, if necessary.

How to prepare a will and make arrangements for surviving family members are issues that need to be dealt with openly among family members and with an attorney, if necessary, so that proper preparations can be made not only legally but psychologically. This would be a great help to the elderly and their adult children from a practical perspective. However, different people and cultures have different attitudes about preparing for the end of life. Clinicians need to explore the cultural views on these sensitive subjects, even though it may be very useful to discuss and prepare for them, and eliminate any anxieties that the elderly might have in relation to the end of their lives.

In summary, elderly persons usually encounter certain psychological problems in their lives that might be considerably different from those of other adults. There is a need to modify the "regular" therapeutic techniques and focus of therapy to meet the individual needs of the elderly in their family situations, taking into account the process of aging and their cultural backgrounds in the past and the present.

## D. WOMEN

### 1. General Issues: Cultural Discrimination against Women

Even though the Earth's population is composed half of men and half of women, differences in treatment between men and women have perhaps existed from the beginning of the history of humankind. Even though politically men and women should be equal, in actual life they are different in many respects. The differences between them are basically related to physical, physiological, and psychological factors. In addition, for the sake of survival, social and domestic revisions of the roles and functions of men and women differ. They are obviously shaped by society and culture. It is considered almost universal that men have more powerful positions than women. From anthropological perspectives, there are exceptions in some cultures. In matrilineal societies, such as Micronesia, women enjoy certain unspoken privileges that men do not, because the lineal system is identified through the female and property is transmitted accordingly.

The truth is that, historically, in many societies, women were, and still are, treated as less favorable than men. There are many examples, which do not necessarily occur as open discrimination, but as unequal treatment. For instance, in Asia, young girls can be sold to others (to serve as maids or prostitutes) for money to help the family resolve financial debts or crises. In China, before the modern revolution, feet binding was practiced for several centuries. For some reason, women with bound feet were considered beautiful (by men), if not sexually appealing (for men). Besides, it enforced women to be bound inside the house so that they could belong only to their husbands or male masters. Based on this, young girls of upper social class were forced to start binding their feet when they were very young, suffering from almost intolerable pain for the sake of men (see Fig. 11(d) in Section 1B5: Customs, Beliefs, and Rituals).

In India, women who become widows are not permitted to have a social life outside of the household for the rest of their lives. They are bound only to take care of their children and to serve their parents-in-law. They are forbidden to have any contact with men, except their fathers-in-law and brothers-in-law. No matter how young they are, they are not permitted to remarry.

In many societies, women are considered significant only for bearing children, particularly sons. If they fail, their husbands have a legitimate reason to dismiss them as their spouses or to have other women. There are no guarantees of "wifely status" in a modern sense (see Case 1: The Muslum Woman with One Foot in the Past, in Section 2A: Culture and Stress). In China, influenced by communist ideology, both women and men work outside of the house. However, in Japan and Korea, it is traditionally considered a woman's job to stay at home, take care of the household, bear children, and serve her husband. Even now, women, after receiving a higher education (such as a college education), once they are married, have to follow the social custom and quit their jobs and stay at home. Therefore, less than 20% of married women work outside of the house in contemporary modern time. Many housewives whose contemporary homes are equipped with modern appliances, making them easy to manage, are bored and develop emotional problems, addressed as the "housewife syndrome" by Korean psychiatrists (Chang & Kim, 1988).

It is well known that even in Western society, which emphasizes basic equality, wages for women have always been less than those for men, although their professional performance and experiences are the same. There is no need to mention that it is women who are usually subject to physical and sexual abuse by men, rarely the other way around. Politically the inequality between men and women is decreasing in most modern societies, however, psychologically, the treatment of women as less important persons by men is still prevalent in many places. There is a need to understand the gender differences in psychiatric problems and to treat women patients differently, with consideration of the bio-psychological-cultural aspects of life, including the role and function of women in contrast to men (Nadelson & Zimmerman 1993). This is particularly true of minority-group women, who suffer from double minority status (Commas-Díaz & Greene, 1994).

## 2. Common Mental Health Problems Relating to Women

*Self-Image Problems.* Associated with a less privileged social status than men, women in general suffer from low self-image, feeling that they are less important, more vulnerable, and no good. This was the basis of the "penis envy complex" proposed by Sigmund Freud in Victorian times. However, such self-image problems still exist in present societies, either explicitly or inexplicitly.

*Sociocultural Discrimination.*   There are endless examples of how women are discriminated against by men on an institutional level, making them feel that they are different from men. Less opportunity for education, employment, and professional careers are commonly observed at the social level, associated with cultural and political views that women do not need such life opportunities. The best-known example is a situation observed not long ago in Afghanistan during the Taliban regime, when all women were forbidden to go to school. Those girls eager to obtain an education could only attend classes provided in secret from the government. Anthropologists informed us that there are different patterns in how sexual life is regarded among various cultures around the world (see Section 4J: Sexual Disorders). If there is a higher degree of male dominance, there will be more complete control over female sexuality. An extreme case is observed in some Islamic African societies, in which males are extremely dominant and attempt to control female sexuality through the required surgical removal of the clitoris during childhood (Castillo, 1997, p. 116).

*Sexual Harassment.*   Although anthropologists have indicated to us that there are various attitudes toward sexual behavior and life, very much based on physiological reasons, in sexual actions, in general, males play dominant roles while females play subordinate ones. For this reason, women always become a target for sexual attacks by men, in the form of rape, in a severe form, or sexual harassment, in a less severe way. It was recently noted that, associated with the increased concern over basic human rights and gender equality, more women are taking legal action against men for sexual harassment in working situations. However, there are still far from satisfactory protections.

## 3. General Psychiatric Problems: Trends for Women

Even though women are "stronger" than men physiologically from the standpoint that they have longer life spans statistically, from a psychiatric point of view, it is generally believed that women suffer more psychiatric problems than men. It is also observed that women tend to seek more psychiatric care than men do. It is suspected that this may be related to illness behavior in the sense that women feel more comfortable than men in seeking professional help from others (Holmshaw & Hillier, 2000). Nevertheless, it is clinically noticed that, in comparison with men, women suffer more from certain psychiatric disorders.

*Depression.*   Either due to biological or psychological factors, it is generally noticed that women suffer more from depression than men. It is indicated that a female to male ratio is about 1.5 to 3.0, with female predominance (Palazidou, 2000). From a psychological perspective, this can be easily attributed to the fact that women encounter more emotional difficulties in their lives, including child-bearing, gender discrimination, and social restrictions.

*Eating Disorders.*   It has been pointed out that eating disorders are quintessentially women's disorders. The improvement of social conditions, an increased tendency toward obesity, and a cultural expectation of slimness as beauty are all associated with the increase of eating disorders among women in European-American societies. However, this is not necessary so in societies (such as most Polynesian societies) in which obesity is considered a sign of health and beauty; or in societies where food deprivation is a reality (see Section 4G: Eating Problems).

*Psychosomatic Disorders.*   It is a salient fact that women's life experiences differ from those of men in many ways, including childbearing and child rearing, women's double shifts at home and at work, and their lack of power in personal, working, economic, social, professional, and political relationships (Stewart et al., 2001). They experience different degrees and natures of stress in their lives and manifest variations in psychosomatic disorders. In the past, women and their physicians have worried about mortality from breast and gynecological malignancies; however, ischemic cardiac disease in becoming the number one killer of women in most Western countries (Abbey & Stewart, 2000).

*Sex-Related Antisocial Behavior.*   Generally speaking, women are less involved in antisocial behavior in a strict sense. However, if they are, it is in different types of antisocial behavior relating to prostitution, or other sex-related crimes. In some societies, many women, particularly the younger ones, are forced by their families or gangs to engage in prostitution as a way of earning income. Needless to say, this indirectly increases their risk of contracting venereal disease and AIDs.

*Physical Abuse.*   Women are often abused by men. Violence against women takes many forms, such as battery, sexual harassment, prostitution, pornography, and rape. Female infanticide is another form of discrimination and abuse of females in the beginning of their lives. Violence by police and security forces in ordinary times and during armed conflict or war are common occurrences. Violence against women refugees and asylum seekers are other examples. However, violence against women in intimate relations is a rather common phenomenon observed cross-culturally. After reviewing research findings from various societies, Krane (1996) reported that 20% to nearly 70% of women have experienced violence in intimate heterosexual relationships.

*Sexual Abuse.*   It is a general pattern that women are abused sexually by men, and not the other way around. Based on an anthropological study of cross-cultural samples published by Murdock (1967), Sanday (1981) reported that the rape of women by men occurred on different level of prevalence among tribal societies. A rape-prone society is one in which the sexual assault of women by men is culturally allowable. In general, in their social lives, men are posed as a social group against women. In contrast to this, a rape-free society is characterized by sexual equality and the notion that the sexes are complementary. Interpersonal violence is uncommon within this society as a whole, and there is recognition of the importance of women's contribution to social continuity. Therefore, Sanday summarized that rape in tribal societies is part of a cultural configuration that includes interpersonal violence, male dominance, and sexual separation. In the urban social environment, characterized by nuclear households and an emphasis on privacy, sexual abuse within private settings is speculated to be high, but it is difficult to reveal unless the victims are willing to report it to public services and seek help. However, many victims are afraid to do so, with the concern of family shame and fear of retaliation from their male partners. This deserves more public health concern and service.

*Suicide.*    Although it is generally noticed that suicide attempts tend to occur more among females than males and completed suicide more among males than females, a reverse situation is observed in China. Epidemiological reports indicate that in mainland China, the suicide rate for females is higher than for males, particularly for young females in rural areas. This hints that life for young women in rural settings is difficult, and suicide is one way to deal with the stress and hardships they encounter in their lives (Pritchard, 1996) (see Section 4H: Suicide Behavior).

*Special Psychiatric Problems.*    Associated with gender and physiological reasons, women are exposed to certain unique psychiatric disorders that men are not. Clinically these include premenstral tension, menopause syndrome, and postpartum depression or psychosis. Even though it is correct to attribute these disorders primarily to biological factors, there is still a room to consider sociocultural factors that may contribute indirectly to the severity and frequency of these female-related disorders. For example, diet (high consumption of vegetable estrogen through *tofu*, or bean curd) may reduce the severity of menopause symptoms. How menopause is regarded by the self and others as a sign of entering a nonreproductive stage for women is a psychological factor that may contribute to the reaction of women facing this syndrome.

## 4. Some Attention Needed for Therapy

*Consideration of the Choice of Gender of the Therapist.*    Because more female healthcare workers now available in the field of medicine, female patients should be given the opportunity to choose female therapists if they wish. This is more true for certain health problems, including psychiatry. It is generally noticed that female physicians are more able to engage with female patients with empathy on an emotional level (Roter & Hall, 1998). In clinical experience, it has been noticed that the matching of gender between therapist and patient is a complex matter. Female patients may prefer to have male therapists over female therapists for many reasons (either healthy or neurotic) and may benefit by doing so. However, for female patients, particularly those who come from cultural backgrounds that have distinct gender separation and feel less natural and comfortable relate to a male, especially in sharing personal matters, it will be more beneficial to work with female therapists.

*Empathetic Understanding of Women's Position and Experience.*   Whether therapists are male or female, they should learn to understand women patients' situation and experience with more empathy: how they, as women, are treated in their culture, the kinds of privileges they may have, the kinds of discrimination they may suffer, and the kinds of harassment or abuse they may have encountered, either emotionally or physically. This is particularly true for patients who come from different cultural backgrounds from the therapist. Cultural knowledge about women in general is useful and essential beyond knowledge about the individual patient under care.

*Careful Management of Intimacy with Female Patients.*   It is generally true that therapists should always be careful to maintain and manage "proper" relation with patients: proper in the sense that they are close but not too intimate, friendly but professional, empathetic but not overinvolved. This is particularly true when therapists are treating patients of the opposite sex. When male therapists are working with female patients, it is very important to know the "proper" relationship that should be maintained from social and cultural perspectives so that it will not be too distant but also not inappropriately too intimate. For example, should male therapists shake hands with female patients, should male therapists comfort female patients in an intimate manner? Those are questions that should be addressed and answered according to the usual norms observed and practiced by female patients in their cultures. The closeness between two persons or the degree of intimacy between male and female is a social matter that is often defined by culture and perceived, interpreted, and reacted to as such. This is a delicate and sensitive matter that needs to be handled carefully to avoid any cultural misunderstanding and error. Otherwise, it may cause unexpected complications in treatment. Patients may develop sex-related transference toward their therapists, not only of an individual nature but also of an ethnic or cultural nature. Ethnic transference may include gender-related transference. For instance, Asian female patients may hold the view that American male therapists are always "gentle, kind, and romantic" to women and develop gender-related ethnic transference accordingly, which needs careful management in the therapeutic course.

*Proper Management of Gender-Related Countertransference.*    It is a general practice among skillful therapists to observe and manage transference as well as countertransference in therapeutic situations. As part of this, competent therapists need to be aware of and handle their own gender-related countertransference toward their patients. For example, American male therapists, based on their limited experience and knowledge, may assume that all Asian women are "kind, subordinate, and obedient" toward men and develop a gender-related ethnic countertransference that brings a bias and complication to the therapy and deserves careful management.

*Relevant Management of Man behind Woman.*    Finally, it deserves to be mentioned that the behavior of men and women are complementary. If we borrow the concept of the system theory, women's behavior does not exist in a vacuum. It occur as part of a system of interaction with their gender partners, men. Their behavior is very much influenced and impacted by the men behind them. To carry out therapy with women patients, it is useful to think how they are influenced by their gender partners, either husbands, boyfriends, brothers, or fathers. Based on the system theory, it is very important to work with men behind women, so that the whole system can be mobilized and changed if necessary. By way of illustration, if a woman is concerned about the use of birth control and feels uncomfortable about it, resulting in anxiety and psychosomatic symptoms, it is not enough to work on the problem merely at the intrapsychic level. It is necessary to be concerned with and explore how her husband views the situation and what kind of reaction he shows to her (his wife). It is definitely necessary to work with him simultaneously; otherwise, the therapy will not be complete. This is particularly true for situations in which, according to the culture, males have strong power over females (see Case 1: The Muslum Woman with One Foot in the Past, in Section 2A: Culture and Stress).

## 5. Special Considerations for Particular Services

In order to provide more suitable psychiatric care for women, special attention in certain services and extra consideration for establishing special service to meet the needs of women are needed. For instance, mother-baby admissions are possible in special inpatient facilities designed for severely mentally ill women who are ready to look after their newborn. Associated with this is the concept of caring for pregnant or postpartum women patients in their homes so that community programs can be set up accordingly (Kohen, 2000a). Although women are less involved in alcohol or substance abuse than men, they do abuse substances. How to provide care for women who abuse substances, particularly when they were pregnant, is a clinical and public health challenge that requires special clincal knowledge and experience. Even though women, in contrast to men, are in general less likely to commit crimes and spend their lives in prison, if they do, they certainly need special concern and care for their basic protection in the confined prison setting. They need special facilities and activities to meet women's needs, and also protection from sexual harassment or abuse from male officers and staff. This is an area of urgent concern (Kohen, 2000a).

In summary, in comparison with men, women are stronger in certain ways but more vulnerable in others. As a subgroup of the population, they need special attention, and special knowledge and skills are necessary to provide psychiatric service for them (Kohen, 2000b). At a theoretical level, it is worthwhile to point out that many psychiatric theories (the Oedipus complex, for example) have evolved mainly regarding males, and females are ignored. There is a need to revise, expand, and add to theories suited for the other half of the population (i.e., females).

## E. COUPLES

From a psychological point of view, men and women are different in some perspectives even when they grow up within the same village or community. When they marry partners of the same cultural background, a so-called "homocultural" marriage, they still have to learn to adjust to the differences that exist between them. If the two partners are from different social or cultural backgrounds, then their marriage is "intercultural" (or "heterocultural"), and the differences that may exist between them are potentially greater, and their marital problems more complicated. One of the main purposes of couple therapy is helping a couple resolve their differences in terms of the way they view or feel about things. From a cultural perspective, couple therapy needs to focus on marital issues that are heavily related to culture. It starts with the basic knowledge about cultural aspects of the system and the nature of marriage that has been elaborated previously (see Section 1B2: Marriage and the Family).

### 1. Culture and Marital Problems

The psychological problems encountered by a married couple can be caused by many factors. Some problems are social, such as financial problems or the separation of the husband and wife due to social demands or war; others are psychological, such as the incompatibility of the personalities of the spouses or an unhealthy motive for marriage. However, at another level, there are numerous ways in which martial problems are related to cultural factors.

### a. Problems Associated with the System of Marriage Itself

Even though the self-selection of marital partners is the most common and favored way to marry in most European-American societies, in many parts of the world, arranged marriages are still practiced. In many Asian societies, gradually shifting from the traditional arranged marriage system toward free marriage, parents still play a significant role in guiding their children in the selection of a mate, at least, the young people still need their parents' agreement or sanction to get married.

Marriage according to free love sounds romantic, but a person not socially sophisticated and experienced in heterosexual interactions may be at a disadvantage, not knowing how to select a proper and suitable mate objectively. In some societies, where love marriage is a newly adopted phenomenon, it has been observed that separation and divorce are relatively frequent among those who wed for love, as opposed to those who marry through parental arrangement. In arranged marriages, parents assist their children in selecting a partner with consideration of objective factors, including the realistic aspects of life, such as level of education, occupational skill, the background of the family of origin, and history of behavior and performance. Besides, theoretically, the relations between in-laws tend to be better from the beginning if the wedded partner has been selected or screened by the prospective in-laws. However, arranged marriages tend to have inherent problems that may emerge after the marriage. The partners selected by the parents may not like each other, and intimate affection may not develop or may be delayed. Unsatisfied with his arranged wife, the husband may seek romance outside of the marriage.

### b. Problems Associated with Relations with the Families of Origin

In an individual-emphasizing society, marriage is considered the binding of two persons. The neolocal residence system, namely living in a new place of their own parting from the parents on both sides, is practiced. The families of origin or marriage-related families are kept at a certain distance from the new couple, according to the nuclear family structure. The relations are characterized by periodic telephone contact supplemented by occasional visits. This is common practice for people living in urban settings who move frequently. However, this is not true in other societies in which either paterlocal or materlocal residence systems are observed and the families of origin or marriage-related family live close together. Even though the families do not live together physically, the nature of a stem or extended family is maintained. Under such circumstances, relations with parent-in-laws, sibling-in-laws, and other members of the family or clan are close, influencing marital relations intensely and significantly. It is almost impossible to ignore the existence and impact of families of origin or families by marriage. No doubt these close, extended ties with families have their advantages.

Often support is available when it is needed. However, there are always certain restraints for married couples as they have to take into consideration the impact of their marital life on their families. This creates certain conflicts, even though harmony may be ideally emphasized in such extended and complicated family ties. (see Case 5 An Indian Woman Who Hanged Herself after Being Beaten by Her Brother-in-Law for Her Unfilial Behavior toward Her Mother-in-Law, in Section 9F: Families).

### c. Conflict due to Prescribed Role Divisions between Spouses

The roles to be performed by a husband and wife are individual and private matters. However, beyond the personal level, they are often influenced by culture in either explicit or subtle ways. While the culturally prescribed role divisions between spouses tends to guide and stabilize their relations and interactions, they may also induce certain conflicts.

In Korea, it is not considered a virtue for a woman to work outside the home after becoming a wife. A wife is expected to stay at home and devote herself primarily to domestic matters, including serving her husband and raising the children. It would be viewed as "disgraceful" for a wife to work outside of the house. Therefore, it is almost a rule that women quit their jobs and become housewives when they are married. It does not matter if the woman is a highly educated professional woman. Less than 20% of women still work as professionals after marriage, even in contemporary Korea. Due to this custom, many young women, as housewives, have to confine themselves to their houses for the rest of their lives. Many Korean wives develop emotional problems in these circumstances, complaining of feelings of loneliness, emptiness, and boredom. This phenomenon, as mentioned earlier, is referred to by Korean psychiatrists as the "housewife syndrome" (Chang & Kim, 1988).

In many parts of the Mideast, Muslim wives are also expected to be subordinate to their husbands, to keep busy with household work, and to not raise their voices to express their opinions, complain, or make demands of their husbands. Some wives suffer as a result of this underprivileged life. They express their unhappiness and satisfy their demands through folk ways, such as participation in the Zar cult. (see Tseng, 2001a, Chapter 32: Culture-Embedded Indigenous Healing Practices. p. 522).

### d. Problems Stemming from Interaction Patterns between Spouses

In contemporary American society, it is common for a husband and wife to communicate openly with each other about how they think and feel. Sharing between spouses is one of the most important elements in maintaining their affection for each other and preserving their relationship. It is also a cultural habit for partners to praise each other as often as possible and to express appreciation whenever it is appropriate. This is a means of offering assurance and making the relationship work.

However, it is important for a marital therapist to know that this concept and habit of open communication to maintain closeness is not necessarily shared by couples in other cultures. In some cultures, it is considered "awkward" for intimate persons, such as a husband and wife, to praise each other verbally and to express gratitude. It is considered necessary to say thank you only to "outsiders," but not to intimate "insiders," particularly spouses. Physical intimacy, such as touching, holding, or hugging, between husband and wife in a public setting is considered impolite or improper behavior. Kissing each other in front of others is considered "disgusting," uncivilized, "animal" behavior. These differences in cultural views and attitudes regarding communication and expression of affection between husband and wife need to be taken into consideration when the therapist assesses the relations between couples from other cultures. Otherwise, a great misunderstanding may take place. Needless to say, there are subtle ways that couples from such cultural backgrounds express their opinions and feelings. These usually involve nonverbal expressions, which can be perceived if the therapist is knowledgeable about and sensitive to them. When subtle ways of communicating are applied, sometimes even the husband and wife themselves fail to perceive the message, confusing or misunderstanding it and feeling frustrated. Such culture-shaped communication patterns can be the source of potential problems.

### e. Difficulties Related to Child-Rearing Patterns

Another source of problems and disagreement may be child-rearing patterns. The husband and wife may not necessarily share the same views on how to raise and discipline their children. This is particularly so if the society is experiencing sociocultural change and parents have lost their values and beliefs on how to raise their children. In many societies, the care and discipline of the children are assigned solely to the wife, while the husband concentrates only on business matters outside of the household. As a result, potential problems may occur. The wife may be overinvolved with the children and neglect her husband, or she may feel overwhelmed by the responsibility of taking care of the children by herself without any help from her husband.

### f. Violence against Wives by Husbands

The physical abuse of wives by their husbands has been documented in almost every culture in the world (Krane, 1996; Levinson, 1989). Women, in their capacities as wives or partners, are not safe. Battered wives often internalize deep feelings of self-blame and shame. Suicide may be one of the ways they react to abuse.

Abuse of women in marital relationships has been identified as possibly the most important precipitant of female suicides cross-culturally (Counts, 1987). In Papua New Guinea, suicide is considered a "reasonable and culturally valid response to abuse" of women by men (Counts, 1987, p. 198). Marital violence is cited as a significant factor in suicide among Fijian Indian families (Lateef, 1992). Similarly, in Egypt, family quarrels were the leading causes of all suicides reported, particularly among young women (Heise et al., 1994). Another consequence associated with physical abuse is homicide. Studies from India, Bangladesh, Kenya, and Thailand verify that murder frequently takes place within the family and most often the victim is a woman (United Nations, 1989). A review of research across the globe found many of the same risk factors. The young wife, in the early years of her marriage, was at great risk (United Nations, 1989). Unfounded sexual jealousy or protest against the woman's threat to terminate the relationship were some other risk factors. It was the real or perceived challenges to the man's possession, authority, and control of his wife that most often resulted in the use of violence. Despite these similarities, there was good reason to speculate that there were sociocultural factors that contributed to the low or high frequency of violence against wives.

### g. Problems Rooted in Views and the Commitment to Marriage

Finally, there may be problems related to the way the couple viewed their commitment to their marriage. Most Western societies believe that marriage should be monogamous. Also, it is basically considered that marriage is a life-long commitment. Therefore, during a religious ceremony, the couple is often officially asked to swear that they will be bonded and take care of each other for the rest of their lives. However, in reality, for couples whose marriages are not working, divorce is a common contemporary solution that is easily entertained and practiced. In contrast, in many other cultures, it is still believed that marriage is a life-long commitment. Even though there are problems, termination of the marriage is seldom considered. When a couple has such a cultural background, separation or divorce as a solution to problems should not be proposed by the therapist. Such a suggestion would be misinterpreted as an attempt to "break up" the marriage, when the couple came to see the therapist with the intention of saving it.

In most monogamous societies, in theory, extramarital affairs are not accepted. However, in some, a husband having affairs outside of the marriage is tolerated. Multiple wives are permitted in some cultures (such as in China in the past and in Muslim societies even in the present), if the husband is affluent enough to support them. The rivalry and conflict between wives may be minimized by certain cultural rules and practices. For instance, the first wife is always respected as the primary spouse, with a certain prestige and power, even though the husband may accumulate other wives or concubines. Still, there is potential competition and conflict in such polygamous situations.

## 2. Intercultural Marriage

"Intercultural marriage" refers to a marriage formed by partners with relatively diverse cultural backgrounds so that different cultural factors, including different views, beliefs, value systems, and attitudes toward couples, become the main issues in their marital adjustment (Tseng, 2001b). The term "intercultural" (rather than "cross-cultural") is used to signify that the *interaction* of the cultures of both partners tends to occur. From a psychological point of view, men and women are different enough that there is always a need for a husband and wife to adjust to each other from the standpoint of gender alone. This is true even in an ordinary "homocultural marriage," when the husband and wife have the same cultural background. The need for adjustment to differences is much greater in a "heterocultural," or "intercultural marriage," when the cultural differences between the husband and wife are considerable or remarkable.

### a. Motivation for Intercultural Marriage

Whether there is a particular motivation for a person to choose a marriage partner of a different ethnic, racial, or cultural background is an often raised and investigated question. Clearly there are many couples who marry interculturally for the same reasons that couples marry homoculturally, simply because they become intimate, find themselves compatible, share a mutual affection, enjoy being together, and so on. However, there are some couples who marry interculturally for special reasons or unique motivations. In speaking of motives, one must appreciate that the conscious reasons given for a culturally mixed marriage might not be the actual ones, and that it is often the result of a combination of several factors, both conscious and unconscious.

Chance and availability are very important factors in the process of mate selection. This is true in all marriages, but probably more so in intercultural marriage. Beyond such nonspecific factors, there are often special psychological factors that lead people to marry partners of diversely different ethnic, racial, or cultural backgrounds. For instance, Davidson (1992) raised some ulterior motives for marrying interracially (specifically blacks and whites), such as rebelling against their families, being sexually curious about people of a different race, seeking economic or class gains, or satisfying the need for exhibitionism. Cohen (1982) mentioned the problems relating to their parents and feeling a great sense of empathy with the foreign partner.

Based on psychoanalytic concepts, one of the psychological reasons for outmarriage is to solve the unresolved triangular complex with parents, particularly with parents of the opposite sex (Char, 1977). According to psychoanalytic theory of personal development, every person needs to resolve the Oedipus complex encountered during the phallic stage of development. If a child is phobic of incest, he is then driven to choose a mate who is very different from his opposite-sex parent, resulting in the extreme situation of "outmarriage."

---

CASE 3
_____

Interracial Marriage as a Way to Rebel against Father

A Japanese girl in Tokyo deliberately dated a black American GI to upset her father. Her father used to say that black men were no good, and she wanted to prove to him that this was not true. Her relationship with her black boyfriend was eventually discovered by her father, who forced it to end. In reaction to this, the girl moved to Hawaii. With the excuse that she was studying abroad, she got her affluent father to send money regularly to "support" her. However, she secretly married a black man she met in Hawaii and had a baby. For several years, she continued to let her father believe that she was still pursuing her college education and relied on his financial support. She needed financial assistance from her father to support her husband, who had drinking problems and difficulty in keeping a job. Her personal history revealed that she was very close to her father when she was little. After puberty, she was sexually involved with her father for several years without the situation being discovered by her mother. Her repeated choice of a nonapproved black mate was a way for her to rebel against her father and, at the same time, try to work out her guilt feelings over having incestuous relations with him. Having a relationship with a man who was physically different from her father was the only way she could allow herself to become sexually aroused. This is a unique case that illustrates complex psychological mechanisms that can lead someone to marry a person of a different race, that is, feelings of superiority-inferiority toward another race, the psychological need for revenge against one's own parent, and the unconscious attempt to resolve a deep-seated Oedipal complex.

---

### b. Adjustment in Intercultural Marriage

*Core Issues in Adjustment.*   In order to adjust to the differences that result from the different cultural backgrounds of two people, there is a need for both sides to recognize the cultural gaps that exist between them, which are beyond personal differences or individual psychological issues. Cultural understanding and empathy are needed next. This means that each partner should try to learn and understand why the other partner thinks, believes, and behaves in certain ways. This requires not only cognitive understanding but also empathy at an emotional level. Cultural empathy refers to psychologically taking the position of the person of the other culture to try to understand how he perceives and feels about the issues. Needless to say, it is a fundamental requirement that one should respect one's partner's ways of viewing things and the emotions attached to them, no matter how they may seem from your point of view—"silly," "strange," "nonsensical." There is no correct or wrong or good or bad from a cultural point of view. There are merely different patterns of thinking, behaving, and reacting. If both partners could take this kind of understanding attitude and culturally egalitarian position, a door would always be open for negotiation and resolution of differences. This would particularly be so if there were a strong affection between the husband and the wife that bound them together and motivated them to work out their problems.

*Patterns of Adjusting to Differences.*    The basic challenge in intercultural marriages is to work out any problematic differences that disturb the couple's lives or interfere with their relations. There are several recognized patterns of solving the problems arising from cultural differences. *Ignoring adjustment* refers to simply denying the existence of troublesome differences between the partners. *One-way adjustment* is asymmetric adjustment. One partner gives up his own cultural behavior and takes on that of the other. Frequently, the proximity to relatives of the dominant culture, relocation to the country of the dominant culture, or previous liking or fascination with the partner's culture helps determine this adjustment. In contrast, *alternating adjustment* is when a wife and husband adopt each other's cultural ways on a trade-about basis. *Midpoint adjustment* means that a compromise is made on specific issues. Sometimes the nature of the differences is such that there is no room for compromise, and differences can only be accepted as they are, allowing *parallel adjustment* (i.e., each partner practices his way on certain issue). Finally, there is *creative adjustment.* This takes place when both partners give up certain individual, cultural behaviors and evolve a new behavioral pattern (Eaton, 1994) so that a totally new way of living gradually ensues. (For details, see Tseng, 2001b, Chapter 46: Intercultural Marriage: Problems and Therapy, pp. 738–739).

*Process of Adjustment.*    From a psychological point of view, it is essential to recognize that the process of intercultural adjustment goes through sequential stages. Similarly to adjusting to a foreign society after migration, the intermarried couple will go through an initial stage characterized by a mixture of excitement and confusion. Excitement is brought about by the curiosity of a new experience. Confusion is the result of the unknown and a lack of preparation. This initial stage will be followed by the next stage, in which the couple tries to separate reality from fantasy, making adjustments according to practical needs. This is the stage in which the spouses discover the differences that exist between them and try to adjust them. Much effort is needed to make this adjustment. Finally, the marriage will reach the stage where a certain balance will be obtained.

Certain differences will be tolerated and accepted, while others will be compromised and adjusted.

The process of adjustment is always dynamic. It involves both cognitive and emotional levels; it is not only conscious thoughts but also unconscious motives that count. It takes psychological work to change oneself and to adjust cognitively and emotionally. From a cultural point of view, it is useful to know that instead of continuous and steady adjustment, it is desirable to have the choice of periodical retreats to one's culture of origin. By allowing a person to return to his culture of origin occasionally, a so-called cultural regression, retreat, or vacation, he will be removed temporarily from the tension of adjustment and, through regratification or reenjoyment of his original lifestyle, will regain the strength for further adjustment and reintegration.

### c. Successful Intermarriage

Even though intercultural marriage is defined as a marriage between two persons of divergently different cultural backgrounds who theoretically need to make more of an effort to adjust to each other, many people are very successful in their adjustment (Crohn, 1995). Advantages and contributions of intermarriage have been noticed, such as a greater degree of commitment, self-other differentiation, the ability to accept, tolerate, and respect each other's differences, and broader opportunities for learning and growth (Ho, 1990). Several factors are essential for success in intermarriage adjustment including sound motivation and positive relations as foundations for marriage, mature personalities with dynamic qualities for adjustment, family and friends who support the marriage, and an accommodating environment that accepts the marriage.

## 3. Cultural Considerations in Working with Couples

In addition to using the fundamental therapeutic strategies and basic techniques utilized in "regular" marital therapy, the following issues need attention when working with couples whose cultural backgrounds are different from the therapist's, the couple is intermarried, or the partners are having culture-related marital problems.

### a. Careful Establishment of the Therapist's Relationship with Spouse-Partners

It is generally the rule for the marital therapist to be careful to maintain a well-balanced relationship between the husband and the wife in treatment, avoiding any possibility of taking sides. The similarities or dissimilarities of personal backgrounds, personalities, and gender are some common factors that may lead to complications in therapy. In terms of gender, the therapist may be seen by the couple in treatment as taking the side of the partner of the same or different gender. As an extension of this, the ethnic or racial background of the therapist and the couple can provoke the "joining" of problems between the husband and wife associated with the tendency of "identification" of the therapist with one of the partners.

In individual therapy, the ethnic or racial background of the therapist could have a significant impact on the therapist-patient relationship, in either a positive or a negative way. In marital therapy, in addition to the impact on the dyad, a forceful influence on the triad relations among the therapist and the two partners deserves careful management. Based on the similarity or differences in the cultural backgrounds of the therapist and the couple-partners, the therapist needs to aware of how their ethnic and cultural background affect the relationships among them and to determine how best to offer the couple therapy, by transcending the cultural barriers that exist between the therapist and the couple.

### b. Relevant Respect of Culturally Defined Roles and Communication Patterns

Based on their cultural backgrounds, the roles of a husband and wife are defined in terms of how they behave, interact, and relate to other people. As a therapist, it is important to recognize the preexistence of such culturally defined roles of the husband and wife and, based on this knowledge, to decide how to relate to the couple, including how to communicate them.

In many cultures, particularly those with Asian or Muslim backgrounds, there is a cultural expectation that the wife should behave submissively toward her husband. If the therapist ignores this cultural expectation and asks the wife too openly and directly to give her opinions, without asking permission from her husband, there is a potential risk of ignoring the culture-defined roles of husband and wife. This goes beyond the matter of communication patterns and is related to respecting the cultural roles expected of the husband and wife in their own cultural systems, even if it is desirable from a therapeutic point of view that they express their own opinions and communicate freely.

### c. Dynamic Understanding of Problems with Cultural Insight

When the therapist does not share the same ethnic-culture with the couple-partners in such interculture marital therapy, as in intercultural psychotherapy in general, he needs to make an effort to understand the nature of the problems presented by the couple with cultural knowledge and insight (Hsu, 2001). After relevant and meaningful understanding of the problems, based on cultural knowledge and insight, culture-relevant coping and solutions can be suggested or prescribed.

---

CASE 4

---

A Mother's Son, but Not Her Husband

A Chinese husband became depressed after his wife deserted him, returning to her family of origin. She complained that her husband was "a mother's son, but not her husband!" The family history revealed that the husband was the only and youngest son, with three elder sisters. As his father was deceased shortly after he was born, he was raised by his widowed mother alone. The mother took extra precautions in raising him and indulged him a lot, and, in return, he became a filial son and almost dependent on her. This situation become more so after his three elder sisters married and moved out, leaving the mother and son living together. He married late. Through a matchmaker, he married a woman older than he. His wife married him thinking that if he was obedient and filial to his mother, he would be a good husband who would be nice to his wife.

Things did not turn out the way the wife wished. Very soon, she found out that the tie between the mother and son was so strong that it interfered with their marital relations. For instance, even though her son was now married, the mother still kept her old habit of coming into his bedroom at night to make sure that he was properly covered with a quilt and not catching cold. The mother-in-law's behavior became intolerable to the wife and upset her more when she discovered that her husband did not have the guts to complain to his mother and stop her intrusion on their privacy.

When the couple and the mother had meals together, the husband, out of respect, would pick out some food to offer to his mother. However, he did not pick out any food for his wife. The turning point came one day when the wife bought a new bicycle. At the time of this story, it was considered an expensive item, and it took a lot of saving to purchase it. She wanted to keep her new bike inside the house when it rained. As the house was rather small, the mother-in-law complained that the bike, which was in the corridor, interfered with her walking. Her husband did not speak up on his wife's behalf. Instead, he advised her to move her new bike outside. She realized that her husband was his mother's son, and not her husband. She packed her belongings and returned to her own family.

---

From a clinical point of view, it can be said that the husband had not mastered his own individualization and was not functioning in his role as a husband. However, from a cultural point of view, the case should not be formulated so quickly. It needs to be considered that filial behavior is considered a virtue in Chinese culture. Close mother-son relationships are not only permitted, but have traditionally been glorified under the concept of filial piety. Even now, it is "morally" and "legally" expected for a child to support his aged parents, particularly a widowed mother who devoted her life to raising her son. It would be hasty for the therapist to suggest that the husband "grow up," "become autonomous," "be a man," and "join his wife as a husband!" His personal background and cultural situation needs to be understood from his perspective. Obviously he needs to restructure his intrapsychic feelings toward his mother and develop his new relationship with his wife as a husband. However, this needs to be done gradually and steadily, not abruptly. To suggest a "mother-sectomy," cutting his bonds with his mother, would be fatal and would only increase his guilt feelings and aggravate his depression. This case illustrates that cultural knowledge is not necessarily an excuse to ignore a psychopathology, but it gives the therapist a more relevant perspective for understanding, reacting to, and dealing with the therapeutic situation.

### d. Delicate Adjustment of Therapeutic Changes between Spouses

It is clear that the therapeutic process needs to be performed at a certain pace, with tenderness and in a correct direction. This is quite true in marital therapy in general. The balance between interpersonal relations and individual intrapsychic homostatis always needs consideration. This is particularly so from a cultural perspective, as emotionally embedded cultural beliefs and attitudes take time to revise. Balancing changes between husband and wife in the therapeutic process needs to be managed delicately (El-Islam, 2001) (see Case 1, The Muslum Woman with One Foot in the Past in Section 2A: Culture and Stress). For conducting marital therapy for a couple with a cultural background characterized by unequal distribution of power and status between husband and wife, even though it might be desirable to improve the wife's status and help her protect her rights and benefits, this would certainly bring about a vigorous reaction and resistance from her husband, as it would challenge his traditional status as a husband and take away his culture-given privileges as a man. Therapy needs to be undertaken in such a way that the change between husband and wife will occur gradually in a delicate and balanced way.

### e. Relevant Application of Special Marital Therapeutic Maneuvers

Based on clinical experiences, Western marital therapists have developed some special marital therapeutic maneuvers, such as "role playing" and "family sculpturing," during therapeutic sessions or the application of "paradox" approaches to deal with therapy-resistant couples of Euro-American backgrounds. However, such special therapeutic maneuvers need careful consideration for application to couples from other cultures. This is not merely because couples from other cultures are often not familiar with such therapeutic maneuvers and need more explanation and preparation before application, but because the cultural background of the couple in therapy may make the application of such special maneuvers technically difficult. It may bring about misunderstanding and negative reactions toward such therapeutic maneuvers; therefore, it may be contraindicated for application. (For details, Tseng, 2001c, Chapter 39: Working with Couples and Spouses, pp. 627–638).

### f. Relevant Concepts and Definitions of "Healthy" Couples

For therapy with an individual patient, the therapist needs to check constantly the definition of normality and health for an individual within his cultural context. In the same way, in marital therapy, the therapist is advised to examine what constitutes a functional, healthy couple within their own culture framework. Otherwise, the therapy may be misdirected.

For most couples in contemporary Euro-American cultures, it is considered desirable to communicate openly, to share their feelings, to maintain affection, and to exercise mutual respect. For couples in other cultures, such as most Eastern societies, it is considered more important to be faithful to each other, to perform complementary roles, and to maintain clear roles with divided functions. Thus, the concept of desirable couples or the definition of a healthy couple varies in different cultural settings. This needs to be examined in therapy with each couple.

### g. Thoughtful Balancing between Cultural Requirements and Professional Theory

Finally, it needs to be mentioned that there should always be a proper balance between what is expected by culture and the theoretic goals suggested by professional therapy. Marital therapy can be viewed as working with a couple suffering from differences existing between them; they can be differences in their ways of viewing things, their belief systems, or their feelings. In a way, the therapist works as a broker between the troubled couple-partners to improve mutual understanding and empathy to promote better and "healthier" relations. This is the general goal of marital therapy, based on the knowledge, experience, and theories accumulated by marital therapists. However, these professional theories are mainly derived from clinical experiences with Euro-American populations, and are embedded in Western culture. It is very important for marital therapists to adjust Western marital therapy theories for application to couples from non-Western backgrounds. The cultural adjustment of therapeutic techniques, approaches, and goals of therapy is essential.

Furthermore, it is necessary to consider the sociocultural environment within which the couple is going to live and function. Compliance and adjustment to the living environment are important parts of life. Depending on whether a Muslim couple is living in the Mideast, in the midst of Muslim culture, or has immigrated to a Euro-American society, the emphasis on adjustment of marital relations can be very different. Cultural compatibility with the living environment needs to be considered and emphasized so that meaningful, culturally relevant marital therapy can be implemented.

## F. FAMILIES

As elaborated previously (see Section 1B2: Marriage and the Family), the family is a special kind of small group that consists of members of different genders (bound by marriage) and generations (related by blood or by adoption), who maintain intense relations for a prolonged period of time. The family is the basic social unit through which culture is transmitted. From a clinical point of view, the family may manifest unique psychological problems or psychopathologies that are different from an individual perspective and need a special approach in treatment.

A clinician must have special knowledge and skills to work with a family that is having problems. Additionally, cultural considerations are essential in family therapy since the family life and behavior of family members are heavily subject to cultural impact (Ariel, 1999; DiNicola, 1985; Falicov, 1983; Mindel & Habenstein, 1981). If the clinician is working with a family of a different cultural background, it is called *intercultural* or *transcultural family therapy*, and the therapist will need a certain cultural orientation and knowledge in order to understand the family transculturally and to deal with its problems in a culturally appropriate way (Kaslow, Celano, & Dreelin, 1995; McGoldrick, Giordano, & Pearce, 1996; Sue & Sue, 1990).

### 1. Formulations of Family and Psychopathology

In order to elaborate on family pathology, it is useful to first clarify from a conceptual point of view the potential relations that may exist between individual and family pathology (Tseng & Hsu, 1991). There are various ways to formulate family psychopathology. The manifested individual abnormality could be a part of the display of the total family psychopathology (Minuchin, Rosman, & Baker, 1978). The family dynamics and environment are the sources of the development of certain individual vulnerabilities, particularly throughout his early life. The expressions of certain observed family behavior patterns are the manifestations of subclinical pathologies of parents or family members who have the same spectrum of genetic predispositions as an individual's identified disorder. Therefore, the pathologies manifested among family members are concomitant in nature, even though they may appear superficially to be different. Thus, the irrational thoughts and pseudomutual communication patterns manifested among the members of a schizophrenic family (Wyne et al., 1958) may be viewed as the concomitant, but subclinical, individual manifestations of the same schizophrenic disorder (Wender et al., 1974). Pathologies or disorders are primarily related to an individual predisposition, yet the unique environment and dynamic of the family provoke, maintain, or aggravate the individual psychopathologies. Situations may occur when family problems or dysfunctions are manifested as secondary reactions to the presence of the disorder or malfunction of an individual family member. Finally, there could be a situation in which there is both an individual pathology and a family pathology that have little interactional relation and occur coincidently. An example is the presence of an epileptic child in a substance-abusing family.

## 2. Culture-Related Family Problems: Common Issues

From a family psychiatric point of view, there are various recognized family pathologies that are difficult to describe exhaustively. Following are some examples of family problems closely related to cultural factors.

*Wide Cultural Differences between Generations.*    It is common for certain differences in viewpoint and opinion between parents and children to be brought about by age, developmental factors, and the different environments in which each generation has grown up. However, when a family faces a rapidly changing cultural environment in its own society or encounters a different sociocultural environment after migrating to an alien culture, the differences between parents and children can become great and create a large schism between generations, resulting in serious family problems. In general, the parents still stick to the traditional ways of viewing and doing things, finding it difficult to adjust to the new changes, whereas the young generation adopts the new ways of life and value systems rather quickly, tending to ignore or even despise the old views and style of life, creating a wide difference between the parents and the children. In association with this, confusion and conflict about how to raise and discipline children threatens the function and role of the parents.

*Culturally Uprooted Families among Deprived Minorities.*    When the sociocultural system of a group of people has been rapidly destroyed, families within that system will suffer from a loss of their cultural roots, resulting in deterioration of the family as a whole. This is usually manifested by parents losing their cultural methods of organizing the family and subsequently experiencing confusion about how to perform their parental functions properly. The children, meanwhile, often dissociate themselves from their parents both cognitively and emotionally and are unsure of their identities and directions in life. Such families have lost not only their own identity but also their cultural guidelines for functioning. This culture-uprooted phenomenon is observed frequently among families of many ethnic minority groups in the United States, including Native Americans, African-Americans, and south Asian refugees, as well as many other ethnic groups around the world who are facing the situation of rapidly losing their traditional culture without establishing a new one.

## 3. Special Family Problems: Some Examples

*Daughter-in-Law Abused in Hindu Family.*    The traditional Hindu family is characterized as a mother-son dyad. Based on this household structure, the daughter-in-law holds an inferior position in the family, not only to her mother-in-law but also to her brother-in-law. This creates a potential situation for the daughter-in-law to be physically and/or mentally abused by members of the extended family.

---

CASE 5

---

An Indian Woman Who Hanged Herself after Being Beaten by Her Brother-in-Law for Her Unfilial Behavior toward Her Mother-in-Law

A daughter-in-law of Hindu background was brought to the emergency room after she was found attempting to hang herself. A physical examination revealed that not only was there a fresh mark around her neck, indicating that she had tried to end her life by hanging, but numerous scars were also found all over her body. Suspecting that she was beaten by others, an inquiry was made by the physician. However, the patient kept her mouth shut, refusing to admit any intention of self-killing and denying any abuse she received. It took a while for the clinician finally to obtain information through other family members. The patient had just given birth several weeks before. As was the custom, her mother-in-law came to visit her and to see the newborn baby. The mother-in-law decided to stay with them for a couple of days. As the new mother felt weak, she asked her mother-in-law to do the laundry for her. When this was discovered by her brother-in-law, he became upset. According to custom, it was not polite for the daughter-in-law to ask the mother-in-law to do household work, even if she had just given birth and was physically weak. The brother-in-law beat the patient (his sister-in-law) severely as punishment for her impolite and unfilial behavior toward his mother. When her husband found out about this, he felt that his wife had brought disgrace to the family and beat her again. After facing such harsh treatment not only from her brother-in-law but also from her own husband, she was so frustrated that she tried to end her life. This case shows that, culturally, a certain relationship is described between a mother-in-law and a daughter-in-law, and breaking the rules of such a relationship is not tolerated. Also, according to the Hindu family system, even a brother-in-law has the authority to "discipline" his sister-in-law, if the latter does not properly follow the etiquette and rules required by the culture between a mother-in-law and a daughter-in-law.

---

*"Parental Abuse Syndrome" Described in Japan.*    Traditionally, Japanese culture emphasizes the virtue of respecting parents and authority. Therefore, it is almost unbelievable that grown-up children physically abuse their parents nowadays. However, the fact is that this is happening, according to Japanese psychiatrists. After World War II, the number of children in families declined remarkably in

Japan. There were usually only two or three at most. There was a high proba- bility that there was only one boy in the household. As a result, the boy was very indulged by his parents, not to mention his grandparents. The situation was complicated by the fact that the Japanese father was usually busy with his work, leaving early and returning home late, seldom having the opportunity to inter- act with his children. From a cultural point of view, it was considered the mother's job to raise the children. Thus, boys were raised and disciplined mostly by their mothers. According to Yoshimatsu (1984), even when the fathers were at home, the authority of the father was generally questioned and weakened; after the war, the generation of middle-age fathers lost its confidence in providing dis- cipline for its teenage sons. The mother, who seldom had the opportunity to be with her husband, usually devoted her attention and emotions to her children, especially her son. Thus, there was close contact between mother and son (even though from an anthropological point of view, the Japanese family had been described theoretically as a father-son dyad family). As a result, some boys were raised exclusively by their mothers and indulged without a prominent father figure in the household. When these boys reached adolescence, they psycholog- ically felt the need to develop a distance from their parent of the opposite sex (namely, their mothers) and tended to react violently when approached by their mothers, reacting to them with repelling action and aggression, resulting in the so-called "parent-abuse" phenomenon (see Case 1: A Japanese Adolescent Who Hit Her Mother, in Section 9B: Adolescents).

This culture-related, unique family pathology was observed not only in Japan, but was also becoming rather frequent in China, due primarily to the fact that, under the one-child-per-couple official policy, many boys were spoiled by their parents and grandparents when they were small and became violent toward their parents when they became teenagers and their demands at home were not satisfied.

*Collective Family Mental Disorder.*   Psychiatric literature has shown that occa- sionally more than one member of a family may become mentally ill through a process of contagion, forming a so-called "double insanity" or "family insanity" (*folie á deu* or *folie á familie*, in French). This psychiatric condition may take the form of dissociation, conversion, delusion, or abnormal behaviors. Although the phenomenon of *folie á familie* is considered rare, sporadic occurrences have been reported from Malaysia (Woon, 1976), Taiwan (Tseng, 1969), and the Philippines (Goduco-Angular & Wintrob, 1964) (see Section 3B: Epidemic or Collective Mental Disorders).

A review of such contagious collective family mental disorders made it apparent that in addition to the existing premorbid personality of the family members, a strong emotional bond between family members facilitated the occurrence of a collective psychiatric condition in the family, particularly when it faced a stressful situation together. To share and be involved in a similar psy- chiatric condition appeared to be an alternative way for family members to deal with the common crisis they encountered. It was speculated that such an unusual contagious family reaction tended to be observed in societies where family ties were stressed.

*Family Suicide Observed in Japan.*    Another unique family pathology is family suicide in Japan (Ohara, 1963). Family suicide refers to situations in which suicidal behavior involves multiple members of a family, occurring as the double suicide of the parents coupled with the murders of their children. It happens usually when one of the parents encounters a culturally unbearable situation, such as severe debt or an incurable disease, or becomes involved in socially disgraceful events and decides to solve the problem by ending his life. The spouse, upon learning of the contemplated suicide, consents to die also. Eventually the parents kill their young children and finally kill themselves, or they make plans for the whole family to die together, perhaps by taking poison (see Fig. 6, in Section 3A: Culture-Related Specific Syndromes).

## 4. Cultural Considerations of Family Therapy

*Applicability of Family Therapy.*    Family therapy should be considered and applied whenever it is indicated and necessary, as long as the problems are dynamic or closely related to family relations, or there is a need to mobilize family resources and make good use of the input of family members to cope with and adjust to problems. It has been suggested that family therapy is particularly appropriate and indicated for ethnic-cultural groups that emphasize family structure in their life patterns, such as the Italians, Portuguese, or Chinese. Clinical experience, however, has shown that an emphasis on family and close family interrelations does not directly favor the family therapy approach. As pointed out by Moitoza (1982), Portuguese families' closed family system prevents them from actively seeking family therapy; instead, they attempt to solve their problems via their own family resources and support systems. When a close family seeks therapy, the family's values and tight intermember relations can be utilized; it will usually take considerable effort, however, for a therapist to work on the intense and complicated family dynamics. Alternatively, it cannot be assumed that family-oriented therapy is unsuitable for families of cultural groups that deemphasize the family system and place more relative value on an individual system. Family therapy may actually prove to be particularly useful to such unlikely candidates by providing an opportunity for self-examination of the relatively neglected aspects of their lives (i.e., the family system) as well as by encouraging them to place more value on the function of the family.

*Therapist-Family Relationship.*    When the family to be treated has a different cultural background than the therapist, cultural effects on the therapist-family relationship need to be closely examined from the very beginning of contact. Three areas need special attention. First, ethnic/racial/cultural transference in the therapist-client relationship needs to be evaluated and addressed. The same principle and management applied in individual therapy may be extended to family therapy (see Section 7A: Intercultural Psychotherapy: Challenges and Competency). Second, there is a need to respect and utilize the culturally defined and sanctioned family hierarchy and relations already existing within the family. Who is the ultimate authority in the household (father, mother, grandmother)? Who needs to be respected and needs to utilize his power to control the family behavior? Does any hierarchical relation exist between the husband and wife, or do they relate and function equally? These things need to be found out, and caution needs to be taken not to ignore them. Even among children, does any hierarchy exist due to gender or birth order? It would be a mistake to allow a younger sister to make comments that indicated a lack of respect toward older brothers if a gender/age hierarchy is valued among the siblings (see Section 1B2 Marriage and Family). Finally, there is a need to be aware of and carefully manage the effect of the therapist's own cultural background and value system on the process and direction of treatment, particularly if the therapist and the family have ethnic/cultural differences. These include basic family issues, such as how family members should relate to each other, how to make decisions, who has the final authority, and what kind of coping is considered functional, all subject to cultural impact and bias beyond therapeutic choice (Hsu, 1983).

*Matching of Treatment Methods.*    Many different schools or modalities of therapy have been described and emphasized by various groups of therapists (Crespi, 1988; F. W. Kaslow, 1982). Is there any particular fit between the family types and the choice of treatment? Unfortunately, this issue has not yet been thoroughly examined, particularly from a cross-cultural perspective. However, there are some suggestions derived from clinical experience. For example, Falicov (1982), investigating Mexican families, and Minuchin and co-workers (1967), working with Chicano families, have proposed that the cultural emphasis on hierarchies within these families lends itself to a structural family therapy approach. In contrast, Herz and Rosen (1982) mentioned that the Jewish family closely relates to a cultural tendency of treasuring suffering as a shared value. By emphasizing the verbal expression of feelings in family therapy, the focus of therapy on this process and interaction can motivate Jewish families to see talking and insight as relevant solutions. Zuk (1978) has pointed out that Jews generally do well in family therapy. The favorable response of Jewish families stems from their cultural emphasis on high familism, high egalitarianism, maternal intrusiveness, verbal rather than physical aggressiveness, an assertive stance toward problem solving, and the maintenance of a scapegoat theme. Zuk suggested that, in treating Jewish families, it is important to keep this entire set of values in mind rather than any one particular value.

In summary, the purpose of family therapy can be described from a cultural perspective as working on the cultural system of the family in various ways, with the aim of promoting the function of the family. In the treatment of an individual, it is necessary to define what is considered a "healthy" or "functional" persona as a standard to guide the course of therapy. Analogously, in family therapy, it is necessary to visualize a well-functioning, normal family as the final goal toward which treatment is directed. The concept of a "functional" or "healthy" family needs to be defined carefully and elaborated further in therapy for families of different cultural groups so that it is consistent with the relevant cultural background.

## REFERENCES

### A. Children

Americal Psychiatric Association. (1994). *Diagnostic and statistical manual of mental disorders* (4th ed.). Washington, DC: American Psychiatric Association.

Canino, I., Canino, G., & Arroyo, W. (1998). Cultural considerations for childhood disorders: How much was included in DSM-IV? *Transcultural Psychiatry, 35*(3), 343–355.

Canino, I., & Spurlock, J. (1994). *Culturally diverse children and adolescents: Assessment, diagnosis, and treatment.* New York: Guilford Press.

Fish, J. E., & Larr, C. J. (1972). A decade of change in drawings by black children. *American Journal of Psychiatry, 129*(4), 421–426.

Greefield, P. M. (1994). Independence and interdependence as developmental scripts: Implications for theory, research, and practice. In P. M. Greenfield & R. R. Cocking (Eds.), *Cross-cultural roots of minority child development.* Hillsdale, NJ: Erlbaum.

Greenfield, P. M., & Cocking, R. R. (Eds.). (1994). *Cross-cultural roots of minority child development.* Hillsdale, NJ: Erlbaum.

Griffith, E. E. H. (1995a). Culture and the debate on adoption of Black children by White families. In J. M. Oldham & M. B. Riba (Eds.), *American psychiatric press review of psychiatry* (Vol. 14) (pp. 543–564). Washington, DC: American Psychiatric Press.

Griffith, E. E. H. (1995b). Forensic and policy implications of the transracial adoption debate. *Bulletin of the American Academic Psychiatry and Law, 23*(4), 501–512.

Griffith, E. E. H., & Silverman, I. L. (1995). Transracial adoptions and the continuing debate on the racial identity of families. In H. W. Harris, H. C. Blue, & E. E. H. Grifith (Eds.), *Racial and ethnic identity: Psychological development and creative expression.* New York: Routledge.

Hill, M., & Peltzer, J. (1982). A report of thirteen groups for White parents of Black children. *Family Relations: Journal of Applied Family and Child Studies, 31*(4), 557–565.

Hsu, C. C., Yang, Y. K., Yeh, T. L., Chen, S. J., & Luo, J. M. (1995). Reading success and failure in logographic writing systems: Children learning to read Chinese do evidence reading disabilities. In T. Y. Lin, W. S. Tseng, & Y. K. Yeh (Eds.), *Chinese societies and mental health* (pp. 93–105). Hong Kong: Oxford University Press.

Hsu, J. (1983). Asian family interaction patterns and their therapeutic implications. *International Journal of Family Psychiatry, 4*(4), 307–320.

Joe, J. R. (1994). Revaluing native-American concepts of development and education. In P. M. Greenfield & R. R. Cocking (Eds.), *Cross-cultural roots of minority child development.* Hillsdale, NJ: Erlbaum.

Johnson, R. O. (1981). The socioeconomic context of child abuse and neglect in native South America. In J. E. Korbin (Ed.), *Child abuse and neglect: Cross-cultural perspectives* (pp. 56–70). Berkeley: University of California Press.

Korbin, J. E. (Ed.). (1981). *Child abuse and neglect: Cross-cultural perspectives.* Berkeley: University of California Press.

Krugman, R. D. (1996). Child abuse and neglect: A worldwide problem. In F. Lih Mak & C. C. Nadelson (Eds.), *International Review of Psychiatry* (Vol. 2) (pp. 367–377). Washington, DC, American Psychiatric Press.

LeVine, S., & LeVine, R. (1981). Child abuse and neglect in Sub-Saharan Africa. In J. E. Kobin (Ed.), *Child abuse and neglect: Cross-cultural perspectives* (pp. 35–55). Berkeley: University of California Press.

Littlewood, R., & Lipsedge, M. (1989). *Aliens and alienists: Ethnic minorities and psychiatry* (2nd ed.). London: Unwin Human.

Makita, K. (1968). The rarity of reading disability in Japanese children. *American Journal of Orthopsychiatry, 38,* 599–614.

Maitra, B. (1996). Child abuse: A universal 'diagnostic' category? The implication of culture in definition and assessment. *International Journal of Social Psychiatry, 42*(4), 287–304.

Mann, E. M., Ikeda, Y., Mueller, C. W., Takahashi, A. H., Tao, K. T., Humris, E., Li, B. L., & Chin, D. (1992). Cross-cultural differences in rating hyperactive-disruptive behaviors in children. *American Journal of Psychiatry, 149*(11), 1539–1542.

Meston, C. M., Heiman, J. R., Trapnell, P. D., & Carlin, A. S. (1999). Ethnicity, desirable responding, and self-reports of abuse: A comparison of European- and Asian-ancestry undergraduates. *Journal of Consulting and Clinical Psychology, 67*(1), 139–144.

Moghal, N. E., Nota, I. K., & Hobbs, C. J. (1995). A study of sexual abuse in an Asian community. *Archives of Diseases in Childhood, 72*(4), 346–347.

Poffenberger, T. (1981). Child rearing and social structure in rural India: Toward a cross-cultural definition of child abuse and neglect. In J. E. Korbin (Ed.), *Child abuse and neglect: Cross-cultural perspectives* (pp. 71–95). Berkeley: University of California Press.

Powell, G. J. (Ed.) (1983). *The psychosocial development of minority group children.* New York: Brunner/Mazel.

Simon, R. (1993). Transracial adoption: Highlights of a twenty-year study. *Reconstruction, 2*(2), 130–131.

Stevenson, H., & Stewart, E. (1958). A developmental study of racial awareness in young children. *Child Development, 29,* 399–409.

Tseng, W. S., & Hsu, J. (1972). The Chinese attitude toward parental authority as expressed in Chinese children's stories. *Archives of General Psychiatry, 26,* 28–34.

Uribe, F. M. T., Levine, R. A., & Levine, S. E. (1994). Maternal behavior in a Mexican community: The changing environments of children. In P. M. Greenfield & R. R. Cocking (Eds.), *Cross-cultural roots of minority child development.* Hillsdale, NJ: Erlbaum.

Vargas, L. A., & Koss-Chioino, J. D. (1992). *Working with culture: Psychotherapeutic interventions with ethnic minority children and adolescents.* San Francisco: Jossey-Bass.

Wagatsuma, H. (1981). Child abandonment and infanticide: A Japanese case. In J. E. Kobin (Ed.), *Child abuse and neglect: Cross-cultural perspectives* (pp. 120–138). Berkeley: University of California Press.

Wu, D. Y. H. (1981). Child abuse in Taiwan. In J.E. Korbin (Ed.), *Child abuse and neglect: Cross-cultural perspectives* (pp. 139–165). Berkeley: University of California Press.

## B.  Adolescents

Bar-On, D. (1993). Children as unintentional transmitters of undiscussable traumatic life events. Presented at the Congress on Children—War and Persecution, Hamburg, Germany.

Becker, D., Lira, E., Castillo, M. I., Gomez, E., & Kovalskys, J. (1990). Therapy with victims of polit-ical repression in Chile: The challenge of social reparation. *Journal of Social Issues, 46*(3), 133–149.

Gibbs, J. T. (1987). Identity and marginality: Issues in the treatment of biracial adolescents. *American Journal of Orthopsychiatry, 57*(2), 265–278.

Mead, M. (1928). *Coming of age in Samoa.* New York: Morrow.

National Institute on Drug Abuse. (1995). *Drug use among racial/ethnic minorities.* Rockville, MD: National Institute of Health.

Nguyen, N., & Willams, H. (1989). Transition from East to West: Vietnamese adolescents and their parents. *Journal of the American Academy of Child and Adolescent Psychiatry, 28*, 505–515.

Smart, R., Murray, G. F., & Arif, A. (1988). Drug abuse and prevention programs in 29 countries. *International Journal of the Addictions, 23*, 1–17.

Vargas, L. A., & Koss-Chioino, J. D. (1992). *Working with culture: Psychotherapeutic interventions with ethnic minority children and adolescents.* San Francisco: Jossey-Bass.

## C. Aged Persons

Baker, F. M., & Takeshita, J. (2001). The elderly. In W. S. Tseng & J. Streltzer (Eds.), *Culture and psy-chotherapy: A guide for clinical practice.* Washington, DC: American Psychiatric Press.

Butler, R. N. (1974). Successful aging and the role of the life review. *Journal of American Geriatrics Society, 22*(12), 529–535.

Grant, R. W. (1995). Interventions with ethnic minority elderly. In J. F. Aponte, R. Y. Rivers, & J. Wohl (Eds.), *Psychological interventions and cultural diversity.* Boston: Allyn and Bacon.

Niederehe, G. T. (1994). Psychosocial therapies with depressed older adults. In L. S. Schneider, C. F. Reynolds III, B. D. Lebowitz & A. J. Friedhoff (Eds.), *Diagnosis and treatment of depression in late life.* Washington, DC: American Psychiatric Press.

## D. Women

Abbey, S. E., & Stewart, D. E. (2000). Gender and psychosomatic aspects of ischemic heart disease. *Journal of Psychosomatic Research, 48*, 417–423.

Castillo, R. J. (1997). Sexual and gender identity disorders. In R. J. Castillo, *Culture and mental illness: A client-centered approach* (pp. 113–147). Pacific Grove, CA: Brooks/Cole.

Chang, H. I., & Kim, H. W. (1988). The study of the "house-wife syndrome" in Korea—With special concern with neurotic symptoms and family strains. *Asian Family Mental Health* (pp. 194–204). Tokyo: Psychiatric Research Institute of Tokyo.

Commas-Díaz, L., & Greene, B. (Eds.). (1994). *Women of color: Integrating ethnic and gender identities in psychotherapy.* New York: Guilford Press.

Kohen, D. (2000a). Psychiatric services for women. In D. Kohen (Ed.), *Women and mental health* (pp. 218–232). London: Routledge.

Kohen, D. (Ed.). (2000b). *Women and mental health.* London: Routledge.

Krane, J. E. (1996). Violence against women in intimate relations: Insight from cross-cultural analysis. *Transcultural Psychiatric Research Review, 33*(4), 435–465.

Holmshaw, J., & Hillier, S. (2000). Gender and culture: A sociological perspective to mental health problems in women. In D. Kohen (Ed.), *Women and mental health* (pp. 39–64). London: Routledge.

Murdock, G. P. (1967). *Ethnographic atlas.* Pittsburgh: University of Pittsburgh Press.

Nadelson, C. C. & Zimmerman V. (1993). Culture and psychiatric care of women. In A. C. Gaw (Ed.), *Culture, ethnicity, and mental illness* (pp. 501–515). Washington, D.C.: American Psychiatric Press.

Palazidou, E. (2000). Depression in women. In D. Kohen (Ed.), *Women and mental health* (pp. 106–132). London: Routledge.

Pritchard, C. (1996). Suicide in the People's Republic of China categorized by age and gender: Evidence of the influence of culture on suicide. *Acta Psychiatrica Scandinavica, 93,* 362–367.

Roter, D. L., & Hall, J. A. (1998). Why physician gender matters in shaping the physician-patient relationship. *Journal of Womens Health, 7*(9), 1093–1097.

Sanday, P. R. (1981). The socio-cultural context of rape: A cross-cultural study. *Journal of Social Issues, 37*(4), 5–27.

Stewart, D. E., Rondon, M., Damiani, G., & Honikman, J. (2001). International psychosocial and systemic issues in women's mental health. *Archives of Women's Mental Health. 4,* 13–17.

# E.  Couples

Chang, H. I., & Kim, H. W. (1988). The study of the "house-wife syndrome" in Korea—with special concern with neurotic symptoms and family strains. *Asian Family Mental Health Conference Proceedings.* Tokyo: Psychiatric Research Institute of Tokyo.

Char, W. (1977). Motivations for Intercultural Marriage. In W. S. Tseng, J. F. McDermott, Jr. & T. W. Maretzki (Eds.), *Adjustment in intercultural marriage* (pp. 33–40). Honolulu: University of Hawaii School of Medicine, Department of Psychiatry.

Cohen, N. (1982). Same or different? A problem in identity in cross-cultural marriages. *Journal of Family Therapy, 4*(2), 177–199.

Counts, D. A. (1987). Female suicide and wife abuse: A cross-cultural perspective. *Suicide and life Threatening Behavior, 17*(3), 194–204.

Crohn, J. (1995). Mixed matches: How to create successful interracial, interethnic, and interfaith relationships. New York: Fawcett Columbine.

Davidson, J. R. (1992). Theories about Black-White interracial marriage: A clinical perspective. *Journal of Multicultural Counseling and Development, 20*(4), 150–157.

Eaton, S. C. (1994). Marriage between Jews and non-Jews: Counseling implications. *Journal of Multicultural Counseling and Development, 22*(4), 210–214.

El-Islam, F. M. (2001). The woman with one foot in the past. In W. S. Tseng & J. Streltzer (Eds.), *Culture and psychotherapy: A guide to clinical practice* (pp. 27–41). Washington, DC: American Psychiatric Press.

Heise, L., Raikes, A., Watts, C., & Zwi, A. (1994). Violence against women: A neglected public health issues in less developed countries. *Social Science Medicine, 39*(9), 1165–1179.

Ho, M. K. (1990). *Intermarried couples in therapy.* Springfield, IL: Charles C. Thomas.

Hsu, J. (2001). Marital therapy for intermarried couples. In W. S. Tseng, & J. Streltzer (Eds.), *Culture and psychotherapy: A guide to clinical practice* (pp. 225–242). Washington, DC: American Psychiatric Press.

Krane, J. E. (1996). Violence against women in intimate relations: Insight from cross-cultural analysis. *Transcultural Psychiatric Research Review, 33*(4), 435–465.

Lateef, S. (1992). Wife abuse among Indo-Fijians. In D. A. Counts, J. Brown, & J. Campbell (Eds.), *Sanctions and sanctuary: Cultural perspectives on the beating of wives.* Boulder, CO: Westview Press.

Levinson, D. (1989). *Family violence in cross-cultural perspective.* Newbury Park, CA: Sage Publications.

Tseng, W. S. (2001a). Culture-embedded indigenous healing practices. In W. S. Tseng, *Handbook of cultural psychiatry* (pp. 515–537). San Diego, CA: Academic Press.

Tseng, W. S. (2001b). Intercultural marriage: Problems and therapy. In W. S. Tseng, *Handbook of cultural psychiatry* (pp. 729–746). San Diego, CA: Academic Press.

Tseng, W. S. (2001c). Working with couples and spouses. In W. S. Tseng, Handbook of cultural psychiatry (pp. 627–638). San Diego, CA: Academic Press.

United Nations. (1989). *Violence against women in the family.* New York: United Nations Publication.

## F. Families

Ariel, S. (1999). *Culturally competent family therapy: A general model.* Westport, CT: Greenwood.

Crespi, T. D. (1988). Specifications and guidelines for specialization in family therapy: Implications for practicum supervisors. *International Journal of Family Psychiatry, 9,* 181–191.

DiNicola, V. F. (1985). Family therapy and transcultural psychiatry: An emerging synthesis. Part II: Portability and cultural change. *Transcultural Psychiatric Research Review, 22,* 151–180.

Falicov, C. J. (1982). Mexican families. In M. McGoldrick, J. K. Pearce, & J. Giordano (Eds.), *Ethnicity and family therapy* (pp. 134–163). New York: Guilford Press.

Falicov, C. J. (Vol. Ed.). (1983). *Cultural perspectives in family therapy.* Rockville, MD: Aspen.

Goduco-Angular, C., & Wintrob, R. (1964). *Folie á famille* in the Philippines. *Psychiatric Quarterly, 38,* 278–291.

Herz, F. M., & Rosen, E. J. (1982). Jewish families. In M. McGoldrick, J. K. Pearce, & J. Giordano (Eds.), *Ethnicity and family therapy* (pp. 364–392). New York: Guilford Press.

Hsu, J. (1983). Asian family interaction patterns and their therapeutic implications. *International Journal of Family Psychiatry, 4*(4), 307–320.

Kaslow, F. W. (Ed.). (1982). *The international book of family therapy.* New York: Brunner/Mazel.

Kaslow, N. J., Celano, M., & Dreelin, E. D. (1995). A cultural perspective on family theory and therapy. *Psychiatric Clinics of North America, 18*(3), 621–633.

McGoldrick, M., Giordano, J., & Pearce, J. K. (1996). Overview: Ethnicity and family therapy. In M. McGoldrick, J. Giordano, & J. K. Pearce (Eds.), *Ethnicity and family therapy* (2nd ed.). New York: Guilford Press.

Mindel, C. H., & Habenstein, R. W. (Eds.). (1981). *Ethnic families in America: Patterns and variations* (2nd ed.). New York: Elsevier.

Minuchin, S., Montalvo, B., Guerney, B. G., Rosman, B. L., & Schumer, B. G. (1967). *Families of the slums.* New York: Basic Books.

Minuchin, S., Rosman, B. L., & Baker, L. (1978). *Psychosomatic families: Anorexia nervosa in context.* Cambridge, MA: Harvard University Press.

Moitoza, E. (1982). Portuguese families. In M. McGoldrick, J. K. Pearce, & J. Giordano (Eds.), *Ethnicity and family therapy* (pp. 412–437). New York: Guilford Press.

Ohara, K (1963). Characteristics of suicides in Japan, especially of parent-child double suicide. *American Journal of Psychiatry, 120*(4), 382–385.

Sue, D. W., & Sue, D. (1990). Cross-cultural family counseling. In D. W. Sue & D. Sue, *Counseling the culturally different: Theory and practice.* New York: Wiley.

Tseng, W. S. (1969). A paranoid family in Taiwan: A dynamic study of *folie á famille. Archives of General Psychiatry, 21,* 55–63.

Tseng, W. S., & Hsu, J. (1991). *Culture and family: Problems and therapy.* New York: Haworth Press.

Wender, P. H., Rosenthal, D., Kety, S. S., Schulsinger, F., & Welner, J. (1974). Crossfostering: A research strategy for clarifying the role of genetic and experiential factors in the etiology of schizophrenia. *Archives of General Psychiatry, 30,* 121–128.

Woon, T. H. (1976). Epidemic hysteria in a Malaysian Chinese extended family. *Medical Journal of Malaysia, 31,* 108–112.

Wyne, L. C., Ryckoff, I. M., Day, J., & Hirsch, S. I. (1958). Pseudo-mutuality in the family relations of schizophrenia. *Psychiatry, 21,* 205–220.

Yoshimatsu, K. (1984). *Parent abuse in Japanese culture.* Presented at the Japanese Culture and Mental Health Conference. East-West Center, Honolulu.

Zuk, G. H. (1978). A therapist's perspective on Jewish family values. *Journal of Marriage and Family Counseling, 4,* 103–110.

# CHAPTER 10

# Culture-Oriented Care of Different Ethnic Groups

In order to perform culturally competent psychiatric care, a clinician should have several qualities, including cultural sensitivity, cultural knowledge, cultural empathy, the ability to establish culture-relevant relations and interactions, and the ability to provide culture-suitable guidance (see Section 5A: The Need for Cultural Competence). Regarding cultural knowledge, it is essential to know the cultural aspects of human behavior in general (see Section 1B: How Does Culture Impact Mind and Behavior?), including the impact of culture on stress and coping (see Section 2: Culture, Stress, and Illness Reaction). It is also desirable to have specific knowledge about the social, ethnic, and cultural background of the patient.

It would be impossible for a mental health care provider to have all existing medical anthropological wisdom. However, in the United States, it would be preferable for a clinician to have fundamental cultural and mental health knowledge of at least the main ethnic-cultural groups recognized. Studying some, if not all, of the major ethnic groups would sensitize and stimulate clinicians regarding the need for knowledge of diverse cultures. This is the reason that, in this chapter, several ethnic groups are chosen for examination, including African-American, Asian-American, European-American, Hispanic-American, and Native-American.

It would be difficult to discuss inclusively all the ethnic or cultural groups in our society. Even within the identified ethnic or cultural group, there usually exist many subgroups, with variations. This is compounded by additional social factors, such as language used, level of education, degree of acculturation to the host society, religious background, and socioeconomic status, as well as individual, gender, family, and generational factors. However, describing "cultural commonalities" or "ethnic characteristics" for each group and examining some basic differences among those major groups will be sufficient for the clinician to start recognizing the similarities and variations existing among them. Based on such sensitivity and awareness, it is hoped that more detailed studies can be carried out and knowledge expanded, depending on the individual clinical situations encountered.

Before we start to examine each representative major group present in the United States, several issues need to be clarified. As has been discussed earlier (see Section 1B1: What Is Culture?), culture is usually addressed on different levels (i.e., the ideal, practical, stereotypical, and deviated). It will be useful for us to be aware of the level on which the subject is described and discussed. It is also important to be aware that even the same cultural group is subject to change associated with time and geographic modification. There is always considerable diversity observed within a group rather than differences between groups. We can only discuss the most common patterns or the most usual modes, leaving a clinician to make a judgment based on the individual concerned. Overgeneralization or stereotyping should be minimized. What is discussed here should serve merely as a guide for further examination and elaboration.

Finally, it needs to be pointed out that it is not the primary intention of this chapter to deal extensively with all ethnic groups in the United States or other parts of the world. There are numerous publications that have appeared with descriptions of them in detail, particularly from the perspective of historical and demographic backgrounds, which deserve further reading (Cuéllar & Paniagua, 2000; Department of Health and Human Services, 2001; Gaw, 1993; McGoldrick, Giordano, & Pearce, 1996; Paniagua, 1998; Powell et al., 1983—see Suggested Further Readings). Here, after a brief introduction to the various ethnic groups, the thrust is toward mental health problems and therapeutic suggestions for clinical application.

## A. AFRICAN-AMERICAN GROUPS

### 1. General Issues

#### a. Demographic Information

African-American refers to the descent of the people who were brought to the America from Africa during the era of slavery between the 16th and 19th centuries (Black, 1996). It also includes the recent immigrants from the African continent (Egypt, Ethiopia, Ghana, Nigeria), the Caribbean (Barbados, Haiti, Tinidad), and Central America (Panama).

According to Lindsey and Cuéllar (2000, p. 196), the African-American population is growing at 1.3%, one of the slowest rates of all ethnic populations in the United States. The percentage of them in the United States in the year 2000 was 11.9% (U. S. Bureau of the Census, 2000); nevertheless, it is projected to be 14.0% in 2020 and 15.4% in 2050 (U. S. Bureau of the Census, 1997). In spite of the Great Migration to the North, a large African-American population remained in the South. According to a survey (U.S. Census Bureau, 2001), 53% of all African-Americans live in the South, 37% in the Northeast and Midwest, mostly in metropolitan areas, and 10% in the West. Even though many African-American are successful in professional careers and are becoming affluent economically, when considered in aggregate, they are relatively poor. In 1999, about 22% of African-American families had incomes below the poverty line, compared to only 10% of all U.S. families (U.S. Bureau of the Census, 2001). Many African-Americans still live in segregated neighborhoods.

### b. Cultural Considerations

*Compound and Conflicting Values.*   In order to comprehend African-American culture, it is necessary to understand its three sources, namely, the residual culture from Africa, the main culture of America, and the culture relating to the adaptation and responses to the "victim" system that they encountered through the history of slavery associated with racism, poverty, and oppression (Pinderhughes, 1979). Traditionally, African values stress the importance of collectivity, sharing, affiliation, obedience to authority, belief in spirituality, and respect for the elderly and the past. This is different from and conflicts with the mainstream culture, which emphasizes individualism, independence, autonomy, ownership of material goods, efficiency, achievement, performance, and success. The victim system is a circular feedback process. Barriers to opportunity and education limit the chance for achievement, employment, and attainment of skill. This limitation can, in turn, lead to poverty or stress in relationships, which interferes with the adequate performance of the individual and the family (Pinderhuges, 1982).

*Valuing Religion and Spirituality.*   A strong religious orientation and emphasis on spirituality were major aspects of the lives of black people in Africa and during the era of slavery. Actually, spirituality sustained African-Americans during their time of servitude as slaves. The church was of key importance in the escape of blacks from the oppression of slavery (Hines & Boyd-Franklin, 1982). When their native religions were forbidden, they adopted the religion of their captors and found support in that. In some places, the African gods were cleverly blended with the Christian God and saints, and so preserved aspects of the "Old Country" faith (Black, 1996). Outlets for expression of feelings about their humiliation, pain, and anger were few during the era of slavery, and music and the ecstatic celebration of salvation provided a means of expressing these feelings. The church continues to serve numerous functions for members of the African-American community in present times, but people are currently represented in a number of different religious groups, such as Baptist, African Methodist, Jehovah's Witness, Church of God in Christ, Seventh Day Adventist, and Nation of Islam. The impact of these religious groups on the lives of African-Americans is a complex phenomena (Hines & Boyd-Franklin, 1982).

*Women's Role and Work.*    People of African descent are usually more accepting of women working outside the home. The tradition existed in Africa, where it was recognized that women's contributions to the family and the village life went beyond childbearing and child rearing. Women were also providers of food, organizers of community life, and, in some societies, leaders and rulers (Black, 1996, p. 61). In the contemporary Americas, it has been easier for women of African descent to find work than for the men.

*Differences within Subgroups.*    Although the people of African descent who live in the United States share many similarities, they also have distinct differences, which derive from the myriad cultures they have experienced across the generations, coupled with their particular migration patterns. For instance, those who came from the former British Caribbean islands will have incorporated aspects of English culture, manifesting formal manners and reserved behavior. They are less likely to think of themselves as minorities than African-Americans because where they grew up they were the numerical majority. Black people from the former Spanish colonies of Central and South America and the Carribean will exhibit the influence of Spanish culture. There are also people from French and Dutch colonies; the beliefs and cultural styles of a person from Haiti will be as different from those of a person from Brazil as a white French person's are from a white Portuguese person's (Black, 1996, pp. 63–64).

## 2. Mental-Health-Related Problems

### a. Common Psychological Issues

*Effects of Slavery, Racism, and Discrimination.*    In seeking to understand the common characteristics of people of African descent, it is important to know what makes them different from all other immigrants to the New World. Psychologically they have experienced the history of slavery, a deliberate attempt to destroy the core and soul of the people, while keeping their bodies in enforced servitude. They have encountered racism and discrimination, ongoing efforts to continue the psychological and economic subjugation started during slavery. They have suffered from the victim system, a process by which individuals and communities are denied access to the instruments of development and advancement, and then blamed for low levels of accomplishment and achievement (Black, 1996, p. 59).

*Defensive Behavior against Discrimination.*    In order to deal with discrimination from the majority group, historically African-Americans developed certain coping patterns which, even now, comprise a part of the character of some of the them. "Healthy paranoia" shared by ordinary African-Americans (i.e., feelings and thoughts that others are conspiring to do one harm) is seen as (ordinary) defensive behavior in response to racism (Lindsey & Cuéllar, 2000, p. 202). "Withdrawal strategy" is another coping mechanism when they are dealing with the majority (i.e., withdrawing from interaction with the majority group).

*Issues Relating to Ethnic Identity and Self-Confidence.*    Ethnic identity refers to the psychological way in which a person identifies with his own ethnic background and how he feels about his own ethnicity. Ethnic or racial identity can be changed over the time. Due to the inferior position that African-Americans have experienced in the past, they have suffered from negative ethnic identity and, consequently, low self-confidence. However, this is changing remarkably in association with the emphasis on basic human rights and the "Black is beautiful" movement. Recently, African-American children have had a more positive image of themselves as African-Americans than they did several decades ago (Fish & Larr, 1972). In the 1950s, studies of racial preference of children consistently showed black children choosing white models and rejecting dark models. However, since the 1960s, a reversal of this position has been observed, with blacks choosing more dark models. This means that African-American children are more positively aware and accepting of their racial and ethnic background now than they were before (Harris, Blue, & Griffith, 1995).

### b. Psychiatric Disorders

As mentioned previously (see Section 4B: Depression Disorders) studies in the Epidemiologic Catchment Area carried out in the 1980s, it was found that there were higher rates of all mental disorders studied among African-Americans than among Caucasian-Americans or Hispanic-Americans (Regier & Kelber, 1995). However, when socioeconomic status (SES) was controlled, rates for African-Americans were not higher than for Caucasian-Americans.

Mauer (1999) reports that nearly half of the prison inmates nationally are African-American, even though they occupy only about one-tenth of the total population. This suggests that a relatively large number of African-Americans, males in particular, have major problems navigating and benefiting from the existing educational, employment, financial, and legal systems.

### c. Mental Health Service Utilization

African-American patients have shown consistently higher admission rates to inpatient services in the public system than Europeans and other ethnic groups in the past half century. African-Americans are also disproportionately misdiagnosed on admission, with more diagnoses of severe mental disorders (Manderscheid & Sonnenschein, 1987). It has also been pointed out that African-Americans tend to enter mental health treatment services at a later stage in the course of their illness and tend to drop out of service.

---

CASE 1

An African-American Law School Student Struggling with Race and Class Tension (abstracted from Blue & Griffith, 2001).

Mr. Robinson is a 25-year-old, single, African-American man, a first-year student in law school. He was referred by his professor to the counseling clinic for his serious doubts about his future and feeling completely out of place. He presented the complaint that he was in a state of "academic paralysis." He described the law school, unlike his previous college, as inflexible. Additionally, he reported sensing "racial" and "economic class" tension between himself and his classmates, who were almost all white.

He was born and reared in the South and was the oldest and the only male of three children. His father worked as a janitor and his mother was an unskilled farm laborer. Neither parent had completed school beyond junior high. His father was functionally illiterate. Despite this, his parents encouraged him to pursue higher education, and he always felt that he needed to be a "model of success." He was a stellar student and graduated at the top of his high school class. Although he was accepted by a number of a Ivy League schools, he chose to attend one of the historically black colleges, where he did well. Again he excelled and was convinced by a college mentor to pursue an academic career. When his father become ill, he felt that he needed to pursue a "more sure career sooner rather than later." When he applied to a law school at a predominantly white college, his problems started.

In therapy, the counselor helped him to recognize that his emotionally charged intellectual discourse about race and racism, although valid and important, served to mask other core psychological concerns and prevented him from exploring other important themes. He became more aware of long-standing feelings of marginalization that resulted from the extreme poverty he had experienced and from the increasing distance he felt between himself and his family. This insight helped place in context his feelings of alienation in relation to his classmates, with whom he admittedly had not pursued closer relationships.

## 3. Therapeutic Considerations and Clinical Suggestions

When treating African-American patients, the first thing that the therapist needs to consider is his own ethnic or racial background, his attitude toward African-Americans in general, and his understanding of them. The matter of ethnic or racial transference and countertransference needs to be assessed and dealt with from the very beginning of therapy and any time it becomes necessary. If it is sensed that the issues of racism have a strong impact on the therapist–patient relationship, they need to be dealt with right away. Otherwise, therapy will go nowhere and tend to fail. In other words, developing trust in the working therapeutic relationship is crucial when the patient is treated by a therapist of a different ethnic background, particularly by a white therapist.

It is very important for the therapist to be aware of the diversity that exists among African-Americans in term of their socioeconomic status, level of education, degree of acculturation to the main stream, religious background, and their attitudes toward the therapist's ethnic or cultural background, so that the individual patient can be understood beyond the stereotype.

In general, besides the common clinical issues presented by the patient, it is always important to pay attention to and assess matters relating to the patient's self-image and any problems relating to ethnic identity. It is also useful to focus and work on any anger and hostility that they may have toward the mainstream and society as a whole (Vontress & Epp, 1997).

## B. ASIAN-AMERICAN GROUPS

### 1. General Issues

#### a. Demographic Information

Asian-Americans include people originally from Eastern Asia of China, Japan, and Korea, or Southeast Asia, such as the Philippines, Vietnam, Laos, Cambodia, Thailand, and India. Sometimes Pacific Islanders from Micronesia (Guam), Hawaii, and Samoa are included. Outsiders refer to all as "Asian," because they look alike, but actually they belong to diverse groups with different languages and cultures, histories of migration, and levels of acculturation to the host society and are characterized by continuity, diversity, and change (Kitano & Maki, 1996).

There has been a remarkable increase in the populations of many Asian-American groups during the last three decades. For instance, from 1970 to 1990, the number of Chinese has increased 3.8 times (from 435,062 to 1,645,472); Filipinos, 4.1 time (from 343,060 to 1,406,770); and Koreans, 11.6 times (from

69,130 to 798,849) (Kitano & Maki, 1996). Between 1990 and 2000, there was a continuous increase in the number of Filipinos (to 1,819,444) and Koreans (to 1,063,326) (U.S. Bureau of the Census, 2000). This was the combined result of birth increases and the arrival of new migrants. The only group with a moderate population increase was the Japanese, whose influx of new residents through immigration was minimal.

Asian-Americans (and Pacific Islanders) are heavily concentrated in the western United States. According to statistics, in 2000 more than half of this group (54%) lived in the West, while a good number of them live in the South (17%) and Northeast (18%) (U.S. Census Bureau, 2001). The largest proportion of nearly every major Asian-American ethnic group lives in California.

### b. Common Cultural Traits

Many scholars have described "cultural commonalities" (Chung, 1992) or common values that are generally emphasized by Asian people in their behavior (Ho, 1992). Following are some examples. Caution is necessary as they describe their values on an ideal level and not necessarily on a level practiced by ordinary people in their daily lives.

*Self and Relations with Others.*    With a cultural emphasis on collectivism, rather than individualism, Asian people tend to see the "self" as a part of the group. Instead of autonomy and independence, interdependence is stressed. As a result, a person needs to be aware of and sensitive to the opinions and feelings of others. The behavior manifested is rather situation-oriented, depending on how others relate to you (Markus & Kitayama, 1991).

*Shame Orientation.*    Shame is utilized as a method of reinforcing proper behavior. Improper behavior brings shame and a loss of face to the self and significant others, including the family (Ho, 1992). This is in contrast to guilt orientation, whose main concern is with right and wrong in and of themselves. Behavior in front of people with whom one is acquainted and strangers is different, with more politeness and humility shown to the former than to the latter.

*Humbleness and Restraint.*    Humbleness in expressing one's desires and appropriate hesitation in communicating one's own opinions is stressed. Self-restraint is practiced rather than asserting the self in dealing with things. This is reflected by the saying, "The nail sticking out will be hit back." Associated with this is respect for authority. Confrontation with authority is considered ill behavior.

*Indirect Communication.*    When Asians are exposed to verbal communication, from the standpoint of mainstream America, they often appear quiet and passive, making a great effort to avoid offending others, sometimes answering all questions affirmatively to be polite, even when they cannot understand the question asked by an authority figure (including the therapist) (Chung, 1992; Paniagua, 1998, p. 60). In general, they do not encourage members of the group to express publicly their problems to others outside the group (Sue & Sue, 1990). They learned how to communicate in a subtle and indirect way to avoid insulting or offending others. This pattern of communication is culturally shaped and is regarded as "ideal"; however, occasionally, particularly when a person is under stress or emotionally very upset, he may lose control, and negative emotional material may burst out. This is observed in a quarrel in social life and can occur in family or group sessions.

*Assumption of a Middle Position.*    Facing a dilemma or conflict, compromise is encouraged with an attempt to take a middle position between the extremes. This approach should not be seen as a lack of assertive behavior but rather as a process that fosters an individual's sense of belonging and togetherness. An effort is often made not to take either side to avoid offending anyone. This attitude is extended into relations with nature. Conquering nature is not a common concept for Asians. Complying with nature is more desirable. This is coupled with the belief system that individuals are powerless and have little control over their own lives (Ho, 1992; Kitano & Maki, 1996).

### c. Ethnic Relations within

Even though Asian people share common cultural traits and physically look alike to outsiders, it should not be considered that all Asians are alike. Besides, it is important to know that, for various historical reasons, some subtle gaps or conflicts exist among the different ethnicities within the larger Asian group. For instance, some Chinese still resent the Japanese for invading China and refuse to buy any Japanese products, such as cars; whereas, fearing retaliation, some Japanese are afraid to go to Nanjing in China, where Japanese soldiers massacred many Chinese civilians during the Sino-Japanese War prior to World War II. Many aged Koreans still remember bitterly that the Japanese destroyed their dynasty and mistreated Koreans during their occupation before World War II and refuse to speak Japanese even when they are fluent in it.

Some tensions or discrimination exists even among subgroups within the same ethnic group. For example, some Japanese still look down on Okinawans, even though Okinawa has been included as a part of Japanese territory for many centuries. There are still mutual feelings of inferiority among a few members of different Chinese subethnic groups, such as between the Bendi (local) people and the Hakka (guest) people, or mainland Chinese and Taiwan-Chinese. Likewise, there are still suspicions among Vietnamese refugee groups, with unresolved hostility among those who were pro- or anticommunist during the Vietnam War. Such intergroup tensions or discrimination often affect interpersonal relations and social involvement in a subtle way or induce conflicts between them in an explicit way.

## 2. Mental-Health-Related Problems

### a. Common Psychological Issues

*Culture Gap and Change.*   It is common for immigrants to face a cultural gap between their own and the host society. Asian-Americans are no exceptions. This is especially true regarding their concepts and value, particularly how they relate to authority, emphasize filial piety, stress individuality, speak out in a group, and so on. There also exists (beyond the ordinary general gap) a cultural gap between parents and children, who experience different degrees of acculturation to the host society. Associated with different levels of acculturation, these cultural gaps differ among different generations of immigrants, often making it useful to distinguish among first-, second-, and third-generation immigrant (referred to as *isei*, *nisei*, and *sansei* in Japanese).

*Struggle against Underprivilege.*   Most Asians, as new immigrants to America, always face problems of underprivilege. This is related to problems of language, negative stereotypes people have toward Asians, and unfamiliarity with the social system in the host society. These problems accumulate if they stay within their own community such as in Chinatown or in Little Tokyo, continue to speak their own language, and socialize solely within their own group, reliving their own culture.

*Suffering from Culture Loss.*   The aged person usually suffers more from problems of cultural loss. This is particularly true for newly migrated Asian parents or grandparents. For many Asian elderly, access to their original culture is fading away, while their contact with the host society seldom improves, mainly due to language problems. They suffer from a sense of loss of their cultural roots.

*Stress from Expectation of Success.*   Immigrant young adults and children face a different kind of problem, namely, the expectation to succeed in the host society. For the sake of their families, they are expected to achieve in education, employment, and finances. These are often expectations they had in their home country, but they are aggravated after they enter the host society, as their success becomes the only hope for their families to solve their problems and improve in the future.

### b. Psychiatric Disorders

Due to the size of the population, there is a lack of formal epidemiological data to indicate the mental health situation of Asian-Americans. Clinical impressions support the view that Asian-Americans share many of the mental health disorders of other ethnic groups, contrary to the layperson's impression that they are happy and immune from mental problems. Although historically, conduct disorders, delinquent behavior, and substance abuse problems were considered few among Asian youngsters, there is currently a tendency for problems in these areas to increase. Alcohol-related problems are generally low for most Asian-Americans. Clinicians' and scholars' reports indicate a prevalence of posttraumatic stress disorders, with depression very high among Southeast Asian refugees (Kinzie et al., 1990). Many Korean-Americans often use the folk term *hwa-byung* (fire sickness) to communicate their psychosomatic problems (Lin, 1983). However, the culture-related specific disorders *of taijinkyuofusho* (a special form of social phobia) and family suicide among Japanese nationals are almost unheard of among Japanese-Americans, as is *koro* (penis-shrinking anxiety) among Chinese-Americans (see Section 3A: Culture-Related Specific Syndromes).

### c. Mental Health Service Utilization

Many investigations conducted in the United States have pointed out that, in contrast to the majority group of Caucasian-Americans, Asian-Americans, as many other minority groups, tend to underutilize the existing (modern) mental health system (K. M. Lin et al., 1982; T. Y. Lin et al., 1978; Sue, 1977) and also tend not to adhere to the services even if they do connect with it. For example, Sue and Zane (1987) reported that more than 50% of Asian-Americans dropped psychotherapeutic treatment after their first appointment. The stigma attached to mental disorders, problems of language, and unfamiliality toward the mental health system and the practice of psychiatry are among the major reasons contributing to the underutilization of mental health services (Sue & Sue, 1990).

## 3. Therapeutic Considerations and Clinical Suggestions

How to deal with stigma related to psychiatric disorders is the first issue that needs to be considered when a therapist is treating Asian-American patients. The therapist should be aware that Asian-American patients may see many other therapists simultaneously, including traditional medical physicians or folk healers. Many Asian-American people still utilize the concepts and practices of traditional medicine in coping with illness. Therefore, it would be useful for the therapist to be familiar with and have some knowledge of traditional medicine.

Asian-American patients often present somatic symptoms even when they encounter psychological problems. The pattern of overly presenting somatic compliant needs dynamic understanding. It needs to be differentiated as merely a prelude to the presentation of emotional problems, simply following a cultural patten of making such complaints to a "physician," or resisting acknowledging and dealing with psychological problems (Tseng, 1975). In general, Asian-Americans tend not to make sharp distinctions between mind and body, thus, determining how to work with the matter of mind and body is a delicate issue that requires skillful treatment.

Because harmonious interpersonal relations are highly valued by Asian-Americans, direct confrontation is avoided whenever possible in therapeutic situations (Okazaki, 2000). In interpersonal psychotherapy, such as family therapy, a structural approach, with an emphasis on active restructuring of the interactions in the family to create change is more useful than relying on direct and open expressions of feeling. Parental authority needs to be respected and not insulted. Otherwise, therapy will be doomed to failure.

## C. EUROPEAN-AMERICAN GROUPS

### 1. General Issues

#### a. Demographic Information

European-American refers to the group of people in the United States who are descendents of (western) European nationals (mainly German, French, British, Italian, and Greek). Because of their fair skin, they are called "white" in contrast to other non-white ethnic groups. In the academic field, they are often categorized as "Caucasian," because of their Caucasoid roots. European-American is the major and most dominant group in the United States. According to the 1990 U.S. Census, whites make up 80% of the total population of 250 million. There are 53 categories of European-Americans, of which the largest are German-Americans (58 million), those of English ancestry (British, English, Welsh, and Scottish, 41 million), and Irish-American (39 million) (Giordano & McGoldrick, 1996, p. 427).

Most families from European-American groups have been in the United States for three generations or more, and the immigration generation's struggles against discrimination and for satisfactory education, occupations, and residence have largely faded. An increasing number have intermarried with other ethnic groups and often are unaware of and uninterested in their mixed European heritage, thinking of themselves simply as "Americans" (Giordano & McGoldrick, 1996, p. 427).

#### b. Common Cultural Traits

Even though European-Americans are composed of many ethnic groups, they are regarded by others mainly as white, or even as "Westerners" by "Easterners," and are considered as having some common cultural traits. In general, they have been described as being oriented to the individual (in contrast to situationally or collectively oriented); oriented to the present or future (rather than to the past); oriented to meeting actively and aggressively solving problems (rather than passively or submissively tolerating or accepting them); oriented to meeting challenges and trying to conquer in their relations with nature (rather than trying to comply or be in harmony with nature).

### c. Ethnic Differences within the Group

The clinical importance of understanding and addressing the ethnic differences among European-American groups cannot be overestimated. However, clinicians, as do laypeople, have generally ignored these differences, except as they pertain to "minority" groups.

As family therapists who are interested in ethnicity and culture, Giordano and McGoldrick (1996) studied how the ethnicity of mental health professionals influenced their lives (particularly relating to family) and revealed that the therapists themselves differed significantly in characterizing their values and practices. They summarized their findings about ethnic differences as follows (pp. 437–438).

*Anglo-Americans.*    The study indicated that Anglo-Americans were raised in families in which men and women are expected to be independent, strong, and able to make it alone. Exploration of the world was encouraged, self-control was highly valued, suffering was to be borne in silence, and conflicts were covered over, especially in public.

*Jewish-Americans.*    It was reported that in Jewish-American families, children were encouraged to discuss and express their opinions on family problems. They learned that talking about problems is the best way to solve them, success is more highly valued than anything else, and suffering is more easily borne when expressed and shared. A person will get attention when he is sick. In general, they were not supposed to marry outside the group. In their experience, guilt was considered one of the best ways to shape a child's behavior.

*Italian-Americans.*    It was learned that nothing was more important than the family, and that eating was a symbol of nurturing and family connectedness and a wonderful source of enjoyment. In their homes, roles were separate and defined; men, who were always dominant, protected, and women nurtured. Family members believed personal connections were the way to get things done.

*Irish-Americans.*    It was revealed that Church rules were paramount; suffering, which was to be handled alone, was punishment for sins; drinking was an important part of social engagements; and complaining about problems was "bad form." Being self-controlled, strong, and psychologically tough was highly valued. Sex was viewed as dangerous and not to be discussed. As a consequence of sexual repression, they also avoided tenderness, affection, and intimacy between husband and wife (McGoldrick, 1982, p. 314). Within a family, traditionally fathers have been shadowy or absent figures, and husbands dealt with wives primarily by avoidance. In the final analysis, women were expected to take care of things.

*Greek-Americans.*  It was described that, in Greek-American families, males were always dominant, and women were expected to know their place. Older family members were respected for their wisdom. Sex was not discussed. Parents warned children about the dangers in the outside world and wanted nothing more than for them to be successful.

Clearly, even European-Americans, who are collectively called white or Caucasian, have considerable subgroup variations among them. It is also important to know that the ethnic or cultural background of the patient, will not significantly affect the nature, content, and process of psychotherapy, but rather that the outcome depends more on how the therapist interacts with the patient.

## 2. Mental–Health–Related Problems

### a. Common Psychological Issues

Due to their lifestyles and common values, European-Americans are vulnerable to certain psychological problems. Because they emphasize the concepts of individualism and autonomy and are encouraged to leave their families early in their young adulthood, learning how to cope with situations by themselves, rather than with help from others, they acquire the virtue of independence. However, they also could be vulnerable to depression when they fail in their lives. A shortage of support from immediate family members is one contributing factor. This is particularly true when a family is broken by parental separation or divorce.

Coupled with the issue of striving for independence, most of the young people put a heavy emphasis on man and woman relationships. Dating is very important, attraction and affection between a man and a woman is very highly regarded. This adds stress in competing for and maintaining a man and woman relationship. This continues even after marriage. Affection is considered the main force that keeps the relationship between the husband and wife together. If there is a problem in the relationship, it threatens the couple's emotional life very severely.

Love and enjoyment of life are centered around young adulthood. Aging is viewed as undesirable. This creates a certain stress when entering late adulthood, creating aging problems for many, particularly those who have failed to build a family and achieve a strong financial foundation during middle adulthood.

### b. Psychiatric Disorders

It needs to be pointed out that the official American psychiatric classification (DSM) system is a product of professional experiences with the mainstream population, namely, the European-American, or Caucasian, group, and the data from epidemiological studies reflect the characteristics of this ethnic group. Therefore, if we need to describe the characteristics of psychiatric disorders of European-Americans, it is necessary to rely on how they are different from the other ethnic groups studied in the United States or in other non-Western societies.

Even among the European-American group, there are some subgroup differences among different ethnic groups within this overall group. For instance, the Irish, both in Ireland and in the United States, continue to have a very high incidence of alcoholism. Alcoholism is tolerated as "a good man's weakness" (McGoldrick, 1982, p. 318).

### c. Mental Health Service Utilization

In general, compared to other ethnic groups, European-Americans utilize the mental health service system without hesitation. This is because they have less of a stigma toward mental illness, and there is no language problem when they seek service from mental health workers. The only problem is when they have no adequate health insurance system, making it difficult for them to utilize private psychiatric facilities and necessary to rely on public ones. Many psychiatrists working in public mental health services are of minority ethnic group backgrounds.

## 3. Therapeutic Considerations and Clinical Suggestions

*Reversed Ethnic Transference and Countertransference.*    When European-American patients are treated by nonmainstream therapists, there is a need to watch for and deal with carefully reversed ethnic transference and countretransference. This is rather common, as many psychiatrists belong to minority ethnic backgrounds, particularly in public settings. There is a need for a therapist of a minority group to learn and understand the culture of European-Americans, as well as the differences among different subgroups of white people.

*Psychologizing the Problems.*    Associated with improvements in mental health work and laypeople becoming familiar with psychiatric knowledge and the practice of psychotherapy, there is a tendency for patients to be concerned with and present their problems in a psychological way, rather than in a more natural way. This is observed particularly among patients of European-American backgrounds. This is in contrast to patients of other ethnic groups, such as Asian-Americans, who tend to somatize their problems. Even though, in general, in psychotherapy, it is more favorable for patients to be able to carry out intrapsychic examinations and to focus primarily and directly on their psychological problems, if the problems are overpsychologized, there is a need for caution. It may not reflect the actual problems, and turn therapy into nothing but intellectualization, with psudo-insight, omitting emotional aspects.

---

CASE 2

A Jewish Male Patient Requested Therapy with a Jewish Therapist (abstracted from Bernstein, 2001)

Mr. Goldberg, a 55-year-old Jewish male, went to a mental health clinic with a chief complaint that he was experiencing a diminished enjoyment of his work and was worried that he was not realizing his full potential. He specifically requested psychodynamic psychotherapy with a Jewish therapist "to explore general philosophical issues relating to achieving my life's goal."

His developmental history included high scholastic achievement that culminated in a master's degree in business administration from an Ivy League school. He related that, despite being raised in an orthodox Jewish household, he never felt particularly religious, and he did not practice Judaism. His father, a successful merchant, pushed Mr. Goldberg to become a rabbi, believing this would be a noble use of his intellectual gifts. Although he was educated in *Yeshiva* (Jewish religious schools) until graduation from high school, to the great disappointment of his father, Mr. Goldberg insisted on a secular college education. After completing his master's degree, he began working for a series of finance-related firms, eventually rising to a middle-management position.

In the therapy, when asked why he wanted a Jewish therapist, he responded that he wanted someone with a *Yiddishe kup* (a Jewish head), a common Jewish expression, meaning that Jews think differently from non-Jews. The therapist noted him to be cooperative yet controlling in the sessions, using intellecturalization and obsessional thinking as major defense mechanism. The therapist was struck by Mr. Goldberg's narcissism and the adolescent qualities of his conflicts regarding rebellion against his past, yet insecurity about having chosen the wrong career path, as evidenced by his self-described "mediocre performance at work." He often came to sessions with pages of "important information," such as descriptions of dreams or cinema critiques. His speech during sessions was replete with Yiddish expressions, and he expressed a sense of enjoyment if he had to explain their meaning to the therapist. He completed the allotted 20 sessions, which he viewed as a positive experience. At the termination, he stated, "If I need a tune-up in the future, I'll contact you again."

# D. HISPANIC-AMERICAN GROUPS

## 1. General Issues

### a. Who Are Hispanics or Latinos?

"Hispanic" and "Latino" are terms used to refer to Cubans, Chicanos, Mexicans, Puerto Ricans, Argentinians, Colombians, Dominicans, Brazilians, Guatemalans, Cost Ricans, Nicaraguans, Salvadorians, and all the other nationalities that comprise South America, Central America, and the Caribbean. Their basic similarities are, except for Brazilians who speak Portuguese, that most of them speak Spanish, they use Spanish surnames, they are mostly Roman Catholic, and they have common values and beliefs rooted in a history of conquest and colonization. Associated with Latin American history, Latinos are the descendants of the oppressors and the oppressed, and for generations they have struggled for liberation (Garcia-Preto, 1996, pp. 141–142).

In the United States, they are officially categorized as "Hispanic" by the U.S. Census, whereas some of them regard the term as an English word without gender and prefer the terms "Latino" and "Latina". The term "Latino" is used with the implication that a person is from a Latin American country (e.g., from Cuba). Mexican-Americans tend to prefer the term "Latino" because it does not signify a conqueror Spain (Paniagua, 1998, p. 39). Some descendants of early Mexican and Spanish settlers, particularly those in Mexico and Colorado, refer to themselves as "Hispanos."

### b. Demographic Information

Presently, in the United States, Mexicans, Puerto Ricans, and Cubans continue to be the three largest Latino groups, however, there has been an increase in the number of Dominicans, Central Americans, and some South American groups, especially Brazilians. As of the year 2000, their population is about 12.7% of the total population of the United States (U. S. Bureau of the Census, 2000). However, it is projected that Hispanic-Americans will become the largest non-European-American ethnic group in the United States by the year 2020 (Davis, Haub, & Willete, 1988).

Hispanic are highly concentrated in the U.S. Southwest. In 2000, 60% lived in five southwestern states (California, Arizona, New Mexico, Colorado, and Texas). Approximately half live in two states, California and Texas (U. S. Census Bureau, 2001). Their economic status differs to some extent among the three main subgroups, paralleling their educational status. Cuban-Americans are more affluent than Puerto Ricans and Mexican-Americans. The percentage of persons below the poverty line are 31% for Puerto Ricans, 27% for Mexicans, and 14% for Cubans (U. S. Census Bureau, 2000).

### c.  Common Cultural Traits

As indicated by Romeros (2000), the collectivistic culture is more representative of Latino culture and construes the self as more interdependent with other important people within one's social realm. Latino social interactions are guided by *personalismo* or the establishment of trust and rapport through developing warm friendly relationships (Cuéllar, Arnold, & González, 1995).

Associated with the collectivistic culture is the understanding and value in the family. There is a deep sense of family commitment, obligation, and responsibility. The nuclear family is embedded in an extended family network (Falicov, 1982). Associated with "familism," affiliation and cooperation are stressed, whereas confrontation and competition are discouraged. The family guarantees protection and caretaking for life as long as the person stays in the system. The family is usually an extended system that encompasses not only those related by blood and marriage, but also *compadres* (godparents) and *hijos de crianza* (adopted children, whose adoption is not necessarily legal) (Garcia-Preto, 1996, pp. 151).

The complementarity of roles between male and female is a cultural ideals rooted in Spanish antecedents and expressed in hierarchies of male dominance and female submission. The ideal of *machismo* dictates that men be aggressive, sexually experienced, courageous, and protective of their women and their children. The female counterpart of this ideal is a humble, submissive, and virtuous woman, devoted to her home and children. However, it is important to realize that this is often a social fiction. In the reality of their private lives, the situation may vary, including those husbands who are submissive and dependent on their wives for major decisions (Falicov, 1982, p. 139).

## 2.  Mental–Health–Related  Problems

### a.  Common Psychological Issues

Concerning Mexican families, it has been indicated that (Falicov, 1982, p. 139), during the early stages of family formation, boundary problems and loyalty conflicts with the families of origin are common. Also associated with the practice of patrilocal residence (brides go to live with their husbands' families after marriage), it is crucial to work out mother-in-law and daughter-in-law relationships for the success of the marriage. Because of the large number of children, their relatively late departure from the family, and their intense connectedness with the parents during adulthood, the parenthood cycle is prolonged and allows the marital couple to maintain a focus on parental and grandparental functions (Falicov, 1982, p. 140). In general, the ties among siblings are very strong in the Mexican family tradition, however, quarrels and resentments among adult siblings are common. They may be caused by favoritism of the parents for one sibling over another, by disagreements about inheritance, by unpaid debts, or by the persistence of a controlling attitude on the part of an older sibling that is no longer acceptable to a younger one (Falicov, 1982, p. 142).

### b. Mental Health Service Utilization

Well and co-workers (1987) reported that less-acculturated Mexican-Americans tended to use outpatient mental health services less frequently (one-seventh as much) than non-Hispanic Caucasian-Americans in the Los Angeles area. Many explanations have been offered for this phenomenon. For instance, Karno and Edgerton (1969) have pointed out that due to their perception and definition of mental illness, Mexican-Americans tend to seek treatment for obviously psychiatric disorders from family physicians. The patients' orientation to and understanding and expectation of psychiatric therapy affect their patterns of utilization. Cultural incongruities between the patient and treatment are considered to play a role in the results among Hispanic patients. Language barriers are always cited as major problems. The utilization of interpreters in psychiatric settings, particularly in psychotherapy, tend to disrupt and delay the work, making it difficult. Finally, therapists' cultural insensitivity is another reason that needs to be considered.

### c. Psychiatric Disorders

According to the Epidemiologic Catchment Area Study (ECA), which examined rates of psychiatric disorders in five selected communities in the United States and conducted interviews in English and Spanish (if indicated), Mexican-Americans (mainly from the Los Angles area) and European-Americans overall had very similar rates of psychiatric disorders. However, when Mexican-Americans were divided into those born in Mexico and those born in the United States, it was found that the former had higher rates of depression and phobias (Burnam et al., 1987). Another epidemiological study, namely, the National Comorbidity Survey, pointed out that despite very low educational and income levels, Mexican-Americans had lower rates of lifetime psychiatric disorders than reported for the total U.S. population. Psychiatric morbidity among Mexican-Americans is primarily influenced by cultural variance rather than socioeconomic status or urban vs. rural residence.

Concerning the psychiatric disorders among Hispanic-Americans, a clinician needs to be aware that some patients and their families may use folk terms to describe their emotional problems. The term "*susto*" means loss of soul and describes how a person feels and behaves after encountering psychological shock or stress, incliuding anxious, depressed, agitated, or emotional, possibly with many somatic symptoms as well. It needs to be understood that the term is used by people to describe and interpret a mental condition. Similarly the term "*ataques de nervios*," which literally means an attack of nerves, may be used. It refers to a stress-induced, culturally shaped unique emotional reaction with mixed anxiety-hysterical features (see Section 3A: Culture-Related Specific Syndromes).

## 3. Therapeutic Considerations and Clinical Suggestions

*Basic Expectation for Therapy.*     In general, patients of Hispanic background want the therapist to be casual about keeping appointments, to take the initiative for change, and to give advice or educate them as to the solution to their problems. Mexican-American families of lower socioeconomic levels appear to respond best to a brief and problem-oriented approach that redefines the problem in interactional terms centered on the relationship between parents and children (Falicov, 1982, pp. 146 & 148).

---

CASE 3

---

A Mexican-American Women Continues to "Talk" to Her Deceased Husband (abstracted from Martinez, 1993)

Mrs. T. is a 54-year-old Mexican-American woman whose husband died suddenly in her arms of a stroke. Following his death, she became withdrawn and intermittently mute. She talked to him and saw him in her mind. In addition, she reported headaches, weakness, and continued "trances." Several weeks later, she was admitted to a hospital, continuing to report that she "saw" her husband and that he was with her. Staff and family repeatedly emphasized to her that her was husband was dead. Her children even showed her videotapes of the funeral. An antidepressant was prescribed and, after 3 weeks, she was released to a day-hospital program in the same condition, without improvement. Finally, a pastoral counselor (a Mexican-American woman) began seeing the patient. Mrs. T. explained to the counselor that she did not want to let go of her husband as she had not said goodbye and was resistant to do so. Working patiently yet persistently, the pastoral counselor told Mrs. T. that her loved one was in heaven and that she needed to wave goodbye to him. A half-hearted but definite wave of the hand occurred, followed by uncontrollable crying and then relief.

---

*Suggested Family Therapy.*     Based on clinical experiences, family therapists have commented that the cultural emphasis on hierarchies within the family lends itself to a structural family therapy approach. It is further suggested that, because cultural norms emphasize the importance of the parent-child dyad over the marital dyad, during the initial stages a focus on parent-child interactions is more readily accepted than a focus on marital issues or on issues concerning the parents' families of origin (Falicov, 1982, pp. 148–149). During the family therapy sessions, in moving to a discussion of the presenting problem, addressing questions to the father first, then to the mother, then to other adults, and finally to the older and younger children, respecting traditional age and sex hierarchies and conveying *respeto* is an important therapeutic skill to be considered (Falicov, 1982, p. 151).

# E. NATIVE-AMERICAN GROUPS

## 1. General Issues

### a. Demographic Information

"Native-American" refers broadly to American Indians, Alaska natives, Native Hawaiians, and those who were pre-Columbian inhabitants of North America, including Alaska. These groups are enormously diverse; however, they share a common historical path in that they suffered from loss of ancestral lands, massive decimation of their people, and destruction of their languages, cultures, and religions (Norton & Manson, 1996). The loss of more than 90% of their populations was due to wars, genocide, and disease (such as smallpox and influenza) (Trimble et al., 1996).

According to censuses (U.S. Bureau of the Census, 1995), at present, American-Indians and Native Alaskans comprised slightly less than 1% of the American population. However, there are more than 250 federally recognized American-Indian tribes and 225 Alaska native villages. Most American-Indians live in the Western states, including California, Arizona, New Mexico, South Dakota, Alaska, and Montana, with 42% residing in rural areas, compared to 23% of whites (Department of Health and Human Services, 2001). Over half of American Indians live in urban areas, and those on the reservations may spend time away looking for education, jobs, and other opportunities. Therefore, major cities have a substantial Indian population (Sutton & Nose, 1996).

Following the devastation of these once-thriving Indian nations, the social environments of native people have remained plagued by economic disadvantage. Many American Indians and Alaska natives are unemployed or hold low-paying jobs (Department of Health and Human Services, 2001). About 26% of Americans and Alaskan natives lived in poverty, compared with 13% for the United States as a whole and 8% for white Americans (U.S. Bureau of the Census, 1999).

### b. Common Cultural Traits

In general, Native Americans are culturally "sociocentric" rather than "egocentric" individuals who are part of an interdependent collective. Cooperation and humility are often more valued than competition or individual success (Richardson, 1981). Harmony with nature is also emphasized.

An emphasis on extended family relationships is typical of American Indians. In many Native American languages, cousins are all referred to as brother and sister. The primary relationship is not that of the parents but rather that of the grandparents (Tafoya, 1989). Many Indian cultures do not have a term for in-law; a daughter-in-law is called a daughter; a sister-in-law, a sister. This means that once one marries into an Indian family, no distinctions are made between natural and inducted family members. Families are blended, not joined (Sutton & Nose, 1996).

For Native Americans, traditionally when strangers meet, they often identify themselves through their relatives, such as: "I am a Navaho. My name is Tiana Bighorn. My hometown is Tuba City, Arizona. I belong to the Deer Springs Clan, born of the Rocky Gap Clan" (Benet & Maloney, 1994, p. 9).

*Time Orientation.*    Native Americans perceive time differently, viewing it as cyclical rather than linear. It may encompass days, months, even years, and is geared to personal and seasonal rhythms rather than being ordered and organized by external mechanical clocks and calendars. They take the view that "time is always with us (Indian time)." It may mean showing up half an hour after a meeting is scheduled. Milestones in the individual life cycle are seen in terms of the rhythmic quality of life (Sutton & Nose, 1996, pp. 39–40).

*Spiritual Relationship of Man and Nature.*    Animals, plants, mountains, and bodies of water may be considered sacred beings, part of the universal family and, as such, involved in a reciprocal system; Native people believe that "we care for mother earth and she nurtures us." The basic philosophy and belief is that all life forces are valuable and interdependent. Instead of taking an attitude of control over nature (as is Western civilization's orientation) the native people take the opposite view. Acceptance of overwhelming natural events that cannot be controlled is an integral part of life (Sutton & Nose, 1996, p. 40).

*Communal Sharing.* Sharing among people in the community is greatly emphasized among native people. From childhood they are enculturated that "what is yours is mine and what is mine is everybody's." Traditionally, Indians accord great respect to those who give the most to other individuals and families, and then to the band, tribe, or community. "Giveaways," an ancient custom according to which many gifts are presented to others for their help or achievements, are a way of marking such climactic events in the life cycle as birth, naming, marriage, and death, still persist in many tribes (Sutton & Nose, 1996, p. 40). This value of sharing contrasts sharply with the dominant culture's capitalist emphasis on acquisition and can make it difficult for Indians on reservation to operate businesses. Similar issues often occur when the head of an urban

Indian family finds steady work or a student receives a stipend or fellowship. Whereas white culture focuses on carefully managing cash flow and savings for the individual's sake, American-Indians are prone to share liquid assets with families and others.

## 2. Mental-Health-Related Problems

### a. Common Psychological Issues

American Indians are less likely to separate aspects of themselves such as their physical, mental, and social selves (Richardson, 1981). Commonly, affect is more contextual and related to interpersonal difficulties rather than the "ego-oriented context-less self-statements of dysphoria or worry presented in more egocentric cultures" (Manson, 1995). Therefore, it might be more helpful for the clinician to first inquire how things have been socially for the client and than ask how any difficulties noted have affected him or her in a feeling or emotional way. They are more likely to express affective concerns in somatic terms given the lack of differentiation between somatic and other aspects of one's being (Manson, 1995).

As part of their culturally patterned behavior, when they encounter the therapist they may present with a subdued manner and lack of eye contact that seems "withdrawn," "passive," or indicative of "flat affect" to the inexperienced clinician. Downcast eyes and a composed demeanor are cultural expressions of interpersonal respect within many tribes and groups (Dillard & Manson, 2000).

### b. Some Psychiatric Disorders Needing Clarification

Among all psychiatric disorders, there are two disorders that stand out among Native Americans that need clarification. They are drinking problems and suicide.

*Alcohol Problems.*    Although high alcoholism rates are widely reported in the literature, the stereotype of the "drunken Indian" is as inaccurate as the stereotype of the "suicidal Indian." As mentioned previously (see Section 4E: Alcohol-Related Problems), there are no systematic data to indicate the nature and extent of the problem. There is only some indirect information. Brod (1975) cited some studies relating to Native Americans and indicated that the alcohol-related arrest rate is 12 times the national average; the alcoholism-related death rate is 4.3 to 5.5 times the U.S. rate for all races. However, it is generally considered that the rate of alcohol problems differs among different tribes, and overall generalization should be avoided.

The etiology of alcoholism in Indians has been written about extensively, but no convincing conclusions have been reached. Although biological theories have been suggested, there is no proof of genetic, metabolic, or other differences in Indians that would negatively affect the processing of alcohol (May & Smith, 1988). High unemployment is considered one possible factor for substance abuse, but it is not clear whether this is the cause or the result of alcoholism (Westermeyer, Walker, & Benton, 1981).

Westermeyer (1972) reported that the Native-American Chippewa of Minnesota practice two types of drinking, which they themselves call "white" and "Indian." The "white" type refers to drinking with restrained behavior, often observed among white people. The "Indian" type means drinking which, after one or two drinks, results in noisy behavior, often precedes fighting, or leads to heavy drinking and a stupor. Indian drinking is an accepted, expected way to maintain in-group relationships and tribal or familiar loyalties.

*Suicide.*   As mentioned previously (see Section 4H: Suicide Behavior), another stereotypical view was that suicide rates were high among culturally uprooted indigenous people. This may have been true in many cases, but there is a need to distinguish between fact and fantasy. High suicide rates among tribes with relatively small population bases have received widespread publicity and have been generalized to include all Native Americans. In fact, there are considerable differences among tribes, with suicide rates varying between 8 and 120 per 100,000 population. Therefore, tribal differences should be recognized, and overgeneralization should be avoided (Shore, 1975).

*Some Culture-Related Specific Syndromes.*   In the past, scholars have described Arctic hysteria as a culture-related specific syndrome among the native people of the North Pole. It refers to when a person suddenly goes into emotional turmoil, behaving strangely for a while, such as taking off their clothes and running outside in cold weather or lying in the snow (see Section 3A: Culture-Related Specific Syndromes). The cause of this mental condition is still not clear. Some scholars interpret it as merely a modification of an hysterical outburst, while others speculate that it may be caused by biological reasons, such as calcium imbalance due to Vitamin D deficiency associated with lack of exposure to sunlight. Another syndrome, *witigo* psychoses, occurs when a hunter, starving in cold weather, without success in hunting, may become occupied with a delusion that he is a cannibal hungry for human flesh. However, no clinicians have actually ever observed such a case; therefore, the existence of this disorder is questionable.

### c. Mental Health Service Utilization

*Variations of Stigma of Mental Illness.*   Because of the diversity of Indian peoples, there exist different stigma associated with mental illness. Some tribal groups attach very little stigma to mental disorders because they make little distinction between mental and physical symptoms; others attach a great deal of stigma to mental disorders such as psychoses, but not to alcoholism. Still others attach stigma to particular events, such as suicide, in part because of the enormous amount of media attention that has been directed toward suicide among Indian youth (Thomson, Walker, & Silk-Walker, 1993, p. 204).

*Hesitation in Utilization of Service.*   There are several reasons that contribute to the reluctance to see mental health workers. One is that the common problem of sharing one's innermost thoughts with a psychiatrist is compounded by the general distrust of federal medicine and doctors (Lockart, 1981). Another problem is the matter of confidentiality. In small, close-knit Indian communities, there are realistic concerns about confidentiality. Indeed, relatives and acquaintances may work in the medical records room of the hospital or clinic. The patient may not want to reveal his or her "secrets" (Thomson, Walker, & Silk-Walker, 1993, p. 205).

*Folk Concepts and Practices of Healing.*   Many Indian people subscribe to the idea that illness is a state of imbalance with the world and express this idea in physical, psychological, and/or spiritual terms. In other words, the mental, physical, and spiritual are all seen as influencing the health of an individual, and all must be considered when treatment is planned. The healing remedies taken by Indian people take many forms. They include herbal medicine, "sweat," and other ceremonies, feasts, and the use of natural phenomena, such as mineral springs. Many Indian patients may use both traditional and modern (Western) medicine simultaneously. Most Indian people are extremely pragmatic. They want to do what will work and see no problem with combining modern and traditional treatments.

## 3. Therapeutic Considerations and Clinical Suggestions

*Proper Social Greeting and Connecting.*   Following the traditional custom of identifying persons through their place of birth and personal connection, in the beginning of the clinical situation it is important for the therapist to introduce who he is, where he comes from, in an accessible, nonthreatening way, and then, after that, ask the patient, "What about you? Would you like to share something about yourself?" so that, based on this social greeting and mutual introduction, a culturally proper relationship and rapport can start to be built (Sutton & Nose, 1996, pp. 36–37).

*Communication by Listening.*   A good therapist always knows how to listen. This is particularly true when working with Native-American patients. Native cultures value listening. Long periods of silence by Indian clients can be confusing for non-Indian therapists. Silence may connote respect, that the client is forming thoughts, or that the client is waiting for signs that it is the right time to speak. Indian people may be very indirect (Sutton & Nose, 1996, p. 37). On the one hand, the therapist should be aware that a directive approach is more comfortable for them than a nondirective approach. Therefore, it is suggested that the therapist take an active role in directing the process of counseling and offering suggestions for improvement. This active approach does not necessarily conflict with the skill of listening carefully to the patient.

*Here-and-Now Sessions with Flexibility.*    Given the cultural emphasis on living in the here and now, native people often present with significant distress and a highly pressing issue to discuss when they contact mental health workers. The "ordinary" weekly sessions lasting for 1 hour might not be an effective option for many Native Americans. Allowing for more lengthy sessions on an as-needed basis with flexibility may be more suitable and appealing to them (Dillard & Manson, 2000). One of the major obstacles encountered in treating Alaska natives is the need to cross great distances. The clinician may be the only trained person within many miles. Using self-help groups and identifying and recruiting of the healthiest member of the family as a "co-therapist" is useful (Richards & Oxereok, 1978).

*Establishment of Trust and Rapport.*    How to develop rapport and establish trust between the therapist and the patient is a major task. This is particularly true if the therapist is of European-American background, representing the majority and the federal government. Prolonged facilitation and clarification to allow patients time to tell their story and express their feelings is important. Gentle confrontation is important, lest the patient interpret this as the same rejection that he has experienced with non-Indians in other majority institutions (Westermeyer & Walker, 1982).

*Provision of Positive Role Models.*    The therapist must assist Native American clients to grow and move toward health and wellness by providing positive, concrete, well-articulated, and well-defined role models as mental health professionals and human beings and, at the same time, assist them in identifying elements of personal mental well-being and to design their own model based on healthy traditional values and practices (Tafoya & Vecchio, 1996, p. 53).

*Work on Denial as Coping Strategy.*    The therapist must work with Native American clients to recognize when denial is used as a strategy to avoid dealing with the consequences of the historical trauma. It would be useful for the therapist to assist clients properly to discharge anger, shame, and fear associated with oppression and historical trauma (Tafoya & Vecchio, 1996, p. 53).

*Involvement of Network and Family.*    Network or system therapy is very useful. Bringing in all of the people important in the treatment process may be more effective than individual therapy.

*Group Therapy.*    Because of the cultural emphasis on "others," therapy in the form of a group may fit better for Native Americans. In fact, many Indian and Native Alaskan cultures have a long tradition of employing groups for social and religious activities, which have strong similarities to the techniques used in group therapy (Dillard & Manson, 2000; Neligh, 1990).

According to Jilck-Aall (1981) Western-style Alcoholics Anonymous meetings have not been successful among North American Indian populations. However, incorporating important indigenous cultural elements, the transformed "AA" groups have been quite successful in attracting and rehabilitating alcohol-abusing persons among native populations. The Amerindian AA groups reject the concept of anonymity. Instead, the open identification of participants is practiced, and family members, including children, are invited to the meetings. A formal set of rules and procedures, including time frame, is abandoned. Instead, more traditional ways of congregating, without predetermined times of arrival or departure of the participants, are practiced (Jilek, 1994). These culturally transformed AA groups are becoming widely accepted among the Amerindian population.

*Collaboration with Indigenous Healers.*    Rather than exclusively focusing on how to use and/or adapt Western perspectives of healing for work with Indians and Native Alaskans, many clinicians are describing models of healing from a Native American perspective. Collaboration with an indigenous healing system may take the forms of actively referring clients to indigenous healers and actively working with healers (Trimble et al., 1996, p. 195). This approach is well illustrated by the following case.

---

CASE 4

---

An American-Indian Woman Who Could Not Escape Her Spirit Song
(abstracted from Jilek-Aall & Jilek, 2001)

Irene was a 46-year-old woman of Coast Salish Indian background of the Pacific Northwest in Canada. She had been treated for arthritis and depression by her general practitioner, who referred her to a Euro-Canadian psychiatrist. Irene had been twice widowed and was now married to her third husband, who pursued a "native" lifestyle; he was often away hunting and fishing with his friends. Irene had five children from her previous marriages and five with her present husband.

*(continues)*

Irene was a small woman, leaning heavily on a cane, and walked slowly, with obvious pain. In the first session, she had a fearful expression and hardly lifted her eyes from the floor, avoiding eye contact with the therapist. She did not speak spontaneously, answered questions hesitatingly, with only a few words, in a low voice, nearly a whisper. In a moment of silence after questions, she began to cry. Irene was left to cry for a while by the therapist to show respect for her feelings. When Irene's crying abated, she was asked whether the arthritis caused her much pain. It was the therapist's effort, at this early stage of session, to focus on emotionally less threatening (medical) problems. After her apprehension was over, she could be induced to talk about her daily life problems, her worries about some of the older teenagers using street drugs and being in trouble with the police, and one of her teenage daughters being pregnant.

In the second session, which started in a more relaxed atmosphere, Irene related something that seemed to be of great importance to her. One evening not long before, when driving home, she was stopped by police because of unsteady driving. She had perhaps taken too many pain killers, and when she stumbled out of the car, the officers, assuming she was under the influence of alcohol, arrested her and placed her in the "drunk tank." No explanation or protest helped. Overwhelmed by shame, pain, and sorrow, Irene cried in her cell. When her crying turned into a strange sing-song, the (white) officers thought she was mentally disturbed and sent her to the mental hospital, where she was diagnosed to have psychotic depression and electroshock treatment was given.

In the remaining treatment sessions, Irene's personal background (of being sent to an Indian residential school at the age of 7) was explored, her supernatural beliefs were brought into the discussion, and her husband was brought in for family sessions to seek his support for the patient. Finally, for the long term, a traditional healer was recommended for culturally meaningful support and dealing with acculturation stress. Initially Irene was surprised to hear such suggestion made by the white therapist. However, after learning that the therapist had been acquainted with a local healer for many years and trusted the healer, Irene was very glad to follow the suggestion. It helped tremendously for her to make a connection with her original cultural roots and to get support from the people in the community as well as from the local healer.

In closing, it should be pointed out that, in this chapter, arbitrarily several ethnic groups are chosen for discussion. There are many other ethnic groups in the population of the United States, such as Americans of Scandinavian, Slavic, or Middle Eastern backgrounds, or Asian Indians, all of which are not elaborated here. Even among the European–American group, there are several unique ethnic groups such as the Amish and Hutterite groups and others. For those various ethnic groups not reviewed here, it is suggested that the reader refer to the literature listed at the end of this chapter.

As explained at the beginning of this chapter, the goal here is to highlight the need for cultural sensitivity and cultural knowledge. Hopefully, it will lead to the promotion of cultural empathy and an increase in the ability of therapists to perform culturally relevant interpersonal interaction with clients and to provide meaningful cultural guidance for patients. These are basic qualities needed for culturally competent clinical care (see Section 5A: The Need for Cultural Competence).

## REFERENCES

### A. African–American Groups

Black, L. (1996). Families of African origin: An overview. In M. McGoldrick, J. Giordano, & J. K. Pearce (Eds.), *Ethnicity and family therapy* (pp. 57–65). New York: Guilford Press.

Blue, H. C., & Griffith, E. E. H. (2001). The African American. In W. S. Tseng & J. Streltzer (Eds.), *Culture and psychotherapy: A guide to clinical practice* (pp. 137–155). Washington, DC: American Psychiatric Press.

Fish, J. E., & Larr, C. J. (1972). A decade of change in drawings by black children. *American Journal of Psychiatry, 129*(4), 421–426.

Harris, H. W., Blue, H. C., & Griffith, E. E. H. (Eds.).` (1995). *Racial and ethnic identity: Psychological development and creative expression.* New York: Routledge.

Hines, P. M., & Boyd-Franklin, N. (1982). Black families. In M. McGoldrick, J. K. Pearce & J. Giordano (Eds.). *Ethnicity and family therapy* (pp. 84–107). New York: Guiford Press.

Lindsey, M. L., & Cuéllar, I. (2000). Mental health assessment and treatment of African American: A multicultural perspective. In I. Cuéllar & F. A. Paniagua (Eds.), *Handbook of multi-cultural mental health: Assessment and treatment of diverse populations* (pp. 195–208). New York: Academic Press.

Manderscheid, R. W., & Sonnenschein, M. A. (1987). *Mental health, United States, 1985.* Rockville, MD: National Institute of Mental Health.

Mauer, M. (1999). *The crisis of the young African male and the criminal justice system.* U.S. Comission on Civil Rights Cenference, Washington, DC.

Pinderhughes, E. (1979). Afro-Americans and economic dependency. *The Urban and Social Change Review, 12*(2), 24–27.

Pinderhughes, E. (1982). Afro-American families and the victim system. In M. McGoldrick, J. K. Pearce, & J. Giordano (Eds.), *Ethnicity and family therapy* (pp. 108–122). New York: Guiford Press.

Regier, D. A., & Kelber, C. T. (1995). The Epidemiologic Catchment Area (ECA) Program: Studying the prevalence and incidence of psychopathology. In M. T. Tsung, M. Tohen, & G. E. P. Zahner (Eds.) *Textbook in psychiatric epidemiology* (pp. 135–155). New York: Wiley.

U.S. Bureau of the Census. (1997). *Statistical abstract of the United States.* Middle series projections. Washington, DC: Government Printing Office.

U.S. Bureau of the Census. (2000). *Statistical abstract of the United States.* Washington, DC: Government Printing Office.

U.S. Bureau of the Census. (2001). *Profiles of general demographic characteristics: 2000 census of population and housing, United States.* Washington, DC: U.S. Bureau of the Census.

Vontress, C., & Epp, L. R. (1997). Historical hostility in the African American client: Implications for counseling. *Journal of Multicultural Counseling and Development, 25*, 170–184.

## B. Asian-American Groups

Chung, D. K. (1992). Asian cultural commonalities: A comparison with mainstream American culture. In S. M. Furuto, R. Biswas, D. K. Chung, K. Murase, & F. Ross-Sheriff (Eds.), *Social work practice with Asian Americans* (pp. 27–44). Newbury Park, CA: Sage.

Ho, M. K. (1992). *Minority children and adolescents in therapy.* Newbury Park, CA: Sage.

Kinzie, J. D., Boehnlein, J. K., Leung, P., Moore, L., Riley, C., & Smith, D. (1990). The prevalence rate of posttraumatic stress disorder and its clinical significance among Southeast Asian refugees. *American Journal of Psychiatry, 147*(7), 913–917.

Kitano, H. H. L., & Maki, M. T. (1996). Continuity, change, and diversity: Counseling Asian Americans. In P. B. Pedersen, J. G. Draguns, W. J. Lonner, & J. E. Trimble (Eds.), *Counseling across cultures* (4$^{th}$ ed.) (pp. 124–145). Thousand Oaks, CA: Sage.

Lin, K. M. (1983). *Hwa-byung*: A Korean culture-bound syndrome? *American Journal of Psychiatry, 140*(1), 105–107.

Lin, K. M., Inui, T. S., Kleinman, A. M., & Womack, W. M. (1982). Sociocultural determinants of the help-seeking behavior of patients with mental illness. *Journal of Nervous and Mental Diseases, 170,* 78–85.

Lin, T. Y., Tardiff, K., Donetz, G., & Goresky, W. (1978). Ethnicity and patterns of help-seeking. *Culture, Medicine and Psychiatry, 2,* 3–14.

Markus, H. R., & Kitayama, S. (1991). Culture and the self: Implications for cognition, emotion, and motivation. *Psychological Review, 98,* 224–253.

Okazaki, S. (2000). Assessing and treating Asian Americans: Recent advances. In I. Cuéllar & F. A. Paniagua (Eds.), *Handbook of multi-cultural mental health: Assessment and treatment of diverse populations* (pp. 171–193). New York: Academic Press.

Paniagua, F. A. (1998). *Assessing and treating culturally diverse clients* (2$^{nd}$ ed.). Thousand Oaks, CA: Sage.

Sue, D. W., & Sue, D. (1990). *Counseling the culturally different: Theory and practice* (2$^{nd}$ ed.) New York: Wiley.

Sue, S. (1977). Community mental health services to minority groups: Some optimism, some pessimism. *American Psychology, 32,* 616–624.

Sue, S., & Zane, N. (1987). The role of culture and cultural techniques in psychotherapy: A critical reformulation. *American Psychology, 42,* 37–45.

Tseng, W. S. (1975). The nature of somatic complaints among psychiatric patients: The Chinese case. *Comprehensive Psychiatry, 16*(3), 237–245.

U.S. Bureau of the Census. (2000). *Statistical abstract of the United States.* Washington, DC: Government Printing Office.

U.S. Bureau of the Census. (2001). *The Asian and Pacific Islander population in the United States: March 2000 (Update).* Washington, DC: Government Printing Office.

## C. European-American Groups

Bernstein, D. M. (2001). Therapist-patient relations and ethnic transference. In W. S. Tseng & J. Streltzer (Eds.), *Culture and psychotherapy: A guide to clinical practice* (pp. 103–121). Washington, DC: American Psychiatric Press.

Giordano, J., & McGoldrick, M. (1996). European families: An overview. In M. McGoldrick, J. Giordano, & J. K. Pearce (Eds.), *Ethnicity and family therapy* (pp. 427–441). New York: Guilford Press.

McGoldrick, M. (1982). Irish families. In M. McGoldrick, J. K. Pearce, & J. Giordano (Eds.), *Ethnicity and family therapy* (pp. 310–339). New York: Guilford Press.

U.S. Bureau of the Census. (1990). Census data for United States. Washington, DC: Government Printing Office.

## D. Hispanic-American Groups

Burnam, M., Hough, R., Karno, M., Escobar, J., & Telles, C. A. (1987). Acculturation and lifetime prevalence of psychiatric disorders among Mexican Americans in Los Angeles. *Journal of Health & Social Behavior, 28*, 89–102.

Cuéllar, I., Arnold, B., & González, G. (1995). Cognitive referents and acculturation: Assessment of cultural constucts in Mexican American. *Journal of Community Psychology, 23*(4), 339–356.

Davis, C., Haub, C. & Willete, J. L. (1988). U.S. Hispanics: Changing the face of America. In E. Acosta-Belen & B. R. Sjostrom (Eds.), *The Hispanic experience in the United States: Contemporary issues and perspectives* (pp. 3–55). New York: Praeger.

Falicov, C. J. (1982). Mexican families. In M. McGoldrick, J. K. Pearce, & J. Giordano (Eds.), *Ethnicity and family therapy* (pp. 134–163). New York: Guilford Press.

Garcia-Preto, N. (1996). Latino families: An overview. In M. McGoldrick, J. Giordano, J. K. Pearce (Eds.), *Ethnicity and family therapy* (pp. 141–154). New York: Guilford Press.

Karno, M., & Edgerton, R. B. (1969). Perception of mental illness in a Mexican-American community. *Archives of General Psychiatry, 20*, 233–238.

Martinez, Jr., C. (1993). Psychiatric care of Mexican Americans. In A. Gaw (Ed.), *Culture, Ethnicity, and Mental Illness* (pp. 431–466). Washington DC: American Psychiatric Press.

Paniagua, F. A. (1998). *Assessing and treating culturally diverse clients* (2nd ed.). Thousand Oaks, CA: Sage.

Romeros, A. (2000). Assessing and treating Latinos: Overview of research. In I. Cuéllar, & F. A. Paniagua (Eds.), *Handbook of multi-cultural mental health: Assessment and treatment of diverse populations* (pp. 210–223). New York: Academic Press.

U.S. Bureau of the Census. (2000). *States ranked by Hispanic population, July 1, 1999.* Washington, DC: Government Printing Office.

U.S. Bureau of the Census. (2001). *The Hispanic population: Census 2000 brief.* Washington, DC: Government Printing Office.

Well, K., Hough, R. L., Golding, J. M., Burnam, M. A., & Karno, M. (1987). Which Mexican-Americans underutilize health services? *American Journal of Psychiatry, 144*(7), 918–922.

## E. Native-American Groups

Benet, N., & Maloney, S. (1994). *Keeper of the culture. Intertribal America*, Collectors Edition.

Brod, T. M. (1975). Alcoholism as a mental health problem of Native Americans: A review of the literature. *Archives of General Psychiatry, 32*, 1385–1391.

Department of Health and Human Services (2001). Mental health care for American Indians and Alaska Natives. In *Mental health: Culture, race, and ethnicity.* A supplement to mental health; A report to the surgeon general (pp. 77–104). Washington, DC: U.S. Public Health Service.

Dillard, D. A., & Manson, S. M. (2000). Assessing and treating American Indians and Alaska Natives. In I. Cuéllar & F. A. Paniagua (Eds.), *Handbook of multi-cultural mental health: Assessment and treatment of diverse populations.* (pp. 226–248). New York: Academic Press.

Jilek, W. G. (1994). Traditional healing in the prevention and treatment of alcohol and drug abuse. *Transcultural Psychiatric Research Review, 31*(3), 219–258.

Jilek-Aall, L. (1981). Acculturation, alcoholism and Indian-style Alcoholics Anonymous. *Journal of Studies on Alcohol, (Suppl. 9)*, 143–158.

Jilek-Aall, L., & Jilek, W. (2001). The woman who could not escape her spirit song. In W. S. Tseng & J. Streltzer (Eds.), *Culture and psychotherapy: A guide to clinical practice* (pp. 43–56). Washington, DC: American Psychiatric Press.

Lockart, B. (1981). Historic distrust and the counseling of American Indians and Alaska Natives. *White Cloud Journal, 2*(2), 31–34.

Manson, S. M. (1995). Culture and major depression: Current challenges in the diagnosis of mood disorders. *The Psychiatric Clinics of North America, 18*(8), 487–503.

May, P. A., & Smith, M. B. (1988). Some Navajo Indian opinions about alcohol abuse and prohibition: A survey and recommendations for policy. *Journal of Studies on Alcohol, 49*, 324–334.

Neligh, C. (1990). Mental health programs for American Indians: Their logic, structure, and function. *The Journal of the National Center Monograph Series, 3*(3).

Norton I. M., & Manson, S. M. (1996). Research in American Indian and Alaska Native communities: Navigating the cultural universe of values and process. *Journal of Consulting and Clincal Psychology, 64*(5), 856–860.

Richards, B., & Oxereok, C. (1978). Counseling Alaskan Natives. In G. R. Walz & L. Benjamin (Eds.), *Transcultural counseling: Needs, programs, and techniques.* New York: Human Sciences Press.

Richardson, E. H. (1981). Cultural and historical perspectives in counseling American Indians. In D. W. Sue (Ed.), *Counseling the culturally different: Theory and practice* (pp. 216–255). New York: Wiley.

Shore, J. H. (1975). American Indian suicide: Fact and fantasy. *Psychiatry, 38*, 87–91.

Sutton, C., & Nose, M. A. B. (1996). American Indian families: An overview. In M. McGoldrick, J. Giordano, & J. K. Pearce (Eds.), *Ethnicity and family therapy* (pp. 31–44). New York: Guilford Press.

Tafoya, T. (1989). Coyote's eyes: Native cognition styles. *Journal of American Indian Education: Special Issues*, 29–40.

Tafoya, N., & Vecchio, A. D. (1996). Back to the future: An examination of the Native American holocaust experience. In M. McGoldrick, J. Giordano, & J. K. Pearce (Eds.), *Ethnicity and family therapy* (pp. 45–54). New York: Guilford Press.

Thomson, J. W., Walker, R. D., & Silk-Walker, P. (1993). Psychiatric care of American Indians and Alaska Natives. In A. Gaw (Ed.), *Culture, Ethnicity, and Mental Illness.* Washington, DC: American Psychiatric Press.

Trimble, J. E., Fleming, C. M., Beauvais, F., & Jumper-Thurman, P. (1996). Essential cultural and social strategies for counseling Native American Indians. In P. B. Pedersen, J. G. Draguns, W. J. Lonner, & J. E., Trimble (Eds.), *Counseling across cultures* (4th ed.) (pp. 177–209). Thousand Oaks, CA: Sage.

U.S. Bureau of the Census. (1995). *Statistical abstract of the United States.* The National Data Book. Washington, DC: Government Printing Office.

U.S. Bureau of the Census. (1999). *Statistical abstract of the United States.* The National Data Book. Washington, DC: Government Printing Office.

Westermeyer, J. (1972). Chippewa and majority alcoholism in the Twin Cities: A comparison. *Journal of Nervous and Mental Disorder, 155*, 322–327.

Westermeyer, J., & Walker, D. (1982). Approaches to treatment of alcoholism across cultural boundaries. *Psychiatric Annals, 12*, 434–439.

Westermeyer, J., Walker, D., & Benton, E. (1981). A review of some methods for investigating substance abuse among American Indians and Alaska Natives. *White Cloud Journal, 2*(2), 13–21.

## Suggested Further Readings

Cuéllar I., & Paniagua, F. A. (Eds.). (2000). *Handbook of multi-cultural mental health: Assessment and treatment of diverse populations.* New York: Academic Press.

Department of Health and Human Services (2001). *Mental health: Culture, race, and ethnicity.* A supplement to mental health; A report to the surgeon general (pp. 77–104). Washington, DC: U.S. Public Health Service.

Gaw, A. (Ed.). (1993). *Culture, ethnicity, and mental illness.* Washington, DC: American Psychiatric Press.

McGoldrick, M., Giordano, J., & Pearce, J. K. (Eds.). (1996). *Ethnicity and family therapy* (2nd ed.). New York: Guilford Press.

Paniagua, F. A. (1998). *Assessing and treating culturally diverse clients* (2nd ed.). Thousand Oaks, CA: Sage.

Powell, G. J., Yamamoto, J., Romero, A., & Morales, A. (Eds.). (1983). *The psychosocial development of minority group children.* New York: Brunner/Mazel.

# CHAPTER 11

# Some Social Phenomena and Therapeutic Considerations

This last chapter briefly addresses several kinds of sociocultural phenomena of which clinicians need to be aware, and about which they need to be equipped with adequate knowledge. At a microscopic level, the phenomena may look as if they have no direct relation to the clinical cases with which clinicians deal on a daily basis. However, when they are examined at a macroscopic level, it becomes clear that these sociocultural issues cannot be ignored because they often have a significant impact on the clinicians' individual cases. No one can live without a social context. Any social phenomena or cultural issues that shape the life of an individual or a family, either directly or indirectly, deserve sufficient attention by competent clinicians. In this chapter, several selected topics related to sociocultural change, minorities, group violence and collective homicide, and religion will be reviewed in relation to mental health issues and discussed from the perspective of therapy and care.

## A. SOCIOCULTURAL CHANGE, MIGRATION, AND REFUGE

### 1. Cultural Change

Although a society normally undergoes a certain degree of change in any given time frame, occasionally sociocultural change of a great magnitude may occur within a relatively short period of time, significantly impacting the lives of people. Therefore, sociocultural change has been a popular subject of study in the social sciences (Berry, 1980) as well as in cultural psychiatry (Beiser, 1980; Favazza, 1980; Foulks, 1980; Tseng et al., 2001; Zilber & Lerner, 1996).

In this century, in contrast to earlier times, large-scale sociocultural change has been taking place rapidly around the globe. This has been due to the remarkable improvement of communication systems as well as the incredible improvement of transportation and the subsequent ease of travel and migration. These developments have increased transcultural encounters much faster and to a far greater extent than in the past. As pointed out by Zwingle (1999), "Goods move. People move. Ideas move. And cultures change." It is a worldwide phenomenon.

Cultural psychiatrists are interested in the social phenomenon of cultural change for theoretical and practical reasons. It is a phenomenon that allows clinicians and scholars to examine the explicit effects of culture on human behavior and psychology. Rapid and extensive sociocultural change has a strong impact on human life and a significant influence on the mental health of those who experience it (Murphy, 1961). There is certainly a clinical need to pay attention to such a phenomenon.

The pattern of reaction toward cultural change is not static and often occurs in a dynamic way. However, several basic patterns can be recognized, that is, rejection of the other (or new) culture, preservation of traditional (or native) culture, integration of native and foreign cultures, assimilation into the other (more powerful) culture, and cultural uprooting. (For details, see Tseng, 2001a, Chapter 43: Cultural Change and Coping, pp. 684–685.) As a reaction to cultural change, various patterns of reaction can occur at the individual, family, small group, or institutional level.

*Individual Level.* It is generally considered that the cultural system introjected through the process of enculturation in early life tends to remain unchanged, even when new cultural subsystems are acquired in adulthood through acculturation. Throughout life, many new things will be incorporated and endless layers of cultural subsystems will be added, so that, analogically, the personality will become like an onion with multiple layers. In general, the various components of the self (the different layers of the "onion") do not differ greatly, allowing interaction among them. They become integrated parts of the total personality manifested as unique patterns of reaction and behavior.

However, if the different cultural subsystems that are absorbed differ widely, or are even oppositional, it is possible for ambivalence, conflict, or confusion to develop within a person's mind. This is often the case with individuals who experience drastic changes in their cultural systems in a short period of time. Shifting from very restrictive views about man-woman relations to very liberal ones, converting from very rigid moral views to very permissive ones, and changing from a loose life orientation to a goal- and achievement-oriented life are some examples of cultural change that can have a serious impact on the psychology of an individual. In the extreme, a person will suffer from cultural confusion and loss of cultural identification. This often results in the formation of various mental health problems.

*Family Level.*    Rapid sociocultural change in a society will cause certain psychological disturbances to the family unit. Due to differences in reaction to the new value systems and ways of viewing things, the generation gap between parents and children will be wider than usual. Added to differences between the spouses, fragmentation and confusion could occur in the family as a whole. For instance, when a conservative Muslim family is exposed to outside Euro-American cultures through the media, whether or not the youngsters should be allowed to watch Western movies can become a serious family issue. The father may not permit any of the children to watch; the mother may secretly allow the sons to watch, but not the daughters, creating a split in the family (El-Islam, 2001) (see Case 1: The Woman with One Foot in the Past, in Section 2A: Culture and Stress).

In a stem or extended family, with the presence of a grandparent(s), the gaps among three generations complicates family functioning even further. For example, a three-generation Asian family migrated to the United States. The grandmother stayed at home most of the time, devoting herself to prayer and the worship of Buddhism, and ate only vegetarian food; the adult children, who worked outside the home, went to church on the weekends, where they simply wanted to meet and spend time with their Asian friends; the grandchildren watched TV and played computer games after school, making noise while the grandmother was meditating. There was hardly any conversation between the grandmother and grandchildren because the grandmother hardly spoke English and the grandchildren did not speak their native language. The adult children had difficulty comprehending the kind of education their children were receiving at school and were often upset by their children, who developed the habit of talking back to them. Cultural disconnection and confusion were illustrated in this transculturally migrated stem family.

*Group or Institutional Level.*    Sociocultural change often occurs in different directions and at different paces among various subgroups. Unless there is a clear goal and direction, and a powerful administrative organization, the change may result in social confusion, imbalance, and disintegration. At the social level, when people have difficulty following and adjusting to changes, such as modernization, revolution, or reformation, certain social phenomena may be observed. For instance, youth movements may arise that stress antimodernization, antidevelopment, or antiauthority (as exemplified by the Hippie movement in the 1960s in the United States, triggered by reactions to the Vietnam War). Sociologists have noticed the frequent emergence of new cults or peculiar religious groups, or the revitalization of indigenous practices, in reaction to sociocultural change that calls for modernization or mechanization. These special groups or social movements may indicate that the sociocultural change is occurring too fast for many people and needs to be slowed down.

## 2. Migration

Migration occurs when a person or a group of people move from one place to another, with the intention of staying in the new place for a considerable period of time. Moving to a new place usually causes considerable disruption in life, including changes in work, social relations, community networks, and lifestyle, and requires extra effort for successful adjustment to take place. If the migration is transcultural, that is, to a foreign country or diversely different sociocultural environment, with remarkable differences in language, life patterns, value systems, or social customs, it usually involves considerable cultural change and calls for special cultural adjustments.

The cultural change and adjustment associated with migration often causes psychological stress, emotional strain, and even mental complications while the migrant is adjusting to the new situation. A certain process is involved in coping, either at an intrapsychic, interpersonal, or social level. Migration impacts not only a person but also a family, a community, and a society. It challenges clinicians on how to provide suitable care for people experiencing mental health problems associated with transcultural migration (Westermeyer, 1989).

*The Impact of Migration on Mental Disorders.*    The subject of migration and mental health has been studied by cultural psychiatrists for several decades (Al-Issa & Tousignant, 1997). Attention was focused on the prevalence of mental illness among immigrants. This was stimulated by the early clinical impression that there were more admissions to mental hospitals among immigrants of certain ethnic groups. Later, many investigations were carried out by Ödegaard (1932), Astrup and Ödegaard (1960), and Murphy (1973) concerning mental disorders and immigrants. (For details, see Tseng, 2001b, Chapter 44: Migration, Refuge, and Adjustment, pp. 696–697.) The many conflicting results obtained from various investigations prompted scholars to realize that migration is not a singular phenomenon. The person who migrates, the motives for and circumstances of migration, the relationship between the hosting and the original society, and the ways the immigrant is received by the new society, are all factors that significantly affect the immigrant's adjustment after migration (Mezey, 1960; Murphy, 1961). Furthermore, it is understood that the process of migration, which is psychologically stressful, might be one of the precipitating factors in the development of certain minor psychiatric disorders, such as anxiety or psychosomatic disorders, but it is not the main reason for the development of major psychiatric disorders (i.e., psychoses), such as schizophrenia.

*Stress, Support, and Coping Styles.*   From the standpoint of psychology and mental health, migration can be viewed as a process of adjustment to the stresses and difficulties encountered in the new cultural setting. Contemporary concepts of stress and coping take the view that stress does not act alone on an individual in a simple manner, but as a part of an interactional system. Conceptually, it can be grasped from several perspectives, that is, the nature of the stress encountered by the subject, the stress perceived by the subject, the support systems available, the environmental conditions within which the stress needs to be coped, and the coping mechanisms utilized by the subject. Thus, all of these factors need to be considered in discussing the process of adjustment.

The usual stresses faced by an immigrant are various in nature. They may be practical, such as difficulty finding a place to live, obtaining a job, arranging for education, establishing a social network, and being accepted by the host society. If the language is different from the home country, there is the additional challenge of learning a new language. Establishing basic security and functioning as an individual or as a family are the main tasks for the new immigrant in the early stages of settlement.

Simultaneously with practical stresses, the immigrant also has to face psychological stresses. These involve the feeling of separation from the home setting, a sense of nostalgia, and a sense of strangeness or unfamiliarity in the new setting. Even though some immigrants may be delighted with and enjoy the new things in the host society and become busy incorporating the new conditions into their lives, learning new behavior patterns, and accepting the new value systems, there is still a process of change. Such change is always accompanied by hemostatic pressure and requires a process of adjustment at the intrapsychic level.

Ethnic or cultural identification may become an issue and a challenge after settlement in the foreign society. This may occur after some time, or soon after the move. A person needs to go through a delicate, ambivalent process, including debating and negotiating with his own mind. The process may take forever, without any final settlement.

These are the means that are available to provide support and assistance when a person faces a problem. Family members, friends, colleagues, neighbors, or various social organizations can be sources of support. The support can be given at the psychological level, such as empathy, emotional encouragement, or advice, or at a mechanical and practical level, such as providing a loan, introducing the migrant to a social network, and offering assistance in the search for a job.

Support systems can be discussed from two different perspectives: the availability of resources and the utilization of resources. Different resources for support are offered in different societies, depending on their structures and systems. In some societies, resources are more personal and private, whereas, in others, they may be more public and official. However, it is quite true that cultural background will significantly influence the pattern of utilization of the supporting systems, in turn, making a difference on the resulting adjustment. McKelvey and Webb (1996), in their survey of Vietnamese-Americans, found that the availability of like ethnic community support was critically important in preventing depressive symptoms in this group of immigrants.

Very much determined by individual personality, group relations and social environment, immigrants may follow different patterns and courses of adjustment. For instance, a group of immigrants may congregate among themselves, in terms of residential patterns, using their maternal language and socializing and doing business mainly with people of their ethnic kind. This is exemplified by the formation of a "Little Italy," "Little Tokyo," or "China Town" in some cities in the United States. Through such local congregations, the immigrants try to recreate and maintain their original sociocultural settings. Although such communities may provide a place where the immigrants can retreat or regress into their cultures of origin as needed, adherence to such a nest of their original cultures will certainly delay the process of assimilation into the larger host society. Even after several generations, the immigrants may still not be able to speak the language of the host society effectively or properly.

In contrast to this, some individuals may choose a course of isolation from (or even rejection by) their original cultures. They try to move far away from people of their own ethnic groups, trying to mix in the middle of the majority of the host society. They make an effort not to speak their own maternal languages in order to become fluent as soon as possible in the new language. They may try not to observe any cultural behavior from their homeland. Instead, they try to learn and imitate as quickly as possible their new way of life. If they are successful, they will experience a relatively rapid acculturation; if not, they may encounter cultural imbalance and emotional frustration.

Another pattern is to take a guarded position in the new environment. The immigrants may become suspicious and defensive and have difficulty relating with the majority people in the host society. This pattern of adjustment is occasionally observed among immigrants who are faced with less favorable situations in the host societies, such as illegal immigrants, reacting in this way to avoid being deported. Paranoid phenomena are common in some immigrant groups (Ndetei, 1988).

## 3. Refugees

By definition, a refugee is an individual or a group of people who, in order to escape from dangers in their home countries, seek temporary safety elsewhere, including foreign countries far away, in times of war or persecution. In a way, they experience a special kind of migration. What has been said about migration in the previous sections can be applied generally to the refugee; however, because of his unique nature, the refugee differs from ordinary migrants in many ways.

*Unique Nature of Refuge.*   First of all, a refugee usually migrates to escape from risks or dangers, often related to political, religious, ethnic, or racial persecution; civil or international war; or natural disasters. Second, seeking refuge usually occurs suddenly, without proper planning and preparation. Third, in many cases, the refugees have encountered killing, robbing, rape, death, and other serious situations that may lead to psychological trauma. Family members are often separated or lose contact. It is thus often grave hardship, suffering and starvation, endless fear, or risk of life that leads to taking refuge. Finally, after arriving in the place of refuge, the problems do not end; rather, new difficulties begin, associated with adjusting to a foreign place. Generally, refugees face more difficulties than ordinary migrants, who planned to migrate. The challenges include adjusting to their new lives from practical social perspectives: finding a place to live and resources for living, and worrying about the family members from whom they are separated or with whom they have lost contact. Thus, there is a series of psychological traumas and burdens that they have to face at different stages of before, during, and after refuge (Beiser, Turner, & Ganesan, 1989). If they take refuge in a foreign culture, dealing with transcultural adjustment presents another level of problems they have to face and with which they have to cope (see Case 1: A Laotian Man Overidentified with America, in Section 1 B4: Personality and Ethnic Identity).

*Working with Traumatized Refugees.*   Clinicians and scholars are newly interested and concerned with understanding the specific nature of the problems encountered by refugees, including those who have been tortured and experienced other traumas, and providing them with suitable care. However, knowledge and experience regarding culturally relevant treatment for these specific populations are still lacking and await further study and improvement (Draguns, 1996; Friedman & Jaranson, 1994; Varvin & Hauff, 1998; Vesti & Kastrup, 1992).

The first thing that needs to be recognized by clinicians is that most refugees have gone through terrible psychological traumas, either prior to, during, or even after they seek refuge. This is true whatever the main reason for taking refuge.

The traumas often are caused by war; are associated with interethnic conflict, political torture, and flight from dangerous places; or are the result of transcultural migration (Jaranson & Popkin, 1998). Mostly the traumas are multiple, severe, and chronic, beyond what ordinary human beings could take (Kinzie, 2001). Witnessing family members, friends, or neighbors being severely threatened, persecuted, raped, injured, or murdered causes most of these refugees to suffer from posttraumatic stress disorders (Kinzie et al., 1990). Many studies report that nearly 80 to 90% of the refugees manifest such clinical conditions. Treating posttraumatic stress disorders becomes almost synonymous with dealing with refugees.

Psychiatrists tend to take the general view that a person has the potential to recover from psychological trauma if proper care and treatment are provided. However, such an optimistic view is not held for many war refugees. These people, who have encountered multiple, repeated, severe psychological traumas, have difficulty improving even with long-term, intensive treatment. It needs to be understood that when the trauma is so severe, a person could suffer from it for the rest of his life. This means that clinically the therapist should not build false hope for himself or for the patient. He needs to be realistic.

It needs to be understood that severe psychological trauma will take a very long time to heal, if healing ever occurs. Longitudinal studies have indicated that it takes a long time to adjust to the host society (Kinzie & Manson, 1983; Sack, Him, & Dickson, 1999; Westermeyer, Neider, & Calliew, 1989). The clinical condition will be up and down, depending on the condition of the individual and the situations he encounters in life. Any trivial matter may provoke a stressful reaction and make the refugee vulnerable. Therapy could be offered mainly in the form of support and guidance, rather than trying to push the patient for a "cure."

Although it is basic for the therapist to provide support for the patient under treatment, this is particularly true when the treatment is for patients who have suffered from severe trauma. Based on his clinical experience with Southeast Asian refugees, Boehnlein (1987, p. 527) commented on the key issues involved in therapeutic work with such patients. The therapist can communicate a sense of warmth, genuineness, and competence by being direct, yet compassionate; by being assertive in the recommendation of a treatment approach, yet responsive to possibly conflicting cultural concepts of illness and healing; and by allowing the patient to report difficult historical information or express intense emotion without a sense of shame.

After working with torture victims, Somnier and Genefke (1986) suggested that by penetrating his most painful experiences, the victim has an opportunity to work with them in a new context. When the victim eventually comes to understand what was done to him and that he was broken down in a predictable way by torture, distorting normal psychological mechanisms, the memories no longer cause the victim the same fear as before.

Regarding model of therapy, Kinzie and colleagues (1980), whose clinical services have focused on Indochinese refugees for many years, have emphasized that instead of a conventional psychiatric approach, the medical approach of a physician, familiar to Indochinese patients, works better for them. Even though many models of psychotherapy are available for caring for the general population, experiences working with refugees from Southeast Asia have pointed out that family and group-oriented approaches, which focus more on occupation, recreation, or other activities, work better for them. There are many reasons for this. These patients are not familiar with individual psychotherapy, not to mention the language obstacle that limits such an approach. They feel more comfortable in a group, as it is in line with their culture to do things together. This not merely provides mutual group support and the opportunity to share the same life experiences and traumas, but also encourages them to feel safer exploring and examining their traumas in group therapy. Groups of the same gender and similar ages work better. Any recreational or social activity, including cooking, sewing, or learning how to prepare things for a cultural festival, for instance, helps them to work together and feel and identify themselves as a group, more important elements in therapy for them than exploring their traumas simply by "talking." Working with these refugees certainly requires bold ideas and revised approaches from a cultural point of view.

As for major therapeutic work, there is clinical debate among clinicians whether a past trauma needs to be psychologically "explored" or whether the patient should simply be encouraged to "repress" the traumatic experience. This is certainly a clinical judgment that needs be applied case by case. However, from a cultural point of view, particularly for those patients who are not used to expressing their private feelings in public, or to strangers, including a therapist, and who suffered from traumas of a very severe nature without the possibility of resolution for the past, it is considered inappropriate to try to explore the trauma if no resolution can be offered for it. For many kinds of trauma, the goal of therapy is to help the patient suppress or repress the trauma rather than bring it up to a conscious level. This is true for patients suffering from certain kinds of psychopathology, such as psychoses or borderline disorders. The same thing could be said for people of certain cultural backgrounds. In many cultures, repression and suppression are regarded as more suitable, if not more "mature," coping mechanisms.

Finally, it needs to be mentioned that many therapists who have worked with refugees with massive traumas year after year, hearing all the miserable and traumatic events that they have encountered, become "infected" by the hopelessness of their patients and feel overwhelmed by the horror of their personal stories (Mollica & Lavelle, 1988). Many therapists develop a certain countertransference, not toward the patients as persons, but toward their lives as human beings. They begin to wonder how life could so full of pain, trauma, injury, damage, and why so many people have to suffer repeatedly from severe traumas, which are almost impossible to bear (Kinzie, 2001). It is not a matter of the therapists becoming "numb" to human experiences, but "nihilistic" to some extent in their world-view. Taken to a severe degree, the therapist might become discouraged and his clinical work with traumatized patients compromised. This is a challenge for clinicians to face. As usual, therapists are advised to share such experiences with their colleagues and to offer mutual support among team workers.

## B. MINORITIES

"Minority" refers to a group of people that is smaller in number than the majority of people in a society and is customarily treated as less important, with less privilege, in the social system. A minority is considered to be of lower status and may even be discriminated against by other groups for various reasons, such as its political, religious, socioeconomic, ethnic/racial, or cultural background or its unusual physical conditions (including handicaps) or merely because it has fewer numbers or is "different." "Minority" is a term used in opposition to "majority," which implies a group of people of remarkably larger size, with an inherited, more dominant or higher social position, customarily with the tendency to exercise privilege and power over the minority group. Thus, it is a social and political term that has significant mental health implications.

When people of a minority group are treated unfairly by the majority and severely discriminated against for a long time, they tend to suffer from psychological feelings of inferiority, inadequacy, or powerlessness. They often have unspoken feelings of fear and resentment toward the majority, which looks down on them and treats them as inferior. Members of the minority tend to be deprived of opportunities for progress and achievement in the social environment. This may affect their self-image and confidence, resulting in negative group identification (Lott & Maluso, 1995).

Caution is necessary not to regard the minority as having more psychiatric disorders than the majority. It depends on the kinds of psychiatric disorders that are concerned. For instance, females (as the less privileged gender), in general, have a higher rate of suicidal attempts but a lower rate of suicide than males. African-Americans (as a minority group in the United States) have lower suicide rates in contrast to the majority Caucasian-Americans. The status of a minority may not necessarily have a more negative effect on psychology. In contrast, persecution of the minority group (by the majority) may lead to a tight bond among minority group members, such as the Irish response to the British or bombing by Basque separatists. The challenges in the lives of the minority may stimulate more creativity in them (Griffith, 1998; Harris, Blue, & Griffith, 1995).

However, a minority may be associated with certain kinds of mental health problems, may be vulnerable to particular behavior problems, and may tend to show certain kinds of psychopathology that warrant special attention (Moffic & Adams, 1983). At the same time, its members often underutilize the mental health care system that is set up for the majority and may not be treated properly and adequately by mental health services. Thus, it is relevant to pay attention to people of such backgrounds from social and cultural perspectives.

Many different kinds of people are perceived and treated as "minorities." For the sake of convenience, they can be subgrouped according to the main reasons that they became minorities.

## 1. Race or Ethnicity

A race or ethnic minority is commonly recognized socially and politically. Race or ethnicity is a powerful factor that leads people to identify certain groups as unique, with their members treating themselves or being treated by others as such. This is particularly true if the group emphasizes a distinct way of life, including how they address themselves or their unique appearance (such as Armenian people, a group that originally migrated from Germany, living in some parts of the United States, who emphasize a very conservative way of life; or orthodox Jewish people in many parts of the world) or obvious physical characteristics such as different facial or physical features, including color of skin. Racism is based on racial difference. Ethnicity or race is one of the main factors for distinguishing one group from another and is often associated with negative treatment. It has been pointed out that racism is more than prejudice. Racism is associated with the overt and covert forceful establishment and maintenance of power by one social group over another (Moore, 2000).

A race can be identified as a "different" group based on external appearance, but the history associated with the group and their past relations with the so-called majority is a more important key. For instance, that African-American people's were brought by Caucasian-Americans to the United States as slaves was the historical root for segregation and discrimination: African-Americans, for example, were not allowed to use the same restrooms or enter the same restaurants and were required to sit in the back of the bus, phenomena that were still observed not too long ago in a country that was originally built on the spirit of freedom and the fundamental principles of human rights and equality.

Native Americans are associated with the historical fact that they, as the original inhabitants of the American continent, which was "discovered" by a European (Columbus) several centuries ago and followed by the "invasion" of European people, lost their land and their way of life, as well as their dignity. Even though they were the native people, the newcomers, with greater military power, not only forced them to move and live on remote reservations but also treated them as people of lower status, socially and culturally. For instance, as children, many of them were taken away from their homes and placed in boarding schools for the sake of their "education" and health and were not allowed to speak their own native language or to live their indigenous, "savage" style of life (Jilek-Aall & Jilek, 2001). They were programmed to lose (or be uprooted from) their culture.

When there has been a negative relationship or severe discrimination between different ethnic or racial groups, the anger, hate, and fear last for a long time, transmitted from generation to generation. Unless special efforts are made to resolve the damage or scars that have resulted, the negative relationship will persist. There are often long-term effects associated with racism on educational and employment opportunities, which, in turn, induce a feeling of chronic despair and unhealthy ways of living, as exemplified by the West Indians in Britain (Burke, 1984). Ethnism or racism will even seriously affect mental health service, particularly in terms of the utilization of service and the therapist-patient relationship (Willie et al., 1995).

## 2. Gender

Differences in treatment between men and women have perhaps existed around the world. It is basically related to the physical and physiological differences between them. However, there are associated psychological factors that cause one to be regarded as superior to the other. Men are mostly regarded as more powerful, warranting a dominant position (not only physically but psychologically), whereas women are considered more vulnerable and therefore assume a subordinate status. In many societies, women are considered significant only for bearing children, particularly sons. If they fail, their husbands have a legitimate reason to dismiss them as their spouses or to have other women. There are no guarantees of "wifely status" in a modern sense.

Even in modern societies that emphasize basic equality, wages for women have always been less than those of men. Women usually are subject to physical and sexual abuse by men. Violence against women takes many forms, such as battery, sexual harassment, prostitution, pornography, or rape. Female infanticide is another form of discrimination and abuse of females at the beginning of life. Violence by police and security forces in ordinary times and by soldiers during war are common occurrences. Violence against women refugees and asylum seekers is another example. However, violence against women in intimate relations is a rather common phenomenon observed cross-culturally. After reviewing research findings from various societies, Krane (1996) reported that 20% to nearly 70% of women have experienced violence in intimate heterosexual relationships. From a therapy point of view, special consideration is necessary in treating women patients (Commas-Díaz & Greene, 1994; Nadelson & Zimmerman, 1993) (see Section 9D: Women).

## 3. Sexual Orientation

One social phenomenon that has been observed since the 1970s is advocacy for people with different sexual orientations. In the past, gay and lesbian people were regarded as sick. Even psychiatrists categorized them as mentally disordered. It was only in the 1970s that such categories were removed from the official classification system (DSM-III) and in 1980 from the internal classification system (ICD-9). However, there is still a stigma attached to homosexuality, and some negative attitudes are manifested by laypeople as well as professionals (Cabaj & Stein, 1996; Greene, 1997; Krajeski, 1993). This was partly due to the reason that newly arisen AIDS crisis in Europe and North America was associated with gay people and their sexual practices.

Campbell and associates (1983) pointed out that as long as there is a social stigma against homosexuality, certain adaptational demands will continue to be made on the members of this minority. The quality of mental health care traditionally provided to this group has often been inferior, resulting in the determination of many homosexuals to provide better care for themselves through growing numbers of gay-staffed and gay-oriented mental health centers. Campbell and colleagues suggested that much remains to be learned about homosexuality. However, the most important recent development is a growing trend toward the reexamination of countertransference distortions influencing the basic attitudes of the psychiatric profession toward homosexuality. Kitzinger (1997) stressed the importance of promoting the study of lesbian and gay psychology and seeking to counter discrimination and prejudice against lesbians and/or gay men.

## 4. Physical Condition

*Physical Handicaps.*  Some minorities are based on physical handicaps, such as deaf or blind people, or have other conditions they were either born with or have acquired. People with physical handicaps or deformities often suffer from limitations of sensation, communication, or the ability to move around freely. They have to endure different kinds of socialization and life experiences. Unfortunately, some of them are mistreated by ordinary people. The majority people are beginning to pay more attention and give more consideration to them in daily life, for instance, building roads in such a way that a handicapped person can get around by wheelchair or having braille in public facilities, such as elevators or automatic bank tellers, for blind people. However, not too many people know how to use sign language to communicate with deaf persons. The reality is that very few, if any, psychiatrists are trained to provide special services for deaf patients.

*Physical Sickness.*   Due to limitations in medical knowledge and lack of proper and effective treatment, patients with certain communicable diseases, such as leprosy and tuberculosis, were historically treated badly by ordinary people out of fear. Severe psychiatric disorders were no exception. Isolation and segregation were often effected by institutions built in remote areas for custodial care. Even family members, not to mention friends, were reluctant to visit the patients. In Asian countries, when arranged marriage was practiced, it was the responsibility of the matchmakers to check and assure the families that there was no history of severe illness such as leprosy or tuberculosis or problems such as drinking, gambling, or criminal behavior. In the contemporary society, being infected with HIV or having AIDS elicits social stigma and practical liabilities, regardless of a person's race and socioeconomic status. AIDS frequently forces significant social changes, including loss of job, denial of insurance, denial of public services, and loss of social and financial support systems. For ethnic minorities who may already face ostracism and economic limitations, the social changes associated with AIDS can be particularly catastrophic (Fernandez, Ruiz, & Bing, 1993, p. 575).

## 5. Young and Old Age

Without noticing it, young children or aged persons are often treated by adults as minorities due to their age. Young children are powerless to protect themselves if they are abused or neglected by their parents. They can be sold as if they are the property of the adults. They may be forced to serve as laborers without proper consideration of their health. Similarly, aged persons, when they become unable to take care of themselves, can potentially be neglected or abused either by their own family members or by care providers in public facilities. They are a minority and less protected in that sense (see Sections 9A: Children; 9B: Adolescents; and 9C: Aged Persons).

## 6. Social Discrimination

*Caste or Social Class.*   In many societies, people are divided into distinct subgroups with different statuses, hierarchies, and social privilege. The groups are determined not by economic factors but by heritage. In such a caste system, not only are clear boundaries recognized, but there is also no possibility of moving among castes. A person is born in a particular caste and is restricted to it for life. In ancient times, Egypt was well known for such a social caste system, which distinguished among priests, administrators, ordinary people, and slaves, in hierarchical order. A similar caste system was observed in most of the Pacific island societies, including Hawaii. It was only a century ago, after the arrival of Westerners, that the caste system was abandoned in Hawaii.

However, the artificial subdivision of castes is still practiced in many societies. India is one example. Marriage among castes is forbidden, which may cause tragedy. For instance, there was news from a rural area in India that a young man of a lower caste had eloped with a young woman of a higher caste. When the father of the young woman found out, he expressed his anger by raping and murdering the mother of the young man, while the villagers watched. Nobody dared to stop him until the police arrived because his actions were considered permissible against a person of a lower caste. Although this is a rare instance occurring in a remote, rural area, it reflects in an extreme way how a caste system may become the source of discrimination and mistreatment.

Instead of recognized social castes, there are invisible subdivisions among people according to different economic and social status or other factors in many societies. There are many stories in the East and West describing marriages that were obstructed because of a wide gap in financial status or personal past history. In Japan, the very popular movie, *Aizenkatsura*, written at the end of the Meiji era, described the love story of a doctor and a nurse. The affair met with strong disapproval from the doctor's family because he was the eldest son of the superintendent of a private hospital and was expected to inherit the post. The woman, while she was very pretty and nice, was a widow with a son. Her ex-husband had died in a traffic accident. A woman who had previously had another man and a son by another man was considered unacceptable for an important man in traditional Japanese culture. Thus, the woman was considered unfit to be the wife of a physician and superintendent-to-be. Strong psychological factors associated with cultural beliefs made her an "unqualified" person. This is quite different from the modern Western movie, *Pretty Woman*, a love story with a happy ending between a wealthy young man and a pretty, charming prostitute. However, it needs to be pointed out that, in a society such as America, even though the existence of social class due to economic factors is denied superficially due to the spirit of equality, in actual life there is still invisible segregation (and, in some instances, clear discrimination) observed. It is only in a movie that a lower class woman can happily marry an affluent man without any resistance from family, friends, or society.

*Immigrants.*    A group of people may be socially discriminated against when they migrate to a host society. Simply because they are newcomers, not yet assimilated into the host society, they suffer from less privilege in education and occupation and are even denied opportunities due to potential competition with the original inhabitants. "Minority" vs. "majority" status can result simply from migration, without other factors, such as ethnicity or race. However, the situation can be aggravated if the migrants are of different ethnic or racial backgrounds than the majority people in the host society. Difficulties in language, differences in faith, different ways of observing social rules and etiquette, make it more difficult for them to adjust to the majority. The combined effects are the formation of an invisible or apparent wall between the migrants and the host society. The migrants are often treated as "aliens" and are even severely discriminated against or persecuted by the majority in the host society.

With the improvement of transportation, the ease of moving far distances, the need for sociopolitical refuge, and a search for better economic or educational opportunities, there is an increase in migration in many parts of the world. The recent increase of migrants from Eastern Europe, the Mideast, and Africa to Western Europe is causing new social tensions between the migrating minorities and the host majorities. This has certainly raised mental health concerns (Littlewood & Lipsedge, 1989). The problems are not centered around only the adult migrants but also often extend into and are magnified in the next generation, calling for special attention to younger migrants (Powell, 1983; Vargas & Koss-Chioino, 1992).

*Occupation and Historical Roots.*   The *Burakumin* in Japan is a unique example of a group of people that is collectively treated as an "untouchable minority" and regarded by the majority as outcasts, not for ethnic or racial reasons, but simply based on social factors (DeVos & Wagatsuma, 1969). This group was originally called *Eta*, a slang term meaning "excessively dirty," or *Hi-ning*, which literally means "not a human person." Some scholars have speculated that they might have originally belonged to a certain lord who lost a war and had to escape from persecution by his enemy. Others think that the prejudice came from the occupations of the group's members; the earliest *Eta* were butchers, tanners, saddle makers, caretakers of the dead, or grave diggers. They touched dead bodies or flesh. In Shinto belief, death was the worst form of pollution; therefore, the *Eta* were regarded as polluted. Later, the group of prejudicial occupations was expanded, and the "no-person" status became hereditary. The classification was abolished by law in 1870, and the term *Buraku-min* (literally, people of the village) was used more often, but the social discrimination continued. Recently, there has been a movement among them to improve their own self-image.

The existence of an "untouchable" group of people is observed in India as well. This is a group belonging to the lowest level of the caste system. Generation after generation, people of this group engaged in cleaning of toilets or collection of garbage, so-called dirty jobs. They usually live in slum areas outside of the city and are not allowed to live with "ordinary" people. They are allowed to marry only their kind, and there is no channel available for them to escape from their discriminated position, by education or any other means.

*Religion.*   There is no shortage of stories about how people regard others as different, inferior, or improper because of differences in religion. Instead of treating people of other faiths as merely different, sometimes actions of opposition and conflict, discrimination, and even elimination may take place. Many interethnic or interracial conflicts that originated with differences of religion have occurred and still occur today, in every corner of the globe. The Crusades, which started in the beginning of the 11th century in Eastern Europe and continued in several waves over a couple of centuries, are obvious examples. The elimination and crucification of Christians in Japan before the Meiji era and the persecution of Jews in Italy in Roman times and in Nazi Germany are well-known parts of history. It cannot be denied that the present, ongoing conflict in the Mideast is rooted in religious matters in addition to historical interethnic relationships and politics. One of the major reasons people in Tibet were persecuted by Chinese soldiers was that they would not give up their religious beliefs and practices in compliance with the Communists' atheistic ideology.

Thus, there are many reasons that persons can be treated unfairly, with discrimination and even persecution. As a minority group, in a broad sense, they have one thing in common: they are considered less important and less favorable by others and, often, as a result, they perceive themselves in the same way. This leads to an unfavorable mental health condition.

## 7. Therapeutic Implications

*Utilization of Psychiatric Service.*   Existing mental health services are generally established primarily for the care of people of the majority. This situation may not be intentional, but it often results in unsuitable conditions for minority people. For instances, the language used is not familiar to migrants from other countries, and often there are no staff available for translation. Because there are almost no staff who understand sign language, there is no way to communicate with deaf people. The existence and function of the services are often not familiar to people from foreign countries or indigenous people. It is almost impossible for financially underprivileged people to follow the appointment system involved in care delivery because they do not have telephones or access to transportation.

The unfamiliarity, unsuitability, and inaccessibility of the services make the existing mental health facilities underutilized by people of minority backgrounds. While some improvements have been made recently in many facilities, with instruction in multilanguages, the utilization of interpreters for certain languages, outreach programs that offer services in the community rather than at a clinic, and so on, there is still a lot of room for improvement.

*Therapist-Patient Relationship.*   The therapist–patient relationship is characterized by a wide gap and certain transference/countertransference issues in relation to the treatment of minorities. Depending on the nature of the existing majority-minority relationship, the therapist-patient relationship may be characterized by problems of trust, feelings of inequality, resentment, or hatefulness. Certainly it involves the displacement of the social majority–minority situation into the therapeutic relationship. It is a special kind of transference and countertransference that could have a negative impact on therapy and needs to be clarified, managed, and resolved from the very beginning. If the negative ethnic or racial transference and countertransference is very intense and negative, a change of therapists may need to be considered.

The gap or differences between therapist and patient is certainly an important issue that cannot be ignored. Often an extra effort is required to minimize potential obstacles. If the obstacles are attributed to issues related to majority-minority status, beyond personal, educational, socioeconomic differences, they need be brought up openly and managed carefully from the very beginning of such interethnic, -racial, or -cultural therapy (see Sections 5B1: Therapist-Patient Relations; 7A: Intercultural Psychotherapy: Challenges and Competency).

In summary, the therapist faces many challenges that need to be addressed whenever there is a gap between the therapist and the patient in terms of personal conditions, privileges of various kinds, life experiences, social status, culture, or race (Carter, 1995). This basic issue was elaborated previously in a broader sense in the chapter on intercultural psychotherapy (see Section 7A), which, in principle, can also be applied to the treatment of minority patients. It is a basic assumption that there are certain psychological issues associated with being a minority, beyond social, economic, ethnicity, race, or cultural differences, that deserve special attention and management in psychiatric therapy (Ho, 1987; Powell, 1983).

## C. GROUP VIOLENCE AND COLLECTIVE HOMICIDE

Although violent or homicidal behavior carried out by an individual against others or a group of people has been elaborated earlier (such as *amok* behavior in Section 3A: Culture-Related Specific Syndromes), here we will discuss massive violent or homicidal behavior undertaken collectively by one group of people against another group of a different ethnic, racial, or cultural background. Therefore, it is a social phenomena beyond individual psychopathology and needs to be comprehended from the standpoint of group psychology and social dynamic. It is relevant to examine these social occurrences from a cultural perspective as well. From a clinical point of view, many victims of group violence or their remaining families are often in need of clinical care relating to the trauma. Group violent behavior occurs in many forms. For the sake of convenience here, it is reviewed under the categories of ethnic conflict, racial riot, terrorism, massacre, and holocaust.

### 1. Various Phenomena

*Ethnic or Racial Conflict.*   Due to historically accumulated hate between groups of different ethnic or racial backgrounds, open conflict exists between them either as constant tension or occasional outbursts of violent or even homicidal behavior toward each other. Many-decades-long open conflict between the Irish and the British people in Ireland (Heskin, 1994) or the Jews and Muslims in the Mideast are representative examples.

*Ethnic or Racial Riot.*   This refers to the public outburst of violent behavior by a group of people against others primarily due to ethnic or racial tension. When a minority is severely discriminated against and mistreated by the majority for ethnic or racial reasons, the accumulated anger may burst into collective violent action. The riot is usually precipitated by some incident, but the collective action of a riot tends to happen without organization. The racial riots of black people against white people in the 1970s in the United States are typical examples.

*Terrorism.*   This refers to the phenomenon of a group of people carrying out terrifying or destructive actions against another group of people with the intention of threatening or retaliation. In contrast to riots, the terrorist action is often carried out by an organization with a plan and under a leader's command (Wilson, 2000). The cause of terrorism could be due to ethnic or racial conflict, financial gain, religious or political purpose, or a mixture of these (Dishman, 2001). In psychology research literature, it has been pointed out that terrorists possess many of the traits of pathological personalities, but rarely possess actual clinically identified psychiatric disorders (Silke, 1998). The use of poisonous gas to kill people in the subway by a member of a religious sect in Tokyo, Japan; suicide bombings in Israel by Palestinian people; or the hijacking of airplanes and crashing into the World Trade Center towers in New York (9/11 event) are some terrible examples.

*Massacre.*   The indiscriminate, merciless killing of a large number of human beings (usually civilians) by another group of people, usually with weapons, is called a massacre. Such large-scale killing often occurs in war. Hundreds or thousands of victims may be killed within a short period of time. However, the massacre of Chinese people by Japanese soldiers in Nanjing, the capital of China, in 1937, during the Japanese-Chinese War, was an atrocity on a scale seldom ever seen in the world. After the war, the Chinese government claimed that, in less than seven weeks after the capital fell, nearly 300,000 people were killed (Hata, 1986) (see Fig. 1). Some Japanese have insisted recently that the number of reported victims of the massacre was exaggerated, implying that China falsified the claim (Takemoto & Ohara, 2000).

*Holocaust.*   The massive homicide of people of other ethnic or racial groups according to an organized plan, with the intension of destroying or eliminating a discriminated ethnic or racial group, is referred to as a holocaust. The

FIGURE 1    Nanjing Massacre of Chinese by the Japanese Army. (a) A Japanese solider uses a sword to kill a Chinese civilian youth. (b) A Japanese newspaper (*Tokyo Daily News*) reported a competition for the killing of Chinese, with two Japanese second lieutenants decapitating more than 100 Chinese victims in a day, and promising to compete for an even better record. (c) Nanjing people killed by the Japanese army were thrown into the Yangtze River. (d) Dead bodies were collectively buried by the Red Cross. [From *A Photo Group Reflecting the Japanese Army's Massacre of Nanjing People*; courtesy of The Editorial Board of Historical Data of Nanjing Massacre]

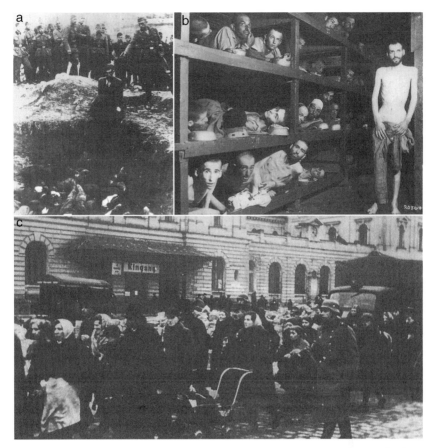

FIGURE 2    Holocaust of Jews by Nazi Germany. (a) Mass execution of Russian Jews by the SS. (b) Undernourished inmates in an overcrowded concentration camp. (c) Jews being marched to the railway station for deportation to a death camp. [From the U.S. Holocaust Memorial Museum]

systematic destruction of over 6 million European Jews by the Nazis before and during World War II is a widely known human tragedy (see Fig. 2).

## 2. Ethnic or Racial Conflict as the Cause

Collective violent behavior or massive homicidal behavior needs to be comprehended from a social viewpoint, with consideration of various social factors, including religion, finances, or politics, as well as from the perspective of group psychology. Beside this, it is important to recognize that there is one common cause for those group violent behavior, namely, the fear and hate between groups of different ethnicity, race, or culture. This is quite true, no matter what form of collective violent behavior is undertaken.

The hate and fear of other ethnic groups may simply be driven by basic human psychology. As a small child, a baby goes through a developmental stage of fear reaction toward a stranger (any person other than familiar the face of a caretaker). Later, as teenagers, instead of showing sympathy, children sometimes laugh at and mistreat people who are handicapped or different from them. This is understood as a defense against fear of those people who look physically different from them. As an extension of this developmental psychology, people carry with them the emotion of fear toward others who are "different" from them. They may show curiosity or interest in people who are different, in terms of their physical appearance or behavior, but underneath they are associated with fear and suspicion, resulting from the feeling of guarding against "strange" people.

Based on this basic human psychology, if there is an incidence of misunderstanding or conflict, fear, anger, and hate develop. If the conflict recurs, the fear, anger, and hate accumulate and are aggravated. Based on the actual experience of trauma from conflict between "them" and "the others," the fear, anger, and hate are imprinted and transmitted generation after generation. They become historically accumulated fear, anger, and hate between them through the process of enculturation. This becomes a feeling that is difficult to erase from the brain.

This basic fear, anger, or hate toward "others" who are different from "us" can be easily be reinforced and intensified, and even justified by social force, including political ideology or religious belief. Violence toward others as a mean for solution can be supported by cultural belief (Hoffman, 1999). The action of collective violence or even massive homicide can be carried out through political organization and often by military power. It has been revealed that some of the terrorists were socialized to violence from childhood through special circumstances, such as in refugee camps (Post, 2000), so that violent acts toward others is a part of their personalities and unswerving belief regarding the solution to problems.

## D. RELIGION

Religion is one of the ways we understand the world and give meaning to our lives. There are numerous religions in different societies and even within the same society that directly or indirectly shape our lives and influence our thoughts and behavior. They also impact psychopathology, on the one hand, and influence therapy, on the other. From a clinical point of view, it is important for therapists to know the religious background of the patients and provide accordingly relevant care. Thus, it is essential for clinicians to understand the nature of religion and how to deal with the important cultural aspects of belief and faith. For this reason, there is a renewed interest among psychiatrists and behavior and social scientists in the interrelation of religion, psychiatry, and mental health (Bhugra, 1996; Boehnlein, 2000a; Koenig, 1998; Neeleman & Persaud, 1995; Pattision, 1984). It is very natural for cultural psychiatrists to be concerned with the religious aspects of our lives and behavior, as they are closely tied to culture.

## 1. Major Religions

In here, "major" religion refers simply to the fact that they have existed for a relatively long time and have a relatively large number of adherents. Therefore, they are conveniently regarded as religions of the mainstream. Several such major religions observed around the world have impact on the people living in the United States in one way or another. Therefore, it is considered important for clinicians to have a basic knowledge about these major religions for relevant clinical care.

### a. Buddhism

Buddhism began with the son (Siddhartha Gautama, born 563 B.C.) of a ruler of a small kingdom in Nepal. Despite his wealth and promised future, he became aware of human pain, suffering, aging, and death. At the age of 29, he left home, plunging into the forest to search for the truth. After his Great Awakening under the *Bodhi* (enlightenment) tree, he became known as the Buddha (the Enlighted One or the Awakened One). He taught that life is dislocation or out of joint being full of pain, conflict, and suffering. He explained that the desire or drive for fulfillment is the cause of the suffering. He pointed out that suffering can be relieved by the path of enlightenment, namely, release from narrow self-interest, overcoming the egoistic drive for separate existence. The way to the resolution is through the Eightfold Path, right knowledge, aspiration, speech, behavior, livelihood, effort, mindfulness, and absorption. The ultimate goal is to reach the state of Nirvana, which literally means "cessation," or "extinction " (of the desire of fire), meaning to void desire.

From a religious point of view, it has been pointed out that Buddhism teaching has evolved as a reaction to the existing Hinduism that partly provoked it (Smith, 1965). Buddha taught a religion devoid of the common elements observed in most religions, that is, authority (he never claimed his status as the leader of religion), ritual (no worship or statues), speculation (no explanation of the origin and the nature of the universe nor the life after death), tradition (no relation with past existing belief systems), and the supernatural (never claimed the existence of supernatural beings in the form of god). The primary goal of enlightenment is wisdom. Even though there was constant pressure during his lifetime to turn him into a god, he insisted that he was merely a human in every respect. A century later, his followers created his statue for worship and a sect concerned with the existence of "paradise" (The Pure Land) after the death.

Although Buddhism originated in Nepal, in northern India, it had little impact on the Indian continent and spread to Asia (China, Japan, and Korea), south Asia (Thailand, Burma, Cambodia), and its neigbor island of Sri Lanka. Associated with time, Buddhism was subdivided into two major schools: Theravada Buddhism and Mahayana Buddhism. Theravada (the Way of the Theras) Buddhism is more conservative in its approach, reflecting the earliest and most authentic Buddhist beliefs and practices. Mahayana (Great Vehicle, or Great Way) Buddhism emphasizes the variety of paths for reaching the final state of enlightenment. The types of Buddhism that Mahayana embraces include Tibetan Buddhism, Chan (Zen in Japanese, or Son in Korean) Buddhism, and Pure Land Buddhism (Morgan, 1993).

As one of the Eightfold Path, Buddhists observe the need to have right behavior. This includes not harming living things, not taking anything that is not given, not misusing the bodily senses, refraining from wrong speech, and abstaining from intoxicants that cloud the mind. Regarding the prohibition of killing, most Buddhists extend this proscription to animals; the strict ones, consequently, are vegetarian. Regarding chastity, for monks and the unmarried, this meant continence; for the married it meant restrant in proportion to one's interest in and distance along the Path.

### b. Christianity

Christianity began with Jesus, a Jewish carpenter who was born in Palestine about two thousand years ago. He stressed Yahweh's compassion and preached to all members of society across social barriers. He opposed the holy codes of the Jewish authorities, which he felt created social division. His teachings were parallel to the Old Testament, inherited with the Jewish vision of a God, but were fresh and appealed to ordinary men's imagination. He preached two most important facts about life: God's overwhelming love for man, and the need for man to receive this love, then let it flow outward again toward his neighbors. Many of the words of Jesus as reported in the New Testament, have become the most repeated words in the world, such as "Love your neighbor as yourself" and "Whatsoever ye would that men should do unto you, do ye also unto them." It is believed that by releasing them from guilt, fear, and self, it could give men a new birth into life.

The Christian religion was institutionalized, and the theology of the church developed over several centuries. It hinges on several key concepts: the original sin of sexuality, God's relief from sin, how God became human, and the Trinity concept of God as the Father, the Son, and the Holy Ghost.

Of all the religions of man, Christianity is the most widely spread geographically and has a large number of adherents. Nearly two thousand years of history have brought an astonishing diversity to this religion. The first great division occurred in the middle of the 11th century (1054) between the Eastern Orthodox Church in the East (with Constantinople as its center) and the Roman Catholic Church in the West (with Rome as its headquarter). This division happened as the culmination of differences in the cultural, linguistic, spiritual, and political traditions that had grown between the Western and Eastern halves of Christendom. The Roman Catholic Church views the Church as Teaching Authority and Sacramental Agent; it was held that in the final analysis those functions belong to the Pope. In contrast, the Eastern Orthodox Church takes the view that god's truth is disclosed through "the conscience of the church."

Later, in the middle of the 16th century, led by a German monk, Martin Luther, the Protestant Reformation happened. It was based on differences of theological views. There are two distinctive features of Protestantism. The first one is Justification by Faith. It holds the view that faith is a personal phenomena that requires a movement of the total self, in mind, will, and affections. The second one is the Protestant Principle. Stated philosophically, it warns against absolutizing the relative; stated theologically it warns against idolatry (Smith, 1965, pp. 343–344). Later, Protestantism followed four main courses: Baptist, Lutheran, Calvinistic, and Anglican, which further subdivided into now more than 250 denominations in the United States alone. About 85% of Protestants belong to 12 major denominations.

### c. Hinduism

Hinduism has a long history and is tied to the metaphysical concepts of Indian mythology. It took its original form in pre-Vedic times, dominated by animistic beliefs and the belief that an extensive world of demons and evil spirits causes illness to humankind. It is characterized by the symbols, myths, and multiple images of gods. It has no founder, no single scripture or creed, but there are many gods. Thus, a better way of describing it is the aggregate of practices and beliefs of some 1.4 billion Hindus living in the Indian subcontinent and other parts of the world (Kanitkar, 1993, p. 125). The term "Hindu" comes from the word coined by ancient Persians to describe those who lived opposite them on the other side of the Indus River. Modern Hindus prefer the phrase *sanatana dharna* to describe their religion, which can be translated as "the eternal way of conduct."

Hindus hold the concept of three gods in one image, illustrating the continuity and change that is an important feature of their religion. The three gods—Brama (the creator), Vishnu (the preserver), and Shiva (the destroyer and regenerator)—are considered to be aspects of Braman, the one God (universal soul). Although there is a great diversity within their religion, there are some common beliefs. Hindus believe that their lives are governed by *samsara*, a cycle of birth, death, and rebirth. Hinduism traces an individual's journey through reincarnation. A person's present life is the product of what he has done in the past. Thus, every action has an inexorable consequence that affects even future life cycles. The Hindus's ultimate goal is to attain personal liberation from the cycle of *samsara*. This can be achieved by following a sacred code of conduct, performing certain rituals, and behaving in a moral way to oneself, one's family, and society. In addition, they go through specific traditional paths of devotion, action, and knowledge.

Most Hindus accept the authority of the ancient scriptures known as the Veda. Hindus share a body of beliefs and knowledge of traditional paths to follow toward the realization of ultimate reality. They would also all emphasize the importance of striving to attain purity and avoiding pollution, as well as the regular practice of worship both in the home and in the temple (Kanitkar, 1993, p. 126). According to orthodox Hinduism, man may desire the acquisition of wealth or sensual pleasures, but they cannot really satisfy him. He needs to tap into the infinite power, which may be accomplished through yoga, a method of training to help unite the power within.

Hindus attach great importance to purity and pollution, in terms of both physical cleanliness and spritual well-being. On the physical side, it affects the preparation and eating of food. Vegetarian food is popular among many Hindus because it is free from blood. Indian society subdivides and ranks people hierarchically in a rigid caste system. In descending order of superiority, they are Brahmins (priest, professionals), Kshatriyas (rulers, administrators, soldiers), Vaishyas (peasant-farmers, mechants), and Shudras (artisans). In addition, there is an additional caste termed "untouchables," who were obliged by their masters to carry out the "unclean" jobs within society. Hinduism believes that through multiple reincarnations all souls migrate through all the castes except the untouchables.

### d. Islam

The prophet Mohammed was born in A.D. 570 in the leading tribe of Mecca in Koreish. His early life was cradled in tragedy, for his father died a few days before he was born, his mother when he was 6, and his grandfather, who cared for him after his mother's death, when he was 9 (Smith, 1965, p. 219). Upon his maturity in need of deep solitude, he frequently visited a cave in a huge rock on the outskirts of Mecca, where he repeatedly heard a voice commanding him to cry, which his wife interpreted to mean that he would be the Prophet from the God. He came to believe that Allah, the high God of the Arabic pantheon, was the one and only God, and started to serve as the Prophecy.

Islam brought a vast change to the moral and social order of Arabia and established a specific social order in which faith, politics, and society were joined. At present, the believers of Islam are estimated at 860 million in the world, comprising nearly one-quarter of the world's population. They form nearly total majorities in countries of the Middle East, northern Africa, central Asia, and

Indonesia, and also substantial minorities in the West and many other parts of the world (Clarke, 1993, p. 85).

The name of this religion, Islam, derived from the word *salam*, which means primarily "peace," but in a secondary sense "surrender." Its full connotation is "the perfect peace that comes when one's life is surrendered to God" (Smith, 1965, p. 217). The classic of Islam teaching, the Koran, proclaimed the omnipotence and mercy of God and man's total dependence on Him. According to the strictly orthodox view, the Koran's every letter was directly dictated by God. The Koran is perhaps the most read book in the world, and certainly the most often memorized one, exerting the most influence on those who read it.

For Muslims, there are five main observances, known as the pillars of Islam. The first is a profession of faith in the oneness of God. This belief in one God, Allah, is the cornerstone of Islam. The second pillar is compulsory prayer, five times a day, facing toward the holy city of Mecca at dawn, noon, midafternoon, evening, and night. The third pillar is to give alms or charity to the poor. It is of two kinds, legal (one-fourtieth of a person's income) and voluntary. The fourth pillar is fasting. During Ramadan, the ninth month of the Islamic year, all adult Muslims in good health, excluding pregnant women, fast from dawn until sunset for the whole month (20 or 30 days, depending on the length of the lunar month). It is intended to foster obedience to God and unity among Muslims. The final pillar is the pilgrimage to Mecca, the holy city, which all Muslims are expected to make once in a lifetime (Clarke, 1993, p. 86).

### e. Judaism

The religion of the Jewish people, Judaism, was the first great faith to hold that there is only one God. This monotheism is not only its cornerstone, but also that of Christianity and Islam, both of which derived much of their spiritual traditions from Judaism. Central to Judaism is the Hebrew Bible, known to Christians as the Old Testament, which tells of the origins and development of the Jewish people beginning from God's creation of the World (Shah, 1993, p. 17).

The Jewish God, Yahweh, evolved from a personal and tribal deity to the ultimate and only God. This God is described as passionate and very involved in human affairs. Judaism conceives God and His creations, the world and its people, as good and righteous. Therefore, the present life is considered important, and humanitarian activities are emphasized. The Jewish culture has a strong moral code that emphasizes justice as a basic value. Jewish people emphasize practices and traditions that are rooted in sharing life with God. The Jews considered themselves to have been chosen not primarily to receive special privilege but to serve and to suffer the ordeals service entails (Smith, 1965, p. 290).

It is estimated that there are approximately 14.5 million Jews in the world today. They are broadly divided between Ashkenazi (German, Central European, and Russian Jews) and Sepjardi (Spanish, Portuguese, northern Africa, Greek,

Italian, Ethiopian, Yemenite, and Syrian) Jews. From biblical times, there has been a creative tension between Jews living in the land of Israel and those outside it. Presently the most dynamic centers of Jewish life are the state of Israel (founded in 1948) as well as the United States, where there are almost 6 million Jews (Shah, 1993, p. 17).

## 2. Other Religions or Movements in America

There are many other religions found in the United States, which, in contrast to the major religions elaborated previously, are practiced and observed by relatively fewer adherents or worshipers. Those that have relative importance to culture and mental health or medical practice will be described briefly here. Some are closely related to parent religions, whereas some are products of new thoughts or religious movement. They are categorized and described accordingly to their backgrounds (Clarke, 1993, pp. 202–211).

### a.  Christianity-Related Religions

*Christian Science.*    Founded by Mary Baker Eddy in the late 19th century in New Hampshire, following a trend observed then, the movement aimed to make Christianity "scientific." It denied the orthodox doctrines of creation, sin, and redemption. Physical illness was viewed as a reflection of discord in a person's spirituality.

*Hutterian Brethren.*    Originally founded in the 1530s in Switzerland by the pastor Jacob Huntter, Hutterites believe that true Christianity can be practiced only in communal living, sharing all possessions. They take little interest in education beyond the primary level, except in the study of their own works and traditions. When the membership of a community reaches a certain number (about 150), it is split, and a new colony is formed.

*Jehovah's Witnesses.*    Founded by Charles Taze Russell in late 19th century in Pittsburgh, Pennsylvania, the Witnesses believe that the final battle of the nations depicted in the biblical books is imminent and Jehovah's Witness will reign with Christ in a future millenarian of blessedness. They reject the belief in the Trinity (three persons in one God). They also reject the belief that Jesus was God by nature and, instead, insist that Jesus received the status of Son of God. The believers have a simple lifestyle. They prohibit blood transfusion as well as stimulants.

*Mormons.*    This movement was founded in New York in 1830 by the visionary Joseph Smith, who claimed to have translated the revealed Book of Mormon, an ancient text containing wisdom that supplemented the Bible. Smith's successor established Mormon headquarters in Salt Lake City, Utah. Believers place an emphasis on missionary work so that young people, always in pairs, with neckties, go out in the community for such work. They are banned from smoking and drinking alcohol, coffee, and tea, whereas sports, recreation, and education play an important part in their lives.

*Olde Order Amish.* This movement emerged as a distinctive branch of the Mennonites in Switcherland in the 1690s. Amish colonies endorse the principle of *meidung* (separation) from society. They believe that salvation can be gained only within the community. They practices nonresistance, obedience to the Bible and church, and the avoidance of all worldly pleasures, amusement, and vanities.

*Seventh-Day Adventists.* This group grew up in the United States in the 19th century as Adventist. They believe Christ will return and inaugurate a millennial reign in heaven, at the end of which the wicked will be annihilated along with Satan, and believers will lead a blessed life on Earth. The group observes the seventh day of the week (Saturday) as the Sabbath (rather than Sunday), when it strictly forbids work. Seventh-Day Adventists are forbidden to use alcohol, tobacco, and meat.

### b. Hinduism-Related Religions

*Hare Krishna.* Founded in the United States in 1966 as a new religion of Indian origin, this religious group focuses it worship to the god Krishna (rather than Vishnu in traditional Hinduism). The followers practice a form of yoga and devotion to a personal god through love. The principal form of devotion is the congregational chanting of the names of God. There is also devotional service, which involves worship as well as teaching, cooking, gardening, and distributing literature in exchange for donations.

*Transcendental Meditation.* Founded by a monk, Maharishi Mahesh Yogi, in 1958 in India transcendental meditation (TM) aims to improve through meditation both the individual and society in general. The movement was popularized by the Beatles rock group in the late 1960s. After a simple rite of initiation, the members meditate daily to induce a feeling of deep relaxation, leading to greater vitality and creativity.

### c. Other New Religions

*Unification Church.* Founded in Korea in 1954 by the Reverend Sun Myung Moon, its teachings offer their own unique interpretation of the Bible. Followers claimed that Jesus's mission was in part a failure because he did not marry and so was only able to offer spiritual and not physical salvation to the world.

They focused on creating the perfect family and saving the human race. The leader, Moon, arrived in the United States in the early 1970s for lecture tours, large rallies, and mass weddings. The unmarried followers were assigned a mate by the leader. Due to the alleged means of recruitment, involving brainwashing techniques, it is popularly viewed as a sinister cult that breaks up families.

*Voodoo.*   Similar to several African-Catholic systems of belief and practice found in the Caribbean and North, Central, and South America (such as Candomblé and Santería), the *voodoo* cult was found in Haiti. The belief is based on the numerous African gods and the Catholic saints. Special songs and dances are performed in honor of each individual diety. Respect for the dead is extremely important. They also believe that breaking a taboo will lead to death.

Finally, from a cross-cultural perspective, it should be pointed out that many people have an atheistic worldview and live without religions. This is attributed to their lifestyle and beliefs, on a voluntary basis; rooted in their childhood encultural experiences; or related to official ideology and policy, such as in mainland China, where more than one-fifth of the world's population lives. As an extension of the traditional Confucian atheistic view and present political ideology, the Chinese people in mainland China are presently instructed not to believe in any supernatural beings.

## 3. Religion and Psychopathology

### a. Distinction between "Healthy" and "Pathological" Religions

Even though it is difficult to distinguish between "healthy" and "pathological" religions, there is a practical need for such a distinction. Perhaps it would be easier to examine certain cults that society has considered to be clearly "unusual," "strange," or "pathological."

Still fresh in our memories is the collective suicide of 39 members of the Heaven's Gate cult, who lived in a rented mansion in Rancho Santa Fe, California. Following their leader, Marshall Applewhite, a former mental patient, the cultists ended their lives in a planned, organized way: taking sleeping pills mixed in pudding and lying on their bunk beds with plastic bags over their heads to await the holy spaceship. This incident occurred when the comet Hale-Bopp appeared in the sky in March 1997. The members believed that they were escaping a revamping of the Earth by hitching a cosmic ride to heaven (see Fig. 17, in Section 3B: Epidemic or Collective Mental Disorders).

Another tragic religious incident was the massive suicide of the members of the People's Temple in late 1978. Following the Reverend Jim Jones, their religious leader, nearly 900 members moved from California to Guyana, South America, to establish a new life in the jungle. Following their leader's order, as part of a routine religious ritual, all of them swallowed the fatal substance, cyanide, and died together (see Fig. 6, in Section 3B).

The belief in death as one of the ultimate ways to fulfill their religious mission was also found in such other cults as the Sun Cult in Europe. This cult tends to keep its religious affiliations and activities secret and is not well-known to outsiders. Occasionally, a small group of members commits ritual collective suicide as a part of its religious practice.

There is no shortage of examples of cult leaders predicting the end of the world and persuading their believers to prepare for salvation. Many believers sell their properties, quit their jobs, and make all necessary "preparations" for the end of the world. These kinds of religious episodes have occurred in the East as well. In Korea in 1997, a cult leader predicted the end of the world and caused social turmoil. This also happened in Taiwan. In early 1999, several hundred people followed their leader to the United States to await the appearance of God who was to appear on television on a certain day to give his instructions on how to deal with the end of the world.

Another kind of cult involves sexual relations between cult members, or with cult leaders, as part of its religious rituals, in the belief that such sexual acts will enhance the blessings of God (Kim, 1972). It was suspected that the leader of the Branch Dividiens had sexual relations with female children of cult members. However, the most terrifying aspect of the Branch Dividiens was their plan to start an antigovernment military movement. They purchased and stored a huge number of weapons in their attempt to achieve their religious goal, and the plan ended in tragedy in Waco, Texas.

In ancient times, it was common for people to sacrifice human beings in religious rituals to please a supernatural power, particularly when the society suffered natural disasters, believing it would relieve the god's anger or induce his favor. Stories are heard in many places of human sacrifices made to appease a supernatural power, such as throwing a young virgin into an erupting volcano or into a river during a flood or killing someone when there was a drought. Such rituals would be despised by contemporary, humanistic men, but they were practiced by many cults in the not too distant past.

What are the common characteristics of these cults that are easily labeled "pathological" or as "sinister" religions? Usually, there is a charismatic leader who is very powerful and convincing and demands absolute obedience from the members. The cult is often tightly organized, and members' behavior is strictly controlled. The goal of the religion is rationalized in such a way that it is convincing to the members, who have a strong faith in their leader. As a result, the members lose their ego functions and their rational judgment and are willing to follow the leader's orders blindly.

Aside from extremely pathological cults, there is a borderline normality in many religious groups. For instance, a cult leader matching marital partners (as in the Unification Church or so-called Moonies) raises a question from a modern mental health perspective. A religious group fighting with different sects of the same religion, with other religious believers, or with nonbelievers, whether in occasional physical fights or formal wars institutionalized at a national level, poses questions from humanistic and religious points of view. Religions involved in politics, politicized religious movements, or religious organizations that seek economic gain are some examples.

The question is "What are the requirements of a 'healthy' religion?" "What about people who choose not to believe in any religion?" "Are they right in taking an atheistic view of the world?" These questions deserve careful consideration before any subjective or biased judgment is made.

### b. Religion and Mental Disorders

Concerning the relationship between religion and serious mental illness, Koenig, Larson, and Weaver (1998) reported that religious delusions are not rare in psychotic disorders and may be present in as many as 10 to 15% of patients hospitalized with schizophrenia. Wilson (1998) commented that these delusions, however, are thought to be culturally driven: a manifestation of psychotic illness rather than a cause of it.

Mental phenomena that are significantly colored by religion and require judgments from both religious and psychiatric perspectives may present a real challenge. For instance, if a person believes that he has a mission to deliver a message from God, or claims that he is sent from God, it is difficult to assess whether this is a religious delusion or a religious phenomenon based on the belief alone. The presence of other mental symptoms or signs indicating a mental breakdown often serve as clues for clinical diagnosis.

A traditional healer, such as a shaman, often enters a possessed state, claiming that he is possessed by a supernatural being for the purpose of healing. He is able to leave the state of possession and return to an ordinary mental state when the healing ritual is over. This is in contrast to a mental patient, whose possession by a supernatural being may be beyond his control, occurring at any time. He may have difficulty coming out of the possessed state, which may last days or months.

## 4. Religion, Mental Health, and Therapy

### a. Religion and Mental Health

Aside from its negative aspects, religion may have certain positive elements from the standpoint of mental health. Frequent claims are made, particularly by those who are devoted to religions, that religious beliefs are beneficial to mental health, providing faith, hope, and calm to a person's mind.

Larson and co-workers (2000) pointed out that numerous national surveys established the central role of religion in the lives of many Americans. Nearly 95% of Americans reported a belief in god (of whatever nature). They also indicated that many studies found that higher levels of religious commitment are associated with enhanced feelings of well-being and a lower prevalence of mental illness (particularly evidenced by self-destructive behaviors such as drug and alcohol abuse). Religion has also been identified as a potential buffer against stress. Religious commitment also often plays a role in reducing suicide rates.

According to Griffith and Mahy (1984), the Spiritual Baptist Church is a black Christian movement of long standing in the English-speaking West Indies. Recently its religious activities have blossomed among African-Americans in urban communities in the United States. Its members engage in a ceremony called "mourning," which involves praying, fasting, and the experiencing dreams and visions while in isolation. Members who had undergone these special experiences cited the benefits of the practice: relief of depressed moods, the ability to foresee and avoid danger, improvement in decision-making ability, heightened facility to communicate with God and to meditate, a clearer appreciation of their racial origins, identification with the church hierarchy, and physical cures. Griffith and Mahy commented that mourning appears to be a viable psychotherapeutic practice for these church members.

Despite the general belief that religion is the fountainhead of all the moral tenets of a society, Sanua (1969) pointed out that a number of empirical studies do not support this view. He commented that religious education as it is taught in the United States today does not seem to ensure healthier attitudes, despite its emphasis on ethical behavior.

### b. Religious Healing Practices

Some religions offer healing practices for certain behavior problems. They usually provide the explanation that the causes of the problems are related to supernatural matters and recommend utilizing supernatural power to heal the problems. Examples of healing practices or ceremonies observed in various forms of folk religion are including shamanism, *zar* ceremonies, *umbanda* healing cult (see Fig. 3), or *voodoo* cult (see Fig. 4). Suggestion, sacrifice, exorcism (see Fig. 5), and authoritative instruction for behavioral changes (see Fig. 6) are some of the therapeutic mechanisms utilized. It needs to be pointed out that religious healing practices are observed not only in folk religion in developing societies but also rather commonly in developed societies in mainstream religions. On TV programs in the United States, we can easily see demonstrations of healing. Believer-patients who have had various kind of sicknesses for many years, such as hearing problems, back pain, and difficulty walking, are called to the stage in front of an audience of many hundreds or thousands, and after being touched by the priest, fall back down on the floor and claim that they are "healed."

FIGURE 3    *Umbanda* healing cult, Rio de Janeiro, Brazil. Participants lie on the floor in a deep trance state. [Courtesy of Wolfgang Jilek, M.D.]

### c. Religious Counseling

It is common for religious persons to provide mental healing practices for believers. This is observed in different types of religions, from ancient shamanism to contemporary religions. In many Western societies, Jewish and Christian clergy are often called upon to act as front-line mental health providers, especially regarding personal problems. In America, many clients who have consulted clergy have been satisfied with the service they received and felt they were helped, even though most clergy are not trained to offer professional counseling (Larson et al., 2000).

American cultural psychiatrist Joseph Westermeyer (1973), after working in Laos, indicated that there were no mental health professionals in Laos when he was there. He pointed out that in the absence of mental health workers, the people of Laos effectively supported one another through crises and role changes. They accomplished this by employing their social institutions and traditions. The main social resources were religious rituals, community elders, and home-centered religious activities involving the extended family, neighbors, and friends, indicating the contribution of religion to the mental health of the people.

Clinical experiences generally indicate that patients prefer to be counseled by therapists who share the same religious background. After an intensive review of the literature on religion and psychotherapeutic processes and outcomes, Worthington and colleagues (1996) pointed out that nonreligious and religious counselors shared most counseling-relevant values but differed in the value they

FIGURE 4    *Voodoo* cult healer (*houngan*) in a trance, Haiti. [Courtesy of Wolfgang Jilek, M.D.]

placed on religion. They commented that these religious differences affected clinical judgment and behavior, especially with religious patients.

Perhaps the comments just described apply differently to various religious groups under different circumstances. When Wikler (1989), through semistructured, in-person interviews, examined the preferences of Orthodox Jewish clients in the New York area regarding the religious identities of their therapists, he found a wide range of meanings attached to a therapist's religious identity, and some clients did not care about the religious backgrounds of their counselors. Keating and Fretz (1990) found that religiously committed patients often had more reservations about being counseled by therapists with nonreligious or different religious backgrounds because they feared that the therapists would ignore their spiritual concerns and view their religious or spiritual beliefs as bizarre, if not pathological, rejecting the idea of communicating with a higher power.

### d. Religion and Psychotherapy

Lukoff, Lu, and Turner (1995) stressed the importance of cultural considerations in the assessment and treatment of religious and spiritual problems in clinical

FIGURE 5  *Phan yak* chanting treatment ceremony in Thailand. (a) Participants hold a sacred thread in a Buddhist temple to get in touch with a supernatural power for treatment. (b) One of the participants (center) fell into dissociated and convulsionlike behavior, indicating that her evil spirit was being chased away by the monk's chanting. [Courtesy of Sangun Suwanlert, M.D.]

settings. Beyond that, they also stressed that clinicians need to have religious knowledge and orientation in their clinical work.

Counseling psychologists Fukuyama and Sevig (1999), through their clinical experiences, pointed out that there are positive and negative expressions of

FIGURE 6    Treatment of drug addicts at a Buddhist temple, Thailand. (a) Performance of "purifi-cation" by herb-induced vomiting. (b) After abstinence is accomplished, a monk instructs patients on how to start new lives. [Courtesy of Wolfgang Jilek, M.D.]

spirituality among people. Pastoral counselor Clinbell (1995) defined spiritual growth as that which "aims at the enhancement of our realistic hope, our mean-ings, our values, our inner freedom, our faith systems, our peak experiences, and our relationship with God." Further, Clinbell described pathological or unhealthy religion or spirituality as growth blocking and resulting from rigidity, idolatry, authoritarianism, and practices that constrict life or deny reality. A therapist needs to help his clients distinguish between healthy and unhealthy spirituality, an essential part of therapy that involves religion.

In ordinary psychotherapy, therapists need to consider patients' religious beliefs. This is particularly true for clinicians working in multiethnic, multireligious societies. Turbott (1996), a psychiatrist from New Zealand, pointed out that recent psychiatric literature suggested a need to reconsider the place of religion and spirituality in the practice of psychiatry. He explained that, in New Zealand, the politically mandated bicultural approach to mental health demanded an understanding of the spirituality of the indigenous Maori. He suggested that psychiatry would benefit if the vocabulary and concepts of religion and spirituality were more familiar to trainees and practitioners.

As pointed out by Boehnlein (2000b), psychiatry and religion both draw upon rich traditions of human thought and practice. Although it is a branch of medicine, in contrast to the main trend of medicine's reliance on natural science, psychiatry incorporates the humanities and social sciences in its scientific base to understand and treat mental illness. Psychiatry often needs to go beyond the world of natural science into the philosophical realm. However, in the past, in general, psychiatrists have shied away from religion.

As an extension of cultural psychiatry, which emphasizes the importance of understanding and respecting a patient's lifestyle and value system, it is natural to consider the religious aspects of a patient's life and respect the patient's beliefs, whether spiritual or atheistic, rather than imposing the views and judgments arising from the therapist's own religious views and attitudes (Post, 1993). In order to meet the demands of patients of diverse cultures, it is essential to add the dimensions of religion and spirituality to the training of future psychiatrists.

## REFERENCES

### A. Sociocultural Change, Migration, and Refuge

Al-Issa, I., & Tousignant, M. (Eds.). (1997). *Ethnicity, immigration, and psychopathology.* New York: Plenum Press.

Astrup, C., & Ödegaard, Ö. (1960). Internal migration and mental disease in Norway. *Psychiatric Quarterly Supplement, 34,* 116–130.

Beiser, M. (1980). Coping with past and future: A study of adaptation to social change in West Africa. *Journal of Operational Psychiatry, 11*(2), 140–155.

Beiser, M., Turner, R. J., & Ganesan, S. (1989). Catastrophic stress and factors affecting its consequences among Southeast Asian refugees. *Social Science and Medicine, 28*(3), 183–195.

Berry, J. W. (1980). Social and cultural change. In H. C. Triandis & R. W. Brislin (Eds.), *Handbook of cross-cultural psychology: Vol. 5. Social psychology* (pp. 211–279). Boston: Allyn & Bacon.

Boehnlein, J. K. (1987). Culture and society in post-traumatic stress disorder: Complications for psychotherapy. *American Journal of Psychotherapy, 16,* 519–530.

Draguns, J. G. (1996). Ethnocultural considerations in the treatment of PTSD: Therapy and service delivery. In A. J. Marsella, M. J. Friedman, E. T. Gerrity, & R. M. Scurfield (Eds.), *Ethnocultural aspects of posttraumatic stress disorder: Issues, research, and clinical application* (pp. 459–482). Washington, DC: American Psychological Association.

El-Islam, M. F. (2001). A women with one foot in the past. In W. S. Tseng & J. Streltzer (Eds.), *Culture and psychotherapy: A guide to clinical practice* (pp. 27–41). Washington, DC: American Psychiatric Press.

Favazza, A. R. (1980). Culture change and mental health. *Journal of Operational Psychiatry, 11*(2), 101–119.

Foulks, E. F. (1980). Psychological continuities: From dissociative states to alcohol use and suicide in Arctic populations. *Journal of Operational Psychiatry, 11*(2), 157–161.

Friedman, M., & Jaranson, J. (1994). The applicability of the posttraumatic stress disorder concept to refugees. In A. J. Marsella, T. Bornemann, S. Ekblad, & J Orley (Eds.), *Amidst peril and pain: The mental health and well-being of the world's refugees.* Washington, DC: American Psychological Association.

Jaranson, J., & Popkin, M. (Eds.). (1998). *Caring for victims of torture.* Washington, DC: American Psychiatric Press.

Kinzie, J. D. (2001). Southeast Asian refugees: Legency of trauma. In W. S. Tseng & J. Streltzer (Eds.), *Culture and psychotherapy: A guide for clinical practice* (pp. 173–191). Washington, DC: American Psychiatric Press.

Kinzie, J. D., Boehnlein, J. K., Leung, P., Moore, L., Riley, C., & Smith, D. (1990). The prevalence rate of posttraumatic stress disorder and its clinical significance among Southeast Asian refugees. *American Journal of Psychiatry, 147*(7), 913–917.

Kinzie, J. D., & Manson, S. (1983). Five-years' experience with Indochinese refugee psychiatric patients. *Journal of Operational Psychiatry, 14*(2), 105–111.

Kinzie, J. D., Tran, K. A., Breckenridge, A., & Bloom, J. D. (1980). An Indochinese refugee psychiatric clinic: Culturally accepted treatment approaches. *American Journal of Psychiatry, 137*(11), 1429–1432.

McKelvey, R. S., & Webb, J. A. (1996). Premigratory expectations and postmigratory mental health symptoms in Vietnamese Amerasians. *Journal of the American Academy of Child & Adolescent Psychiatry, 35*(2), 240–245.

Mezey, A. G. (1960). Psychiatric aspects of human migrations. *International Journal of Social Psychiatry, 5*, 245–260.

Mollica, R. F., & Lavelle, J. (1988). Southeast Asian refugees. In L. Comas-Díaz & E. E. H. Griffith (Eds.), *Clinical guidelines in cross-cultural mental health* (pp. 262–304). New York: Wiley.

Murphy, H. B. M. (1961). Social change and mental health. *Milbank Memorial Fund Quarterly, 39*(3), 385–445.

Murphy, H. B. M. (1973). The low rate of hospitalization shown by immigrants to Canada. In C. A. Zwingmann & M. Pfister-Ammende (Eds.), *Uprooting and after.* New York: Springer-Verlag.

Ndetei, D. M. (1988). Psychiatric phenomenology across countries: Constitutional, cultural, or environmental? *Acta Psychiatrica Scandinavica, Supplementum, 344*, 33–44.

Ödegaard, Ö. (1932). Emigration and insanity: A study of mental disease among the Norwegian born population of Minnesota. *Acta Psychiatrica Neurologica, Supplementum, 4*.

Sack, W. H., Him, C., & Dickson, D. (1999). Twelve-year follow-up study of Khmer youths who suffered massive war trauma as children. *Journal of the American Academy of Child and Adolescent Psychiatry, 38*(9), 1173–1179.

Somnier, F. E., & Genefke, I. K. (1986). Psychotherapy for victims of torture. *British Journal of Psychiatry, 149*, 323–329.

Tseng, W. S. (2001a). Cultural change and coping. In W. S. Tseng, *Handbook of cultural psychiatry* (pp. 683–694). San Diego, CA: Academic Press.

Tseng, W. S. (2001b). Migration, refuge, and adjustment. In W. S. Tseng, *Handbook of cultural psychiatry* (pp. 696–697). San Diego, CA: Academic Press.

Tseng, W. S., Ebata, K., Kim, K. I., Krahl, W., Kua, E. K., Lu, Q. Y., Shen, Y. C., Tan, E. S., & Yang, M. J. (2001). Asia mental health: Improvement and challenge. *International Journal of Social Psychiatry*, *47*(1), 8–23.

Varvin, S., & Hauff, E. (1998). Psychotherapy with patients who have been tortured. In J. Jaranson & M. Popkin (Eds.), *Caring for victims of torture.* Washington, DC: American Psychiatric Press.

Vesti, P., & Kastrup, K. (1992). Psychotherapy for torture survivors. In M. Basoglu (Ed.), *Torture and its consequences: Current treatment approaches.* Cambridge: Cambridge University Press.

Westermeyer, J. (1989). *Psychiatric care of migrants: A clinical guide.* Washington. DC: American Psychiatric Press.

Westermeyer, J, Neider, J., & Calliew, A. (1989). Psychosocial adjustment of Hmong refugees during their first decade in the United States: A longitudinal study. *Journal of Nervous and Mental Disease*, *177*(3), 132–139.

Zilber, N., & Lerner, Y. (1996). Psychological distress among recent immigrants from the former Soviet Union to Israel. I. Correlates of level of distress. *Psychological Medicine*, *26*(3), 493–501.

Zwingle, E. (1999). A world together. *National Geographic*, *196*(2), 6–33.

## B. Minorities

Burke, A. W. (1984). Racism and psychological disturbance among West Indians in Britain. *International Journal of Social Psychiatry*, *30*(1&2), 50–68.

Cabaj, R. P., & Stein, T. S. (Eds.). (1996). *Textbook of homosexuality and mental health.* Washington DC: American Psychiatric Press.

Campbell, H. D., Hinkle, D. O., Sandlin, P., & Moffic, H. S. (1983). A sexual minority: Homosexuality and mental health care. *American Journal of Social Psychiatry*, *3*(2), 26–35.

Carter, R. T. (1995). *The influence of race and racial identity in psychotherapy: Toward a racially inclusive model.* New York: Wiley-Interscience.

Commas-Díaz, L., & Greene, B. (Eds.). (1994). *Women of color: Integrating ethnic and gender identities in psychotherapy.* New York: Guilford Press.

DeVos, G. A., & Wagatsuma, H. (1969). Minority status and deviance in Japan. In W. Caudill & T. S. Lin (Eds.), *Mental health research in Asia and the Pacific* (pp. 342–357). Honolulu: East-West Center Press.

Fernandez, F., Ruiz, P., & Bing, E. G. (1993). The mental health impact of AIDS on ethnic minorities. In A. C. Gaw (Ed.), *Culture, ethnicity, and mental illness* (pp. 573–586). Washington, DC: American Psychiatric Press.

Greene, B. (Ed.). (1997). *Ethnic and cultural diversity among lesbians and gay men.* Thousand Oaks, CA: Sage.

Griffith, E. E. H. (1998). *Race and excellence: My dialogue with Chester Pierce.* Iowa City: University of Iowa Press.

Harris, H. W., Blue, H. C., & Griffith, E. E. H. (Eds.). (1995). *Racial and ethinc identity: Psychological development and creative expression.* New York: Routledge.

Ho, M. K. (1987). *Family therapy with ethnic minorities.* Newbury Park, CA: Sage.

Jilek-Aall, L., & Jilek, W. (2001). A woman who sing spirit song. In W. S. Tseng & J. Streltzer (Eds.), *Culture and psychotherapy: A guide for clinical practice* (pp. 43–56). Washington DC: American Psychiatric Press.

Kitzinger, C. (1997). Lesbian and gay psychology: A critical analysis. In D. Fox & I. Prilleltensky (Eds.), *Critical psychology: An introduction.* London: Sage.

Krajeski, J. P. (1993). Cultural considerations in the psychiatric care of gay men and lesbians. In

A. C. Gaw (Ed.), *Culture, ethnicity, and mental illness* (pp. 553–572). Washington, DC: American Psychiatric Press.

Krane, J. E. (1996). Violence against women in intimate relations: Insight from cross-cultural analysis. *Transcultural Psychiatric Research Review, 33*(4), 435–465.

Littlewood, R., & Lipsedge, M. (1989). *Aliens and alienists: Ethnic minorities and psychiatry* (2nd ed.). London: Unwin Human.

Lott, B., & Maluso, D. (1995). *The social psychology of interpersonal discrimination.* New York: Guilford Press.

Moffic, H. S., & Adams, G. L. (Guest Ed.). (1983, Spring). The psychiatric care of "minority" groups [Special issue]. *American Journal of Social Psychiatry, 3*(2).

Moore, L. J. (2000). Psychiatric contributions to understanding racism. *Transcultural Psychiatry, 37*(2), 147–1822.

Nadelson, C. C., & Zimmerman, V. (1993). Culture and psychiatric care of women. In A. C. Gaw (Ed.), *Culture, ethnicity, and mental illness* (pp. 501–515). Washington, DC: American Psychiatric Press.

Powell, G. J. (Ed.). (1983). *The psychosocial development of minority group children.* New York: Brunner/Mazel.

Vargas, L. A., & Koss-Chioino, J. D. (1992). *Working with culture: Psychotherapeutic interventions with ethnic minority children and adolescents.* San Francisco: Jossey-Bass.

Willie, C. V., Rieker, P. P., Kramer, B. M., & Brown, B. S. (Eds.). (1995). *Mental health, racism, and sexism.* Pittsburgh: University of Pittsburgh Press.

## C. Group Violence and Collective Homicide

Dishman, C. (2001). Terrorism, crime and transformation. *Studies in Conflict and Terrorism, 24*(1), 43–58.

Hata, Y. (1986). *Nankin jiken: Giakusatsu no kozou* (Nanking incidence: The structure of massacre). Tokyo: Chuokoronsha. (In Japanese.)

Heskin, K. (1994). Terrorism in Ireland: The past and the future. *Irish Journal of Psychology, 15*(2–3), 469–479.

Hoffman, B. (1999). The mind of the terrorist: Perspectives from social psychology. *Psychiatric Annals, 29*(6), 337–340.

Post, J. M. (2000). Terrorist on trial: The context of political crime. *Journal of the American Academy of Psychiatry and the Law, 28*(2), 171–178.

Silke, A. (1998). Cheshire-cat logic: The recurring theme of terrorist abnormality in psychological research. *Psychology Crime and Law, 4*(1), 51–69.

Takemoto, T., & Ohara, Y. (2000). The alleged "Naking Massacre"—Japan's rebuttal to China's forged claims. Tokyo: Meisei-shia.

Wilson, M. A. (2000). Toward a model of terrorist behavior in hostage-taking incidents. *Journal of Conflict Resolution, 44*(4), 403–424.

## D. Religion

Bhugra, E. (Ed.). (1996). *Religion and psychiatry: Context, consensus and controversies.* London: Routledge.

Boehnlein, J. K. (Ed.). (2000a). *Psychiatry and religion.* Washington, DC: American Psychiatric Press.

Boehnlein, J. K. (2000b). Introduction. In J. K. Boehnlein (Ed.), *Psychiatry and religion* (pp. xv–xx). Washington, DC: American Psychiatric Press.

Clark, P. B. (Ed.). (1993). *The world's religions: Understanding the living faiths.* Pleasantville, NY: The Reader's Digest Association.

Clark, P. B. (1993). Islam. In P. B. Clarke (Ed.), *The world's religions: Understanding the living faiths* (pp. 84–120). Pleasantville, NY: The Reader's Digest Association.

Clinbell, H. (1995). *Counseling for spiritually empowered wholeness: A hope-centered approach.* New York: Haworth Pastoral Press.

Fukuyama, M. A., & Sevig, T. D. (1999). *Integrating spirituality into multicultural counseling.* Thousand Oaks, CA: Sage.

Griffith, E. E. H., & Mahy, G. E. (1984). Psychological benefits of spiritual baptist "mourning." *American Journal of Psychiatry, 141,* 769–773.

Kanitkar, V. P. (1993). Hinduism. In P. B. Clarke (Ed.), *The world's religions: Understanding the living faiths* (pp. 124–147). Pleasantville, NY: The Reader's Digest Association.

Keating, A. M., & Fretz, B. R. (1990). Christians' anticipations about counselors in response to counselor descriptions. *Journal of Counseling Psychology, 37,* 293–296.

Kim, K. I. (1972). New religions in Korea: The sociocultural consideration. *Korean Neuropsychiatric Association, 11*(1), 31–36 (In Korean.) (Reviewed in *Transcultural Psychiatric Research Review, 10,* 30–31 [1973].)

Koenig, H. G. (Ed). (1998). *Handbook of religion and mental health.* San Diego, CA: Academic Press.

Koenig, H. G., Larson, D. B., & Weaver, A. J. (1998). Research on religion and serious mental illness. *New Directions for Mental Health Services, 80,* 81–95.

Larson, D. B., Milano, M. G., Weaver, A. J., & McCullough, M. E. (2000). The role of clergy in mental health care. In J. K. Boehnlein (Ed.), *Psychiatry and religion* (pp. 125–142). Washington, DC: American Psychiatric Press.

Lukoff, D., Lu, F. G., & Turner, R. (1995). Cultural considerations in the assessment and treatment of religious and spiritual problems. *Psychiatric Clinics of North America, 18*(3), 467–485.

Morgan, P. (1993). Buddhism. In P. B. Clarke (Consulting editor), *The world's religions: Understanding the living faiths* (pp. 148–171). Pleasantville, NY: The Reader's Digest Association.

Neeleman, J., & Persaud, R. (1995). Why do psychiatrists neglect religion? *British Journal of Medical Psychology, 68*(2), 169–178.

Pattision, E. M. (1984). Towards a psychosocial cultural analysis of religion and mental health. In R. C. Nann, D. S. Butt, & L. Ladrido-Ignacio (Eds.), *Mental health, cultural values, and social development: A look into the '80s.* Dordrecht, The Netherland: D. Reidel.

Post, S. G. (1993). Psychiatry and ethics: The problematics of respect for religious meanings. *Culture, Medicine, and Psychiatry, 17*(3), 363–384.

Sanua, V. D. (1969). Religion, mental health, and personality: A review of empirical studies. *American Journal of Psychiatry, 125*(9), 1203–1213.

Shah, N. (1993). Jainism. In P. B. Clarke (Ed.), *The world's religions: Understanding the living faiths.* Pleasantville, NY: The Reader's Digest Association.

Smith, H. (1965). *The religions of man.* New York: Harper & Row. (Original work published in 1958.)

Turbott, J. (1996). Religion, spirituality and psychiatry: Conceptual, cultural and personal challenges. *Australian and New Zealand Journal of Psychiatry, 30*(6), 720–727.

Westermeyer, J. (1973). Lao Buddhism, mental health, and contemporary implications. *Journal of Religion and Health, 12*(2), 181–188.

Wikler, M. (1989). The religion of the therapist: Its meaning to Orthodox Jewish clients. *Hillside Journal of Clinical Psychiatry, 11*(2), 131–146.

Wilson, W. P. (1998). Religion and psychosis. In H. H. Koenig (Ed.), *Handbook of religion and mental health.* San Diego, CA: Academic Press.

Worthington, Jr. E. L., Kurusu, T. A., McCullough, M. E., & Snadage, S. J. (1996). Empirical research on religion and psychotherapeutic processes and outcomes: A 10-year review and research prospectus. *Psychological Bulletin, 119*(3), 448–487.

# Subject Index